628883850/6334279

Novell®

ZENworks® 7 Suite

Administrator's Handbook

BRAD DAYLEY
RON TANNER

Novell
PRESS™
Novell®

Published by Pearson Education, Inc.
800 East 96th Street, Indianapolis, Indiana 46240 USA FEB 2 2 2007

Novell® ZENworks 7 Suite Administrator's Handbook

International Standard Book Number: 0-672-32846-1

Library of Congress Catalog Card Number: 2005928288

Printed in the United States of America

First Printing: November 2005

08 07 06 05   4 3 2 1

Trademarks

Warning and Disclaimer

Bulk Sales

Pearson offers excellent discounts on this book when ordered in quantity for bulk purchases or special sales. For more information, please contact

U.S. Corporate and Government Sales
1-800-382-3419
corpsales@pearsontechgroup.com

For sales outside of the U.S., please contact

International Sales
international@pearsoned.com

Acquisitions Editor
Jenny Watson

Development Editor
Emmett Dulaney

Managing Editor
Charlotte Clapp

Project Editor
Seth Kerney

Production Editor
Heather Wilkins

Indexer
Erika Millen

Technical Editor
John Bate

Publishing Coordinator
Vanessa Evans

Multimedia Developer
Dan Scherf

Book Designer
Gary Adair

Page Layout
Brad Chinn

Novell Press is the exclusive publisher of trade computer technology books that have been authorized by Novell, Inc. Novell Press books are written and reviewed by the world's leading authorities on Novell and related technologies, and are edited, produced, and distributed by the Que/Sams Publishing group of Pearson Education, the worldwide leader in integrated education and computer technology publishing. For more information on Novell Press and Novell Press books, please go to www.novellpress.com.

Associate Publisher
Mark Taber

Program Manager, Novell, Inc.
Darrin Vandenbos

Marketing Manager
Doug Ingersoll

Contents At a Glance

Table of Contents

Chapter 3 Getting ZENworks Desktop Management 7 Working in Your Environment **151**

Chapter 4 Getting ZENworks Server Management 7 Working in Your Environment **165**

Chapter 5 Getting Asset Inventory 7 Working In Your Environment **173**

Chapter 31 Using ZENworks Server Management to Manage Servers 907

Chapter 32 Making the Most of ZENworks Server Management Reporting 955

Preface

IT professionals are constantly asked to get more done with fewer resources. Our lives are often spent doing mundane tasks such as hauling mounds of CDs around so we can install applications on our user's computer, re-installing operating systems, or trying to figure out where all of our assets are. We could get on with the more strategic things that will make our companies better if we could just have a system that takes care of these operational tasks.

ZENworks is just such a solution. ZENworks will help you manage your systems through their entire lifecycles. With ZENworks the system will automatically track assets; deliver applications; keep your laptops, workstations, handhelds, and servers up-to-date on the latest approved patches; and keep the user's data safe, all through policies that tell the system how to behave and allow ZENworks to manage itself. ZENworks will even deliver images to those systems that need restoring or upgrading. ZENworks includes secure remote management capabilities to help you diagnose and control computers in your WAN or across the Internet.

ZENworks will deliver all of these features into your enterprise regardless of your preferred platform. ZENworks can function in a Windows-only environment or mixed environments including Windows, NetWare, and Linux. All of the capabilities of ZENworks are delivered via a web server, allowing you to support your users over the Internet. In this latest release of ZENworks, you now have full freedom of choice of back-end servers. You can even manage Windows desktops from a Linux server.

This book is about installing and getting ZENworks working in your environment, from small to enterprise levels. We will try to point out all of the tips and gotchas to watch for to make your installation and deployment of ZENworks a success.

We thank you for purchasing this book and hope that it is useful to you.

About the Authors

Brad Dayley is a software engineer in Novell's Nterprise Development Group. He has 14 years of experience installing, troubleshooting, and developing Novell's products. He co-developed an advanced debugging course used to train Novell's engineers and customers and is the co-author of *Novell's Guide to Resolving Critical Server Issues* as well as seven other Novell Press titles on the ZENworks suite. When he is not writing books or software, he can be found biking, hiking, and/or Jeeping somewhere in the remote regions of the Pacific Northwest with his wife, DaNae, and four sons.

Ron Tanner is currently a director of product management for Novell ZENworks, defining the future of the product. Ron has been associated with ZENworks since its inception and led software development as director of engineering through the invention and first releases of ZENworks. He has 18 years of experience in developing software and leading engineering teams into exciting, cutting-edge technology. Prior to working at Novell, Ron worked at AT&T Bell Laboratories developing advanced networking systems. Ron has co-authored seven other ZENworks Novell Press titles. If Ron has some free time he is often found with his wife, CheRee, cheering for their four children at football games, competitive cheering events, karate, and hula championships. Sometimes Ron sneaks away for some quiet time with a book.

Dedication

For D, A & F!

—Brad Dayley

To the family, thanks for your support. To my sweetheart, thanks for everything; you are a great wife and mother. And to my engineering, product management, and marketing buddies; thanks for the heated debates that make the product better. I love it when a plan comes together.

—Ron Tanner

Acknowledgments

Our sincere gratitude goes out to the following persons, without whom this book could not have happened:

To the ZENworks team that keeps working hard to make a great product even better. We're looking forward to the next version. We hear it will be amazing.

To everyone at Novell who allowed us to pick their brains, including but not limited to (with apologies to any whose names we have forgotten): Ken Muir, Kevin McGill, Kelly Norman, Dale Asay, Scott Blake, Blain Ogden, Ron Ulloa, Steve Wootton, Wes Butler, Larry Supino, Anand Sinha, Mark Schouls, Kevin Wilkins, and Ty Ellis.

To our editors who made the book readable, checked us on our technical accuracy, and kept us on track, you all are great (and picky). It seems that nothing gets by you. Thanks to Seth Kerney, Jenny Watson, and Emmett Dulaney. Special thanks to John Bate, who kept us honest.

We Want to Hear from You!

As the reader of this book, *you* are our most important critic and commentator. We value your opinion and want to know what we're doing right, what we could do better, what topics you'd like to see us cover, and any other words of wisdom you're willing to pass our way.

You can email or write me directly to let me know what you did or didn't like about this book—as well as what we can do to make our books better.

Please note that I cannot help you with technical problems related to the topic of this book and that due to the high volume of mail I receive I may not be able to reply to every message.

When you write, please be sure to include this book's title and author as well as your name and email address or phone number. I will carefully review your comments and share them with the author and editors who worked on the book.

Email: feedback@novellpress.com

Mail: Mark Taber
            Associate Publisher
            Novell Press/Pearson Education
            800 East 96th Street
            Indianapolis, IN 46240 USA

Reader Services

For more information about this book or others from Novell Press, visit our website at www.novellpress.com. Type the ISBN or the title of a book in the Search field to find the page you're looking for.

## CHAPTER 1

The ZENworks Family

This book discusses features of the ZENworks 7 Suite. It is important to understand that the Suite is actually a bundle of several, independently available ZENworks products that include the following:

- ▶ ZENworks Desktop Management (formerly ZENworks for Desktops)—A desktop management system that manages many workstation aspects. ZENworks Desktop Management also includes ZENworks Patch Management, ZENworks Data Management, Instant Messenger, ZENworks Personality Migration, and ZENworks Software Packaging.

- ▶ ZENworks Server Management (formerly ZENworks for Servers)— A system that enables you to manage servers and to distribute files and applications across the network. ZENworks Server Management also includes ZENworks Patch Management.

- ▶ ZENworks Handheld Management (formerly ZENworks for Handhelds)—A system that enables you to manage policies, applications, and inventory on PDA devices.

- ▶ ZENworks Asset Management—A system that enables you to discover devices on your network and then perform inventory scans, track software usages, and reconcile licenses to those discovered applications.

All ZENworks products rely significantly on the directory—specifically Novell eDirectory—to provide a greater capability to securely share management responsiblities and a greater ease of management for each component in the network. All the ZENworks products are cross-platform and can run not only in NetWare environments but also in Windows, Linux, and Solaris environments (without the need for NetWare or the Novell Windows client).

With the release of ZENworks 7, all products in the ZENworks family include the full collection of software shipped in the ZENworks 7 Suite. The included software functions as a 90-day trial.

What Is ZENworks Desktop Management?

ZENworks Desktop Management is designed to minimize the cost of deploying and managing desktops in the enterprise. The *ZEN* in ZENworks Desktop Management stands for *Zero Effort Networks* and is named to reflect the zero effort required for end-users and the minimum effort necessary for administrators to manage the desktops in their systems.

ZENworks Desktop Management is segmented into three desktop management and maintenance areas, discussed in the following sections. These include Application Management, Workstation Management, and Remote Management.

Application Management

The ZENworks Application Management area for Desktop Management is designed to easily deploy applications from the network to individual desktops. These applications can be automatically installed on the workstation, cached for later installation, or just have an icon applied to the desktop that references a software executable or installation bundle on a server. All the applications deployed to the desktop enable the administrator to control when they are deployed, how they are applied, and who or which desktops get certain applications.

ZENworks Desktop Management also enables you to customize the settings for each individual user by referencing values in Novell eDirectory and embedding them in the registry keys and files for the application. When that application is deployed to the desktop, these values are then customized for the particular user. In addition to customization, the ZENworks Desktop Management Application Management portion includes the capability to help you equalize usage through its load balancing features, and attempts to make the application always available with its fault-tolerance features.

ZENworks Desktop Management keeps applications working, providing self-healing capabilities to automatically fix applications that become broken. ZENworks provides all its features to laptop users who are even disconnected from the network.

With the integration of eDirectory, ZENworks Desktop Management Application Management makes sure that the applications follow the user to whichever desktop he uses in the network, keeping the user's connection to the network always functioning in a familiar way. ZENworks Application Management has features that enable you to distribute and assign applications to users, thus making the management of applications for desktops and your users on the desktop simple and consistent.

Application Management features are currently provided for the Windows 98, Windows NT, Windows 2000, and Windows XP platforms.

Workstation Management

Workstation Management refers to the administrator's ability to make direct changes on the desktop and manage the registry, Novell clients, desktop images, printers, and Windows group policies. With the Novell eDirectory advantages, you can make changes to a configuration object that affect the configuration of a program or registry, for example, and then have that configuration applied to all or a portion of the workstations in your entire organization. Due to the inheritance rules of eDirectory, and the introduction of workstation objects into the tree, these configuration objects can be applied to many users and workstations in the tree by their associations with objects, groups, or containers.

To illustrate the usefulness of this, a customer was told by support that to fix the reported problem he needed to change only one registry key of each client. The customer was not happy because he had more than 10,000 clients of that type, and he determined that it would take years with the current staff to make that change. Now, with ZENworks Desktop Management, one administrator can make the change in one configuration object, and the change can be forwarded and made to all associated workstations. This one change can be done in minutes instead of years.

In addition, the ZENworks Desktop Management Workstation
Management feature includes workstation hardware and software inventory. This inventory can be useful to the administrator in understanding
the capabilities of each workstation as she manages and maintains the
desktop. Reports are also included with ZENworks Desktop Management
that provide useful, tabular information of what is stored in the scanned
database. Now you can quickly find out who has a copy of Office
installed anywhere in the enterprise.

Scheduled Actions in Workstation Management allow the administrator
to schedule the launch of scripts and applications at any specified time or
interval. This proves useful in performing regularly required tasks such as
backups, scans, transmissions, and so on. All this is performed automatically, through policies that enable you to configure settings and then let
the system take care of itself.

Workstation Management features are currently provided for the
Windows 98, Windows NT, Windows 2000, and Windows XP platforms.

Remote Management

The ZENworks Desktop Management Remote Management feature
includes the capability to discover information about the workstation and
to do some remote diagnostics and repairs on that workstation. As mentioned earlier, ZENworks Desktop Management introduces into the tree a
new object representing the workstation. This object is associated with
the physical desktop and is a repository for information about the specific desktop. The administrator can use this information in determining
how to most effectively maintain and repair that desktop.

In addition to the introduction of the workstation object, the Remote
Management feature of ZENworks Desktop Management provides the
administrator with the capability of eDirectory Authenticated Remote
Control. The eDirectory Authenticated Remote Control feature keeps
anyone who does not have rights to remotely control a particular workstation from being able to do so. This assures administrators and end-
users that only authorized personnel can remotely control their desktops.
Should this extra security not be needed, ZENworks Desktop
Management provides the capability to enact password-based remote
control, and you can choose to encrypt remote control communications.

To help in workstation diagnostics and repair, Remote Management of
ZENworks includes remote diagnostics and file transfer capabilities. For

security reasons, these also require proper rights in the eDirectory tree or passwords to perform the tasks.

To assist in your diagnostics, ZENworks includes Instant Messenging that allows you to communicate with your users to assist in determining the issues and problems. The instant messaging system allows messaging between any of your eDirectory users.

ZENworks Desktop Management Remote Management features are currently provided for the Windows 98, Windows NT, Windows 2000, and Windows XP platforms.

What Is ZENworks Server Management?

ZENworks Server Management provides easier management of your server environments. With ZENworks Server Management, you can install applications and configure and manage your Windows, Linux, Solaris, and NetWare servers. ZENworks Server Management is broken into two major components: Policy and Distribution Services and Management and Monitoring Services.

Policy and Distribution Services

ZENworks Policy and Distribution Services provides a highly scalable, bandwidth-aware transmission capability that can send configuration and file data to all the servers in your enterprise, or even across the Internet into a completely different environment.

ZENworks Distribution Services can package any content and compress it—encrypted if you want—and send that content efficiently to any number of servers. With advanced features such as checkpoint restart, bandwidth throttling, and digital signatures, ZENworks Distribution Services provides the most effective way to keep your data moving throughout the network.

Management and Monitoring Services

ZENworks Management and Monitoring Services provides traditional SNMP management and monitoring. With ZENworks Management and Monitoring Services you can have the system watch your network traffic and servers and alert you should any threshold be reached. This allows you to respond to network needs before they become a problem.

ZENworks Management and Monitoring also manages any SNMP-enabled devices by allowing you to compile into the system any needed MIBs to provide management and trending analysis.

What Is ZENworks Asset Management?

ZENworks Asset Management provides the ability to automatically discover devices on the network. After devices are discovered you can deploy specialized agents that scan for software and hardware components using a special fingerprinting technology to accurately determine bundles and suites on the devices. ZENworks Asset Management also includes the ability to track use of all software on each device and to reconcile licenses to those installed systems. Additionally, ZENworks Asset Management includes the ability to keep track of all changes in your system and generate reports that show you how your systems are evolving.

With ZENworks Asset Management you can keep track of these valuable resources and accruately understand where software is being used.

What Is ZENworks Handheld Management?

ZENworks Handheld Management is a system that provides delivery of security and configuration policies along with data and software to the PDA systems in your environment. ZENworks Handheld Management supports Palm, Windows CE, PocketPC, and Rim BlackBerry devices.

With ZENworks Handheld Management you can be sure that the corporate data stored on those PDA devices is secure and up-to-date.

Additionally, with ZENworks you can synchronize users' passwords, ensuring that the password on their PDA devices matches their eDirectory passwords. And to help you with troubleshooting those devices, ZENworks even provides the ability to remote control online PDA devices.

What's New for ZENworks 7?

In general, the new features for the entire ZENworks 7 family line now include support for Windows XP tablet, Windows XP SP2, SLES servers, and NetWare OES servers. With this release of ZENworks you can now support your Windows servers and desktops from a Linux server back-end.

The following sections briefly mention the new features that have been added in each of the components of ZENworks.

Desktop Management

ZENworks Desktop Management continues to improve and add new features to help make Desktop Management more efficient. Like its predecessor, ZENworks 7 does not require NetWare or the Novell client on the workstations. ZENworks 7 only requires that an agent be present on the device. This agent performs all the functions that ZENworks provides.

Application Management

The ZENworks Application Management agents have been enhanced for Applications to be able to deliver entire directories and subdirectories from the server to the workstation.

Workstation Imaging

ZENworks Desktop Management 7 imaging system has been updated to use the latest Linux kernel. Not only is the update Linux kernel used in the imaging system, but the initial SUSE boot sequence is now being used for the booting of Linux on workstations. This allows you to have maximum support for more drivers and whenever SUSE adds a driver to the system, ZENworks will be updated as well.

Workstation Inventory

The following new features for workstation inventory have been added:

▶ Additional enhancements to the software dictionary and interface have been included.

▶ Inventory of additional antivirus products including Symantec, Network Associates, Central Command, Sophos, and Trend Micro products.

▶ Quick reports have been added that can quickly query your database and provide tabular output that can then be viewed, saved, or printed.

What's New for ZENworks Server Management 7?

ZENworks Server Management has added the following capabilities:

▶ Replication of Association attributes in application distributions. This allows you to synchronize and maintain whether an application should be shown on the Desktop, Start menu, or window on all your copies of an application across the tree.

▶ Notification of when the maximum number of revisions is being approached. When the maximum number of revisions is achieved, ZENworks Server Management resends an entire package rather than just deltas. This can have significant bandwidth impact. By notifying you before this happens you can delay the distribution and prepare for the work.

▶ Tiered-distribution visual presenation of distributions in the browser may now drill down into the extraction results. From the browser you can directly communicate with the remote system and discover if your distribution was successful and, if not, why.

What's New for ZENworks Handheld Management 7?

ZENworks Handheld Management has added the following enhancements:

▶ The ability to remote control a handheld device.

▶ Access Point failover by introducing multiple Access Points and, when one is not available, automatically forwarding all handhelds to another in the system.

▶ Password synchronization between eDirectory and the PDA device. When your password changes in eDirectory, it can automatically be synchronized and placed on the device as the device password.

▶ Application and file uninstallation from the device.

What Are the New ZENworks 7 Components?

Several components that accompany the ZENworks product have been updated. They include new ZENworks Patch Management, ZENworks Data Management, ZENworks Personality Migration, and ZENworks Software Packaging. Additionally, ZENworks now includes an Instant Messenger component. These are discussed briefly in the following sections.

What Is ZENworks Patch Management?

ZENworks Patch Management is powered by PatchLink and tracks all the systems in your network and identifies all the patches that the systems require. Then, when you specify, the Patch Management server automatically transmits and installs all the approved patches to the systems that require them. With ZENworks Patch Management you can keep up with the many patches for your systems and get them where they need to be.

What Is ZENworks Data Management?

ZENworks Data Management is a delivery of Novell iFolder and provides synchronization and encryption of data from the workstation to a back-end web server. This way, all the user's data is safely tucked back on the server and can be updated and restored to your workstations.

What Is ZENworks Personality Migration?

ZENworks Personality Migration is powered by Miramar and provides the capability to capture the unique configurations that a user performs on his system, making it his own. Personality includes settings, fonts, background bitmaps, dictionaries, browser favorites, and data files. ZENworks Personality Migration can capture all these settings and apply them to a newly restored or updated workstation.

What Is ZENworks Software Packaging?

ZENworks Software Packaging is a special ZENworks delivery of InstallShield's AdminStudio. InstallShield AdminStudio ZENworks edition provides three components: Repackager, Tuner, and Distribution Wizard. The additional features of AdminStudio can be activated with an additional purchase.

The Repackager tool allows you to capture installations, much like snAppShot, but with additional features. The Repackager generates an MSI installation package that can be delivered to systems via ZENworks.

The Tuner tool allows you to construct Microsoft transform (MST) files to configure the installation of MSI files on workstations. Unique MST files can be created and delivered with the MSI files, giving a unique experience for each associated user or device. The Tuner may also be used to drill into, analyze, and modify MSI files directly.

Finally, the Distribution Wizard has been enhanced to deliver the MSI files to the ZENworks system, automatically creating application or distribution objects. The wizard copies the files to the servers and creates the objects associated with them.

What Is ZENworks Instant Messenging?

An Instant Messaging component is now being delivered as part of ZENworks. This Instant Messager component is a delivery of GroupWise Instant Messenger. This messenger discovers the users in the directory and allows secure communication between two users. Unlike other instant messaging solutions, the GroupWise Instant Messenger ensures that the person to whom you are talking is who she says she is and all communications are encrypted to eliminate eavesdropping.

Summary

ZENworks is a complete management system that can help you become more effective and efficient in managing all the desktops, laptops, servers, and handheld devices in your environment.

The next chapters walk you through the steps that you need to follow to properly install ZENworks into your environment.

## CHAPTER 2

Installing ZENworks 7 Suite

This chapter provides a walk-through for getting all the components of ZENworks working in your environment. The chapter is organized into several main sections to help you easily install ZENworks. It will be most effective to follow the steps in order; however, if you are not installing some optional components, skip that section and move on to the next.

The installation steps are written to aid in installing ZENworks in either a Windows-only or a NetWare environment. Sections unique to the specific operating system will be marked.

Prerequisites to Installing ZENworks Components

The first step to install ZENworks is to make sure that your network hardware and software meet the requirements. The following sections discuss the hardware and software requirements that must be met on your servers to install ZENworks on them. Preinstall checklists are given for you to verify that you are ready to begin the install. Taking the time to review the hardware and software requirements will help you resolve any deficiencies in your network and help eliminate problems during and after installation.

ZENworks Desktop Management

The ZENworks Desktop Management portion of ZENworks is composed of the server services, middle-tier web services, and the agents on the workstations. Table 2.1 lists the requirements for the ZENworks server, Table 2.2 lists the requirements for the ZENworks Middle-Tier Server, and Table 2.3 lists the managed workstation requirements.

Table 2.1   ZENworks Desktop Management Server Requirements

REQUIREMENT	NETWARE 6	NETWARE 6.5	WINDOWS 2000	WINDOWS 2003	SLES 9 SP1	OES LINUX 1.0
Free disk space	290MB	290MB	290MB	290MB	190GB for <100 users, 290GB for 100–500 users	190GB for <100 users, 290GB for 100–500 users
Processor	Pentium III	Pentium III	Pentium III	Pentium III	Pentium III	Pentium III
Memory	256MB for 200 users, 1GB above	512MB for 200 users, 1GB above	256MB for 200 users, 1GB above	256MB for 200 users, 1GB above	512MB for 200 users, 1GB above	512MB for 200 users, 1GB above
Updates	Support Pack 4	Support Pack 1.1	Service Pack 4	None	Samba version 3.0.9-2.6 installed	Samba version 3.0.9-2.6 installed
JVM	Version 1.4.1	Shipped with 6.5	N/A	N/A	N/A	N/A
eDirectory	eDirectory 8.7.3	eDirectory 8.7.3	Access to eDirectory 8.7.3	Access to eDirectory 8.7.3	Access to eDirectory 8.7.3	Access to eDirectory 8.7.3
Inventory database included	100MB–25GB additional disk space	100MB–25GB additional disk space	100MB–25GB additional disk space	100MB–25GB additional disk space	100MB–25GB additional disk space	100MB–25GB additional disk space

Table 2.2   ZENworks Desktop Management Middle-Tier Server
Requirements

REQUIREMENT	NETWARE 6	NETWARE 6.5	WINDOWS 2000	WINDOWS 2003	SLES 9 SP1	OES LINUX 1.0
Free disk space	160MB	160MB	160MB	160MB	190GB for <100 users 290GB for 100– 500 users	190GB for <100 users 290GB for 100– 500 users
Processor	Pentium III	Pentium III	Pentium III	Pentium III	Pentium III	Pentium III
Memory	256MB for 200 users, 1GB above	256MB for 200 users, 1GB above	256MB for 200 users, 1GB above	256MB for 200 users, 1GB above	512MB for 200 users, 1GB above	512MB for 200 users, 1GB above
Updates	Support Pack 4	Support Pack 1	Service Pack 4	None	None	None
Novell International Cryptographic Infrastructure (NICI)	Client 2.4.0, if SSL connections will be used	Client 2.4. 0, if SSL connections will be used	Client 2.4. 0, if SSL connections will be used	Client 2.4. 0, if SSL connections will be used	N/A	N/A
IIS	N/A	N/A	Version shipped with Windows 2000	Version shipped with Windows 2003	N/A	N/A
Domain requirements (if in a domain)	N/A	N/A	Same domain as ZENworks server	Same domain as ZENworks server	N/A	N/A
Apache web server	Version 1.3.22	Version shipped with NetWare 6.5	N/A	N/A	N/A	N/A

Table 2.3   ZENworks Desktop Management Workstation Agent
Requirements

REQUIREMENT	WINDOWS 98SE	WINDOWS NT4	WINDOWS 2000	WINDOWS XP
Free disk space	20MB	20MB	20MB	20MB
Processor	Pentium 32-bit	Pentium 32-bit	Pentium 32-bit	Pentium 32-bit
Internet Explorer	5.5 SP2	5.5 SP2	5.5 SP2	Shipping version
Microsoft Windows Installer	Version 1.11	Version 1.11	Version 1.11	Shipping version

If you are placing ZENworks in a Windows only environment, it is
expected that the workstations, servers, and middle-tiers are all in the
same domain.

Confirmed Windows and NetWare Server Platform Combinations

Table 2.4 shows the Desktop Management combinations (that is, the
ZENworks Middle-Tier Server platform connecting to the Desktop
Management Server platform) that have been fully tested and are fully
supported by Novell ZENworks 7 Desktop Management for Windows
and NetWare servers.

Table 2.4   ZENworks Desktop Management Middle-Tier Combinations

MIDDLE-TIER SERVER PLATFORM	DESKTOP MANAGEMENT SERVER PLATFORM	NOTES
Windows 2000 SP4	Windows 2000 SP4	Both of these servers must be members of the same Microsoft domain.
		If you want to install the Middle-Tier Server software on the same machine with the Novell Client, the client must be installed first.
		The ZENworks Middle-Tier Server must have Microsoft Internet Information Server (IIS) installed (the version shipping with Windows 2000 Server).
		The Desktop Management Server on Windows 2000 must have the following:

MIDDLE-TIER SERVER PLATFORM	DESKTOP MANAGEMENT SERVER PLATFORM	NOTES
		▶ Novell ConsoleOne 1.3.6 and Novell eDirectory 8.7.1 (minimum) or 8.7.3 (recommended) installed ▶ Novell Client 4.9 SP1a installed and configured to use the IP protocol, not IPX ▶ The current location of eDirectory (usually c:\novell) shared using the name SYS This configuration is supported only when both the Middle-Tier Server and the Desktop Management Server are installed on the same machine.
	Windows 2000 SP4	Both of these servers must be members of the same Microsoft domain. If you want to install the Middle-Tier Server software on the same machine with the Novell Client, the client must be installed first. The ZENworks Middle-Tier Server must have Microsoft Internet Information Server (IIS) installed (the version shipping with Windows Server 2003). The Desktop Management Server on Windows 2000 must have the following: ▶ Novell ConsoleOne 1.3.6 and Novell eDirectory 8.7.1 (minimum) or 8.7.3 (recommended) installed ▶ Novell Client 4.9 SP1a installed and configured to use the IP protocol, not IPX ▶ The current location of eDirectory (usually c:\novell) shared using the name SYS

Table 2.4   Continued

MIDDLE-TIER SERVER PLATFORM	DESKTOP MANAGEMENT SERVER PLATFORM	NOTES
Windows Server 2003 Standard Edition	Windows Server 2003 Standard Edition	Both of these servers must be members of the same Microsoft domain. If you want to install the Middle-Tier Server software on the same machine with the Novell Client, the client must be installed first. The ZENworks Middle-Tier Server must have Microsoft Internet Information Server (IIS) installed (the version shipping with Windows Server 2003). The Desktop Management Server on Windows Server 2003 must have the following: ▶ Novell ConsoleOne 1.3.6 and Novell eDirectory 8.7.3 installed ▶ Novell Client 4.9 SP1a installed and configured to use the IP protocol, not IPX ▶ The current location of eDirectory (usually c:\novell) shared using the name SYS This configuration is also supported when both the Middle-Tier Server and the Desktop Management Server are installed on the same machine.
Windows Server 2003 Enterprise Edition	Windows Server 2003 Enterprise Edition	Both of these servers must be members of the same Microsoft domain. If you want to install the Middle-Tier Server software on the same machine with the Novell Client, the client must be installed first.

MIDDLE-TIER SERVER PLATFORM	DESKTOP MANAGEMENT SERVER PLATFORM	NOTES
		The ZENworks Middle-Tier Server must have Microsoft Internet Information Server (IIS) installed (the version shipping with Windows Server 2003). The Desktop Management Server on Windows Server 2003 must have the following: ▶ Novell ConsoleOne 1.3.6 and Novell eDirectory 8.7.3 installed ▶ Novell Client 4.9 SP1a installed and configured to use the IP protocol, not IPX ▶ The current location of eDirectory (usually c:\novell) shared using the name SYS This configuration is also supported when both the Middle-Tier Server and the Desktop Management Server are installed on the same machine.
Windows Server 2003 Standard/ Enterprise Edition	NetWare 6 SP4	If you want to install the Middle-Tier Server software on the same machine with the Novell Client, the client must be installed first. The ZENworks Middle-Tier Server must have Microsoft Internet Information Server (IIS) installed (the version shipping with Windows Server 2003). The Desktop Management Server must have the latest versions of the JVM, ConsoleOne, and eDirectory installed.

Table 2.4   Continued

MIDDLE-TIER SERVER PLATFORM	DESKTOP MANAGEMENT SERVER PLATFORM	NOTES
Windows Server 2003 Standard/ Enterprise Edition	OES NetWare 1.0/ NetWare 6.5 SP3	If you want to install the Middle-Tier Server software on the same machine with the Novell Client, the client must be installed first. The ZENworks Middle-Tier Server must have Microsoft Internet Information Server (IIS) installed (the version shipping with Windows Server 2003). The Desktop Management Server must have the latest versions of the JVM, ConsoleOne, and eDirectory installed. This configuration is also supported when both the Middle-Tier Server and the Desktop Management Server are installed on the same machine.
OES NetWare 1.0/NetWare 6.5 SP3	NetWare 6 SP4	The Desktop Management Server must have the latest versions of the JVM, ConsoleOne, and eDirectory installed.
OES NetWare 1.0/NetWare 6.5 SP3	OES NetWare 1.0/ NetWare 6.5 SP3	The Desktop Management Server must have the latest versions of the JVM, ConsoleOne, and eDirectory installed. This configuration is also supported when both the Middle-Tier Server and the Desktop Management Server are installed on the same machine.

Confirmed Linux and Other Server Platform Combinations

Table 2.5 shows the Desktop Management combinations (that is, the ZENworks Middle-Tier Server platform connecting to the Desktop Management Server platform) that have been fully tested and are fully supported by Novell ZENworks 7 Desktop Management.

No Network Firewall

When there is no firewall in place, the agents have direct access to CIFS file systems.

Table 2.5   ZENworks Middle-Tier Combinations with Linux

MIDDLE-TIER SERVER PLATFORM	DESKTOP MANAGEMENT SERVER PLATFORM	NOTES
SLES 9 SP1	SLES 9 SP1	Middle-Tier and Desktop Management Servers operating on the same Linux machine.
SLES 9 SP1	SLES 9 SP1	Middle-Tier and Desktop Management Servers operating on different Linux machines. ZENworks for Desktops 4.0.1 Desktop Management Agent does not work (does not copy files). You must use a mapped drive from the desktop to a NetWare or Windows server outside of the Middle-Tier or Desktop platform.
SLES 9 SP1 OES (Linux) 1.0	OES (Linux) 1.0	
OES (Linux) 1.0	SLES 9 SP1	
OES (Linux) 1.0	Windows 2000 SP4	ZENworks for Desktops 4.0.1 Desktop Management Agent does not work (does not copy files). You must use a mapped drive from the desktop to a NetWare or Windows server outside of the Middle-Tier or Desktop platform.

Table 2.5   Continued

MIDDLE-TIER SERVER PLATFORM	DESKTOP MANAGEMENT SERVER PLATFORM	NOTES
OES (Linux) 1. 0	OES (Linux) 1.0	Middle-Tier and Desktop Management Servers operating on the same Linux machine.
OES (Linux) 1.0	OES (Linux) 1.0	Middle-Tier and Desktop Management Servers operating on different Linux machines.
OES (Linux) 1.0	NetWare 6 Support Pack 5	
OES (Linux) 1.0 OES	(NetWare) 1.0/ NetWare 6.5 Support Pack 3	Desktop Management Server operating in a Novell Cluster Services environment.
Windows Server 2003	SLES 9 SP1	
Windows Server 2003	OES (Linux) 1.0	
OES (NetWare) 1.0/NetWare 6.5 SupportPack 3	OES (Linux) 1.0	

Network Firewall in Place

With a firewall in place between the Middle-Tier server and the Desktop Server, this limits the choices you have because the files must be delivered to the workstation through the Middle-Tier server, as shown in Table 2.6.

Table 2.6   ZENworks Multiple Platform Combinations

MIDDLE-TIER SERVER PLATFORM	DESKTOP MANAGEMENT SERVER PLATFORM	NOTES
Windows Server 2003	OES (Linux) 1.0	Reference a Samba share on the OES server
Windows Server 2003	SLES 9 SP1	Reference a Samba share on the OES server

MIDDLE-TIER SERVER PLATFORM	DESKTOP MANAGEMENT SERVER PLATFORM	NOTES
OES (Linux) 1.0	OES (Linux) 1.0	Middle-Tier and Desktop Management Servers operating on the same Linux machine
OES (NetWare) 1.0/NetWare 6.5 Support Pack 3	OES (Linux) 1.0	
OES (Linux) 1.0	OES (NetWare) 1.0/ NetWare 6.5 Support Pack	

ZENworks Server Management

ZENworks Server Management is composed of Policy and Distribution Services (PDS), inventory, and inventory agents. The following tables list the hardware and software requirements for each of these components.

Any server running the inventory components requires a minimum of 5GB free disk space. The root server requires a minimum of 20GB free disk space. Table 2.7 lists the requirements for the back-end ZENworks policy and distribution server, Table 2.8 lists the ZENworks management and monitoring back-end server requirements, and Table 2.9 lists the requirements for the managed device.

Table 2.7	ZENworks Server Management PDS Server Requirements						
REQUIREMENT	**NETWARE 5.1**	**NETWARE 6**	**NETWARE 6.5**	**WINDOWS 2000**	**WINDOWS 2003**	**LINUX**	**SOLARIS**
Processor	Pentium III	Pentium III	Pentium III	Pentium III	Pentium III	200Mhz Pentium	SPARC
Memory	384MB minimum, 512MB recommended	512MB	512MB	512MB	512MB	128MB minimum, 256MB recommended	256MB
Free disk space	35MB	35MB	35MB	35MB	35MB	150MB	195MB
Updates	SP6	SP4	SP1a	SP4	None	None	None
eDirectory	8.6.2 or 8.7.1, 8.7.3	8.6.2 or 8.7.1, 8.7.3	8.6.2 or 8.7.1, 8.7.3	Access to 8.7.3	Access to 8.7.3	Access to 8.7.3	Access to 8.7.3
DNS/NIS	Yes	Yes	Yes	Yes	Yes	Yes	Yes

The supported Linux distributions are

- ▶ SUSE LINUX Enterprise Server 8
- ▶ SUSE LINUX Enterprise Server 9
- ▶ SUSE LINUX Standard Server 8
- ▶ SUSE LINUX Standard Server 8
- ▶ Red Hat Advanced Server 2.1
- ▶ Red Hat Enterprise Server 2.1
- ▶ Red Hat Enterprise Linux AS 3
- ▶ Red Hat Enterprise Linux ES 3

Table 2.8   ZENworks Server Management, Monitor and Management Server Requirements

REQUIREMENT	NETWARE 5.1	NETWARE 6	NETWARE 6.5
Processor	Pentium III	Pentium III	Pentium III
Memory	384MB	512MB	1GB
Free disk space	170MB	170MB	170MB
Updates	SP6	SP3	None
eDirectory	8	8	8.6.2 or 8.7.1, 8.7.3
DNS/NIS	Yes	Yes	Yes

* Management and Monitoring back-end services may only be installed on a NetWare Server. The trending agents may be installed on a Linux server.

The supported Linux distributions are

- ▶ SUSE LINUX Enterprise Server 8
- ▶ SUSE LINUX Enterprise Server 9
- ▶ SUSE LINUX Standard Server 8
- ▶ SUSE LINUX Standard Server 9
- ▶ Red Hat Advanced Server 2.1
- ▶ Red Hat Enterprise Server 2.1
- ▶ Red Hat Enterprise Linux AS 3
- ▶ Red Hat Enterprise Linux ES 3

Table 2.9   ZENworks Server Management, Management and Monitoring Agent Requirements

REQUIREMENT	NETWARE 5.1	NETWARE 6	NETWARE 6.5	WINDOWS 2000	WINDOWS 2003	LINUX
Memory	128MB	128MB	128MB	128MB	128MB	128MB
Free disk space	2.5MB	2.5MB	2.5MB	2.5MB	2.5MB	10MB
Updates	SP6	SP3	None	SP4	None	None
DNS/NIS	Yes	Yes	Yes	Yes	Yes	Yes

* Management and Monitoring back-end services may only be installed on a NetWare Server. The trending agents may be installed on a Linux server.

The supported Linux distributions are

▶ SUSE LINUX Enterprise Server 8

▶ SUSE LINUX Enterprise Server 9

▶ SUSE LINUX Standard Server 8

▶ SUSE LINUX Standard Server 9

▶ Red Hat Advanced Server 2.1

▶ Red Hat Enterprise Server 2.1

▶ Red Hat Enterprise Linux AS 3

▶ Red Hat Enterprise Linux ES 3

The agents in Table 2.9 include the server management agent, traffic analysis agent, and advanced trending agent.

Asset Inventory

Asset Inventory is composed of the discovery, scanning, and reporting components of ZENworks Asset Management (a separater ZENworks product). When you purchase ZENworks Suite, you are entitled to the Asset Inventory components of ZENworks Asset Management. Tables 2.10 and 2.11 identify the hardware and software requirements for Asset Inventory.

Stand-alone Deployment

With stand-alone deployment of Asset Inventory, all of the scanning, management, and control of inventory collection is performed by a single server and an MSDE installation is placed on that server as part of the installation. This server must have the minimum requirements shown in Table 2.10.

Table 2.10   Stand-alone Deployment Minimum Requirements

RESOURCE	MINIMUM REQUIREMENTS
Hardware requirements	Pentium 4 1.4GHz processor, 1GB of memory, 2GB hard disk storage (plus 2GB for database expansion). **Note:** The disk space noted is for a base installation. Additional space is required for expansion over time.
Display setting	A minimum display resolution of 1024 × 768, small fonts
Operating systems	Windows 2000, Windows XP, Windows Server 2003
Conflicts and limits	If you are running ZENworks Handheld Management using the default MSDE installation, you cannot run ZENworks Asset Management on the same machine. A Standalone Deployment can support up to 1,000 workstations. Novell does not support Standalone Deployment installation on virtual machines.

Enterprise Deployment

With Enterprise deployments of Asset Inventory, scanning, management, and control of inventory collection is performed by a several collection servers. These servers must have the minimum requirements shown in Table 2.11.

NOTE Before you can install any ZENworks Asset Management applications, a Microsoft SQL Server or Oracle server must already be installed. All servers must be installed on actual machines. Novell does not support installations of servers on virtual machines.

Table 2.11   ZENworks Enterprise Deployment Minimum Requirements

SYSTEM	PROCESSOR		MEMORY		HARD DISK	
Devices	<= 5,000	> 5,000	<= 5,000	> 5,000	<= 5,000	> 5,000
Database	P4 1.3GHz	P4 2.4GHz	1GB	2GB	2GB	4 GB
Collection server	P4 1.3GHz	P4 2.4GHz	512 MB	1GB	100MB	100MB
Task servers	P4 1.3GHz	P4 2.4GHz	512 MB	1GB	100MB	100MB
Web console	P4 1.3GHz	P4 2.4GHz	2 GB	2GB	100MB	100MB
Manager	P4 1.3GHz	P4 2.4GHz	512 MB	1GB	100MB	100MB

ZENworks Handheld Management

ZENworks Handheld Management is composed of the following components: Management Server, Access Point, and Handheld Client. The following tables identify the hardware and software requirements for each of these components.

Table 2.12 lists the requirements for the back-end ZENworks Handheld Management server; Table 2.13 lists the requirements for the Handheld Management Access point server; and Table 2.14 shows the requirements for the PDA device to hold the client.

Table 2.12   ZENworks Handheld Management, Management Server Requirements

REQUIREMENT	WINDOWS 2000 SERVER OR WORKSTATION	WINDOWS 2003 SERVER	WINDOWS XP WORKSTATION
Processor	Pentium	Pentium	Pentium
Memory	64MB	64MB	64MB
Free disk space	20MB	20MB	20MB

Table 2.13   ZENworks Handheld Management, Access Point Requirements

REQUIREMENT	WINDOWS 2000 SERVER OR WORKSTATION	WINDOWS 2003 SERVER	WINDOWS XP WORKSTATION
Processor	Pentium	Pentium	Pentium
Memory	64MB	64MB	64MB
Free disk space	20MB	20MB	20MB

Table 2.14   ZENworks Handheld Management, Handheld Client Requirements

REQUIREMENT	WINDOWS SYNCHRONIZATION DESKTOP	WINDOWS CE	PALM OS RIM	BLACKBERRY
Processor	Pentium	N/A	N/A	N/A
Memory	64MB	N/A	N/A	N/A
Free disk space	20MB	N/A	N/A	N/A
Software	Palm Hotsync 3.0, Microsoft Activesync 3.1	Windows CE version 2.11 or later	Palm OS version 3.x or later	DataTAC or Mobitex network

ZENworks Linux Management

ZENworks Linux Management consists of two components: ZENworks Linux Management Server and ZENworks Linux Management agents. Table 2.15 specifies the hardware and software requirements for these components.

Table 2.15   ZENworks Linux Management, Management Server Requirements

REQUIREMENT	SUSE LINUX ENTERPRISE SERVER 8	RED HAT LINUX 7.3 OR 9	RED HAT ENTERPRISE LINUX 2.A AS	RED HAT ENTERPRISE LINUX 3 AS OR ES
Processor	Pentium, 1Ghz	Pentium, 1Ghz	Pentium, 1Ghz	Pentium, 1Ghz
Memory	512MB	512MB	512MB	512MB
Free disk space	17GB	17GB	17GB	17GB
Updates	Service Pack 3	Up-to-date Kernel errata	Up-to-date Kernel errata	Update 1
Software	Mozilla 1.4 or greater	Mozilla 1.4 or greater, Rpm 4.2.1	Mozilla 1.4 or greater, Rpm 4.2.1	Mozilla 1.4 or greater, Rpm 4.2.1

ZENworks Linux Management agents function on any system that meets the Linux OS requirements.

ZENworks Data Management

The ZENworks Data Management system consists of a ZENworks Data Management Server and ZENworks Data Management agents installed on

Windows workstations. Table 2.16 identifies the hardware and software requirements for these components.

Table 2.16   ZENworks Data Management Server Requirements

REQUIREMENT	NETWARE 6.5	WINDOWS 2000 SERVER	WINDOWS 2003 SERVER	RED HAT LINUX 8
Processor	Pentium II	Pentium II	Pentium II	Pentium II
Memory	512MB	512MB	512MB	512MB
Free disk space	15MB and space for users	15MB and space for users	15MB and space for users	15MB and space for users
Updates	Support Pack 1	Service Pack 3	None	None
Software	Apache 2.0.43	IIS 6.0	IIS 6.0	Apache 2.0.43
LDAP Access	eDirectory	eDirectory or Active Directory	eDirectory or Active Directory	eDirectory

The ZENworks Data Management client functions and installs properly on any supported Windows (98, NT4, 2000, XP) configuration.

ZENworks Patch Management

ZENworks Patch Management consists of two components: ZENworks Patch Management Server and a ZENwork Patch Management agent installed on the managed device. Table 2.17 identifies the hardware and software requirements for these components.

ZENworks Patch Management requires a dedicated server with the following requirements.

Table 2.17   ZENworks Patch Management Server Requirements

REQUIREMENT	WINDOWS 2000 SERVER OR ADVANCED SERVER	WINDOWS 2003 SERVER
Processor	500Mhz	500Mhz
Memory	512MB	512MB
Free disk space	5GB	5GB
Updates	Service Pack 2 or higher	None
Software	IIS	IIS, ASP.NET services
Internet access	Yes	Yes

The ZENworks Patch Management agent functions in any supported Windows or NetWare configuration.

ZENworks Software Packaging

ZENworks software packaging can be installed on any of the systems shown in Table 2.18 meeting the specified hardware and software minimum requirements.

Table 2.18   ZENworks Software Packaging Requirements

REQUIREMENT	WINDOWS 98	WINDOWS 2000	WINDOWS XP	WINDOWS SERVER
Processor	Pentium II	Pentium II	Pentium II	Pentium II
Memory	256MB	256MB	256MB	256MB
Free disk space	1.1GB	1.1GB	1.1GB	1.1GB
Updates	None	None	None	None
Software	Microsoft Internet Explorer 5.01 or higher	Microsoft Internet Explorer 5.01 or higher	Microsoft Internet Explorer 5.01 or higher	Microsoft Internet Explorer 5.01 or higher

ZENworks Personality Migration

The ZENworks Personality Migration tool can be installed or executed on any of the supported ZENworks Windows platforms. Each Windows system must have Microsoft XML Parser 3 installed.

Installing eDirectory and IDM 2

If your ZENworks system is installed in a Windows-only (Active Directory or NT Domain) network and you don't already have eDirectory installed, you will need to install eDirectory (to hold ZENworks objects) and Identity Manager (formally DirXML, to synchronize users and passwords into the ZENworks eDirectory tree).

If you have NetWare systems only, or a mixed NetWare and Windows network, eDirectory is already in your system, and no installation is required. If you will be using Active Directory or NT domains for identity management, you will need to install IDM to synchronize your users.

The Windows server that runs eDirectory must be in the same domain as the server running ZENworks Middle-Tier server. Although the ZENworks servers can be on the domain server, it is not recommended.

As you set up ZENworks in a Windows network environment, you need to access one of the two Novell ZENworks Companion CDs. You need the following components from the Companion CDs:

- ► IDM 2 for Windows Server 2003, available on the Novell ZENworks Companion 2 CD in the `\novell dirxml starter pack` folder.

- ► Novell eDirectory 8.7.3 for Windows Server 2003. eDirectory 8.7.3 is available from the Novell ZENworks Companion 1 CD in the `\novell edirectory for windows 2k` folder.

- ► Novell iManager 2.5 for configuring and administering the IDM 2 drivers is available from the Novell ZENworks Companion 1 CD in the `\novell edirectory for windows 2k` folder.

Creating an eDirectory Evaluation License Diskette

ZENworks provides a one-for-one license of eDirectory for Windows. You can obtain an eDirectory 8.7.x evaluation license from the Novell eDirectory 8.7.x Evaluation License Download website (http://www.novell.com/products/edirectory/licenses/eval_87.html). You are required to complete some contact information to enable Novell to send you an email with two files attached: an .NFK file and an .NLF file.

Although not required, we recommend that you format a diskette, create a \license directory off the root of this diskette, and save the two files in this directory. You are prompted for this diskette/file during the product installation.

Running the eDirectory Installation Program

To start the eDirectory installation program for the server in your Windows network environment (for example, ZENSVR), perform the following steps:

1. Log on to the Windows Server 2003 as the administrator and launch the eDirectory installation program from the Novell ZENworks Companion 1 CD. A startup screen, like that shown in Figure 2.1, appears.

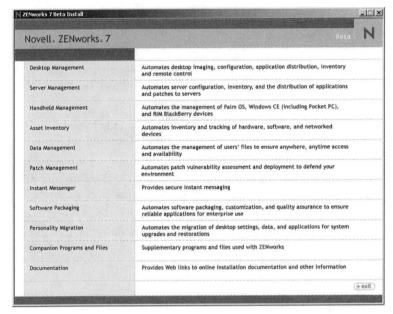

FIGURE 2.1
ZENworks Install startup screen.

2. Select Companion Programs and Files. Select Novell eDirectory to launch a program that unpacks the eDirectory installation files into a specified directory, specify the c:\edir873 directory to unzip the files, and then click Close when the files are extracted.

3. Browse to the c:\edir873 directory and launch `setup.exe`. Select Install Novell eDirectory and Install Novell Client; then click Install.

Now that you have completed the initial installation of eDirectory, the installation of the Novell Client automatically begins. The following section describes this portion of the installation process.

The Novell Client Subinstallation
The first subinstallation of the eDirectory product is for the Novell Client, which is executed by the Novell Client Installation Wizard. The following steps walk through this:

1. In the Novell Client license agreement dialog box, click Yes.

2. Select Custom Installation; then click Next.

3. Verify that only the client is selected on the modules list; then click Next.

4. Verify that NMAS and NICI are selected; then click Next.

5. Select IP Only and Remove IPX (if present); then click Next.

6. Select NDS to instruct the client to default to using NDS connections. Click Next and then click Finish.

Now that the client is installed, the eDirectory installation will proceed. This is discussed in the next section.

The eDirectory License Subinstallation

When theNovell Client has been installed, the Novell eDirectory License Installation Wizard helps you install the server license for eDirectory. The steps to follow are

1. On the Welcome page of the License Installation Wizard, click Next to view the license agreement.

2. Read the license agreement; then click I Accept if you agree with the terms of the license agreement.

3. In drive A:, insert the license diskette you created in the section "Creating an eDirectory Evaluation License Diskette" earlier in the chapter.

4. Select Specify Path to License File, browse to and select the .NFK license file in the directory you created on the diskette, and then click Next.

5. In the Licensing Success dialog box, click Close.

After the licensing portion of the installation is complete, the NICI portion of eDirectory is installed. The following sections discuss this installation.

The NICI Subinstallation

When the Novell Client and the eDirectory license are installed, the Novell International Cryptographic Infrastructure (NICI) Installation Wizard automatically runs. When the NICI installation is complete, the Windows server prompts for a reboot. Follow these steps to complete the NICI subinstallation:

1. Remove the licensing diskette from drive A:; then click OK in the reboot request dialog box. The server reboots, and the eDirectory installation sequence continues.

2. At the Novell Client login dialog box, press Ctrl+Alt+Delete.

3. In the login dialog box, select Workstation Only, log on to the server as the administrator, and then click OK.

After the first portion of the eDirectory system is installed, the server reboots and continues the eDirectory installation as described in the next section.

The eDirectory Subinstallation

When the Novell Client, the eDirectory license, and NICI are installed, the eDirectory installation continues. Continue with the installation of eDirectory by following these steps:

1. At the eDirectory Installation Welcome dialog box, click Next.

2. Read the license agreement; then click I Accept if you agree with the terms of the license agreement.

3. Select a language for the installation; then click Next.

4. Click Next to accept the default installation path.

5. Click Yes to create a new directory that does not exist.

6. Select Create a New eDirectory Tree; then click Next.

7. Set up the access to the new tree and server (see Figure 2.2) by specifying a name for the new tree, such as ZENTREE, and specifying a server object context, such as ZENSVR.SERVICES.ZEN.

8. Specify the name of the Admin user object, such as Admin.

NOTE This document assumes that you are creating an organization container in eDirectory named ZEN, an organizational unit container named SERVICES where ZENSVR will reside, and an organizational unit container named USERS where the Admin user object will reside.

9. Specify the password of the Admin user object, such as Novell; then click Next.

10. On the HTTP Server Port Configuration page, accept the HTTP Stack Ports as default because there will be no conflicting ports on this server; then click Next.

11. On the LDAP Configuration page, specify which LDAP ports to use. Because eDirectory must not interfere with default Active Directory ports 389 and 636, you need to choose other LDAP ports (see Figure 2.3).

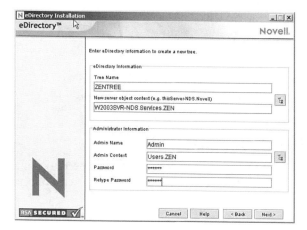

FIGURE 2.2
Specify the new tree parameters.

12. Change the Clear Text Port number to 388, and change the SSL Port to 635.

13. Deselect Require TLS for Simple Bind with Password to allow password synchronization to function; then click Next.

14. Click Next to accept the default NMAS login method.

15. Click Finish to complete the eDirectory installation.

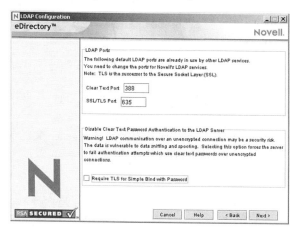

FIGURE 2.3
Configure the eDirectory LDAP ports.

16. The eDirectory installation program performs the installation on the ZENSVR server. When the program completes successfully, click Close in the Success dialog box.

Now that you have completed the installation of eDirectory. To manage ZENworks, you must install the ConsoleOne management tool. Follow the instructions in the next section to install ConsoleOne.

The ConsoleOne Installation

When the eDirectory installation is complete, you need to manually install ConsoleOne on ZENSVR. Use the following steps to install ConsoleOne:

1. Insert the Novell ZENworks Companion 1 CD into the CD drive of ZENSVR2. If the CD does not automatically start, run `winsetup.exe` from the root of the CD.

2. Select Companion Programs and Files; then select Novell ConsoleOne.

3. On the WinZip self-extractor dialog box, click Setup to launch the extraction and to start the ConsoleOne installation program.

4. On the ConsoleOne Installation Wizard welcome page, click Next.

5. Read the license agreement; then click I Accept if you agree with the terms of the license agreement.

6. Accept the default installation path; then click Next.

7. Accept the default components for installation; then click Next.

8. On the Additional Languages page, select any additional languages you want to install; then click Next.

9. Read the JInfoNet Licensing Agreement page; then click I Accept if you agree with the terms of the license agreement.

10. On the ConsoleOne Installation Summary page, click Finish to install ConsoleOne on the ZENSVR server.

11. On the ConsoleOne Installation Success page, click Close.

Now that the ConsoleOne installation is completed, you need to verify that your tree is working properly by following the steps of the next section.

Running the iManager 2.5 Installation and Setup

The iManager tool is required for configuring NSure Identity Manager DirXML drivers that are used to synchronize Active Directory and eDirectory.

NOTE We recommend that you install Novell iManager on a server where the Microsoft IIS Web server has already been installed. Although iManager can run on Windows 2003 servers without IIS installed, the absence of IIS requires that you install the Apache Web server with the Tomcat servlet.

When the eDirectory installation is complete, you need to manually install and set up Novell iManager. Use the following steps to install iManager:

1. Insert the Novell ZENworks 7 Companion 1 CD into the CD drive. If the CD does not autorun, run `winsetup.exe` from the root of the CD.

2. Select Companion Programs and Files, and then select Novell iManager.

3. On the Novell iManager Installation Wizard welcome page, click OK.

4. On the iManager Introduction page, click Next.

5. Read the License agreement, click I Accept if you agree with the terms of the License Agreement, and then click Next.

   If you do not agree with the terms of the license agreement, do not install the software. Click Cancel.

6. On the Detection Summary page, make sure that the IIS Web server is already installed (version 6 on Windows Server 2003), visually check the other default values, and then click Next.

NOTE If the IIS Web server is not already installed, the iManager installation program installs the Apache Web server with the Tomcat servlet.

7. On the Choose Install Folder page, accept the default on the installation path, and then click Next.

8. On the Get User and Tree Names page, fill in the fields

   ▶ Username—Specify the username and context (for example, `admin.users.novell`) of the administrative account with which you will configure iManager and its modules.

   ▶ Tree Name—Specify the name of the eDirectory Tree that iManager will primarily manage, for example ZENTREE.

9. On the Pre-Installation Summary page, click Install.

10. On the Install Complete page, click Done to finish the iManager installation on the server.

Setting Up iManager for Launch

Use the following steps to complete the setup of iManager for launching:

1. From the Windows desktop, double-click the Novell iManager shortcut to launch Internet Explorer and display the Getting Started with Novell iManager help page.

2. In Internet Explorer, click Tools→Internet Options to open the Internet Options dialog box.

3. From the Internet Options dialog box, click Security, click Trusted Sites, and then click Sites to open the Trusted Sites dialog box.

4. In the Add This Website to the Zone field of the Trusted Sites dialog box, specify the URL of the server (for example, http://*server_IP_address*), click Add, click Close, and then click OK to open the iManager Login page.

5. From the iManager Login page, make sure the username, tree name, or IP is supplied, and then enter the user password to launch iManager.

6. From the iManager Home page, click the View Objects icon, and then click the Browse tab in the left pane to locate the tree (ZENTREE) and to verify that the Admin object and the server are present.

Verifying the Viability of the Directory Tree

When the installation of eDirectory and ConsoleOne is complete, verify that the tree is viable by performing the following steps:

1. Log in to eDirectory.

2. From the Windows server desktop, right-click the red N in the taskbar and select Login.

3. Type `Admin` in the Username field (see Figure 2.4).

4. Type in the password of the admin user in the Password field.

5. Click Advanced to open the NDS page of the login dialog box.

6. Type `ZENTREE` in the Tree field.

7. Type `USERS.ZEN` in the Context field.

8. Type `ZENSVR` in the Server field; then click OK to log in to eDirectory.

9. To verify that you are logged in to the tree as Admin, right-click the red N in the taskbar, select NetWare Connections, and verify that a resource is listed for ZENTREE and for the username (CN=Admin). The authentication state for this connection should be listed as Directory Services.

10. Click Close to close the NetWare Connections dialog box.

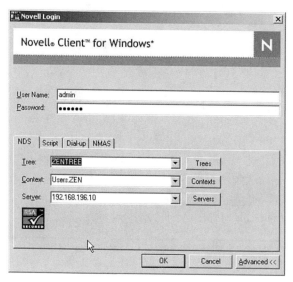

FIGURE 2.4
Novell Client 32 login dialog.

11. In ConsoleOne, verify that the tree object is visible, that the Admin user is visible in the Users container, and that the ZENSVR server is visible in the Services container.

12. Create a shortcut on your server for c:\novell\nds\ndscons.exe.

NOTE NDSConsole is a utility that lets you view the state of the eDirectory tree and the services that are running.

13. Click the NDSConsole shortcut and verify that at least ds.dlm and nldap.dlm are running.

You now have an eDirectory tree running on your Windows Server 2003.

Installing IDM 2

When eDirectory is running and stable, you need to install IDM 2 so that users can be synchronized between your Active Directory domain and eDirectory. The following steps are used to accomplish this:

NOTE Make sure that no ZENworks services are running on the Windows server when you install IDM 2.

1. Log on to the SRV-02 Windows Server 2003 as administrator and into eDirectory as admin.

2. Insert the Novell ZENworks 7 Companion 2 CD into the CD drive of the server, and then use Windows Explorer to browse to the Nsure Identity Manager 2 Bundle Edition folder.

3. Double-click `setup.bat` to launch the IDM2 installation program.

4. On the DirXML Welcome page, click Next.

5. Read the License agreement, and then click I Accept if you agree with the terms of the license agreement.

CAUTION If you do not agree with the terms of the license agreement, do not install the software. Click Cancel.

6. On the DirXML Overview page, click Next twice.

7. On the component selection page, select DirXML Server, select DirXML Web Components, deselect Utilities, and then click Next.

8. On the Select Drivers for Engine Install page, click Clear All, select DirXML Engine, select Active Directory (in the DirXML Drivers list), and then click Next.

9. (Conditional) On the DirXML Warning: Activation Notice dialog box, you are reminded to license DirXML. Click Next.

NOTE If you continue without activating the license, these components function only for a 90-day evaluation period. A license for the DirXML engine and Active Directory driver is included as part of the overall ZENworks 7 license.

10. (Conditional) In the Password Synchronization Upgrade Warning dialog box, you are informed that older versions of Password Synch need to be upgraded. Read the information in the dialog box if applicable, and then click OK.

11. On the Schema Extension page, verify that the tree is appropriate (ZENTREE), type or browse to and select the fully distinguished name (DN) of the admin user and the user's password (admin user-name is CN=admin,OU=Users,O=ZEN), and then click Next.

12. On the Select Components to Install page, retain the selected defaults, and then click Next.

13. Read the Summary page, and then click Finish.

14. On the Installation Complete dialog box, click Close for DirXML to finish the installation.

15. Reboot the server to allow the drivers to be properly registered.

When you have finished installing Nsure Identity Manager 2.02 Bundle Edition, you must configure the DirXML drivers before synchronization can occur.

Configuring DirXML Drivers

When you have finished installing eDirectory and DirXML on the server, you need to configure the DirXML drivers to begin synchronization between Active Directory Domain and eDirectory by following these steps:

1. Log on to the SRV-01 server as the Active Directory administrator.

2. Insert the ZENworks 7 Companion 2 CD into the server's CD drive, browse to the `nsure identity manager 2 bundle edition\nt\` `dirxml\utilities\ad_disc` folder, and then double-click `admanager.exe` to run the Active Directory Driver Preparation Tool.

2a. Click Discover. The tool runs and discovers data for the fields on the tool window.

2b. In the Proposed DirXML Driver Account grouping of the tool window, locate the Password field, type the password, locate the Re-enter Password field, type the password again, and then click Update.

2c. In the Create Account Notification dialog box, click OK.

2d. Copy and paste the Domain, Domain DN, Domain Controller, and Account DN into a text file, and then save the file to the desktop so you can have access to the data later.

NOTE If you prefer, you can leave the tool running. You will then be able to retrieve (copy) this data directly from the tool one field at a time for pasting into the fields of another configuration tool.

2e. Click Done to close the Preparation tool.

3. Complete the security setup for the DirXML account user.

3a. From the Windows desktop, click Start→Programs→Administrative Tools, and then select Domain Controller Security Policy.

3b. In the Tree view, click Security Settings→Local Policies→User Rights Assignment.

3c. Double-click Log on As a Service. Click Security→Add User or Group→Browse→Advance→Find Now.

3d. Select the user you created (ADDriver_zendemo), click OK, and then click OK again in the three succeeding dialog boxes.

3e. Close the Domain Controller Security Policy.

4. At the server, extend the eDirectory schema to accommodate the new Active Directory driver.

4a. In the Windows Control Panel, double-click Novell eDirectory Services.

4b. In the Novell eDirectory Services dialog box, select `install.dlm`, and then click Start.

4c. Click Install Additional Schema Files, and then click Next.

4d. Type the eDirectory admin login name (**admin**), type the context (**ZEN\Users**), type the password (**novell**), and then click OK.

4e. Browse to and select `c:\novell\nds\dvr_ext.sch`, and then click Open.

4f. Click Finish to apply the schema.

4g. Click the close (X) button in the Novell eDirectory Services dialog box.

5. At SRV-02, launch iManager and then click the Roles and Tasks icon to open the iManager Roles and Tasks pane of the main iManager page.

6. From iManager, create a new organizational unit (OU) container under the ZEN organizational container, and then name this OU container **DIRXML**.

7. In the Roles and Tasks pane, click DirXML Utilities, and then click New Driver to open the Create New Driver Wizard.

8. On the Create Driver Wizard opening page, click In a New Driver Set, and then click Next to open the Create Driver page.

9. On the Create Driver page, fill in the fields

 ▶ Name—Type a driver set name, for example **ADDriverSet**.

 ▶ Context—Browse to and select the DirXML container.

 ▶ Server—Browse to and select the SRV-02 server.

10. Click Next. The wizard creates the objects for the driver set, and then displays the ADDriver Set page.

11. Select Import a Driver Configuration from the Server (.XML file), browse to and select Active Directory from the drop-down menu, and then click Next to display the Active Directory Driver Set page of the Create Driver Wizard.

12. Configure the driver parameters that are listed (visible by scrolling) on the Create Driver Wizard by filling in the fields

 ▶ Driver Name—Leave the name of the driver as the default.

 ▶ Authentication Method—Use the default value (Negotiate).

 ▶ Authentication ID—Type the AD Domain Name (NetBios) followed by a forward slash and the Driver Account User that was created earlier. You can obtain the Driver Account User from the Account DN name you copied.

For example, enter **ZENDEMO/ADDriver_zendemo** on this line.

▶ Authentication Password—Use the same password used to create the Proposed DirXML Driver Account in the admanager.exe tool.

▶ Reenter the Password—Re-enter the password you used in the field above.

▶ Authentication Server—Copy and paste the Domain Controller name from the line items that you saved in a text file as you used admanager.exe.

▶ Domain Name—Copy and paste the Domain DN name from the line items that you saved in a text file as you used admanager.exe.

▶ Domain DNS Name—Copy and paste the domain name from the line items that you saved in a text file as you used admanager.exe.

▶ Driver Polling Interval—Specify the polling interval you want. In a lab environment, the interval should be set at approximately one minute. In a production environment, you should set the interval at approximately 15 minutes.

▶ Password Sync Timeout (minutes)—Retain the default value (five minutes).

▶ Base Container in eDirectory—Specify the container where you want your users to be created and synchronized with Active Directory (for example, users.zen). You can browse for this container by clicking Browse. If you are going to mirror the Active Directory containers, this would be the top container in eDirectory.

▶ Base Container in Active Directory—Type the name of the base container in Active Directory. This is the container where you want users to be synchronized with eDirectory (for example, CN=Users,DC=zendemo,DC=com).

▶ Configure Data Flow—Retain the default value (bidirectional).

▶ Publisher Placement—Select Flat or Mirror. If you choose Flat, all user objects coming from Active Directory are placed in the same container. If you choose Mirror, all user objects and containers are re-created in eDirectory.

- ▸ Subscriber Placement—See the Publisher Placement field to choose your placement.

- ▸ Password Failure Notification User—Leave the field blank.

- ▸ Support Exchange 2000/2003—Retain the default value (No).

- ▸ Enable Entitlements—Retain the default value (No.)

- ▸ Driver Is Local/Remote—Retain the default value (Local).

13. Click Next to launch the Security Equivalences page of the Create Driver Wizard.

14. Click Define Security Equivalences to launch the Security Equals window.

15. Click Add to launch the browser window, browse to and select the Admin.Users.ZEN user, add this user to the Selected Objects list, click OK, and then click OK again.

16. On the Security Equivalences page of the Create Driver Wizard, click Exclude Administrative Roles.

17. In the Security Equals window, click Add, browse to and select all users that are administrators of eDirectory, and then click OK.

This prevents the users from being created in the Active Directory domain and synchronized later. The Summary—Current Driver Configuration page of the wizard is displayed.

18. Click Finish.

Before the DirXML driver can run, you need to install the Password Synchronization software. For more information, see the next section, "Installing Password Synchronization."

Before the DirXML driver can run, you need to install the Password Synchronization software. This is discussed in the next section.

Installing Password Synchronization

Password synchronization allows each user object automatically created in IDM 2 to have the same password as the corresponding user you created in Active Directory. This is necessary to allow for single-login to both Active Directory and eDirectory when users log in to their workstations.

Password synchronization requires that platform-specific password policies are not in conflict with each other. Password policies that are in conflict will prevent successful password synchronization. For example, if eDirectory passwords are required to be at least eight characters in length and Windows passwords have no length requirements, users could create shorter Windows passwords that would not be accepted by eDirectory. Password Synchronization does not override platform policies.

IDM 2 lets you generate an initial password for an account based on the account's attributes or other information available through Java services. For instance, you can generate a password based on a user's surname plus a four-digit number. Generating an initial password requires driver customization, but it is a good way for you to manage passwords when you provision an account through an existing personnel management toolset.

ConsoleOne lets you set an initial password when you create a user account if you select Assign NDS Password and then select Prompt During Creation. In this case, ConsoleOne sets the password before an account is associated in NT or Active Directory accounts. This prevents the initial password from being synchronized. Passwords are synchronized only after the first password change. To avoid this delay, you can do one of the following things:

▶ Deselect Assign NDS Password During User Creation and assign the password later. A brief delay allows account associations to be completed.

▶ Select Prompt User on First Login so that password setting is delayed until the account is actually used.

The Microsoft Management Console (MMC) lets you set an initial password on a user account by typing the password when you create the account. The password is set before Password Synchronization can associate an eDirectory account with the Active Directory account, so the Password Synchronization service cannot update the eDirectory account immediately. However, the service will retry the password update, and the account will be properly updated within several minutes.

To install Password Synchronization on your servers, make sure that ConsoleOne is not running and then follow these steps:

1. Log in to the SRV-02 server as an administrator, and then log in to eDirectory as Admin.

2. In iManager, click the Roles and Tasks icon. Then in the left pane, click Passwords, click Password Policies, and then click New to open the Password Policy Wizard.

3. Configure the Password Policy.

3a. In the Policy Name field, enter a name for the policy (such as DirXML UnivPassword), and then click Next to display the Step 2 page of the wizard.

3b. On the Step 2 page of the wizard, click View Options to open the password synchronization options.

3c. Select Synchronize Simple Password When Setting Universal Password, and then click Next.

3d. On the Advanced Password Rules page, click Next.

3e. On the Step 4 page of the wizard (Enable Forgotten Password Feature), retain the default (No), and then click Next.

3f. On the Step 7 page of the wizard (Assign the Password Policy), select Browse to open the browse window, select the Users.ZEN container, click OK, and then click Next to display the Step 8 page of the wizard (Summary of the Password Policy).

3g. Click Finish, and then click Close.

4. From the Windows desktop, click Start→Settings→Control Panel, and then double-click DirXML PassSync.

5. In the PassSynchConfig dialog box, click Yes to the question Is This Machine Where the DirXML Driver Is Configured to Run? The Password Synchronization dialog box is displayed.

6. In the Password Synchronization dialog box, click Add. The Password Synchronization—Add Domain dialog box is displayed.

7. In the Password Synchronization—Add Domain dialog box, open the drop-down list in the Domain field, select ZENDEMO from the list, and then click OK. Do not add information to the Computer field.

8. On the PassSyncConfig dialog box, click Yes.

9. Highlight the Domain DNS Name, and then click Filters to display the Password Filters dialog box.

10. In the Password Filters dialog box, select the Domain Controller name, and then click Add. This option copies files to the Domain Controller. After the copy is complete, the status changes to Installed—Needs Reboot.

11. Click Reboot, and then wait until the server reboots and the dialog box shows that it is running. Click Refresh after SRV-01 restarts (if the status has not changed).

12. Click OK, and then click OK again.

13. Make sure to reboot the SRV-02 server to complete the installation.

Finalizing DirXML Driver Configuration

When you have installed and configured both the DirXML drivers and the PasswordSync driver, you need finalize the configuration so these drivers start automatically and function properly. Use the following steps to finalize the configuration:

1. Log on to the SRV-02 server as administrator.

2. From the Windows Server 2003 desktop, click Start→Settings→Control Panel→Novell eDirectory Services to open the Novell eDirectory Services dialog box.

3. Click Services, select the dstrace.dlm service, and then click Start to display the Novell eDirectory Trace window.

4. In the Novell eDirectory Trace window, click Edit→Options to open the Novell eDirectory Trace Options dialog box.

5. On the Events page of the dialog box, click Clear All, select DirXML, select DirXML Drivers, and then click OK.

NOTE Make sure you leave the Novell EDirectory Trace window open.

6. Launch iManager, and then click the server link to log in as Admin.

7. In iManager, click the Roles and Tasks icon to open the Roles and Tasks left pane, click DirXML, and then click DirXML Overview to open the DirXML Overview utility in the right pane.

8. In the DirXML Overview utility, select Search Entire Tree, and then click Search to open the Active Directory—eDirectory configuration page.

9. Click the icon to open a menu options list and then select Start Driver. When you start the driver, the Novell eDirectory Trace window displays red messages as errors, yellow messages as warnings, and green messages as successful processes. Although there might be initial errors and warnings, the final message should be green and the status shown as Success for the Active Directory DirXML log event. When the driver is running successfully, the icon changes to the icon.

10. Click the icon, and then select Edit Properties to open the Modify Object window.

11. In the Modify Object window, select the DirXML tab, click Driver Configuration, scroll to the Startup Option section of the window, select Auto Start, and then click OK. A message dialog box displays the question, "Do you want to restart the driver to put your changes into effect?"

12. Click OK on the message dialog box to restart the driver.

13. Roll your mouse pointer over the icon to reveal the status message Driver Is Running. Now that the IDM 2 is completely configured, you need to test the system to make sure that it is functioning properly.

Verifying that eDirectory, DirXML, and Password Sync Are Working Properly

To verify that eDirectory, DirXML, and password synchronization are working properly in your environment, you need to create a few users in Active Directory to verify that they are automatically created in eDirectory with the proper passwords. The following steps allow you to verify that these elements are working properly:

1. Log on to Domain Server as the administrator of the Active Directory domain.

2. Launch the Active Directory administration tool and create a test user in Active Directory—for example, TestUser1@zendemo.com.

3. Log in to ZENSVR as the administrator of the domain and as admin in eDirectory.

4. Open ConsoleOne; then verify that TestUser1 has been created in the administered container. You might have to wait for a synchronization cycle to complete before the user is listed in eDirectory.

5. Log in to eDirectory as TestUser1, verify that the password is the same as the one given in Active Directory, and then verify that you successfully authenticated to eDirectory. Another synchronization cycle might be necessary before the password is updated.

6. For completeness, create a user in eDirectory (using ConsoleOne while logged in as Admin); then verify that the user is now in the domain and that you can log in to the domain as that user using the password you specified in eDirectory.

The default synchronization rules do not create an Active Directory user until the full name attribute field is populated in eDirectory. Check this in ConsoleOne→User_object→Properties→General.

Installing ZENworks Desktop Management

This section assumes that you have already installed eDirectory and have it properly functioning in your environment. ZENworks Desktop Management is constructed of three components: ZENworks Desktop Management Server, ZENworks Middle-Tier Server, and ZENworks Management Agents.

You will install ZENworks Desktop Management components by completing the following sections. The installation is performed on a Windows 2000/XP workstation with a Novell Client 4.9 SP1a or later installed.

Installing ZENworks Desktop Management Server

Use the following steps to get the Novell ZENworks Desktop Management Server up and running on a NetWare or Windows server:

1. Select a Windows 2000/XP workstation (or a Windows 2000/2003 server) to run the Desktop Management installation. You can install from any of these systems as long as they have access to the eDirectory tree you created previously.

2. At a Windows workstation, insert the Novell ZENworks Desktop Management CD. The winsetup.exe program runs automatically. If it does not start automatically, launch the program from the root of the CD.

NOTE If you remove the Novell ZENworks Desktop Management CD from the CD drive during the installation, the installation program will stop and will not proceed. To terminate the installation process, in the Windows Task Manager, click Processes, select javaw.exe, and then click End Process.

3. Click Desktop Management to display a page with options to install in various languages.

4. Click English to display a page with Desktop Management installation options.

From this page, you can choose to either extend the schema before you actually install the new Desktop Management product, or you can choose to extend the schema as part of the installation procedure.

Extending the Schema Before the Installation

If the network environment where you want to install the Desktop Management Server is a large tree, you might want to extend the schema and let the Novell eDirectory tree stabilize before you actually install the new Desktop Management product. To extend the schema first, follow these steps:

1. Select Schema Extension and Product Licensing to launch the ZENworks Desktop Management Schema Extension and Product Licensing Wizard.

2. After you accept the terms of the license agreement and click Next, complete the eDirectory Tree for Creating Objects page of the wizard by browsing to or entering the name of an eDirectory tree where you want to add ZENworks Desktop Management schema extensions, select Extend Schema, and then click Next (see Figure 2.5).

You need to extend the schema on a tree only once. You can authenticate to a tree by clicking the Login button and entering a user ID and password with the appropriate rights.

The duration of the schema extension operation depends on the size and complexity of your tree.

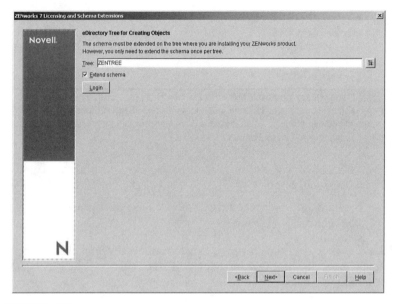

FIGURE 2.5
Extend schema install dialog for Desktop Management.

3. On the ZENworks License page, enter the license code that was emailed to you as part of the SmartCert product registration package; then click Next (see Figure 2.6).

If you do not enter a license code on this page, the wizard considers this installation of ZENworks Desktop Management to be an evaluation version. If you install for an evaluation, you will be reminded to license the product at periodic intervals. After 90 days, the product evaluation will no longer function.

When the schema extension operation is complete, you can view a log file stored in c:\novell\zfdtemp\zwextsch.log.

Performing the Full Installation (Including Schema Extension)
If you want to install the Desktop Management Server software after extending the schema, or if you want to extend the schema of the tree as part of the installation, use the following steps:

1. Click Desktop Management Services to launch the Desktop Management Server Installation Wizard (see Figure 2.7).

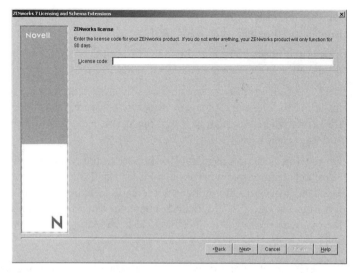

FIGURE 2.6
The License page appears during the Desktop Management installation
process.

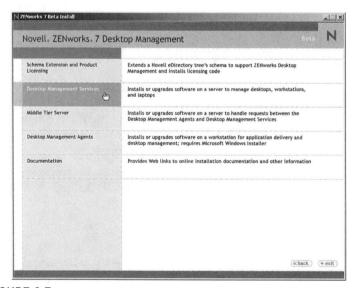

FIGURE 2.7
The Desktop Management installation selections.

2. On the first Installation page, read the details about running the installation program; then click Next.

3. Read the license agreement; then click Accept if you agree with the terms of the license agreement.

4. On the Installation Requirements page, read the requirements for installing the Desktop Management Server software, make sure that the server where you plan to install meets the listed requirements, and then click Next.

5. On the Tree Selection page, type or browse to the name of the Novell eDirectory tree where you want to install the Desktop Management Server. If you have not already extended the schema for this installation, select Extend Schema to extend the schema on the tree where you will be installing Desktop Management Server software; then click Next.

NOTE You cannot install Desktop Management Server software on multiple trees at the same time.

You need to extend the schema on a tree only once. You can authenticate to a tree by clicking the Login button and entering a user ID and password with the appropriate rights.

6. On the ZENworks Desktop Management Licensing page, specify the license code that was emailed to you as part of the SmartCert product registration package.

   If you do not specify a license code on this page, the wizard considers this installation of ZENworks Desktop Management to be an evaluation version. If you install for an evaluation, you will be reminded to license the product at periodic intervals. After 90 days, the product evaluation version no longer functions.

7. On the Server Selection page, click Add Servers to browse to the names of the servers where you want to install Desktop Management Server software (see Figure 2.8).

   You can select servers only from the tree you selected in step 5. You can install up to seven servers at a time.

8. (Optional) In the Add Servers dialog box, you can list servers by their eDirectory tree names. To install to a server, select eDirectory Trees, browse to and click the name of the server you want to

install to. Or click Add All Servers to select all the servers in a container, click the right-arrow button to move your selected servers to the Selected Servers pane, and then click OK.

NOTE If you want to add a Windows server that you might not be authenticated to, you can double-click the server icon to display a dialog box where you can enter credentials to allow for Windows authentication.

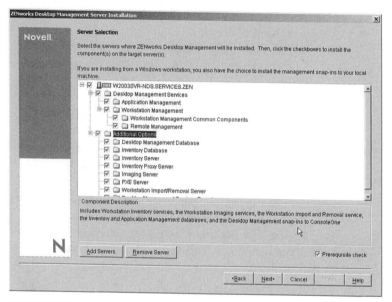

FIGURE 2.8
Server Selection page of the Desktop Management installation.

9. (Optional) In the Add Servers dialog box, you can specify the hostname or IP address of a server in the Add Server Via Hostname/IP Address field. The value that you provide must be resolvable to the name of a server. Click to begin the name resolution process and add the server to the Selected Servers list.

10. On the now-populated Server Selection page, you can further specify the services you want to install for the Desktop Management components you previously selected and then click Next to save your settings. The list of settings includes the following:

▶ Local Workstation—Even though the ConsoleOne 1.3.6 installation program lets you install ConsoleOne files to a local hard drive, such an installation will not include the Desktop Management Services snap-ins. You have the option of installing Desktop Management Services snap-ins to your local workstation by selecting Desktop Management Service Snap-ins under the Local Workstation option. ConsoleOne must be installed on the workstation before the snap-ins can be added.

▶ Desktop Management Services—Desktop Management Services (collectively referred to as the Desktop Management Server) are commonly used files and programs that enable the configuration and distribution of workstation applications and policies. These services provide automatic management of Windows applications, user and workstation configurations, processes, and behaviors.

▶ Application Management—Select this option to install software that enables the automated application distribution, launching, and healing.

▶ Workstation Management Common Components—Select this option to install workstation-resident modules that are used to authenticate the user to the workstation and network, and used to transfer configuration information and policies from eDirectory.

▶ Remote Management—Select this component to install files and programs that enable the remote management of workstations from a central console; including remote control, remote file transfer, remote execute and remote diagnostics. Make sure that the selected servers do not have the ZENworks for Servers 3.0.2 (or earlier) Remote Management component already installed.

▶ Additional Options—If you want to customize your deployment of Desktop Management Services, there are a number of services to choose from, each with a specialized purpose:

    ▶ Desktop Management Database—Select this option if you want to install a network database to be used by the Novell Application Window as a repository for data about application events (install, launch, cache, and so forth) that have occurred.

▶ Inventory Database—Select this option if you want to install
a network database to be used by Workstation Inventory as a
repository for hardware and software inventory information
collected from inventoried workstations.

▐ **NOTE** ▐ If you want to use the Inventory database with an existing Oracle or MS SQL
setup, do not select this option during the Server Inventory installation.

▶ Inventory Server—Select this option if you want to install
files and programs to enable the gathering and viewing of
hardware and software inventory information for managed
workstations. If the selected servers have the Server Inventory
component of ZENworks for Servers 3.0.2 or earlier installed,
you must upgrade the component to ZENworks Server
Management.

▶ Inventory Proxy Server—Select this option if you want to
install a proxy service that enables the roll-up of inventory
scan data to an inventory server located across a network
firewall. Make sure that the selected servers do not have the
ZENworks for Servers 3.0.2 (or earlier) Inventory component
already installed.

▶ Imaging Server—Select this option if you want to install a
Linux imaging environment to be used to create, store, send,
or restore workstation image files to a workstation.

▐ **NOTE** ▐ Install the Imaging Server service and the PXE Server service on the same server; do not install the PXE Server service separately.

▶ PXE Server—Select this option if you want to install Preboot
Execution Environment (PXE) protocols and programs to be
used by the server to communicate with a PXE-enabled
workstation and to enable sending imaging tasks to that
workstation. When you install Preboot Services, one of the
components installed is the Proxy DHCP server. If the
standard DHCP server is on the same server where you are
installing the Proxy DHCP server, you must set option tag 60
in DHCP services.

NOTE Install the Imaging Server service and the PXE Server service on the same server; do not install the PXE Server service separately.

▶ Workstation Import/Removal Server—Select this option if you want to install files and programs that add workstation objects into eDirectory (or remove those already added), where they can be managed to receive applications or computer settings.

▶ Desktop Management Services Snap-Ins—Select this option if you want to install additions to ConsoleOne to enable you to launch Desktop Management tools and utilities, to view Desktop Management object property pages in eDirectory, and to browse and configure those objects.

NOTE You can perform a custom selection by selecting one or more servers and right-clicking to display a pop-up menu with options to add Database Services, Inventory Services, or Imaging Services to all the servers you have selected. The Default option returns the selections to their initial state. The custom selection launches another dialog box that you can use to select specific components for all the selected servers. This selection overrides any other selections you might have made.

11. (Optional) The Prerequisite Check check box is selected by default. Retain the selection if you want the installation program to verify that the server or servers meet the installation requirements for ZENworks Desktop Management Services. The installation program checks the version of the server's network operating system (including any required service or support packs), the presence and version of the Novell Client (4.9 SP1a) on Windows servers and on the installing workstation, and the presence of ConsoleOne (1.3.6).

If the server operating system and support/service packs are not the correct version, the installation displays a warning message and does not continue until the required software is installed and detected or until you deselect the check box.

12. (Optional if Workstation Inventory or Remote Management is selected.) On the File Installation Location page, select one or more target servers in the Selected Servers list; then browse for or enter the volume or drive where you want the Workstation Inventory or Remote Management files to be installed. The default is SYS: for Novell NetWare and C: for Windows servers (see Figure 2.9).

NOTE If a previous installation of ZENworks Workstation Inventory or Remote Management component is detected on the machine, the existing path is displayed and dimmed. The current installation installs all the files in the same path.

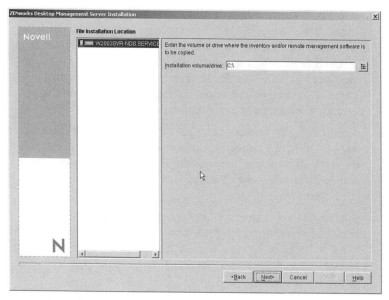

FIGURE 2.9
File installation location in the Desktop Management Installation Wizard.

13. (Optional) The Database Location Installation page is displayed if you choose to install the Inventory database or the Desktop Management database. Select a previously designated server in the left pane. Then in the Database Path field, browse for or type in the name of the volume or drive where the database file will be installed; then click Next.

You can provide a different volume or drive for each database server. For example, the volume names might be different on your various NetWare servers. However, you cannot have multiple instances of the database files on the same server because you can run only one instance of the database engine per server. For NetWare servers, this path cannot include extended or double-byte characters.

NOTE SYS: is the default for NetWare servers. We recommend that you do not select SYS: on NetWare servers because the database file can become large.

14. (Optional) The Inventory Standalone Configuration page is displayed if you choose to install the Inventory server and the Inventory database on the same server. If you want the installation program to automatically create the server package and the database location policy within the server package, and to start the inventory service on the server, configure the settings on the Inventory Standalone Configuration page.

   Select Configure Standalone, select the server or servers that you want to point to a common database location search policy, type in the name or browse to the tree container where you want to create and configure the Server Package containing this policy, and then click Next.

15. (Optional) On the Inventory Proxy Service Configuration page, select the server or servers with a port you want to designate as one to allow XMLRPC requests to pass through to the Inventory Proxy service. Then in the Proxy Port field, designate the port you want to use.

   You can configure the same port number for all servers by selecting all of them, or you can define the values individually by selecting the servers one at a time. If you want to change the Port 65000 default, specify a value between 0 and 65535. Make sure that the port number is not used by other services on the server.

16. On the Summary page, review the list of components and their parts to be installed. If the summary is correct, click Finish to launch the installation program. You can click Back as many times as necessary to make changes. If you click Cancel, no installation information is saved.

   You can review the installation log file after the installation has completed. The log filename is *datestamp_timestamp_*`zdmserver_install.log` (for example: **20040304_024034_**`zdmserver_install.log`). The log file is located in the \novell\zfdtemp directory on the machine you are installing from. This log file indicates whether any component failed to install.

You can also review the installation summary to review the selections you made. The summary is saved in a log file named `datestamp_timestamp_zdmserver_installsummary.log` (for example: `20040304_024034_zdmserver_installsummary.log`). The summary log file is also located in c:\novell\zfdtemp.

If you install Sybase on a NetWare server that has CIFS as a default component, the server IP address or DNS name of the Inventory database *server name* object might not be configured correctly after the Sybase installation. To configure the database object correctly, follow these steps:

1. Open ConsoleOne and double-click the inventory database object.

2. At the ZENworks Database page of the database object, enter the server IP address or DNS name of the server where the inventory database is installed.

Installing the ZENworks Middle-Tier Server

The ZENworks Middle-Tier server allows the ZENworks features to be delivered to device agents via this web server. Use the following steps to get the ZENworks Middle-Tier Server up and running on a NetWare or Windows server.

The workstation used to install the Middle-Tier Server must be a Windows 2000/XP workstation with a Novell Client 4.9 SP1a install. The installation is accomplished through the following steps:

1. At a Windows workstation or server, insert the Novell ZENworks Desktop Management CD. The winsetup.exe program will autorun. If it does not autorun, launch the program from the root of the CD.

NOTE If you remove the Novell ZENworks Desktop Management CD from the CD drive during the installation, or if you lose your connection to the server you are installing to, the installation program stops and will not proceed. To terminate the installation process, in the Windows Task Manager click Processes, select javaw.exe, and then click End Process.

2. Click Desktop Management to display a page with options to install in various languages.

3. Click English to display a page with Desktop Management installation options.

4. Click Middle-Tier Server to launch the Middle-Tier Server installation program.

5. On the first Installation page, read the details about running the installation program; then click Next.

6. Read the license agreement; then click Accept if you agree with the terms of the license agreement.

7. On the Installation Requirements page, read the requirements for installing the Middle-Tier Server software, make sure that the server where you plan to install meets the listed requirements, and then click Next.

8. On the eDirectory Location and Credentials page, fill in the following fields (see Figure 2.10):

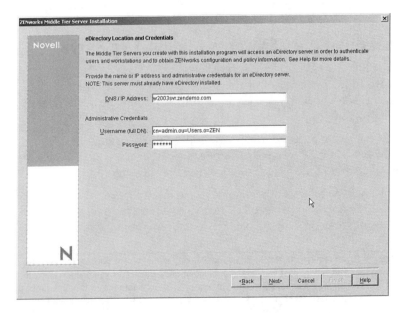

FIGURE 2.10
eDirectory Location and Credentials page of the Desktop Management Installation Wizard.

▶ DNS/IP Address—Specify the DNS name or IP address of the server where eDirectory is installed.

▶ Username (full DN)—Specify the fully qualified distinguished username of the Middle-Tier proxy user account (for example, midtier-proxy.org-unit.org). To ensure that these credentials remain secure, you can set up an arbitrary user with specific administrative rights.

▶ Password—Specify the eDirectory password for the Middle-Tier proxy user.

9. On the ZENworks User Context page (User Context field), specify the eDirectory context where the Middle-Tier Server can look for user objects that will be used by Desktop Management.

Use the context of the highest-level container where user objects reside. This value is passed to the ZENworks Middle-Tier Server, which will use it as a starting point in searching for a user.

For example, if users exist in many subcontainers, specify the context of the container that holds all those subcontainers. When a user logs in through the ZENworks Middle-Tier Server, the server begins searching for a user in the designated eDirectory container and then searches subcontainers in that container until the correct user is found.

For any Middle-Tier Server you designate during this installation, currently configured authentication domains (for example, the authentication domain configured for NetStorage) are replaced by a single authentication domain having the context that you specify here.

After the installation, you can reconfigure this authentication domain context using the NSAdmin utility. You can open the utility in a web browser (http://*middle_tier_server_name*/oneNet/nsadmin).

NOTE The installation program verifies the existence of the context (that is, the container) before continuing.

10. On the ZENworks Files Location page, select the network location where you will access application and policy files managed by ZENworks (see Figure 2.11).

The ZENworks Middle-Tier Server requires access to ZENworks files installed elsewhere on your network. As the ZENworks administrator, you define the location of these files when you create policies or applications for distribution. The information you provide on this page is used to help the Middle-Tier Server determine how to access different file systems. This decision is necessary for the installation now, even if you have not yet created any ZENworks files. The two choices available to you are as follows:

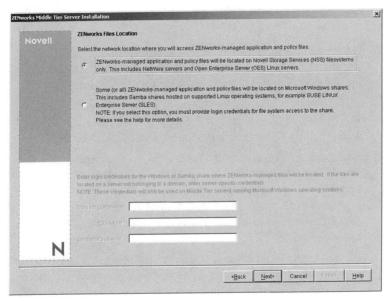

FIGURE 2.11
ZENworks Files Location page of the Installation Wizard.

▶ Select the first option button if your ZENworks-managed application and policy files will be located on NetWare servers only.

▶ Select the second option button if some or all of your ZENworks-managed application and policy files will be located on Microsoft Windows servers.

If your ZENworks files will be located in a Windows file system, the Middle-Tier Server might not be able to access them using a username and password for Novell eDirectory; instead, it requires Windows domain credentials to access the files.

If the files are located on a server not belonging to a domain, enter server-specific credentials:

▶ Domain Username—Specify the username of any user in the Microsoft domain who has Windows file system rights to the ZENworks file locations.

▶ Password—Specify the password for the user in the Microsoft domain who has file system rights to ZENworks files.

▶ Confirm Password—Specify the same password to confirm that it was entered correctly.

11. On the Server Selection page, you need to build a list of target servers that you want to function as Middle-Tier Servers. The Add Servers button opens a dialog box used to find and add servers to the list. The Remove Servers button lets you delete servers from the target list after they are added. Click Add Servers.

12. (Optional) Prerequisite Check is selected by default. You can retain this selection if you want the installation program to verify that the server or servers meet the installation requirements for ZENworks Middle-Tier Servers.

The installation program checks the version of any previously installed Middle-Tier Server software, the server's network operating system (including any required service or support packs), the presence and version of the IIS web server on Windows servers, the presence and version of the appropriate web server on NetWare servers, and the presence and version of NetStorage (2.6.0) on target servers.

If the server operating system and support/service packs are not the correct version, the installation displays a warning message but can continue. If other requirements are not met, the installation displays a warning and does not continue until the required software is installed and detected.

13. On the Add Servers dialog box, open the List Servers By drop-down list to show the options of listing the servers according to their location in Novell eDirectory trees, in Microsoft Windows Network structures, or in Microsoft Active Directory trees.

You can install the ZENworks Middle-Tier Server software to several servers during the installation. After you finish adding servers to the list, click OK.

14. (Conditional if you want to list servers in eDirectory trees.) In the List Servers By drop-down box, select eDirectory Trees to list all the eDirectory trees to which you are currently authenticated, browse the tree to the server of your choice, and then click the double right-arrow to move it to the Selected Servers list box. Other options in this dialog box include the following:

- ▶ You can click Browse Unlisted Tree to open a dialog box listing all the trees in your network. Double-clicking any one of these trees moves it to the Available Servers list, even though you are not authenticated to that tree.

- ▶ You can specify the hostname or IP address of a server in the Add Server via Hostname/IP Address field. The value that you enter must be resolvable to the name of a server.

Click to begin the name resolution process and add the server to the Selected Servers list.

To remove a server from the Selected Servers box and return it to the Available Servers list box, click the server name in the Selected Servers box; then click the double left-arrow. You can remove multiple servers from the Selected Servers box by selecting them with the Shift and Ctrl keys.

15. (Conditional if you want to list servers in Microsoft Windows Network structure.) In the List Servers By drop-down list, select Microsoft Windows Network to list all the Windows workgroups and Microsoft domains to which you are currently authenticated, browse the structure to the server of your choice, and then click the double-right arrow to move it to the Selected Servers list. Other options in this dialog box include the following:

- ▶ You must be an administrative user for a server to add it to the Selected Servers list. If you are not authenticated to a server, the object is designated by a question mark. You can double-click the question mark to authenticate to the server, and then click the double-right arrow to move the server to the Selected Servers list, provided it is a supported server platform for ZENworks Desktop Management.

- ▶ When you list servers in Microsoft domains, NetWare servers are not listed for browsing because ZENworks files located on a Windows server cannot be obtained through a Middle-Tier Server installed on NetWare.

- ▶ You can specify the hostname or IP Address of a server in the Add Server via Hostname/IP Address field. The value that you enter must be resolvable to the name of a server located in the designated operating environment.

Click to begin the name resolution process and add the server to the Selected Servers list.

If you are using multiple hostname aliases for a Windows server, the first alias must be the physical name of your Windows server. Other things to note:

- ▶ If the credentials you provided for authentication to the server are not administrative credentials, you can add it as a target server, but you will be reprompted for Administrative credentials when you close the Add Servers dialog box.

- ▶ Click Add All Servers to add all the servers in a selected domain or workgroup. Selecting a domain or workgroup selects all the authenticated servers in that domain or workgroup.

- ▶ To remove a server from the Selected Servers list and return it to the Available Servers list, click the server name in the Selected Servers list; then click the double left-arrow. You can remove multiple servers from the Selected Servers box by selecting them with the Shift and Ctrl keys.

16. (Conditional if you want to list servers in a Microsoft Active Directory.) In the List Servers By drop-down list, select Microsoft Active Directory. If your workstation is a member of an Active Directory, the domains in the Active Directory trees are displayed.

You can browse to all the servers listed in Active Directory (on a per-domain basis), browse the structure to the server of your choice, and then click the double right-arrow to move it to the Selected Servers list. Other options in this dialog box include the following:

- ▶ You can also click Browse Unlisted Tree to open a dialog box where you can specify the name of the domain you want to add and then authenticate to it with the proper credentials prior to displaying its servers in the List Servers By drop-down list.

- ▶ You can specify the hostname or IP address of a server in the Add Server Via hostname/IP Address field. The value that you enter must be resolvable to the name of a server located in the designated operating environment.

Click to begin the name resolution process and add the server to the Selected Servers list. Right-click a domain object to select one of three search methods:

▶ Search Standard Locations—Lists the computers and domain controllers at the root of the domain. This is the default search method.

▶ Search Entire Directory—Lists all directory containers where computers are located.

▶ Browse Directory Hierarchy—Lists all the containers in the directory, which you can expand and browse one at a time to find the computer you want. This search method might be useful if you have computers in a nonstandard location of a large directory.

Click Add All Servers to add all the servers in a selected domain or container. Selecting a domain or container selects all the servers in that domain or container.

To remove a server from the Selected Servers box and return it to the Available Servers list box, click the server name in the Selected Servers box; then click the double left-arrow. You can remove multiple servers from the Selected Servers box by selecting them with the Shift and Ctrl keys.

17. On the Summary page, review the location where you have chosen to install the ZENworks Middle-Tier Server software and the Desktop Management Server to which it is associated; then click Finish to begin the installation process if the summary is correct.

The Middle-Tier Server Installation Wizard launches another installation program. Wait until this program is completed.

NOTE You can review the installation log file after the installation has completed. The log file name is *datestamp_timestamp_zdmmidtier_install.log* (for example: *20040304_024034_zdmmidtier_install.log*). It is located in the \novell\zfdtemp directory on the machine you are installing from. This log file indicates whether any component failed to install.

You can also review the installation summary to review the selections you made. The summary is saved in a log file named *datestamp_timestamp_zdmmidtier_installsummary.log* (for example: *20040304_024034_zdmmidtier_installsummary.log*). It is also located in c:\novell\zfdtemp.

18. In ConsoleOne pointing to eDirectory on the Desktop Management Server, make sure that you have set up the Desktop Management Server to allow clear text passwords.

19. Reboot the server where you installed the ZENworks Middle-Tier Server software.

20. Verify that the ZENworks Middle-Tier Server is installed and running by entering one of the following URLs at a browser on the workstation:

   ▶ If the ZENworks Middle-Tier Server is running, this URL opens a web page where server statistics are displayed. You should be able to see where the request count increases by clicking the Refresh button on your browser. The URL is http://Middle_Tier_Server_DNS_or_IP/oneNet/xtier-stats.

   ▶ This URL launches a dialog box that prompts for user credentials: http://Middle_Tier_Server_IP_address/oneNet/zen.

   ▶ This URL launches a web page where a message is displayed stating that XZEN (the Xtier module in the Middle-Tier Server) is running: http://Middle_Tier_Server_IP_address/oneNet/xzen.

Installing All ZENworks Features on a Linux Server

The information in this section includes a procedure for installing all Novell ZENworks Desktop Management features on a SLES 9 or OES Linux server.

Use the following steps to install all of the ZENworks 7 Desktop Management features on a SLES 9 or OES Linux server:

1. From the terminal console, use the **su** command to switch to the root user.

2. Run mount */CD_mount_point* to mount the ZENworks 7 Desktop Management Installation program CD or CD recorder.

3. Change to the CD mount directory, and run ./setup to display the first page of the installation program that looks as follows:

```
==========================================================

Introduction

------
```

InstallAnywhere will guide you through the installation
of ZENworks Desktop Management.

It is strongly recommended that you quit all programs
before continuing with this installation.

Respond to each prompt to proceed to the next step in
the installation. If you want to change something on a
previous step, type 'back'.

You may cancel this installation at any time by typing
'quit'.

PRESS <ENTER> TO CONTINUE:

4. Read the introduction, and then press Enter to display the
   Installation Prerequisites page.

5. Read the prerequisites, pressing Enter to page down as you read. At
   the end of the prerequisites, press Enter to display the License
   Agreement page.

6. Read the terms of the license, pressing Enter to page down as you
   read. At the end of license agreement, enter **Y** if you accept the
   terms of the license.

NOTE Enter **back** on any page of the installation program to go back to the previous
page. Enter **quit** on any page to cancel the installation program.

The first page of the installation is displayed:

```
============================================================
Choose Install Set
— — — — — — — —

Please choose the Install Set to be installed by this
installer.
->1- All Features
2- ZENworks Desktop Management Server
3- ZENworks Middle Tier Server
4- Customize...
ENTER THE NUMBER FOR THE INSTALL SET, OR PRESS <ENTER>
TO ACCEPT THE DEFAULT
:
```

7. Enter **1** or press Enter to accept the default. The tree information is prompted for next:

```
============================================================
Tree information

— — — — — — —

Please enter authentication information for the tree
where you want to configure ZENworks.
Tree (zentree):
```

8. On the Tree Information page, enter the name of the local host (that is, this server's) tree where you want to configure ZENworks. This field is not case sensitive.

9. Enter the eDirectory distinguished name (DN) for the Administrative User. This field is not case-sensitive.

10. Enter the password for the Administrative User. This field is case sensitive.

NOTE Pressing Enter at any prompt causes the installation program to accept the default, which is the value shown in parentheses.

After your credentials are validated, the ZENworks License Key page is displayed:

```
============================================================
ZENworks License Key Information

— — — — — — — — — — — — — — — —

Please enter a valid ZENworks license code. (90 Day
Trial):
```

11. Enter the license code that you received in an email from Novell after you purchased Novell ZENworks. You are periodically reminded to license the product until you provide this license code. If you don't enter an appropriate code, ZENworks Desktop Management functions for only 90 days.

The Middle-Tier Server Configuration Information page is displayed:

```
============================================================
Middle Tier Server Configuration Information
— — — — — — — — — — — — — — — — — — — — — — —
The Middle Tier Server you configure with this program
will access an eDirectory server in order to
authenticate users and workstations and to obtain
ZENworks configuration and policy information.
Please provide the name or IP address and administrative
credentials for an eDirectory server.
Server Name/IP Address (zenmidt):
```

12. Enter the DNS name or IP address of the server where eDirectory is installed:

```
Enter Administrative Credentials:
Proxy User (admin.myCompany):
```

13. Enter the full distinguished username of the Middle-Tier proxy user account (for example, admin.mycompany):

```
Password():
```

14. Enter the eDirectory password for the Middle-Tier proxy user. The ZENworks Middle Tier software searches for ZENworks user objects in a specified eDirectory context and below.

```
Please Specify the ZENworks user context.
NOTE: This context must already exist.
Users Context (users.novell):
```

15. Enter the eDirectory context where the Middle-Tier Server can look for user objects that will be using Desktop Management.

The installation program verifies the existence of the context (that is, the directory container) before continuing. The Inventory Standalone Configuration page is displayed:

```
============================================================
Inventory Standalone Configuration
— — — — — — — — — — — — — — — — — —
Do you want to configure as a Standalone? (Y/N) (Y):
```

16. (Optional) The Inventory Standalone Configuration page is displayed if you choose to install the Inventory Server and the Inventory Database on the same server. If you want the installation program to automatically create the Server Package and the Database Location policy within the Server Package, and to start the Inventory Service on the server, configure the settings on the Inventory Standalone Configuration page.

Enter **Y** to select Inventory Standalone configuration:

```
Inventory Server Context (novell):
```

17. Enter the context for the standalone inventory server. The Inventory Proxy Configuration page is displayed:

```
===========================================================
Inventory Proxy Configuration
— — — — — — — — — — — — —·
XML Proxy port (65000):
```

18. Enter the port number you want to designate as one to allow XML-RPC requests to pass through to the Inventory Proxy service. If you want to change the Port 65000 default, specify a value between 0 and 65,535. Ensure that the port number is not used by other services on the server. The SSL Configuration page is displayed:

```
===========================================================
SSL Configuration
— — — — — — — —·
Do you want to configure SSL? (Y):
```

19. (Optional) If you want the ZENworks 7 Inventory server to establish a secure connection with eDirectory using LDAP, enter **Y**, and then enter the complete path and the filename of the SSL certificate. The NetBIOS Configuration page is displayed:

```
===========================================================
NetBIOS Configuration
— — — — — — — — — —·
NetBIOS Name (NetBIOS_name):
```

20. (Conditional). The NetBIOS Configuration page is displayed only if the NetBIOS name is not present in `/etc/samba/smb.conf`, and the Linux server name where you run the ZENworks installation is more than 13 characters.

If the NetBIOS name is not present in `/etc/samba/smb.conf` and the Linux server name is more than 13 characters, the installation program generates a NetBIOS name using the first 13 characters of the Linux server name where you run the installation. This name is displayed as the default value during the ZENworks Linux installation:

```
==========================================================
NetBIOS Configuration
— — — — — — — — — —.

NetBIOS Name(NetBIOS_name_generated_by_the_ZENworks_
installation_program):
```

You can either accept the default value or enter a new value, but make sure that the NetBIOS name is unique.

21. The Pre-Installation Summary page is displayed:

```
Pre-Installation Summary
— — — — — — — — — — —

We are ready to install ZENworks to your server. Press
<Enter> to continue, type "back" to change your choices
or "quit" to exit this install.
Product Name:
ZENworks Desktop Management
Product Components:
Inventory Server,
Remote Management,
Application Management,
Inventory Proxy,
Inventory Database,
NAL Database,
Autoworkstation Import/Removal,
PXE,
Imaging,
Middle Tier,
ZENworks Desktop Agent Installer
```

```
ZENworks License Key:
90 Day Trial
Schema Extensions:
Schema extensions will be applied.
PRESS <ENTER> TO CONTINUE:
```

22. Press Enter to begin the installation. When the installation process is complete, InstallAnywhere creates an installation log file. Press Ctrl+C to abort the creation of the log file. If the installation is successful, the View Readme page is displayed:

```
============
View Readme
— — — — — ·

Do you want to view the readme file?
->1- YES
2- NO
ENTER THE NUMBER FOR YOUR CHOICE, OR PRESS <ENTER> TO
ACCEPT THE DEFAULT:
    :
```

23. (Optional) Enter **1** to open the readme file. Read the file, pressing Enter to page down as you read. At the end of the readme, press Enter to display the Installation Complete page.

24. (Optional) Enter **2** to display the Installation Complete page:

```
=========================================================
Installation Complete
— — — — — — — — — ·

Congratulations. ZENworks Desktop Management has been
successfully installed to:
/opt/novell/zenworks/
All installed ZENworks services have been started.
Please see the log file (/var/log/ZENworks_Desktop_
Management_InstallLog.log)
for more details.
PRESS <ENTER> TO EXIT THE INSTALLER:
```

25. Press Enter to exit the installation program.

Breathe a huge sigh. You have now successfully finished the installation.

Installing and Configuring the Desktop Management Agent

The workstation functionality afforded by Novell ZENworks Desktop Management components is available only if you install the Desktop Management agent. This is true even if you currently have the Novell Client installed on a workstation. The Desktop Management agent installation removes the ZENworks features previously installed by the Novell Client and replaces them with selected ZENworks workstation features.

The installation program utilizes Microsoft Windows Installer functionality. For detailed information about Microsoft Windows Installer, see the MSI website (http://www.microsoft.com/windows2000/techinfo/administration/management/wininstaller.asp).

The Desktop Management agent installation program, zfdagent.msi, requires a minimum of Microsoft Windows Installer (MSI) version 1.11 on each workstation during the installation process.

If you are installing the Desktop Management Agent on a workstation that already has MSI 1.11 (or later) installed (such as a Windows 2000 or Windows XP system), the Agent MSI installation program runs normally.

Manually Installing the Desktop Management Agent

This section includes information about installing the Desktop Management agent using the Novell ZENworks Desktop Management CD or images you create yourself from a downloaded copy of zfdagent.msi.

Use the following steps if you want to manually install the Desktop Management agent to individual workstations from the Novell ZENworks Desktop Management CD:

1. At a Windows workstation, insert the Novell ZENworks Desktop Management CD. The winsetup.exe program autoruns. If it does not automatically start, launch the program from the root of the CD.

NOTE If you remove the Novell ZENworks Desktop Management CD from the CD drive during the installation, or if you lose your connection to the server you are installing to, the installation program stops and does not proceed. To terminate the installation process, in the Windows Task Manager select Processes→javaw.exe→End Process.

2. Click Desktop Management to display a page with options to install in various languages.

3. Click English to display a page with Desktop Management installation options.

4. Click Desktop Management Agents to launch the ZENworks Desktop Management Agent Installation Wizard.

5. On the first Installation page, read the details about running the installation program; then click Next.

6. Read the License Agreement. If you agree to the terms of the license, click I Accept the Terms in the License Agreement.

7. On the Custom Setup page, select the features that you want to install to the workstation; then click Next. The features you can install include the following:

   ▶ Application Management—Uses the Novell Application Window to provide users access to workstation applications that the administrator can install and then manage.

NOTE Application Management is installed by default, even if it is not selected, to accommodate future updates to the Desktop Management agent.

   ▶ Workstation Manager—Lets administrators configure and manage workstations through policies.

   ▶ Workstation Inventory—Helps administrators collect hardware and software inventory information from scanned workstations.

   ▶ Remote Management—Lets an administrator manage remote workstations from a management console.

   ▶ Mirror Driver—Provides video adapter independence and coexistence with other remote control solutions. If this feature is selected, the MSI installation overrides video driver checks and suppresses any Windows messages. If you do not want this driver, you can deselect it (optimization will be disabled).

   ▶ Workstation Imaging—Lets an administrator take an image of a workstation's hard drive and put it on other workstations over the network.

8. On the General Settings page, fill in the fields and then click Next.

   Enter the DNS Name or IP Address of the Middle-Tier Server: Specify the DNS name or IP address of the ZENworks Middle-Tier Server that this workstation will use. If you are running ZENworks in a NetWare server environment where a Novell Client will be installed on the workstation, this field may be left empty because eDirectory and the files should be accessible through the Novell client.

Enter the Port Value Used by the Middle-Tier Server: Specify the HTTP or HTTPS port number that the Apache web server (NetWare) or the IIS web server (Windows) will use to listen for the agent login.

NOTE When designating a secure (HTTPS) port, you must use port 443.

The IP address or DNS name and the port number let the workstation access the Apache web server running alongside the Middle Tier, which passes on the authentication credentials to the Desktop Management Server. The IP address or DNS name is optional if the Novell Client is installed.

9. (Conditional) If you are installing to a workstation that does not have a Novell Client installed, the Workstation Manager Settings page is displayed. Customize the settings for the Workstation Manager feature by selecting either Display ZENworks Middle-Tier Server Authentication Dialog or Allow Users to Change Middle-Tier Server Address, or both. Then click Next and click Next again to display the Novell Application Window/Windows Startup Options page.

10. Choose to launch either the Application Explorer or Application Window (or neither) on startup; then click Next.

11. (Conditional) If you are installing the Workstation Manager or the Application Window, the ZENworks Tree page is displayed. Select Limit Application Window to One Tree Only if you want to limit the user of that workstation to accessing applications available on the eDirectory tree you designate in the field.

If you want to limit the user to receiving applications on one tree, specify the name of that eDirectory tree in the ZENworks Directory Tree field; then click Next to display the Ready to Install the Program page.

If you did not select Limit Application Window to One Tree Only, you can still specify the name of a tree in the ZENworks Tree field.

This tree is recognized by the Workstation Manager as the tree where policies are accessed and applied to workstations. Click Next to display the Ready to Install the Program page.

12. Click Back if you want to review the settings you have selected for the Desktop Management agent installation. If the settings are correct, click Install to launch the installation program.

13. On the InstallShield Wizard Completed page, click Finish.

This completes the installation of the agents on a managed workstation.

Installing ZENworks Server Management

ZENworks Server Management has two main components: Policy and Distribution Services and Management and Monitoring. The following sections identify how to install these components.

Installing Policy and Distribution Services

The following steps identify how to install the ZENworks Server Policy and Distribution Services:

1. On the installation machine, insert the ZENworks Server Management Program CD. The main menu is displayed. If it is not automatically displayed after inserting the CD, run `winsetup.exe` at the root of the CD.

2. Select the Server Management option.

3. The schema must be extended on the eDirectory tree where you want to create the ZENworks objects. This menu option can also be used to update a 90-day evaluation license to a full license by identifying the tree where ZENworks objects have been created and entering a license code. To extend the schema, select the Server Management option to display the ZENworks Server Management menu.

4. To extend the schema for ZENworks Server Management objects, click Schema Extensions and Product Licensing to display the ZENworks License Agreement page.

5. If you agree with the software license agreement, click Accept; then click Next to display the eDirectory Tree for Creating Objects page; otherwise, click Decline and Cancel to exit.

6. Select the tree where you want the ZENworks objects created and then click OK to display the ZENworks Server Management Licensing page.

7. The Login button allows you to log in to the tree if you are not already authenticated. ZENworks Server Management schema extensions need to be done only once for a tree. If you have multiple trees, you need to extend the schema only on the trees where you will be installing ZENworks objects.

   Schema extensions for all ZENworks Server Management components (Policy and Distribution Services, Server Inventory, Remote Management, and Management and Monitoring Services) are installed at the same time when extending the schema.

8. Enter a license code, or leave the field blank and click Next to display the Summary page. If you leave the field blank, the 90-day evaluation license goes into effect. You can return to this page at a later date to enter a license code.

NOTE You should receive the license code when you purchase the product.

9. To extend the schema, click Finish. After the schema extension process is complete, the main installation menu is displayed.

10. Click Policy-Enabled Server Management to start the installation program. The License Agreement page is the first installation page displayed when the program has loaded.

11. If you agree with the Software License Agreement, click Accept and then click Next to display the Installation Type page; otherwise, click Decline and click Cancel to exit.

12. On the Installation Type page, click Next to perform a new installation and display the Installation Options page.

    or

    To install from a saved installation configuration file, click Template Installation, browse for or specify the path and the filename, and then click Next.

13. On the Installation Options page, click Next to accept the defaults and display the eDirectory Tree for Creating Objects page, or configure the options and then click Next (see Figure 2.12).

Three check boxes appear beneath the installation options:

▶ Create eDirectory Objects—For a first-time installation, this check box must be selected.

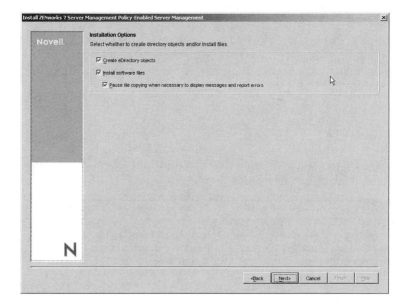

FIGURE 2.12
Installation Options page of the ZENworks Server Management Installation Wizard.

NOTE Select this check box if you want to install additional subscribers. This creates the subscriber's eDirectory object, installs its subscriber software, and assigns its trusted tree to be the tree that you select in the next installation page.

Deselect this check box if you only want to install subscriber software to a server that does not have a server object in any eDirectory tree, such as a Windows server that is in a Microsoft domain. You can identify its trusted tree in a later installation page.

If you install or reinstall the Inventory server or database, you must select the Create eDirectory Objects check box.

▶ Install Software Files—Must be selected to install the distributor or subscriber software.

▶ Pause File Copying When Necessary to Display Messages and Report Errors—By default, this check box is selected. If you want to have an unattended installation (and check the installation logs later), deselect this check box.

eDirectory Tree for Creating Objects

The eDirectory Tree for Creating Objects page is displayed only if you select the Create eDirectory Objects option on the Installation Options page. If this is displayed, you need to browse for the target tree, click OK, and then click Next to display the Server Selection page.

This is the tree where you want the ZENworks objects to be created during installation. This installation page displays only if you selected installation of ZENworks Server Management objects.

This automatically becomes the trusted tree for all subscriber servers selected in the next installation page. The trusted tree is where the subscriber receives its configuration updates.

NOTE If you select the Create eDirectory Objects check box on the Installation Options page, both NetWare and Windows servers will have eDirectory subscriber objects created in the tree that you identified in the eDirectory Tree for Creating Objects page. However, if you deselected this check box, you should identify a trusted tree for each subscriber in the File Installation Paths and Options page.

File Installation Paths and Options

On the File Installation Paths and Options page, you can create different configurations for different sets of objects. Therefore, you can select objects that might have different installation paths and different trusted trees.

Server Selection Page

Clicking Next advances the wizard to the Server Selection page. If you installed ConsoleOne on your installation machine, enable the ConsoleOne Snap-ins check box for Local Machine on this page (see Figure 2.13).

Local Machine refers to the Windows machine you are using to perform the installation, or to the Windows machine where you intend to install ZENworks Server Management locally.

If the local machine is a Windows 2000/XP workstation, you can install only the ZENworks Server Management ConsoleOne snap-ins for Policy and Distribution Services, Server Inventory, and Remote Management. If the local machine is a Windows 2000 server (with or without eDirectory installed), you can install the following:

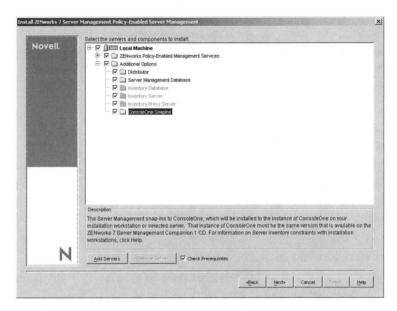

FIGURE 2.13
Server selection page of ZENworks Server Management Installation Wizard.

▶ ZENworks Server Management ConsoleOne snap-ins for Policy and Distribution Services, Server Inventory, and Remote Management

▶ Remote Management agent

▶ Inventory agent

▶ Inventory proxy service

▶ Inventory database

NOTE The Inventory server can only be installed on a Windows server that also has eDirectory installed.

On the server selection page, click Add Servers to display the Add Servers dialog box.

NOTE For more information on using the Add Servers dialog box, click its Help button.

Browse for the servers where you want to install Server Management software; then click OK. The selected servers are displayed below the Local Machine option on the server selection page. The Add Servers option displays the Add Servers dialog box, where you can browse for both NetWare and Windows servers by selecting either NetWare trees or Microsoft domains from a drop-down box. You can select servers individually or in multiples (using Ctrl and Shift). You can also select groups of servers by selecting eDirectory containers, Windows workgroups, and Microsoft domains.

To install to a Windows server that does not have Novell Client running on it (and therefore you cannot install to it locally), browse for and select the Windows server that doesn't have the client so that you can install ZENworks Server Management to it.

The Inventory server can only be installed on a Windows server that also has eDirectory installed.

You can choose to install the Inventory database on a server that does not have eDirectory installed, but the database objects will not be created automatically. You must manually create the database objects.

Make sure that you have selected all the NetWare and Windows servers before exiting the Add Servers dialog box. Also browse for the workstations where you want the ConsoleOne snap-ins installed. You must have previously installed ConsoleOne to each of these workstations.

The installation program requires an eDirectory context for placing subscriber objects. If you add a Windows server from a Microsoft domain that does not have an eDirectory object, in another installation page you are asked to browse and select an eDirectory context where the subscriber object can be created and associated with the Windows server.

If you intend for this Windows server to be used only as an external subscriber, however, do not install the subscriber object and software at this time. Instead, you can later install the subscriber software locally on that machine (which will not have a subscriber object) and then create the external subscriber object for it in ConsoleOne.

You next need to configure each server listed on the server selection page (refer to Figure 2.13).

NOTE To quickly configure a specific role or set of roles for one or more servers, select the servers, right-click the selection, and then select the role for the server. The options that apply to that role are automatically selected. Repeat for additional roles.

The following three options are all selected by default. If you want to install the inventory agent, you must also select to install the policy and distribution server.

- ▶ Policy and Distribution Server—For each server that you want to be a subscriber, select this check box.

- ▶ Inventory Agents—Select this check box for each server that you want to inventory.

- ▶ Remote Management—Select this check box for each server that you want to remotely manage.

Additional options are also available. The installation program detects whether these options are already installed on a target server and dims the option label. You can still select the check box to reinstall the component. The choices are

- ▶ Distributor—The subscriber service is installed automatically to all target servers. Select this check box to also make a server a distributor.

- ▶ Server Management Database—This is the Policy and Distribution Services database that the distributor logs to. Install it on the same server as the distributor to minimize network traffic for database logging.

NOTE You can install the database to multiple servers per run of the installation program; however, you can only install one database per server. On the Database Settings page, you can individually configure each database being installed. On the Database Logging page, you identify which of the databases being installed is to be the one database for initial logging.

- ▶ Inventory Database—Select this check box for the servers where you want to install the Inventory database to run on Sybase.

- ▶ Inventory Server—Select this check box for the server where you want to run the inventory services.

NOTE If you choose to install on servers not residing in the tree, but you have logged in to the tree and chosen to create eDirectory objects, the installation program also creates eDirectory objects in this tree.

▶ Inventory Proxy Server—Select this check box for the servers where you want to install and configure an XML proxy server. If you want to send or roll up the scan data to an Inventory server across the firewall, you must configure a NetWare or Windows server to run the XML Proxy service.

▶ ConsoleOne Snap-ins—For any server where you installed ConsoleOne, enable the ConsoleOne Snap-ins check box.

NOTE ZENworks Server Management does not support using a server's console to run ConsoleOne installed on that NetWare server. To use the server's installation of ConsoleOne, you must map a drive from a workstation to that server and run ConsoleOne from the workstation.

You can configure a group of selected servers with the same options by selecting the group and right-clicking the group. This displays the Custom Selection dialog box.

After you finish configuring the selected servers, click Next to display the File Installation Paths and Options page.

NOTE If you have invalid DNS names, you could receive an error message asking whether to continue installing using IP addresses. Either fix the DNS name problems, or continue by using IP addresses for the affected servers. If you continue with only IP addresses, you must manually enter the correct DNS hostname on the Other tab in the server object properties of these servers to use Server Management.

File Installation Locations and Options

The File Installation Locations and Options page is displayed only if you chose the ZENworks Policy-Enabled Management Services option for one or more servers. This includes Policy and Distribution Services, Server Inventory, and Remote Management.

You can click Next to accept the defaults on the File Installation Paths and Options page and display the Distributor Object Properties page. If you change the beginning of the path to a different volume or drive, all subsequent paths displayed in the installation program automatically match your changes. Each field on this page is configurable per server. You can make configuration changes server by server, or select multiple servers and make the same configuration changes to all of them. For example, you might want the same installation volume for all of your NetWare servers.

If you deselected installation of eDirectory objects for ZENworks Server Management, an empty Trusted Tree field is displayed and must be filled in. When you install the subscriber software to a server in another tree or in a Microsoft domain, and you do not want to create a subscriber object in your distributor's tree, you must identify the trusted tree for the subscriber server.

The trusted tree has two purposes:

▶ To locate a distributor that can give the Tiered Electronic Distribution configuration information to the Subscriber

▶ To indicate which tree to accept policies from

If you do not select a tree to be recognized as the subscriber server's trusted tree during installation of only the subscriber software (no object installation), your policy package distributions cannot extract and be enforced on that subscriber server because policies often point to objects in a tree.

Leave the Launch Policy and Distribution Services on Startup check box selected to have the installation program configure the startup processes to automatically launch Policy and Distribution Services any time a server is started.

Leave the Start Services When the Installation Is Finished check box selected because the subscribers' passwords are reset when the service starts.

Distributor Object Properties

The Distributor Object Properties must be configured, as shown in Figure 2.14.

This page is displayed only if you chose the ZENworks Policy-Enabled Management Services option for one or more servers.

You can change the default settings for distributors individually or in groups by selecting multiple distributors listed in the left pane.

To change the defaults for any of the distributors, select one or more distributors in the left pane; then edit the following fields as necessary:

▶ Object Name—The default distributor object name includes the server's name. If you want to rename the distributor objects, Novell recommends that you maintain the servers' identities in their names, including the fact that they are distributors.

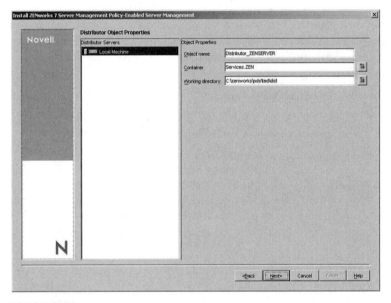

FIGURE 2.14
Distributor Object Properties page of the ZENworks Server Management Installation Wizard.

▶ Container—The location of the distributor server's NCP server object is the default. Novell recommends that you use the containers that you may have created for distributor objects. Where eDirectory is not installed on a Windows server, that server will not have a default container object displayed. You must select a container for the distributor object.

▶ Working Directory—For NetWare servers, the default working directory is on the SYS: volume.

If you change any part of the default path, such as a directory name, and that new entry does not yet exist on the server, the distributor creates that new path the first time it needs to use it.

The default volume on a NetWare server is SYS:. If the working directory has the potential to become large because you expect to have many large distributions and/or many revisions of large distributions for this distributor, we recommend that you specify a different volume. For most distributors, you can retain the SYS: volume.

Click Next to display the Subscriber Object Properties page.

Subscriber Object Properties

The Subscriber Object Properties are shown in Figure 2.15. This page is displayed only if you chose the ZENworks Policy-Enabled Management Services option for one or more servers.

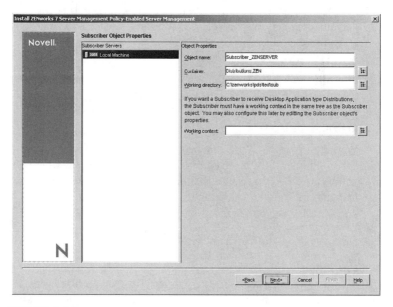

FIGURE 2.15
Subscriber Object Properties page of the ZENworks Server Management Installation Wizard.

You can change the default settings for subscribers individually or in groups by selecting multiple subscribers listed in the left pane. To change the defaults for any of the subscribers, select one or more subscribers in the left pane; then edit the following fields as necessary:

▶ Object Name—The default subscriber object name includes the server's name. If you want to rename the subscriber objects, Novell recommends that you maintain the servers' identities in their names, including the fact that they are subscribers.

▶ Container—The location of the subscriber server's NCP server object is the default. If you created containers for subscriber objects, Novell recommends using these containers. You should use the same context for all subscriber servers of the same operating system type. For example, place all NetWare subscriber servers' objects under a NetWare container, and all Windows subscriber servers' objects under a Windows container. Where eDirectory is not installed on a Windows server, that server does not have a default container object displayed. You must select a container for the subscriber object.

▶ Working Directory—For NetWare servers, the default working directory is on the SYS: volume. If you change any part of the default path, such as a directory name, and that new entry does not yet exist on the server, the subscriber creates that new path the first time it needs to use it.

▶ Working Context—If you anticipate Desktop Application Distributions will be received by a subscriber, browse for where you want related objects to be stored. You can add a working context later in ConsoleOne for any subscriber that receives Desktop Application Distributions.

Click Next to display the Database Settings page.

Database Settings

Figure 2.16 shows the Database Settings page. This page is displayed only if you chose to install the Policy and Distribution Services database (the Server Management Database option) or the Server Inventory database (the Inventory Database option) on a server.

Click Next to accept the defaults, or—for each database being installed—edit the applicable fields:

NOTE You can multiple-select databases to provide the same information for each of them.

▶ Database Path—The default for NetWare servers is SYS: and for Windows servers is C:, which you can change.

▶ Object Name—The default name is Server Management Database *server name*, which you can change. However, if you select the same container for all database objects, each must have a unique object name. A database object is not created for the Server Inventory database.

▶ Container—The default container is where the server's NCP server object resides. Novell recommends that you use the container that you created for database objects. For ease of management, Novell also recommends that you place all database objects in the same container.

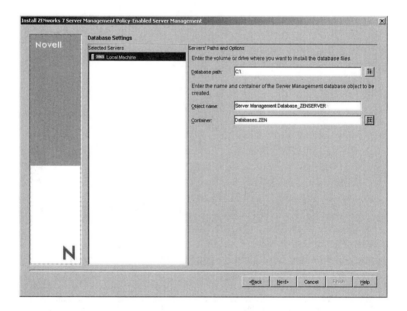

FIGURE 2.16
Database Settings Properties page of the ZENworks Server Management Installation Wizard.

Click Next and continue with the applicable section for the installation page that is displayed next.

Inventory Standalone Configuration

The Inventory Standalone Configuration page is shown in Figure 2.17. This page is displayed only if you chose to install Inventory Server and the Inventory Database on the same server.

To automatically create the server package and start the Inventory Services, click the Configure Standalone box to enable it. You can select one or more Inventory servers in the left pane to have the same configuration.

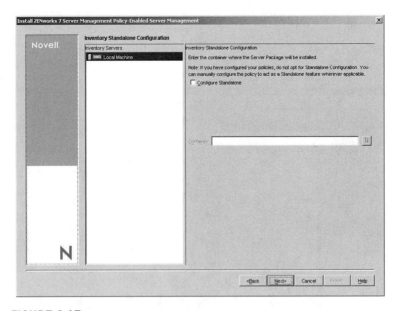

FIGURE 2.17
Inventory Standalone Configuration page of the ZENworks Server Management Installation Wizard.

> **NOTE** If you have already configured server package policies for these servers, do not enable the Configure Standalone check box. You can manually configure the policy to act as a standalone feature wherever applicable.

To specify the container for the server package object, browse for and select the container. You can select one or more Inventory servers in the left pane to assign the same container for creating the server package.

Inventory Proxy Service Configuration

This page is displayed only if you chose the Inventory Proxy Server option for one or more servers. To configure the port number of the inventory proxy service, specify the port number in the Proxy Port field, if you will not use the default port of 65000.

You can select one or more inventory proxy servers in the left pane to assign the same port number. You must specify a value between 0 and 65535. Make sure that the port number is not used by other services on the server.

Remote Management Configuration

The Remote Management Configuration options are shown in Figure 2.18. This page is displayed only if you chose the Remote Management option for one or more Windows servers.

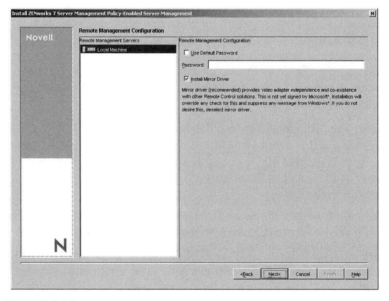

FIGURE 2.18
The Remote Management Configuration page of the ZENworks Server Management Installation Wizard.

Use this dialog box to configure the password for the Remote Management agent and install Mirror Driver on the managed server. You can either use the default password or specify a password. This password is used for establishing a Remote Management session with the managed servers.

To set the default password for the Remote Management agent, select the Use Default Password check box. The default password is novell.

To use a password other than the default password, specify another password in the Password field.

You should use a password of 10 or fewer ASCII (nonextended) characters. The password is case sensitive and cannot be blank. You can choose to proceed without specifying any password, but you will not be able to establish the remote control session with the server.

NOTE If a previous installation of ZENworks Remote Management agent is detected on the machine and a password is set, the Password field is not displayed.

You can install Mirror Driver only if your target server is a Windows 2000/2003 server. Mirror Driver provides video adapter independence and coexistence with other remote control solutions. If this check box is selected, InstallShield overrides video driver checks and suppresses any Windows messages. If you do not want this driver, you can deselect it (optimization will be disabled).

Policy and Distribution Services Database Logging

The Policy and Distribution Services Database Logging options are shown in Figure 2.19. This page is displayed only if you chose to install the Policy and Distribution Services database (the Server Management Database option) on a server.

This page eliminates the need to configure a ZENworks database policy (in the service location package), so that Server Management can begin logging to a database immediately after installing.

At your convenience after installation, you can set up the other installed databases by configuring service location packages for each of them so that their distributors can use them.

To determine logging for a Server Management database that you configured in a previous installation page, select one of the following:

▶ Log to an Existing Server Management Database—Select an existing database file for logging by browsing for and selecting the database object instead of logging to one of the databases being installed.

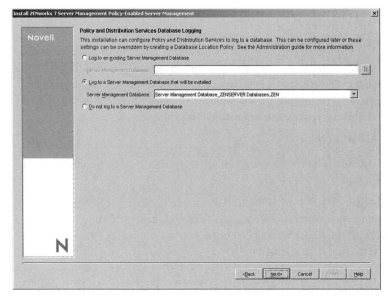

FIGURE 2.19
Policy and Distributions Services Database Logging page of the ZENworks
Server Management Installation Wizard.

▶ Log to a Server Management Database That Will Be Installed—One
of the database objects that you configured in a previous installation page is displayed. However, you can select a different database
object that is being installed by clicking the down arrow.

▶ Do Not Log to a Server Management Database—You can elect to
not log to a database at this time, even though you have configured
a database in the previous installation page.

After making your choice, click Next.

Installation Summary

To save the current installation configuration for future use, click the
Save the Following Configuration check box; then specify a path and filename for the template file.

NOTE You can use this template file to repeat the ZENworks Server Management
installation. It can save time in re-entering information and reselecting servers. When
you rerun the installation using a template, you can make changes to the fields and
selected servers in the installation pages populated by the template.

On the Installation Summary page, click Finish to begin the installation process. You can click Back to make changes if you discover errors or omissions in the summary.

After the installation program has finished, review the installation log file to determine whether any components failed to install. The log file is located in the installation machine's temporary directory as determined in its Windows environment settings. For example:

```
c:\temp\_resnnn.txt
```

where *nnn* is increased incrementally each time a new installation log is created.

After successfully installing the software, click Exit to close the main installation program. At this time, Server Management objects have been created, the software has been installed, and the Server Management agents should be starting.

Web-based Management for Policy and Distribution Services

You can use Novell iManager 2.0.2 in addition to ConsoleOne 1.3.6 to make some of the Tiered Electronic Distribution administration and agent monitoring tasks easier. iManager enables you to perform Policy and Distribution Services tasks from any location where a supported version of Internet Explorer is available.

To install the Policy and Distribution Services plug-ins for iManager, follow these steps:

1. On the installation machine, insert the ZENworks Server Management Program CD. The startup page is displayed. If the startup page is not automatically displayed after inserting the CD, run `winsetup.exe` at the root of the CD.

2. Click Web-Based Management Components to display the License Agreement page.

3. Accept the license agreement; then click Next to view the Login Information page.

4. Fill in the following fields (see Figure 2.20):

   ▶ DNS/IP Address—Specify the address of the server where iManager is installed.

▶ Port—Specify the port number to use when communicating with iManager. It will most likely be 443 if SSL is used; if not, use 8080.

▶ Use SSL—By default, this check box is not selected. If you have iManager configured to use SSL, you should enable this check box.

▶ iManager Username—Specify the iManager (fully distinguished) login name of the user with rights to iManager. This must be entered in the format indicated (for example, cn=admin.o= novell). Installation cannot continue if the username cannot authenticate.

▶ iManager Password—Specify the iManager password of the user running the installation program.

▶ Install the Policy and Distribution Services Plug-ins to Novell iManager—Select the check box to install the Remote Web Console and Tiered Electronic Distribution plug-ins to iManager so that you can manage these components from a web browser.

▶ Install the ZENworks Certificate Authority—Select the check box to install the ZENworks certificate authority servlet for interserver communications security. This provides additional security to ensure that data received from outside your secured network is from a trusted source, that it has not been tampered with en route, and that the data received can be trusted by other machines. This is accomplished through the use of signed security certificates and digital signatures.

5. Click Next to view the Summary page. The installation summary indicates that the selected web components are installed to the Tomcat installation directory.

6. Click Finish.

7. When the installation is complete, click Yes to view the installation log file.

8. After successfully installing the iManager plug-ins, close the log file.

9. For iManager to recognize the new plug-ins, stop Tomcat and then restart Tomcat.

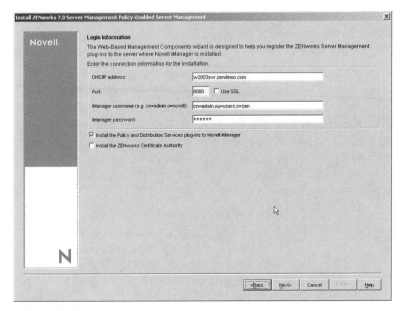

FIGURE 2.20
Login Information page for the installation of web-based components of ZENworks Server Management.

This completes the installation of the Server Management web components into iManager.

Installation on Linux and Solaris

This section provides instructions for installing Novell ZENworks Server Management on Linux or Solaris servers. The Policy and Distribution Services component is supported on the Linux and Solaris platforms; however, the Server Inventory and Remote Management components are not.

If your network also includes NetWare and Windows servers, it is easiest to install Policy and Distribution Services to one of those platforms first because the database files must be created on NetWare or Windows servers. The database stores log messages for reporting purposes, detailing the successes and failures of distribution processing. If necessary, you can install the Policy and Distribution Services software on the Linux or Solaris servers first and then create the databases afterward on the NetWare or Windows servers.

An installation script on the ZENworks Server Management Program CD is used to install the Linux or Solaris version of the software on a single Linux or Solaris server. It also creates the necessary ZENworks objects in Novell eDirectory.

The most straightforward way to run this script is to insert the Program CD into the CD drive of the Linux or Solaris server where you want to install Policy and Distribution Services. Installation solutions that eliminate physically moving from server to server are left to the discretion of the Linux or Solaris administrator.

The Linux or Solaris server where you install Policy-Enabled Server Management can function as a distributor, subscriber, or both.

At the Linux or Solaris server where you want to install Policy and Distribution Services, do the following:

1. Log in as root.

2. If you are running X Windows on the Linux or Solaris server, open an XTerm window.

3. Place the ZENworks Server Management Program CD in the server's CD drive.

4. To run the Policy and Distribution Services installation script, do one of the following in an XTerm window (*platform* is either Linux or Solaris):

   ▶ Red Hat Linux—/mnt/cdrom/ZfS/TedPol/*platform*/zfs-pds-install

   ▶ SUSE LINUX—/media/cdrom/ZfS/TedPol/*platform*/zfs-pds-install

5. Change to the directory where the Policy and Distribution Services installation script is located (*device_directory* represents the mount point for the CD device and *platform* is either Linux or Solaris):

   `cd /device_directory/ZfS/TedPol/platform`

   Then enter

   `./zfs-pds-install`

6. Press Enter to display the license agreement, press the spacebar to scroll through the license agreement, press Y, and then press Enter to accept the license agreement. The script installs software from the j2re and novell-zen-zfs RPM files.

7. To configure Server Management, respond to the prompts as they are displayed. Any information displayed within parentheses and before the colon represents defaults accepted if you press the Enter key. However, you can specify your own information before pressing Enter if the displayed default is not correct.

NOTE If you are using an XTerm window, it should be opened wide enough so that any entry you might make will fit on one line. If your entry wraps, and you need to backspace to change it, you can only backspace to the beginning of the wrapped line. If that happens, press Enter to display the script prompt again if the information you had entered does not represent an acceptable entry.

8. Specify the DNS name of a server where a replica of the eDirectory tree exists.

9. Enter the user DN that has admin rights to the root of the tree.

10. Enter the admin user's password. Nothing is displayed as you type the password to indicate the characters you are typing.

11. If you have specified a correct username and password, the message "Authentication successful" and the tree's name are displayed.

12. If the correct DNS name is displayed within the parentheses, press Enter to accept it. If the correct name is not displayed, enter the correct DNS name before pressing Enter.

NOTE If you have DNS set up correctly, the DNS name of the Linux or Solaris server where this script is running should be displayed within the parentheses.

13. If you want this server to be a distributor, press **Y** and then press Enter.

14. Enter the distributor object's name.

15. Enter an existing eDirectory container where the distributor object can be created.

16. Enter the subscriber object's name.

17. Enter an existing eDirectory container where the subscriber object can be created.

18. If you already have a ZENworks database installed in your network and want this server to log to it, enter the DN of the database object.

19. Review the information displayed for how to start the Policy and Distribution agent and how to reconfigure if the service does not start.

20. To verify that the agent is running, enter the following:

    `/etc/init.d/novell-zfs status`

    The following agent should be listed:

    Novell ZENworks Server Management

    If the agent does not start, review the zfs-startup.log file in the /var/opt/novell/log/zenworks directory.

If the installation is successful, repeat these steps on each Linux server.

Installing ZENworks Server Management and Monitoring Services

This section provides instructions to help you install Novell ZENworks Management and Monitoring Services on NetWare and Windows platforms. The steps to accomplish this are as follows:

1. If you haven't already done so, log in with Admin or equivalent rights to the target management server and the container containing the target management server.

2. If Sybase is running on the server on which the database is installed, quit the Sybase engine. To quit Sybase, go to the server console, and enter **Q** on the Sybase screen.

3. Insert the ZENworks Server Management Program CD. The startup page appears. If the startup page is not automatically launched after inserting the CD, you can launch it by running **winsetup.exe** at the root of the CD.

4. If you have not already done so, extend the schema. The schema must be extended on the eDirectory tree where you want to create the ZENworks objects.

5. Click Management and Monitoring Services→Site Management Services and Agents. If you restart the target Management server after you mapped a drive at the workstation, the installation might no longer recognize the mapped drive. Detach the tree from NetWare connection, disconnect the mapped drive, and remap the volume.

100

NOTE Novell recommends that you do not install on the SYS: volume of your target Management server.

6. Click Next at the Welcome screen.

7. If you agree with the software license agreement, click Yes; otherwise, click No and then click Exit Setup to exit.

8. Select the desired ZENworks Server Management components.

NOTE You need Admin or equivalent rights to target servers. Create a shared folder on all Windows 2000/2003 servers where you are installing the ZENworks agents.

9. Click Next.

10. Select a NetWare server to a management site server, specify the location (volume and path) where the software should be installed, and then click Next.

11. Enter the license code if you have not already done so when extending the schema; then Click Next.

12. Specify the database file path.

NOTE If the selected server has 4GB RAM or more, the following error message might be displayed: "Management Site Server requires a minimum of 512 MB of RAM for proper functioning. The server you have selected does not have 512 MB of RAM." Ignore the message.

13. If you are installing Management and Monitoring Services for the first time, select the option to provide the copy of the empty database files. If you want to copy Management and Monitoring Services Novell ConsoleOne snap-ins to the Management Site Server ConsoleOne, select the option to copy the ConsoleOne snap-ins to the Management Site Server.

14. If you do not need to reconfigure your discovery parameters beyond the default settings (for example, using SNMP community names other than PUBLIC), start the autodiscovery process and the back-end services:

    ▶ To start the autodiscovery process, select Start the Autodiscovery Process.

    ▶ To start the back-end services, select Start the Backend Services on the Server.

15. Specify a name for the service locator object and specify the context. Other management objects also need to be created in this context. If multiple management sites are used, specify a context that is readily accessible. The default name and context are provided based on the management server you selected in step 10.

16. Click Next.

17. If you selected to install only Server Management Agent, Traffic Analysis Agent, or Advanced Trending Agent in step 8, you need to select the site server or specify the IP address, which is used for updating the destination of the traps.

18. Select the NetWare and Windows 2000/2003 servers, the agents to install on each server, and the destination folder for the software; then click Next.

19. Review the summary list of selections you made in the preceding steps. To change a setting, click Back. Otherwise, click Finish to start the installation.

NOTE For managed servers on NetWare, the ZENworks agents are automatically started. For managed servers on Windows 2000/2003, you must restart Windows 2000/2003 after you install the agents.

20. If you chose not to start all the back-end services and the autodiscovery process during installation, you need to manually start the back-end services and the autodiscovery process after the installation is complete. To manually start the services, enter `startmms` at the command prompt.

This completes the installation of the Management and Monitoring services. Now you need to install the snap-ins into the Novell ConsoleOne management tool to manage the system.

Installing the ConsoleOne Snap-Ins

You can install multiple management consoles for accessing data on a management server. You must have Admin rights to the workstation to install the management console software on a Windows 2000/XP workstation.

To install the ZENworks Server Management ConsoleOne software, follow these steps:

1. If you want to install to a remote server, you need to log in as an administrator or a user with Admin equivalent rights.

2. Insert the ZENworks Server Management Program CD. If the start-up page is not automatically launched after inserting the CD, you can launch it by running `winsetup.exe` at the root of the CD.

3. Click Management and Monitoring Services→Site Management ConsoleOne Snap-ins.

4. Specify a destination folder for the snap-ins or click Next to accept the default destination folder. The snap-in files are installed.

5. Select to view the Readme file; then click Finish.

This completes the installation of the plug-ins into ConsoleOne.

Installation on Linux

This section provides instructions for installing the following agents of Management and Monitoring Services on Linux servers: Server Management agent and Advance Trending agent.

You can install Management and Monitoring Services' agents on Linux servers using the Linux installation script on the ZENworks Server Management Program CD. The installation script is used to install on a single Linux server.

This section provides basic instructions on installing the Management and Monitoring Services' agents on Linux servers. Before you begin this process, you should thoroughly understand and plan your implementation.

You can use the Management and Monitoring Services installation script to install the following agents on a single Linux server:

▶ Linux Management agent—Manages and monitors Linux servers. This includes fault management and performance management.

▶ Advanced Trending agent—Collects the trend data for SNMP variables. This includes threshold configuration and SNMP Trap generation.

All the examples provided in the installation steps are case sensitive. Make sure that you copy the values as written in the installation steps.

After you install Management and Monitoring Services' agents on Linux, you must configure the SNMP service on your Linux machine.

At the Linux server where you want to install Management and Monitoring Services' agents, follow these steps:

1. Log in as root.

2. Place the ZENworks Server Management Program CD in the CD drive. If automount does not occur, mount the CD drive manually.

3. If you are running X Windows, open an XTerm window on the Linux server console.

4. In the server prompt, change to the directory where the Management and Monitoring Services installation script is located:

   cd /*device_directory*/ZfS/SvrMgmt/mms/*platform*

   where *device_directory* represents the mount point for the CD device, and *platform* is Linux.

   The installation script is named

   MMS_Linux_Install.pl

NOTE The capitalization used for the examples in this step is used throughout this section for case-sensitive text that must be typed exactly as provided in the example.

5. To run the Management and Monitoring Services installation script, enter the following:

   ./MMS_Linux_Install.pl

6. The Welcome page displays; press Enter to display the next page.

7. Press Enter to display the license agreement, press the Spacebar to scroll through the license agreement, type **Y**, and then press Enter to accept the license agreement.

8. Type one of the following numbers, separated by a space or a comma, to specify what you want to install:

   ▶ 1 Linux Management agent

   ▶ 2 Advanced Trending agent

   ▶ 3 Both

For example, type **3** and then press Enter. The Linux Management agent, Advanced Trending agent, or both are installed based on the option you select.

9. To confirm your selection, type **Y** and then press Enter. The installation script uses the Red Hat Package Manager (RPM) to install the program files. Installation progress displays on the page.

10. If you selected to install the Advanced Trending agent in step 8, at the end of installation, specify the IP address of the server and the community string where the traps need to be sent; then type **Q** to quit. You can also add multiple trap targets.

    You can manually add the trap targets by editing the snmpd.conf file used by the snmpd master agent. For you to manage alarms from ConsoleOne, you must specify the IP address of the destination machine that will be your site server. You can also specify multiple IP addresses.

    For Linux Management agent, you need to manually edit the configuration file.

11. Press Enter to continue.

12. Review the log file to determine the success or failure status of the installation. The installation script logs all the actions in the /var/opt/novell/zenworks/log/zfs-mms-install.log file. Open this log file to verify whether Management and Monitoring Services is installed successfully on the Linux server.

13. If the installation was successful, repeat these steps for each Linux server.

This completes the installation of the services on a Linux system.

Installing ZENworks Patch Management

ZENworks Patch Management requires a dedicated server and is installed by doing the following:

1. Place the product CD into your computer, and you will see an AUTORUN screen. Select Patch Management. Select ZENworks Patch Management.

2. Click the Next button at the Welcome Screen to begin the installation process.

3. The System Requirements for Installation screen details the system requirements. The installation program checks many of these requirements automatically and does not allow you to continue if the minimum requirements are not met. Click Next to continue (see Figure 2.21).

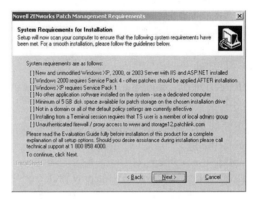

FIGURE 2.21
System Requirements for ZENworks Patch Management Installation Wizard.

4. Read the license agreement for the Update Server software and Patch Subscription Service. Click Yes to acknowledge the agreement.

5. Complete all the information within the Subscription Information (see Figure 2.22) area fully because this will be used by PatchLink to identify you through your automatic subscription. Your serial number is delivered as part of the purchase of ZENworks Patch Management. If you are performing a product evaluation, you need to obtain your own unique product serial number from Novell. Before proceeding, make note of your product serial number and keep it in a safe place. You will be required to use it to reinstall your server in the future when hardware upgrades occur, as well as to install Update agents across your network. Click Next to continue.

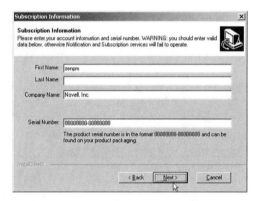

FIGURE 2.22
Subscription Information dialog for the ZENworks Patch Management
Installation Wizard.

6. By default your ZENworks Patch Management Server will be installed into the Program Files directory on your operating system drive. To place it elsewhere, click the Browse button next to the Destination Location to identify your new preferred install location. The target drive is the location where all packages will be downloaded, and because Service Packs can take up a lot of space, the drive must continue to have a large amount of available space over time for the system to cache new critical packages as they become available. Click Next to continue.

7. In the Email Address field enter the person who will be used as the primary contact person to receive email notifications from the PatchLink Update Server after it is completely installed (see Figure 2.23).

   SMTP Host is the name of your Internet mail server, usually mail.company.com or similar, which must have SMTP relay capability enabled. This mail server will be used to distribute email notifications from the system to one or more network administrators who use the system. If you don't know this information, you can leave it blank; however, no email notifications can be sent until this information is completed after installation. Click Next to continue.

8. Enter the password for the PatchLink user, which will be automatically created and can be used to log in to this machine to manage patch updates to all computers. Make sure that the password chosen meets your current effective policy restrictions for Local Computer user accounts. Click Next to continue.

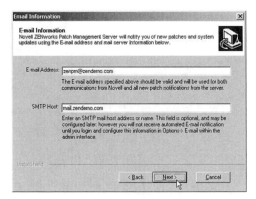

FIGURE 2.23
Email Information dialog in the ZENworks Patch Management Installation Wizard.

NOTE Make a note of your password at this time. After the product is installed, log in with username PatchLink and your password to start managing your network's patch configuration.

---

9. If your local area network uses a proxy server to access the Internet, the Web Browsing Requires Proxy Server option should already be checked and your proxy server address and port number pre-filled. This information must be supplied correctly at this time so that your Update Server can communicate to the Novell Patch Subscription Server correctly.

Should your Internet connection be using the Auto-Proxy feature, you will need to enter the static IP address and port of a valid proxy server before continuing.

Firewall authentication agents must be disabled for this computer because there will be nobody logged on to the server overnight when it is time for subscription replications to occur.

Click Next to continue.

10. In the Agent Installation screen, ZENworks Patch Management Server creates a new website within your Internet Information Server on the computer that allows you to administer and manage the system. This page contains all the configuration information required to correctly set up the new website (see Figure 2.24).

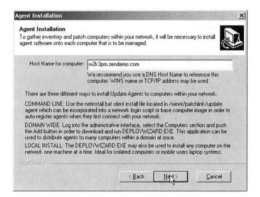

FIGURE 2.24
Agent Installation dialog of the ZENworks Patch Management Installation
Wizard.

The Host Name for Computer is the name by which other
machines on the network can address this computer. By default,
this field is filled in.

It is recommended that you use a name for your server that will
not be changed over time. This is why a DNS name is recommended—such as update.mycompany.com—which all agents can use to
obtain their updates in the future, even if the underlying Update
Server hardware is changed to another box elsewhere in the network infrastructure.

Click Next to continue.

11. The advanced settings in the Advance Configuration page can be
ignored for an evaluation installation; however, for production use
in a secure environment or on the public Internet, it is likely you
may want to use an SSL certificate.

In this release of the product, your connection to the Patch
Subscription Server always points to Novell update servers and the
connection is fully secure using 128-bit SSL connections on port
443. This option is always checked and cannot be modified.

(Optional) Should you want to use SSL between your update server
and all your update agent computers to guarantee authentic and
fully encrypted communications, you may check the Use SSL
Security option. However, note that you will be required to supply
a valid website certificate at the end of this installation process to

allow your update server to function correctly. You may obtain your website certificate from any trusted provider, Verisign Inc., your own Enterprise PKI system such as Entrust, or even the Microsoft Certificate Server built into Windows 2000. However, all your computers within the network must trust that certificate automatically before the update agent will function correctly. Also remember that the issued name of your certificate *must* match the DNS Host Name you provided previously.

Your web certificate must be installed before continuing. This can take several days to be issued by a public trusted CA, so it is good to plan ahead if you intend to use an SSL certificate for your production patch server.

Click Next to continue.

12. In the Installation Summary page, verify all the basic install information. If there are errors, or information that you did not know, click the Back button to correct them, or click Cancel to abort the installation process and try again later.

Click Next to begin the installation process.

13. For the next few minutes, your system will be copying files and installing dependencies needed to make your ZENworks Patch Management Server function properly and communicate with the Novell Patch Subscription Server.

14. At the end of installation, you are prompted to restart your computer. This reboot is required for your Patch Subscription service to start and also for update agent computers to be able to register. By default the Yes, Restart Now option is preselected for you.

(Optional) If you chose the Use SSL Security option, you are now required to manually install your trusted website certificate. To do this, launch the Internet Services Manager from your Start menu (click Programs→Administrative Tools→Internet Services Manager). Now locate the website called PLUS and then right-click. Select Properties from the context menu and then choose the Directory Security tab in the resulting properties dialog.

At this point, click the Server Certificate button to start the IIS Web Server Certificate Wizard, which guides you through the process of importing your trusted certificate into the website. As mentioned before, you should install your *existing* server authentication certificate now—don't request a new certificate at this time.

Note that this step is *not optional* if you have chosen to employ SSL security because absolutely no socket-level communications can occur with your newly installed update server until a trusted certificate has been installed. If you don't have a certificate, abort installation at this time and reinstall without checking the SSL security option.

Click Finish to restart your computer and complete the installation process.

Log in to your computer immediately after it restarts because a brief registration process runs that installs the PatchLink Update agent on this computer, starts the web server, and initiates your patch subscription.

NOTE The update agent is automatically installed on the ZENworks Patch Management Server computer. Do not modify its configuration or remove the agent from the update server because all subscription activities will then cease.

Installing ZENworks Data Management

ZENworks Data Management can be installed on a Windows, NetWare, or Linux server. These instructions differ slightly based on the platform, and the following sections describe how to install on a NetWare and Windows server.

Installing on a NetWare Server

After you meet all the prerequisites for installing iFolder on NetWare, you are ready to install Novell iFolder. To accomplish this, follow these steps:

1. On your installation workstation, map a drive to the SYS: volume on the destination server where you want to install the iFolder server. Map the drive, using one of these methods:

   ▶ If you use CIFS on the destination NetWare server, map a drive, using Windows Explorer.

   ▶ If you do not use CIFS on the destination NetWare server, map a drive, using the Novell Client.

2. On your NetWare server, you must bring the Apache website down to install, upgrade, repair, or uninstall the iFolder server. For Apache 1.3.26 and 1.3.27, enter the following command from the NetWare command prompt:

   `nvxadmdn.ncf`

3. To start the installation, insert the ZENworks Data Management CD and click Data Management when the CD autostarts. The iFolder Installation Wizard opens on the desktop of your installation workstation.

4. Choose New Installation. Click Continue.

5. For new iFolder 2.1 installations, read the End User License Agreement; then click Yes to agree.

6. Specify the directory on the destination NetWare server where you want iFolder server to be installed. Browse to select the drive letter that you mapped previously in step 1.

7. Configure the global settings for the eDirectory LDAP server that your iFolder server uses; then click Next. The settings include the following:

   ▸ LDAP hostname or IP—Enter the DNS name (such as ldap1.your-domain-name.com) or IP address (such as 192.168.1.1) of the server that acts as your LDAP server. This might be the same server that you are configuring as your iFolder server.

NOTE If you use a DNS name, that name must already exist as an entry on your DNS server and point to the IP address of the destination server.

   ▸ Port—Select the port type, based on your security needs, for data exchanges between your LDAP server and your iFolder server.

   ▸ Clear Text—Specify any valid TCP port number to use for clear text exchanges. By default, Port 389 is used for clear text. Use clear text if you want to use LDAP without SSL encryption or if your LDAP server does not support SSL. Clear text is also a good choice if iFolder and LDAP are running on the same server. Because no communication or data is being transferred across network connections, no encryption is necessary. If you use clear text, the LDAP group object must be able to allow clear text passwords. To verify this, launch ConsoleOne, locate the context where your server resides, right-click the LDAP Group object, click Parameters, and make sure that the Allow Clear Text Passwords check box is checked.

▶ SSL—Specify any valid TCP port number to use for SSL exchanges. By default, Port 636 is used for SSL. Select SSL if you want to use SSL exchanges to provide your network with encryption and security when data is transferred across network connections.

▶ LDAP Context Where iFolder Admin User Is Located—Enter the LDAP context where your iFolder Admin User objects are located. For example, o=all. If you are entering more than one context, separate them with semicolons and with no spaces. For example:

```
o=all;o=novell
```

Do not include spaces between delimiters in the context. For example:

```
o=novell;ou=users,o=novell
```

8. Configure the iFolder settings for the NetWare server that will be your iFolder server; then click Next. The settings include the following:

▶ iFolder Server Host Name or IP—Enter the DNS name (such as nif1.your-domainname.com) or the IP address (such as 192.168.1.1) to use for your iFolder server.

NOTE If you use a DNS name, that name must already exist as an entry on your DNS server and point to the IP address of the destination server.

To specify a port, append the IP address of the server with a colon followed by the port number. For example, 192.168.1.1:80.

▶ iFolder Admin Names—Specify the default user ID for the iFolder administrator for this iFolder server. For example:

```
admin
```

The iFolder Admin Names are the users who have permission to manage the iFolder server, using the iFolder Management Console. You can assign more than one user ID to be an iFolder administrator. If you have multiple user IDs, separate them with semicolons and with no spaces. For example:

`admin;jsmith;acatt`

NOTE All the users identified here must exist in the context identified in step 7.

▶ Local iFolder User Database Path—Specify the path to the directory on the iFolder server where user data for all the iFolder accounts will be stored. For example:

sys:\iFolder or *nif-user:*\iFolder

where *sys:* or *nif-user:* is the name of the preexisting volume and *iFolder* is the location of iFolder user data.

The default location is SYS:\iFolder because a SYS: volume is the only NSS volume known to exist prior to the definition of your storage architecture solution for the NetWare server. By using a separate volume for user data, you can avoid filling up your SYS: volume.

NOTE The iFolder installation creates a directory on an existing volume, but it does not create a new volume. You must create the alternate volume prior to installing iFolder. Otherwise, the installation will fail. To keep it from failing, do one of the following:

▶ Specify the preexisting volume other than SYS: and the directory where you want to store user data. For example, *nif-user:*\iFolder, where *nif-user* is the name of the preexisting volume, and *iFolder* is the location of iFolder user data.

▶ Specify the default location of SYS:\iFolder for now. If you want, you can change the location later by editing the value in the Apache\iFolderServer\ httpd_ifolder_nw.conf file.

9. Review the settings on the summary screen. To return to previous pages and change the settings, click Back and repeat the steps, as necessary. When you are finished, click Next.

10. To exit the Installation Wizard, click Finish.

11. After the software is installed on your NetWare server, you must bring the Apache website down and up again to make the changes permanent. For Apache Web Server 1.3.26 and 1.3.27, at the command prompt, enter

    `nvxadmdn.ncf`

    Allow enough time for the web server to shut down gracefully; then at the command prompt, enter the following:

    `nvxadmup.ncf`

    After the server restarts, iFolder is active on your system.

12. If this is a new installation, you must extend the eDirectory schema before you can use the iFolder server.

To open the iFolder Management Console, do one of the following:

▶ Select the Administer iFolder option on the last window of the iFolder installation process.

▶ From a web browser on your installation workstation, go to the iFolder Management Console, select File[ra]Open; then enter the following URL (replace *nif1.your-domain-name.com* with the actual DNS name or IP address of your iFolder server):

   `https://nif1.your-domain-name.com/iFolderServer/Admin`

NOTE This URL is case sensitive.

On completion, log in to the Global Settings page. On successful login, iFolder extends the eDirectory schema. This can take several seconds, so expect a 10- to 30-second delay in the response.

When the browser opens to the Global Settings General Information page, the installation is complete.

Installing Data Management on Windows 2000/2003 Server

After you meet the prerequisites for this configuration, you are ready to install iFolder. The steps to accomplish this are

1. If you plan to use LDAP over SSL, locate a self-signed root certificate (rootcert.der) for your iFolder server. You can export a self-signed root certificate from your certificate server. For information, see your Windows 2000/2003 Server documentation or visit the Microsoft website (http://www.microsoft.com).

   Save the rootcert.der file to a location on the iFolder server or to a floppy disk. For example, a:\rootcert.der. Remember this location; you need it in step 8.

2. If your IIS server is not currently running, start your IIS server.

3. To start the installation, insert the ZENworks Data Management CD and select Data Management when the installation program autostarts.

4. The iFolder Installation Wizard opens on your desktop. Select New Installation.

5. For new iFolder installations, read the End User License Agreement; then click Yes to agree.

6. To select Novell eDirectory as your LDAP server, click eDirectory (see Figure 2.25).

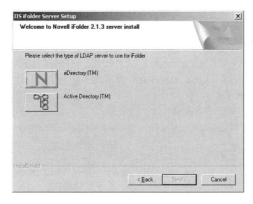

FIGURE 2.25
iFolder Server Setup dialog in the ZENworks Data Management Installation Wizard.

NOTE If you have an Active Directory LDAP server and want to install the iFolder server on a Windows 2000 server, follow the installation procedures in the section "Installing iFolder on Windows/IIS/Active Directory" later in this chapter.

7. Specify the directory on the destination server where you want iFolder server to be installed. Browse to select the drive letter that you mapped in step 1.

8. Configure the global settings for the eDirectory LDAP server that your iFolder server uses; then click Next (see Figure 2.26). Settings you can configure include the following:

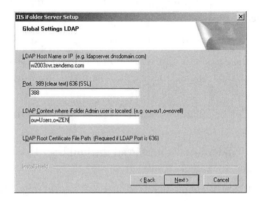

FIGURE 2.26
Global Settings LDAP dialog in ZENworks Data Management Installation Wizard.

▶ LDAP Host Name or IP—Specify the DNS name (such as *ldap1.your-domainname.com*) or IP address (such as 192.168.1.1) of the server that acts as your LDAP server. Replace *ldap1.your-domain-name.com* or 192.168.1.1 with the actual DNS name or IP address of your LDAP server. This can be the same server that you are configuring as your iFolder server.

NOTE If you use a DNS name, that name must already exist as an entry on your DNS server and point to the IP address of the destination server.

▶ Port—Select the port type, based on your security needs, for data exchanges between your LDAP server and your iFolder server.

▶ Clear Text—Specify any valid TCP port number to use for clear text exchanges. By default, Port 389 is used for clear text. Use clear text if you want to use LDAP without SSL encryption or if your LDAP server does not support SSL. Clear text is also a good choice if iFolder and LDAP are running on the same server. Because no communication or data is being transferred across network connections, no encryption is necessary.

▶ SSL—Specify any valid TCP port number to use for SSL exchanges. By default, Port 636 is used for SSL. Use SSL if you want to use SSL exchanges to provide your network with encryption and security when data is transferred across network connections.

▶ LDAP Root Certificate File Path—If you selected the SSL option, provide the full directory path to your self-signed root certificate you created or identified in step 1. For example, type **a:\rootcert.der** if you exported the certificate to a floppy disk.

▶ LDAP Context Where iFolder Admin User Is Located—Specify the LDAP context. For example: o=all.

9. Configure the iFolder settings for the Windows 2000/2003 server that will be your iFolder server; then click Next (see Figure 2.27). Settings include the following:

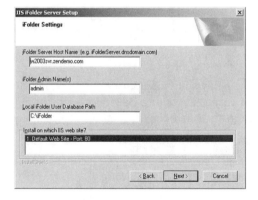

FIGURE 2.27
iFolder Settings page from the ZENworks Data Management Installation Wizard.

▶ iFolder Server Host Name—Specify the DNS name (such as nif1.*your-domainname*.com) or the IP address (such as 192.168.1.1) to use for your iFolder server.

NOTE If you use a DNS name, that name must already exist as an entry on your DNS server and point to the IP address of the destination server.

> ▶ iFolder Admin Names—Specify the default user ID for the iFolder administrator for this iFolder server—for example, admin.
>
> The iFolder Admin Names are the users who have permission to manage the iFolder server. You can assign multiple users to be iFolder administrators. For multiple Admin Names, separate them with semicolons and with no spaces. For example
>
> ```
> administrator;jsmith;acatt
> ```

NOTE All the users identified here must exist in the context identified in step 8 under the LDAP context.

> ▶ Local iFolder User Database Path—Specify the path on the iFolder server where user data for all the iFolder accounts will be stored. For example, `e:\iFolder`, where `e:` is the preexisting volume, and `iFolder` is the directory. If you want, you can edit the value later in the Windows Registry.

NOTE The volume you specify must already exist on the Windows server. The iFolder installation program does not create it for you.

10. Review the settings in the summary screen. To return to previous pages and change the settings, click Back and repeat the steps, as necessary. When you are finished, click Next.

11. To exit the Installation Wizard, click Finish.

12. Extend the eDirectory schema. Open the iFolder Management Console and do one of the following:

> ▶ Select the Administer iFolder option on the last window of the iFolder installation.
>
> ▶ From a web browser on your installation workstation, go to the iFolder Management Console by selecting File→Open and then entering the following URL: https://*nif1.your-domain-name.com/*iFolderServer/Admin (replace *nif1.your-domain-name.com* with the actual DNS name or IP address of your iFolder server).

NOTE This address is case sensitive.

13. Click the Global Settings icon.

14. Log in to the Global Settings page as the Admin user with schema extension privileges.

On successful login, iFolder extends the eDirectory schema. This can take several seconds, so expect a 10- to 30-second delay in the response. When the browser opens to the Global Settings page, the installation is complete.

Installing iFolder on Windows/IIS/Active Directory

After you meet all the prerequisites for this configuration, you are ready to install Novell iFolder. This is accomplished through the following steps:

1. If you plan to use LDAP over SSL, locate a self-signed root certificate (rootcert.der) for your iFolder server. You can export a self-signed root certificate from your certificate server. For information, see your Windows 2000 server documentation or visit the Microsoft website (http://www.microsoft.com). Save the rootcert.der file to a location on the iFolder server or to a floppy disk. For example, a:\rootcert.der. Remember this location; you need it later as you specify the root certificate.

2. If your IIS server is not currently running, start your IIS server.

3. To start the installation, go to the temporary directory where you saved the installation program; then double-click the installation program icon.

4. The iFolder Installation Wizard opens on your desktop. Choose New Installation by pressing Continue.

5. Read the End User License Agreement and click Yes to accept the agreement.

6. To select Microsoft Active Directory as your LDAP server, click Active Directory.

NOTE If you have an eDirectory LDAP server and want to install the iFolder server software on a Windows 2000 server, follow the installation procedures in "Installing Data Management on Windows 2000/2003 Server" earlier in the chapter.

7. Select to extend the Active Directory schema, install iFolder, or both by selecting one of the following options:

   ▶ Complete Install—Install the iFolder server and extend the Active Directory schema. This option requires that you have the necessary credentials as the iFolder administrator and as the schema administrator.

   ▶ Install iFolder Server Only—Install the iFolder server. Before you install iFolder server, you must extend the schema. Run the iFolder installation program with the appropriate schema administrator credentials and follow the Extend Directory Schema Only path.

   ▶ Extend Directory Schema Only—Extend the Active Directory schema for an LDAP server. This option only extends the schema. It does not install the iFolder server software to your iFolder server. Before you can use the iFolder server, you must repeat the installation with the appropriate iFolder administrator credentials to follow the Install iFolder Server Only path. If a secondary Active Directory LDAP server exists outside the forest where the primary Active Directory LDAP server is installed, you must run the iFolder installation program again and select this option to extend the schema for the secondary Active Directory LDAP server.

8. If you chose the Complete Install or Extend Directory Schema Only options in step 7, verify your credentials to extend your Active Directory schema by specifying your schema administrator distinguished name and password:

   ▶ Distinguished Name—Type the full context using commas with no spaces as delimiters. For example: cn=administrator,cn=users, dc=your-domainname,dc=com.

   ▶ Password—Type your schema administrator password in this case-sensitive field.

9. Configure the global settings for your Active Directory LDAP server that your iFolder server uses; then click Next:

▶ LDAP Host Name—Specify the DNS name (such as
ldap1.your-domain-name.com) of the server that acts as your
LDAP server (replace *ldap1.your-domain-name.com* with the
actual DNS name of your LDAP server). This might be the same
server that you are configuring as your iFolder server.

NOTE The DNS name you use must already exist as an entry on your DNS server and
point to the IP address of the destination server.

▶ Port—Select the port type, based on your security needs, for
data exchanges between your LDAP server and your iFolder
server.

▶ Clear Text—Specify any valid TCP port number to use for clear
text exchanges. By default, Port 389 is used for clear text. Use
clear text if you want to use LDAP without SSL encryption or if
your LDAP server does not support SSL. Clear text is also a
good choice if iFolder and LDAP are running on the same
server. Because no communication or data is being transferred
across network connections, no encryption is necessary.

▶ SSL—Specify any valid TCP port number to use for SSL
exchanges. By default, Port 636 is used for SSL. Use SSL if you
want to use SSL exchanges to provide your network with
encryption and security when data is transferred across network
connections.

▶ LDAP Context Where iFolder Admin User Is Located—Specify
the LDAP context. For example: cn=administrator,cn=users,
dc=your-domain-name,dc=com.

NOTE Make sure that the first context in the list is the one that the iFolder administrator is in.

10. Configure the iFolder settings for your iFolder server; then click
Next:

▶ iFolder Server Host Name or IP—Enter the DNS name (such as
nif1.*your-domainname*.com) or the IP address (such as
192.168.1.1) to use for your iFolder server.

NOTE If you use a DNS name, that name must already exist as an entry on your DNS server and point to the IP address of the destination server.

▶ iFolder Admin Names—Specify the default user ID for the iFolder administrator for this iFolder server. For example, administrator. The iFolder Admin Names are the users who have permission to manage the iFolder server, using the iFolder Management Console. You can assign more than one user ID to be an iFolder administrator.

If you have multiple user IDs, separate them with semicolons and with no spaces. For example: administrator;jsmith;acatt.

NOTE All the users identified here must exist in the context identified in the specified LDAP context.

▶ Local iFolder User Database Path—Specify the path on the iFolder server where user data for all the iFolder accounts will be stored. For example, *e:\iFolder*, where *e:* is the volume and *iFolder* is the directory. You can edit the value later, if you want, in the Windows Registry.

NOTE The volume you specify must already exist on the Windows server. The iFolder installation program will not create it for you dynamically.

▶ Install on Which IIS Web Site?—If multiple websites are on your server, select where you want to install iFolder.

11. Review the settings on the summary page. To return to previous pages and change the settings, click Back and repeat the steps, as necessary. When you are finished, click Next.

12. Log in to Global Settings in the iFolder Management Console to finalize the installation.

13. Open the iFolder Management Console. Do one of the following:

▶ Select the Administer iFolder option on the last window of the iFolder installation process.

▶ From a web browser on your installation workstation, go to the iFolder Management Console, select File→Open, and then enter the URL https://*nif1.your-domain-name.com*/iFolderServer/ Admin (replace *nif1.your-domain-name.com* with the actual DNS name or IP address of your iFolder server).

NOTE This address is case sensitive.

14. Click Global Settings; then log in. When the browser opens to the Global Settings page, the installation is complete.

15. To exit the Installation Wizard, click Finish.

This completes the installation of Data Management into the system.

Installing ZENworks Handheld Management

ZENworks Handheld Management is composed of two components: ZENworks Handheld Server and ZENworks Handheld Access Points.

The following sections discuss how to install these components on your servers.

Creating the ZENworks Handheld Management Server's Windows User Account

The ZENworks Handheld Management Server requires a valid Windows user account that is a member of the Administrators group on the local machine to log in as a service and to access the ZENworks Handheld Management database and application data.

To create the server user account in the Administrators group, follow these steps:

1. On a Windows NT/2000/XP computer, log in as the Administrator or as a member of the Administrators group.

2. Click Start→Settings→Control Panel.

3. Double-click Users and Passwords.

4. Click Add. If the Add button is disabled, select the Users Must Enter a User Name and Password to Use This Computer check box.

5. Type the username, full name, and description for the new account; then click Next.

6. Type a password for the new account, confirm the password by retyping it, and then click Next.

7. Select the Other button, click Administrators in the drop-down list, and then click Finish.

You must configure the newly created user account's password so that it never expires. If you allow the password to expire, the service cannot load until you reconfigure the password.

To configure the password so that it never expires, follow these steps:

1. On a Windows NT/2000/XP computer, log in as the Administrator or as a member of the Administrators group.

2. Click Start→Settings→Control Panel.

3. Double-click Administrative Tools.

4. Double-click Computer Management.

5. Expand Local Users and Groups under System Tools.

6. Click Users.

7. In the right pane, right-click the user account you created previously; then click Properties.

8. Deselect the User Must Change Password at Next Logon check box.

9. Select Password Never Expires.

10. Click OK.

This completes the creation of the administrator account that will be used by the system during its normal functions.

Creating the Service Object's User Account

The ZENworks Handheld Management service object requires a valid user account to access eDirectory through LDAP. You create this user in ConsoleOne.

Make sure that you use a nonexpiring password for this account.

The rights you assign to this user account depend on whether you want to access NetWare volumes for application data or to store retrieved files.

If you want to access objects or copy retrieved files on a NetWare volume, the user should have at least Read, Write, and Create rights on the NetWare server.

If access to a NetWare volume is not needed, this user account should have at least Read, Write, Create, Rename, Compare, and Delete rights on all tree areas that will contain ZENworks Handheld Management objects and policies.

Creating a MAPI Profile (BlackBerry Device Support Only)

If you want to manage BlackBerry devices using ZENworks Handheld Management, you need to create a MAPI profile on the ZENworks Handheld Management Server machine to connect to your email system.

ZENworks Handheld Management supports the same groupware/email systems supported by RIM, including Novell GroupWise, Microsoft Exchange, Lotus Notes, and any POP3- or IMAP-compliant email system.

Before creating the MAPI profile, log in using the user account you created in the section "Creating the Service Object's User Account" earlier in the chapter. Refer to Windows help or to your email system help for step-by-step information on creating the MAPI profile.

Schema Extension and Product Licensing

Before installing the ZENworks Handheld Management Server, you must prepare the directory by extending the eDirectory schema for ZENworks Handheld Management.

To extend the schema, you must have root level admin privileges to the tree, and you must have the Novell Client installed.

Before running the schema extension tool, make sure that you are logged in to the tree that you want to extend.

To extend the schema, follow these steps:

1. Insert the ZENworks Handheld Management CD on a machine that has the Novell Client running. The installation program will autorun. If it does not, run `winsetup.exe` from the root of the CD.

2. Click Handheld Management.

3. Click English.

4. Click Schema Extension and Product Licensing.

5. In the software license agreement, select the language, select Accept, and then click Next.

6. Click to select the eDirectory tree for creating the objects; then select the Extend Schema check box.

7. Click Next.

8. Provide the license code. If you do not provide the license code, you can use the product for only 90 days.

9. Review the installation summary. To make any changes, click Back. Click Finish to complete the schema extension and product licensing.

This completes extending the schema. Now the system is prepared to have the software installed.

Installing the ZENworks Handheld Management Server

This section discusses how to install the back-end ZENworks Handheld Management server, which is used to manage handheld devices.

1. Insert the ZENworks Handheld Management Product CD in the CD drive on a Windows NT/2000/XP machine where you want to install the ZENworks Handheld Management Server. The installation program autoruns. If it does not, run `winsetup.exe` from the root of the CD.

2. Click Handheld Management.

3. Click English.

4. Click Handheld Management Services.

5. Click ZENworks Handheld Management Server.

6. Click Next.

7. Read the license agreement; then click Yes if you agree with the terms of the license agreement.

8. Review the destination location where the installation program will install the ZENworks Handheld Management Server software (browse to a different location, if you want); then click Next.

9. In the Select Components page, select the components you want to install (see Figure 2.28):

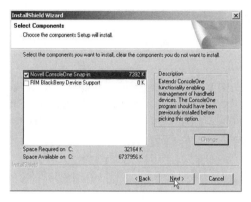

FIGURE 2.28
The Select Components page of the ZENworks Handheld Management Server Installation Wizard.

▶ Novell ConsoleOne Snap-In—Extends ConsoleOne functionality to allow you to manage handheld devices. This option is enabled by default. You should have previously installed ConsoleOne 1.3.6 or later on at least one workstation or server before you install the ZENworks Handheld Management Server.

▶ RIM BlackBerry Device Support—Adds support for managing RIM BlackBerry devices. If you select this option, you must have set up a MAPI profile for email access.

10. Click Next.

11. In the Start Copying Files page, review the settings; then click Next.

12. (Optional) Select Display Readme File to review the Readme file for installation notes and product issues that you need to know as you install and use ZENworks Handheld Management.

13. (Optional) Select the Configure Access Point HTTP and SSL Settings check box if you want to enable HTTP encapsulation, configure secure sockets layer (SSL), or change the default port settings.

NOTE

If the ZENworks Handheld Management Server is running on the same machine as Novell eDirectory, the ZENworks Handheld Management Server will fail to start when enabling HTTP unless the HTTP port is changed. By default, eDirectory uses port 80, which is the same default port the ZENworks Handheld Management Server uses. Both services cannot listen on the same port.

14. Click Finish.

15. (Conditional) If you selected the Configure Access Point HTTP and SSL Settings check box in step 13, the remaining steps must be completed. The Configure Access introduction screen appears.

16. Click Next.

17. Select Internal ODBC-Compatible Database if you want ZENworks Handheld Management to create a database for you (see Figure 2.29). Alternatively, you can select Microsoft SQL Server, specify the machine name, and then specify the database name. To use a SQL database, SQL Server must already be installed.

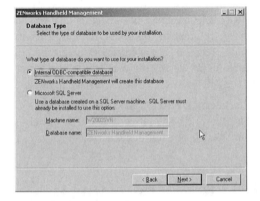

FIGURE 2.29
Database Type page of the ZENworks Handheld Management Installation Wizard.

NOTE If you are currently using ZENworks Desktop Management, you cannot extend the ZENworks Desktop Management database to include the handheld inventory information; the inventory databases for ZENworks Handheld Management and ZENworks Desktop Management are currently separate.

18. Click Next.

19. In the Service User dialog box, specify the domain name, account name, and password for the account you created in the "Creating the ZENworks Handheld Management Server's Windows User Account" section earlier in the chapter and then click Next (see Figure 2.30).

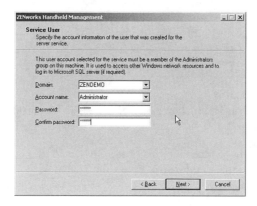

FIGURE 2.30
The Service User dialog box in the ZENworks Handheld Management Installation Wizard.

20. In the Directory User Information dialog box, specify the server name where eDirectory is installed, the username, and password for the account that you created in the section "Creating the Service Object's User Account" earlier in the chapter and then click Next (see Figure 2.31).

NOTE The user needs rights to create the service object in the container you specify and rights to create handheld objects and to access application and policy objects in the tree. Browse to the user in the tree and specify the full context name.

21. (Conditional) In the Product Activation dialog box, select the Activated option and provide a license code for the product. Alternatively, if you want to use the evaluation version of the product for 90 days, select Evaluation.

22. Click Next.

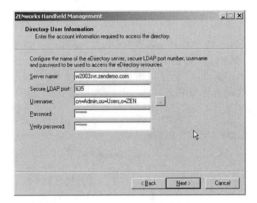

FIGURE 2.31
The Directory User Information dialog of ZENworks Handheld Management
Installation Wizard.

23. If you want to access objects or store retrieved files on a NetWare
volume in the specified tree, select the Enable Access to NetWare
check box.

24. Click Next.

25. Select the container where you want the service object created;
then click Next. To browse to a container you must have a valid
LDAP user configured.

26. (Optional) In the Global User Authentication Settings page, select
the Enable User Authentication check box to require that users
type in their eDirectory usernames and passwords on the handheld
device, click Add, specify the container to add to the container list,
and then click OK.

Select the Enable User Authentication check box if you want to use
user-based management rather than device-based management.

27. Click Next.

28. (Conditional) If you chose to enable RIM BlackBerry support, type
the service user's email address to be used by the BlackBerry client
software. Then select the MAPI profile that you created in the section "Creating a MAPI Profile (BlackBerry Device Support Only)"
earlier in the chapter and click Finish.

29. Click Finish.

30. On the computer where you installed the ZENworks Handheld Management Server software, create a share to the installation directory. The default location is c:\program files\novell\zfh.

This completes the installation of the ZENworks Handheld Management back-end server.

Installing the Access Point on Additional Computers

When you install the ZENworks Handheld Management Server using the installation program, the ZENworks Handheld Management Access Point is installed on the same computer.

You can install the Access Point on additional computers to distribute the communication load and provide better support for WAN environments. These machines must be able to communicate to the ZENworks Handheld Management Server through TCP/IP.

You can also install the Access Point on the laptops or desktops that are usually not connected to the network but are used by Windows CE devices for synchronization. If you install the Access Point on these com-puters, the synchronizing Windows CE devices can communicate to the Access Point even when the ZENworks Handheld Management server is not connected to the network. The communication between the Access Point and the ZENworks Handheld Management Server happens when you connect these laptops or desktops to the network.

NOTE If computers that are disconnected from the network do not have an IP address, the Windows CE devices must be configured to use PPP_PEER as the Access Point name so that connections to the Access Point are successful.

If you are installing the Access Point, you must log in as a member of the Administrators group.

To install the Access Point on additional computers, follow these steps:

1. Insert the ZENworks Handheld Management CD in the CD drive. The installation program will autorun. If it does not, run `winsetup.exe` from the root of the CD.

2. Click Handheld Management.

3. Click English.

4. Click Handheld Management Services.

5. Click Access Point (Optional).

6. In the Welcome page, click Next.

7. Read the license agreement, then click Yes if you agree with the terms of the license agreement.

8. Review the destination location where the installation program will install the Access Point (browse to a different location, if you want); then click Next.

9. In the Customer Information page, specify your name and your company name.

10. In the Server Configuration page, specify the name or the IP address of the machine where the ZENworks Handheld Management Server is installed.

11. (Optional) If you are using user-based management of handheld devices, on the eDirectory Server Information page, specify the server and secure the LDAP port number that ZENworks Handheld Management should use when validating users' credentials; then click Next.

12. In the Start Copying Files page, review the information; then click Next.

13. Ensure that the Start Access Point check box is selected.

14. (Optional) Select the Configure Access Point HTTP and SSL Settings check box.

15. Click Finish.

You can install the Access Point on users' desktop or laptop machines using ZENworks Desktop Management.

Installing ConsoleOne Snap-Ins on an Existing ConsoleOne Installation

ConsoleOne and the ZENworks Handheld Management ConsoleOne snap-ins can be installed on any number of computers so that you can give other administrators or help desk staff access to ZENworks Handheld Management from multiple locations on your network.

To install the ConsoleOne snap-ins on an existing ConsoleOne installation, follow these steps:

1. On a machine where ConsoleOne is installed, insert the ZENworks Handheld Management CD in the CD drive. The installation program autoruns. If it does not, run `winsetup.exe` from the root of the CD.

2. Click Handheld Management.

3. Click English.

4. Click Handheld Management Services.

5. Click ConsoleOne Snap-ins (optional); then follow the instructions in the wizard.

This completes the installation of the Handheld Management snap-ins into the Novell ConsoleOne management tool.

Installing the Handheld Clients

ZENworks Handheld Management provides IP clients for Windows CE and Palm OS devices that can make TCP/IP connections, a RIM BlackBerry Client, and Desktop Synchronization software for handheld devices that use Palm HotSync or Microsoft ActiveSync to synchronize.

Working with Windows CE IP Client

ZENworks Handheld Management provides an IP client for Windows CE that can make TCP/IP connections.

The Windows CE IP client supports multiple types of Windows CE devices. ZENworks Handheld Management provides a wizard that creates CAB files for all supported devices. The appropriate CAB file must then be installed on the device.

When running the wizard, you are prompted for the name of the computer (or IP address) of the ZENworks Handheld Management Server or the computer with the Access Point installed.

The computer name or IP address is built into the CAB file so that when the CAB file is installed on the handheld device, it is ready to communicate.

NOTE If Windows CE devices use Microsoft ActiveSync on a computer that has the Access Point or Desktop Synchronization software installed, the appropriate CAB file is configured and automatically installed on the device when you synchronize the Windows CE device using ActiveSync. In this situation, the following procedure is not necessary.

Creating CAB Files for the Windows CE IP Client

Windows CE devices must have CAB files to install the IP client. These steps show how to have the installation system create and extract these CAB files so that they can be installed on the Windows CE devices:

1. Insert the ZENworks Handheld Management CD in the CD drive. The installation program will autorun. If it does not, run `winsetup.exe` from the root of the CD.

2. Click Handheld Management.

3. Click English.

4. Click Handheld Clients; then click Windows CE IP Client.

5. Click Next.

6. Review the destination location where the installation program will install the Windows CE IP client (browse to a different location, if you want); then click Next.

7. In the Access Point text box, type the computer name or IP address of the server or computer to which your handheld devices will connect (where the Access Point is installed). You can leave this text box empty if you want to configure this setting on the handheld device.

   If you are using an IP address to specify the location of the ZENworks Handheld Management Server or Access Point computer, the IP address should remain constant (for example, it doesn't change because of DHCP).

8. (Optional) Select the Enable HTTP Encapsulation check box.

9. (Optional) Select the Enable SSL check box; then check the Accept Next Root Certificate from Access Point (And Then Disable) check box, if you want.

   You can also configure the Access Point settings (HTTP, SSL, and ports) using the cfgip.exe program (in the /program files/novell/zfhap directory, by default). If you select the Publish Root Certificate for Client Download check box using cfgip.exe, the root certificate will be automatically downloaded. For this root certificate to be accepted, you must select the Accept Next Root Certificate from Access Point (And Then Disable) check box.

10. (Optional) If you want to change the default port that ZENworks Handheld Management uses, deselect the Use Default Port check box and then type the desired port number in the Port text box. If you change the default port number, you must also change it at the computer where the IP conduit is installed.

11. Click Next.

12. (Optional) Select the Create Shortcut to the Client Console on CE Device check box; then click Next.

13. Review the information on the Start Copying Files page; then click Next.

14. Click Finish.

The wizard creates CAB files for the following types of devices and copies them to the program files\novell\zfh ceipclient directory by default:

▶ CE 3.0 (Handheld 2000) client for ARM-based Handheld PCs zfhipclientforce.hpc2000_arm.cab

▶ CE 3.0 (Handheld 2000) client for MIPS-based Handheld PCs zfhipclientforce.hpc2000_mips.cab

▶ CE 2.11 client for SH3-based Handheld PCs zfhipclientforce.hpc211_sh3.cab

▶ CE 2.11 client for ARM-based Handheld PCs zfhipclientforce.hpc211_arm.cab

▶ CE 2.11 client for MIPS-based Handheld PCs zfhipclientforce.hpc211_mips.cab

▶ MIPS-based Pocket PC 2000s (some Cassiopeia models) zfhipclientforce.ppc_mips.cab

Installing the Windows CE IP Client

The following steps walk through the process of installing the Windows CE IP clients onto the Windows CE handheld devices:

1. Find the CAB file appropriate for your device in the directory where the CAB files were created (program files\novell\zfh ceipclient by default).

2. Copy the CAB file to the device, using the method most appropriate for your environment (for example, Microsoft ActiveSync).

3. After the CAB file is on the device, run it by clicking it.

The Windows CE IP client is installed on the handheld device.

Installing the Palm OS IP Client

If you have Palm OS devices that can make a TCP/IP connection, you can install the ZENworks Handheld Management Palm OS IP client on each device.

To install the Palm OS IP client, follow these steps:

1. Insert the ZENworks Handheld Management CD in the CD drive. The installation program will autorun. If it does not, run `winsetup.exe` from the root of the CD.

2. Click Handheld Management.

3. Click English.

4. Click Handheld Clients; then click Palm OS IP Client.

5. Click Next.

6. Review the destination location where the installation program will install the Palm OS IP client (browse to a different location, if you want); then click Next twice.

7. In the Handheld Configuration page, type the computer name or IP address of the ZENworks Handheld Management Server (or the computer on which you installed the Access Point).

   If you are using an IP address to specify the location of the ZENworks Handheld Management Server (or Access Point, if it is installed on a computer other than the server), the IP address of the computer should remain constant (for example, it doesn't change because of DHCP).

8. (Optional) Select the Enable HTTP Encapsulation check box.

9. (Optional) Select the Enable SSL check box.

10. (Optional) If you want to change the default ports that ZENworks Handheld Management uses, deselect the Use Default Ports check box; then type the desired port number in the TCP Port and SSL Port text boxes. If you change these port numbers, you must also

change them at the computer where the Access Point is installed (the ZENworks Handheld Management Server or the computer on which you installed the Access Point).

11. Click Next. The device type CAB files to install are

   ▶ SH3-based Pocket PC 2000s (some Jornada models)
   zfhipclientforce.ppc_sh3.cab

   ▶ ARM-based Pocket PCs (iPAQ and all PPC2002 models)
   zfhipclientforce.ppc_arm.cab

   ▶ Pocket PCs running Windows Mobile 2003
   zfhipclientforce.ppc2003_arm.cab

12. In the Connections Options page, fill in the following fields:

   ▶ Client Should Auto Connect to Server—Select an option from the drop-down list:

      ▶ Never—The Palm OS IP client never automatically connects. The user must manually connect the Palm OS IP client by clicking the ZENworks Handheld Management Console icon on the Palm OS device and then clicking Connect Now.

      ▶ When IP Connection Exists—The Palm OS IP client automatically connects whenever an IP connection exists and it is time to connect. For example, if the device is cradled using an Ethernet cradle, the device has Bluetooth running on the device, or if the device dials up using a modem, and it is time to connect (as specified in the Client Should Connect Every option), the Palm OS IP client automatically connects.

      ▶ Always—The Palm OS IP client tries to establish an IP connection and connect to the IP conduit automatically if it is time to connect. Client Should Connect Every specifies how often (in hours or minutes) the Palm OS IP client should connect.

   ▶ At Connection Time, Display to User—Specify an option from the drop-down list:

      ▶ Nothing (Just Connect)—The Palm OS device user sees a visual indication that the Palm OS IP client has connected, but the user is not prompted to do anything.

▶ Flashing Icon (Subtle)—A flashing icon displays on the Palm OS device when it is time to connect. The user can connect by clicking the reminder icon and then clicking OK.

▶ Dialog—A dialog box displays on the Palm OS device whenever it is time to connect. The user can connect by clicking Connect.

▶ Dialog with Timeout—A dialog box with a timeout value displays on the Palm OS device whenever it is time for the Palm OS IP client to connect. If the user does not respond by clicking Connect or Cancel during the timeout period, the Palm OS IP client connects. For example, if the device is cradled using an Ethernet cradle and you are away from your desk when it is time for the Palm OS IP client to connect, the Palm OS IP client waits until the timeout period has passed and then connects.

13. If you want, click Advanced Settings and then fill in the following fields:

▶ Connection Timeout (Seconds)—The number of seconds you specify determines how long the Palm OS IP client tries to connect before it stops trying if a connection cannot be established.

▶ Session Timeout (Seconds)—The number of seconds you specify determines the length of time that the Palm OS IP client stays connected. If the session reaches the limit you specify, the Palm OS IP client session terminates. For example, if you lose an IP connection, the Palm OS IP client session terminates after the number of seconds that you specify has passed.

▶ Connect Retry (Seconds)—Specify the number of seconds that you want the Palm OS IP client to wait after a failed connection before trying to connect again.

▶ Maximum Connect Retries—Specify the maximum number of retry attempts you want the Palm OS IP client to attempt.

▶ Timeout (Seconds)—Specify the number of seconds you want to allow before closing the alarm dialog box before trying to make the connection.

▶ Message—Type a message to be displayed on the Palm OS device when it is time for the Palm OS IP client to connect.

14. Click OK.

15. Click Finish twice.

The wizard creates Palm OS IP client files and copies them to the program files\novell\zfh palm ip client directory by default.

Instead of running the ZENworks Handheld Management installation program to install the Palm OS IP client, you can also copy the contents of the program files\novell\zfh palm ip client directory to a Palm OS device using the HotSync Manager Install Tool.

Installing the RIM BlackBerry Client

The ZENworks Handheld Management RIM BlackBerry client is the software that manages BlackBerry devices that use the BlackBerry wireless platform.

NOTE If BlackBerry devices use RIM Desktop Manager on a computer that has the Access Point or Desktop Synchronization software installed, ZENworks Handheld Management automatically creates the necessary installation files for the RIM BlackBerry client and adds them to the BlackBerry Application Loader. In this situation, the following procedure is not necessary.

To install the RIM BlackBerry client, follow these steps:

1. Insert the ZENworks Handheld Management CD in the CD drive. The installation program will autorun. If it does not, run `winsetup.exe` from the root of the CD.

2. Click Handheld Management.

3. Click English.

4. Click Handheld Clients; then click RIM BlackBerry Client.

5. Click Next.

6. Review the destination location where the installation program will install the RIM BlackBerry client (browse to a different location, if you want); then click Next twice.

The RIM BlackBerry client files that will be copied to the destination location include two client .DLL files: one file for devices that use the Mobitex network and one file for devices that use the DataTAC network. The copied files also include the .ALX installation file that will be used by the BlackBerry Application Loader and the configuration application file.

NOTE If your RIM Desktop Manager software is not at least version 2.1.3 (2.1 SP3), it might not recognize .ALX files. If this is the case, you must use the BlackBerry Application Loader to copy the appropriate .ALI file to your BlackBerry devices (zfhbbmtexclient.ali for the Mobitex network or zfhbbdtacclient.ali for the DataTAC network). The two .ALI files are found in the \blackberryclient directory on the ZENworks Handheld Management CD.

7. Type the email address of the ZENworks Handheld Management back-end server that will be used by the BlackBerry client to communicate to the back-end server.

8. Click Finish. The installation program copies the RIM BlackBerry IP client files to the program files\novell\zfhblackberryclient directory.

9. In the InstallShield Wizard Complete page, click Add Client to BlackBerry's Application Loader to have ZENworks Handheld Management automatically add the necessary files to the BlackBerry Application Loader.

   Enable the Add Client to BlackBerry's Application Loader option if you are running the BlackBerry Client Installation Wizard from the machine on which the BlackBerry device synchronizes.

10. Click Finish.

This completes the creation and installation of the BlackBerry client.

Desktop Synchronization Integration

You must install the ZENworks Handheld Management Desktop Synchronization Integration software on users' desktops if

► Handheld devices use Palm HotSync or Microsoft ActiveSync to synchronize and connect to the network (no IP access).

► You want to use ZENworks Handheld Management to distribute applications to BlackBerry devices that use RIM Desktop Manager software. ZENworks Handheld Management lets you distribute software to BlackBerry devices that are synchronized with a cradle; software distribution to BlackBerry devices using wireless synchronization is not supported.

► You want to distribute applications to desktop computers where handheld devices synchronize (for example, installation programs that integrate with Microsoft ActiveSync or Palm HotSync).

NOTE When you install ZENworks Handheld Management Server using the installation program, the ZENworks Handheld Management Desktop Synchronization Integration software is automatically installed on the same computer.

To install the Desktop Synchronization Integration software, follow these steps:

1. Insert the ZENworks Handheld Management CD in the CD drive on a user's computer. The installation program will autorun. If it does not, run `winsetup.exe` from the root of the CD.

2. Click Handheld Management.

3. Click English.

4. Click Handheld Clients; then click Desktop Synchronization Integration Software.

5. Click Next.

6. Read the license agreement; then click Yes if you agree with the terms of the license agreement.

7. Review the destination location where the installation program will install the Desktop Synchronization Integration software; then click Next. By default, the installation program copies the files to the program files\novell\zfhds directory.

8. Enter the username and company information; then click Next.

9. Make sure that the components you want to install are selected; then click Next.

10. Enter the name or IP address of the computer where the ZENworks Handheld Management Server is installed; then click Next. If you are using an IP address, the IP address of the computer where the ZENworks Handheld Management Server is installed should remain constant (for example, it doesn't change because of DHCP).

    If you are using a DNS or computer name, make sure that your handheld devices can resolve the name if the devices are being cradled and using a third-party synchronization package.

11. Type the name or IP address of the computer where the Access Point is installed (the ZENworks Handheld Management Server or the computer on which you installed the Access Point). If you are

using an IP address to specify the location of the computer that the Access Point is installed on, the IP address should remain constant (for example, it doesn't change because of DHCP).

If you are using a DNS or computer name, make sure that your handheld devices can resolve the name if the devices are being cradled and using a third-party synchronization package.

12. (Optional) Select the Enable HTTP Encapsulation check box.

13. (Optional) Select the Enable SSL check box; then select the Accept Next Root Certificate from Access Point (and Then Disable) check box, if you want.

You can also configure the Access Point settings (HTTP, SSL, and ports) using the cfgip.exe program (in the /program files/novell/zfhap directory, by default). If you select the Publish Root Certificate for Client Download check box using cfgip.exe, the root certificate is automatically downloaded. For this root certificate to be accepted, you must select the Accept Next Root Certificate from Access Point (and Then Disable) check box.

14. (Optional) If you want to change the default port that ZENworks Handheld Management uses, deselect the Use Default Port check box; then type the desired port number in the Port text box. If you change this port number, you must also change the port number at the computer where the Access Point is installed (the ZENworks Handheld Management Server or the computer on which you installed the Access Point).

15. Click Next.

16. Review the information in the Start Copying Files page; then click Next.

17. After the files are copied, make sure that the Start Desktop Sync check box is selected; then click Finish.

This completes the installation of the handheld synchronization software used on the client machine that synchronizes the handheld device.

Installing GroupWise Instant Messenger

ZENworks now includes GroupWise Instant Messenger to allow you to have secure communications.

To install GroupWise Instant Messenger, insert the Novell ZENworks Data Management and Instant Messenger CD into the drive. The CD should autolaunch. If it does not, launch the `winsetup.exe` program at the root of the drive.

Select Instant Messenger and do the following to install:

1. Read the license and click Next.

2. Select Create or Update a System from the wizard. See Figure 2.32 for a sample of this screen.

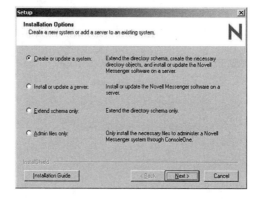

FIGURE 2.32
Installation Options dialog for Instant Messenger.

3. Choose If You Are Installing onto a NetWare or Windows Server. The rest of the steps follow the Windows server path. Figure 2.33 is a sample of this screen.

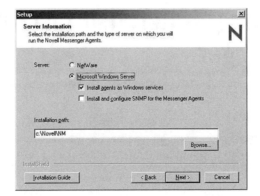

FIGURE 2.33
Server information dialog for Instant Messenger.

4. Continue the wizard until the System Configuration dialog appears (a sample is shown in Figure 2.34). Enter the eDirectory tree and the user context where user accounts may be found. Leave the object names and context as the default. Click Next.

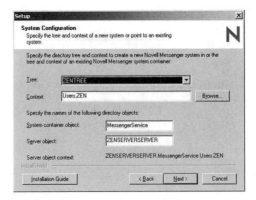

FIGURE 2.34
System Configuration dialog for Instant Messenger.

5. Continue the wizard and then select all desired agents from the Install Components dialog. The agents include Messaging Agent (a service that allows messaging communication), Archive Agent (a service that will periodically archive communications), and Administration Files (a service that allows you to manage the Messenger through ConsoleOne). Click Next.

6. On the Windows Service Option enter either a local administrator account or a Windows account that has administrative privileges. These will be the accounts that are used by the Messenger services.

7. On the Directory Access screen, determine if the agents should communicate and discover users from eDirectory through direct eDirectory access or through LDAP protocols.

8. On the Directory Authentication screen, enter the admin account Distinguished Name and password to allow administrative access to eDirectory to create new objects.

9. On the User Configuration screen (shown in Figure 2.35) enter all of the containers where users may be found in the eDirectory tree.

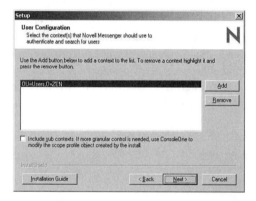

FIGURE 2.35
User Configuration dialog for Instant Messenger.

10. On the next page, the Server Address, enter the address of this server where the Messaging Agent will be running.

11. Continue through the wizard to complete the installation of the Instant Messenger server.

After the instant messenger server is installed, you need to install the client on the devices. The client may be found on the CD and can be installed from the CD, from the server, or through ZENworks Desktop Management.

Installing Asset Inventory Components of ZENworks Asset Management

ZENworks now allows you to install the Asset Inventory components of ZENworks Asset Management as part of your purchase.

To install the Asset Inventory components, insert the Novell ZENworks Asset Management CD into the drive. The CD should autolaunch. If it does not, launch the `winsetup.exe` program at the root of the drive.

Select Asset Inventory and do the following to install:

1. Proceed through the installation wizard until the Choose the Installation Type dialog appears (shown in Figure 2.36). On this dialog you need to decide if you will have one server or multiple servers doing collections of inventory data. The difference between Standalone and Enterprise deployments is the ability to have more than one server collecting and controlling inventory scanning.

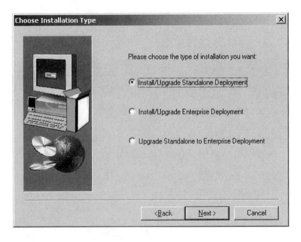

FIGURE 2.36
Choose the Installation Type dialog.

2. Continue through the installation wizard until the Choose the Method of Installation dialog appears (shown in Figure 2.37).

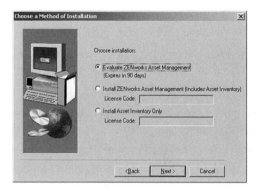

FIGURE 2.37
Choose the Method of Installation dialog.

3. Choose Install Asset Inventory Only to install those components. Enter the license code for the Asset Inventory that was delivered with your ZENworks license.

4. Continue through the installation wizard to complete the installation. The defaults should be good for most any installation.

After the Asset Inventory is installed you need to deploy the agent that will scan the hardware and software information on these devices. For access to the Asset Inventory web page and console, the default account is entadmin with a password of enterprise.

Installing ZENworks Personality Migration

You can run Novell ZENworks Personality Migration from a Windows server or from a Windows workstation. You use either the server or the workstation to open the Desktop DNA Template Editor to create the personality templates that collect users' workstation personalities.

To install Personality Migration, follow these steps:

1. Insert the ZENworks Personality Migration CD into the CD drive.

2. Click Personality Migration.

3. Click ZENworks Personality Migration.

4. Click Install ZENworks Personality Migration, review the information on the Welcome page, and then click Next.

5. Review the license agreement, click I Accept the Terms of the License Agreement, and then click Next.

6. Fill in the fields in the Customer Information page; then click Next.

7. Click the type of installation you want: Typical, Compact, or Custom; then click Next.

8. On the Ready to Install the Program page, click Install.

9. On the Select Options page, click the options you want: View Readme, Run ZENworks Personality Migration, or Add Shortcut to Desktop.

10. Click Next; then click Finish.

This completes the installation of the Personality Migration software onto the system.

Installing ZENworks Software Packaging

ZENworks Software Packaging is a ZENworks Edition of InstallShield's AdminStudio. The components of AdminStudio ZENworks Edition include Repackager, which allows the snapshot and capture of an installed application; Tuner, which allows the creation of MST files; and Deployment Wizard, which places the captured files onto the server and creates ZENworks application and distribution objects.

To install ZENworks Software Packaging, insert the Novell ZENworks Software Packaging CD into the drive. The CD should autolaunch. If it does not, launch the `winsetup.exe` program at the root of the drive.

Select Software Packaging And select AdminStudio ZENworks Edition. Follow the wizard's instructions to install the product on the current Windows device.

You need to register with InstallShield to receive a serial number to activate the program.

Summary

This completes the installation of the software packaging component of ZENworks that allows you to create and capture MSI and MST files.

Now that ZENworks is installed on your system, we can now talk about how to use the system to manage your desktops, servers, and handhelds.

## CHAPTER 3

Getting ZENworks Desktop Management 7 Working in Your Environment

This chapter provides a step-by-step walk-through of how to get ZENworks Desktop Management up and running quickly in your environment. This chapter assumes that you have previously installed eDirectory into your environment. If you are installing ZENworks into an Active Directory environment, you need to follow the information described in Chapter 2, "Installing ZENworks 7 Suite," on how to install ZENworks into an Active Directory environment.

Before beginning this chapter, verify that the following components of ZENworks Desktop Management 7 have been installed:

- ▶ Desktop Management
- ▶ Workstation import and removal services
- ▶ Inventory
- ▶ Sybase database
- ▶ Middle-tier server

When you are sure that all these are installed, you can begin working through this chapter.

Set Up the ODBC Driver

You will want to get reports, views, and queries out of the Desktop Management system, so you need to install the ODBC drivers to access the Sybase database or the external database that you may supply.

Assuming that you are using the embedded Sybase installed when ZENworks Desktop Management 7 was installed, you must perform the following steps:

1. Insert the Companion CD 2 and browse the CD to the Database Drivers directory.

2. Unzip the `SybaseODBC.zip` file onto your `c:\` directory. This creates a directory called `Sybase` on your drive.

3. Browse to this directory and copy the `c:\Sybase\Sybase\Program Files\sybase` subdirectory into your `c:\Program Files directory`.

4. Run the `Sybase8ODBC.reg` file located at `c:\Sybase\Sybase`. This updates the registry keys so that you can use the drivers.

5. Start up your ODBC Data Source Administrator by choosing Start→Settings→Control Panel→Administrative Tools→Data Sources. You should see a display similar to Figure 3.1.

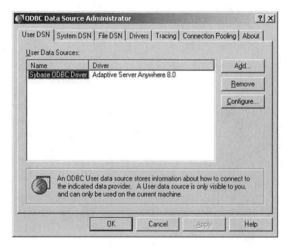

FIGURE 3.1
The ODBC Data Source Administrator.

To continue, highlight the Sybase ODBC Driver configuration module and click the Configure button. Click on the Database tab and fill in the IP address of the server holding the Sybase database. Click on the Network tab and change the TCP/IP field to be `host=<IP Address of your Sybase Database>`.

Go to the ODBC tab and click on the Test Connection button. You should receive a "connection successful" message. When this is done, you can move on to the next step.

Register Workstations into eDirectory

You are going to want workstation objects in the tree so that you can send content and policies to them and run a secure remote control. To get these objects into the tree, you need to set some registry keys on the workstations. You can have the registry key set as part of a corporate image that you place on your corporate machines, for example, or you can do it automatically when any user logs in to those workstations. Let's do it automatically when a user logs in to ZENworks.

You need to create an application object that will create the appropriate registry key for the workstation and associate it with all users. Additionally, you need to create an import policy to tell ZENworks how to name these newly created workstations and where to put them.

The following steps configure the settings in your ZENworks tree:

1. Log in to eDirectory as admin and launch ConsoleOne.

2. Optionally create an Applications container and browse to that container.

3. Choose the Application Object Creation Wizard on the toolbar, or select the container, right-click, and select New→Application.

4. Create a new simple application object called Workstation Registration. Define no path and system requirements, and don't associate it with anyone yet. On the last page of the wizard select Display Details After Creation and click Finish.

5. Select the Distribution Options→Registry page and enter the following registry key:

   ```
   HKEY_LOCAL_MACHINE\Software\Novell\ZENworks\zenwsreg\Imp
   ortServer = IP/DNS
   ```

   Figure 3.2 illustrates this process.

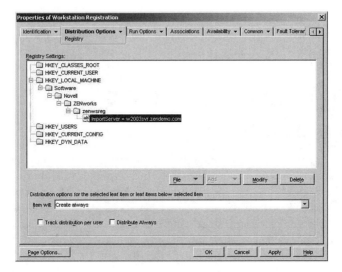

FIGURE 3.2
The registry key for Workstation Registration object.

6. Select the Associations tab and associate this new application object with all users in the system. Make sure that the association has Force Run turned on and all the other settings turned off so that the application will not show up on the user's desktop.

7. Click OK.

ZENworks attempts to register the workstation at boot time and user login or logout. If you want to manually force it to register immediately, just call `zwsreg.exe` in the postdistribution script of the Workstation Registration application object.

You now need to set up a workstation import policy to tell the system how to name the workstation objects when they are automatically created. This can be done by executing the following steps:

1. Open the server package created when you installed ZENworks Desktop Management on the server. (This will most likely be found in the container where the server is located in the tree.) Enable the workstation import policy.

2. Select the import policy and click Properties.

3. Select the Containers tab and click Add to add to the list the container where you want the workstations to be created. If they are going to be scattered around the tree (because you want them in the user's or relative container), you need to select on this screen a container in the tree that is higher than any of the potential locations of the workstation objects.

4. Select the Platforms→General tab and fill in the container where you want the workstation objects to be placed (under the Location tab on page).

5. Select the Naming tab and enter the rules for the names of your workstations.

6. Select the Groups tab and enter the groups you want the workstations to be added as members.

7. Select the Limits tab and enter the value of the user login number that you want. This value causes ZENworks to create the object only after the user has logged in the specified number of times.

8. Click OK.

9. Verify that the server package is associated with the server running the installed Import process.

10. Click OK.

You are now set on both the server side and configuration, and ready for the next step.

Set Up Policies to Take Inventory and Provide Remote Management

You are going to need workstation objects in the directory so that you can activate inventory scanning to retrieve hardware and software information about the workstation. This step instructs ZENworks when to take an inventory of the workstations and sets the security of remote management to use eDirectory security.

Set up the inventory and remote policy by executing the following steps:

1. Launch ConsoleOne.

2. Make a Policies container to hold your policies. (You don't techni-
cally need to do this, but I like to try to be organized.)

3. With the Policies container highlighted, click the Package Wizard
toolbar button. This launches the policy package creation tool.

4. Select Create a Workstation Package and click Next. Enter a name
for the package and click Next. Select Define Additional Properties
and click Finish.

5. Select Remote Control Policy under the Policies→General tab.
Click the Properties button.

6. Configure the properties on the various tabs to configure such
items as Password Enabled and whether to allow encrypted sessions. After the policy is configured as you want, click OK.

7. Select a platform to configure the inventory policy by selecting
Policies→Windows XP (for example). Enable the inventory policy
by selecting the policy and then clicking Properties.

8. Under the General tab, browse and select the inventory service created at installation time. This object will most likely be in the container where the server is located and will be named something like
`Inventory Service_SERVERNAME`.

9. Configure the policy by selecting the Hardware and Software Scan
tabs and selecting the desired configuration.

10. Select the top Policy Schedule tab and choose when you want the
inventory scanning to take place on the workstations. Click OK.

11. Select the Associations tab in the policy package and associate the
policy with workstations or with containers that hold workstations.
Click OK.

You have now configured the policy to describe how inventory and
remote management will behave for the associated workstations.

Deliver the ZENworks Management Agent to the Workstations

You are now ready to get the agents on the workstations in your network and start managing them. This can be done by adding the agent install to a login script, group policy (delivered by Active Directory), or website.

ZENworks includes a tool called the Agent Distributor that uses the information in an Active Directory to locate and install the agent directly on attached workstations.

To install the agent using the Agent Distributor, do the following:

1. Log in as a member of the Active Directory domain.

2. Launch the Agent Distributor (this is typically found in `c:\novell\consoleone\1.2\bin\AgentDistributor.exe`).

3. Enter the administrator username and password. This account will be used to authenticate and install the agent to the selected workstations. Click OK.

4. Browse to and select the ZENworks agent. This is typically located (on a Windows server) at `c:\novell\public\zenworks\ZfDAgent\English\ZfDAgent.msi`.

5. Click the Configure Agent button to bring up another dialog that lets you set what components are installed and where the middle-tier server is located. Fill in all the appropriate and desired configurations and click OK (see Figure 3.3).

6. Click the Add button. Browse to and add all the workstations from Active Directory for which you want the Agent Distributor to install the agent. Give it a little time to get connected with the workstation and install the agent.

FIGURE 3.3
The Agent Distributor installation configuration screen.

Create an Application Object

The next step is to create an application object to deliver to the workstation. There are two types of application objects: an MSI and a URL. Both can be created with the following steps:

1. Launch ConsoleOne.

2. Browse to and select your Applications container. Click the Create Application Object button on the toolbar. This launches the Application Object Wizard.

3. Select a Web application option and click Next.

4. Give the object a name, such as ZENworks Web Page, and click Next.

5. Enter the URL for the desired web page (for example, www.novell.com/zenworks). Click Next.

6. Add any rules for workstation requirements for this application object. The assumption can be made that everyone will have a browser, so just click Next.

7. Associate the application with all your users and click Next.

8. Click Display Details After Creation and click Finish.

9. Modify the Application Icon for the application object by clicking on Modify, Browse and then browsing to `iexplorer.exe` and selecting an appropriate icon for a web page. Click OK.

Now it is time to create the MSI application. First, you must make sure that the MSI files are available to the user or workstation. To do so, copy the MSI file to a Windows Share or NetWare volume where users will have rights to read the files. After the MSI files have been properly placed on the server, do the following:

1. Launch ConsoleOne.

2. Browse to and select your Applications container. Click the Create Application Object button on the toolbar. This launches the Application Object Wizard.

3. Select the MSI Application option and click Next.

4. Browse to the MSI file on the server. If you are going to use a mapped drive that all workstations will know, then use that; otherwise, make sure that the path is a full UNC path. Click Next.

5. Give the object a name and click Next.

6. Add any rules for workstation requirements for this application object. This could be free disk space or other requirements. Click Next.

7. Associate the application with all your users and click Next.

8. Click the Display Details After Creation check box and click Finish.

9. Select Run Options→Applications. You can change the path to file attribute to be the executable on the local workstation after the MSI is installed. If you do, ZENworks automatically launches the application after the MSI install is complete. Click OK.

You have now completed all the steps to deliver any application, perform remote management functions, and collect inventory on all of workstations running the ZENworks management agents.

Checking It All Out

Now it is time to see whether everything is working properly. To do so, first log in to a workstation that has the ZENworks agent installed. If you are in a Windows environment, the ZENworks management agents will automatically log in to eDirectory behind the scenes and will not prompt the user, as long as the username and password for the domain are the same as the username and password for eDirectory.

Launch Application Launcher or Explorer on the workstation, if you did not set it to launch automatically. Notice that when launched it automatically runs the Workstation Registration application object and then displays the other two applications in the window or on the desktop.

You should be able to click on the applications and have them installed and launched. When the schedule for the inventory hits, the scanner should start up and send the inventory to the server to be placed in the Sybase database.

When the inventory scanner is running a service, `ZfDInvScanner.exe` will show up in the services list. When it is completed, it will be sent to the server. You can open the ZENworks Inventory icon on the taskbar of the server and see what is happening on the inventory store functions. You will eventually see that the workstation inventory is imported into the database.

While waiting for the inventory, you can try some remote management functions by doing the following:

1. Launch ConsoleOne.

2. Browse to the Workstations container and see your workstation object. Select the workstation object and right-click. Select Actions→Remote Control from the pop-up menu.

3. If you have rights, ZENworks will allow you to remotely control the workstation.

If you don't have a workstation object or want to perform remote control based on a password, do the following:

1. Launch ConsoleOne.

2. Select the Tools→ZENworks Remote Management→Remote Console→Windows from the menu. You are presented with a dialog to enter an IP address and a password.

3. On the workstation, right-click on the Remote Control icon in the systray; choose Security, Set Password from the menu; and enter a password.

4. In the dialog box on ConsoleOne, enter the IP address of the workstation and the password that was entered on the workstation. Choose the Remote Control operation. Click OK.

By now the inventory should be done. You can look at a brief history of the inventory by opening the workstation object and looking at the Minimal Inventory on the Inventory tab. If you want to look at all the information, click the More Workstation Information button on the Minimal Inventory tab. This launches the interface to display all the scanned information, as shown in Figure 3.4.

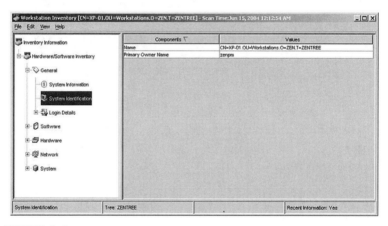

FIGURE 3.4
Workstation inventory information.

To generate a printable report, do the following:

1. Launch ConsoleOne.

2. Select Tools→ZENworks Inventory→Configure DB from the menu.

3. Browse to and select the Database that contains the inventory (this database object was created when the Sybase database was installed).

4. Click OK.

5. Choose Tools, ZENworks Inventory, ZENworks Reports. You are given a dialog box with the list of reports previously defined by ZENworks (see Figure 3.5). Choose a report and view the output, as illustrated by Figure 3.6.

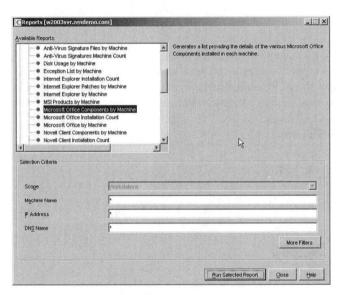

FIGURE 3.5
Choose the report you want to run.

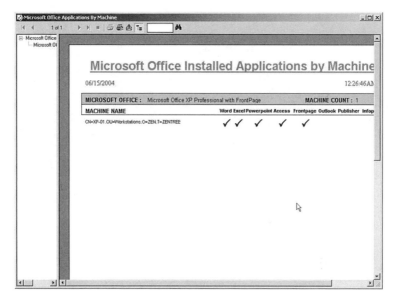

FIGURE 3.6
Microsoft Office analysis report on the workstations.

Congratulations! You have now successfully installed ZENworks Desktop Management, delivered applications, run an inventory, generated reports, and performed remote management functions.

Summary

Now that you know the basics of installing, configuring, and setting up basic Desktop Management, we will move on to understanding how to get Server Management started in your environment.

## CHAPTER 4

Getting ZENworks Server Management 7 Working in Your Environment

This chapter provides a step-by-step walk-through of how to get ZENworks Server Management up and running quickly in your environment. This chapter assumes that you have previously installed eDirectory into your environment. However, if you are using Active Directory, you can refer to Chapter 2, "Installing ZENworks 7 Suite," for information on how to install ZENworks in an Active Directory environment.

Before beginning this chapter, verify that the following components of ZENworks Server Management 7 have been installed:

- ▶ Policy and Distribution Services
- ▶ Server Inventory
- ▶ Remote Management
- ▶ Management and Monitoring Services

Set Up the ODBC Driver

You will want to get reports, views, and queries out of the Server Management system, so you need to install the ODBC drivers to access the Sybase database, or the external database that you may supply.

Assuming that you are using the embedded Sybase installed when ZENworks Server Management 7 was installed, you must perform the following:

1. Insert the Companion CD 2 and browse the CD to the `Database Drivers` directory.

2. Unzip the `SybaseODBC.zip` file onto your `c:\` directory. This creates a directory called `Sybase` on your drive.

3. Browse to the directory and copy the `c:\Sybase\Sybase\ Program Files\sybase` subdirectory into your `c:\Program Files` directory.

4. Run the `Sybase8ODBC.reg` file located at `c:\Sybase\Sybase`. This updates the registry keys so that you can use the drivers.

5. Start your ODBC Data Source Administrator by choosing Control Panel→Administrative Tools→Data Sources. You should see the screen shown in Figure 4.1.

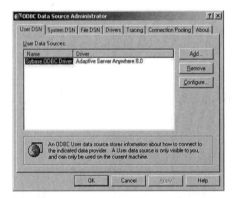

FIGURE 4.1
The ODBC Data Source Administrator.

6. Select the Sybase ODBC Driver configuration module and click the Configure button. Click on the Database tab and fill in the IP address of the server holding the Sybase database. Click on the Network tab and change the TCP/IP field to be `host=<IP Address of your Sybase Database>`.

7. Select the ODBC tab and click the Test Connection button. You should receive a connection successful message.

After this is completed, you can move on to the next step.

Start the ZENworks Server Management Console

After the ZENworks Management and Monitoring Services are installed, start the management console to begin monitoring your network.

> **NOTE** If you did not start the autodiscovery process and the back-end services during installation, you cannot expand the site and use the Atlas view until you complete the discovery process. You must manually start the services on NetWare, at the command prompt by entering the STARTMMS command.

To start the management console, do the following:

1. Log in to the eDirectory tree containing the Management server.

2. Start ConsoleOne by selecting ZfS Console in the ZfS program group of the Windows Start menu.

3. Select ZfS Sites to begin managing your network.

4. Expand the site and select Atlas.

From the Atlas view, you can begin monitoring your managed servers. For example, you can configure and monitor alarms on servers and segments or check the utilization of the IP protocol. These, and many other features of ZENWorks Server Management and Monitoring Services, will be discussed in later chapters of this book.

Create a TED Distribution

Another step in getting started with ZENworks Server Management is to set up a TED channel. This can be done by first creating a TED distribution, which is a collection of files that you want distributed across the network.

Use the following steps to create a TED distribution:

1. From within ConsoleOne, create a container for TED distributions.

2. Create a TED distribution object in the new container.

3. From the Type tab in the properties window of the new TED distribution object, shown in Figure 4.2, set the distribution type to File.

4. Add files to the distribution, set a schedule, and specify a TED distributor.

5. Click Apply to save the settings.

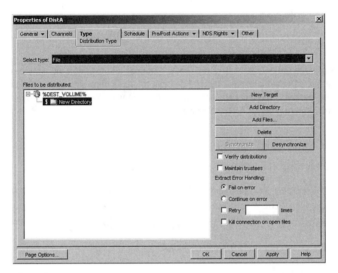

FIGURE 4.2
The Type tab in the properties window of a TED distribution object.

After you create a TED distribution, you need to set up the TED channel to distribute the distribution to servers in your network. To set up the TED channel, first configure a TED channel object by using the following steps:

1. From within ConsoleOne, create a TED channel object.

2. From the Distributions tab of the new channel object, shown in Figure 4.3, add the TED distribution created earlier to the new TED channel object.

3. Add at least one subscriber object to the Subscribers panel, shown in Figure 4.4, of the new TED channel object.

After the TED distribution object is associated with a channel object and subscribers are added to the channel, the distribution is ready to be distributed.

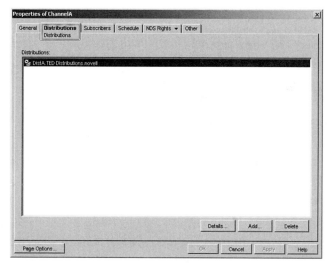

FIGURE 4.3
Distributions tab in the properties window of a TED channel object.

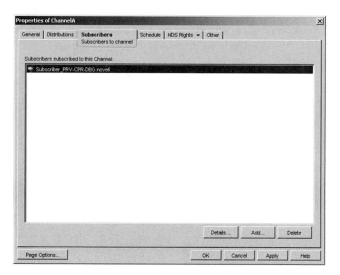

FIGURE 4.4
Subscribers tab in the properties window of a TED channel object.

> **NOTE** When changes are made to channels, distributions, or subscribers, administrators will be prompted to resolve certificates. You need to resolve the certificates for the distribution changes to be completed.

Checking It All Out

Now it is time to see whether everything is working properly.

If the network discovery has finished, you should be able to view information about managed servers and segments. Use the following steps to view the Segment Dashboard of a managed segment:

1. Launch ConsoleOne.
2. Select ZfS Sites.
3. Select a site management object and expand the view by clicking the '+' sign.
4. Right-click on a segment object and then select Views→Segment Summary to display the Segment Summary window shown in Figure 4.5.

The segment summary displays information about alarms, protocols, and packet distribution actively being monitored on the segment.

Now that you've verified that your management and monitoring services are in place and available, you need to verify the server distribution channel. The easiest way to verify the server distribution channel is to send distribution to be sent immediately.

Use the following steps to send the distribution immediately:

1. Launch ConsoleOne.
2. Open the properties window of the TED distribution object you created earlier.
3. Select the Schedule tab.
4. Set the Schedule type to Run Immediately.
5. Check the Send Distribution Immediately After Building option.
6. Click the Apply button, and the distribution will be sent when the distributor is refreshed.

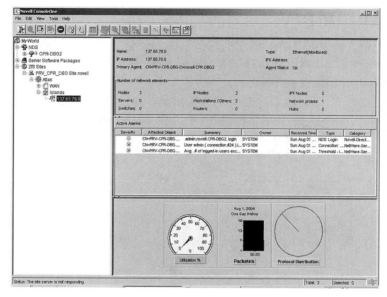

FIGURE 4.5
Segment Summary view of a monitored segment in the ZENworks Site Management Atlas.

After the distribution is sent, you can run a report that shows whether the distribution was successful. This also allows you to test the ZENworks reporting mechanism.

Use the following steps to run a distribution report:

1. Launch ConsoleOne.

2. Select Tools→ZENworks Reports from the main menu.

3. Expand the Tiered Electronic Distribution Reports option.

4. Select the Distribution Detail report and click the Run Selected Report button to generate the report.

The report should show the date, time, and status of the distribution you started.

Summary

You have now successfully installed ZENworks Server Management, accessed the server management console, delivered a server software distribution, and generated reports.

Chapter 6, "Getting ZENworks Handheld Management 7 Working in Your Environment," walks you through getting your ZENworks Handheld Management system up and functioning.

## CHAPTER 5

Getting Asset Inventory 7 Working In Your Environment

This chapter will provide a step-by-step walkthrough on how to get ZENworks Asset Inventory up and running quickly in your environment.

Step One—Install ZENworks Asset Management

Install ZENworks Asset Management (Asset Inventory only) by following the instructions specified in Chapter 2, "Installing ZENworks 7 Suite." As part of ZENworks suite you are entitled to the inventory portions of ZENworks Asset Management. To have the other components, including software usage tracking and license compliance, you must purchase ZENworks Asset Management separately.

This how-to assumes that you have installed the Asset Inventory components of ZENworks Asset Management. There are several ways to get the agent onto the devices in order to begin collecting inventory. You can install the agent from the ZENworks Asset Management CD, through a login script, through a group policy (delivered by AD), through a website, or by using ZENworks Desktop Management. In this how-to we will discuss a new method that has not been available to previous ZENworks Desktop Management customers: Network Discovery.

NOTE In order to perform Asset Inventory functions, the default ports 7460 and 7461 must be open on any firewall that may be running on the devices.

Step Two—Discover Devices on the Network

ZENworks Asset Management can find workstations, servers, printers, routers, hubs, and other devices on the network. From this list of possible devices, you can select the devices to receive the agent. After they are selected, the agent will be installed and will collect its first inventory scan.

To get the most information about the devices through Network Discovery, you need to have SNMP and/or WMI installed and enabled on the devices.

To configure and start Network Discovery, complete the following:

1. Launch the ZENworks Asset Manager and log in as the enterprise administrator.

2. Click on the Management tab (next to the Query and Report tabs).

3. Expand Public Network Discovery Tasks.

4. Double-click on the Default Network Discovery Task. This opens a window similar to Figure 5.1.

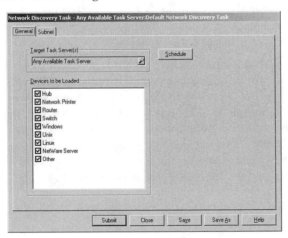

FIGURE 5.1
The Default Network Discovery Task dialog.

5. Select the Subnet tab (see Figure 5.2).

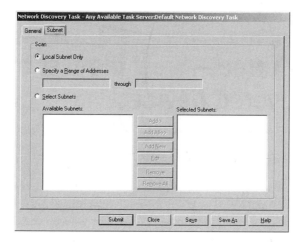

FIGURE 5.2
The Default Network Discovery Task dialog with the Subnet tab.

6. Select one of the following to scan:

▶ Local Subnet Only—To scan the subnet that is the same as the server.

▶ Specify a Range of Addresses—Enter the beginning and ending IP address values.

▶ Select Subnets—From the list of available subnets, select the ones you desire.

NOTE Limit your initial Network Discovery to one or two subnets, as each subnet can take up to 40 minutes to scan.

7. Click on the General tab.

8. Click on the Schedule button to set the schedule for the network scan. Choose Immediately from the drop-down menu, and then click OK to save. Click Submit to start the network discovery task on the server and then click Yes to save the information.

9. To see the status of Network Discovery, click the Tasks tab at the bottom of the ZENworks Asset Manager window. You might need to press F5 in that window to get it to update with the task list.

The system now scans each of the possible IP addresses and attempts to discover if there is a device with that address and, if there is, what kind of device is found.

Step Three—View the List of Discovered Devices

You can view the list of discovered devices from the Web Console. Complete the following to see the list of discovered devices along with collected information:

1. Launch the Web Console and log in as the enterprise administrator.

2. Click on the Network Discovery tab. This displays a set of expandable folders on the left that contain reports that can be run.

3. Click on the plus sign next to the Device List branch. This opens up that part of the branch and displays it. Click on the All Types branch label.

4. This displays on the screen a brief report that lists a count of all devices, Windows devices, and other devices.

5. Click on the number on the right in the row you are interested in. For this how-to, click on the All row. This displays a list of IP addresses discovered to have a device, along with some basic OS product information.

6. Drill in further by selecting the IP address. This displays the SNMP or WMI information discovered about this device.

Now that you are discovering devices, you need to place the ZENworks Asset Management agent on the devices about which you want to collect more detailed inventory.

Step Four—Remote Client Installation

From the ZENworks Asset Manager application you can push out the Asset agent to the selected devices. Complete the following to push the agent to a device:

1. Launch and log into the Manager application as the enterprise administrator.

2. Click on the Tools→Remote Client Install menu. This displays a screen similar to Figure 5.3.

FIGURE 5.3
The Remote Client Install dialog.

3. Expand the Entire Network, Network Discovered (Windows machines) part of the tree. This displays the list of IP addresses that represent Windows machines.

4. Select an IP address root and expand that to display the devices that have been discovered in that subnet.

5. Select the device under this list. After it is highlighted, choose the Edit→Add to Workstation List menu item. This places that device on the list to install the agent.

6. Select the workstation in the list and then press the Install→Start Install menu item. This brings up a dialog similar to what is shown in Figure 5.4.

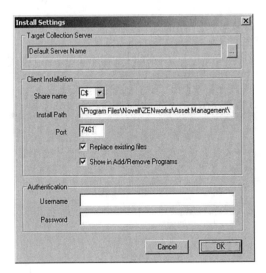

FIGURE 5.4
The Install Settings dialog.

7. Enter an administrator account and password that will be accepted by the remote device. Click OK to begin the installation process.

Now the installation begins. After the installation has completed, an inventory scan will be taken and sent to the ZENworks Asset Management server.

Step Five—Checking It All Out

Now it is time to see if the scanning is occurring and begin looking at the reports that show the scanned devices in your network. You can view the inventory reports by completing the following:

1. Launch the Web Console and log in as the enterprise administrator.

2. Click on the Reports tab.

3. Click on the plus sign next to the System List folder item on the left.

4. Click on the All Departments entry and you see a count list of inventoried devices.

5. Click on a hot-linked number to the right to display those devices. You can drill into those devices by selecting the specific device and seeing the collected inventory.

Explore other reports that are available under the Reports folder to see additional ways to explore your collected inventory information.

Summary

Congratulations! You have now successfully installed ZENworks Asset Management, discovered devices, installed the agent, run an inventory scan, and generated reports.

## CHAPTER 6

Getting ZENworks Handheld Management 7 Working in Your Environment

This chapter provides a step-by-step walk-through of how to get ZENworks Handheld Management up and running quickly in your environment. This chapter assumes that you have previously installed eDirectory into your environment. If you are installing ZENworks into an Active Directory environment, you need to follow the information described in Chapter 2, "Installing ZENworks 7 Suite," on how to install ZENworks in an Active Directory environment.

Before beginning this chapter, verify that you have installed the following components of ZENworks Handheld Management 7:

- ▶ Handheld Management
- ▶ Access Point (optional)
- ▶ Desktop synchronization integration software (if you are using the desktop to hotsync your PDA device)
- ▶ PDA client on the desktop

When you are sure that all these are installed, you can begin configuration.

Complete Handheld Server Configuration for Inventory

You will most likely want to get inventory information and reports from your PDAs in the network. To get at this information you must complete the configuration of the handheld service object that was placed into eDirectory at installation time.

You can configure the service object with the following steps:

1. Open Explorer and browse to the installation directory of ZENworks Handheld Management (this is typically `c:\Progam Files\Novell\ZfH`) and make the `ZfH` directory a Windows share.

2. Launch ConsoleOne.

3. Browse to where the handheld service object was placed (it will most likely be called `<HANDHELDSERVER>_ZfHService`). Open the object to look at its properties.

4. Modify the Remote Path attribute to point to the `ZfH` share that you created in step 1. Click OK.

After this is done, you can move on to the next step of creating a handheld policy to import.

Create a Handheld Policy for Import

It is important to have the handheld objects imported into the eDirectory tree so that you can associate policies and applications with them, and it is possible to retrieve their inventory.

The following steps are necessary to get the import policy up and running in your ZENworks tree:

1. First make sure that you are logged in to eDirectory as admin and launch ConsoleOne.

2. Create a Handhelds container, if you are going to put them all in the same place.

3. Browse to the container where you want the handhelds import policy to be placed. This can be any container in the tree even if it is different from the Handhelds container.

4. Select the Policies container and select the Create Policy Package Wizard.

5. On the first page of the wizard select Handheld Service Package and click Next.

6. Select the container (that you defined in step 3) where you want it and click Next.

7. Select Define Additional Properties and click Finish. ConsoleOne creates the policy package and then opens the properties of that package.

8. Enable the Handheld Import policy by checking the check box and click the Properties button.

9. Select the Platforms→General tab for all PDAs, or administer different policies for each different type of device. These policies allow you to specify where you want the handheld object created (that represents the physical device), the rules the system should use to name the object, and any specifications on which groups you want the created handheld objects to be members of. After you have completed all these specifications, click OK.

10. Select the Associations tab and click Add; then browse to and select the ZENworks Handheld Service object created at installation and modified in a step 3 of the "Complete Handheld Server Configuration for Inventory" section.

After the handheld agents are installed on the handheld device, when the device attempts to perform synchronization, ZENworks will register the device and create a handheld device object in eDirectory. When that object is present, any associated applications and policies will be applied (on the next synchronization).

ZENworks Handheld Management always takes an inventory of the handheld device so that no additional inventory policy is required to be created and associated.

Now we are set on the server side and the configuration.

Deliver the ZENworks Handheld Agent to the Workstations

If your handheld devices are not going to synchronize via a desktop, the agents must be installed via your wireless synchronization point. After those agents are delivered to the device, they will connect via IP into the Access Points or directly to the ZENworks Handheld Server to get their policies and applications and to deliver their inventory.

The ZENworks Handheld Management clients and synchronization software must be installed on each of the workstations where a PDA device will be synchronizing from the cradle. Installing the agents via a group policy, login script, or other mechanisms can do this. If ZENworks Desktop Management is in the system, ZENworks can deliver these clients to the proper workstations. Proceed with the following steps to get the synchronization software and agents to the workstations via ZENworks Desktop Management:

1. Copy the `Proxy` directory (under a language directory of the ZENworks Handheld Management CD) to your `ZfH` share on the server. This is the proxy client that needs to be installed on the workstations where synchronization is done.

2. Log in as an eDirectory admin and launch ConsoleOne.

3. Browse to your Applications container, select that container, and select the Application Wizard.

4. Give the application object a name. Let's call it Handheld Synchronization Client.

5. The path to the executable file should be a UNC path to the `setup.exe` file in the `Proxy` directory of the `ZfH` share you created earlier—for example, `\\w2003svr.zendemo.com\ZfH\Proxy\Setup.exe`. Click Next.

6. The next page asks for rules that have to be satisfied before this application is delivered to the desktop. Specify the rules that tell whether HotSync or ActiveSync is installed on the desktop.

   This can be done with a rule that checks to see whether the HotSync Manager or ActiveSync programs are in the Start menu of the user. The rule can be something like

```
File exists(%*ProgramFiles%\Palm\Hotsync.exe) exists OR
(File exists(%*ProgramFiles%
\Microsoft ActiveSync\WCESMgr.exe) exists)
```

Click Next.

7. Associate the application object with all users in the system. You will probably want it to be a force run so that it will automatically install and also to uncheck the App Launcher configuration so that it will not show up on the desktop. Click Next.

8. Select Define Additional Properties and click Finish. ConsoleOne creates the application object and opens the properties of that object.

9. Select the Run Options tab and turn on the Run Application Once field. This way the application object will only be run one time and not every time the application launcher is started.

10. Click OK.

This application object will now deliver and install the Handheld Synchronization Client to those desktops with ActiveSync or HotSync installed, when the user logs in to her workstation.

If you want to also deliver the IP clients for wireless connectivity to other desktops, you can create another application object just as we did for the synchronization client and associate it with your users. The synchronization client then delivers the IP client with it.

The way we have configured this application object will launch the installer from the server, and the user will need to walk through the installation interface. If you want, you could run Snapshot to capture the install and provide this as a Microsoft Installer package (MSI) or Application Object Template (AOT) package that would remove the user interface installation. (See Chapters 10, "Creating Application Packages with snAppShot," and 11, "Creating and Using Application Objects," for more information on Snapshot and application object creation.)

Open Firewall Ports for Synchronization with the Workstations

From the previous step, you will have created an application object for the synchronization software required to run on the workstation where the handheld will run. If you have workstations that are Windows XP workstations with SP2 installed, there could be a firewall running on these workstations. ZENworks Handheld Management requires that certain ports be opened for communication between the synchronization workstation and the Access Points.

If ZENworks Desktop Management is in the system, ZENworks can deliver the proper registry key changes to the clients to open these ports and allow handheld communication. Proceed with the following steps to get the firewall ports opened properly on these workstations via ZENworks Desktop Management:

1. Log in as an eDirectory admin and launch ConsoleOne.

2. Browse to your Applications container, select that container, and select the Simple Application Wizard.

3. Give the application object a name. Let's call it Open Handheld Firewall.

4. Leave the path to the executable file blank. Click Next.

5. The next page asks for rules. Leave the page blank and press Next.

6. Leave the associations page blank as well and press Next.

7. Select Display Details After Creation and click Finish. ConsoleOne creates the application object and opens the properties of that object.

8. Select the Distribution Options tab and then the Registry submenu from there.

9. Create the following registry keys by adding each component of the registry tree to the list and finishing with the proper key and value:

   ```
   Key Tree:

   HKEY_LOCAL_MACHINE\SYSTEM\CurrentControlSet\Services\
   SharedAccess\
   ```

```
➥Parameters\FirewallPolicy\DomainProfile\
➥GloballyOpenPorts\List
Value Name = Value Data
"2398:TCP"="2398:TCP:*:Enabled:ZENworks Handheld TCP"
"2398:UDP"="2398:UDP:*:Enabled:ZENworks Handheld UDP"
```

10. Select the Run Options tab and turn on the Run Application Once and Install Only fields. This way the application object will only be ran one time for the user.

11. Select OK to close the application object.

12. Select the application object you created above for the handheld agent and open its properties.

13. Select the Run Options tab and Application Dependencies submenu.

14. Click Add. Browse to and select the Open Handheld Firewall application object. This will cause the firewall application to be delivered any time that the synchronization client is delivered.

15. Click OK to save and close the application.

This application object will now deliver and install the registry keys required to open the firewall on the workstation. This allows the handheld synchronization client on desktops with ActiveSync or HotSync installed to communicate back to the Access Points.

Create a Handheld Application Object

You can create a handheld application object to deliver applications to the handheld device by following these steps:

1. Place the files destined for the handheld device in the **ZfH** share that you created. You may want to create an **Apps** subfolder for your files.

2. Launch ConsoleOne.

3. Browse to and select the container where you want to create your handheld application object.

4. Right-click and select New→Object from the pop-up menu.

5. Select Handheld Application from the list of available objects and click OK.

6. Enter a name for the handheld application. In this example, we call it ListDB because that is the name of the Palm application we will demonstrate. Select Define Additional Properties and then click OK.

7. Click on the Files tab.

8. Click Add to add the files. Browse to the directory and select the files that you need to deliver to the device as part of the application.

9. Click the drop-down for Destination and select what is appropriate. For the Palm, we will select Copy the Files to a Palm Device.

10. Select the Associations tab and then click Add. Browse to and select any containers of devices or a specific device. Click OK.

11. Click OK again to save the handheld application object.

Now we have an application to deliver to any new Palm devices introduced into the system. The next step illustrates how policies also can be applied.

Creating and Applying a Handheld Policy

In this step we create a handheld policy for our Palm device. You can also create policies for Windows CE or PocketPC devices as well as RIM Blackberry devices.

To create a new handheld policy and hand it out to your devices, do the following:

1. Log in as admin and launch ConsoleOne.

2. Browse to and select the container where you want to keep your policies for handhelds—it does not have to be in the container where the actual handheld objects reside.

3. Select the Create Policy Package Wizard on the toolbar.

4. Select Handheld Package on the first page of the wizard and click Next.

5. Enter a package name for the object and the container where you want this object. Click Next.

6. Click Define Additional Properties and click Finish.

7. On the Policies tab, select the device type, and enable the policy you want. For this example, enable Palm Security Policy, as shown in Figure 6.1.

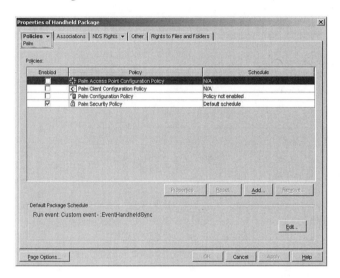

FIGURE 6.1
Select Palm Security Policy.

8. Click on the Security tab and activate Require a Password to Be Set on the Handheld. For this example, also activate Additional Password Settings and then Enable Auto Lock Configuration On Power Off, as shown in Figure 6.2.

9. Click on the Self-Destruct tab and enable self-destruct after the specified number of failed attempts. Click OK.

NOTE When the user fails to log in properly, immediately after the specified failed login the device will be reset and will remove all applied software and content.

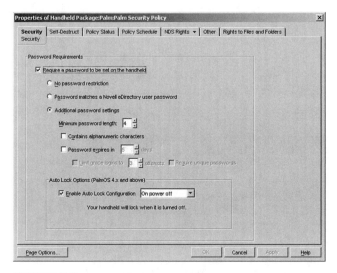

FIGURE 6.2
Configuring the handheld security policy.

10. Select the Associations tab and then click Add. Browse to and select the handheld devices or containers of handheld devices that you want to receive and enforce this policy. Click OK.

11. Click OK.

Now you have an application and a policy to deliver to your new handheld objects when they are created.

Checking It All Out

Now it is time to see whether everything works properly.

Log in to a workstation that has the ZENworks agent installed. If you are in a Windows environment, the ZENworks Management agents will automatically log in to eDirectory behind the scenes and will not prompt the user as long as the username and password for the domain are the same as the username and password for eDirectory.

Launch the Application Launcher or Explorer on the workstation, if you did not set it to automatically launch. ZENworks should display the associated applications. The Force Run installation of the Open Handheld

Firewall application and the Handheld Synchronization application should happen automatically. When installed on the laptop or desktop where the device is synchronized, the clients will be automatically placed on the handheld device at the next synchronization.

Synchronize the handheld device. You should see some ZENworks Handheld Management agents being installed on the device. The first synchronization places the agents on the device.

Synchronize the device again. This time the agents will communicate with the Access Point installed on the ZENworks Handheld Server. Notice that because user associations are active for Handheld Management, you are prompted for a username and password for eDirectory. After the agents have communicated with the server, a handheld object will automatically be created in the directory along with full inventory information.

Go to the server and launch ConsoleOne. Browse to the container where you told the import policy to place handheld devices. You should see the handheld device that was just created. Look into its properties and see the general and inventory information about the device. Notice that the application and security policy has still not been sent to the device. The last synchronization just created the object.

Synchronize the Palm device yet again. This time you will see that the list application is automatically installed. You will also see that the policy is delivered—the Palm automatically prompts you for a password. Enter a password and click OK. Power off the Palm and power it back on—note that the password is now enforced on power-on of the device.

Check out the policy. Enter the correct password at the power-on prompt. Enter some addresses in the address book. Power off the Palm device. Power it back on, but enter an incorrect password the number of times you specified in the policy (default is 5). After the fifth incorrect password, enter the correct one. Notice that the address book is empty, and the list application is gone. Reset and synchronize to restore your Palm device.

Go to the server and look at the properties of the Palm device. Click on the ZENworks Inventory tab and click the Advanced Inventory button at the bottom. Another inventory tool opens up and shows you the full details of the handheld scan as shown in Figure 6.3.

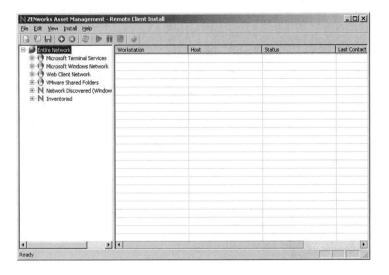

FIGURE 6.3
Advanced inventory tools for handhelds.

From this Advanced Inventory view you can create and run reports. From the menu, select Reports→Software Inventory→Applications→For a Client, for example. Select the Palm device that was just imported and click OK. This brings up the report for that handheld device as illustrated in Figure 6.4.

Congratulations! You have now successfully installed ZENworks Handheld Management, delivered applications and policies, and run an inventory report.

Summary

Now that you have successfully configured the basic features of ZENworks Handheld Management, you are prepared to continue to explore handheld and other features of ZENworks.

The next chapter walks you through getting your ZENworks Patch Management system up and functioning.

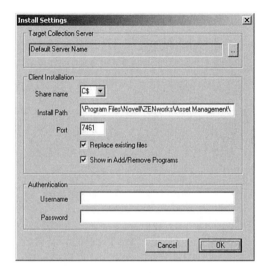

FIGURE 6.4
Software inventory report for Palm handheld device.

## CHAPTER 7

Getting ZENworks Patch Management Working in Your Environment

This chapter provides a walk-through of how to get ZENworks Patch Management up and running quickly in your environment. ZENworks Patch Management is powered by PatchLink software, which analyzes each workstation to determine the patches needed and then delivers those patches. ZENworks Patch Management determines all the patches that may be required through connectivity and publications of patches from PatchLink back-end servers over the Internet.

Before beginning this chapter, verify that you installed ZENworks Patch Management by following the instructions specified in Chapter 2, "Installing ZENworks 7 Suite."

Deploying the PatchLink Agent to Managed Workstations

After you install the ZENworks Patch Management server, you need to deploy the agents that determine whether a patch is required, retrieve the patch, and then install the patch onto the workstation. The agent can be deployed in a number of ways. Choose what is most appropriate for your environment. The agent can be delivered to the workstation via

▶ A ZENworks application object associated with a workstation or with a user.

▶ An image applied to workstations in your environment.

▶ Launching a browser from the local machine and connecting to the ZENworks Patch Management server. Then click on the Computers link and click the Install button.

▶ Running the Deployment Wizard using information in a domain environment. This can be launched by opening the ZENworks Patch Management administration browser page, clicking the Computers link, clicking the Install button, and selecting the Domain-wide Agent Deployment Wizard for Windows link.

For the example in this chapter, we will run the Deployment Wizard by clicking the computer's link on the Patch Management Administration browser page. When you click on the link, the system downloads an installation program that installs the Deployment Wizard. The wizard must be run on a Windows computer that is a member of the domain.

To accomplish this, walk through the wizard as outlined in the following steps:

1. Enter the Host URL. This is the URL for the ZENworks Patch Management Server that provides the patches to the workstation agent (see Figure 7.1).

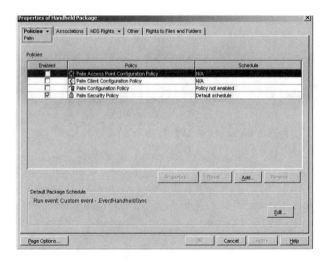

FIGURE 7.1
Initial screen of the Deployment Wizard.

2. Enter the Serial Number. This is the unique number entered when the ZENworks Patch Management Server was installed. This number is displayed on the home page of the administration browser tool.

3. Choose the Domain Wide Install/Uninstall option and click Next.

4. You are prompted for, and need to supply, the Domain Administrator password. You also must select whether you want all computers in the domain to be listed and then selected or whether you will enter the computers manually. For this example, you only need to select a small set of computers to receive the agent. Click Next (see Figure 7.2).

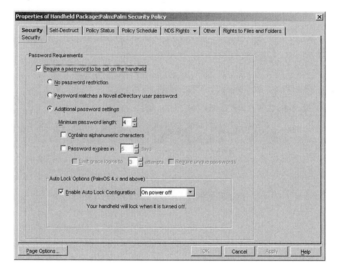

FIGURE 7.2
Deployment Wizard prompt for domain administrator account.

5. Select the computer or computers you want to have the agent installed on and click Install.

6. Click Begin on the summary screen. The wizard will authenticate to each of the workstations as a domain administrator, and the files will be copied to the workstation and then installed. A process called *agent rollout* will be launched on that workstation. When the agent is installed, this is reported back to the wizard.

Now that the agents are properly deployed and running on the workstations in your environment they will begin to analyze the systems. After each workstation is examined, this information is sent to the ZENworks Patch Management server.

Reviewing Reports of Required Patches

After the agents have reported their information back to the ZENworks Patch Management Server, the server generates reports to display what patches are required in your environment.

These reports can be seen by selecting the Vulnerabilities hotlink on the home page (see Figure 7.3).

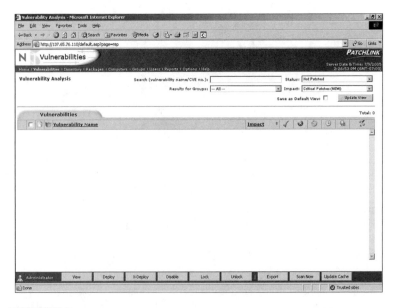

FIGURE 7.3
Vulnerabilities page of ZENworks Patch Management system.

As you can see, the Vulnerabilities page lists each of the patches that are available and needed in your environment. A green check mark identifies the number of systems that have this patch installed, whereas a red X identifies the count of systems that do not have the patch installed.

You can drill down into the report by selecting the report name. This displays the actual systems in the environment that have reported not having this patch installed.

From this screen, you can manually deploy the patch to your selected machines as explained in the next section.

Manually Deploying a Patch to a Workstation

From the detail listing of the patch report, you are shown a list of computers that require this patch. On this screen, you can select the computers you want to receive the patch and then click the Deploy button at the bottom of the screen. Clicking the Deploy button launches the Schedule Deployment Wizard (see Figure 7.4).

FIGURE 7.4
The Schedule Deployment Wizard offers a number of choices.

This wizard walks you through the following configuration items:

▶ The Welcome screen appears first and gives you an overview of the tasks the wizard performs.

▶ The Schedule screen is used to identify when you want the system to send and install the patch. The default values of the current time are automatically entered into the fields.

▶ The Deployment Options screen (see Figure 7.5) enables you to specify whether the system should send the patch to 25 computers at a time or blast it out to all servers. Remember that performance demands on the server will increase based on the number of computers it communicates with.

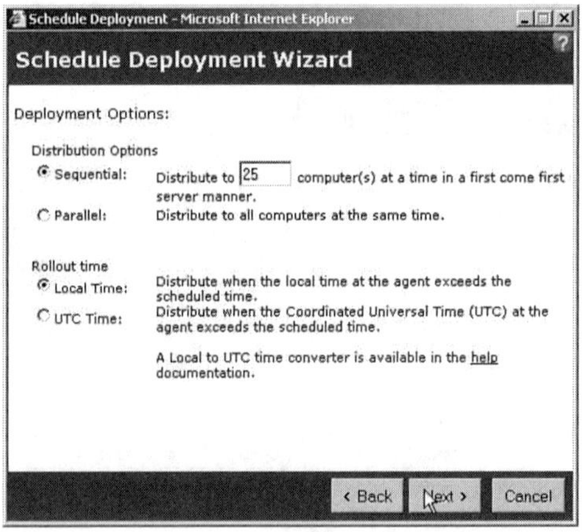

FIGURE 7.5
Specify whether to send to all computers immediately and the time to base patch application on.

You can also specify whether the time you gave on the previous screen is based on the local time of the computer or Universal time.

▶ Following this, several screens appear that ask you about rebooting the workstation and accepting license agreements; then the summary screens appear. Clicking Finish on the last screen of the wizard begins the process of sending the patch to the specified computers.

This method can be used to manually send a particular patch to one or more specified machines, either fulfilling an immediate need or for testing purposes. This can become cumbersome, however, if you have many machines in your environment.

ZENworks Patch Management has the capability to automatically send patches to machines based on grouped criteria. The next section examines the method for automatically deploying patches.

Automatically Deploying Patches

When a computer receives the agent and connects into the ZENworks Patch Management Server, the system automatically places the computer into a group based on its operating system. These operating system groups are automatically defined and exist by default in the system. You can create additional groups and modify the requirements for membership.

When a computer is in a group, you can view reports and look at membership and scheduled deployments. In addition to these features, you also have the ability to define mandatory patches. When a patch is defined as mandatory for a group, any computer that is, or becomes, a member of the group automatically receives and installs the mandatory patches if they don't already have the patch applied.

You can configure a patch to be mandatory by performing the following steps:

1. Click the Groups hotlink at the top of the administration browser page.

2. Select the operating system group you are interested in. For this example, select WinXP.

3. On the next screen, you are presented with the criteria that defines membership in the group. Select the Mandatory tab.

4. To place a patch into the mandatory list, click the Manage button at the bottom of the screen.

5. You are presented with a screen that shows the list of available patches on the system. Browse through the list of patches and select the patches you want to place as mandatory; then click the Assign button (see Figure 7.6).

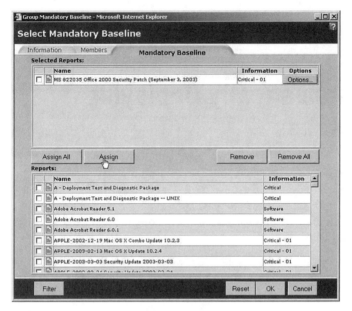

FIGURE 7.6
Screen showing mandatory patches to a group.

> Click OK to place the assigned patches into the system. If the patch
> requires accepting a license agreement, that agreement will be dis-
> played on the screen. If so, accept the agreement by clicking the
> Accept button.

After the patch is placed in the mandatory list, ZENworks Patch
Management applies the patch automatically to any member of the group
that does not have the patch installed.

Congratulations! You have now successfully installed ZENworks Patch
Management, delivered a patch, and configured the system to make sure
that all workstations receive the patch when necessary.

Summary

Now that you have gotten your ZENworks Patch Management to the
basic level and delivering a patch to your test machines, the next chapter
explores how to get ZENworks Data Management functioning in your
environment.

## CHAPTER 8

Getting ZENworks Data Management 7 Working in Your Environment

This chapter provides a step-by-step walkthrough of how to get ZENworks Data Management up and running quickly in your environment. This chapter assumes that you have previously installed eDirectory into your environment. If you are using Active Directory, you can refer to Chapter 2, "Installing ZENworks 7 Suite," for information on how to install ZENworks in an Active Directory environment. If you are using Linux servers, you can also refer to Chapter 2 for information on how to install ZENworks in a Linux environment.

Start the iFolder Management Console

To access the iFolder management console, do the following:

1. Open a supported web browser.

2. Enter the following URL in the Address box of the web browser to bring up the iFolder management console shown in Figure 8.1:

   ```
   https://<ip_address_or_dns_name>.<domain_name>.com/
   iFolderServer/Admin
   ```

After you have successfully opened the management console, you are ready to configure your first iFolder server.

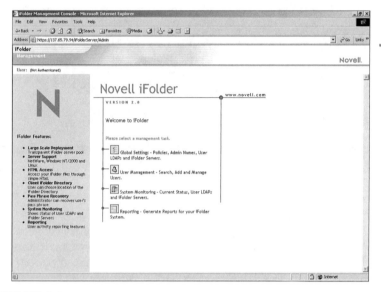

FIGURE 8.1
ZENworks iFolder management console.

Configure the iFolder Server User Context

The first task you need to perform in the iFolder management console is to define a context where user objects are stored. All user objects in this context will then show in the iFolder management console.

To define the user context, use the following steps:

1. Click Global Settings and enter the admin ID and password.

2. Click User LDAPs from the Global Settings screen shown in Figure 8.2.

3. Select the iFolder Server.

4. Select the contexts where user objects reside in the Contexts To Search list shown in Figure 8.3.

5. Enable the Search Subcontexts option if you need LDAP to search for users below the selected context.

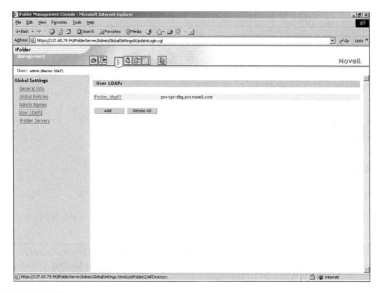

FIGURE 8.2

Global settings in iFolder management console.

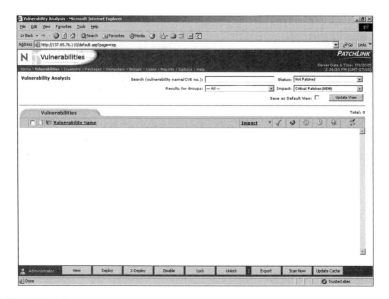

FIGURE 8.3

User search context list for LDAP in the iFolder management console.

6. Click Add to add any additional contexts.

7. Click Update to save the new settings.

After you define the user context, you can begin provisioning user objects to be able to use the iFolder services.

Enable iFolder Services for Users

Use the following steps to enable iFolder services for users:

1. From the iFolder management console, click User Management.

NOTE The first time you log in to User Management, iFolder extends the schema. Make sure that you log in as a user with sufficient rights to make the schema extension.

---

2. Use the Advanced Search for Users tool, shown in Figure 8.4, to locate the users you want to enable.

3. Enable iFolder services for users using one of the following methods:

   ▶ Single user—Enable only a single user by clicking on the user link.

   ▶ Multiple users—Enable all users that meet the search criteria by clicking the Enable button.

   ▶ Subset of users—Enable a subset of users by selecting the check box next to each user you want to enable; then click the Enable button.

   ▶ Subset of users on a specific iFolder server—Enable a subset of users on a specific server by selecting the server from the drop-down menu and then clicking the Enable button.

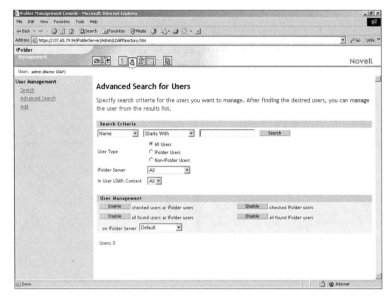

FIGURE 8.4
Advanced Search for Users in the User Management section of iFolder management console.

Check It Out

After you access the iFolder management console and configure the iFolder server and users, it is time to see whether everything is working properly. Use the following steps to verify whether iFolder is properly configured:

1. Install the iFolder client on a user workstation.

2. Log in to the iFolder server as one of the users you enabled.

3. Copy files to the user's iFolder home directory.

4. Access the iFolder website for users by typing the following URL into a web browser:

   ```
   https://<ip_address_or_dns_name>.<domain_name>.com/
   iFolder
   ```

5. Click the login link and type in the user's name and password.

6. Verify that the files copied to the user's home directory are available from the iFolder user web interface, shown in Figure 8.5.

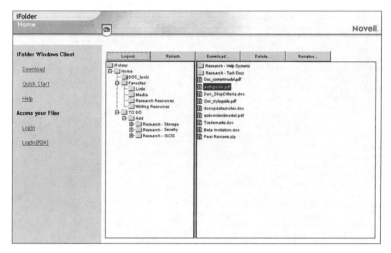

FIGURE 8.5
Web interface for iFolder.

Summary

You have now successfully installed ZENworks Data Management, configured an iFolder server, enabled services for users, and synchronized user data using both the iFolder client and the web interface.

CHAPTER 9

Creating Application Packages with New Software Packaging

ZENworks has added a new software packaging tool to its suite to enhance the creation of application objects. That tool is a limited version of AdminStudio that ships with the ZENworks suite.

The limited edition includes the following tools shown in Figure 9.1:

- ▶ Repackager—Used to create and modify software packages
- ▶ Tuner—Used to create transforms for the software packages
- ▶ Distribution Wizard—Used to create ZENworks application and server distribution objects

The following sections describe how to use AdminStudio to create ZENworks software distribution objects.

FIGURE 9.1
AdminStudio ZENworks edition.

Creating a Software Package Using the Monitoring Method

There are two methods to create software packages inside AdminStudio. The first is using a monitoring method, in which the utility watches lower-level system activities and records related changes made by one or more setup programs.

After the changes have been monitored, they are analyzed and stored in an output file that can be converted into a ZENworks software object.

Use the following steps to create a software package using the monitoring method from AdminStudio:

1. Open the Repackager.

2. Select InstallShield Repackaging Wizard from the main Repackager screen shown in Figure 9.2.

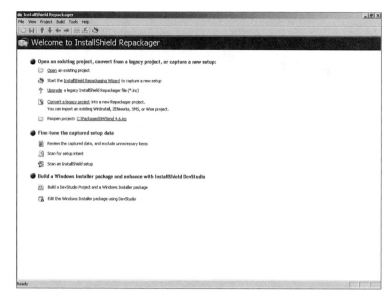

FIGURE 9.2
The InstallShield Repackager.

3. Click Next.

4. Select Installation Monitoring and click Next.

5. Specify a set of programs to execute to install the software package as shown in Figure 9.3. All programs executed will be packaged together in one software package.

6. Specify the product information for the software package and click Next.

7. Specify the path to store the package in.

8. Click Edit to modify the Analysis Options, as shown in Figure 9.4, and click OK. Any items not checked are not monitored.

9. Click the Start button, and the install programs begin to execute in order.

10. Complete the install of all install programs.

11. Click Process to begin analysis of the monitored changes.

12. Review the summary and click Finish to complete the creation of the software package.

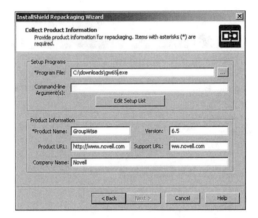

FIGURE 9.3
Repackaging Wizard Collect Product Information screen.

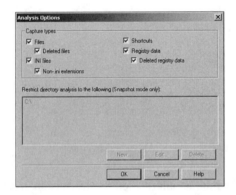

FIGURE 9.4
Repackaging Wizard Analysis Options dialog box.

After AdminStudio finishes creating the software package, you can import it into eDirectory and use it to distribute the software using ZENworks.

Creating a Software Package Using the Snapshot Method

The second method of creating a software package is using a snapshot method, in which the utility takes an initial snapshot of the local system and then takes a second snapshot after the program installation is complete.

The differences between the two snapshots are analyzed and stored in an output file, which can be converted into a ZENworks software object.

Use the following steps to create a software package using the snapshot method from AdminStudio:

1. Open the Repackager.

2. Select InstallShield Repackaging Wizard from the main Repackager screen shown previously in Figure 9.2.

3. Click Next.

4. Select Snapshot and click Next.

5. Select Single Step. The single step takes the initial snapshot, runs the installation programs, and then takes the second snapshot all in one pass.

NOTE You also have the option to select Multistep, where only the initial snapshot is taken. Then at some point in the future, after the product install has occurred, you run the second pass. However, you would really only ever want to use this if the application install and the Repackaging Wizard were not compatible, or if a workstation reboot must take place.

6. Specify whether you want to be prompted before executing the setup program and click Next.

TIP Only check this if you need to be prompted before running the install. On some workstations it takes a lot of time to run each snapshot, and, if the option is not checked, you can walk away from the workstation and come back after the installation is finished.

7. Specify a set of programs to execute to install the software package as shown previously in Figure 9.3. All programs executed will be packaged together in one software package.

8. Specify the product information for the software package and click Next.

9. Specify the path to store the package in.

10. Click Edit to modify the Analysis Options, as shown previously in Figure 9.4, and click OK. Any items not checked are not monitored.

11. After the install is complete, click Process to begin analysis of the monitored changes.

12. Review the summary and click Finish to complete the creation of the software package.

After AdminStudio finishes creating the software package, you can import it into eDirectory and use it to distribute the software using ZENworks.

Modifying a Software Package

After the Repackager creates a software package, administrators can modify the package to include only the components necessary for distribution. This feature allows administrators to trim applications to a smaller size as well as remove any file or Registry conflicts that might occur during distribution.

Use the following steps to modify a software package from AdminStudio:

1. Open the Repackager from the Start Page tab of AdminStudio, shown in Figure 9.1.

2. Select Open from the main Repackager screen, shown previously in Figure 9.2.

3. Find the software package you want to modify and click Open to bring up the Repackager editor shown in Figure 9.5.

The following sections describe modifying different parts of the software package.

Modifying Files and Folders

The Repackager editor allows administrators to exclude and include specific files and folders of a software package. This feature can be useful if the software install added a lot of unnecessary files to the system.

Unnecessary files and folders can be excluded from being distributed with the package by using the following steps from the Repackager editor:

1. Select Files and Folders as shown in Figure 9.6.

2. Select the files or folders you want to exclude.

3. Click the Exclude button.

4. Select File→Save from the main menu.

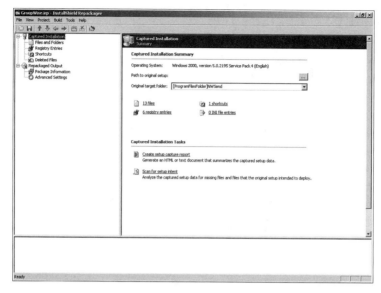

FIGURE 9.5
The InstallShield Repackager editor.

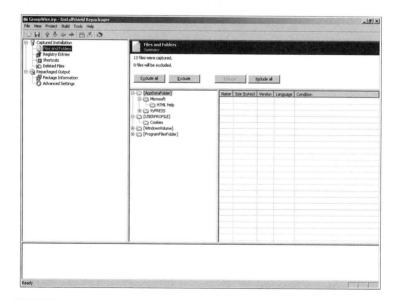

FIGURE 9.6
Files and Folders screen of the InstallShield Repackager editor.

Modifying Registry Entries

The Repackager editor also allows administrators to exclude and include specific Windows Registry entries from a software package. This feature can be useful if the software install added Registry entries that are not necessary and have the potential of conflicting with other Registry entries.

Unnecessary Registry entries can be excluded from being distributed with the package by using the following steps from the Repackager editor:

1. Select Registry Entries as shown in Figure 9.7.

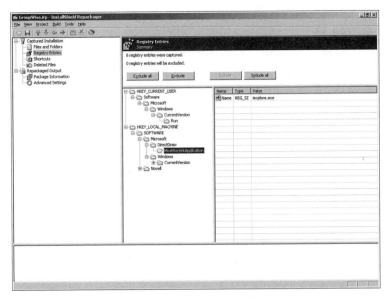

FIGURE 9.7
Registry Entries screen of the InstallShield Repackager editor.

2. Select the Registry entries you want to exclude.

3. Click the Exclude button.

4. Select File→Save from the main menu.

Modifying Shortcuts

The Repackager editor also allows administrators to exclude and include shortcuts from being created by a software package.

Unnecessary shortcuts can be excluded from being distributed with the package by using the following steps from the Repackager editor:

1. Select Shortcuts.

2. Select the Shortcut you want to exclude.

3. Click the Exclude button.

4. Select File→Save from the main menu.

Modifying Deleted Files

The Repackager editor allows administrators to exclude the deletion of files by a software package. This feature can be useful if the software install removes data files that you want to be kept intact when the software is distributed.

Unnecessary file deletion can be excluded from being distributed with the package by using the following steps from the Repackager editor:

1. Select Deleted Files as shown in Figure 9.8.

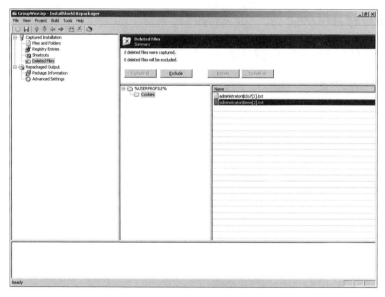

FIGURE 9.8
Deleted Files screen of the InstallShield Repackager editor.

2. Select the files you want to exclude from deleting.

3. Click the Exclude button.

4. Select File→Save from the main menu.

Creating ZENworks Objects

After a software package has been created and modified it can be built into an .MSI file and then turned into either a ZENworks application or server distribution object.

To build the .MSI file select Build→Build from the main menu of the Repackager editor shown in Figure 9.8. The .MSI file will be created in the same folder the software package is located in.

The following sections describe how to turn the .MSI file into a ZENworks object that can be distributed using the ZENworks distribution methods.

Creating a ZENworks Application Object

The Distribution Wizard, included with AdminStudio, can be used to turn an .MSI file into a ZENworks application object that can be distributed to managed workstations.

Use the following steps to create the ZENworks application object:

1. Open the Distribution Wizard from the Start Page tab of AdminStudio, shown previously in Figure 9.1.

2. Select ZENworks Desktop Application from the drop-down list, shown in Figure 9.9.

3. Select the .MSI file and any transforms or additional properties and click Next.

4. Specify the login information in the ZENworks Login Screen shown in Figure 9.10 and click Next.

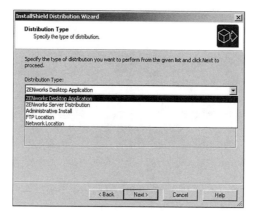

FIGURE 9.9
Distribution Type screen of the Distribution Wizard.

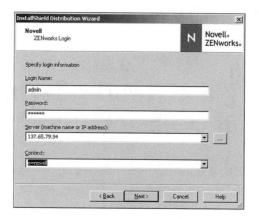

FIGURE 9.10
ZENworks Login screen of the Distribution Wizard.

5. Specify the object name, context, version, source path, and Administration Package Path in the application object properties screen shown in Figure 9.11 and click Next.

6. Review the application object summary and click Next.

7. Review the status of the distribution for any problems creating the application object and then click Finish.

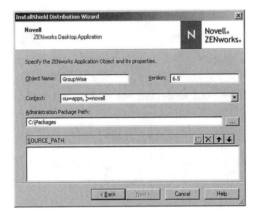

FIGURE 9.11
Application object properties screen of the Distribution Wizard.

After you complete the preceding steps, a ZENworks application object is placed in the location you specify and can be distributed to workstations on the network.

Creating a ZENworks Server Distribution Object

The Distribution Wizard, included with AdminStudio, can also be used to turn an .MSI file into a ZENworks server distribution object that can be distributed to managed servers.

Use the following steps to create the ZENworks server distribution object:

1. Open the Distribution Wizard from the Start Page tab of AdminStudio, shown previously in Figure 9.1.

2. Select the .MSI file and any transforms you want to perform on it and click Next.

3. Select ZENworks Server Distribution from the drop-down list shown previously in Figure 9.9.

4. Specify the login information in the ZENworks Login Screen shown previously in Figure 9.10 and click Next.

5. Specify the object name and context in the server distribution object properties screen shown in Figure 9.12 and click Next.

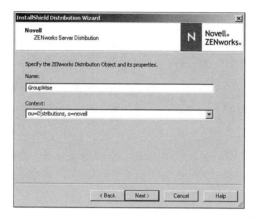

FIGURE 9.12
Server distribution object properties screen of the Distribution Wizard.

6. Specify the name and context of the distributor object you want to use to distribute the server distribution, as shown in Figure 9.13.

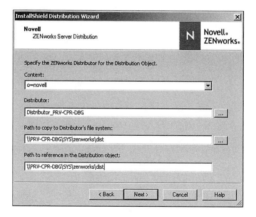

FIGURE 9.13
Distributor object properties screen of the Distribution Wizard.

7. Specify the path to the distributor's file system and the path that should be referenced in the distribution object and click Next.

8. Review the server distribution object summary and click Next.

9. Review the status of the distribution for any problems creating the server distribution object and then click Finish.

After you complete the preceding steps, a ZENworks distribution object is placed in the location you specify and can be distributed to servers on the network.

Summary

This chapter examined the new software packaging tool that ZENworks added to its suite to enhance the creation of application objects. The tool is a limited version of AdminStudio that ships with the ZENworks suite.

## CHAPTER 10

Creating Application Packages Using snAppShot

One of the most useful tools provided in ZENworks Desktop Management is the snAppShot utility. As an administrator installing and updating applications on client workstations, the snAppShot utility saves you an extensive amount of time by enabling you to create a template during a single install that can be used to easily distribute applications and upgrades to several workstations on your network.

This chapter familiarizes you with the snAppShot utility and shows you how to use it to create application packages. The following topics are discussed:

- ▶ Understanding snAppShot
- ▶ When to use snAppShot
- ▶ How snAppShot works
- ▶ Advanced features of snAppShot
- ▶ Limitations of snAppShot
- ▶ Using snAppShot
- ▶ snAppShot application packages versus .MSI files

Understanding snAppShot

The first step in using the snAppShot utility is to understand what it is. Simply put, snAppShot is an application used to create before-and-after images of a model workstation when installing or upgrading an application to it.

snAppShot discerns the differences between the two pictures. It saves the differences and can use them later to upgrade or install applications to other workstations on the network.

When To Use snAppShot

Now that you understand what snAppShot is, you need to know when to use it. By default, snAppShot is generally used to package an application to distribute to several other users based on eDirectory and the application properties.

snAppShot captures changes made to a workstation during install; however, many situations exist in which you can use it to save time. The following sections describe how snAppShot is useful in three situations.

Complex Installations or Upgrades

Using snAppShot to aid in complex installations or upgrades can save you a considerable amount of time spent repeating the same steps. By using snAppShot, you simply need to perform the complex installation or upgrade once, record the differences, and then apply those differences to the other workstations.

One example of where snAppShot is useful in a complex upgrade is installing and configuring a printer driver on a Windows XP client. To do so, use the following steps:

1. Enter the network path to the printer or browse the network to find the appropriate queue.

2. Use the Windows XP CD-ROM or the path to the CAB files that have the necessary files to install the printer driver.

3. Configure the printer drivers for the desktop.

4. Make the appropriate configuration changes for the printer.

The preceding steps are tolerable if it is for one or two workstations. If a hundred or more workstations need the printer set up, however, the task becomes monumental.

Using snAppShot on one Windows XP machine to "package" a printer installation enables you to create an application object template that you can use to create an application object. After the application object is created for the printer installation, other Windows XP clients can install the printer, with drivers, without having to use CAB files, use the Windows XP CD-ROM, or make configuration changes!

Numerous Installations or Upgrades

Using snAppShot to aid in installations that must be done on numerous workstations can also save you a lot of time. Often, application upgrades or installations are simple to perform and only take a short time on one workstation. That time is multiplied, however, by the number of clients you have on your network. Many companies have thousands of clients, and, although installing an application takes only a few minutes on one client, the installation takes days to complete on all network clients.

snAppShot enables you to configure the upgrade or install to be automatically performed throughout the network. Instead of running the install or upgrade on workstation after workstation, you simply perform it once on the model workstation and use snAppShot to record the differences. When recorded, the changes can be made to several other workstations easily and efficiently.

Using snAppShot to record the changes during the update and packaging into an application object enables you to have the upgrade performed automatically as the users log in to the network. This saves a lot of time and effort in upgrading many users and also guarantees that every client is upgraded.

Verifying Changes Made During an Install or Upgrade

Another situation where snAppShot is useful is to verify or view the changes made by an application install or upgrade. Although snAppShot was not designed for this purpose, it works well because it captures the changes made during the install.

Several times, the installation of one application has been known to create difficulties for other applications. Using snAppShot enables you to detect what the application install did to your client and enables you to correct it without uninstalling or reinstalling an application.

A good example of where snAppShot can help with reviewing an application install is installing a new application that updates shared DLLs in the SYSTEM directory for Windows 98. The application replaces a working DLL with a newer DLL that has bugs.

After the new DLL is installed, the new application works fine, but a previously installed application fails to load properly. Normally you would have two options: to either reinstall the application that is failing to unload, or to uninstall the new application and hope that its uninstall mechanism backed up the old DLLs before copying over them.

Using snAppShot, however, enables you to see which DLLs were replaced by the new application install, so that you can simply replace them from a backup, CD-ROM, or other source.

How snAppShot Works

Now that you know what snAppShot is, and what it is for, you need to understand how it works. This section discusses how snAppShot analyzes and stores the changes made by an installation or upgrade.

Files Created by snAppShot

When snAppShot is used to determine the changes made by an installation or upgrade, many files are created to store information. These files are used later when the installation or upgrade needs to be performed again. They contain all the information needed to update other clients without having to run the installation program or upgrade again.

The following sections describe the file types created by snAppShot when recording the changes during an installation or upgrade.

.AXT Files

AXT stands for *Application Object Text Template*, meaning that the .AXT file is written in human-readable, text format. Therefore, you can open it in a text editor and edit the contents.

NOTE The .AXT file takes longer to import into an application object than an .AOT file (discussed in the following section) and is prone to inaccuracies if certain .AXT file format standards are not followed.

An .AXT file is a collection of information about what happened on a workstation when an application was installed to it. You can also think of it as a *change log* that contains the differences between the pre- and postapplication installation states of a workstation. snAppShot discovers these differences and records them in an .AXT file, shown in Figure 10.1, that is named after the application object specified when snAppShot is run.

FIGURE 10.1
Sample excerpt from a snAppShot .AXT file.

You use the .AXT file when creating and setting up application objects using Application Window for large-scale distribution. The .AXT file delivers the information about the application to the new application object.

.AOT Files

AOT stands for *Application Object Template*. The .AOT file is written in binary format and cannot be edited in a text editor.

NOTE .AOT files import faster into an application object and can be more accurate than their text-based counterpart, the .AXT file.

An .AOT file is a collection of information about what happened on a workstation when an application was installed to it. You can also think of it as a *change log* that contains the differences between the pre- and postapplication installation states of a workstation. snAppShot discovers these differences and records them in the .AOT file named after the application object specified when snAppShot is run.

You use the .AOT file when creating and setting up application objects using Application Window for large-scale distribution. The .AOT file delivers the information about the application to the new application object.

.FIL Files

One .FIL file represents one application file installed to a workstation. Just as there can be hundreds of files installed to a workstation during an application's installation or upgrade, there can also be hundreds of .FIL files representing that application.

Think of .FIL files as the application object's copy of the originally installed application files.

> **TIP** For convenience, it's recommend that you store .FIL files in the same place as the .AOT file. If you place these files in a network location, it is easier to access them as you build and distribute the application object.

A list of the .FIL files that need to be copied to run an application is kept in the .AOT file. This list can be viewed from the Application Files property page in the application object in ConsoleOne.

FILEDEF.TXT

The FILEDEF.TXT file is a *legend* that compares originally named installed files with the newly named .FIL files. snAppShot copies the FILEDEF.TXT file to the same directory where the .FIL files are created. You then use it to compare .FIL files to the originally installed files. Figure 10.2 shows a sampling from the FILEDEF.TXT file.

Information Saved by snAppShot

snAppShot saves information before and after an installation or upgrade and then determines the differences. Installations and upgrades can change many different files and settings on a workstation; therefore, snAppShot saves many different types of information about the configuration of the workstation.

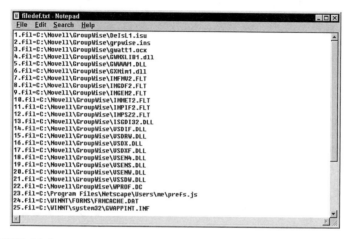

FIGURE 10.2
Sample excerpt from a snAppShot `filedef.txt` file.

The following sections describe system configuration information that snAppShot stores before and after an installation or upgrade, and then uses to determine changes to the workstation.

Files and Folders

First and foremost, snAppShot saves a list of all files added or modified during the installation or upgrade. It also saves a copy of the file named as a .FIL file to be used in later installations or upgrades.

INI Files

snAppShot saves any changes to application or system INI files so that those files can be modified when the application object is used later. The following are some of the files snAppShot monitors for changes:

▶ WIN.INI—Contains information about the Windows workstation setup, such as desktop settings, file types, and so on.

▶ SYSTEM.INI—Contains information about device and driver settings for the Windows workstation.

▶ PROTOCOL.INI—Contains information about the network settings for the Windows network protocols.

System Configuration Text Files

snAppShot records any changes to system configuration text files as well. Any changes to drivers being loaded, paths being set, or environment variables being added or changed are recorded and can be applied to other systems when the application object is used to install or upgrade the workstation.

The following are the two files snAppShot monitors for system configuration changes:

- ▶ `AUTOEXEC.BAT`
- ▶ `CONFIG.SYS`

Windows Shortcuts

Any changes to Windows shortcuts are also recorded by snAppShot. If an application installation or upgrade adds a new shortcut to the desktop or Start menu or modifies the path in an existing shortcut, those changes are applied to other systems as well, along with the application object.

Registry

snAppShot also records any changes made to a Windows workstation's Registry by an installation or upgrade. This is important later because even if you copy all files installed by an installation or upgrade and make the appropriate changes to configuration files, the application often fails to run because Registry settings have not been made.

Using snAppShot to save the Registry settings fixes that problem by saving the changes to the Registry and then applying them when the application object is used to install or upgrade the application on a new workstation.

Advanced Features of snAppShot

Although snAppShot is a relatively easy program to run, some advanced features make it a powerful tool. This section discusses the following advanced features included in the snAppShot utility.

Using snAppShot Preferences

If you think of snAppShot as a camera and the .AOT file as the developed "picture," you can think of snAppShot preferences as the adjustments you make to the camera (for example, aperture settings, film speed, or focus) before you take the picture.

snAppShot preferences let you control what snAppShot "sees" as it discovers the changes made to a workstation as a result of installing an application. In other words, you can specify or control information recorded about the certain items (described in the following sections) during an installation or upgrade.

Files/Folders

Using snAppShot preferences, you can include or exclude the recording of certain changes to particular folders and files. This enables you to protect certain directories that you do not want altered on other workstations when the application object is used on them to install or upgrade an application.

Windows Shortcuts

Using snAppShot preferences, you can exclude particular Windows shortcut files from being recorded. This allows you to protect certain application shortcuts from being created or altered on other workstations during the installing or upgrading of an application.

INI Files

Using snAppShot preferences, you can exclude particular application INI files from being recorded. This enables you to protect certain application INI files from being created or altered on other workstations when the application object is used on them to install or upgrade an application.

System Configuration Files

Using snAppShot preferences, you can define which system configuration file changes are recorded. This enables you to set which system configuration changes should be recorded and created or altered on other workstations when the application object is used on them to install or upgrade an application.

Registry Entries

Using snAppShot preferences, you can also include or exclude changes from particular portions of the Windows Registry from being recorded. This enables you to protect certain areas of the Windows Registry that you do not want to be altered on other workstations when the application object is used on them to install or upgrade an application.

Special Macros

Special macros are built-in machine and user-specific values that the snAppShot utility uses to control how application object templates are created. These special macros read from the Registry, enabling for the customization of application objects in snAppShot. This customization enables you to distribute the same application to several machines that might have Windows installed or configured differently.

The following is a list of some common macros:

- ▶ WinDir—Directory containing the Windows OS, typically C:\Windows or C:\WINNT
- ▶ WinSysDir—Directory containing the Windows system files (DLLs)
- ▶ TempDir—Windows temporary directory, typically C:\Windows\temp
- ▶ Favorites—File system directory that serves as a common repository for the user's favorite items
- ▶ Fonts—Virtual folder containing system fonts
- ▶ Personal—File system directory that serves as a common repository for personal documents

---

TIP The online help that appears when you click the help button on the Application Object Macros property page in ConsoleOne gives a detailed list and explanations of the macros available to snAppShot.

When snAppShot starts, it asks the client library for a list of the special macros. This list combined with the user macros (created in the custom mode) make up the complete list of macros, which are then placed in order from the longest value to shortest.

While snAppShot runs, it records the differences between the preinstallation scan and the second scan. It then creates an entry in the AOT file, during which snAppShot calls the routine that searches and replaces data with the macro's name. Later, when the Application Window is used to distribute the object, it gets the macro values from the .AOT file.

The Application Window receives the values and names for these special macros by looking in the Registry under the key:

```
HKEY_CURRENT_USER
+Software
+Microsoft
+Windows
+CurrentVersion
+Explorer
+Shell Folders
```

The Application Window client creates a special macro using the name and value.

NOTE If the value does not exist, the special macro is returned, and the data value is set to blank.

For example, let's say that a special macro is defined for a directory containing temporary files. The entry in the Windows Registry would appear as

```
HKEY_CURRENT_USER
+Software
+Microsoft
+Windows
+CurrentVersion
+Explorer
+Shell Folders
TempDir=C:\DATA\TEMP
```

This Registry entry would correspond to the special macro

```
%*TempDir%
```

Therefore, when snAppShot adds the creation information for the Registry entry in the .AOT or .AXT file, it writes an entry similar to the following:

```
[Registry Value Create]
Type=String
Flag=Write Always
Key=HKEY_CURRENT_USER\Software\Microsoft\Windows\CurrentVersi
on\Explorer\Shell
Folders
Name=TempDir
Value=%*TempDir%
```

When the Application Window tries to distribute the settings, it sees the special macro value and then, in an attempt to set this Registry key, tries to read the value from this exact Registry key.

If the Registry value was set before the application is distributed, this works beautifully; however, if it is not set until after the application is distributed, the Application Window tries to use data from the same Registry entry that it is trying to create.

This problem can be remedied in two ways:

▶ The first way to resolve this problem is to set the Registry value before the user clicks on the icon (perhaps using ZENworks Desktop Management workstation policies discussed later in this book). Then when the Application Window client reads the data for these special macros, it reads the correct value and knows how to replace the special macro correctly.

▶ The second better and more difficult solution is to manually edit the .AXT file created for the application object template. Instead of using the macro you are trying to create, add in an additional entry with a different macro name but the same value.

Partial Install Detection

If your application needs to reboot the workstation to finish the installation, snAppShot recognizes this and picks up where it left off before the reboot. All snAppShot data is stored in a hidden directory on the c: drive. Furthermore, snAppShot is automatically run after the machine is restarted. When snAppShot restarts, it detects a partial installation, and a window pops up and allows you to continue with the previous installation.

Limitations of snAppShot

Now that you know how snAppShot works and understand some of its advanced features, you need to know the limitations it has. snAppShot is a powerful tool; however, it cannot be used for the tasks described in the following sections.

Capturing Install Logic

snAppShot cannot capture the "logic" of an installation involving choices based on existing hardware, software, or other settings. For example, if the application's setup program installs a particular video driver or modem setting file to a workstation, these settings may not be valid when transferred to another workstation.

The following sections describe some of the things you should be aware of when using snAppShot to create application packages.

Hardware-Specific Drivers

Some applications query the computer system to find out what hardware is installed and only install necessary drivers for the hardware that actually exists. This often results in problems if you distribute the application to clients that do not have the same hardware as the computer in which the application package was created. You can use the hardware inventory feature of ZENworks Desktop Management, discussed later in this book, to quickly determine what specific hardware is installed on clients.

Available Disk Drives

Occasionally an application install prompts the user to input additional paths of locations to store files. When you use snAppShot to create an application package, make sure that any additional paths you specify, both local and network, exist on all clients you want to distribute the application to. For example, if you specify a path on the D: drive, all clients must have a D: drive on their computer. If necessary, you can use macros and user prompts when distributing the application to handle this as well; however, that must be defined in the application object itself.

Prerequisite Drivers and Applications

Another thing you should watch for when creating application packages using snAppShot is prerequisites for application installs. For example, if the application detects to see which version of DirectX is installed on the computer, it may determine that the current version is correct and then not install needed DirectX drivers. This results in the drivers not being included in the application object. If a client receiving the application from ZENworks Desktop Management does not have the correct version of DirectX drivers, the application may not function.

Guaranteeing Impact on All Workstations

Although, snAppShot can be used to install or upgrade applications on all workstations, it cannot guarantee the impact the application install or upgrade will have on all workstations. The following sections describe some rare occasions when an application distributed to a client might result in problems.

Conflicting Local Applications

It is possible that an application distributed with ZENworks Desktop Management could conflict with a local application installed by the user of that workstation. An example of such an occurrence might be if you distribute a corporate virus scanner down to all workstations, and an existing application cannot open files correctly because the virus scanner believes it is a virus that is trying to modify the files. Another possibility is that the workstation already has another virus scanner installed that is not compatible with the corporate virus scanner.

Most companies have at least some sort of standard for applications that can be installed on clients. This standard usually ensures that applications being distributed with ZENworks Desktop Management do not conflict with any other applications on the users' systems.

Specialized Shared DLLs

When an application object is delivered to a workstation, it can be configured to copy files only if they are newer. This usually protects shared DLLs because the older functionality is usually available in newer versions.

However, some applications have DLLs that have functionality written specifically for them. This functionality does not exist in newer versions, and, if they are overwritten with a newer file, the application they supported may no longer function.

Hardware Requirements

Many applications are written for computer systems that have a high level of CPU speed, RAM, video memory, disk speed, and so on. If this type of application is distributed down to a client workstation that does not have the hardware capability to support them, they will not function properly.

This can be controlled somewhat by configuring the application object to check for hardware levels before installing (discussed in Chapter 11, "Creating and Using Application Objects"). You can use the hardware inventory feature of ZENworks Dekstop Management, discussed in Chapter 20, "Using ZENworks Workstation Inventory," to quickly determine what hardware is installed on clients.

Imaging an Entire Workstation

snAppShot is designed to record changes made by a single application install, and, therefore, it cannot image an entire workstation for disaster recovery purposes. When snAppShot discovers a workstation, it only saves some information about the files, such as the date, time, and size of the files. It does not save a copy of all the files on the workstation.

If you need to image an entire workstation, see Chapter 22, "Imaging a Workstation."

Using snAppShot

After you are familiar with when and why to use the snAppShot utility and some of its advanced features, you are ready to begin using it to create application objects.

The snAppShot utiltity can be started by executing `snapshot.exe` located by default in the `\\<server>\public\snapshot` directory. When you start snAppShot, you see a screen similar to the one in Figure 10.3.

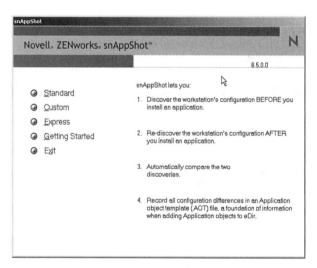

FIGURE 10.3
Select which discovery mode to use from the main menu.

This startup screen for snAppShot allows you to select from among standard, custom, or express modes (explained in detail in the following sections) depending on your needs and whether you already have a preference file ready.

Standard Mode

You should use the standard mode in snAppShot to discover the application installation changes on a workstation using default settings. If you have never run snAppShot before and are unfamiliar with the available settings, this is the best option. It requires little intervention.

To use the standard mode, simply select it and perform the following operations to create the needed files:

Name the Application Object Icon Title

After you select the standard mode installation from the main screen in snAppShot, a window similar to the one shown in Figure 10.4 is displayed. From this screen you need to input the name that the application object has in the eDirectory tree and a title for the icon that represents the application object.

TIP It is recommended that you choose names for the object and its icon that are descriptive enough to distinguish which application, and often, which version. This saves confusion and time later.

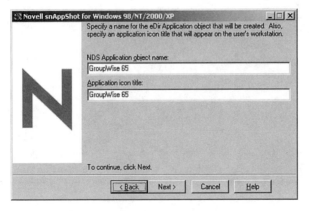

FIGURE 10.4
Name the application object and the application's icon.

Specify the Network Location of the Application Source (.FIL) Files

After you set the name for the application object and title for its icon in the standard mode install, a screen similar to the one in Figure 10.5 enables you to set the network location to store the application source files (.FIL).

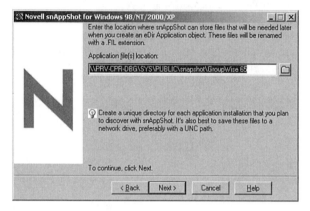

FIGURE 10.5
Specify the location to store the application source files.

When setting this location, remember the following:

▶ Make sure that you select a location that all users who must use the application object have access to.

▶ Make sure that there is enough disk space in the network location that you set to store the entire application.

Specify the Network Location of the Application Template (.AOT and .AXT) Files

After you specify a network location for the .FIL files, and checked or unchecked the Create 6.5 Application Object Template file, click the Next button. The next screen enables you to set a network location for the application template (.AOT and .AXT files). Set the network location by either entering it into the text window or by clicking on the folder button and navigating to the appropriate directory.

Specify the Drives That Will Be Discovered

After you select the network location to store the application object support files, you are given the option to select which disk drive to scan on the workstation to determine changes, as shown in Figure 10.6.

You can add drives to the list by clicking on the Add button and selecting the drives you want to scan. Conversely, you can remove drives from the list by selecting the drive and then clicking on the Remove button. You can select network drives as well but only if they are mapped. This allows you to install applications to a larger network drive if needed and still discover the changes.

FIGURE 10.6
Specify which disk drives—network and local—are scanned during discovery.

> **NOTE** Make sure that you select all drives that the application install or upgrade affects. If you do not select a drive and the application install or upgrade adds, removes, or modifies files on that drive, the changes will not be discovered.

Read the Prediscovery Summary to Check Settings

After you have all the drives you want to select added to the list of drives to be scanned, click Next, and a summary of the preferences are displayed in the next window, as shown in Figure 10.7. The information displayed includes

- ▶ Application object name
- ▶ Application icon title

- ▶ Template filename
- ▶ Application files directory
- ▶ snAppShot's working drive
- ▶ Scan options
- ▶ Disks to scan
- ▶ Directories to exclude
- ▶ Files to exclude
- ▶ System text files to scan

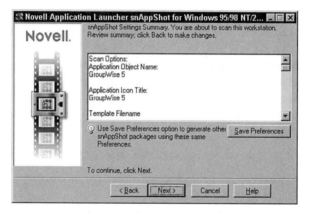

FIGURE 10.7
Review the current preference settings before starting the first discovery.

TIP Click Save Preferences to save the snAppShot preferences you have defined thus far to a file. Later, during a similar snAppShot session, you can choose the preferences you save now to accelerate the process.

Run the First snAppShot Discovery

The first snAppShot discovery is run when you click Next from the Preference Summary window. A screen shows the status of the discovery and a count of the following items that have been discovered:

- ▶ Folders and files
- ▶ Windows shortcuts
- ▶ INI files

► System configuration files

► Registry entries

Run Application's Installation or Upgrade

After the first snAppShot discovery is complete, a Run Application Install button becomes available. When you select the Run Application Install button, a file pop-up menu appears, and you can navigate to the application install executable and execute it.

After the application install is complete, you can continue with the discovery process of the snAppShot application.

NOTE Write down where the installation program installs the application's executable file. It will be useful later when creating and distributing the application object.

Enter the Path to the Application's Executable

After you complete the application install, snAppShot gives you the option to specify a path to the application's executable on this workstation. You can enter the location of the installed application files on this workstation in the text field.

Of course, if you do not want snAppShot to set a target distribution location, leave this field blank and continue.

Run the Second snAppShot Discovery

After you are finished setting the path to the application's executable and click Next, snAppShot runs the second discovery. Once again, you can monitor the status of the discovery by noting the count of the same items as before.

When the discovery is finished, snAppShot begins generating an object template. This is where the actual differences between the two discoveries are discerned and the template files created.

NOTE Depending on the number of folders, files, and Registry entries on your workstation, the second discovery process can take a considerable amount of time. However, both the discovery and the template generation screens have status counters to let you know how far along they are.

Read the Completion Summary

When the second snAppShot discovery is completed and the template files generated, a completion summary of what took place is displayed in the window shown in Figure 10.8. The completion summary contains information about the application template creation, including

- ▶ Location of the new application object template (.AOT)
- ▶ Location of the new .FIL files
- ▶ Location of the textual version of the application object template (.AXT)
- ▶ Steps to take to create the application object
- ▶ Statistical totals from the second discovery
- ▶ Statistical totals from entries added to the application object template (.AOT)

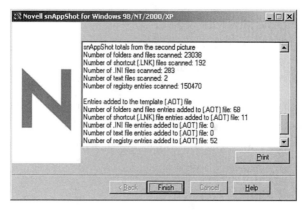

FIGURE 10.8
Review the summary of the application object template generation.

TIP You have the option from this window to print out the summary. It is recommend doing so and keeping it as a record to aid in troubleshooting future problems if they occur.

Custom Mode

Use the custom mode in snAppShot to set specific options when discovering the application installation or upgrade changes on a workstation. Custom mode is much like standard mode except that it gives you the added opportunity to specify the drives, files, folders, Registry hives, and shortcuts that you want to include or exclude in the discovery process.

You can save these settings in a preference file for later use if you need to run snAppShot for a similarly configured application.

Only in custom mode are you able to see and use all of snAppShot's features. To use the custom mode, simply select it and perform the following operations to create the needed files:

1. Choose the snAppShot preferences file.

2. Name the application object and icon title.

3. Specify the network location of the application source (.FIL) files.

4. Specify the network location of the application template (.AOT and .AXT) files.

5. Specify which parts of the workstation to include or exclude.

6. Specify the drives that will be discovered.

7. Read the prediscovery summary.

8. Run the first snAppShot discovery.

9. Run the application's installation or upgrade.

10. Specify how to handle the creation of files, folders, .INI file entries, and Registry settings.

11. Enter the path to the application's executable file.

12. Define macros for distribution automation.

13. Run the second snAppShot discovery.

14. Read the completion summary.

The following sections discuss the choices available.

Choose the snAppShot Preferences File

The first window that comes up after you select the custom mode in snAppShot is the Choose snAppShot Preferences window. From this window you have the option of either using a previously saved preference file or using the snAppShot default settings.

If you have previously created and saved a preferences file in a previous custom mode, you can navigate to that file or enter the path to it into the text field as shown in Figure 10.9.

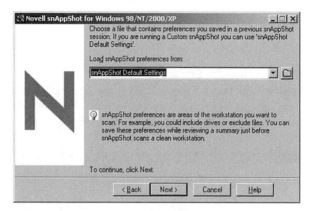

FIGURE 10.9
Specify a precreated preference file or use the default settings.

Name the Application Object and Icon Title

After you select the preference file option in custom mode in snAppShot, a window is displayed. From this screen you need to input the name that the application object will have in the eDirectory tree and a title for the icon that represents the application object.

Specify Location of Source Files

After you set the name for the application object and title for its icon in the custom mode install, a screen enables you to set the network location to store the application source files (.FIL).

When setting this location, remember the following:

▶ Make sure that you select a location that all users who must use the application object will have access to.

▶ Make sure that there is enough disk space in the network location that you set to store the entire application.

Specify Location of Template Files

After you specify a network location for the .FIL files, snAppShot enables you to set a network location for the application template (.AOT and .AXT files). Set the network location either by entering it into the text window or by clicking on the folder button and navigating to the appropriate directory. Then select the Create 7 Application Object Template File option if you want snAppShot to create a 7 version of the .AOT.

NOTE If files already exist with the same object name, you are given the option of whether to overwrite the older ones.

Specify What to Include or Exclude

After you select the network location to store the application object support files, you are given the option to select which of the following parts of the workstation you want to include, as shown in Figure 10.10:

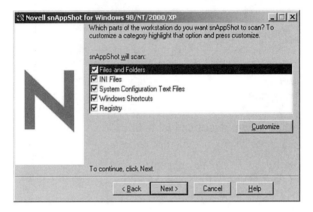

FIGURE 10.10
Specify which parts of the workstation to include or exclude.

▶ Files and Folders—From the Workstation Scan Customization menu in snAppShot, you can modify which files and folders you want to include or exclude. Simply select the Files and Folders option and click the Customize button. A window similar to the one shown in Figure 10.11 pops up, and you can select which folders and files to ignore.

TIP Wildcards are completely valid here. Therefore, if you want to exclude all .DAT files, you could specify *.DAT in the list of files to ignore.

▶ INI Files—From the Workstation Scan Customization menu in snAppShot, you can modify which .INI files to exclude. Simply select the INI Files option and click the Customize button. A window pops up, and you can select which .INI files to ignore.

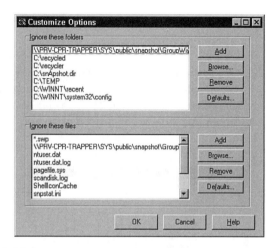

FIGURE 10.11
Specify how and which folders and files are to be created.

▶ System Configuration Text Files—From the Workstation Scan
  Customization menu in snAppShot, you can modify which system
  configuration text files you want to include in the scan. Simply
  select the System Configuration Text Files option and click the
  Customize button. A window similar to the one shown in Figure
  10.12 pops up, and you can select which system configuration text
  files you want to include.

FIGURE 10.12
Specify which system configuration files are created in the template.

▶ Windows Shortcuts—From the Workstation Scan Customization
  menu in snAppShot, you can modify which Windows shortcuts to
  exclude. Simply select the Windows Shortcuts option and click the

Customize button. A window pops up, and you can select which Windows shortcuts to ignore.

▶ Registry—From the Workstation Scan Customization menu in snAppShot, you can modify which Registry hives you want to include or exclude. Simply select the Registry option and click on the Customize button. A window similar to the one shown in Figure 10.13 pops up, and you can select and deselect from a list of hives to include.

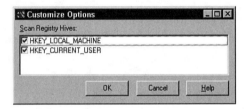

FIGURE 10.13
Indicate which Windows Registry hives will be created in the template.

Specify the Drives That Will Be Discovered

After you specify which parts of the workstation to include or exclude, you are given the option to select which disk drive to scan on the workstation to determine changes.

You can add drives to the list by clicking on the Add button and selecting the drives you want to scan. Conversely, you can remove drives from the list by selecting the drive and then clicking on the Remove button.

NOTE You can select network drives as well, however, only if they are mapped. This enables you to install applications to a larger network drive if needed and still discover the changes.

Read the Prediscovery Summary

After you have all the drives you want to select added to the list of drives to be scanned, click Next, and a summary of the preferences is displayed. The information displayed includes

▶ Application object name

▶ Application icon title

▶ Template filename

- ▶ Application files directory
- ▶ snAppShot's working drive
- ▶ Scan options
- ▶ Disks to scan
- ▶ Directories to exclude
- ▶ Files to exclude
- ▶ System text files to scan

> **TIP** Click Save Preferences to save the snAppShot preferences you have defined thus far to a file. Later, during a similar snAppShot session, you can choose the preferences you save now to accelerate the process.

Run the First snAppShot Discovery

The first snAppShot discovery is run when you click Next from the Preference Summary window. A screen shows the status of the discovery and a count of the following items that have been discovered:

- ▶ Folders and files
- ▶ Windows shortcuts
- ▶ .INI files
- ▶ System configuration files
- ▶ Registry entries

Run the Application's Installation or Upgrade

After the first snAppShot discovery is complete, a Run Application Install button becomes available. When you select the Run Application Install button, a file pop-up menu appears, and you can navigate to the application install executable and execute it.

After the application install is complete, you can continue with the discovery process of the snAppShot application.

> **TIP** Write down where the installation program installs the application's executable file. It is useful later when creating and distributing the application object.

Set Option Settings

After the application's installation or upgrade is complete, snAppShot enables you to specify how to handle the creation of entries for the application object. From the screen shown in Figure 10.14, you can set the additional criteria for the entries described in the following list:

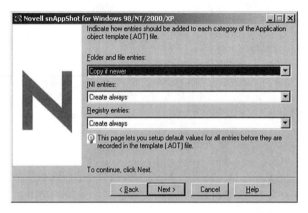

FIGURE 10.14
Specify how snAppShot handles the creation of entries in the template.

▶ Folder and File Entries—From the Application Object Entry Addition window in snAppShot, you can choose whether files and folders will be added to the application object. Click the down arrow under the Folders and Files option and select one of the following additional criteria, as shown in Figure 10.15:

  ▶ Copy Always

  ▶ Copy If Exists

  ▶ Copy If Does Not Exist

  ▶ Copy If Newer

  ▶ Copy If Newer and Exists

  ▶ Request Confirmation

  ▶ Copy If Newer Version

  ▶ Copy If Different

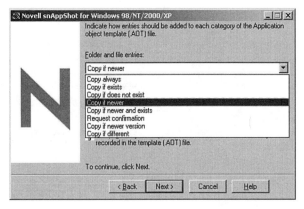

FIGURE 10.15
Specify how snAppShot handles the creation of file and folder entries in the template.

▶ INI Entries—From the Application Object Entry Addition window in snAppShot, you can configure whether .INI files are added to the application object by clicking the down arrow under the INI Entries option and selecting one of the following additional criteria, as shown in Figure 10.16:

  ▶ Create Always

  ▶ Create If Does Not Exist

  ▶ Create If Exists

  ▶ Create or Add to Existing Section

▶ Registry Entries—From the Application Object Entry Addition window in snAppShot, you can configure whether Registry entries will be added to the application object. Click the down arrow under the Registry Entries option and select one of the following additional criteria, as shown in Figure 10.17:

  ▶ Create Always

  ▶ Create If Does Not Exist

  ▶ Create If Exists

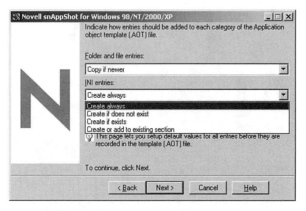

FIGURE 10.16
Indicate how snAppShot handles the creation of .INI file entries in the template.

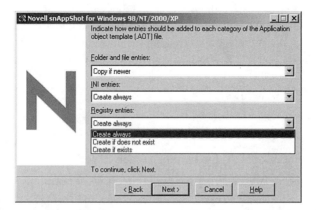

FIGURE 10.17
Specify how snAppShot handles the creation of Registry entries in the template.

Enter the Path to the Application's Executable File

After you define the additional criteria for entries into the application object, snAppShot gives you the option to specify a path to the application's executable on this workstation. You can enter the location of the installed application files on this workstation in the text field.

If you do not want snAppShot to set a target distribution location, leave this field blank and continue.

Define Macros for Distribution Automation

After you are finished setting the path to the application's executable and have clicked Next, you have the option to define macros to control the distribution of application objects. A screen similar to the one shown in Figure 10.18 enables you to add, edit, or remove macros to control automation of application distribution.

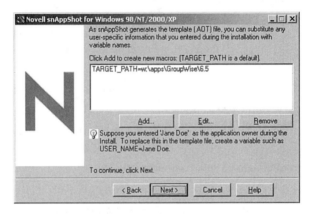

FIGURE 10.18
Add, edit, or remove macros to be used in the template.

When you click the Add button in the Macro Definition window, you are given the option to specify a variable name and a string that it is replaced within the template data, as shown in Figure 10.19.

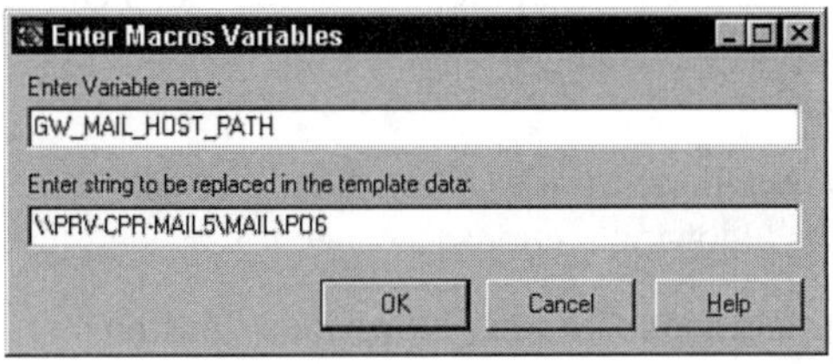

FIGURE 10.19
Specify a variable name and string in macros.

Run the Second snAppShot Discovery

When you are finished with defining macros to automate application object distribution, click Next, and snAppShot runs the second discovery.

Once again, you can monitor the status of the discovery by noting the count of the same items as you had before.

When the discovery is finished, snAppShot begins generating an object template. This is where the actual differences between the two discoveries are discerned and the template files created.

Read the Completion Summary

After the second snAppShot discovery is complete and the template files generated, a completion summary of what took place is displayed. The completion summary contains information about the application template creation, including

- ▶ Location of the new application object template (.AOT)
- ▶ Location of the new .FIL files
- ▶ Location of the textual version of the application object template (.AXT)
- ▶ Steps to take to create the application object
- ▶ Statistical totals from the second discovery
- ▶ Statistical totals from entries added to the application object template (.AOT)

Express Mode

Use express mode when you've already saved a snAppShot preference file from a previous discovery process. By choosing this file, you can skip most of the standard or custom mode settings, which enables you to discover a new application installation much more quickly than in standard or custom mode.

To use the express mode, simply select it and perform the operations described in the following sections to create the needed files.

Choose the Preferences File from a Previous Session

The first window that comes up after you select the express mode in snAppShot is the Choose snAppShot Preferences window. From this window you have the option of using a previously saved preference file.

If you have previously created and saved a preferences file in a previous custom mode, you can navigate to that file or enter the path to it into the text. If you have not previously created and saved a preference file, you must do so before selecting the express mode.

Read Summary Page to Verify Discovery Settings

After you select a preference file from a previous application package, click Next, and a summary of the preferences are displayed in the next window. The information displayed includes

- ▶ Application object name
- ▶ Application icon title
- ▶ Template filename
- ▶ Application files directory
- ▶ snAppShot's working drive
- ▶ Scan options
- ▶ Disks to scan
- ▶ Directories to exclude
- ▶ Files to exclude
- ▶ System text files to scan

Run the First snAppShot Discovery

The first snAppShot discovery is run when you click Next from the Preference Summary window. A screen shows the status of the discovery and a count of the items that have been discovered, including

- ▶ Folders and files
- ▶ Windows shortcuts
- ▶ .INI files
- ▶ System configuration files
- ▶ Registry entries

Run Application's Installation Program

After the first snAppShot discovery is complete, a Run Application Install button becomes available. When you select the Run Application Install button, a file pop-up menu appears, and you can navigate to the application install executable and execute it.

Run the Second snAppShot Discovery

After the application install or upgrade is finished, click Next, and snAppShot runs the second discovery. Once again, you can monitor the status of the discovery by noting the count statistics of the same items as you had before.

When the discovery is finished, snAppShot begins generating an object. This is where the actual differences between the two discoveries are discerned and the template files created.

Read the Completion Summary

When the second snAppShot discovery is completed and the template files generated, a completion summary of what took place is displayed. The completion summary contains information about the application template creation, including

- ▶ Location of the new application object template (.AOT)

- ▶ Location of the new .FIL files

- ▶ Location of the textual version of the application object template (.AOT)

- ▶ Steps to take to create the application object

- ▶ Statistical totals from the second discovery

- ▶ Statistical totals from entries added to the application object template (.AOT)

Super Express (Command Line) Mode

Use super express (command line) mode to discover changes to a workstation in the fastest possible way. The super express mode of snAppShot enables you to run snAppShot from a command prompt, which enables you to discover changes to a workstation faster than the other available modes.

To use this mode of snAppShot, which you do exclusively from the command line, you must use a preferences file from a previous snAppShot session. To use the super express mode, simply select it and perform the operations described in the following sections to create the needed files.

Change to the Directory Where snAppShot Is Located

The first step to use the super express (command line) mode in snAppShot is to enter DOS and change to the following directory where the snAppShot utility is located:

```
\\Server\public\snapshot
```

Enter the snAppShot Command

After you are in the directory of the snAppShot utility, enter the following command from the DOS prompt:

```
snapshot /u:<filename>
```

`<filename>` is the name of a snAppShot preferences file you defined and saved earlier when running snAppShot in custom or express mode.

Specify Whether to Overwrite a Previous snAppShot Discovery

After you execute the snAppShot command from the DOS session, a window appears that gives you the option to overwrite the existing application object template, as shown in Figure 10.20. You must select Yes to continue.

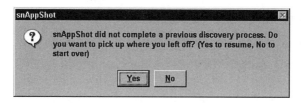

FIGURE 10.20
Overwrite the previous snAppShot discovery when using super express mode.

After you select Yes, the application object template creation continues the same as in regular express mode by displaying the prediscovery summary screen, followed by the first discovery.

snAppShot Application Packages Versus .MSI Files

Now that the creation of application object packages using snAppShot has been discussed, it is useful to know how they compare to Microsoft Windows installer (.MSI) package files. The files involved are described as follows:

▶ .MSI files—An .MSI file is a storage file containing the instructions and data required to install an application. .MSI files are used by the Microsoft Windows Installer to deploy and install applications to computers with 32-bit versions of Windows on them.

▶ .MSM files—A merge module (.MSM) file, referred to as a *merge package file*, is a single package that includes all files, Registry changes, and setup logic to install a shared component. Merge modules are contained inside .MSI files.

How .MSI Files Are Created

The information .MSI files contain depends on how they are created. The following sections describe the ways that .MSI files are typically created.

Development Tool Method

The most complete way of creating .MSI files is by using development tools to create .MSM and .MSI files and then configuring them with the files, Registry changes, resources, and logic to perform a complete install of the application.

Most application developers prefer this method because it gives them the greatest control over how and what information and logic actually goes into the .MSI file.

Discovery Method

The discovery method of creating .MSI files is similar to the way snAppShot creates its application object templates. The discovery method works in one of two ways. The first way is by using a double discovery process to accumulate changes made by an install. The second way is to monitor the changes on the system as they occur during application install. Chapter 9, "Creating Application Packages with New Software Packaging," covers both of these methods available in the AdminStudio product that ships with ZENworks.

How Do .MSI Files Work with ZENworks Desktop Management?

Now that you understand what .MSI files are and how they are created, you need to understand what role they can play in creating application objects instead of using .AOT or .AXT files.

The ZENworks snap-ins to ConsoleOne allow you to use .MSI files to create application objects in exactly the same way that .AOT or .AXT files are used. Therefore, if an .MSI file is already available for an application object, you can save yourself time and effort by simply using the .MSI file to create the application object (discussed in Chapter 11). Additionally, with ZENworks you can also apply .MST files along with the .MSI files to your desktops.

Summary

This chapter focused on the snAppShot utility and showed you how to use it to create application packages. Understanding snAppShot and when to use it were examined first. This was followed by an explanation of how snAppShot works and an overview of the Advanced features.

The coverage of snAppShot was rounded out by looking at some of its limitations and comparing snAppShot application packages against .MSI files.

## CHAPTER 11

Creating and Using Application Objects

Now that you have an understanding of how to create an application object template from Chapter 10, "Creating Application Packages Using snAppShot," we need to discuss how to use that template to create an actual application object and distribute it to users. This chapter covers the following main points in taking you through the process of application object creation and distribution:

► Creating the application object

► Setting properties for the application object

► Setting up application distribution

► Distributing the application

Creating the Application Object

The first step in using ZENworks Desktop Management to distribute applications to users is to create an application object. The application object is an actual object in the eDirectory tree. ZENworks Desktop Management uses this object to distribute the application to users based on the properties the object is created with. This section guides you through the following methods for creating application objects:

► Creating an application object using an .AOT/.AXT file

► Creating an application object using an .MSI file

▶ Creating a simple application object without an .AOT, .AXT, or .MSI file

▶ Creating an application object using an existing application object

▶ Creating a web application

▶ Creating a terminal server application

NOTE We highly recommend starting with an .MSI, .AOT, or .AXT file, or duplicating an existing application object because it greatly simplifies the setup, distribution, and management of applications on users' workstations. You create .AOT and .AXT files using snAppShot, which is a component of Application Window.

Creating an Application Object Using an .AOT/.AXT File

Creating an application object with an .AOT or .AXT file usually creates more complex application objects. In other words, objects that make changes to Registry settings, .INI files, text configuration files, and so on.

To use an .AOT or .AXT template file to create an application object, follow these steps:

1. Open ConsoleOne, browse the eDirectory tree, and right-click in the container in which you want to create the application object.

2. From the menu, select New→Application. This launches the New Application Object Wizard.

3. From the New Application Object dialog, select An Application That Has an .AOT/.AXT File, and then click Next as shown in Figure 11.1.

4. Browse for the .AOT or .AXT file, select it, and then click Open. A window appears that displays the path to the .AOT or .AXT file. From this window, click Next.

5. Type the object name of the application object in the Object Name text box.

6. Check (and change, if necessary) the target and source directories of the application object as shown in Figure 11.2; then click Next.

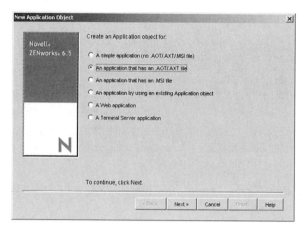

FIGURE 11.1
The New Application Object Wizard offers numerous creation options.

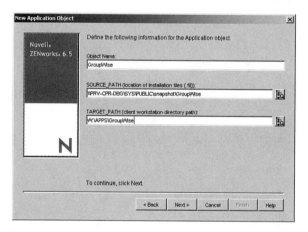

FIGURE 11.2
Within the New Application Object Wizard, choose the target and source directories.

7. You have the option to add application distribution rules to set workstation requirements to be able to receive the application. These settings can also be modified or added after the application object has been created. Add any rules you know are necessary and click Next.

8. Add any associations you know are necessary and click Next.

9. Review the information about the application object (click the Back button to make any changes).

10. You have the option to select Display Details After Creation to access the property pages of this application object. This is recommended to ensure that the application object was correctly created.

11. You also have the option to select Create Another Application Object After This One if you want to create another after finishing with the current one.

After you make your selections from this window, click Finish, and the application object is created.

Creating an Application Object Using an .MSI File

ZENworks Desktop Management also enables you to create and administer an application object from an .MSI file. This makes it possible for you to use your existing .MSI files to roll out applications to users without having to create a fresh object or .AOT file.

Creating an application object with an .MSI file is similar to creating one with an .AOT or .AXT template file. Use the following steps to create an application object for an .MSI file:

1. Open ConsoleOne, browse the eDirectory tree, and right-click in the container in which you want to create the application object.

2. From the button bar, select the Create Application Object button. This launches the New Application Object Wizard.

3. From the New Application Object dialog, select An Application That Has an .MSI File and then click Next.

4. Browse for the .MSI, select it, and then click Open. A window appears that displays the UNC path to the .MSI file. From this window click Next.

5. Enter the object name of the application object in the Object Name text box and a UNC path in the Administration Package Path box; then click Next.

6. You have the option to add application distribution rules to set workstation requirements to be able to receive the application.

These settings can also be modified or added after the application object has been created. Add any rules you know are necessary and click Next.

7. Add any associations you know are necessary and click Next.

8. Review the information about the application object (click the Back button to make any changes).

9. You have the option to select Display Details After Creation to access the property pages of this application object. This is recommended to ensure that the application object was correctly created.

10. You also have the option to select Create Another Application Object After This One if you want to create another after finishing with the current one.

11. After you have made your selections from this window, click Finish and the application object is created.

Objects created from .MSI files are not managed exactly the same way other application objects are. The following are ways that an application object created from an .MSI file can be managed (they are discussed in more detail later in this chapter):

▶ View package information—Enables you to view specific information about the MSI package.

▶ Set properties for MSI package—Enables you to modify the public properties of the MSI package.

▶ Set transform file list—Enables you to create a list of transform files to be applied to the MSI object prior to distribution.

▶ Set fault tolerance options—Normal fault tolerance and load balancing options for applications can also be applied to application objects created from an .MSI file.

Creating a Simple Application Object Without an .AOT, .AXT, or .MSI File

The process of creating an application object without an .AOT or .AXT file is usually employed to create simple application objects that do not make any changes to Registry settings, such as .INI files, text configuration files, and so on.

A good example of when to use the process of creating an application object *without* an .AOT or .AXT file is creating an application object for a corporate calendar program. Many corporations have small home-grown calendar applications that contain information specific to their business. These programs rarely modify the Registry or change system .INI files and therefore are great candidates for this option.

To create a simple application object, use the following steps:

1. Open ConsoleOne, browse the eDirectory tree, and right-click in the container in which you want to create the application object.

2. From the button bar select Create Application Object. This launches the New Application Object Wizard.

3. From the New Application Object dialog, choose A Simple Application (No .AOT/.AXT/.MSI File); then click Next.

4. From this window, type the name of the application object in the Object Name dialog box. Click Next.

5. Use the browse button to specify the location of the executable in the Path to Executable text box. Click Next.

6. You have the option to add application distribution rules to set workstation requirements to receive the application. These settings can also be modified or added after the application object has been created. Add any rules you know are necessary and click Next.

7. Add any associations you know are necessary and click Next.

8. You have the option to select Display Details After Creation to access the property pages of this application object. This is recommended to ensure that the application object was correctly created.

9. You also have the option to select Create Another Application Object After This One if you want to create another after finishing with the current one.

After you make your selections from this window, click Finish, and the application object is created.

Creating an Application Object Using an Existing Application Object

Use the Duplicate an Existing Application Object method if the object you want to create has already been created, but you want to create another of the same application, say, to allow for different properties and distribution options.

A good example of when to duplicate an existing application object would be if you are setting up application fault tolerance and need several nearly identical application objects. The fastest method to accomplish this is to create the primary application object and then create as many duplicate application objects as needed. You can then adjust each duplicated application object as necessary (for example, specify different application source [.FIL] locations for each).

To use the Duplicate an Existing Application Object method to create an application object, use the following steps:

1. Open ConsoleOne, browse the eDirectory tree, and right-click in the container in which you want to create the application object.

2. From the button bar, select Create Application Object. This launches the New Application Object Wizard.

3. From the New Application Object dialog, choose An Application by Using an Existing Application Object and then click Next.

4. From this window browse the eDirectory tree and identify the reference application object by its distinguished name. After the reference application is selected, click Next.

5. Modify the name of the application object—default is the `<original name> #<iteration number>`—and then specify a custom source path (where the .FIL files are stored) and target path (where the files are copied during a distribution, usually a workstation's `c:` drive).

6. You have the option to add application distribution rules to set workstation requirements to receive the application. These settings can also be modified or added after the application object has been created. Add any rules you know are necessary and click Next.

7. Add any associations you know are necessary and click Next.

8. Review the new, duplicated application object's summary and click Back to make changes.

9. You have the option to select Display Details After Creation to access the property pages of this application object. This is recommended to ensure that the application object was correctly created.

10. You also have the option to select Create Another Application Object After This One if you want to create another after finishing with the current one.

After you make your selections from this window, click Finish, and the application object is created.

Creating a Web Application

ZENworks Desktop Management allows you to create an application object for an application stored and executed on the web through a URL. This feature is an integral piece for companies wanting to create an internal as well as external web presence.

A good example of when you would want to create a web application object would be if you had a corporate servlet that tracks login information. Every time a user logged in, the servlet could be executed, and information about the login gathered and stored.

Another example of how a web application could be used would be if you had a corporate statement or newsletter that you wanted every employee to read. You could create a web application with a URL that pointed to that page, and it would be displayed to users in their browser as they logged in.

Use the following steps to create a web application object:

1. Open ConsoleOne, browse the eDirectory tree, and right-click in the container in which you want to create the application object.

2. From the button bar, select Create Application Object. This launches the New Application Object Wizard.

3. From the New Application Object dialog, choose Create a Web Application and then click Next.

4. From this window, type the name of the application object in the Object Name dialog box and click Next.

5. Specify the URL (web location where the application is stored) for the web application, test the URL by clicking the Test the URL button, and then click Next.

6. You have the option to add application distribution rules to set workstation requirements to receive the application. These settings can also be modified or added after the application object is created. Add any rules you know are necessary and click Next.

7. Add any associations you know are necessary and click Next.

8. Review the new, duplicated application object's summary and click Back to make changes.

9. You have the option to select Display Details After Creation to access the property pages of this application object. This is recommended to ensure that the application object was correctly created.

10. You also have the option to select Create Another Application Object After This One if you want to create another after finishing with the current one.

After you make your selections from this window, click Finish, and the Application object is created.

Creating a Terminal Server Application

ZENworks Desktop Management allows you to create an application object for an application to be stored and executed on a Citrix MetaFrame or Microsoft terminal server. This feature is useful if you implement terminal servers on your network.

Use the following steps to create a terminal server application object:

1. Open ConsoleOne, browse the eDirectory tree, and right-click in the container in which you want to create the application object.

2. From the button bar, select Create Application Object. This launches the New Application Object Wizard.

3. From the New Application Object dialog, choose Create a Terminal Server Application and then click Next.

4. From this window, type the name of the application object in the Object Name dialog box and click Next.

5. Specify the session type (ICA/RDP). For ICA sessions, specify the Published Application Name and Servers Hosting the Application. For RDP Sessions, specify the Terminal Server Address, Port, and Domain as well as the Application Path and Working Directory. Then click Next.

6. You have the option to add application distribution rules to set workstation requirements to receive the application. These settings can also be modified or added after the application object is created. Add any rules you know are necessary and click Next.

7. Add any associations you know are necessary and click Next.

8. Review the new, duplicated application object's summary and click Back to make changes.

9. You have the option to select Display Details After Creation to access the property pages of this application object. This is recommended to ensure that the application object is correctly created.

10. You also have the option to select Create Another Application Object After This One if you want to create another after finishing with the current one.

After you make your selections from this window, click Finish, and the Application object is created.

Setting Properties for the Application Object

After you create the application object, you need to set the application object's properties to define how it will behave. The following sections cover using ConsoleOne to define the identity, distribution behavior, run behavior, availability, fault tolerance, and existence of the application object.

Setting Up the Application Object Identification

The first step in setting up the application object in ConsoleOne is to access the Identification property page to control the application icon, description, folders, contacts, and notes used to define the application. Use the following steps to select which set of options you want to modify:

1. Right-click the Application object and click Properties.

2. Click the Identification tab.

3. Click the down arrow on the Identification tab to access the available Identification property pages, as shown in Figure 11.3, and then click OK.

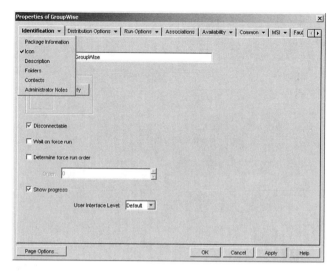

FIGURE 11.3
The application Identification tab options in ConsoleOne.

From the application object's Identification property tab, you can access the individual property pages to configure the application identity options described in the following sections.

Setting Application Icon Properties

To set application icon properties, first select the Icon property page from the Identification tab. A page similar to the one shown in Figure 11.4 is displayed, and you can configure the following options for the application object.

Configure the Application Icon Title

Type in the title you want to use for the application in the Application Icon Title box. The application icon title, which is mandatory, can be different from the application object name (the name that eDirectory uses to identify the application) and might contain periods and other special characters. You can also use the Description property page for longer descriptions of the application. The title you select here is displayed to a user when he accesses the application object (for example, the name that shows up in the Start menu if the application is set up to appear there).

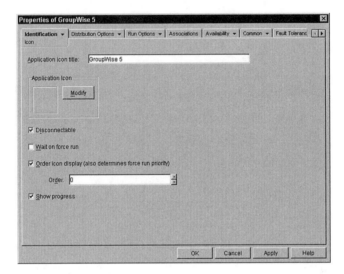

FIGURE 11.4
The Icon property page in ConsoleOne.

TIP If icon titles do not appear in their entirety, you might need to increase your icon spacing. Do this using Windows. After you have adjusted the icon spacing in Windows, exit Application Window or Application Explorer and restart for the changes to take effect. You can also use the Description property page for longer descriptions of the application.

Configure the Application Icon

To configure the application icon, you use the Application Icon option to assign an icon for the application object. The icon you choose appears in Application Window or Application Explorer, depending on what you have specified on the Associations property page. If you do not specify an icon, a default Application Window icon is used.

Configure the Disconnectable Option

The Disconnectable option enables you to control what happens to the icon when the user disconnects from the network. If this option is set, the icon remains present when the user disconnects; otherwise, it does not appear.

Configure the Wait on Force Run Option

The Wait on Force Run option enables you to specify whether the icon appears before the application has been run, if the force run option is set.

If you enable this option, the icon won't appear until the force run is complete for the application.

Configure the Order Icon Display

From this page you also have the option to set the Order icons are displayed and set the force run sequence. This option performs two useful functions. First, it organizes the icons in Application Window and Application Explorer. Second, it dictates the order in which application objects set as force run are used.

To set ordering, enter a numeric value into the Order text box. All Application objects you want to order must have a numeric value. The value of zero gives the icon the highest priority and thus the highest prominence in the list. The maximum value is 999. If you do not order application objects, they are ordered alphabetically (the default order).

For example, suppose that you have 10 icons (applications A, B, C, D, E, F, G, H, I, and J) that you want to organize in Application Window. You specify an order number of "0" for application G, "1" for application F, "2" for application E, and "3" for application D. You specify an order number of "4" for applications C, B, H, and I. You do not order the remaining applications, A and J.

The result is that the first four applications are ordered with G being the first in the list followed by F, E, and D. After this, applications C, B, H, and I are gathered together and arranged alphabetically. The last two icons, A and J, come at the end of the list and are arranged alphabetically (the default order).

If users (who have been associated with these application objects) run Application Window, they will see a list of icons according to this order. If these applications have all been set to force run, they will run in this order as soon as Application Window has loaded itself into memory.

NOTE Ordered and force run applications run in sequential order without waiting for the last force run application to terminate.

Configure the Show Progress Option

The last thing you can configure from the Icon property page is the Show progress option. Select this option if you want an easy-to-read progress bar to be displayed to users the first time they distribute an application to their workstations.

TIP Turn off the Show Progress option if you are distributing only a small change to the application, such as a Registry modification. Turn it on if you are distributing a large application and want to give the user a general idea of how long the distribution will take. By default, the Show Progress option is on.

Setting Application Description

The second setting available for Application object identification is the ability to enter text into the Description property page to give users more complete information than the application icon caption allows. Select the Description property page from the Identification tab. A page similar to the one shown in Figure 11.5 is displayed, and you can set the description for the application object.

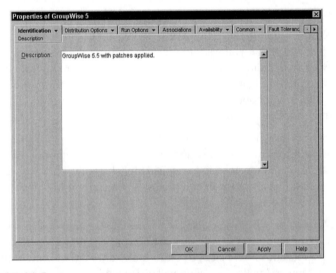

FIGURE 11.5
The Description property page for application objects in ConsoleOne.

After the description is set, users can right-click an application object in Application Window or Application Explorer to see details containing both the descriptive name of the application and the more lengthy description that you provide here.

An example of when to use the Description option for Application objects is if you have additional information about the application that users need. This might include information such as which new features are available in the application.

NOTE The text you type in the Description property page is the same text the user sees if you have enabled the Prompt User Before Distribution option on the Distribution property page.

Setting Up Application Folders

The next setting available for application object identification is the Folders property page. The Folders property page lets you specify the folder object you want the application to reside in for the Application Window and Start menu. Select the Folders property page from the Identification tab. A page similar to the one shown in Figure 11.6 is displayed, and you can set up the application folder for the application object.

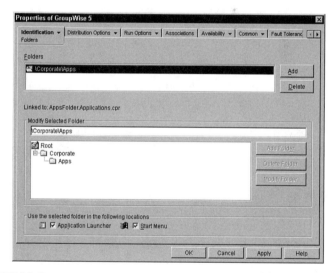

FIGURE 11.6
The Folders property page for application objects in ConsoleOne.

In the Folders property page you can set up which folders the application icon will reside in by using the following steps:

1. From the Folders property page, click the Add button.

2. From the Add menu select Custom Folder or Linked Folder. If you select Custom Folder, name the folder with a meaningful name. If you select Linked Folder, navigate the eDirectory tree and select the application folder object you want the application to reside in.

3. In the Modify Selected Folder window, shown in Figure 11.6, add, delete, or modify the selected folder. This controls the location where the application appears in the Start menu and Application Explorer window.

4. Select whether you want the application to appear in the folder for the Application Window, Start menu, or both.

You can select multiple application folder objects for the application to reside in by following the preceding steps. You may want to do this if a difference exists in behavior or availability defined in different application folders. For example, you have an application folder for Accounting, Development, and Sales, but you only want the application to appear for accounting and sales. You handle this by adding the Accounting and Sales folders, but not the Development folder, to the application. That way the application does not show up in the developers' Start menu, but it does show up for the accountants and salespersons.

Contact Setting for Applications

From the pull-down list under Identification for application objects, you can also specify a contact list of people to contact for help if a problem occurs when deploying the application. To create the contact list, select Contacts from the Identification tab and click the Add button on the Contacts property page. Then type in the username or select the user object by browsing the eDirectory tree.

Adding Administrator Notes to Applications

From the pull-down list under Identification for application objects, you can also specify administrator notes for administrators to keep track of important items pertaining to the application object. To create administrator notes, simply type in the message you want users to see if they view the information about applications available through the Application Window.

Viewing MSI Package Information for MSI Objects

Application objects created from an .MSI file enable you to select Package Information from the Identification drop-down menu. The package information page for MSI application objects displays the following information about the MSI package:

▶ The Administration package path

▶ The version of the MSI package

▶ The vendor who created the MSI package

▶ The locale (language) the MSI package is in

▶ Any help link associated with the MSI package

▶ The path to the MSI package

Setting Distribution Options for Application Objects

After you set up the application objects identification, the next step in setting up the distribution options for the application object in ConsoleOne is to configure the application's shortcuts, Registry settings, files, INI settings, text files, distribution scripts, preinstall schedule, Pre-Distribution Process Termination, and general options. Use the following steps to select which set of options you want to modify:

1. Right-click the Application object and click Properties.

2. Select the Distribution Options tab.

3. Click the down arrow on the Distribution Options tab, and a screen similar to the one shown in Figure 11.7 is displayed.

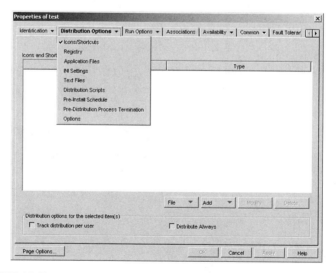

FIGURE 11.7
The Distribution Options property page in ConsoleOne.

From the application object's Distribution Options property tab, you should access the individual property pages to configure the application distribution options described in the following sections.

NOTE If this application object has been distributed previously, note that many of the changes on distribution will not go into effect until you change the Version Stamp value. Changing the Version Stamp value signals Application Window to redistribute the application.

Configuring Application Icons/Shortcuts

The top page accessible from the Distribution Options tab is the Icons/Shortcuts property page. The Icons/Shortcuts property page enables you to add, change, or delete the Program Groups, Program Group Items, and Explorer shortcut icons that appear in Windows Explorer (Windows98, Windows NT 4.x, and Windows 2000/XP) when the application distributes to workstations.

You need to specify the following settings when you add Explorer shortcut items:

- ▶ Shortcut Option—Allows you to specify the following creation options for the shortcut: Create Always, Create Only If It Does Not Exist, and Delete the Shortcut If It Exists.

- ▶ Shortcut Name—Name to identify the shortcut.

- ▶ Shortcut Location—Path where the shortcut is located.

- ▶ Target File—Path to the application that should be executed.

- ▶ Parameters—Parameters to be passed into the target file.

- ▶ Start In—Working directory for the application.

- ▶ Icon Filename—Path to the icon that represents the application.

- ▶ Run—Allows you to specify whether to run the application in a normal, minimized, or maximized window.

You need to specify the following settings when you add a program item group:

- ▶ Icon Option—Allows you to specify the following creation options for the icon: Create Always, Create Only If It Does Not Already Exist, and Delete the Icon If It Exists.

- ▶ Icon Name—Name to identify the group icon.

- ▶ Program Group—Specifies the program group to store the item in.

▶ Shortcut Option—Allows you to specify the following creation options for the shortcut: Create Always, Create Only If It Does Not Already Exist, and Delete the Shortcut If It Exists.

▶ Target File—Specifies the location of the file to execute when the item is selected.

▶ Parameters—Specifies parameters to be added to the command line when executing the target file.

▶ Start In—Specifies the location used to start the target file in.

▶ Icon Filename—Specifies the name of the file that stores the icon to be displayed for the item or shortcut.

▶ Icon Index—Specifies the index of the icon inside the icon file specified in the Icon Filename option.

▶ Run—Specifies whether to start the application in a normal, maximized, or minimized window.

One example of when you might modify the icons and shortcuts for an application object is if you wanted to use special icons for all applications that users run on their workstations. Using the Icons/Shortcuts property page for this application object, you can change icons of other applications that might or might not have anything to do with this application object.

Configuring Application Registry Settings

The next page accessible from the Distribution Options tab is the Registry Settings property page. This page enables you to add, change, and delete Registry keys and values when the application object distributes to the workstation. Several Registry types are supported, including binary format, default strings, DWORD values, Expand Strings (`REG_EXPAND_SZ`), and Multi-Value Strings (`REG_MULTI_SZ`). You can import and export Registry settings, either as .AOT or .AXT files, or using the standard Registry (.reg) format.

For each Registry setting you create, you have the option of specifying the following options:

▶ Create Always

▶ Create If It Does Not Exist

▶ Create If It Does Exist

▶ Delete

▶ Append If Exists Otherwise Create

▶ Prepend If Exists Otherwise Create

▶ Track Distribution Per User

▶ Distribute the Change Always

NOTE Make sure that you need to track changes before checking the Track Distribution Per User box. Tracking too many items can use a lot of resources and can make it difficult to wade through the data to gather the information you need.

Configuring Application Files

The next page accessible from the Distribution Options tab is the Application Files property page. This page is used to add, change, or delete application files and directories. You can also import new template information about files and directories.

From the Application Files page, you click Add and then select a file or directory. If you are adding a file, you are prompted to enter a source and target path and specify whether the target file should be deleted first.

If you are adding a directory, you are prompted to enter a directory name and specify whether the directory should be created, deleted, or copied. If you select to copy a directory, you can enter a source path and specify if you wish to to copy subdirectories as well. ZENworks Desktop Management 7 enables you to specify wildcard characters in the source path enabling you to only copy specific sets of files. For each file entry you create, you have the option of specifying the following options:

▶ Copy Always

▶ Copy If It Does Not Exist

▶ Copy If It Does Exist

▶ Copy If Newer

▶ Copy If Newer and Exists

▶ Copy If Newer Version

▶ Request Confirmation

▶ Copy If Different

▶ Delete

▶ Track Distribution Per User

▶ Distribute Always

▶ Shared File

▶ Include Subdirectories

Configuring .INI File Settings for Applications

The next page accessible from the Distribution Options tab is the INI Settings property page. This page enables you to add, change, and delete .INI files, sections, and values when the application object distributes to the workstation. Not only can you order the changes within the .INI file, you can also import or export .INI files and settings using the .AOT or .AXT file format or the standard .INI file format.

For each INI entry you create, you have the option of specifying the following options:

- ▶ Create Always
- ▶ Create If It Does Not Exist
- ▶ Create If It Does Exist
- ▶ Create or Add to Existing Section
- ▶ Create or Append to Existing Value
- ▶ Delete
- ▶ Delete or Remove from Existing Value
- ▶ Track Distribution Per User
- ▶ Distribute Always

.INI file configuration changes can be useful if you want to add a specific version stamp that can be read later by the application to determine its current version. For example, Figure 11.8 shows that a specific version for the GroupWise Application object of 5.5 is made to the `GW.INI` file in the Windows directory when the application is distributed. The next time GroupWise is run, it could use the version stamp to determine its current revision.

Configuring Text File Options

The next page accessible from the Distribution Options tab is the Text Files property page. This page enables you to add, change, or delete workstation text files (such as `config.sys` and `autoexec.bat`).

After you add a file to be modified, you can specify an entry by selecting the file and clicking the Add button. The Edit Text File window allows you to specify whether to simply add the text to the file, remove the text from the file, or find and replace the text in the file. If you select Add Text, you can specify whether to add the text at the beginning or the end of the file. If you select Delete Text, you can specify whether to simply search for the text in the file or search for an entire line in the file. If you select Find and Replace, you can specify whether to search for text or search by line as well as the replacement text.

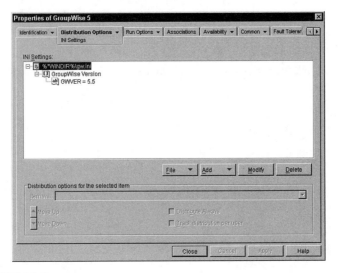

FIGURE 11.8
The INI Settings property page for application objects in ConsoleOne.

For each text file change, you can specify whether the workstation needs to be rebooted if the change is made.

One example of when to use the Text Files properties page to modify the application object is if users experience problems due to an incorrect text string found in their workstation's `config.sys` file. Rather than visit and change each workstation or run the risk of users incorrectly and inconsistently implementing a change, you can set up a text file that finds, deletes, modifies, or adds text strings to the text file of your choice. The text file implements the changes the next time the application runs.

NOTE If you set the Prompt User for Reboot Setting on the Options property page of the Distribution Options tab to Always, that setting overrides the setting you make here.

Configuring Application Distribution Scripts

The next available option to control distribution is setting up distribution scripts executed automatically each time the application is distributed to a workstation. Unlike environment parameters, scripts can overwrite existing drive mappings and printer ports.

The two types of distribution scripts are the Run Before Distribution script and the Run After Distribution script. Run Before Distribution scripts are executed before the application is distributed. Run After Distribution scripts are executed after the application is closed and before the network resources are cleaned up. Distribution scripts enable you to provide dynamic mappings beyond those defined, run other applications, log in to other servers or eDirectory trees, and perform other tasks that must be done before and after an application is distributed. The scripts support the same commands and syntax as the Novell Client by default. However, ZENworks Desktop Management allows you to specify your own script engine and file type extension. This allows you to create much more extensive and powerful scripts by using another script engine, such as a Perl parser.

To set up distribution scripts use the following steps:

1. Right-click the Application object and click Properties.

2. Select the Distribution Options tab and select Distribution Scripts from the drop-down list.

3. Create the Run Before Distribution and the Run After Distribution scripts in the text boxes shown in Figure 11.9.

4. Specify the location of the script engine. If you do not specify a script engine, then the Novell Client is used as the script engine.

5. Enter or select a file extension for the script file.

NOTE On Windows NT/2000/XP, distribution scripts are run in the secure system space, which means that users do not see any of the script commands or the command results. Therefore, you should not use any commands that require user interaction because the script will be halted at that point.

Configuring a Pre-Install Schedule for Application

The next available option to control distribution is setting up a pre-install schedule for local availability for the application. The pre-install can be useful in deploying applications to many workstations.

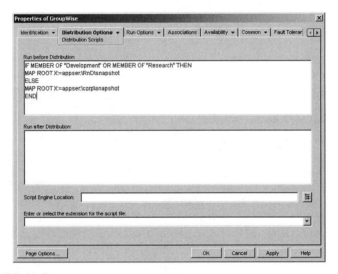

FIGURE 11.9
The Distribution Scripts property page in ConsoleOne.

For example, if you have an application that needs to go out to 1,000 workstations all on the same day, having ZENworks Desktop Management deliver the application all at the same time could cause the network and server to be overutilized. If you know in advance that you need to deploy the application, you can set up a pre-install schedule to deliver the application to the workstations over a period of time before the day it needs to be installed. After this, all 1,000 workstations can install the application at the same time, without causing network problems, because they have a local copy of the application to work from.

To configure an application pre-install, select Pre-Install Schedule from the Distribution Options tab drop-down list, and the Pre-Install Schedule page appears. If you want to have the application pre-installed prior to having it deployed, select the Pre-Install Application box. The next step is to specify the schedule type you want to use for the pre-install.

The None option is selected by default; however, you *can* configure the application object to pre-install the application to workstations based on a set of specific days or a range of days as described in the following sections.

Set Schedule by Specified Days

You can schedule application pre-installs by specifying the Specified Days option as shown in Figure 11.10. This enables you to select specific dates during which you want the application to be available for pre-install.

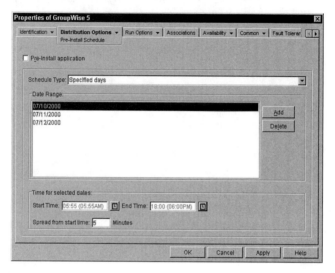

FIGURE 11.10
The Pre-Install Schedule availability for specified days property page in ConsoleOne.

The application is only visible to be pre-installed to workstations on the specific dates and times you specify in this option. For example, if you select the dates June 7, 2005, and June 10, 2005, and start and end times of 8:00 a.m. and 5:00 p.m., the application is available to be pre-installed to a workstation from 8:00 a.m. to 5:00 p.m. on each of the days selected. The application is not available to be pre-installed to the workstation at any other time.

Set Schedule by Range of Days

You can set a schedule by specifying a range of days to make the application available for pre-install, as shown in Figure 11.11. An example would be if you select a start date of June 12, 2005, and an end date of June 16, 2005, with a start time of 6:00 a.m. and an end time of 6:00 p.m. The application object icon would be able to be pre-installed to workstations from June 12 at 6:00 a.m. until June 16 at 6:00 p.m.

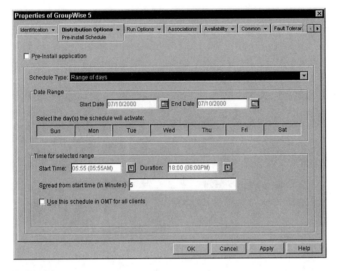

FIGURE 11.11
The Pre-Install Schedule availability for a range of days property page in
ConsoleOne.

Spread from Start Time

You also have the option to specify a spread of time in which the application becomes available to users. This is useful if you don't want all users
to run the application at the same time for fear that the load and traffic
may bring down the network. The Spread from Start Time option literally
"spreads out" user access times over the number of minutes specified so
that they don't all run the application at once.

An example of how to use the Spread from Start Time option is to set it
to 120 minutes; the application then becomes available, on a random
basis, between the hours of 10:00 a.m. and 12:00 noon. This spreads the
demand for the application out over a longer period of time, and network traffic is minimized.

NOTE If users access applications after the spread time is expired but before the end
time of the application object, they access the application at that time, and the spread
variable has no effect.

GMT (Greenwich Mean Time)

The final option available on the scheduling pages is to specify that all application scheduling that you do with the application property page is based on the workstation's time zone.

In other words, if your network spans different time zones and you schedule an application to run at 4:00 p.m., it would normally run at 4:00 p.m. in each time zone. However, by selecting the Use This Schedule in GMT for All Clients check box, workstations run applications at the same time worldwide (according to GMT). Although, you should be aware that GMT time is not available if you are filtering out days of the week when in the Specified Days mode.

Configuring Pre-Distribution Process Termination

The next page accessible from the Distribution Options tab is the Pre-Distribution Process Termination property page. This page allows you to specify processes and/or services that must be terminated prior to distributing the application.

This feature allows you to halt processes or service running on a client workstation that will interfere with the distribution of an application. For example, if you are distributing a new version of an application that cannot install if an older version is running, you can have ZENworks halt the application's process prior to installing the new version.

Configuring General Application Distribution Options

The next page accessible from the Distribution Options tab is the Options property page. This page, shown in Figure 11.12, enables you to configure the general distribution options for application objects discussed in the following sections.

Distribute Always

Use the Distribute Always option to force a distribution of the entire application object every time the user runs the application or the application is set for a force run on the workstation (see the user or container object's Applications property page). This option is useful to ensure that all application settings are updated every time the application runs.

You can also update settings on a case-by-case basis. For example, if you want to always distribute a particular Registry key and value, you can set the Distribute Always option on the Registry Settings property page for that particular key and value. The Distribute Always option on the Options property page of the Distribution Options tab overrides the Distribute Always option on the Registry Settings, INI Settings, Application Files, Icons/Shortcuts, and Text Files property pages.

288

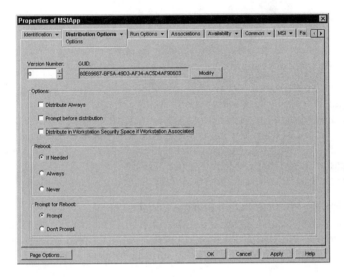

FIGURE 11.12
The Options property page for application objects in ConsoleOne.

Prompt Before Distribution

Next, use the Prompt before distribution option to display a message to users after they have clicked an Application Window-distributed application for the first time. This message asks them to confirm whether they want to distribute the application to their workstations. This option is turned off by default.

> **TIP** To better inform users, the text that you enter in the application object's Description property page is displayed in the distribution confirmation dialog box. For example, you might write a note to the user such as "This is an essential application for your workstation that takes approximately 10 minutes to distribute. Please answer Yes to distribute it now."

Distribute in Workstation Security Space if Workstation Associated

Enable the Distribute in Workstation Security Space if Workstation Associated option (available on MSI Application objects only) to force the Application Launcher to distribute the application in the workstation security space using the workstation's credentials. Enabling this option allows you to distribute the application even if the user is not logged in at the workstation and restrict access to the application's source .MSI files to the workstation, not the user.

Reboot Options

Next, use the options in the Reboot group box to control how a workstation reboot should occur according to the following options:

- ▶ If Needed—(the default setting) Only prompts for reboot if Application Window or Application Explorer needs to make changes that cannot occur while Windows is running (such as replacing open DLLs).

- ▶ Always—Prompts the user to reboot every time a distribution takes place.

- ▶ Never—Does not prompt the user to reboot. In this case, the changes take effect the next time the workstation reboots.

- ▶ Prompt—Prompts the user before rebooting the system.

- ▶ Don't Prompt—Does not prompt the user before rebooting the system.

Use Version Number to Trigger Redistribution

Use the Version Number option to trigger a redistribution of the application. A *version number* is simply a text string representing the version of the application used to customize the application object's GUID. In fact, any change you make to the version number is like changing the GUID.

NOTE The version number might not have anything to do with the actual version of the software. It is a tool to help you upgrade applications. It helps you control the version of Application Window-delivered applications.

If the Run Once option is checked and you change the version number, the Run Once option causes the application to run again once. This is useful when upgrading application software to a new or different version.

For example, suppose that you purchased new application software and want to update an application object. By changing the version number and selecting the Run Once option, the application runs once after installation even though a previous version might have already run once.

Use GUID for Troubleshooting

The application GUID is stamped in the workstation's Registry when ZENworks Desktop Management distributes an application to a workstation. The GUID is a randomly generated number for tracking, such as {5A0511440-77C5-11D1-A663-00A024264C3E}.

TIP Use GUIDs to track and troubleshoot distributed applications. For example, if you want to ensure that a particular application has been distributed to a workstation, you can compare the GUID as recorded in the application object's Options property page of the Distribution Options tab with the GUID currently stamped in the workstation's Registry.

You can make several application objects use the same GUID by using the Synchronize Distributed GUIDs option. This is useful if you are distributing a suite of applications. You can also "regenerate" or "re-randomize" the GUIDs for those same applications.

You can also modify the GUID by clicking on the Modify button to bring up the GUID Manager. The GUID Manager allows you to create new GUIDs and assign them to application objects.

Setting Run Options for Application Objects

After you set up the distribution options for an application, you need to set the run options. Setting the run options for an application object enables you to control the behavior, environment, and licensing of an application as it is distributed to users. To access the options on the Run Options property tab, use the following steps to select which set of options you want to modify:

1. Right-click the Application object and click Properties.

2. Select the Run Options tab.

3. Click the down arrow on the Run Options tab, and a screen similar to the one shown in Figure 11.13 is displayed.

From the application object's Run options property tab, you can access the individual property pages to configure the application run options described in the following sections.

Configuring Application Run Options

The top page accessible from the Run Options tab is the Application property page. The Application property page enables you to set the path, parameters, and behavior of an executable that needs to run when the application is distributed. Use this page, shown previously in Figure 11.13, to configure the following options.

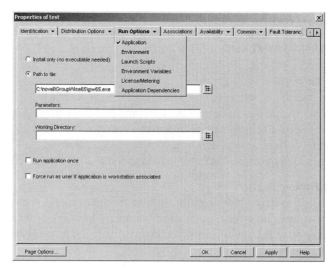

FIGURE 11.13
The Run Options property page in ConsoleOne.

Install Only (No Executable Needed)
If you just want users to install an application but not run it, check the
Install Only option. An example of this is if the application object's pur-
pose is to just update some files on the workstation. When you select the
Install Only option, the software is installed but not run.

Set Path to File
If an executable file exists that needs to be run for the application distribution, select the Path to File option. Next set the path in the Path to File
text box to the executable to be run when an application object icon is
double-clicked in Application Window or Application Explorer. Use the
browse button to browse the file directory structure to find the executable you want. UNC pathnames are permitted. For example:

- ▶ server\volume:path

- ▶ \\server\volume\path

- ▶ volume_object_name:path

- ▶ directory_map_object_name:path

- ▶ driveletter:\path

NOTE If you don't want to run an application (for example, this application object's purpose might be to just update some files on the workstation), use the Install Only option and do not specify a path.

Specify Parameters

You can specify parameters to be passed into the executable file specified in the Path to File field. This can be useful in controlling the application being executed. For example, if you wanted the application to run silently and that option is controlled by a command-line parameter, you could specify that parameter in Path to File field to force silent execution.

Specify Working Directory

You can also specify a working directory for the application to be started in. For example, if you wanted to use a temporary location for the application to use as its base directory, you could specify a temporary directory such as `c:\temp`.

Run Application Once

The next option you have from the Applications property page is to set the Run Application Once option. This runs the application once and then removes the icon from the workstation.

Check this option when an application object's purpose is to install software to a workstation. It can be confusing and annoying to users if an install icon remains in the Application Window or in Application Explorer after the software has already been installed.

NOTE If you selected Run Application Once and also specified a version number for this application, the application runs once until the next time you change the version number, whereupon the application runs once one more time. This latter method is useful for upgrading applications.

Force Run as User if Application Is Workstation Associated

The final option you have from the Application property page is Force Run As User If Application Is Workstation Associated.

This feature allows you to force the application to be installed for each user who logs in from a workstation. This can be useful if an application applies settings to a workstation based on a user directory or program group.

Configuring Environment Options for Running Application

The next run option configurable for application objects is the
Environment option. The Environment property page, shown in Figure
11.14, lets you set up information about the environment the application
is run in.

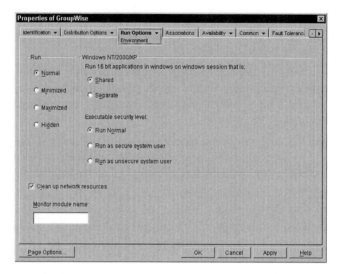

FIGURE 11.14
The Environment property page in ConsoleOne.

The Run section on the Environment property page enables you to select
one of the following window types with which to deploy the application:

▶ Normal—Pulls up the default window and deploys the application
in it.

▶ Minimized—Pulls up the window and begins the application
deployment; then minimizes it so that it is out of the view of the
user. This is the most commonly used option because the user has
access to the application deployment; however, it is not cluttering
up the user's screen.

▶ Maximized—Pulls up and maximizes the window for application
deployment. This is used if you want the user to be aware of the
application deployment so that the user waits until it is finished.

▶ Hidden—Hides the window that the application is deployed in
from the user. This can be used for an application that you want

users not to know about as well as to seamlessly provide a silent update that users are not affected by or aware of.

The Windows NT/2000/XP section of the Environment property page lets you specify whether 16-bit applications are run in Shared or Separate mode. It also enables you to configure the following application security levels:

▶ Run Normal—The default for applications being deployed to Windows NT/2000/XP.

▶ Run As Secure System User—Makes the application run at a secure system level. Use this option if you need the application to be installed even on workstations that have a high security level set up.

▶ Run As Unsecure System User—Makes the application run at a non-secure system level. Use this option if you want workstations that have a high security level set up to be protected from applications being deployed to them.

▶ Monitor Module Name—Allows you to specify the name of a module that remains running after the launched executable has finished. In cases where the launched executable is actually a wrapper module that launches another executable and then ends, this feature allows ZENworks to wait until the actual module has finished before cleaning up network resources.

The Environment property page also lets you select the Clean Up Network Resources option. If this is selected, any mapped drives or ports made by the application deployment will be cleaned up when it is finished.

Configuring Application Launch Scripts

The next run option configurable for application objects is launch scripts that are executed automatically each time the application is launched on a workstation. Unlike environment parameters, scripts can overwrite existing drive mappings and printer ports.

The two types of launch scripts are the Run Before Launching script and the Run After termination script. Run Before Launching scripts are executed before the application is launched. Run After Termination scripts are executed after the application is closed and before the network resources are cleaned up.

Launch scripts enable you to provide dynamic mappings beyond those defined, run other applications, log in to other servers or eDirectory trees, perform special termination options, and perform other tasks that must be done before and after an application is launched. The scripts support the same commands and syntax as the Novell Client by default. However, ZENworks Desktop Management allows you to specify your own script engine and file type extension. This allows you to create a much more extensive and powerful script by using another script engine, such as a Perl parser.

To create launch scripts, use the following steps:

1. Right-click the Application object and click Properties.

2. Select the Run Options tab and select Launch Scripts from the drop-down list.

3. Create the Run Before Launching and Run After Termination scripts in the text boxes shown in Figure 11.15.

4. Specify the location of the script engine if necessary. If no script engine is specified, ZENworks uses the Novell Client.

5. Specify or select the extension of the script file.

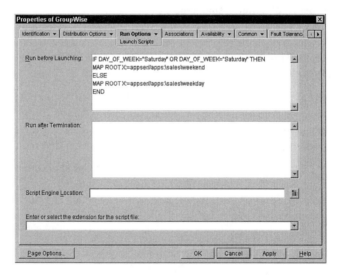

FIGURE 11.15
The application Launch Scripts property page in ConsoleOne.

Configuring Environment Variables for Application Launch

The next run option configurable for application objects is the Environment Variable option. The Environment Variable property page lets you add variables to be applied to the workstation environment when the application is deployed.

For example, if you have an application install that needs a temporary path variable name to be set to a specific location, you could add that variable name and path to the application object. When the application is deployed, the path variable is inserted into the environment on the workstation enabling the install to take place without any intervention from the user.

Configuring Licensing and Metering for Applications

The next run option configurable for application objects is the Licensing/Metering Variable option. The Licensing/Metering Variable property page enables you to specify that you want to use Novell licensing and metering to run the application. If you want to use licensing, you can simply click the browse button and select the license certificate you want to use from the eDirectory tree. You can also specify that you do not want to run the application if NLS is not available.

Configuring Application Dependencies

ZENworks Desktop Management allows you to define applications that the application object is dependent on before it can be executed on a workstation. This can be a useful feature to verify the software requirements for a workstation.

One example of when you would need to define an application dependency would be if an application required a specific Windows support pack to be applied. You could create an application object for the support pack and then use it as a dependency for any application that required it.

Another example of when you would need to define an application dependency would be if you have an application upgrade that will only install on a workstation with the original software installed. You could create an application object for the original application and use it as a dependency for the upgrade.

Other examples might include the need for an Oracle client to be installed on the workstation before the Oracle database application is run. The Application Window ensures that the client is installed properly before running the database application.

ZENworks allows for the nesting of chained applications. For example, application A could depend on B, who depends on C and D, and so on. When A is launched, the Application Window verifies that all the dependent applications up the chain are installed. Also when a verify is launched to repair any applications, the system verifies all applications up the chain.

ZENworks allows you to define the following options for application dependencies:

- ▶ Continue Distributions Immediately—Forces the application dependency object to be applied immediately to the workstation without waiting for the application to finish running before continuing to the next dependent application.

- ▶ Reboot Wait—Applies the application dependency, and, if any application needs to reboot, ZENworks waits until all applications in the chain are finished and then requests a system reboot.

- ▶ Show Chain—Brings up a window that displays the full chain of dependent applications. This can be useful in managing dependencies if you have many applications.

Setting Application Object Associations

After you set up the run options for an application, you need to set the application object associations. Setting the associations for an application object enables you to associate the application with a user, container, workstation, user group, or workstation group, and control the behavior and visibility of the application as it is distributed to users. To access these options, select the Associations tab on the application object, and a screen similar to the one shown in Figure 11.16 is displayed.

From the application object Associations property page, you can click the Add button and then navigate the tree to add objects with which you want to associate the application. If you specify a container object, you are given the option to specify whether to associate the application object with all users within the container, all workstations within the container, or both users and workstations in the container.

After the objects are added, you can check the following items for each object to control the behavior and visibility of the application for that object:

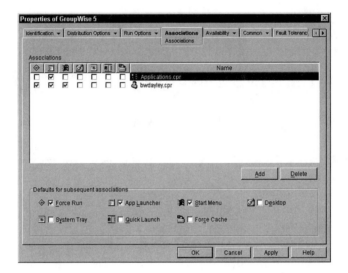

FIGURE 11.16
The Associations property page in ConsoleOne.

▶ Force Run—Specifies that after the application is available to the workstation, meaning that the user has logged in and meets the criteria specified, the application is automatically deployed to the workstation.

▶ App Launcher—Specifies that the application should appear in the Application Window when the user runs it.

▶ Start Menu—Specifies that the application should appear in the Start menu on the workstation.

▶ Desktop—Means that when the application is available, an icon is displayed on the desktop for the user to launch.

▶ System Tray—Specifies that when the application is available, an icon is displayed in the system tray on the workstation for easy launch.

▶ Quick Launch—Puts the icon for the application in the Quick Launch menu for even faster and easier distribution of the object.

▶ Force Cache—Forces the application to be cached to the workstation, where it can be used later the next time it is run and even run when the workstation is not connected to the network.

Setting Application Availability

After you set up the Association options for an application, you need to set the availability options. You can use the Availability tab to access pages used to control when the application icon is available or when the users can install software.

This feature depends on the settings you have set up for the Application Window on a user, workstation, organizational unit, organization, or country object. Be aware of those setting before trying to set up scheduling for the application object.

A good example of how to use the application availability feature is if you want to force run a virus detection application on users' workstations at a certain time, and only one time. You can force users to run the virus check by scheduling the appearance of the application using the Schedule property page and designating the application as Force Run.

NOTE Scheduling cannot deny access to an application outside the schedule because file rights might still exist.

To access the options on the Availability property tab, use the following steps to select which set of options you want to modify:

1. Right-click the Application object and click Properties.
2. Select the Availability tab.
3. Click the down arrow on the Availability tab, and a screen similar to the one in Figure 11.17 is displayed.

From the application object's Availability property tab, you should access the individual property pages to configure the application availability options described in the following sections.

Configuring Distribution Rules for Applications

The top page accessible from the Availability tab is the Distribution Rules property page. The Distribution Rules property page enables you to choose which applications will be available to workstations by making sure that the workstation meets the certain criteria specified. The Distribution Rules page enables you to set requirements on installed applications, authentication, client, connection speed, disk space, environment variables, memory, operating system, processor, Registry entries, file requirements, and terminal server. If workstations do not meet the criteria you specify, the icons do not appear on that workstation.

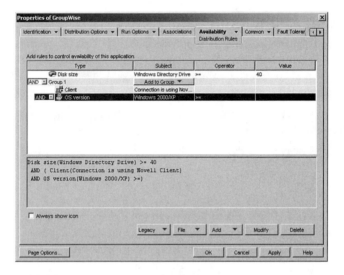

FIGURE 11.17
The Availability Distribution Rules in ConsoleOne.

For example, suppose that you want a GroupWise 5.5 application icon to appear only on workstations that have at least 32MB of RAM, a Pentium processor, 5MB of free disk space on the `c:` drive, and 100MB of free disk space on a temp drive. You can set up those options by clicking on the Add button, shown in Figure 11.18, to select and configure the requirement options described in the following sections.

New Group
ZENworks Desktop Management includes a huge feature to the distribution rules for applications. That feature is the capability to group dependencies based on and/or logic using the New Group option.

When you select New Group, a rule is added to the list with options to set the logic to either AND or OR. If AND is selected, the previous rules must be satisfied AND the new group's rules must be satisfied for the application to be distributed. However, if OR is selected, only the previous rules OR the new group's rules must be satisfied for the application to be distributed.

You can add as many rules to the new group as you need by clicking the Add to Group button and selecting the rule type from the drop-down list.

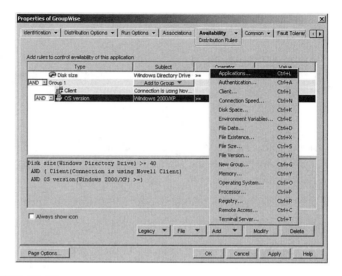

FIGURE 11.18
The Distribution Rules choices for application objects in ConsoleOne.

ZENworks allows you to chain together as many groups or individual rules as you need to control the application distribution properly.

Applications

The Distribution Rules tab for application objects enables you to filter applications based on the existence of other applications on the client. To filter workstations by installed applications, click the Add button from the Distribution Rules propety page and then select Application from the pop-up menu. A window is displayed that enables you to navigate the directory services tree to find specific applications that should or should not exist.

To filter on a specific application, simply navigate to that application object in the eDirectory tree and then select it. Next click either the Application Object Is Installed or the Application Object Is NOT Installed option. You want to use this option if an application is dependent on the existence of another one. For example, if you want to deploy an application update, you can check for the existence of the original application before making it available to the workstation.

Authentication

The Distribution Rules property page for application objects enables you to filter applications based on the type of authentication that they have.

You can filter on whether they have or do not have either a local worksta-tion or a network authentication.

To filter on the authentication type, select Authentication from the menu shown in Figure 11.18. Next, from the pop-up window, select either Local Workstation Authentication or Network Authentication from the drop-down menu.

Client
The Distribution Rules property page for application objects enables you to filter applications based on the availability of Novell client. This can be useful for applications that require a Novell client connection.

To filter on terminal server availability, select Client from the menu shown in Figure 11.18. Next, from the pop-up window, select either Connection Is Using Novell Client or Connection Is Not Using Novell Client from the drop-down menu. Then select the criteria option of True or False.

Connection Speed
The Distribution Rules property page for application objects enables you to filter applications based on the speed of the connection that they have. This rule allows you to hide applications from workstations that are too slow to run them.

To filter on the connection speed, select Connection Speed from the menu shown in Figure 11.18. Next, specify the speed in kilobits per sec-ond. Then specify the logic in terms of greater than, less than, greater than or equal to, or less than or equal to.

Remote Access
The Distribution Rules property page for application objects enables you to filter applications based on the type of remote access that they have. You can filter on whether they have or do not have either a LAN connec-tion or Remote Access connection.

To filter on the remote access connection type, select Remote Access from the menu shown in Figure 11.18. Next, from the pop-up window, select either LAN Connection or Remote Access Connection from the drop-down menu. Then select the criteria option of True or False.

Terminal Server

The Distribution Rules property page for application objects enables you to filter applications based on the availability of a terminal server. This can be useful for applications that require a terminal server.

To filter on terminal server availability, select Terminal Server from the menu shown in Figure 11.18. Next, from the pop-up window, select either Terminal Server Required or Terminal Server Not Required from the drop-down menu. Then select the criteria option of True or False.

Free Disk Space

The Distribution Rules property page for application objects enables you to filter applications based on the amount of free disk space available to the client. You can filter disk spaced on local drives and mapped network drives, as well as the following specific locations:

- ▶ Windows System directory drive
- ▶ Windows directory drive
- ▶ Temp directory drive

To filter workstations by disk space available, click the Add button from the Distribution Rules property page and then select Disk Space from the pop-up menu. A screen similar to the one shown in Figure 11.19 appears. From this screen, first select the location disk, in which space is needed, from the top drop-down list. Next, type in the MB of disk space needed to install and run the application. Next, you have the option of specifying one of the following logical requirements:

- ▶ Less Than
- ▶ Less Than or Equal To
- ▶ Equal To
- ▶ Greater Than or Equal To
- ▶ Greater Than

You can specify multiple locations that require disk space by performing the same steps again.

An example of when to use this is if the application requires a minimum of 5MB free on the Windows directory drive and 100MB free on the TEMP drive. If you specify these settings, the application object icon will only appear on workstations that contain enough free disk space in all three locations.

FIGURE 11.19
The Disk Space Rule dialog box from the Distribution Rules property page
for application objects in ConsoleOne.

Environment Variables

The Distribution Rules property page for application objects also enables
you to filter applications based on specific environment variable settings
on the client. To filter workstations by environment variables, click the
Add button from the Distribution Rules screen and then select
Environment Variables from the pop-up menu. A screen similar to the
one shown in Figure 11.20 appears. From this screen, first type in the
name of the variable and then select whether the name should exist. You
also have the option of filtering on the value of the variable by typing in a
value and selecting a logic operation such as equal to.

You can specify multiple environment variables to check for before displaying and installing the application by following the same process
again.

One example of when to use this is if some users use Netscape as their
browser and some use Internet Explorer. If you only want users who use
Netscape to receive the Netscape object, you could set up a browser environment variable on the workstations and then specify that that variable
be present from the Distribution Rules property page.

Another example of when to filter on environment variables would be if
you wanted to apply an update to users with GroupWise 4 on their systems. You could check the version environment variable on those systems
to make sure that GroupWise is installed and that its version is equal
to 4.

FIGURE 11.20
The Environment Variable Rule dialog box for application objects.

Memory

The Distribution Rules property page for application objects enables you to filter applications based on the amount of memory installed on the client. To filter workstations by memory installed, click the Add button from the Distribution Rules property page and then select Memory from the pop-up menu. A screen similar to the one in Figure 11.21 appears. From this screen, first type in the MB of RAM needed to install and run the application. Next, you have the option of specifying one of the following logical requirements:

- ▶ Less Than
- ▶ Less Than or Equal To
- ▶ Equal To
- ▶ Greater Than or Equal To
- ▶ Greater Than

An example of when to use this option would be if the application requires 32MB of RAM; specify memory is greater than, and then enter 32 in the text box. The application object will not appear on workstations that do not have at least 32MB of RAM.

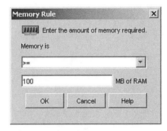

FIGURE 11.21
The Memory Rule dialog box for application objects.

Operating System

The Distribution Rules property page for application objects enables you to filter applications based on the operating system installed on the client. To filter workstations by operating system, click the Add button from the Distribution Rules property page and then select Operating System from the pop-up menu. A screen similar to the one in Figure 11.22 appears. From this screen, select the desired Windows platform. Then you have the option of specifying a version number of the operating system as well as one of the following logical requirements:

- Less Than
- Less Than or Equal To
- Equal To
- Greater Than or Equal To
- Greater Than

FIGURE 11.22
The Operating System Rule dialog box for application objects.

Processor

The Distribution Rules property page for application objects enables you to filter applications based on the speed of the processor installed on the client. To filter workstations by processor, click the Add button from the Distribution Rules property page and then select Processor from the pop-up menu. A screen similar to the one shown in Figure 11.23 appears. From this screen, first select the minimum processor needed to install and run the application from the following list:

- ▶ Pentium
- ▶ Pentium Pro
- ▶ Pentium II
- ▶ Pentium III
- ▶ Pentium IV

FIGURE 11.23
The Processor Rule dialog box for application objects.

Next you have the option of specifying one of the following logical requirements:

- ▶ Less Than
- ▶ Less Than or Equal To
- ▶ Equal To
- ▶ Not Equal To
- ▶ Greater Than or Equal To
- ▶ Greater Than

Registry Entries

The Distribution Rules property page for application objects enables you to filter applications based on specific Windows Registry settings on the client. To filter workstations by Registry settings, click the Add button from the Distribution Rules screen and then select Registry from the pop-up menu. A screen similar to the one shown in Figure 11.24 appears. From this screen, first navigate the Registry to find the specific Registry key to use to filter which workstations will receive the application. Type in the name of the Registry entry or browse to find it. Then set the value of the entry, the data type (String or DWORD), and the logical operation to perform on it. Then you have the option to filter based on the following criteria:

- ▶ Key Exists—Distribute application if key exists in the Registry by selecting this radial button.

- ▶ Key Does Not Exist—Distribute application if key does not exist in the Registry by selecting this radial button.

- ▶ Name—Specify the name of the entry associated with the key.

- ▶ Value Exists—If the Name box is filled out, you can specify to distribute the application only if a name does exist for the selected key.

- ▶ Value Does Not Exist—If the Name box is filled out, you can specify to distribute the application only if a name does not already exist for the selected key.

- ▶ Value—If a value is typed in, ZENworks checks the value against the value of the entry based on the logical operation and data type specified in the Value section.

You can specify multiple Registry entries to check for before displaying and installing the application by following the same process again.

Files

The Distribution Rules property page for application objects enables you to filter applications based on specific files installed on the client. To filter workstations by files, click the Add button from the Distribution Rules property page and then select one of the following file filtering options:

- ▶ File Existence—Provides a window with a box that enables you to specify the name of and location to the file to filter on. At the bottom two radial buttons are present, which enable you to specify whether to filter if the file exists or does not exist.

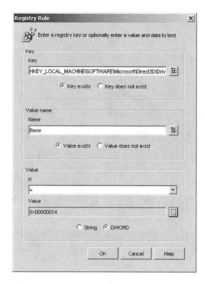

FIGURE 11.24
The Registry Rule dialog box for application objects.

▶ File Version—Provides a window with two text boxes that enable you to specify the name of and location to the file to filter on. At the bottom of this window, you can input a specific version number to filter on as well as the following logical operations: less than, less than or equal to, greater than, greater than or equal to, and equal to.

▶ File Date—Provides a window with two text boxes that enable you to specify the name of and location to the file to filter on. At the bottom you can specify a date for the file based on one of the following: before, on or before, on, on or after, and after.

▶ File Size—Provides a window with two text boxes that enable you to specify the name of and location to the file to filter on. At the bottom you can specify a size for the file based on one of the following: equal to, greater than, less than, greater than or equal to, and less than or equal to.

Configuring Availability Schedule for Application

After you configure the Distribution Rules for application availability, you can move on to setting up a schedule for availability for the application. Select Schedule from the Availability tab drop-down list, and the

Schedule property page appears. The None option is selected by default; however, you can configure the application object to be available only to workstations based on a set of specific days or a range of days as described in the following sections.

For information about setting the schedule options, see the "Configuring a Pre-Install Schedule for Application" section earlier in this chapter.

Configuring Application Termination Options

The final option you have available from the Availability tab is to set termination options for application availability. To configure the termination behavior, select termination from the drop-down menu on the Availability tab. A page similar to the one shown in Figure 11.25 appears.

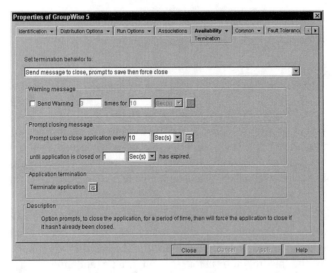

FIGURE 11.25
The Termination property page for application objects in ConsoleOne.

From this page you can configure the following options that control the behavior terminating the application after it has been executed at the workstation.

None

This option (default) enables users to close the application on their own without any intervention from ZENworks. If you require the application to be closed for any reason (such as updates or database indexing), you should not use this option because you will not be able to force users to close the application.

Send Message to Close Application

This option prompts users, at a specified interval, to close the application on their own until the application closes. For example, if you set an interval of 5 minutes, ZENworks sends a message (if one is active) to the user every 5 minutes until the application is closed or the message has been sent the configured amount of times.

To set this option, follow these steps:

1. Specify the time interval between messages in the text box provided.

2. Click the message button next to the seconds drop-down list, and a message window is displayed. From this message window you can select to use the default message, no message, or a custom message. If you select Custom Message, you can type in a message to users that is displayed on their workstations asking them to close the application.

3. Click OK.

Send Message to Close Then Prompt to Save Data

This option, Send Message to Close Then Prompt User to Save Data, enables users a specified period of time to close the application on their own (this action is optional). When that period of time expires, the Application Window attempts to close the application. If users have not saved data, they are prompted to save it. Users can choose not to close the application. If users have no unsaved data, the application closes. After the application is closed, users cannot reopen it.

To set this option, follow these steps:

1. Select the check box next to Send Warning and specify the warning interval and period in the text boxes provided (optional). If you want to specify a custom message, click the message button next to the seconds drop-down list, and a message window is displayed. Select Use Custom and then enter a message in the message text box.

2. In the next group box, specify the Prompt Message Time Interval in the text boxes provided. If you want to specify a custom message, click the message button next to the minutes drop-down list, and a

message window is displayed. Select Use Custom and then enter a message in the message text box.

3. Click OK.

Send Message to Close, Prompt to Save, Then Force Close

The Send Message to Close, Prompt to Save, Then Force Close option prompts users, for a specified period of time, to close the application on their own. When that period of time expires, ZENworks Desktop Management can close the application that is prompting users, at specified intervals, to save their work. If users have still not closed within a specified period of time, the application is forced to close.

To set this option, follow these steps:

1. Select the check box next to Send Warning and specify the warning interval and period in the text boxes provided (optional). If you want to specify a custom message, click the message button next to the seconds drop-down list, and a message window is displayed. Select Use Custom and then enter a message in the message text box.

2. In the next group box, specify the Prompt Message Time interval and period in the text boxes provided. If you want to specify a custom message, click the message button next to the minutes drop-down list, and a message window is displayed. Select Use Custom and then enter a message in the message text box.

3. In the last group box, click the message button next to the Terminate application label, and write a note to users explaining why the application terminated and perhaps when it will be available again.

4. Click OK.

Send Message to Close Then Force Close with Explanation

The Send Message to Close Then Force Close with Explanation termination option prompts users, for a specified period of time, to close the application on their own. When that period of time expires, the application is forced to close.

To set this option, follow these steps:

1. Select the check box next to Send Warning and specify the interval and period in the text boxes provided (optional). If you want to specify a custom message, click the message button next to the

seconds drop-down list, and a message window is displayed. Select
Use Custom and then enter a message in the message text box.

2. In the last group box, click the message button next to the
   Terminate application label, and write a note to users explaining
   why the application terminated and perhaps when it will be available again.

3. Click OK.

Setting Common Options for Application Objects

After you set up the availability options for an application, you need to
set some common options to control some general behavior and configure the application object. To access the options on the Common property tab, use the following steps to select which set of common options you
want to modify:

1. Right-click the Application object and click Properties.

2. Select the Common tab.

3. Click the down arrow on the Common tab, and a screen similar to
   the one shown in Figure 11.26 is displayed.

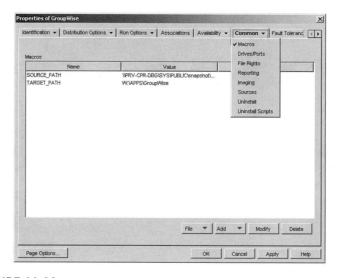

FIGURE 11.26
The Common property tab list in ConsoleOne.

From the application object's Common property tab, you should access the individual property pages to configure some common options for the application as described in the following sections.

Configuring Application Drives and Ports

The first advanced option available for application objects from the Common tab pull-down menu is the Drives/Ports property page. The Drives/Ports property page enables you to specify drives and ports that need to be mapped when the application is being launched on a workstation. This feature requires the existence of the Novell Client on the workstation.

To add a drive to be mapped for the application window, click the Add button under the Drives to be Mapped window to bring up the drive mapping box as shown in Figure 11.27. From this box you can perform the following options:

▶ Specify an option (Drive, Search Drive 1, or Search Drive 16).

▶ Specify a letter.

▶ Specify a network path.

▶ Specify whether it should be a root mapping.

▶ Specify whether it should overwrite existing mappings.

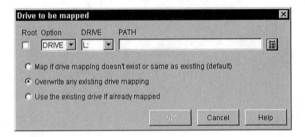

FIGURE 11.27
The Drive To Be Mapped box for Common options.

To add a port to be captured for the application launch, click the Add button under the Port to Be Captured window to bring up the port capturing box as shown in Figure 11.28. From this box you can perform the following options:

▶ Specify a port to capture.

▶ Specify a network printer or print queue.

▶ Specify to use notify flag.

▶ Specify to use form feed flag.

▶ Specify to use banner flag.

FIGURE 11.28
The Port to Be Captured box for Common options.

Configuring File Rights for Application Launch

The next advanced option available for application objects from the Common tab pull-down menu is the File Rights property page. The File Rights property page enables you to grant rights to files, directories, and volumes. This is used when this application object is associated with a user object or with a group, organizational unit, organization, or country object with which the user is already associated.

Use the following procedure to grant file rights to users when an application object is associated with them:

1. Right-click the Application object and click Properties.

2. Click the File Rights property page under the Common tab.

3. Click Add and specify the volume or directory to which users need access when they run the application object.

4. Highlight the volume or directory and specify Supervisor, Read, Write, Create, Erase, Modify, File Scan, and Access Control rights as necessary; then click Apply.

5. Next associate this application object with a user, group, organizational unit, organization, or country object to grant the rights.

Configuring Application Reporting

The next advanced feature available from the Common tab pull-down menu is the Reporting option. When an application is distributed to the workstation, the Application Window records whether the application was properly distributed. A successful distribution is recorded as well, and if there were any errors with the distribution, this is recorded along with the reasons for the failure in the distribution.

This record of distribution is recorded on a local file and results in an event being sent to the centralized database that is also used for hardware and software inventory. These distributions can be set up through the Reporting property page in ConsoleOne.

To access the Reporting property page, follow these steps:

1. Right-click the Application object and click Properties.

2. Select the Common tab.

3. Click the down arrow on the Common tab and select the Reporting option.

4. On the Reporting property page you have the option of performing changes to the application object as shown in Figure 11.29.

From the Reporting property page you can select from the four following destination keys for various events that occur during application deployment:

▶ Enable database reporting—Select the Database box to enable reporting of the event to the database.

▶ Enable log file reporting—Select the Log to File box and specify a location in the text box to the location of where reporting should log events to enable log file reporting.

▶ Enabling SNMP traps—Select the SNMP Traps box if you want the SNMP trap engine to be notified of application distribution events.

▶ Enable XML reporting—Select the XML box if you want the application event to be sent via XML to the web management console. Agents that collect these XML messages and place them in a database are available on the companion CD.

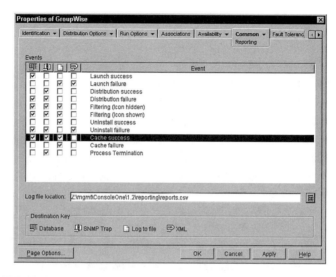

FIGURE 11.29
The Reporting property page for application objects.

You can specify these event keys for the following list of events:

▶ Launch Success

▶ Launch Failure

▶ Distribution Success

▶ Distribution Failure

▶ Filtering (Icon Hidden)

▶ Filtering (Icon Shown)

▶ Uninstall Success

▶ Uninstall Failure

▶ Cache Success

▶ Cache Failure

▶ Process Termination

Configuring Launch Macros

One way to automate application objects is to use the Macros property page to set up special macros that can be used during object distribution and launch. These macros enable you to set up application objects even when the user has a different system setup than what is expected by the administrator.

To access the Macro property page, follow these steps:

1. Right-click the Application object and click Properties.

2. Select the Common tab.

3. Click the down arrow on the Common tab and select the Macros option.

4. On the Macros property page you have the option of adding special macros to the application object as shown in Figure 11.30.

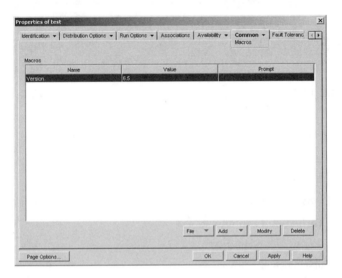

FIGURE 11.30
The Macros property page for application objects.

The following sections describe the special macros that can be added to an application object for use in distribution and launching.

String Macros

The first type of macro available for application objects is the string macro. The string macro can retain a value that remains static during application distribution and launching.

To set up a string macro, access the Macros property page, using the steps described previously, from within ConsoleOne. Then select

Add→String Value. You can set up the following options for the string macro:

▶ Value Name—Name set up for the macro for install scripts, and so on.

▶ Value Data—Specify a value for the macro.

Prompted Drive Macros

The next type of macro available for application objects is the prompted drive macro. The prompted drive macro enables you to prompt the user for a drive that will be used for application distribution and launching.

For example, users may want to put an application on a different drive than what was described in the application object. Prompted drive macros enable the administrator to request that the user be prompted for the information. By using the prompted drive macros feature, the administrator can have the destination drive requested of the end-user, and the resulting distribution goes to the specified drive.

To set up prompted drive macros, access the Macros property page using the previous steps from within ConsoleOne. Then select Add→Prompted→Drive. A window similar to the one shown in Figure 11.31 is displayed. From the Prompted Drive Macros window, you can set up the following options for the prompted drive macro:

▶ Macro Name—Name set up for the macro for install scripts and so on.

▶ Prompt Text—Textual information to be displayed for the user when prompting for the macro.

▶ Default Value—Specify a default value for the drive macro for users to use if they have no need to specify otherwise. The available options are Windows System Directory Drive, Windows Directory Drive, Temp Directory Drive, or letters A...Z.

▶ Minimum Disk Space in MB—Specify a minimum amount of disk space required in setting the macro.

Prompted String Macros

The next type of macro available for Application objects is the prompted string macro. The prompted string macro enables you to prompt the user for a string used for application distribution and launching.

FIGURE 11.31
The Prompted Drive Macros window for application objects.

For example, suppose that you want to ask the user for the user ID he uses to access a corporate database. The macro can then be used by the application install later to access the database and retrieve information necessary for the install.

To set up prompted string macros, access the Macros property page using the previous steps from within ConsoleOne. Then select Add→Prompted→String. You can set up the following options for the prompted string macro:

- ▶ Macro Name—Name set up for the macro for install scripts and so on.

- ▶ Prompt Text—Textual information to be displayed for the user when prompting for the macro.

- ▶ Default Value—Specify a default value for the macro for users to use if they have no need to specify otherwise.

- ▶ Minimum Disk Space in MB—You can specify a minimum amount of disk space required in setting the macro.

- ▶ Maximum String Length—Use this option to specify the maximum number of characters allowed for string macros.

Configuring Application Object Imaging
The next advanced feature available from the Common pull-down menu is the Imaging option. ZENworks enables you to create an Add-on image

of the application by selecting the location of the image file, as shown in Figure 11.32, and then clicking the Create Image button. That image can later be applied to a newly imaged workstation as part of the imaging process discussed in the Chapter 22, "Imaging a Workstation."

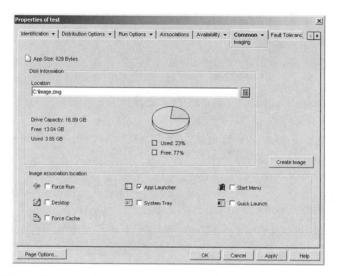

FIGURE 11.32
The Imaging property page for application objects.

Configuring Application Sources

Another advanced feature available from the Common tab pull-down menu is the Sources option. The Sources option enables you to specify network volumes and directories that ZENworks for Desktops uses to find application packages for the application during distribution and launching.

You can add volumes or directories to the list by clicking on the Add button and either typing in the UNC path, or using the browse button and navigating the file system.

Configuring Application Uninstall

One of the most powerful features in ZENworks Desktop Management application distribution is the capability to uninstall applications previously delivered. This provides administrators with control over which applications users have.

Use the following steps to access the application Uninstall page for application objects and configure the uninstall behavior:

1. Right-click the Application object and click Properties.

2. Select the Common tab.

3. Click the down arrow on the Common tab and select the Uninstall option as shown in Figure 11.33.

From the Uninstall property page you have the option to set the following options:

▶ Enable Uninstall—Determines whether the application can be uninstalled.

▶ Enable User to Perform a Manual Uninstall—Determines whether users can uninstall the application.

▶ Prompt User Before Uninstall—Prompts the user prior to performing an application uninstall, allowing the user to save any work being done by the application.

▶ Prompt User Before Reboot—Prompts the user prior to performing a workstation reboot, allowing the user to save any work being done.

▶ Terminate Application Before Uninstall—Forces the application to be terminated prior to uninstalling. This option should be used for any application that requires access to files, directories, or Registry settings removed by the uninstall.

▶ Uninstall Application If Not Used Within x Days—Enables you to specify a number of days the application remains available to users. If the user does not use the application within that number of days, the application is removed.

The following sections describe the options available to specifically control how the uninstall is performed on files, shortcuts, .INI files, and Registry entries.

Files Uninstall

From the application Uninstall property page you can specify the precise criteria of how files are uninstalled. Click the Files tab, and a screen similar to the one shown in Figure 11.33 is displayed. From this screen you can specify to uninstall files with any of the following attributes set:

- ▶ Copy Always

- ▶ Copy If Exists

- ▶ Copy If Does Not Exist

- ▶ Copy If Newer

- ▶ Copy If Newer And Exists

- ▶ Copy If Newer Version

- ▶ Request Confirmation

- ▶ Copy If Different

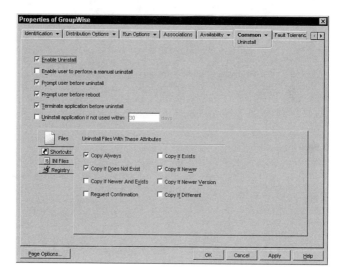

FIGURE 11.33
The Files Uninstall property page for application objects.

Shortcuts Uninstall

From the application Uninstall property page you can specify the precise
behavior of how shortcuts are uninstalled. Click the Shortcuts tab, and a
screen similar to the one shown in Figure 11.34 is displayed. From this
screen you can specify to uninstall shortcuts with either of the following
attributes set:

- ▶ Create Always

- ▶ Create If Does Not Exist

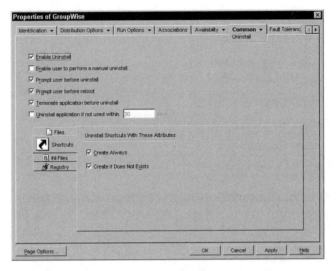

FIGURE 11.34
The Shortcuts Uninstall property page for application objects.

.INI Files Uninstall

From the application Uninstall property page you can specify the specific behavior of how .INI files are uninstalled. Click the INI Files tab, and a screen similar to the one shown in Figure 11.35 is displayed. From this screen you can specify to uninstall .INI files with any of the following attributes set:

- ▶ Create Always
- ▶ Create If Exists
- ▶ Create If Does Not Exist
- ▶ Create or Add to Existing Section
- ▶ Create or Append to Existing Value

Registry Uninstall

From the application Uninstall property page you can specify the specific behavior of how Registry entries are uninstalled. Click to show the Registry tab, and a screen similar to the one shown in Figure 11.36 is displayed. From this screen you can specify how the uninstall of Registry entries with any of the following attributes set will be handled:

- ▶ Create Always

▶ Create If Does Not Exist

▶ Create If Exists

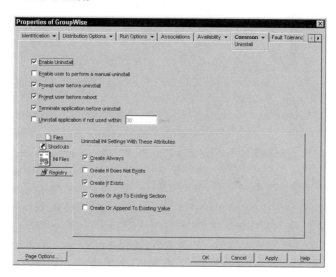

FIGURE 11.35
The INI Files Uninstall property page for Application objects.

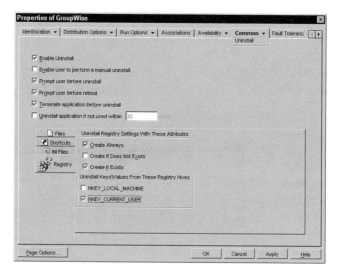

FIGURE 11.36
The Registry Uninstall property page for application objects.

You also need to specify which of the following Registry hives should be uninstalled:

▶ HKEY_LOCAL_MACHINE

▶ HKEY_CURRENT_USER

Configuring Application Uninstall Scripts

Another powerful feature in ZENworks Desktop Management for application distribution is the capability to define uninstall scripts to uninstall applications previously delivered. This provides administrators with greater control over which applications users have access to.

To define an uninstall script for an application, select the Uninstall Scripts option from the Common tab of the application object properties window. Then configure the following options:

▶ Run Before Uninstalling—Allows you to specify the script command to be executed prior to uninstalling the application.

▶ Run After Uninstalling—Allows you to specify the script command to be executed after the application is uninstalled.

▶ Script Engine Location—Allows you to specify the location of the engine that will execute the script. This option is powerful because it allows you to specify your own script engine to handle the uninstall scripts. All you need to do is point to the executable file. If no script engine is specified the Novell Client is used as the script engine.

▶ Script Extension—Allows you to specify the extension that the script should be executed as. This feature is important if your script engine supports multiple script types and uses the file extension to determine which type of script it is.

Setting Up Application Fault Tolerance

Another powerful feature in ZENworks Desktop Management application distribution is the capability to provide fault tolerance and load balancing to application delivery. The Fault Tolerance property page enables you to control the availability of applications to users.

Use the following steps to access the Fault Tolerance property page for application objects and configure the uninstall behavior:

1. Right-click the Application object and click Properties.

2. Select the Fault Tolerance tab.

The following sections describe setting up application fault tolerance and load balancing options from the Fault Tolerance property page.

Configuring Application Fault Tolerance Options

The first option available from the drop-down menu under the Fault Tolerance tab is to set up fault tolerance. The fault tolerance feature enables you to specify alternative forms of the application object to make the application available even if a problem with the current one exists.

From the Fault Tolerance property page you have the ability to enable fault tolerance and then set up the following fault tolerant options discussed in the following sections.

Use Source List

You can define a list of application package sources to use if the current application object is unavailable for any reason. To add additional application package source locations, click the Add button. A window displays the sources that have been defined for this application object (see "Configuring Application Sources" earlier in the chapter). Select the sources you want to use and click OK to add them to the Source List section of the Fault Tolerance property page.

Use Application Objects

You can also define application objects to be used as backup application objects if the current object is unavailable. To add application objects to the list, click the Add button. Then navigate the eDirectory tree to add the additional backup application objects.

Configuring Application Object Load Balancing

The next option available from the drop-down menu under the Fault Tolerance tab is to set up load balancing. The load balancing feature enables you to specify alternative forms of the application object to balance the use for a number of users. This increases the reliability and availability of applications for busy networks.

From the Load Balancing property page, shown in Figure 11.37, you have the ability to enable load balancing for the application and then set up the following load balancing options.

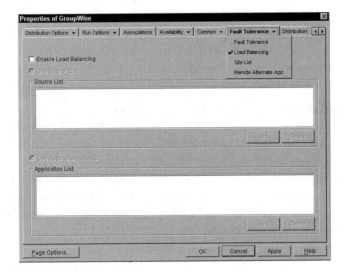

FIGURE 11.37
The Fault Tolerance Load Balancing property page for application objects.

Use Source List

You can define a list of application package sources to distribute the use of the current application object. To add additional application package source locations, click the Add button. A window displays the sources that have been defined for this application object (see "Configuring Application Sources" earlier in the chapter). Select the sources you want to use and click OK to add them to the source section of the Load Balancing property page.

Use Application Objects

You can also define application objects to be used as load balancing options for the current object. To add application objects to the list, click the Add button; then navigate the eDirectory tree to add the additional backup application objects.

Configuring a Site List for Application Objects

The next option you can define from the Fault Tolerance tab is additional sites for the application object. If you need your application to be highly available for users, create multiple copies of the application object and link them to the original object by clicking the Link button. That way you can maintain a list of compatible application sources to use for fault tolerance and load balancing.

Configure Remote Failover

The final option you can define in the Fault Tolerance tab is an application to failover to if you are remote and unable to execute the current one. To add a failover application object, simply click on the browse button on the Remote Alternate App property page and locate the remote backup. You also have the option to select Always Use This Alternate Application When Running Remotely, if you want all remote users to use the failover application.

An example of when to use this feature would be if you have an application that requires a high-speed connection such as a database application. Normally the user, when connected, would launch this application over the LAN connection. You could make an application object that will run the same database application on a Terminal Server. Then you could hook the Terminal Server version into the failover field. Then when the user is connected over a slow link, the system automatically connects them to a terminal services version of the application instead of failing to provide this because they are not on the LAN. This way your users get to their applications no matter where they are connected!

Setting Up MSI-Specific Options for Application Objects

ZENworks Desktop Management provides special options for MSI application objects in addition to the standard ones mentioned earlier in this chapter. The following sections discuss those options and how to configure them.

Configuring and Viewing the Package Information

The first MSI-specific option for application objects is the Package Information property page located under the Identification tab of the application object properties window. The following information is provided about the MSI application object:

- ▶ Administration Package Path—Is configurable and points to the location of the Administration Package.

- ▶ Version—Displays the version of the application.

- ▶ Vendor—Displays the manufacturer name for the application.

- ▶ Locale—Displays the language the application is written to.

- ▶ Help Link—Displays the web address that the vendor intended to be used to support the application.

► Package Path—Is configurable and points to the location of the
   .MSI file.

Configuring the Transform List

The first MSI-specific option for application objects is the Transforms
property page located under the MSI tab of the application object, shown
in Figure 11.38. You can add multiple transform (.MST) files to be
applied the application object. This allows you to add additions to the
MSI object without having to create a new one.

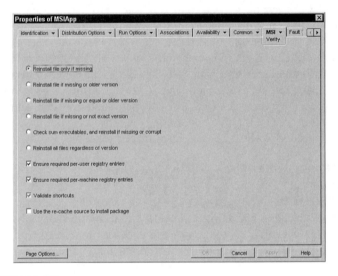

FIGURE 11.38
The MSI tab menu for application objects.

Configuring the MSI Properties

The next MSI-specific option for application objects is the Properties
property page located under the MSI tab of the application object, shown
in Figure 11.38. The Properties list allows you to add and customize
properties of the MSI application object. The properties available depend
on the vendor that created the .MSI file. They include things such as
readme or copyright files, macro data, environment variables, and so on.

To add a property to an MSI application object, click the Add button.
Then select the property value name from the drop-down menu. Finally,
set the correct value of the property and click OK. The property will now
appear in the Properties list.

Configuring the MSI Verify Options

The next MSI-specific set of options for application objects is the Verify property page located under the MSI tab of the application object, shown in Figure 11.38. From this page you can customize the methods ZENworks will use, during application distribution, when verifying different aspects of the MSI application install. The following is a list of the verification settings for MSI application objects:

- ▶ Reinstall File Only If Missing (default)
- ▶ Reinstall File If Missing or Older Version
- ▶ Reinstall File If Missing or Equal or Older Version
- ▶ Reinstall File If Missing or Not Exact Version
- ▶ Check Sum Executables, and Reinstall If Missing or Corrupt
- ▶ Reinstall All Files Regardless of Version
- ▶ Ensure Required Per-User Registry Entries (default)
- ▶ Ensure Required Per-Machine Registry Entries (default)
- ▶ Validate Shortcuts (default)
- ▶ Use the Re-cache Source to Install Package

Configure the MSI Patches List

The final MSI-specific option for application objects is the Patches property page located under the MSI tab of the application object, shown in Figure 11.38. You can add multiple patch (.MSP) files to be applied to the application object. This allows you to add updates/patches to the MSI object without having to create a new one.

Setting Up Terminal Server Specific Options for Application Objects

ZENworks Desktop Management provides special options for Terminal Server application objects in addition to the standard ones mentioned earlier in this chapter. The following sections discuss those options and how to configure them.

To access the Terminal Server options select the Terminal Server Client tab as shown in Figure 11.39.

Depending on the type of terminal server application object created you will see different configuration options on the Terminal Server Client tab.

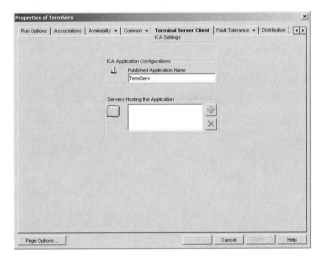

FIGURE 11.39
The Terminal Server Client tab menu for application objects in
ConsoleOne.

For RDP terminal servers, you can configure the server address, port, and
domain as well as the application path and application working directory.

For ICA terminal servers, you can set the published application name
and a list of servers that host the application.

Setting Up Web-specific Options for Application Objects

ZENworks Desktop Management provides a special option for web application objects in addition to the standard ones mentioned earlier in this
chapter. If you select the Web URL property page from the Run Options
tab of the application objects properties window, you will be able to configure the location of the web application. You can also click the Test the
URL button to check the behavior in the local browser.

Summary

This chapter discussed how to use a template to create an actual application object and distribute it to users. This chapter covered the main
points necessary to walk through the process of application object creation and distribution.

## CHAPTER 12

Setting Up Application Distribution

ZENworks Desktop Management has a powerful distribution engine that enables you to distribute your applications throughout your network. After an application object is created in eDirectory, you only need to set up the application distribution environment to apply it to several workstations on your network. This chapter covers using ConsoleOne to set up application users to receive applications and application foldering, as well as automating application object distribution.

Setting Up Application Foldering

The first step in setting up the application environment is to set up application foldering. ZENworks Desktop Management offers powerful foldering capabilities that enable users to organize the applications you deliver to them using Application Explorer. These folders appear in the Application Window, Application Explorer browser view, and on the Start menu.

> **NOTE** If two folders have the same name, their contents are merged together.

The following are the four types of folders available to users in Application Window:

- ▶ Application folder object—An application folder object is an independent object with which you associate application objects. By linking many application objects to one application folder object, you can manage the folder pathnames of many application objects from one object. See the section "Create Application Folder Object and Associate with Application Objects" later in the chapter for more information.

▶ Custom folder—Custom folders are set up on the application object's Folders property page and thus belong exclusively to the application object. A custom folder cannot be shared with another application object. You can name custom folders any way you want and set up folders within folders (subfoldering). Custom folders override any system folders that may exist as the result of application object to container associations. See the "Create Custom Folders for Application Object" section later in the chapter for more information.

▶ Personal folder—Personal folders let users create and name their own folders and place Application Window-delivered applications in them. See the "Enable Personal Folders" section later in this chapter for more information.

▶ System folder—System folders appear in Application Window or Explorer when you associate an application object with a user, group, organizational `unit`, organization, or country object, and you have not created any custom folders for that application object or associated the application object with a linked folder.

To set up application foldering to manage application objects, you need to perform the following tasks discussed in the following sections.

Create Application Folder Object and Associate with Application Objects

The first step in setting up application foldering is to create a folder object that can be linked to application objects. Use the following steps from within ConsoleOne to create an application folder object:

1. Right-click the organization unit, organization, or country object under which you want to create a folder object.

2. Choose New→Object; then select Application Folder in the new object dialog and click OK.

3. Name the folder, select Define Additional Properties, and then click OK.

Custom folders are tied to one application object. Linked folders, however, may contain many application objects. All folders appear in Application Window or Explorer browser view and also in the Start menu.

After the application folder has been created, use the Folders property page on a folder object to create custom or linked folders in which to organize application objects. To set up the folder for applications, use the following steps to access and modify the Folders property page from within ConsoleOne:

1. Right-click the application folder object and select Properties.

2. Click the Folders tab, and a screen similar to the one shown in Figure 12.1 appears.

3. Click Add→Folder and then name the folder.

4. Click Add→Folder and name the folder to put additional folders within the folder you created in step 3.

5. With a folder highlighted, click Add→Application, browse to the application object you want to add, and then click OK. Repeat this process for all the application objects you want to place in this folder.

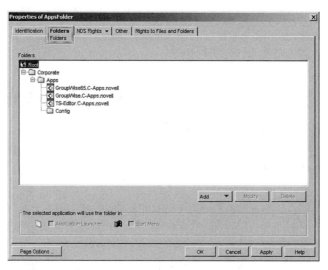

FIGURE 12.1
The Folders property page for application folders in ConsoleOne.

6. Check the Application Window and/or Start menu boxes depending on whether you want to display the folders in Application Window/Explorer browser view or on the Start menu.

Create Custom Folders for Application Object

The next step in setting up application foldering is to use the Folders property page for the application object to create custom folders in which to organize application objects, as described earlier in this chapter. A custom folder is tied to one application object; however, you can have multiple custom folders per application object.

Using custom folders, you can achieve *subfoldering* or placing folders within folders. This is often essential if you have numerous application objects available to users. Custom foldering enables you to organize application objects and control which users see which applications.

TIP Suppose that you have created a folder object that contains several folders linked to several application objects. You now want to clear these folder-application links and start over. One possibility is to delete the folder object, which converts all the linked folders to custom folders, which are then saved in all the relevant application objects. In this case you would have to open each application object and delete the custom folders in them.

A quicker method is to delete the folders and the links to application objects from the folder object but not delete the folder object itself. When the folder object is empty, you can decide whether you want to start over with new folders and links to application objects, or you can delete the folder object.

Customize Application Window Configurations Per User or Container

After you create the folder objects, you need to customize the Application Window configurations. ZENworks Desktop Management enables you to customize the behavior of the Application Window at a user, group, organizational unit, organization, or country object level.

Use the following steps to configure the Application Window for an object in ConsoleOne:

1. Right-click the object and select Properties.

2. Click the ZENworks→Launcher Configuration tab, as shown in Figure 12.2.

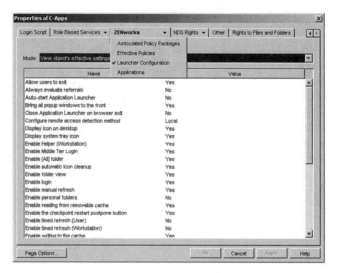

FIGURE 12.2
The Launcher Configuration tab.

3. From this screen select the View/Edit object's custom configuration from the Mode drop-down menu.

4. Click the Add button to bring up the Launcher Configuration window, shown in Figure 12.3.

From the Launcher Configuration window you can set up the Application Window options for users, the Application Window, Application Explorer, and workstations as described in the following sections.

Setting Up User Application Window Options

From the Launcher Configuration window, you can specify configurations that dictate how users view and work with Application Window and Application Explorer desktop software by selecting the User tab as shown previously in Figure 12.3. From this screen, you can set the following options that define how the Application Window behaves for users.

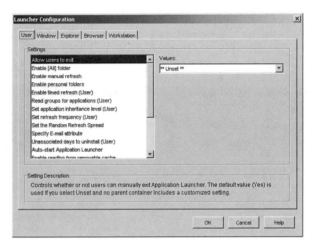

FIGURE 12.3
Launcher Configuration window for user objects in ConsoleOne.

Allow Users to Exit (Default=Yes)

The Allow Users to Exit option determines whether users can exit Application Window or Explorer.

An example of when to use this would be if you were running software at a conference where workstations are available for the attendees of the conference to use.

Enable (All) Folder

The folder view in Application Window might be confusing to some users. By setting Enable (All) Folder to No, the (All) folder is hidden from users in the Application Window.

Enable Manual Refresh (Default=Yes)

Enable Manual Refresh lets users refresh Application Window or Application Explorer manually. This displays any application objects delivered since the last refresh.

Enable Personal Folders (Default=No)

If Enable Personal Folders is set to Yes, users can create their own folders and move the icons around in them as they see fit. However, the icons must originate from an application associated with the user. A user cannot add a new, unassociated application object using personal folders.

TIP Use caution when offering the option to create personal folders. Users might forget where they have placed applications and call you for help. Not allowing personal folders might be a way to exert more strict control and thus reduce support calls.

Enable Timed Refresh (User) (Default=No)

The Enable Timed Refresh option refreshes the application icons automatically, based on the Set Refresh Frequency setting, without the user having to choose View→Refresh or press F5 to manually refresh icons. The Timed Refresh setting affects settings such as the Force Run feature.

Read Groups for Applications (User) (Default=Yes)

If a group object has been associated with application objects, users who are members of that group can run application objects by virtue of their membership. Although this is a convenient way of indirectly associating users with applications, it can also decrease performance. If you want to increase performance, set this option to No.

Set Application Inheritance Level (User) (Default=1)

The Set Application Inheritance Level option specifies how many parent organization or organizational unit objects up the eDirectory tree Application Window, or Application Explorer, will navigate through to search for applications.

For example, if a user object's distinguished name is `user1.dev.la.acme` and this option is set to a value of 2, Application Window or Application Explorer would look at the organization or organizational unit object `dev` and `la` for application objects but ignore `acme`. A value of -1 instructs Application Window or Application Explorer to search all the way up the eDirectory tree.

Set Refresh Frequency (User) (Default=43200 Seconds)

The Set Refresh Frequency option lets you specify the refresh frequency in seconds.

For example, if you set the refresh to 300 seconds, Application Window or Application Explorer updates applications from the network automatically every five minutes and might even run some applications depending on how you have set them up.

NOTE A short timed refresh interval is useful in situations where you want changes to refresh quickly. However, a short timed refresh interval can cause higher network traffic. The Refresh Icons option and Timed Refresh option are not connected in any way except that they both control refresh. One option does not have to be selected for the other to work.

Set the Random Refresh Spread

The Set the Random Refresh Spread option lets you specify a range of time, in seconds, that can be waited before initiating the first refresh.

For example, if you set the refresh spread to 300 seconds, Application Window or Application Explorer will choose a random number within the five minute interval before initiating application updates from the network. This way each workstation will randomly pick a different value within the interval, thus spreading your load on the server.

Specify Email Attribute (Default=Mailbox ID)

This option lets you specify the eDirectory attribute that you want to use to display an e-mail name in the Help Contacts tab (when the user right-clicks an application icon and chooses Properties). If users have problems with applications, they can contact people by email to get help. The email name that appears is pulled from the eDirectory attribute you specify here.

Unassociated Days to Uninstall (User)

The Unassociated Days to Uninstall option enables you to specify the number of days to wait until after the user has been unassociated with an application before the application is uninstalled. The range can be from –1 to 730 days. A value of –1 means that the application will never be uninstalled and is the default value.

You can use this option if you do not want users to be immediately cut off from an application, but you also do not want them to have continual access. An example of this might be if a user is transitioning to a new job inside your company and still needs access to his old applications for a few weeks.

Auto-Start Application Window

The Auto-Start NAL option enables you to control whether the Application Window is automatically started when a user logs in; an example of this might be if you have a new application that needs to go out to users in a specific container. You could associate the application with the container and then specify this option so that the Application Window runs, and the application is delivered to users when they log in to the container.

Enable Reading from Removable Cache

The Enable Reading from Removable Cache option enables you to allow workstations to read application objects from a removable cache.

Enable Writing to the Cache

The Enable Writing to the Cache option enables you to allow workstations to write to the disconnected NAL cache. Disabling this option forces the workstation to wait until the NAL cache has reconnected before writing to it.

Enable the Checkpoint Restart Postpone Button

The Enable the Checkpoint Restart Postpone Button option enables you to specify whether you want Application Window/Explorer to display a Postpone button that enables the user to postpone the distribution of an application to his or her workstation. This can be useful if you are trying to distribute a large application across a slow network link.

If you enable the Postpone button, it will be displayed only when Application Window/Explorer detects that the user's workstation is running in remote mode. If the user clicks the Postpone button, the application distribution is postponed.

The setting values are Yes, No, and Unset. The default value of Yes is used if you select Unset and no parent container includes a customized setting.

Always Evaluate Referrals

The Always Evaluate Referrals option forces ZENworks Desktop Management to always check the validity of protocol referrals, thus increasing the reliability of application deployment to users.

Enable Automatic Icon Cleanup

The Enable Automatic Icon Cleanup option allows you to force removal of application icons when the Application Window exits. If this option is enabled, all application icons are automatically cleaned up when the user exits the Application Window or if Application Window exits automatically.

Configure Remote Access Detection

The Configure Remote Access Detection option allows you to control how the Application window will detect whether the user is at a remote or local location. This option allows you to set the following methods for remote access detection:

▶ Always Assume User Will Be Local—Assumes that the user is local and uses the local setting for the application.

▶ Always Assume User Will Be Remote—Assumes that the user is remote and uses the remote setting for the application.

▶ Prompt—Prompts the user to specify whether he is using a remote or local connection.

▶ Autodetect Using Max Interface Speed—Uses the maximum interface speed for the connection to determine whether the user is using a local or remote connection.

NOTE The Autodetect Using Max Interface Speed option is based on the maximum speed of the card as reported to Windows and not on the speed of the current connection.

▶ Detect Using Network ID—Specifies a mask of the IP address that you will use to determine whether the user is connected remotely. This is useful if you have your remote users coming in over a dial-up connection always assigned an IP address with a particular subnet.

Bring All Pop-Up Windows to the Front (Default=Yes)

This option forces all pop-up windows displayed by the Application Window to be pushed to the front of the window. If not set, these dialog boxes can end up being behind other windows.

Enable Middle-Tier Login (Default=Yes)

This option allows a menu item to exist in the Application Window so that the user can log in to the middle tier if she doesn't already have a middle-tier session.

Setting Up Application Window Options

From the Launcher Configuration window you can specify configurations that dictate how the Application Window behaves by selecting the Window tab as shown in Figure 12.4. From this screen you can set the following options that define availability and behavior of the Application Window.

Enable Folder View (Default=Yes)

For users to be able to see the folders you have created, you must make sure that this option is enabled. If Enable Folder View is set to No, users see only the application icons available to them in Application Window.

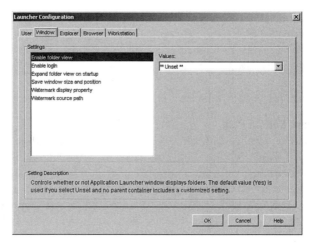

FIGURE 12.4
Configuration for the Application Window in ConsoleOne.

Enable Login

Setting the Enable Login option to Yes activates the Login option found on Application Window's File menu. The user can use this option to run the GUI Login software and log in to the network. This option is not available for Application Explorer.

NOTE When the Enable Login option is selected, and the user is not logged in, Application Window searches for the login executable in the path and, if found, displays a Login icon in Application Window. If the login executable cannot be found, or if the user is already logged in, the Login option is grayed. Make sure that Application Window can find the login program (login.exe or loginw32.exe) on the client workstation before you select the Login option.

Expand Folder View on Startup (Default=No)

The Expand Folder View on Startup option enables you to specify whether the user or container is enabled to view folders. The Expand Folder View on Startup option expands the entire tree of folder when the Application Window starts.

Save Window Size and Position (Default=Yes)

The Save Window Size and Position option enables you to choose whether to save window size and position settings on a local drive. By setting this option to Yes, Application Window is always displayed in the same position for every user.

Watermark Display Property

The Watermark Display Property option allows you to specify how the watermark should be positioned inside the application window. The watermark is displayed as background wallpaper inside the application window. You can specify to use the default, which centers the watermark, or you can specify tiled, which tiles the watermark inside the window.

Watermark Source Path

The Watermark Source Path allows you to determine the path to the watermark file that you want to be displayed in the application window. This can be useful if you want to display different watermarks for different containers, users, or workstations. For example, you could set up a different watermark for Windows 98, Windows 2000, and Windows XP workstations by creating three different workstation containers and assigning each a different source path.

Setting Up Application Explorer Options

From the Launcher Configuration window you can specify configurations that dictate how the Application Explorer behaves by selecting the Explorer tab as shown in Figure 12.5. From this screen you can set the following options that define availability and behavior of the Application Explorer.

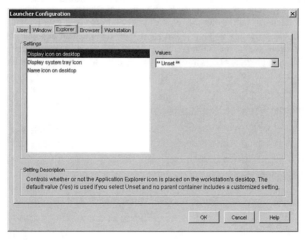

FIGURE 12.5
Launcher Configuration window for the Application Explorer.

Display Icon on Desktop (Default=Yes)

The Display Icon on Desktop option enables you to specify whether you want the Application Explorer icon to appear on the user's desktop. When enabled, an Application Explorer icon appears on the desktop.

Display System Tray Icon (Default=Yes)

The Display System Tray icon enables you to specify whether you want the Application Explorer icon to appear on the user's system tray. When enabled, an Application Explorer icon appears in the user's system tray, from which it is easily launched.

Name Icon on Desktop (Default=Application Explorer)

The Name Icon on Desktop option enables you to change the name of the icon that opens the Application Explorer browser view. For example, you could name it something such as "Corporate Applications."

Setting Up Browser Application Window Options

From the Browser Configuration window you can control how the browser view behaves by selecting the Browser tab shown in Figure 12.5. From the Browser tab you can control the following option to define how the Application Window Browser will behave on workstations.

Close Application Window on Browser Exit (Default=No)

When the browser view of applications is launched by the user going to the `myapps.html` page on the middle-tier server, the `naldesk` executable is automatically launched on the workstation. Without changing this parameter from the default of No, when the user closes the browser, the `nalagent` executable stays active and maintains a connection to the middle-tier server. By setting this configuration flag to Yes, the `naldesk` will be terminated when IE is closed on the workstation.

NOTE If the user is not already logged in to the middle tier, when he launches the browser he will be prompted for the eDirectory login name and password. This prompting occurs each time the browser is opened to `myapps.html` if Close Application Window on Browser Exit is set to Yes.

Setting Up Workstation Application Window Options

From the Launcher Configuration window you can specify configurations that dictate how workstations view and work with Application Window and Application Explorer desktop software by selecting the Workstation tab as shown in Figure 12.6. From this screen you can set the following options that define how the Application Window behaves for workstations.

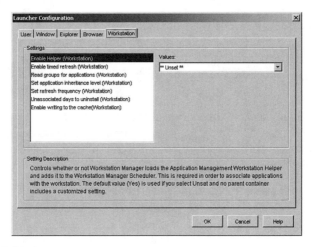

FIGURE 12.6
The Launcher Configuration window for workstation objects in ConsoleOne.

Enable Helper (Workstation)

The Enable Helper option enables the helper DLL by loading and adding it to the WM scheduler for the workstations.

Enable Timed Refresh (Workstation)

The Enable Timed Refresh option refreshes the application icons automatically without the user having to choose View→Refresh or press F5 to manually refresh icons. The Timed Refresh setting also affects settings such as the Force Run feature.

Read Groups for Applications

If a Workstation group object has been associated with application objects, users who are members of that group can run application objects by virtue of their membership. Although this is a convenient way of indirectly associating users with applications, it can also decrease performance. If you want to increase performance, set this option to No.

Set Application Inheritance Level

The Set Application Inheritance Level option specifies how many parent organization or organizational unit objects up the eDirectory tree will be searched for applications.

For example, if a user object's distinguished name is `user1.dev.la.acme` and this option is set to a value of 2, Application Window or Application Explorer would look at the organization or organizational unit object `dev` and `la` for application objects but ignore `acme`. A value of -1 instructs Application Window or Application Explorer to search all the way up the eDirectory tree.

Set Refresh Frequency

The Set Refresh Frequency option lets you specify the frequency in seconds.

For example, if you set the refresh to 300 seconds, Application Window or Application Explorer updates applications from the network automatically every five minutes and might even run some applications depending on how you have set them up.

Unassociated Days to Uninstall

The Unassociated Days to Uninstall option enables you to specify the number of days to wait until after the user has been unassociated with an application before the application is uninstalled. The range can be from -1 to 730 days. A value of −1 means that the application will never be uninstalled and is the default value.

You can use this option if you do not want users to be immediately cut off from an application, but you also do not want them to have continual access. This might happen if, for example, a user is transitioning to a new job inside your company and still needs access to her old applications for a few weeks.

Enable Writing to the Cache

The Enable Writing to the Cache option enables you to control whether Application Window can write information out to the cache.

This option is on by default and saves time because users do not need to access cached applications through eDirectory.

Setting Up Users to Receive Applications

After you set up application foldering, you need to set up users to receive applications via ZENworks Desktop Management. This section covers using ConsoleOne to set up user objects to receive applications by associating their object with an application object, making Application Explorer and Application Window available to them, and setting Application Window configurations.

Associate a User, Group, Workstation, Workstation Groups, or Container Object to Application Objects

The first step in setting up users to receive applications is to use the Applications property page to associate a user, group, workstation, workstation group, organizational unit, organization, or country object to one or more application objects. You could also use the Associations panel for Application objects to individually add users or containers; however, unless you associate applications using one of these two methods, applications are not available to users.

Design your application associations to make it as easy as possible for you to administer. For example, separating applications into company, division, group, and then users levels would enable you to make the fewest associations possible and also reduce the cost of future administration.

In addition to associating applications with other objects, use the Applications property page to specify where and how users access applications on their workstations. For example, you can display application icons in Application Window, Application Explorer, Windows Explorer, the Start menu, the desktop, and the system tray (or in all these areas). You can also force applications to launch when Windows starts.

NOTE The default method of access is Application Window, meaning that users see the application only in the Application Window and Application Explorer browser view (depending on what you have made available).

To add applications to a user or container to specify who sees the application and where it is displayed on workstations, use the following method:

1. Right-click the User, Group, Organizational Unit, Organization, or Country object, and then click Properties.

2. Click the ZENworks→Applications tab.

3. Click Add, browse and select the application object, and then click OK. From container objects, you can add application associations for either users or workstations located within the container.

4. Select an application object and then specify how and where you want the application to work by checking the appropriate check box and clicking OK as shown in Figure 12.7.

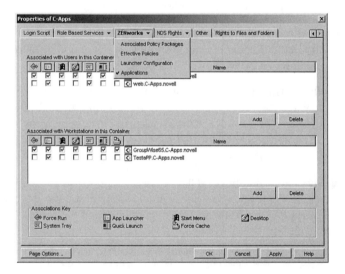

FIGURE 12.7
The Applications property page for container objects in ConsoleOne.

The following sections describe options available from the Applications panel to specify how the application is available to users.

Force Applications to Run

The Force Run option runs applications immediately when Application Window or Application Explorer starts and the application is available.

You can use the Force Run option in conjunction with several other application object settings to achieve unique behaviors.

For example, if you set an application as Run Once (on the application object's Identification property page) and Force Run (on the user, group, or container object's Applications property page), the application runs immediately one time (if available).

Put Applications in the Application Window or Explorer Browser View
The App Launcher option displays application icons in Application Launcher and Application Explorer (browser view) depending on which one you make available to your users.

Put Applications on the Start Menu
When Application Explorer is enabled, the Start Menu option displays icons on the Windows 98 or Windows NT/2000/XP Start menu.

Put Applications on the Desktop
When Application Explorer is enabled, the Desktop option displays icons on the Windows 98 or Windows NT/2000/XP desktop area.

Put Applications on the System Tray
The System Tray option displays icons on the system tray, an area on the Windows 98 or Windows NT/2000/XP taskbar where small icons, representing applications, are placed for easy access. The Application Explorer can display or remove applications on the system tray at any time.

Set Application for Quick Launch
The Quick Launch option puts the icon for the application in the Quick Launch menu for even faster and easier distribution of the object.

TIP If you plan to add the application to the Quick Launcher, use an icon for the application that users can easily recognize. Also the user must have the QuickLaunch toolbar turned on for the application icons to be displayed.

Force Cache the Application
The Force Cache option forces the application to be cached to the workstation, where it can be used later the next time it is run. This can be useful for applications that need to be run more than once or that may need to run when the workstation is disconnected from the network. For example, you could use this option for a virus scanner that is run every

time the user logs in to the network. The workstation would only need to pull down the virus scanner object once and from then on it would be applied out of cache.

Make Application Window/Explorer Available to Users

After you associate the application object with the specific users you want receiving it, you need to make Application Window/Explorer available to them.

Application Window and Explorer are software that run on users' Windows 98 or Windows NT/2000/XP workstations. They display the applications that you distribute to users using the Application Window/Explorer snap-in. You can specify to what degree users control the options in Application Window/Explorer by using a user, organizational unit, organization, or country object's Launcher Configuration window.

Application Explorer displays application icons in a special Application Explorer window, Windows Explorer, Start menu, system tray, or desktop. Use the Applications property page of the user, group, organizational unit, organization, or country object to set up the different Application Explorer access points as discussed earlier in this chapter.

The following sections discuss methods to make applications available to your users through Application Window/Explorer.

Manually Starting Application Window and Explorer

The easiest way for you to make Application Window and Explorer available to users is to have them run them manually.

Choose Start→Programs→Novell ZENworks 7 Desktop Management→Application Management Window to start Application Window manually on a workstation with the ZENworks Desktop Management Agent installed on it.

Choose Start→Programs→Novell ZENworks 7 Desktop Management→Integrated Application Explorer to start application explorer manually on a workstation with the ZENworks Desktop Management Agent installed on it.

You can also set the Launcher/Explorer to start up automatically as part of the installation of the ZENworks Management agent.

Starting Application Window/Explorer from a Login Profile

The most user-friendly method to make Application Window/Explorer available to users is to add the command to launch them to a login profile that the users will run when logging in to the network. This gives the administrator more control over how and where they are run.

Making Application Explorer Available to Users

Make sure that `nalexpld.exe` is in a network directory (such as `sys:\public`) where users have rights and access. The Application Explorer is installed to the `sys:\public` directory when ZENworks Desktop Management is installed on a server, but you may need to copy it to the public directory on other servers that do not have ZENworks Desktop Management installed on them.

Making Application Window Available to Users

1. Make sure that `nal.exe` is in a network directory (such as `sys:\public`) where users have rights and access.

2. Add one of the following commands to the login script of the user object or the user's organizational unit:

   `#\\servername\sys\public\nal.exe`

   Or

   `@\\servername\sys\public\nal.exe`

NOTE The # command requires the external command to complete before executing the next line in the login script. The @ command enables the login script to continue processing while the external command is processed. We recommend using the @ symbol for faster script execution. Do not equate `nal.exe`, a *wrapper* executable that does not stay in memory, with `nalwin32.exe`. If you use # with `nalwin32.exe`, any scripts will wait until the user exits Application Window.

NOTE In ZENworks Desktop Management, the Application Window actually resides in the `C:\Program Files\Novell\ZENworks` directory. The `nal.exe` on the server is replaced with an executable that launches the local copy of the Application Window.

Setting Up Application Window/Explorer as a Shell

The most powerful way for you to make applications available to users via Application Window is to use Application Window as a shell in place of Windows Explorer. This allows you to completely control what applications your users have access to on their local workstations.

Use the following steps to set Application Window as the shell on a Windows 98 workstation with the ZENworks Desktop Management Agent installed on it:

1. Copy the files specified in Table 12.1 from the source location to the destination location.

2. Open the SYSTEM.INI file in a text editor.

3. Replace the SHELL=EXPLOR.EXE line with the following:

   SHELL=C:\NOVELL\CLIENT32\NALWIN32.EXE

4. Save the SYSTEM.INI file.

5. Reboot the workstation.

TABLE 12.1 Files Copied to a Windows 98 Workstation to Create an Application Window Shell

FILE	SOURCE	LOCATION
NALWIN32.EXE	Z:\PUBLIC	C:\NOVELL\CLIENT32
NALRES32.DLL	Z:\PUBLIC\NLS\ENGLISH	C:\NOVELL\CLIENT32\NLS\ENGLISH
NALBMP32.DLL	Z:\PUBLIC\NLS\ENGLISH	C:\NOVELL\CLIENT32\NLS\ENGLISH
NALEXP32.HLP	Z:\PUBLIC\NLS\ENGLISH	C:\NOVELL\CLIENT32\NLS\ENGLISH
NALEXP32.CN	Z:\PUBLIC\NLS\ENGLISH	C:\NOVELL\CLIENT32\NLS\ENGLISH
NWAPP32.DLL	Z:\PUBLIC	C:\NOVELL\CLIENT32

Use the following steps to set Application Window as the shell on a Windows NT/2000/XP workstation with the ZENworks Desktop Management Agent installed on it:

1. Copy the files specified in Table 12.2 from the source location to the destination location.

2. Run REGEDIT.EXE and navigate to the following setting:

   HKEY_LOCAL_MACHINE\SOFTWARE\Microsoft\WindowsNT\CurrentVersion\Winlogon

3. Replace the SHELL value of the entry with the following one:

   SHELL=C:\WINNT\SYSTEM32\NALWIN32.EXE

4. Close REGEDIT.

5. Reboot the workstation.

TABLE 12.2 Files Copied to a Windows NT/2000/XP Workstation to Create an Application Window Shell

FILE	SOURCE	LOCATION
NALWIN32.EXE	Z:\PUBLIC	C:\WINNT\SYSTEM32
NALRES32.DLL	Z:\PUBLIC\NLS\ENGLISH	C:\WINNT\SYSTEM32\NLS\ENGLISH
NALBMP32.DLL	Z:\PUBLIC\NLS\ENGLISH	C:\WINNT\SYSTEM32\NLS\ENGLISH
NALEXP32.HLP	Z:\PUBLIC\NLS\ENGLISH	C:\WINNT\SYSTEM32\NLS\ENGLISH
NALEXP32.CNT	Z:\PUBLIC\NLS\ENGLISH	C:\WINNT\SYSTEM32\NLS\ENGLISH
NWAPP32.DLL	Z:\PUBLIC	C:\WINNT\SYSTEM32

Automating Application Objects

The final step in setting up the application distribution environment is automating application objects. Automating application objects is the process of setting up scripting, scheduling, and macros to remove required interaction with application object distribution. This step is completely optional; however, you may want to use some of the following options to make the application distribution completely seamless for users.

Manage Application Object Macros

One way to automate application objects is to use the Macros property page to manage the application object macros that you create expressly for this application object and that are used on other property pages of the application object. You can use all types of macros (including application object macros) in the following application object locations:

- ▶ Path to Executable (Identification property page)
- ▶ Command Line (Environment property page)
- ▶ Working Directory (Environment property page)

▶ Mapping Path (Drives/Ports property page)

▶ Capture Port Path (Drives/Ports property page)

▶ Registry Settings property page: Key, Name, Value (String only)

▶ .INI Settings property page: Group, Name, Value

▶ Application Files property page: Source/Target, Directory

▶ Text Files property page: Find and Add String

▶ Icons/Shortcuts property page: All locations

TIP You can put macros within macros. For example:

```
%TARGET_PATH%=%*WINDISK%\Program Files
EMAIL_ADDRESS=%CN%@acme.com.
```

To access the Macros property page use the following steps from within ConsoleOne:

1. Right-click the Application object and click Properties.

2. Click the Common tab and select Macros from the drop-down menu.

3. Click Import, browse and highlight the Application Object template (.AOT or .AXT) file that you created with snAppShot, and then click Open.

   Or click Add and then select String to create a new Macro template entry. Name the macro and include a value and then click OK.

   Or click Add When Prompted and then select either String or Drive to create a new Macro template entry. Name the macro and include a default value and prompt string and then click OK.

TIP For best results, we recommend using a UNC pathname for the source path rather than a mapped drive. If you use a mapped drive letter as the source drive, some files might not copy correctly.

Prompted Macros

One way to automate application objects is to use the Macros property page to set up special prompted macros. Sometimes the end-user has a different system setup than what is expected by the administrator.

For example, users may want to put an application on a different drive than what was described in the application object. Prompted macros enable the administrator to request that the user be prompted for the information. By using the prompted macros feature, the administrator can request the destination drive of the end-user, and the resulting distribution goes to the specified drive.

To set up prompted macros, access the Macros property page. From within ConsoleOne, select Add→Prompted→String. A window similar to the one shown in Figure 12.8 is displayed. From the prompted macro window, you can set up the following options for the macro:

▶ Macro Name—Name set up for the macro for install scripts and so on.

▶ Prompt Text—Textual information to be displayed for the user when prompting for the macro.

▶ Default Value—Specify a default value for the macro for users to use if they have no need to specify otherwise.

▶ Minimum Disk Space in MB—Specify a minimum amount of disk space required in setting the macro.

▶ Maximum String Length in Chars—Use this option to specify the maximum number of characters allowed for string macros.

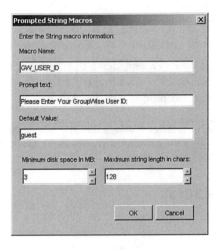

FIGURE 12.8
The Prompted String Macros window for application objects in ConsoleOne.

Special Windows Macros

Another way to automate application distribution is by using special Windows macros. A special Windows macro is one that defines Windows 98 and Windows NT/2000/XP directories. The typical paths, listed following, are based on default installations and may or may not match your specific setup. On Windows 98 workstations, macros behave differently if user profiles are enabled.

The following macros are helpful for redirecting application files that expect Windows directories to be in a particular location:

```
%*WinDir% Windows directory, typically c:windows or c:winnt
%*WinSysDir% Windows system directory, typically
c:\winnt\system32
%*WinDisk% Drive letter (plus colon) for Windows directory,
typically c:
%*WinSysDisk% Drive letter (plus colon) for Windows system
directory c:
%*WinSys16Dir% Windows NT** 16-bit system directory
(c:\winnt\system)
%*TempDir% Windows temporary directory (c:\windows\temp)
```

NOTE The asterisk character (*) is a required syntax for these macros. Don't confuse these asterisk characters with the Novell trademark asterisk.

Login Script Variables

Another way to automate application distribution is by using login script variables. Application Window supports the familiar or traditional login script variables; however, not all login script variables are supported.

Table 12.3 displays a list of supported login script macros and what they mean. Alternative macro names are shown in parentheses.

TABLE 12.3 Login Script Macros

LOGIN SCRIPT MACRO	DEFINITION
DAY	Numeric day of the month. For example: 01, 10, 15, and so on.
FILESERVER (FILE_SERVER)	Name of the NetWare file server of eDirectory monitored connection. For example: APPS_PROD.

TABLE 12.3 Continued

LOGIN SCRIPT MACRO	DEFINITION
FULL_NAME	Full name attribute of the user object. For example: Jane Doe.
HOUR24 (24HOUR)	Time of the day according to a 24-hour clock. For example: 02, 05, 14, 22, and so on.
HOUR (HOURS)	Hour of the day. For example: 0 = 12, 13 = 1, and so on.
LAST_NAME	Last name of the current user (also known as the user's eDirectory Surname attribute).
LOGIN_NAME	First eight bytes of the user's eDirectory object name. For example: jsmith.
MINUTE (MINUTES)	Current minute. For example: 02, 59, and so on.
MONTH	Current month number. For example: 01 for January and so on.
NDAY_OF_WEEK	Numeric day of the week. For example: 1 for Sunday and so on.
NETWORK (NETWORK_ADDRESS)	Workstation network address. For example: 01010120.
OS_VERSION	Version of the OS. For example: v5.00.2195.
OS	OS type. For example: WIN98, WIN2000, WINXP, and so on.
PLATFORM	Platform running. For example: WIN, W98, WNT, and so on.
PHYSICAL_STATION (P_STATION)	MAC address. For example: 0000C04FD92ECA.
REQUESTER_CONTEXT	Context of the requester (for the selected tree).
SECOND (SECONDS)	Number of seconds. For example: 03, 54, and so on.
SHORT_YEAR	Short year number. For example: 97, 04, and so on.
WINVER	Windows version. For example: v5.00, v6.00, and so on.
YEAR	Full year number. For example: 2004 and so on.

eDirectory Attribute Macros

Another useful tool in automating application distribution is using eDirectory attribute macros. Application Window supports macros that pull information from the attributes of the currently logged-in user, the current application object, or from the attributes of other eDirectory objects.

An example of using eDirectory attribute macros would be a GroupWise application object that runs `ofwin.exe` with a command-line parameter:

`/@U-@USERNAME@`

`USERNAME` can be replaced with a macro that uses a user's eDirectory common name (CN):

`/@U-@%CN%@`

If the eDirectory object name is the same as the email login for GroupWise, every user who runs the application has the correct username passed into GroupWise.

Table 12.4 displays variables defined by an attribute in an eDirectory object that can be used as eDirectory attribute macros.

TABLE 12.4   eDirectory Attribute Macros

ATTRIBUTE MACRO	EDIRECTORY OBJECT ATTRIBUTE
%CN%	Common name (user's object name or login name)
%DN%	User's full distinguished name (used with Application Window only)
%Given Name%	Given Name
%Surname%	Last Name
%Full Name%	Full Name
%Telephone Number%	Telephone
%Home Directory%	Home directory
%Email Address%	Email address
%Mailbox ID%	Mailbox ID

Environment Variables

Another useful tool in automating application distribution is using environment variables. The following are some examples of environment variables that Application Window supports:

- ▶ %NWLANGUAGE%

- ▶ %TEMP%

- ▶ %PATH%

NOTE The value of the variable must not exceed the length of the application object name; otherwise, the variable fails.

Schedule Application Pre-Install

Another useful tool in automating application distribution is to schedule application pre-install. In Chapter 11, "Creating and Using Application Objects," we discussed using the Pre-Install property page for application objects to set schedules of when the application will be pre-installed to the workstation. Set up large application distributions to be pre-installed in advance so that the objects are locally available to users. This provides the following safeguards:

- ▶ Low network bandwidth can't inhibit deployment of the application.

- ▶ You know for certain that all workstations are set up and ready to deploy the application.

- ▶ You don't need to stagger workstation installs over a period of time, making the transition much easier for users.

Schedule Application Availability

Another useful tool in automating application distribution is to schedule application availability. In Chapter 11 we discussed using the Scheduling property page for application objects to set schedules of when the application will be available. You can use this to help automate when users will be able to access the application object.

Create Application Scripts

Another useful tool available to automate application distribution is the use of the Scripts property page to set up scripts executed automatically each time the application is launched and closed. Unlike environment parameters, scripts can overwrite existing drive mappings and printer ports.

The two types of application scripts are the startup script and the post-termination script. Run Before Launching (or startup) scripts are executed after the environment is set and before the application is launched. Run After Termination (or post-termination) scripts are executed after the application is closed and before the network resources are cleaned up.

The following are some examples of what you can use application scripts for:

- ▶ Provide extra mappings beyond those defined on the Drives/Ports property page

- ▶ Provide a mapping to override another mapping

- ▶ Run other applications

- ▶ Log in to other servers or eDirectory* trees

- ▶ Terminate applications under certain circumstances

To create application object scripts, use the steps listed for creating pre-install scripts and launch scripts for application objects in Chapter 11.

TIP Commands for cleaning up the changes made by the pre-launch script should be placed in the post-termination script. The post-termination script is run after Application Window detects that the application has terminated.

The following is a list of scripting commands that Application Window does not support:

- ▶ CLS

- ▶ DISPLAY

- ▶ EXIT

- ▶ FDISPLAY

- ▶ INCLUDE

- ▶ LASTLOGINTIME

- ▶ NO_DEFAULT

- ▶ NOSWAP
- ▶ PAUSE
- ▶ PCCOMPATIBLE
- ▶ SCRIPT_SERVER
- ▶ SET_TIME
- ▶ SWAP
- ▶ WRITE

The following is a list of scripting actions that Application Window scripting does not do:

- ▶ Output anything to the screen
- ▶ Display errors

ZENworks also allows administrators to define and use their own scripting engine and scripts, such as Perl, to perform pre- and postinstallation tasks. Refer to Chapter 11 for information on defining your own script engines.

Distribute the Applications

After you create the application object, set up the properties for the object, and set up the distribution options, the final step is to actually distribute the application object to the application users. To do this, you need to do nothing further.

That is what ZENworks Desktop Management application distribution is all about. After you have it set up, ZENworks Desktop Management automatically distributes the application for you according to your application object settings.

Summary

This chapter focused on the distribution engine that enables you to distribute your applications throughout your network. After an application object is created in eDirectory, you only need to set up the application distribution environment within ZENworks Desktop Management to apply it to several workstations on your network.

## CHAPTER 13

Setting Up Handheld Application Objects

This chapter provides a step-by-step walk-through of how to create a handheld application. Following that, it walks through how to get a description of the handheld application object and attributes.

Creating a Handheld Application

With ZENworks Handheld Management, there are no wizards to use when you create a handheld application like those used to create ZENworks application objects. Additionally, the single created handheld application can be used to deliver content and applications to WinCE, PocketPC, Palm, and RIM BlackBerry devices, instead of having to create a unique handheld application object for each device type.

In the handheld application object, you specify some configuration information and then list the files that should be delivered to the device. After this information is placed into the handheld application object, you can associate that object with either a user or a handheld device, and that application will be placed on the device the next time that synchronization occurs.

To create a handheld application object, do the following:

1. Locate the handheld files and place them in a location on a server where the user and device will have access. Some handheld applications are delivered as executables. If this is the case, you need to run the setup executable on a desktop to the point where the handheld files are extracted and placed into a temporary directory.

Following that, you need to copy the files in the temporary directory to a saved location and then cancel the installation.

2. Launch ConsoleOne.

3. Browse to and select the container in eDirectory where you want the handheld application object to reside. Remember that the application object does not need to be in the same container as the handheld objects. You can associate the application object with any other object in the tree, no matter where the application objects are located.

4. Right-click and choose New→Object from the menu. This brings up a dialog box (see Figure 13.1) that allows you to select the object type you want to create.

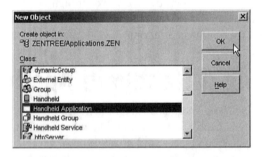

FIGURE 13.1
Select the new object to create in the selected container.

5. Select the Handheld Application object type in the New Object dialog box. Click OK.

6. You are then presented with a New Handheld Application dialog box that asks you for the name of the new object. After you have entered the name, click on the Define Additional Properties check box and click OK.

7. At this point, ConsoleOne creates the new handheld application object and then opens the properties of that newly created application object.

8. Click on the Files tab of the handheld application object. On this tab we identify all the files that need to be delivered to the handheld device.

The Files tab is divided into two sections: Source and Destination. In the Source area, you select all the files that need to be delivered, and in the Destination area, you specify the type of device to send it to or whether it should be placed on the synchronizing desktop.

9. Click Add in the Source area of the Files tab. This brings up a dialog box that allows you to specify the directory path and a file (see Figure 13.2).

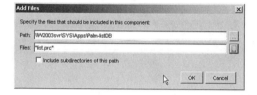

FIGURE 13.2
Specify the files to be delivered to the PDA device.

10. Click on the browse button (the button with three dots on it). Browse to and select the directory on the server where the handheld files are stored.

NOTE Notice that the path to this directory must be a UNC path because ZENworks Handheld Management uses CIFS to connect.

11. Click on the File Browse button and select a single file. Repeat this step for each file you require on the handheld device. Wildcards and multiselection in the browser can be used in the file list to select more than one file with a single entry. Select the Include Subdirectories of This Path check box to get all the files and subdirectory files in the specified directory. Click OK.

12. After you complete the identification of all the files for the PDA, move to the Destination area and select whether these files should be placed on the handheld device or synchronization machine (see Figure 13.3).

13. All the files specified in the object will be placed in the administered destination. Select the Install Files on Storage Cards (If Available) check box if that is what you want. Click Apply.

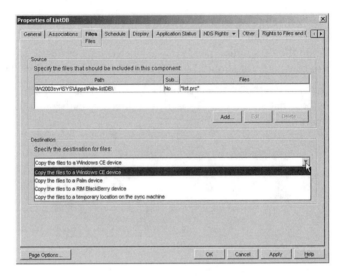

FIGURE 13.3
Specify the source handheld files and their destination on the device.

14. A dialog box pops up reminding you that this application object is not associated with anyone (so it will never be delivered). Click the Yes button, and the Associations tab automatically is selected.

15. Select the handheld devices, handheld group, or handheld container that should receive this application. Click the Add button and browse to a container, group, or device and select it. Click OK. You can associate the application object with any number of devices.

NOTE Don't worry about associating handheld application objects to containers that may contain different types of devices. ZENworks knows (by you specifying the destination on the Files tab) what type of device should receive the handheld application object. It will not attempt to deliver Palm applications, for example, to a WinCE device.

---

16. You now have a handheld application object defined and associated with devices. For the rest of this walk-through, let's assume that we have created an application object called Palm-ListDB and associated it with a container called Handhelds. Now let's switch over to a workstation that has the ZENworks Handheld Proxy agent installed along with a Palm device. (See Chapter 2, "Installing ZENworks 7 Suite," for more information on installing ZENworks Handheld Management and its agents.)

17. Synchronize the Palm device to the synchronization workstation. The first time you synchronize after installing the ZENworks Handheld Proxy agent, the ZENworks device agents are delivered to the device.

18. Synchronize the Palm device again. On the next synchronization, the ZENworks agents on the PDA will attempt to contact the Access Point specified during installation of the Proxy. Through this Access Point, ZENworks will communicate with eDirectory, create the handheld object, and deliver inventory.

If you specified that user authentication (for user-associated PDA objects) is to be used, a prompt appears for the user to authenticate to eDirectory. The Proxy then attempts to authenticate as the user and retrieves any associated PDA applications or policies (see Figure 13.4).

FIGURE 13.4
eDirectory username and password to be prompted for during a HotSync process.

19. The second time you synchronize, the ZENworks agents will collect any associated policies or applications to the handheld through its device object, container, or group membership. In this example, the Palm-ListDB application will be delivered to the Palm device.

You have now successfully imported a PDA device into eDirectory, taken an inventory, and delivered an application to that device. Let's take a closer look at the handheld application object.

Properties of a Handheld Application

ConsoleOne is used as the primary administration tool for ZENworks Handheld Management. The properties of a handheld application object can be administered by double-clicking on the handheld application object or right-clicking on the object and selecting Properties from the pop-up menu.

The following sections discuss each of the property pages and the attributes that can be administered on those pages.

General Handheld Application Property Page

The General property page is where you configure general items for the application object (see Figure 13.5).

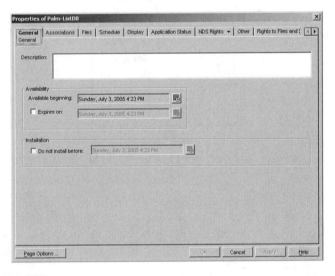

FIGURE 13.5
General handheld application property page.

The following attributes are available on the General property page:

- ▶ Description—Allows you to specify the description of the application that this object represents.

▶ Availability—Specifies when the application is available for delivery to PDA devices. You can specify when a handheld application is no longer available.

▶ Installation—You can specify to not install on the PDA device until the date given has arrived.

> **NOTE** When a handheld application becomes unavailable, it is *not* uninstalled from devices that had previously received the application. It is just no longer delivered to any associated devices.

Associations Handheld Application Property Page

The Associations property page identifies the objects assigned this handheld application (see Figure 13.6).

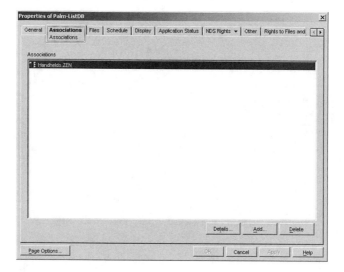

FIGURE 13.6
Associations handheld application property page.

Associations are created when the administrator assigns one object to another. A handheld application object can be assigned to many other objects. Associations of a handheld application can be to handheld objects, containers, and handheld groups. When an association is made, a link is constructed between the associated object and the application.

When the handheld agents connect to eDirectory, they look to see what application objects are associated with the device object, then any associated application objects to any parent containers of the handheld device, and also any application associations to any groups of which the device is a member. All the associated applications are then delivered to the device.

The associated containers, groups, and devices do not have to be in the same container as the actual application object.

Files Handheld Application Property Page

The Files property page identifies the source files that constitute the content or application to be delivered (see Figure 13.7).

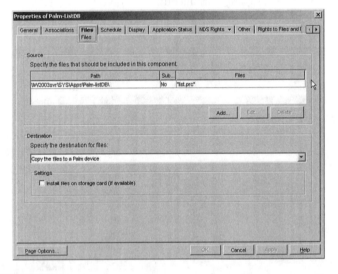

FIGURE 13.7
Files property page identifying the source files to be delivered.

The Files property page has two sections:

▶ Source—Lists the files to be delivered as part of an application object. These files lists can include wildcards. When a file list is added, you can also specify that subdirectories and files should be included.

▶ Destination—Identifies the type of device by specifying that the files are to be delivered to a WinCE, Palm, or BlackBerry device. Additionally, you can specify that the files be delivered to the synchronization machine.

The purpose of delivering to the synchronization machine is that some PDA deliveries require that an application be run on the synchronization machine as part of the delivery of the application to the PDA. These deliveries can be sent to the synchronization machine and then the specified command-line is executed. Additionally, the administrator can check to fail the installation if the execution of the command reports a failure.

ZENworks Handheld Management only delivers to BlackBerry devices when they synchronize with a desktop. Applications cannot currently be delivered wirelessly for these devices.

NOTE If a file as part of a distribution is already on the device, ZENworks overwrites the file. If the file is open and cannot be written, the delivery will fail.

The Novell client must be installed on the ZENworks Management Server to access NetWare files for handheld device applications.

Schedule Handheld Application Property Page

The Schedule property page allows you specify whether the application files should be refreshed periodically onto the device (see Figure 13.8).

The attributes of the page are not activated until the Enable Automatic Updates check box is selected. After this box is selected, the administrator can select the schedule when the application files are refreshed. The schedule choices include

▶ Daily—Every day of the week is automatically selected. The update time specifies when on each day this application is updated.

▶ Weekly—The administrator has the ability to choose the day of the week when the files are scanned for changes.

▶ Monthly—The administrator may enter the numerical day of each month or select to have the files checked on the last day of each month.

▶ Yearly—The administrator can select the date of each year that ZENworks should scan and check the files.

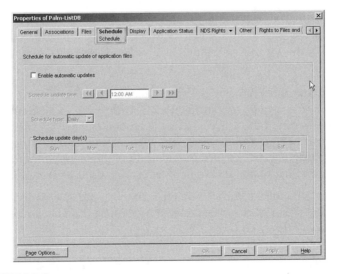

FIGURE 13.8
Schedule handheld application property page.

When the schedule time occurs, ZENworks Handheld Management
checks the files for any changes in the files or for additional files (with
wildcards and subdirectories) and delivers those changed files. If no
changes are detected, nothing is sent to the handheld devices that have
previously received the files.

NOTE Newly associated devices always get the files immediately and not based on the
schedule.

Display Handheld Application Property Page

The Display property page is useful only when the application object is
sent to the synchronization device rather than directly to the PDA (see
Figure 13.9).

With the Display property page, you can specify a dialog box message
that will be displayed on the synchronization desktop after the handheld
application object files are delivered to the temporary file system and
before the specified command is launched.

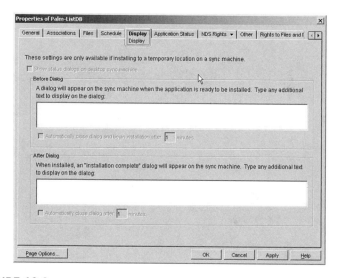

FIGURE 13.9
Display property page of the handheld application object.

The dialog is displayed for the specified number of minutes (or fewer, if the user clicks the Continue button on the dialog box). Then the specified command is executed. When the command completes, the After Dialog is displayed. The user is also notified should the command execution fail.

The After Dialog also has a timer specified and stays onscreen until the specified number of minutes completes or until the user clicks OK.

Application Status Handheld Application Property Page

The Application Status property page shows a report on the delivery of the application to specific handheld devices. Each individual handheld device is listed, even if the association is to a container or group (see Figure 13.10).

The Application Status property page reads the logging information stored in the database associated with the ZENworks Handheld Service. If this is the first time that the screen has been accessed, you need to browse to the ZENworks Handheld Service object that will service these requests. After the ZENworks Handheld Service is specified, click the Display button.

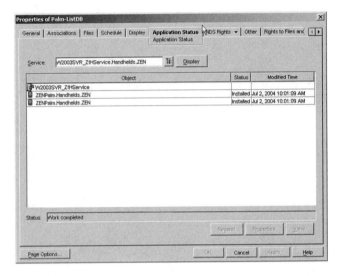

FIGURE 13.10
Application Status property page of the handheld application object.

Clicking the Display button retrieves the logging information and displays the devices that have attempted to receive the application. The status of the delivery of the application may be Installed, Failed, Cancelled, Skipped, or Pending. Along with the status, the time of the last attempt is displayed.

The status has the following definitions:

▶ Installed—The application was successfully installed on the device.

▶ Failed—The application was not able to be delivered to the device or to the synchronization desktop. You can find out more information about this status entry by double-clicking on the entry line.

▶ Cancelled—The application is cancelled because the distribution has been removed.

▶ Skipped—The device already has this application installed.

▶ Pending—The application has not been delivered to the device as of yet. This could be because the device has not yet synchronized, or the event information has not been passed back to the Access Point.

If at some time you want to have the application re-sent and installed again on the device, select the status record and click the Resend button. This causes ZENworks Handheld Management to re-install the application.

> **NOTE** Deleting an application on the handheld device does *not* automatically resend any previously delivered applications. The applications will not be redelivered and reinstalled unless the Resend button is clicked or the device has been reset, and all applications need to be restored.

Summary

This chapter covered the creation of handheld applications and how to get a description of a handheld application object and attributes.

The next chapter discusses the use and creation of user policies. User policies are associated with users and affect their working environment.

## CHAPTER 14

Setting Up User Policies

This chapter discusses the use and creation of user policies. User policies are associated with users and affect their working environment.

User policy packages in ZENworks Desktop Management 7 may be created for any of the Windows 32 environments, namely Windows 98/NT/2000/XP. The support for Windows 95 is available only with the ZENworks 3.x version.

Relationship of User Policies to Users

Users are assigned user policies through associations in any of three ways:

- ▶ Policies can be associated with the user object directly.
- ▶ Policies can be associated with a parent container of the user object.
- ▶ Policies can be associated with a group to which the user is a member.

When a user logs in to the tree, a ZENworks Management agent (Workstation Manager Service) walks up the tree looking for the first user policy package it can find that is associated with the user. Like all agents associated with ZENworks, the order the tree is searched depends on standard Novell eDirectory behavior and any search policies that may be in the tree.

When a policy is being searched within the tree, the ZENworks Management agent walks the tree until it finds the root or a search policy that limits the searching. All the applicable user policies are merged together, and the culmination is applied to the workstation. If any conflicts exist with the policies (such as two user policies both affecting the same parameter), the parameter setting in the first policy found is applied.

The remote control policy, for example, can be created for both the user and the workstation. In instances where a remote control policy exists for both the user and the workstation, the subsystem applies the most restrictive combination of the policies. For example, if one policy says to prompt the user for permission and the other does not, the result is that the system prompts the user.

With ZENworks, a group policy may be associated with a workstation object. This group policy will be directed to administered areas: User Configuration, Workstation Configuration, or Security Settings. The workstation associated group policy can be used in conjunction with any user associated group policy. The two policies either can be merged (user policy is applied last), or the user policy can be ignored and only the workstation policy used for a specific workstation. For more information on this, see the discussion of workstation policy packages in Chapter 18, "Creating Service Location Policies."

General and Platform-Specific Policy Advantages

ZENworks simplifies administration by giving you the ability to select policies in one place (the general page) and have them apply to all types of workstations that your users use. At the same time, you do not lose the ability to have unique policies for each platform—the general policies can be overridden by a platform-specific policy (an alternative to the platform page).

Regardless of the users who log in to the system, each workstation finds the policies associated with itself and applies those policies. The workstation policies applied can come from the General tab of the policy or from the platform-specific tab of the policy.

In some instances, you may want to associate a particular unique policy to a set of users housed in containers along with other users of the same type. In such cases, you can create a group of users and associate specific policies to those users by associating the policy package to the user group. These users then receive the policies from this group rather than from the container.

Creating a User Policy Package

To have a policy that affects users who are logging in to the tree through workstations, you need to create a user policy package. To create a user policy package, do the following:

1. Start ConsoleOne.

2. Browse to the container where you would like to have the policy package. Make sure that you have the container where you want the policy package selected in ConsoleOne. Remember, you do not have to create the policy package in the container where you are doing the associations—you can associate the same policy package to many containers in your tree.

3. Create the policy package by right-clicking and choosing New→Policy Package or by selecting the Policy Package icon on the toolbar.

4. Select the User Package object in the wizard panel and click Next.

5. Enter the desired name of the package in the Policy Package Name field and select the container where you want the package to be located. The Container field is already filled in with the selected container, so you should not have to browse to complete this field. If this is not the case, click the browser button next to the field and browse to and select the container where you want the policy object stored. Click Next.

6. Select the Define Additional Attributes field to go into the properties of your new object and activate some policies. Click Finish.

7. Check and set any policies you want for this user policy package and click OK.

The following subsections describe each of the fields and property pages available in the user policy package.

Policies Property Page

All the policies for users are activated within the Policies property page. Initially, the page appears on the General policies. As other platforms are selected, additional policies are displayed. You can select which platform to display by placing the mouse over the small triangle on the right side of the Policies tab. This activates a drop-down menu that allows you to select which platform-specific page you want to display (see Figure 14.1).

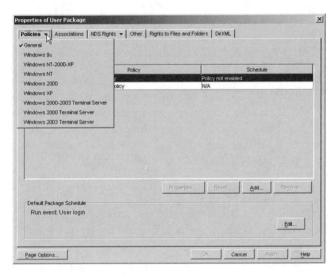

FIGURE 14.1
The user package Policies property page with drop-down menu.

The following sections discuss briefly each of the policy pages, and then we cover the specifics of each policy.

General Policies

When you first go into the properties of the user policy package, you are presented with the policy package property page. The policy package property page first displays the General category. All the policies activated in the General category are active for *all* platforms supported by ZENworks Desktop Management and associated with the logged-in user.

Figure 14.2 shows the initial property page of the user policy package.

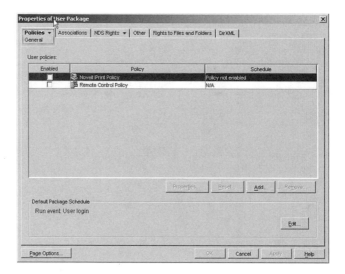

FIGURE 14.2
The user policy package Policies General property page.

As you can see from Figure 14.2, the Remote Control Policy and the Novell iPrint Policy are the only policies available to all the platforms supported by ZENworks Desktop Management. The Remote Control policy and Novell iPrint policy are discussed later in this chapter.

To activate a policy, you simply click in the box to the left of the policy. You can then go into the details of the policy and set additional configuration parameters on that specific policy.

Policies on the General property page will also be on the specific pages for the device. If any policy is activated on the specific OS property page, that policy will supercede the same policy that may have been selected on the General page.

Windows 9x Policies

Within the Policies tab, you can select the Windows 9x policy page. This page displays the policies available for Windows 98 users. These policies include the Windows 98 Desktop Preferences policy, Remote Control policy, Novell iPrint policy, and the User Extensible policies. Figure 14.3 shows the Windows 9x Policies page.

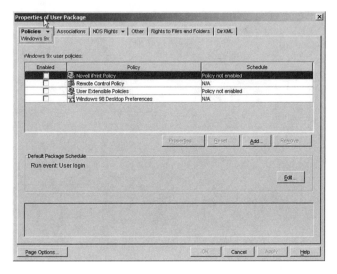

FIGURE 14.3
The Windows 9x Policies page of the user policy package.

Windows NT Policies

Within the Policies tab, you can select the Windows NT policy page. This page displays the policies available for Windows NT users. These policies include the Novell iPrint policy, Dynamic Local User policy, Windows Desktop Preferences policy, Remote Control policy, and the User Extensible policies. Figure 14.4 shows the Windows NT Policies page.

These policies allow you to configure the various aspects of the Windows NT desktop environment. They are discussed in the following sections in more detail.

Windows 2000 Policies

Within the Policies tab, you can select the Windows 2000 policy page. This page displays the policies available for your Windows 2000 users. These policies include the Dynamic Local User policy, Windows Desktop Preferences policy, Novell iPrint policy, Remote Control policy, User Extensible policies, and the Windows Group policy. Figure 14.5 shows the Windows 2000 Policies page.

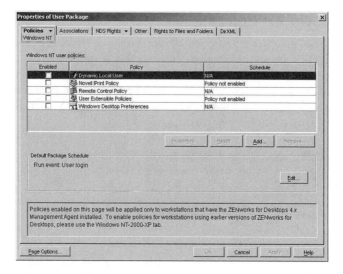

FIGURE 14.4
The User Package Windows NT Policies property page.

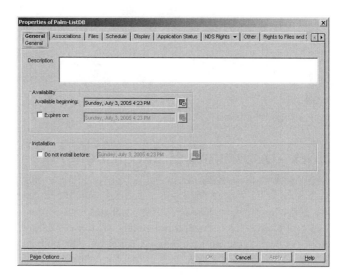

FIGURE 14.5
The User Package Windows 2000 Policies property page.

Windows XP Policies

Within the Policies tab, you can select the Windows XP policy page. This page displays the policies available for your Windows XP users. These policies include the Dynamic Local User policy, Novell iPrint policy, Windows Desktop Preferences policy, Remote Control policy, and the Windows Group policy. Figure 14.6 shows the Windows XP Policies page.

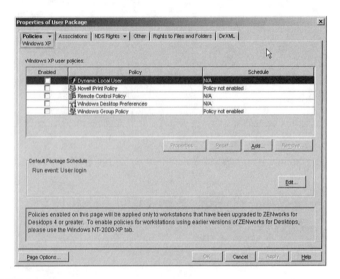

FIGURE 14.6
The User Package Windows XP Policies property page.

Windows 2000 Terminal Server Policies

Within the Policies tab, you can select the Windows 2000 Terminal Server policy page. This page displays the policies available for your Windows 2000 Terminal Server users. These policies include the Dynamic Local User policy, Novell iPrint policy, Windows Desktop Preferences policy, Remote Control policy, User Extensible policies, and the Windows Group policy. Figure 14.7 shows the Windows 2000 Terminal Server Policies page.

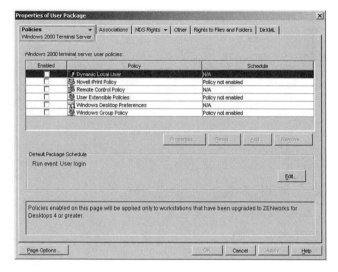

FIGURE 14.7
The User Package Windows 2000 Terminal Server Policies property page.

Windows 2003 Terminal Server Policies

Within the Policies tab, you can select the Windows 2003 Terminal Server policy page. This page displays the policies available for your Windows 2003 Terminal Server users of. These policies include the Dynamic Local User policy, Novell iPrint policy, Windows Desktop Preferences policy, Remote Control policy, and the Windows Group policy. Figure 14.8 shows the Windows 2003 Terminal Server Policies page.

Associations Property Page

The Associations page of the user package displays all the locations in the tree (containers) where the policy package has been associated. These associations do not necessarily reflect where the policy package is located in the directory. The Windows users in or below those containers have this policy package enforced. Additionally, you can associate the package directly with a user or with a user group.

Clicking the Add or Remove buttons allows you to add or remove containers in the list associated with this policy.

FIGURE 14.8
The User Package Windows 2003 Terminal Server Policies property page.

User Policies

The following sections describe, in detail, each of the various policies in the policy packages.

Novell iPrint Policy

The Novell iPrint Policy option is available across all platforms and on the General policy page. It allows you to configure a Novell iPrint client that can be placed on the workstation, allowing it to use Internet printing capabilities.

Client Install Page

This page allows you to specify the path on a server where the iPrint client can be found. Specifying the path on the iPrint policy causes the iPrint client to automatically be installed on the workstation. You can also specify the language and version number of the software. You can also specify whether to install a new client, should an older version be found on the workstation.

Additionally you can specify that the system should Force Reboot to cause the workstation to be rebooted at this time to activate the iPrint client instead of waiting until the user reboots the workstation manually.

Settings Page

This page allows you to specify any set of printers you want to automatically install and configure on the receiving workstation.

Remote Control Policy

The Remote Control Policy option is available across all platforms and on the General policy page.

A Remote Control policy is activated for this policy package by selecting the check box on the Remote Control policy. After this is selected and a check is displayed in the check box, this Remote Control policy is activated for all users associated with the user policy package.

The Remote Control policy controls the features of the Remote Control subsystem shipped with ZENworks. The Remote Management system is comprised of two parts: remote management session manager that makes the connection and is used by the administrator, and the remote management agents installed on the end-user's workstation. The remote control agent is part of the full ZENworks management agents and is installed as part of the agent installation process. Running the `ZfDAgent.msi` in the `public\zenworks\ZfDAgent\<language>` folder installs the agent on the workstation that has MSI (Microsoft System Installer) installed.

The Remote Management system makes a peer-to-peer IP connection between the administrator's workstation and the remote workstation.

Remotely controlling a workstation via ZENworks Desktop Management may also require rights within the workstation object that represents the workstation to be controlled. Without these rights, the administrator is denied access to the remote control subsystem. Both the session manager and the agents validate that the user has rights to remotely control the workstation. You assign the remote control rights through the Remote Management Rights Wizard or in the workstation object in the Remote Operators page.

ZENworks Desktop Management also has the capability to remote control via a password, without any workstation object in the tree. Launching remote control from the Tools menu of ConsoleOne does this (or right-clicking when a workstation is selected). The dialog that comes up requires the IP address of the workstation and a password. This password must match the password entered by the end-user through the Security menu of the remote control agent (on the system tray) of the workstation. The password use of remote control must be configured in the policy as accepted.

Remote Management Page

The Remote Management page identifies the features you want to be activated with the Remote Management system. The following sections describe configuration options available under each of the tabs of the Remote Management policy window shown in Figure 14.9.

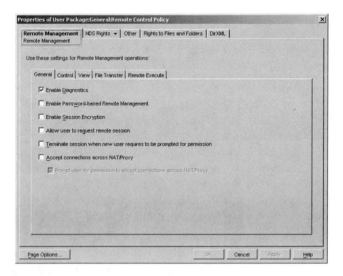

FIGURE 14.9
The Remote Management Policy page.

General Tab

The first tab of the Remote Management page allows you to set the following general system functions:

- ▶ Enable Diagnostics—Allows the agent on the workstations to perform a diagnostics report. This can be done by selecting the workstation and then right-clicking and selecting Actions→Diagnostics on the menu. The Diagnostics utility performs some basic queries on the system and returns the information about the workstation. This information includes memory, environment, and processes running. Additionally, it includes eDirectory and NetWare connection information, client information, network drives, and open file lists, as well as printers, Network protocols, and network services active. You can also view the various event and error logs that have been recorded on that workstation.

▶ Enable Password-Based Remote Management—Allows the operator to establish password-based remote management with the workstation.

▶ Enable Session Encryption—Activates session encryption between the administrative workstation and the remote controlled desktop. The system activates a 168-bit DES algorithm when a password-based remote control session is started, and a 512-bit RSA algorithm session when an eDirectory-enabled session is activated.

▶ Allow User to Request Remote Session—Allows the remote user to request a remote control session of the administrator. This is useful when the remote workstation is behind a NAT (Network Address Translation), and you cannot accurately determine the address and port required.

▶ Terminate Session When New User Requires to be Prompted for Permission—Terminates any ongoing remote management session with the workstation when a new user, whose permission for starting a remote management session is required, logs in.

▶ Accept Connections Across NAT/Proxy—Allows the remote agents to accept connections across a NAT/proxy. This option is valid only for eDirectory-based remote sessions.

▶ Prompt User for Permission to Accept Connections Across NAT/Proxy—Valid only for eDirectory-based sessions and, when selected, causes the user to be prompted when the connection is over a NAT/proxy even if the other policies state not to prompt the user.

Control Tab

The Control tab describes the feature enabling of remote control functions. It allows you to set the following functions:

▶ Enable Remote Control—Activates the remote control subsystem. Without this setting on, no one may remotely control the workstations where the currently logged-in user has this policy associated with his user object.

▶ Prompt User for Permission to Remote Control—Causes a dialog box to be displayed on the end-user's machine when a remote control session is started. The end-user has the option of accepting or denying the remote control request. Within this dialog box, the user is told who wants to remotely control his machine and asks whether this is approved. If the user denies the remote control session, the session is terminated, and the administrator cannot remotely control the workstation.

▶ Give User Audible Signal When Remote Controlled—Provides the end-user a tone periodically while the remote control session is active. This option can be further modified by specifying the number of seconds between beeps.

▶ Give User Visible Signal When Remote Controlled—Displays a dialog box on the end-user's desktop while the remote control session is active. The dialog box displays that the workstation is being remotely controlled and also displays the eDirectory name of the user who is remotely controlling the workstation. You can set the number of seconds that you want to have between flashing the name of the user initiating the remote control session.

▶ Allow Blanking User's Screen—Causes the screen on the remote desktop to be blanked, preventing the end-user from seeing what is being done to the workstation by the administrator. When you enable blanking of the screen, the keyboard and mouse are automatically locked.

▶ Allow Locking User's Keyboard and Mouse—Deactivates the keyboard and the mouse on the remote workstation when the administrator remotely controls the workstation. The end-user may move the mouse or keyboard, but they will not function, and any input from them will be ignored.

View Tab

The View tab describes the feature enabling of the remote view functions. Remote view is the capability for the administrator to view the remote Windows screen of the target machine but not be able to control the mouse or keyboard of the machine. It allows you to set the following functions:

▶ Enable Remote View—Activates the remote view subsystem. Without this setting on, no one may remotely view the workstations where the currently logged-in user has this policy associated with his user object.

▶ Prompt User for Permission to Remote View—Causes a dialog box to be displayed on the end-user's machine when a remote view session is started. The end-user has the option of accepting or denying the remote view request. Within this dialog box, the user is told who wants to remote view their machine and asks whether this is approved. If the user denies the remote view session, the session is terminated, and the administrator cannot remote view the workstation.

▶ Give User Audible Signal When Remote Viewed—Provides the end-user a tone periodically while the remote view session is active. You can also set the number of seconds between each beep.

▶ Give User Visible Signal When Remote Viewed—Displays a dialog box on the end-user's desktop while the remote view session is active. The dialog box displays that the workstation is being remotely viewed and also displays the eDirectory name of the user remotely viewing the workstation. You can set the number of seconds that you want to have between flashing the name of the user initiating the remote view session.

File Transfer Tab

The File Transfer tab describes the feature enabling of the file transfer system. This allows you, the administrator, to send files to the remote workstation. It allows you to set the following functions:

▶ Enable File Transfer—Activates the file transfer subsystem. Without this setting on, no one may send files to the workstations where the currently logged-in user has this policy associated with her user object.

▶ Prompt User for Permission to Transfer Files—Causes a dialog box to be displayed on the end-user's machine when a file transfer session is started. The end-user has the option of accepting or denying the file transfer request. Within this dialog box the user is told who wants to perform the file transfer from her machine and asks whether this is approved. If the user denies the file transfer session, the session is terminated, and the administrator cannot send the files to the workstation.

Remote Execute Tab

The Remote Execute tab describes the feature enabling of the remote execute system. This allows you or the administrator to remotely execute a program on the remote workstation. The output of the program is not displayed on the administrative console. It allows you to set the following functions:

▶ Enable Remote Execute—Enables the administrator to execute applications or files on the remotely managed workstation.

▶ Prompt User for Permission to Remote Execute—Causes a dialog box to be displayed on the end-user's machine when a remote execute session is started. The end-user has the option of accepting or denying the remote execute request. Within this dialog box the user is told who wants to perform the request and asks whether this is approved. If the user denies the remote execution session, the session is terminated, and the administrator cannot execute the program on the workstation.

Desktop Preferences Policy

This policy is an option across all platforms and allows you access to the ZAW/ZAK (Zero Administration for Windows/Zero Administration ToolKit) features exposed by the Microsoft Windows system. Within the ZENworks system, these policies are divided into their logical parts: Desktop Preferences, User System Policies, and Workstation Policies. This policy allows the administrator to set the desktop preferences for any Windows system to which the user is currently connected. This policy follows the user as she moves from workstation to workstation.

Microsoft provides a tool called *poledit* for versions prior to Windows 2000 and *gpedit* with Windows 2000 and later versions. These tools allow an administrator to construct some registry settings (ZAW/ZAK features) and have those settings saved in a set of files. These files can then be applied to any workstation by having the system look for them on the server.

The problem here is that these policy files must be located on every server that any user may use as an initial connection. With ZENworks, the policies are linked into Novell eDirectory, thus making it always accessible to every user who connects to the system without requiring you to place these policy files on every server.

NOTE Editing policies are discussed in more detail later in the chapter when group policies are discussed.

The Desktop Preferences policy allows the administrator to set Control Panel features as well as roaming profile configurations.

Roaming Profile Page

The settings for any particular desktop—such as the desktop icons, screen colors, taskbar selections, and so on—are stored in profiles. These profiles can, with the Roaming Profile feature, be placed into the file system on the network. By doing this, when the user who has a profile saved on the network logs in to any workstation, her profile is retrieved from the network and brought to that workstation. This creates a consistent look and feel for the desktop presented to that user regardless of which workstation she is using. Any changes to the desktop, or preferences, are stored back onto the network and are therefore reflected the next time the user logs in to any workstation. Figure 14.10 is a screen image from the Roaming Profiles page.

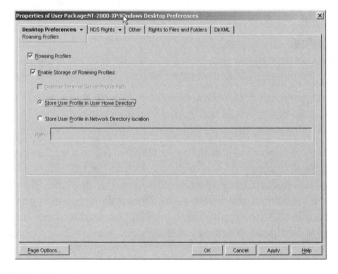

FIGURE 14.10
Roaming Profiles page of a Windows Desktop Preferences policy.

On the Roaming Profile page, the administrator can set whether roaming profiles are available. If they are available, you want to also check the Enable Storage of Roaming Profiles check box. This allows the profiles to be stored on a network server for access from any workstation.

The Override Terminal Server Profile Path option allows you, when checked, to have this user profile override any profiles they may have received via the Terminal Server system available for 2000/2003 servers. This option is grayed for all platforms other than Terminal Services platforms.

After the enabling of storage has occurred, you have the choice of either allowing the profiles to be stored in the user's home directory or in a specified file system directory. By specifying that the profiles be stored in the user's home directory, a subdirectory called Windows Workstation Profile is created in the home directory. Within that directory, the profile information is stored and maintained.

If you identify a specific directory, all users who log into the workstation with that policy store the desktop information directly into that directory and have the profiles shared with all users that log into that workstation. This is why storage into a specific directory is recommended only for profiles that you want applied to all users.

Settings Page

The Settings page is accessed by clicking the drop-down arrow on the Desktop Preferences tab and selecting Settings from the drop-down list.

By clicking on each of the Console and Desktop icons presented in the Settings page of the Windows Desktop Preferences policy, the administrator can configure the properties of each of the Control Panel items.

The standard scenario is that the agent searches the tree for this policy and applies it during the login of the user. This schedule can be changed in the policy package to be another scheduled time or event. To ensure that these preferences are always applied when the user logs in to the tree, regardless of the schedule in the policy, you need to check the Always Update Desktop Settings on eDirectory Authentication check box.

Console

The Console icon, when clicked, brings up the property page that allows you to configure the properties of the Console window (such as the DOS box) for the Windows system. The Console Window properties allow you to set the following:

► Colors tab sets the Console colors for the text and backgrounds.

► Layout tab provides the configuration for the screen buffer size, window size, and the window position.

▶ Options tab allows the setting of console options such as cursor size, display options, command history sizes and buffers, QuickEdit mode, and Insert mode.

From the Console policy you cannot set the font properties of the Console window.

Display

Clicking on the Display icon brings up the property page that allows you to make the following configurations:

▶ Background tab allows setting of the wallpaper. You can specify that no wallpaper be presented or specify a filename of the .BMP file to be displayed for the wallpaper.

▶ Screen Saver page allows you to configure whether a screen saver should be available. You also may specify a particular .SCR or .EXE to be executed for the screen saver. In addition to the screen saver program, you can specify whether the screen should be password protected.

▶ Appearance tab allows you to specify the color scheme that you want applied for this user. You can set the color scheme to any of the following choices: Windows Standard, Brick, Desert, Eggplant, High Contrast Black, High Contrast White, Lilac, Maple, Marine (high color), Plum (high color), Rainy Day, Red White and Blue (VGA), Rose, Slate, Spruce, Storm (VGA), Teal (VGA), or Wheat.

▶ Plus page allows you to set some basic features of the Plus! Package. These features include Use Large Icons, Show Window Contents While Dragging, Smooth Edges of Screen Fonts, Show Icons Using All Possible Colors, and Stretch Desktop Wallpaper to Fit the Screen.

User Extensible Policies

This policy option is available across all but the Windows XP platforms. (For Windows XP, use the group policies.) Microsoft has required that software packages that bear the Windows approved logo provide capabilities to be configured through .POL files. The poledit program allows you to edit these extensible policies and include them into the system .POL file. ZENworks also allows the policies stored in eDirectory to accept these additional extensible polices and provide them to all the users associated with these policies.

Microsoft, in post Windows 95/98 editions of Windows, introduced
.ADM files that allow developers and application vendors to create customized policy files that could be applied to their applications. The User
Extensible policy allows you to import special .ADM files into the
eDirectory tree and have them administered and dispersed to the users
associated with the policy package. After these .ADM files have been
imported into the tree, they can be administered and associated with
users in the eDirectory tree. These settings are applied like the User
System policies.

User Extensible Policies Page

When you first bring up the User Extensible Policies dialog, you are presented with the User Extensible Policies page (see Figure 14.11). This
page is split into three areas: ADM Files, Policies, and a policy-specific
window at the bottom-right corner.

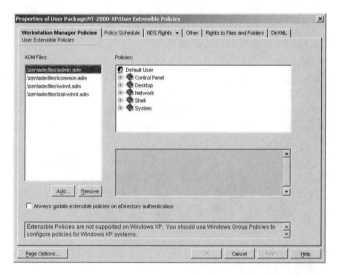

FIGURE 14.11

The User Extensible Policies page.

The files listed in the ADM Files list are the policies applied to the users
associated with this policy. To add a policy file to the list, simply click the
Add button. You are presented with a file dialog box where you can
browse and select the file. Remember that this file should reside on the
server because it is stored there for retrieval by the policy managers.

When you browse and select a file, make sure that it is on the server and that the drive that you use is mapped correctly for all users associated with the policy. You can enter a UNC path in the filename field of the dialog box and thereby get a UNC path for the .ADM file. If you browse and then select, the program puts a drive letter into the path necessitating that each user has the same drive mapping.

When this policy is initialized, four .ADM files are automatically pulled in by the plug-in into ConsoleOne. These include `admin.adm`, `common.adm`, `winnt.adm`, and `zakwinnt.adm`. Each of these files is stored in the `ConsoleOne\bin\zen\admfiles` directory and is considered the default package that will be used.

> **NOTE** The .ADM file must be stored on a server that users can access. The policy references the .ADM file and needs to retrieve it to apply it to the users and to allow the administrators to modify the settings. It would be recommended, therefore, to use a UNC path in specifying the location of the file.

You delete the .ADM file from the applied set by selecting the file and clicking the Remove button.

> **NOTE** Other .ADM files are available depending on which version of Windows you are running on your workstation. For example, Windows 2000 clients also include the `system.adm`, and there is an `inetres.adm` file for restricting Internet Explorer.

You can also modify the settings of the .ADM files by selecting the file in the ADM Files window. When you select the file, its registry content appears in the Policies window. The user interface for this window mimics the poledit program available from Microsoft. The small window underneath the Policies box displays information about the selected registry setting along with any subsetting categories available with the specific key. Selecting the key in the Policies window populates the details fields.

You can browse through the ADM files and turn on (checked), turn off (unchecked and white), or leave as set in the registry (unchecked and gray) each of the keys as you would in the poledit program. After you have made your changes, click Apply or OK to update the ADM files on the server.

Policy Schedule Page

The Policy Schedule page allows you to customize (outside the package default schedule) when you want the ADM files applied to the workstation/desktop of the user.

This page allows you to select when the package should be applied: Event, Daily, Weekly, Monthly, or Yearly.

After you have selected when you want the package applied, you have additional fields to select in the lower portion of the screen. The following sections discuss the various options you have with scheduling the package.

Event

When you choose to have the ADM files applied upon an event that occurs in the workstation, you also need to select which event effects the changes.

The events that you can select are as follows:

- ▶ User Login—Causes the policies to be applied when the user logs in to the system. This happens after the user enters her username and password, but before the user's desktop is shown and the user login scripts have started.

- ▶ User Desktop Is Active—Runs the policies after the user has logged in to the system and all login scripts have been completed, but before the desktop is displayed. This is available with Windows NT/2000/XP only.

- ▶ Workstation Is Locked—Causes the policies to be applied when the workstation is locked (such as when the screen saver is activated and is locked awaiting a password). This is available with Windows XP/2000 only.

- ▶ Workstation Is UnLocked—Runs the policies when the workstation becomes unlocked, after the user has supplied his password to unlock the system. This is available with Windows XP/2000 only.

- ▶ Screen Saver Is Activated—Runs the policies when the screen saver is activated on an idle system.

- ▶ User Logout—Applies the policies when the user logs out of the system.

- ▶ System Shutdown—Applies the policies when a system shutdown is requested.

Daily

When you choose to have the ADM files applied daily on the workstation, you also need to select when the changes are made.

This schedule requires that you select the days when you want the policy applied. You do this by clicking on the days you want. The selected days appear as depressed buttons.

In addition to the days, you can select the times the policies are applied. These times, the start and stop times, provide a range of time where the policies will be applied.

To keep all workstations from simultaneously accessing the servers, you can select Randomly Dispatch Policy During Time Period. This causes each workstation to choose a random time within the time period when the workstation will retrieve and apply the policy.

You can have the policy also reapplied to each workstation within the timeframe every specified hour, minute, or second by clicking on the Repeat the Action Every field and specifying the time delay. This results in a scheduled action being run on every associated user's workstation for the selected repeat time.

Weekly

You can alternatively choose that the policies be applied only weekly. In the Weekly screen you choose on which day of the week you want the policy to be applied. When you select a day, any other selected day is unselected. After you have selected the day, you can also select the time range when the policy may be applied.

To keep all workstations from simultaneously accessing the servers, you can select Randomly Dispatch Policy During Time Period. This causes each workstation to choose a random time within the time period when it will retrieve and apply the policy.

Monthly

Under the monthly schedule, you can select on which day of the month the policy should be applied, or you can select Last Day of the Month to handle the last day because all months obviously do not end on the same calendar date (30 days hath September, April, June, and November; all the rest have 31 except for February...).

After you have selected the day, you can also select the time range when the policy may be applied.

To keep all workstations from simultaneously accessing the servers, you can select the Randomly Dispatch Policy During Time Period. This causes each workstation to choose a random time within the time period when it will retrieve and apply the policy.

Yearly

Select a yearly schedule if you want to apply the policies only once a year. On the Yearly page, you must choose the day that you want the policies to be applied. This is done by selecting the calendar button to the right of the Date field. This brings up a monthly dialog box where you can browse through the calendar to select the date you want for your policies to be applied. This calendar does not correspond to any particular year and may not take into account leap years in its display. This is because you are choosing a date for each year that comes along in the present and future years.

After you have selected the date, you can also select the time range when the policy may be applied.

To keep all workstations from simultaneously accessing the servers, you can select Randomly Dispatch Policy During Time Period. This causes each workstation to choose a random time within the time period when it will retrieve and apply the policy.

Advanced Settings

On each of the scheduling pages you have the option of selecting the Advanced Settings button, which allows you some additional control of the scheduled action placed on each user's workstation. Clicking this button gives you a dialog box with several tabs to set the specific details of the schedule.

When first displayed, the Completion tab is activated. The following sections describe each field on the tabs and how each setting relates to the action.

Completion

The Completion dialog allows you to specify what should happen on the workstation after the scheduled action has completed. You can choose any of the following by selecting the check box next to the appropriate items:

▶ Disable the Action After Completion—Prevents the action from being rescheduled after completion. If you decide that the policy should be applied every hour, choosing this option turns off that action. The policy will not be reapplied. This rescheduling only occurs once and is reset when the user logs off and back on to the system.

▶ Reboot After Completion—Causes the workstation to reboot after applying the policies.

▶ Prompt the User Before Rebooting—Allows the user to be prompted before rebooting. The user can cancel the reboot.

Fault

This dialog tab allows you to specify what should occur if the scheduled action fails in its completion.

The following choices are available to failed actions:

▶ Disable the Action—Results in the action being disabled and not rescheduled or rerun.

▶ Retry Every Minute—Attempts to rerun the action every minute despite the schedule that may have been specified in the policy.

▶ Ignore the Error and Reschedule Normally—Assumes that the action ran normally and reschedules the action according to the policy.

Impersonation

These settings allow you to specify the account that should be used when running the action.

The following choices are available for the user type used to run the scheduled item:

▶ Interactive User—Runs the action with the rights of the currently logged-in user. This should be used if it is acceptable to run this action and not have access to the secure portions of the registry because most local users do not have access to the secured portions of the registry or file system.

▶ System—Runs the action in the background with administrative privileges. This impersonation level should be used only if the action has no user interface and requires no interaction with the user.

▶ Unsecure System—Runs the action as a system described previously, but allows user interaction. This is available only on Windows XP and 2000.

Priority

This tab allows you to specify at which level you want the action to run on the workstation.

The following choices are available within the priority schedule:

▶ Below Normal—Schedules the actions at a priority that is below the normal user activity. This level does not interfere with the behavior of the system and gives the user a normal experience.

▶ Normal—Schedules the action at the same level as any user activity. This can cause the workstation to perform at a slower level because the service is competing with the user for resources.

▶ Above Normal—Schedules the action at a higher priority than the user requests and results in being completed before user activity, such as mouse and keyboard input, is serviced by the system. Using this level allows the action to be completed faster; however, it can impact users by resulting in slow performance on the client.

Time Limit

This tab of the scheduled advanced settings allows you to specify how long the service should be allowed to run before it is terminated. This can be used to protect you from having the action run for long periods of time on the workstation. This terminates the action, which may cause the action to not complete properly. This tab is not normally used because you usually want the action to fully complete.

Dynamic Local User Policy

Often, several users within a company have access to shared Windows XP workstations, and it would be an administrative nightmare to keep up accounts for all users of these shared systems. Consequently, ZENworks has the capability to dynamically create accounts on the local Windows workstation while the user is logging in to the system. The local account is literally created at login time.

By having the system automatically create the account at the time that the user is authenticated to the eDirectory tree, any of these users can log in to any Windows XP workstation and have a local account automatically created on that workstation. To prevent the system from allowing any user to log in to a specific workstation, you can enable the Login Restrictions page of this policy (click the triangle on the Dynamic Local

User tab and view the Login Restrictions page), which allows you to specify which users can or cannot log in to the specific workstation.

Dynamic Local User Policy Page

Figure 14.12 displays the Dynamic Local User Policy page.

NOTE This policy option is available on all platforms excluding Windows 98.

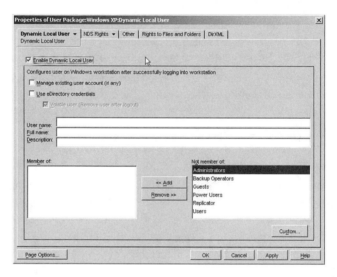

FIGURE 14.12
The Dynamic Local User page.

Checking Enable Dynamic Local User allows the system to start creating accounts on the local system. The following options may be set in this policy:

▶ Manage Existing User Account (If Any)—Allows the ZENworks Desktop Management agents to manage a previously existing account for this user through the Dynamic Local User system. If this is checked, any previously generated accounts are subject to the properties that you administer in this policy.

▶ Use eDirectory Credentials—The system uses the password used for Novell eDirectory Services as the password for the local account.

▶ Volatile User (Remove User After Logout)—Accessible only if you have previously checked the Use eDirectory credentials box. This check box enables the system to remove the local account used for the dynamic user when the user logs out of the system. Having this feature enabled in conjunction with enabling the Manage Existing User Account (If Any) option causes a previously created local account to become volatile and be removed when that person logs out of the workstation.

▶ User Name—Accessible only if Use eDirectory Credentials is disabled. The system uses the specified name for the local account when any Novell eDirectory Services user logs in to the system.

▶ Full Name—Accessible only if Use eDirectory Credentials is disabled. The system uses the specified full name for the local account when any Novell eDirectory Services user logs in to the system.

▶ Description—Accessible only if Use eDirectory Credentials is disabled. The system uses the given description for the local account when any Novell eDirectory Services user logs in to the system.

▶ Member Of/Not member Of—Allow you to specify which local accounts, created or used for these users, are members of which local user groups.

▶ Custom—Allows you to create new custom groups to the list to make the dynamic local users members of these groups.

If the eDirectory credentials are not used for the Dynamic Local User policy—causing the User Username, Full Name, and Description to be used—this account will always be volatile and will be created and removed each time a user logs in to and out of the workstation.

Additionally, if any password restrictions—such as Minimum Password Age or Length or Uniqueness—have been placed in the local workstation policy, the Dynamic Local User system is not activated for that workstation. A dialog box notifying the user that Dynamic Local User features have been disabled is displayed whenever anyone attempts to log in to the workstation.

Login Restrictions Page
On this page, the administrator may either specify the workstations included in activating this policy or list the workstations that are not to activate this policy. There is also a check box that restricts unregistered workstations (workstations that have not been imported into eDirectory).

By checking this attribute, workstations that have the ZENworks Desktop agent on them but have not yet been registered will not support the Dynamic Local User policy and allow users without local accounts to log in.

File Rights Page

On this page, you may specify the path to file system directories and files and grant explicit file rights to DLU users. For example, if the Dynamic Local User policy creates the user as a member of a group that does not give access to a directory required to launch an application, you can use this page to explicitly grant the required directory rights. Or, if the user has Full Control rights to a directory, you can use this page to limit rights to any of the directory's files.

Windows Group Policy

The Windows Group Policy option is available on the Windows 2000 and Windows XP platforms. With Windows 2000 and Active Directory, Microsoft introduced the group policy to its servers. This policy can be applied to a set of users that are part of a container or a subcontainer in Active Directory. Novell ZENworks incorporates this group policy into ZENworks by applying this policy to any group, user, or container in the tree.

The Microsoft Group Policy is nothing more than another .ADM file applied to all the users in the container—in Novell's case, users associated with this policy via direct association, group association, or container association.

Figure 14.13 displays a sample screen of this policy.

After a group policy directory has been specified in the Network Location of Existing/New Group Polices field, all the remaining options become available. The following describes each of the options available on the Windows Group Policies page:

- ▶ Network Location of Existing/New Group Policies—Allows you to specify or browse to the location of the group policy you want like to edit or create.

- ▶ Edit Policies—If you are running on a Windows 2000 or XP workstation, the Microsoft Management Console editor is accessed. You can then edit the user and computer configuration settings.

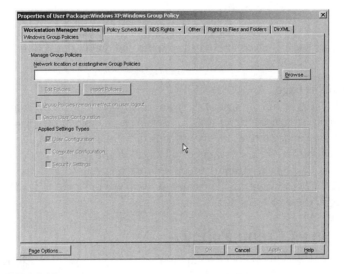

FIGURE 14.13
The Windows Group Policies page.

▶ Import Policies—If you want to create or access a group policy from Active Directory, this allows you to browse to the folder where the Active Directory Group policy or Security Settings are and copy it to the directory specified in the Network Location field.

▶ Group Policies Remain in Effect on User Logout—Indicates that the selected group policies will remain in effect on the local desktop after the user has logged out.

▶ Cache User Configuration—Caching user configuration settings is different than enabling the Group Policies Remain in Effect on User Logout check box.

The Group Policies Remain in Effect on User Logout functionality enables the administrator to retain the group policy settings of the last logged-in user. The limitation with this approach is that any user who logs in locally (workstation only) receives the group policy settings of the last person who logged in to the network on that workstation. If an administrator was the last user to log in to the network on a particular workstation, any subsequent local logins result in the user receiving the administrator's policy settings.

To avoid this situation, you can enable the Cache User Configuration check box to allow each user's settings to be cached.

The Cache User Configuration functionality works with both NetWare or Windows on the back end. If you are using a Windows server on the back end, consider the following:

▶ The user must be logged in with a local user account, not a cached domain account. Windows group policy settings apply to domain accounts as long as the user is logging in to the domain. When the user does not log in to the domain but uses a cached domain account, the Desktop Management Windows group policy settings do not apply.

▶ If you store group policy files on an Active Directory server, the Active Directory username and password must match the eDirectory credentials.

▶ Users must have unique local user accounts. The Windows group policy settings are cached in the local user's profile, so users with different effective Windows group policies need to have different local user accounts.

▶ Each user must have a profile on the machine in which to cache the settings. You can provide this profile by using local user accounts or by using Dynamic Local User accounts; however, the account cannot be removed. If the Dynamic Local User policy removes the local user account (either by a using a volatile user account or by using an expired cached volatile user account), the user cannot log in locally.

▶ Only the settings contained in the `\user\registry.pol` file are cached. This is roughly equivalent to the User Settings in the Group Policy editor with the exception of the logon/logoff scripts (they are stored in the `Scripts` folder under `\User` and are therefore not cached).

▶ Enabling the Cache User Configuration check box causes the user configuration settings of each user's effective Windows group policies to be stored in each user's local profile. When each user logs in locally, the user settings are read from the cached copy of the `registry.pol` file in that user's profile and are applied. The only settings cached are those stored in the `registry.pol` file in the `User` folder. Other settings are not cached, including logon/logoff scripts, computer settings, and security settings.

NOTE Novell does not recommend using both the Group Policies Remain in Effect On User Logout settings and the Cache User Configuration settings in an environment in which the user group policies are pushed to different users on common workstations.

▶ Applied Settings Types—In earlier releases of ZENworks, it wasn't possible to apply computer configuration settings to a user. ZENworks allows you to apply the following settings to be selected with a user policy:

  ▶ User Configuration—Enables the settings under User Configuration with the group policy.

  ▶ Computer Configuration—Enables the settings under Computer Configuration (except security settings) with the group policy.

  ▶ Security Settings—Applies all security settings in the group policy.

Windows Terminal Server Policy

The Windows Terminal Server policy option is available on the Windows 2000/2003 Terminal Server platforms. For a greater compatibility between ZENworks Desktop Management and other systems, ZENworks has included this policy that allows you to administer your user's interaction and the behavior of Terminal Server available on Microsoft servers.

Figure 14.14 displays a sample page of this policy.

In this policy you may administer the various aspects of user policies for when the user is logged in to a Terminal Server.

All the policies for Terminal Services are the same as specified previously for Windows 2000 and Windows XP systems.

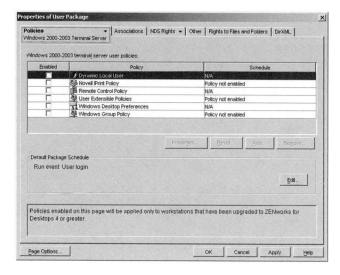

FIGURE 14.14
The Terminal Server policy.

Summary

ZENworks provides significant, feature-rich components to manage all your required policies to manage end-user environments and desktops. Using policies and associating them with your users will provide them their environment wherever they are and on any device that they use to connect into the system.

Setting Up Workstation Policies

This chapter discusses the use and creation of workstation policies. Workstation policies are associated with containers (resulting in all workstations in the container and subcontainers receiving the policy), workstations, and workstation groups and affect their working environment.

Relationship of Workstation Policies to Workstations

Workstations are associated with workstation policies through associations with policies in any of three ways:

- ▶ Policies can be associated with the workstation object directly.

- ▶ Policies can be associated with a parent container of the workstation object.

- ▶ Policies can be associated with a workstation group to which the workstation is a member.

The ZENworks Management agent is activated on a workstation at user login time for Windows 98 systems, and on Windows NT/2000/XP systems, it is activated when the service is started. When the ZENworks Management agent is activated, it logs in to the eDirectory tree as the workstation and walks up the tree looking for the first workstation policy package it can find associated with the workstation. Like all ZENworks agents, the order that the tree is searched depends on standard Novell eDirectory behavior and any search policies that may be in the tree. All the applicable workstation policies are merged together and then the culmination is applied to the workstation. If any conflicts occur with the policies (such as two workstation policies both affecting the same parameter), the parameter setting in the first policy found will be applied.

The Remote Control policy, for example, can be created for both the user and the workstation. In instances where a Remote Control policy exists for both the user and the workstation, the remote control subsystem takes the most restrictive of the policies. For example, if one policy says to prompt the user for permission and the other does not, the system prompts the user.

Advantages of Platform-Specific Policies

ZENworks enables the administration of specific policies for each platform supported in the system. By having a policy categorized for each type of platform, the administrator can make unique policies for each system. Regardless of the users logged in to the system, each workstation finds the policies associated with it and executes the administrative configurations for that platform.

Occasions exist in which you may want to associate a particular unique policy to a set of workstations that may be held in containers along with other workstations of the same type. You can then create a group of workstations and associate specific policies to those workstations. Consequently, these workstations receive the policies from this group rather than from the container.

Setting Up a Workstation Package

To have a workstation policy package, you must first create the policy package. To create a workstation policy package do the following:

1. Start ConsoleOne.

2. Browse to the container where you want to have the policy package. Remember that you do not have to create the policy package

in the container where you are doing the associations. You can associate the same policy package to many containers in your tree.

3. Create the policy package by right-clicking and choosing New→Policy Package or by selecting the Create Policy Package icon on the toolbar.

4. Select the Workstation Package object in the wizard panel and click Next.

5. Enter the desired name of the package in the Policy Package Name field and select the container where you want the package to be located. The Container field is already filled in with the selected container, so you should not have to browse to complete this field. If it is not, click the browser button next to the field and browse to and select the container where you want the policy object stored. Click Next.

6. Select the Define Additional Properties check box to go into the properties of your new object and activate some policies. Click Finish.

7. Check and set any policies you want for this workstation policy package and click OK.

The following subsections describe each of the fields and property pages available in the workstation policy package.

Policies Property Page

All the policies for workstations are activated within the Policies property page. Initially the page is on the general policies. As other platforms are selected, additional policies are displayed. You can select which platform to display by placing the mouse over the small triangle on the right side of the Policies tab. This activates a drop-down menu that enables you to select which platform-specific page you want to display.

The following sections discuss briefly each of the policy pages and then we cover the specifics of each policy.

General Policies

When you first go into the properties of the workstation policy package, you are presented with the Policies property page. The Policies page first displays the General category. All the policies activated in the General category are active for *all* workstation platforms supported by ZENworks and associated with the workstation.

Figure 15.1 shows the initial property page of the workstation policy package.

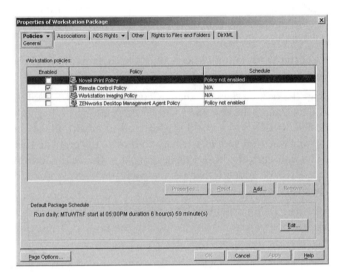

FIGURE 15.1
Workstation package, Policies General property page.

As you can see from Figure 15.1, four policies are available to all the platforms supported by ZENworks. They include the Novell iPrint policy, the Remote Control policy, the Workstation Imaging policy, and the ZENworks Desktop Management Agent policy. These, as well as all the other policies, are discussed later in this chapter.

To activate a policy, click on the box to the left of the policy. You can then go into the details of the policy and set additional configuration parameters on that specific policy.

Windows 9x Policies

Within the Policies tab you can select the Windows 9x Policies page. This page displays the policies available for Windows 9x workstations. These policies include the Computer Extensible policies, the Novell iPrint policy, the Remote Control policy, the Workstation Inventory policy, and the ZENworks Desktop Management Agent policy. Figure 15.2 shows the Windows 9x Policies page.

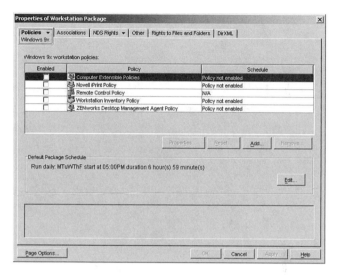

FIGURE 15.2
Workstation package, Windows 98 Policies property page.

Windows NT Policies

Within the Policies tab you can select the Windows NT Policies page.
This page displays the policies available for Windows NT workstations.
These policies include the Computer Extensible policies, the Novell iPrint
policy, the Remote Control policy, the Workstation Inventory policy, and
the ZENworks Desktop Management Agent policy. Figure 15.3 shows the
Windows NT Policies page.

As you can see from Figure 15.3, some of the same policies are under
both the General and the Windows NT Policies page (as well as other
platform-specific pages). When you select a policy in the Windows NT
page, it supercedes any selections that may have been on the General tab
for that platform. The policies are not merged together, and only the
platform-specific policy is used rather than the policy set in the General
category. Also, only the policies selected in the platform-specific tab are
used in place of the general policies. For example, if the Remote Control
policy is selected in the General tab and in the Windows NT tab, agents
on a Windows NT system use the Windows NT Workstation Remote
Control policy rather than the policy in the General tab.

416

CHAPTER 15 Setting Up Workstation Policies

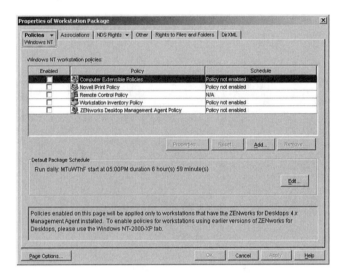

FIGURE 15.3
Workstation package, Windows NT Policies property page.

Windows 2000 Policies
Within the Policies tab you can select the Windows 2000 Policies page. This page displays the policies available for Windows 2000 workstations. These policies include the Computer Extensible policies, the Novell iPrint policy, the Remote Control policy, the Windows Group policy, the Workstation Inventory policy, and the ZENworks Desktop Management Agent policy. Figure 15.4 shows the Windows 2000 Policies page.

Windows XP Policies
Within the Policies tab you can select the Windows XP Policies page. This page displays the policies available for Windows XP workstations. These policies include the Novell iPrint policy, the Remote Control policy, the Windows Group policy, the Workstation Inventory policy, and the ZENworks Desktop Management Agent policy. Figure 15.5 shows the Windows XP Policies page.

Windows NT-2000-XP Policies
The Windows NT-2000-XP tab provides backward compatibility for workstations using previous versions of ZENworks. If you need to set policies for workstations that are using versions of ZENworks previous to ZENworks 6, you will need to set these policies using the Windows NT-2000-XP tab.

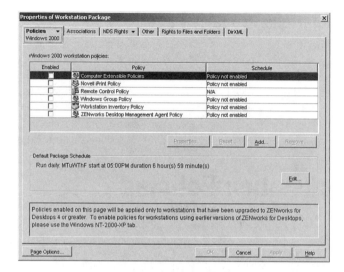

FIGURE 15.4
Workstation package, Windows 2000 Policies property page.

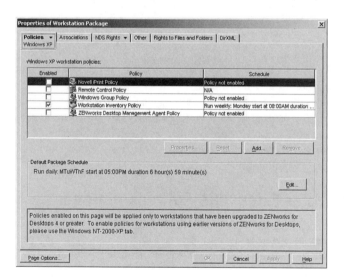

FIGURE 15.5
Workstation package, Windows XP Policies property page.

Associations Property Page

The Associations page of the workstation policy package displays all the locations in the tree (containers and workstations) where the policy package has been associated. These associations do not necessarily reflect where the policy package is located in the directory. The agents associated with users or workstations in or below those containers have this policy package enforced. Clicking the Add or Remove buttons enables you to add or remove containers in the list that are associated with this policy.

Workstation Policies

The following sections describe the various policies available to workstations.

Computer Extensible Policies

Microsoft requires that software packages bearing the Windows approved logo provide the capability to be configured through .POL files. The poledit program enables you to edit these extensible policies and include them in the system .POL file. ZENworks also enables the policies stored in eDirectory to accept these additional extensible polices and provide them to all users associated with these policies.

The Computer Extensible policy enables you to import these special .ADM files into the eDirectory tree and have them administered and dispersed to the users associated with the policy package. After these .ADM files have been imported into the tree, they can be administered and associated with users in the eDirectory tree. These settings are applied like the user system policies.

Computer Extensible Policies Dialog

When you first bring up the Computer Extensible Policies dialog you are presented with the Computer Extensible Policies page under the Workstation Manager Policies tab. Figure 15.6 shows an example of this page.

This page is split into three areas: ADM Files, Policies, and a policy-specific window at the bottom-right corner.

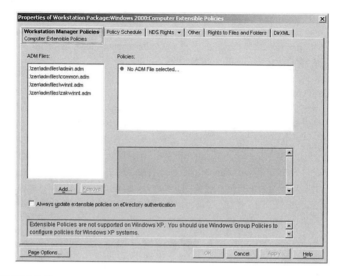

FIGURE 15.6
Computer Extensible Policies page of the workstation policy package.

The files listed in the ADM Files list are the policies applied to the work-stations associated with this policy. To add a policy file to the list, click the Add button, and you are presented with a file dialog box where you can browse and select the file. Remember that this file should reside on the server because it is stored there for retrieval by the policy managers. When you browse and select a file make sure that it is on the server and that the drive that you use is mapped correctly for all users who would be associated with the policy. You can enter a UNC path in the Filename field of the dialog box and thereby get a UNC path for the .ADM file; however, if you browse and then select, the program puts a drive letter into the path necessitating that each user have the same drive mapping.

When this policy is initialized, four .ADM files are automatically pulled in by the plug-in into ConsoleOne. These include `admin.adm`, `common.adm`, `winnt.adm`, `zakwinnt.adm`. Each of these files is stored in the `ConsoleOne\1.2\bin\zen\admfiles` directory, and they are considered the default packages to be used.

NOTE Other .ADM files are available depending on which version of Windows you are running on your workstation. For example, Windows 2000 clients also include the `system.adm`, and there is a `inetres.adm` file for restricting Internet Explorer.

NOTE The .ADM file must be stored on a server on which users have access. The policy references the .ADM file and needs to retrieve it to apply it to the users and to enable the administrators to modify the settings. It would be recommended, therefore, to use a UNC path in specifying the location of the file.

You delete the .ADM file from the applied set by selecting the file and clicking the Remove button. You can also modify the settings of the .ADM files by selecting the file in the ADM Files window. When you select the file, its registry content is displayed in the Policies window. The user interface for this window mimics the poledit program available from Microsoft. The small window underneath the Policies window displays information about the selected registry setting along with any subsetting categories available with the specific key. Selecting the key in the Policies window, by double-clicking, populates this details field.

You can browse through the .ADM files and turn on (checked), turn off (unchecked and white), or leave as set in the registry (unchecked and gray) each of the keys as you would in the poledit program. After you have made your changes, click Apply or OK to update the .ADM files on the server.

Policy Schedule Page

The Policy Schedule page enables you to customize (outside the package default schedule) when you want the .ADM files applied to the workstation.

This page enables you to select when the package should be applied: Event, Daily, Weekly, Monthly, or Yearly.

After you have selected when you want the package applied, you have additional fields to select in the lower portion of the screen. The following sections discuss the various options you have with scheduling the package.

Event

When you choose to have the .ADM files applied upon an event that occurs in the workstation, you also need to select which event effects the changes.

The events that you can select are one of the following:

▶ User Login—Causes the policies to be applied when the user logs in to the system. This happens after the user enters her username and password but before her desktop is shown and the user login scripts have started.

- ▶ User Desktop Is Active (WinNT-2000-XP Only)—Runs the policies after the user has logged in to the system and all login scripts have been completed but before the user desktop is displayed. This is available with Windows 2000/XP only.

- ▶ Workstation Is Locked (WinNT-2000-XP Only)—Causes the policies to be applied when the workstation is locked (such as when the screen saver is activated and is locked awaiting a password). This is available with Windows XP/2000 only.

- ▶ Workstation Is Unlocked (WinNT-2000-XP Only)—Runs the policies when the workstation becomes unlocked, after the user has supplied his password to unlock the system. This is available with Windows XP/2000 only.

- ▶ Screen Saver Is Activated—Runs the policies when the screen saver is activated on an idle system.

- ▶ User Logout—Applies the policies when the user logs out of the system.

- ▶ System Shutdown—Applies the policies when a system shutdown is requested.

Daily

When you choose to have the .ADM files applied daily on the workstation, you also need to select when the changes are made.

This schedule requires that you select the days when you want the policy applied by clicking on the days you want. The selected days appear as depressed buttons.

In addition to the days, you can select the times the policies are applied. These times, the start and stop times, provide a range of time where the policies will be applied.

To keep all workstations from simultaneously accessing the servers, you can select Randomly Dispatch Policy During Time Period. This causes each workstation to choose a random time within the time period when the workstation will retrieve and apply the policy.

You can have the policy also reapplied to each workstation within the timeframe every specified hour, minute, or second by clicking on the Repeat the Action Every field and specifying the time delay. This results in a scheduled action being run on every associated workstation for the selected repeat time.

Weekly

You can alternatively choose that the policies be applied only weekly. In the Weekly screen, you choose on which day of the week you want the policy to be applied. When you select a day, any other selected day is unselected. After you have selected the day, you can also select the time range when the policy may be applied.

To keep all workstations from simultaneously accessing the servers, you can select Randomly Dispatch Policy During Time Period. This causes each workstation to choose a random time within the time period when the workstation will retrieve and apply the policy.

Monthly

Under the monthly schedule, you can select on which day of the month the policy should be applied, or you can select Last Day of the Month to handle the last day because all months obviously do not end on the same calendar date (30 days hath September, April, June, and November; all the rest have 31 except for February…).

After you have selected the day, you can also select the time range when the policy may be applied. To keep all workstations from simultaneously accessing the servers, you can select Randomly Dispatch Policy During Time Period. This causes each workstation to choose a random time within the time period when the workstation will retrieve and apply the policy.

Yearly

Select a yearly schedule if you want to apply the policies only once a year. On the Yearly page you must choose the day that you want the policies to be applied. This is done by selecting the calendar button to the right of the Date field. This brings up a monthly dialog box where you can browse through the calendar to select the date you want for your policies to be applied. This calendar does not correspond to any particular year and may not take into account leap years in its display. This is because you are choosing a date for each year that comes along in the present and future years.

After you have selected the date, you can also select the time range when the policy may be applied. To keep all workstations from simultaneously accessing the servers, you can select Randomly Dispatch Policy During Time Period. This causes each workstation to choose a random time within the time period when the workstation will retrieve and apply the policy.

Advanced Settings

On each of the scheduling pages you have the option of selecting the Advanced Settings button, which allows you some additional control of the scheduled action placed on each workstation. Clicking Advanced Settings gives you a dialog with several tabs to set the specific details of the schedule.

When first displayed, the Completion tab is activated. The following sections describe each field on the tabs and how it relates to the action.

Completion

The Completion dialog allows you to specify what should happen on the workstation after the scheduled action has completed. You can choose any of the following by selecting the check box next to the appropriate items:

- ▶ Disable the Action After Completion—Prevents the action from being rescheduled after completion. If you decide that the policy should be applied every hour, choosing this turns off that action. The policy will not be reapplied. This rescheduling only occurs and is reset when the user logs off and back on to the system.

- ▶ Reboot After Completion—Causes the workstation to reboot after applying the policies.

- ▶ Prompt the User Before Rebooting—Allows the user to be prompted before rebooting. The user can cancel the reboot.

Fault

This dialog tab allows you to specify what should occur if the scheduled action fails in its completion.

The following choices are available to failed actions:

- ▶ Disable the Action—Results in the action being disabled and not rescheduled or rerun.

- ▶ Retry Every Minute—Attempts to rerun the action every minute despite the schedule that may have been specified in the policy.

- ▶ Ignore the Error and Reschedule Normally—Assumes that the action ran normally and reschedules the action according to the policy.

Impersonation

These settings allow you to specify the account that should be used when running the action.

The following choices are available for the user type used to run the scheduled item:

▶ Interactive User—Runs the action with the rights of the currently logged-in user. This should be used if it is acceptable to run this action and not have access to the secure portions of the registry because most local users do not have access to the secured portions of the registry or file system.

▶ System—Runs the action in the background with administrative privileges. This impersonation level should be used only if the action has no user interface and requires no interaction with the user.

▶ Unsecure System—Runs the action as a system described previously but allows user interaction. This is available only on Windows XP and 2000.

Priority

This tab allows you to specify at which level you want the action to run on the workstation.

The following choices are available within the priority schedule:

▶ Below Normal—Schedules the actions at a priority below the normal user activity. This level does not interfere with the behavior of the system and gives the user a normal experience.

▶ Normal—Schedules the action at the same level as any user activity. This can cause the workstation to perform at a slower level because the service is competing with the user for resources.

▶ Above Normal—Schedules the action at a higher priority than the user requests and results in being completed before user activity, such as mouse and keyboard input, is serviced by the system. Using this level allows the action to be completed faster; however, it can negatively impact user productivity by resulting in slow performance on the client.

This tab of the scheduled advanced settings allows you to specify how long the service should be allowed to run before it is terminated. This can be used to protect you from having the action run for long periods of time on the workstation. This terminates the action, which may cause the action to not complete properly. This tab is not normally used because you usually want the action to fully complete.

Time Limit

This tab of the scheduled advanced settings enables you to specify how long the service should be allowed to run before it is terminated. This can be used to protect you from having the action run for long periods of time on the workstation. Terminating the action, though, may prevent the action from completing properly. Therefore, because you usually want the action to fully complete, this tab is not normally used.

Novell iPrint Policy

The Novell iPrint Policy option is available across all platforms and on the General Policies page. It allows you to configure a Novell iPrint client that can be placed on the workstation, allowing it to use Internet printing capabilities.

Client Install Page

This page allows you to specify the path on a server where the iPrint client can be found. Specifying the path on the iPrint policy causes the iPrint client to automatically be installed on the workstation. You can also specify the language and the version number of the software. Also you can specify whether to install the new client, should an older version be found on the workstation.

Settings Page

This page allows you to specify any set of printers you want to automatically install and configure on the receiving workstation.

Remote Control Policy

The Remote Control Policy option is available across all platforms and on the General Policies page.

A Remote Control policy is activated for this policy package by selecting the check box next to Remote Control Policy. After this is selected and a check is displayed in the check box, this Remote Management policy is activated for all workstations associated with the workstation policy Package.

The Remote Control policy controls the features of the Remote Management subsystem shipped with ZENworks. The Remote Management system is comprised of two parts: Remote Management Session Manager, which makes the connection and is used by the administrator, and the remote control agents, which are installed on the end-user's workstation. The remote control agent is part of the full ZENworks management agents and is installed as part of the agent installation process. Running the `ZfDAgent.msi` in the `public\zenworks\ZfDAgent\<language>` folder installs the agent on the workstation that has MSI installed.

The Remote Management system makes a peer-to-peer IP connection between the administrator's workstation and the remote workstation. Remotely controlling a workstation via ZENworks Desktop Management may also require rights within the workstation object that represents the workstation to be controlled. Without these rights, the administrator is denied access to the remote control subsystem. Both the session manager and the agents validate that the user has rights to remotely control the workstation. You assign the remote control rights through the Remote Management Rights Wizard, or in the workstation object in the Remote Operators page.

ZENworks Desktop Management also has the capability to remotely control via a password, without any workstation object in the tree. Launching remote control from the Tools menu of ConsoleOne does this (right-clicking when a workstation is selected). The dialog that comes up requires the IP address of the workstation and a password. This password must match the password entered by the end-user through the Security menu of the remote control agent (on the system tray) of the workstation. The password use of remote control must be configured in the policy as accepted.

Remote Management Page

The Remote Management page identifies the features that you want to be activated with the Remote Management system. The following sections describe configuration options available under each of the tabs of the Remote Management policy window shown in Figure 15.7.

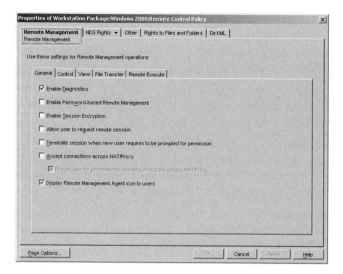

FIGURE 15.7
Remote Management page, General tab of a workstation policy package.

General Tab

The first tab of the Remote Management page allows you to set the following general system functions:

▶ Enable Diagnostics—Allows the agent on the workstations to perform a diagnostics report. This can be done by selecting the workstation and then right-clicking and selecting Actions→Diagnostics from the menu. The Diagnostics utility performs some basic queries on the system and returns the information about the workstation. This information includes memory, environment, and processes running. Additionally, it would include eDirectory and NetWare connection information, client information, network drives, and open file list, as well as printers, Network protocols, and network services active. You can also view the various event and error logs that have been recorded on that workstation.

▶ Enable Password-based Remote Management—Allows the operator to establish password-based remote management with the workstation.

▶ Enable Session Encryption—Activates session encryption between the administrative workstation and the remote controlled desktop.

The system activates a 168-bit DES algorithm when a password-based remote control session is started, and a 512-bit RSA algorithm session when an eDirectory-enabled session is activated.

▶ Allow User to Request Remote Session—Allows the remote user to request a remote control session of the administrator. This is useful when the remote workstation is behind a NAT, and you cannot accurately determine the address and port required.

▶ Terminate Session When New User Requires to Be Prompted for Permission—Terminates any ongoing remote management session with the workstation when a new user, whose permission for starting a remote management session is required, logs in.

▶ Accept Connections Across NAT/Proxy—Allows the remote agents to accept connections across a NAT/proxy. This option is only valid for eDirectory-based remote sessions.

▶ Prompt User for Permission to Accept Connections Across NAT/Proxy—Is valid only for eDirectory based sessions and will, when selected, cause the user to be prompted when the connection is over a NAT/proxy even if the other policies state not to prompt the user.

▶ Display Remote Management Agent Icon to Users—Controls whether an icon will appear on the user's system tray. From this icon the user may set the password and review policy configurations applied to the workstation.

Control Tab

The Control tab describes the feature enabling of remote control functions. The following are the settings that can be managed from this policy:

▶ Enable Remote Control—Activates the remote control subsystem. Without this setting on, no one may remotely control the workstations where the currently logged-in user has this policy associated with his user object.

▶ Prompt User for Permission to Remote Control—Causes a dialog box to be displayed on the end-user's machine when a remote control session is started. The end-user has the option of accepting or denying the remote control request. Within this dialog box, the user is told who wants to remotely control his machine and asks whether this is approved. If the user denies the remote control session, the session is terminated and the administrator cannot remotely control the workstation.

▶ Give User Audible Signal When Remote Controlled—Provides the end-user a tone periodically while the remote control session is active. This option can be further modified by specifying the number of seconds between beeps.

▶ Give User Visible Signal When Remote Controlled—Displays a dialog box on the end-user's desktop while the remote control session is active. The dialog box displays that the workstation is being remotely controlled and also displays the eDirectory name of the user remotely controlling the workstation. You can set the number of seconds that you want to have between flashing the name of the user initiating the remote control session.

▶ Allow Blanking User's Screen—Causes the screen on the remote desktop to be blanked, preventing the end-user from seeing what is being done by the administrator to the user's workstation. When you enable the blanking of the screen, the keyboard and mouse are automatically locked.

▶ Allow Locking User's Keyboard and Mouse—Deactivates the keyboard and the mouse when the administrator remotely controls the workstation. The end-user may move the mouse or keyboard, but they will not function, and any input from them will be ignored.

View Tab

The View tab describes the feature enabling of the remote view functions. Remote view is the capability for the administrator to view the remote Windows screen of the target machine but not be able to control the mouse or keyboard of the machine. The following lists the options available:

▶ Enable Remote View—Activates the remote view subsystem. Without this setting on, no one may remotely view the workstation.

▶ Prompt User for Permission to Remote View—Causes a dialog box to be displayed on the end-user's machine when a remote view session is started. The end-user has the option of accepting or denying the remote view request. Within this dialog box, the user is told who wants to remotely view his machine and asks whether this is approved. If the user denies the remote view session, the session is terminated, and the administrator cannot remote view the workstation.

▶ Give User Audible Signal When Remote Viewed—Provides the end-user a tone periodically while the remote view session is active. You can also set the number of seconds between each beep.

▶ Give User Visible Signal When Remote Viewed—Displays a dialog box on the end-user's desktop while the remote view session is active. The dialog box displays that the workstation is being remotely viewed and also displays the eDirectory name of the user remotely viewing the workstation. You can set the number of seconds that you want to have between flashing the name of the user initiating the remote view session.

File Transfer Tab

The File Transfer tab describes the feature enabling of the file transfer system. This allows you, the administrator, to send files to the remote workstation. The following provides a list of options available:

▶ Enable File Transfer—Activates the file transfer subsystem. Without this setting on, no one may send files to the workstation.

▶ Prompt User for Permission to Transfer Files—Causes a dialog box to be displayed on the end-user's machine when a file transfer session is started. The end-user has the option of accepting or denying the file transfer request. Within this dialog box, the user is told who wants to perform the file transfer from her machine and asks whether this is approved. If the user denies the file transfer session, the session is terminated, and the administrator cannot send the files to the workstation.

Remote Execute Tab

The Remote Execute tab describes the feature enabling of the remote execute system. This allows you or the administrator to remotely execute a program on the remote workstation. The output of the program is not displayed on the administrative console. The following options may be administered:

▶ Enable Remote Execute—Enables the administrator to execute applications or files on the remotely managed workstation.

▶ Prompt User for Permission to Remote Execute—Causes a dialog box to be displayed on the end-user's machine when a remote execute session is started. The end-user has the option of accepting or denying the remote execute request. Within this dialog box, the user is told who wants to perform the request and asks whether this is approved. If the user denies the remote execution session, the session is terminated, and the administrator cannot execute the program on the workstation.

Windows Group Policy

The Windows Group Policy option is available on the Windows 2000 and Windows XP platforms. With Windows 2000 and Active Directory, Microsoft introduced the Group Policy to its servers. This policy can be applied to a set of workstations that are part of a container or a subcontainer in Active Directory. Novell ZENworks incorporates this Group Policy into ZENworks by applying this policy to any workstation, workstation group, or container in the tree.

The Microsoft Group Policy is nothing more than another .ADM file applied to all the users in the container—in Novell's case, users associated with this policy via direct association, group association, or container association.

Figure 15.8 displays a sample screen of this policy.

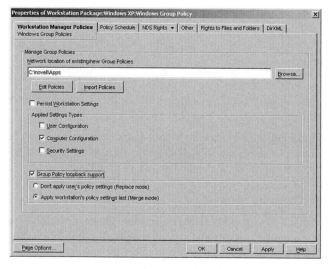

FIGURE 15.8
Windows group policy of the Workstation Policies page.

After a group policy directory is specified in the Network Location of Existing/New Group Polices field, all the remaining options become available. The following describes each of the options available on the Windows Group Policy page:

- ▶ Network Location of Existing/New Group Policies—Allows you to specify or browse to the location of the group policy you want to edit or create.

- ▶ Edit Policies—If you are running on a Windows 2000 or XP workstation, the Microsoft Management Console editor is accessed. You can then edit the user and computer configuration settings.

- ▶ Import Policies—If you want to create or access a group policy from Active Directory, this allows you to browse to the folder where the Active Directory Group policy or Security Settings are and copy it to the directory specified in the Network Location field.

- ▶ Persist Workstation Settings—Check this box to indicate that the selected group policies will remain in effect on the local desktop after the user has logged out or the workstation has rebooted.

- ▶ Applied Settings Type—ZENworks allows you to apply Windows user, computer, and security settings to be selected with a user policy. Each option is discussed in the following list:

    - ▶ User Configuration—Enables the settings under User Configuration with the group policy.

    - ▶ Computer Configuration—Enables the settings under Computer Configuration (except Security settings) with the group policy.

    - ▶ Security Settings—Applies all Security settings in the group policy.

- ▶ Group Policy Loopback Support—Controls how the group policies interact between a workstation (which is applied to all users) and any group policies that may be associated with the user logging in to the workstation. After the loopback support is checked, you may specify the following:

    - ▶ Don't Apply User's Policy Settings (Replace Mode)—Does not apply the user's associated group policy and leaves the workstation associated policy in effect for any users logging in to the workstation.

    - ▶ Apply Workstation's Policy Settings Last (Merge Mode)—Causes the agents to apply the associated user's group policy to the desktop and then apply the workstation's associated group policy onto the desktop. Any settings made in the user's policy will be overwritten by the workstation's policy (if the workstation policy has the same policy key set as the user's policy).

The association of a group policy to a workstation is powerful in that you could lock down a specific workstation regardless of the user logging in. This may be valuable if there are some special hardware or capabilities of the workstation that you want to protect—such as not allowing the users to install software on that particular workstation.

Workstation Imaging Policy

ZENworks has the capability to image a workstation and then to apply that image back to the original or other workstations. See Chapter 22, "Imaging a Workstation," for more detailed information on the functionality of the ZENworks imaging system.

The placement of an image, associated with an image object in the directory, onto a workstation may occur four different ways in ZENworks:

▶ Booting the workstation and allowing the NIC card with PXE (Preboot Execution Environment) capabilities to communicate to the imaging server through PXE.

▶ Booting the workstation with a floppy disk that communicates with the imaging agent on the server.

▶ Placing a special boot partition on an unregistered workstation that communicates with the imaging agent on the server.

▶ Placing a special boot partition on a registered workstation and setting the Put an Image on This Workstation on the Next Boot field in the workstation object.

Each of these ways results in the workstation being imaged. The image being used will either be the image associated with the workstation or determined by the imaging agent (and associated policy) that resides on the server. The workstation finds the imaging server when the imaging boot diskettes are created; the administrator can specify either an IP or a DNS name for the server. This information is saved on the diskettes or in the special boot partition. In the case of PXE, configuration settings are made when the ZENworks PXE system is installed that will direct the workstation to the imaging server.

The Workstation Imaging policy comes into effect if the workstation is to be imaged, no image is associated with the workstation object, and the policy is activated. This policy enables the administrator to create a set of rules that can govern when a particular image should be used, based on some basic information from the workstation. The imaging server follows the list of rules in the policy until one of the rules is satisfied. The rule that is satisfied results in an associated image that is then applied to the workstation.

Rules Page

This page enables the administrator to input the rules and associated images that the system uses to determine the image to place on a specific type of workstation. Figure 15.9 shows a sample of this page.

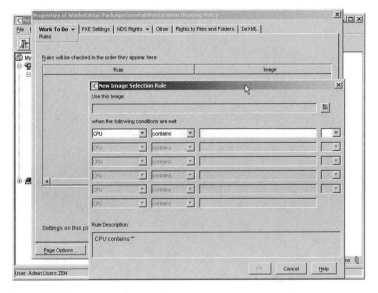

FIGURE 15.9
Rules page for a sample Workstation Imaging policy of a workstation policy package.

You must first click the Add button to add rules to the list. After you have added several rules, you may then select a specific rule, change its order in the list, look at its properties, or remove the rule. When you click Add a dialog box is brought up to add the rule to the policy.

You first click the browse icon button next to the Use This Image field to browse to an image object in the tree associated with an image file on the image server. After the image object is selected, you may identify the rule associated with this image. You may currently have only six key/value pairs to compare about the workstation to determine what image to use.

In the middle of the dialog, you can see the six potential equations that you can generate to determine whether the image should be used. The equation is made up of a series of true/false statements put together with AND and OR logic. You construct the statement by filling in the drop-down statements. (The resulting statement is displayed in a more English-like view to help you understand the equation.)

The logic for the AND and OR operators is strictly left to right in the equation. In the Rule Description box, parentheses are added to the equation to help the administrator understand how the rule is evaluated. You cannot insert the parentheses; they are automatically inserted as part of the explanation of the equation and are not under user control.

You first select the key you want to examine by selecting the key via a drop-down dialog box. The keys that you can choose from are the following:

- ▶ CPU—The reported processor. An example would be GenuineIntel Mobile Pentium MMX 233 MHZ.

- ▶ Video—The type of video adapter in the workstation. An example of this would be Trident Cyber9397 (rev 243).

- ▶ Network—The network adapter for the workstation. An example would be 3Com.

- ▶ Sound Card—The sound card that has been reported. Often this field results in no sound card detected. This is because the system sends out a PCI request, and, if no sound cards respond, you get this even if a sound card is present.

- ▶ Hard Drive Controller—The type of hard drive in the system. If the hard drive is an IDE device, the value for this field is IDE. If the hard drive is a SCSI device, you get the reported name of the device, such as FUJITSU MHJ2181AT.

- ▶ MAC Address—The MAC address of the network card. An example of this value would be 00 60 80 03 C2 E7.

- ▶ IP Address—The assigned IP address of the workstation. This would be reported as the traditional 137.65.237.5.

- ▶ BIOS Asset Number—Any asset value placed in the BIOS of the computer.

- ▶ BIOS Serial Number—The serial number placed in the BIOS of the computer.

- ▶ Hard Drive Size—The disk size in number of megabytes. Therefore, an 8GB hard drive would be reported as 8192MB in this field. The imaging system may not always report the full disk capacity. It is advisable that you use a wide boundary when generating your rules. For example, if you want to look for an 8GB drive, put in the statement `Hard drive size > 8000MB and not equal to an exact number`.

- ▶ RAM—The reported amount of RAM in megabyte units. This would be reported as 64MB. This field also may not always report the exact amount of RAM space that you would expect on your workstation. It is advisable that you use a wide boundary when generating your rules. For example, if you want to look for 16MB of RAM, put in the statement `RAM > 15MB and not equal to an exact number`.

When the workstation is booting the imaging system, it is in reality booting up the Linux operating system and running the tools included in the imaging system. The values for the keys described previously are values that the Linux system can report to the software. To discover what a system reports to Linux, you need to boot a sample workstation with the Imaging system boot disk and run the `Img information` command. This displays the information sent to the image server about the workstation. This information will be the data values that you put into the key comparison equations for your rules. You can also get this information from an image by opening the image in the ZENworks image editor and choosing properties on the image root. See Chapter 22 for more detailed information on the functionality of the ZENworks imaging system.

The next part of the equation is to specify the operator. Two types of operators exist: String and Integer operators. The Hard Drive Size and RAM fields are treated as integers; all the other fields are treated as strings, where a case insensitive string compare is done to determine operator results. The string operators are `contains`, `doesn't contain`, `begins with`, and `equals`. The integer operators are =, <>, >, >=, <, and <=.

These operators perform expected comparisons between the key value supplied by the workstation to the imaging server and the value that you place into the value field of the equation. The following meanings are placed with each operator:

- `contains`—The specified value is a substring anywhere in the reported value.

- `doesn't contain`—The specified value is not equal to or contained in the reported value.

- `begins with`—The specified value is represented in the initial character of the reported value.

- `equals`—The specified value is the same as the reported value.

- = equals—The specified value is numerically equivalent to the reported value.

- <> not equal—The specified value is not equal to the reported value.

- > greater than—The specified value is greater than the reported value.

- >= greater than or equal to—The specified value is numerically equal or greater than the reported value.

- < less than—The specified value is less than the reported value.

- <= less than or equal to—The specified value is numerically less than or equal to the reported value.

The next field in the operation is where you enter the value that you want to compare. The far right field enables you to extend the operation to additional key/value comparisons. Your choices currently are AND and OR.

The Boolean operators are evaluated strictly from left to right. For example, if the following rules were entered into the policy:

- Hard drive size >= 600MB AND

- RAM < 16MB OR

- RAM > 31MB

the resultant evaluation would be (hard drive < 60MB AND RAM < 16MB) OR (RAM > 31MB). This would result in giving the image to any system that has a disk smaller than 200MB with less than 16MB

RAM. This would also give the image to any system that has more than 31MB RAM regardless of the size of the hard drive.

You can view the precedence of the equation, complete with parentheses, on the bottom half of the screen as you introduce new key/value pairs into your rule.

After your set of key/value pairs has been entered and you have reviewed your equation at the bottom of the screen, click the OK button to include the rule into the imaging system. You are returned to the original Rules page with the rule that you entered placed on the screen.

Once again, from this page—after you have entered some rules—you can then specify the order that the rules are evaluated. After selecting a rule, you can move that rule in the order by clicking either the Move Up or the Move Down buttons. As the imaging server is evaluating the rules, the first rule that results in a TRUE evaluation results in that image being supplied to the workstation.

Imaging Partition

The Imaging Partition page allows you to disable the ZENworks imaging partition if it exists. This page is accessed by clicking on the triangle on the Work To Do tab and selecting Imaging Partition from the drop-down list.

This is useful if you want to disable imaging on the workstation because no active imaging is occurring on the workstation. For example, you have a one-time image applied to a workstation annually in January. You need the partition to remain intact, but you can disable it the rest of the year.

NOTE Novell recommends that you disable the imaging partition and use PXE instead to perform preboot work.

Multicast

The Multicast page is accessed by clicking on the triangle on the Work To Do tab and selecting Multicast from the drop-down list.

This page allows you to specify whether the imaging server checks first to see whether the workstation should take part in a multicast session prior to checking the image selection rules within this policy. If the check box is checked, the imaging server checks the image selection rules prior to checking its multicast sessions.

NOTE This check box will have no effect on workstations configured to serve as session masters because that role takes priority over any other imaging setting.

PXE Settings Page

ZENworks Desktop Management ships with PXE-enabled software. You also may set the PXE settings for deploying any images. Novell now recommends that the Linux partition on the workstation be removed, and customers should move to the PXE method of image deployment. On this page you may set whether the PXE menu should appear automatically when PXE is launched, and you may also set the values that appear on the menu.

A PXE menu will display, for example, whether to receive an image or to take an image.

On this page you may select the following options:

- ▶ Always Display the PXE Menu—When checked, this item causes the PXE menu to always be displayed when the workstation is rebooted.

- ▶ Display the PXE Menu Only if Ctrl+Alt Are Held During Reboot— When selected, the PXE boot menu will not be displayed unless the user presses and holds down the Ctrl+Alt keys while the workstation is rebooting.

- ▶ Do Not Display the PXE Menu—This option prevents the PXE menu from being displayed.

- ▶ Read the PXE Menu from This File Instead of Using the Default Menu—This field allows you to browse to and select a file that will be used to display the PXE menu.

NOTE The PXE menu file that you specify must be located in the `tftp` directory on the server (`SYS:\TFTP` for NetWare, `Program Files\ZEN Preboot Services\TFTP\Data` for Windows NT/2000/XP).

To create the menu, you need to run the Menu Editor tool located on the server where the PXE boot services were installed. If you want, they can be run from the ZENworks Desktop Management CD in the `\ZEN Preboot Services\Menu Editor` directory. Run the `MEditor.exe` program.

Image-Safe Data Page

The Image-Safe Data page is a tab composed of four pages. These pages represent information and data placed or retrieved from the system regardless of the image used. The following depicts the pages available by selecting the small triangle drop-down menu on the tab.

An agent exists that may be placed on the workstation called the Image-Safe Data agent. This agent has the responsibility of moving data between a special sector on the disk that is used to store configuration information such as IP address or DHCP configuration along with workgroup information. This information on the disk is not affected by an image taken or placed on the drive.

When the Image-Safe Data agent runs on the workstation it makes sure that the information in the special sector and the operating system are synchronized properly. For example, following an image placement the agent moves the data from the disk into the operating system, setting up the DHCP and computer name. On a workstation that has not just been imaged, the agent moves the information from the operating system into the sector on the disk so that the data can be restored should a new image be placed on the drive. Should the agent not run, the workstation would be an exact mirror of the image (with the same IP and computer name configuration).

The Image-Save Data configuration page enables the imaging server to pass this configuration information to the agent via this disk sector.

IP Assignment Log Page

The IP Assignment Log page displays the IP addresses that the imaging server has assigned to any imaged or reimaged workstations. The set of available IP addresses can be set in the IP Configuration Page described following.

The IP Assignment page displays the log of these addresses that have been assigned.

This page can also be used to place an IP address back into the pool of available addresses. If you have an address that you want to place back into the pool, you can select it in the log list and then click the Remove button.

NOTE When you remove a specific IP address, it may not be properly represented in the IP Configuration range and therefore will not be reused.

If you specify a range in the IP Configuration page to be the set of IP addresses that you will make available for workstations, when the imaging server uses a portion of the range (at the ends), the range is refreshed on the configuration page. For example, if the range 123.65.234.1... 123.65.234.100 was in the configuration and IP address 123.65.234.1-10 was assigned, the range would be changed to 123.65.234.11... 123.65.234.100. Consequently, when you go to the log page and free up IP address 123.65.234.10, the range is not reconfigured, and the freed IP address is not reassigned. You must manually go to the configuration page and modify the range to include the addresses that you have freed.

IP Configuration Page

The IP Configuration page enables you to specify whether the workstations imaged by the imaging server will obtain their IP address from a DHCP server or via a static assignment done as part of the imaging process.

If you select the DHCP option, when the workstation is imaged the windows system is told to get IP addresses from a DHCP server. If, however, you select that you want to specify an IP address, the other fields on the page are activated.

To specify a static IP address you must first enter the subnet mask and default gateway that you want all your imaged workstations (imaged via the image server using this particular policy) to receive. You must also specify the range of IP addresses used by the imaging server and assigned uniquely to each of the imaged workstations. You specify the set of IP addresses by using the Add and Add Range buttons.

When the imaging server is given a request for an image, after the image has been placed onto the workstation, the IP address information is transmitted and assigned to the workstation. That address is then logged in the imaging server and not reused for another workstation.

To remove any address or ranges from the possible set, select the item and click the Remove button. These addresses will no longer be in the pool of available addresses for the imaging server to assign.

Windows Networking Page

In the Windows Networking page you can specify the computer name for the workstation and the workgroup for the system.

The computer name prefix that you enter in the field (maximum of seven characters) is prepended to a randomly generated set of characters and numbers to construct the final 15-character computer name for the workstation.

The Make the Computer a Member of the Following field enables you to specify the workgroup that you want for the workstation. You select which you prefer by selecting the field and entering the workgroup name.

DNS Settings

The DNS Settings page allows you to specify the DNS suffix and name servers that will be used by this policy. Simply type in the suffix you want to use and then click the Add button to bring up an IP address dialog box to specify the addresses of name servers. It is important to use the correct suffix and name servers for the ZENworks Desktop Management imaging engine to process imaging operations on a workstation.

Security Page

As part of the imaging system, the administrator has the ability to request that the workstation have an image taken of itself and placed onto the server. This is done by checking some fields in the workstation object (see Chapter 22, for more details), which causes the workstation to take an image of itself on its next reboot.

When the workstation takes an image of itself, or when an image is taken when a request is made through the Linux boot system, the image is transmitted to the image server. This image server then receives the .ZMG file and places it in the path specified. To protect the system from over-writing any files or by having users place the image files into inappropriate directories, the imaging server takes the information in the Security page and restricts the placement of the image files.

When you check the Allow Imaging to Overwrite Existing Files When Uploading option, you enable the system to overwrite any files that may have the same name as the one specified by the user for the name of the image file.

The Restrict Uploads to the Following Directories check box activates the requirement that all requested uploads must specify one of the directories identified. If the directory portion of the destination path, specified by the user, does not match one of the directories specified in the list on this page, the request to store the uploaded image is refused. To add paths to the list of accepted destinations, click the Add button and enter the acceptable path.

Paths in the directories may be one of the following formats:

Driveletter:path

Volume\path

NTShare\path

The system does not, for example, take any UNC path. When the user enters the location of the file, including the path, this information transmits to the imaging server; the server compares the directory portion of the path given with all the strings in this list. If a match occurs (that is, the directory is listed), the operation is accepted, and the image is taken and stored; otherwise, the operation fails, and the image is not taken.

Workstation Inventory Policy

The ZENworks Workstation Inventory Policy page allows you to configure how workstations associated with this workstation policy package will be inventoried.

See Chapter 20, "Using ZENworks Workstation Inventory," for more detailed information about the inventory system with ZENworks.

With the Workstation Inventory policy, you identify where the collector of the inventory information is located, whether hardware or software scanning is done, and the capability to customize the scan list to identify programs without any identifying header.

Figure 15.10 displays the Workstation Inventory page of the Workstation Inventory policy.

Within the inventory policy, the administrator has the ability to administer the following parameters:

- ▶ Inventory Service—Represents the service object in the tree that represents the service module running on a server in the network. This server agent is responsible for receiving the information from the workstations and processing it, either by placing it in a local Sybase database, or forwarding it on to the next level of the inventory database hierarchy (see Chapter 19, "Creating Server Policies"). All workstations that have this policy associated with them send their scanned information to the specified server agent.

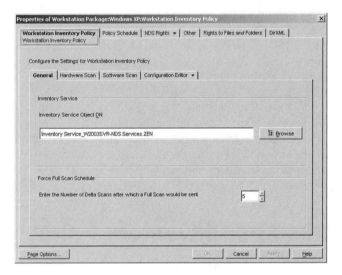

FIGURE 15.10
Workstation Inventory policy within a workstation policy package.

▶ Hardware Scan—Enables DMI (Desktop Management Interface), WMI (Windows Management Instrumentation), and custom scanning as well as configures the custom attributes to scan for.

▶ Software Scan—Enable Software Scan—Turns on ZENworks Desktop Management agents to perform a software scan in addition to the standard hardware scan.

▶ Software Scan—Custom Scan Editor—Brings up a dialog that enables you to configure information about files that may be found on a workstation. You can store the vendor name, product name, product version, filename, and file size in this list. When a file does not have header information, it is found in this table (by filename and size) and reported as the specified program. You can export and import these file lists into the eDirectory policy object.

▶ Configuration Editor—Allows you to import, export, and modify custom scanning configuration settings, such as Zip file extensions to scan for, vendor and product rules, and asset information.

NOTE The Policy Schedule page determines when the hardware and software inventories for associated workstations are run. See the "Computer Extensible Policies" section earlier in the chapter, for a description of this page.

ZENworks Desktop Management Agent Policy

The ZENworks Desktop Management agent is one of the most dynamic features of ZENworks because it provides you with the ability to maintain workstations. The ZENworks Desktop Management Agent policy, shown in Figure 15.11, allows you to configure the following settings that the agent running on workstations associated with the workstation policy package will use:

- ▶ Apply Middle Tier Address—Causes the address specified in this policy to be applied to the associated workstation agents.

- ▶ DNS Name or IP Address of the ZENworks Middle Tier Server— Specifies the IP address or DNS name for the web server running the ZENworks middle-tier server that the ZENworks Desktop Management agent uses to connect the workstation to the network. This field is activated only when the Apply Middle Tier Address check box is selected.

- ▶ eDirectory Refresh Rate (Minutes)—Specifies the amount of time in minutes that the ZENworks agent waits before checking eDirectory for changes in objects of policies. The default is 1380 minutes. Each time the agent refreshes, eDirectory information traffic is generated on your network, so if you have many workstations connecting through the agent, you may need to adjust this time to a larger amount.

- ▶ Display ZENworks Authentication Dialog—Allows you to specify whether ZENworks should present the login dialog rather than the standard Windows dialog.

- ▶ Allow Users to Change ZENworks Middle Tier Address on Authentication Dialog—On the dialog, a field shows the DNS name or IP address of the middle tier that the agents will be contacting. This check box allows users to edit this field, directing the agents to a different middle tier. This field is only accessible when the Display ZENworks Authentication Dialog check box is selected.

- ▶ Resident Workstation Welcome Bitmap (NT/2000/XP Only)— Allows you to specify the bitmap file that should be displayed when the workstation starts up. This file must be present on the workstation. (You can get it there with ZENworks.)

- ▶ Welcome Caption (NT/2000/XP Only)—Allows you to specify the text that will be displayed on the header of the welcome screen.

▶ Login Window Bitmap (NT/2000/XP Only)—Specifies the bitmap file that should be displayed as part of the login. This file must be present on the workstation, in the default Windows directory.

▶ Enable Volatile User Cache—Allows volatile user information that has been cached on a workstation to stay cached on the workstation for the specified period of time.

▶ Cache Volatile User Time Period (Days)—The default time is five days. Because volatile users are not created or removed at every login or logout, this makes login times much faster and makes it possible for a user to continue using the workstation even when the workstation is disconnected from the network and the user is not a registered user on the workstation. Here you can set the number of days before the cached information is removed. This field is available only when the Enable Volatile User Cache check box is activated.

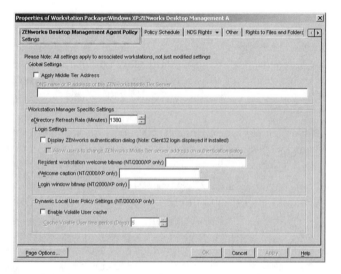

FIGURE 15.11
ZENworks Desktop Management Agent policy within a workstation policy package.

Scheduled Action Policy

The Scheduled Action policy is a plural policy that allows you to specify one or more actions to perform on workstations associated with the workstation policy package based on the policies schedule. Because it is a plural policy, you can create as many Scheduled Action policies for each platform in the workstation policy package as you need.

For example, if you needed all your DNS/DHCP clients to refresh their IP configuration every day at 8 a.m., you could create a Scheduled Action policy that runs the IPCONFIG utility twice, once with the /release and once with the /renew parameter. Then set the policy schedule to run daily at 8 a.m.

You create a Scheduled Action policy by going to the package you want and clicking the Add button on the Policies tab. This brings up a dialog that lists the plural policies available. Schedule Action policy will be one of them. Enter a policy name and click OK to add the policy to the package.

From the Scheduled Action Policy window Actions tab, shown in Figure 15.12, you can configure the following for each action by clicking the Add or Properties button:

- ▶ Name—Full path name to the application that will be executed on the workstation.

- ▶ Working Directory—The working directory the policy will use when applying the action.

- ▶ Parameters—Command-line parameters that will be added to the command line when the action is executed.

- ▶ Priority—The priority assigned to this action when compared to the priority of the user's access to the workstation. You can specify a priority of Action Default, Above Normal, Normal, and Below Normal. Setting the priority to Above Normal helps ensure that the action is performed quickly on the workstation no matter what the user is doing. Setting the priority to Below Normal impacts the user on the workstation less. For example, take into account this priority balance when scheduling actions. You may want to create one Scheduled Action policy for high priority actions and one for low priority.

▶ Terminate Time if Still Running After—The amount of time in minutes that the application will be allowed to run on the workstation before the policy forces its termination. The default is one minute. This can be useful in protecting users from experiencing too big of a performance hit by the scheduled action. It can also be useful in ensuring that all the actions in the policy are able to run.

You can also disable an individual action by selecting the individual action in the list and clicking the Disable button. This allows you to keep the action and its setting available for future use but not have it executed the next time the policy schedule is reached.

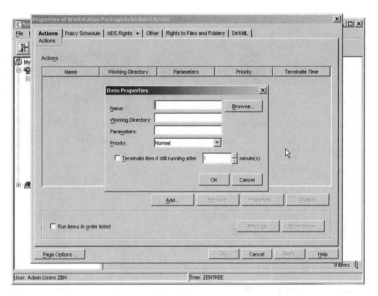

FIGURE 15.12
Scheduled Action policy within a workstation policy package.

The final setting you have on the Actions tab of the Scheduled Actions policy is to enable the Run Items in Order Listed option, shown in Figure 15.12. When enabled, this forces the actions to run one at a time in the order they are listed in the Actions list. This can be useful if you need to run a set of actions in a specific order. The Move Up and Move Down buttons allow you to change the order of the actions if necessary.

Summary

This chapter discussed all the policies that can be applied to workstations in your environment. These policies can manage the operating system of your Windows workstations as well as the behavior of ZENworks features and functions.

With these policies you can cause work to be done on a recurring, scheduled basis; you can apply corporate images and lock down workstations through group policies.

These policies provide you full life-cycle management for your workstations.

## CHAPTER 16

Setting Up Handheld Policies

This chapter discusses the use and creation of handheld policies. Handheld policies are associated with handheld device objects and handheld groups or containers and affect their working environment.

Relationship of Handheld Policies to Handheld Devices

Handhelds are associated with handheld policies through any of three ways:

- ▶ Policies can be associated with the handheld object directly.
- ▶ Policies can be associated with a parent container of the handheld object.
- ▶ Policies can be associated with a handheld group to which the device is a member.

The ZENworks Handheld server periodically scans the eDirectory tree and imports PDA objects as well as discovers any associated policies or applications. When the handheld agent (or proxy on the synchronization device) contacts an Access Point, the services will communicate back to the Handheld server and will be given any associated policies or applications.

There are three unique handheld policy packages:

▶ Handheld package—Holds policies given to the particular PDA to function on the device.

▶ Handheld Service package—Holds policies that direct the functions of the Handheld Server.

▶ Handheld User package—Holds policies that are for a handheld device but associated and based on a user rather than the particular device. These policies follow a user from device to device.

The following section examines how to set up the first of these—the Handheld Package.

Handheld Package

The Handheld package is one of the three types of handheld policy packages. The Handheld package is associated with a handheld device, handheld group, or container and contains policies that are enforced on the associated handheld device.

Setting Up a Handheld Package

To have a Handheld package, you must first create the policy package. To create a Handheld package do the following:

1. Start ConsoleOne.

2. Browse to the container where you want to have the policy package. Remember that you do not have to create the policy package in the container where you are doing the associations. You can associate the same policy package to many containers in your tree.

3. Create the policy package by right-clicking and choosing New→Policy Package or by selecting the Policy Package icon on the toolbar.

4. Select the Handheld Package object in the wizard panel and click Next.

5. Enter the desired name of the package in the Policy Package Name field and select the container where you want the package to be located. The Container field is already filled in with the selected container, so you should not have to browse to complete this field.

If it is not, click the browser button next to the field and browse to and select the container where you want the policy object stored. Click Next.

6. Select the Define Additional Attributes field to go into the properties of your new object and activate some policies. Click Finish.

7. Check and set any policies you want for this handheld policy package and click OK.

The ZENworks Handheld agents search the eDirectory for all associated policies and combine all policies associated with the device, groups, or containers. Should more than one of the same type of policy be accessible by the device, the policy "closest" in search order (device, groups, and then containers) is used.

The following subsections describe each of the fields and property pages available in the Handheld package.

Policies Property Page

The Policies property page displays the policies available and activated in this package. Three platforms are supported by the handheld policy package: Palm, WinCE (which also implies PocketPC), and BlackBerry. You can manage the policies for each of these platforms by selecting the desired platform through the drop-down menu on the tab.

Palm Policies

The Palm policies include the Palm Client Configuration policy, the Palm Configuration policy, and the Palm Security policy, as shown in Figure 16.1. Any number of File Retrieval policies may be included in the list by clicking the Add button.

The Policies tab allows for the configuration and activation of these policies. The Associations tab allows you to assign this policy to a device, container, or group of handheld devices.

Palm Access Point Configuration Policy

The Palm Access Client Configuration policy allows you to specify for the associated Palm devices the set of Access Points that are available for the device. The device will attempt to connect to the first address listed. If that address is unavailable, the device will attempt the next address in the list. This will continue until the device connects with an Access Point.

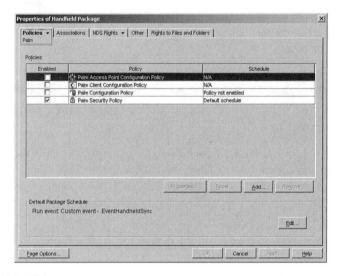

FIGURE 16.1
Palm policies in the handheld policy package.

To add an Access Point DNS name or IP address, activate the policy and click Properties. You will see a policy as shown in Figure 16.2.

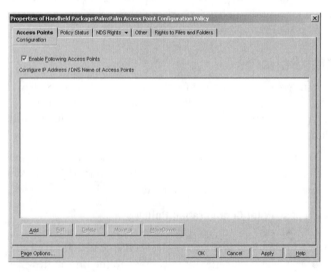

FIGURE 16.2
The Access Point configuration policy in the handheld policy package.

From this page, click the Add button to input a new Access Point address. You will be presented with a screen where you can select the Access Points that are known to the system (see Figure 16.3).

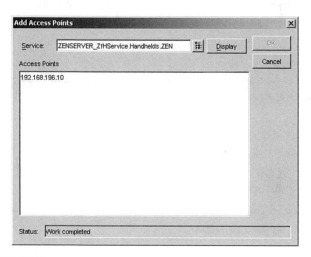

FIGURE 16.3
Palm Access Point entry dialog.

Ensure the field points to the Handheld service object in your system. Then click the Display button to show the known Access Points to this service. From this list select the Access Point you want to add to the policy. Click OK. This will take you back to the administered access point list.

To re-arrange addresses and modify the order, select an entry and click the Move Up or Move Down button. When completed, click the OK button to return to the policy package screen.

Palm Client Configuration Policy

The Palm Client Configuration policy allows the administrator to configure whether the client should prompt the user at synchronization time for his username and password. The configuration to prompt for the user credentials is also located in the handheld service object. This policy, when associated, can override the service object.

Click the Override the Server Configuration check box to have this policy override the server. Click Enable User Authentication on Handhelds to activate the prompting of the user credentials.

When user credentials are given, ZENworks uses LDAP to authenticate to eDirectory and then find any applications and policies that have been associated with the user.

Palm Configuration Policy

The Palm Configuration policy allows the administrator to configure the various parameters, buttons, and applications that should reside on the Palm device.

On the General tab of the Palm Configuration policy, you can configure the following parameters:

▶ Auto-off After—Specify the number of minutes before the Palm device should automatically power off.

▶ Stay on in Cradle—Flag to see whether the Palm device should stay on or off when sitting in the cradle.

▶ System Sound—Set the system sound to off, low, medium, or high.

▶ Alarm Sound—Set the alarm sound to off, low, medium, or high.

▶ Alarm Vibrate—Turn off or on the vibration of the device when an alarm fires.

▶ Alarm LED—Turn off or on the flashing of the Palm screen with an alarm.

▶ Game Sound—Set the game sound to off, low, medium, or high.

▶ Beam Receive—Turn beam receiving off or on.

On the Buttons tab, the policy can be used to configure the following buttons on the Palm device: Date Book, Address, To Do List, Note/Memo Pad, Calculator, HotSync Cradle, and HotSync Modem. Each button can be set to specify the application that should be launched when clicked. If the button is not defined, it remains as set on the handheld device.

Additionally, you can configure a special Pen behavior where dragging the pen from the writing area to the top of the screen causes an administered function to occur. The following functions can be chosen:

▶ Not Specified—Applies no function when the pen is moved.

▶ Backlight—Lights the backlight on the Palm device.

- ▶ Keyboard—Brings up the keyboard to the screen to allow input from the displayed keyboard.

- ▶ Graffiti Help—Displays the Graffiti Help screen, which displays the Graffiti keystrokes and the corresponding text character.

- ▶ Turn Off & Lock—Turns off and locks the Palm device.

- ▶ Beam Data—Beams the selected data or application.

On the Programs tab of the policy, the administrator can specify the applications that should be allowed or removed from the handheld PDA. Clicking the Add button allows the administrator to browse to and select an application found on the file system server. The selected application can then be set to be allowed or removed from the PDA device.

The Policy Status tab allows the administrator to click the Display button and query the Handheld Service running on the ZENworks Handheld server to determine whether the policy has been delivered and applied to associated devices.

The Policy Schedule tab allows you to select when the policy is applied to the associated Palm devices. The policy is always applied at synchro-nization time, but you can also specify a time or date when the policy will be effective. Advanced settings allow you to specify what should hap-pen if there was a fault attempting to send or apply the policy.

Palm Security Policy

The Palm security policy provides configuration settings that give a greater security to the palm data, through power-on passwords and enforcement of data and application removal should security be compromised.

The Security tab allows you to configure whether a password is to be required on the Palm device. On this screen, you can specify some addi-tional requirements to provide a greater measure of security when it comes to the password set on the device. This feature is not available natively on the PDA device and includes minimum password length, alphanumeric mix, password expiration, and unique passwords. Additionally, the policy can specify whether the password should be set as part of power-on sequence after inactivity for a specified time or at a specified time. ZENworks enforces this on the PDA device. ZENworks also remembers the last eight passwords to prevent the user from reenter-ing any of these last eight passwords.

The Self-Destruct tab allows you to specify when the data and applications should be destroyed on the PDA device through a system reset. The self-destruct can be set to occur should the user fail to enter the correct password after a specified number of attempts and/or number of days since the last time the device has synchronized. Should the device not be synchronized after the specified time, or the password fails, the device will be reset and factory restored—removing all data and installed applications.

NOTE The Self-Destruct feature causes the Palm device to perform a factory reset, removing all data and applications that have been placed on the device. This could result in all or some of your data being lost. You can restore from your last synchronization, but any changes since then will be lost.

The policy status can display how this policy has been deployed across associated devices. The policy schedule allows the specification of when the policy will be enforced.

This policy can be effective in protecting any sensitive corporate data from being lost or stolen. Should some problem arise and the device be reset inadvertently, the user need only resynchronize with ZENworks to have all associated applications and data restored either through ZENworks or HotSync features.

File Retrieval Policy

The File Retrieval policy is included in the package by clicking the Add button. You can have multiple File Retrieval policies in the package.

On the Files tab, the policy allows the specification of the files that should be collected from the handheld device. The filenames are case sensitive and can include wildcards. Additionally, this policy specifies the destination directory of the files. As part of the destination path, the policy may refer to specific values, including

- ▶ Device CN—Common name in eDirectory for the handheld device.
- ▶ Device DN—Distinguished name of the eDirectory object for the device.
- ▶ Device User—Username of the device.
- ▶ Retrieval Date—Date when the file was retrieved from the device.
- ▶ Retrieval Time—Time stamp of when the file was retrieved from the device.

▶ Device GUID—Unique GUID of the device that is automatically generated when the agents are placed on the device and the device is imported into the system.

▶ Server Name—Windows Name of the server that received the data.

The destination filename may also be set as the same as the original or then renamed to another name.

WinCE Policies

The WinCE policies include the WinCE Client Configuration policy, the WinCE Configuration policy, and the WinCE Security policy, as shown in Figure 16.4. Any number of File Retrieval policies may also be included in the list by clicking the Add button.

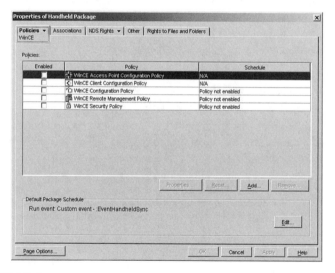

FIGURE 16.4
WinCE policies in the handheld policy package.

The Policies tab allows for the configuration and activation of these policies. The Associations tab allows you to assign this policy to a device, container, or group of handheld devices.

WinCE Access Point Configuration Policy

The WinCE Access Client Configuration policy allows you to specify for the associated Palm devices the set of Access Points that are available for the device. The device will attempt to connect to the first address listed. If that address is unavailable, the device will attempt the next address in the list. This will continue until the device connects with an Access Point.

To add an Access Point DNS name or IP address, activate the policy and click Properties. From this page, click the Add button to input a new Access Point address. To re-arrange addresses and modify the order, select an entry and click the Move Up or Move Down button. When completed, click the OK button to be return to the policy package screen.

WinCE Client Configuration Policy

The WinCE Client Configuration policy allows the administrator to configure whether the client should prompt the user at synchronization time for her username and password. The configuration to prompt for the user credentials is also located in the handheld service object. This policy, when associated, can override the service object.

Click the Override the Server Configuration check box to have this policy override the server. Click Enable User Authentication on Handhelds to activate the prompting of the user credentials.

When user credentials are given, ZENworks uses LDAP to authenticate to eDirectory and then find any applications and policies that have been associated with the user.

WinCE Configuration Policy

The WinCE Configuration policy allows the administrator to configure the various parameters, buttons, and applications that should reside on the WinCE device.

On the Buttons tab of the WinCE Configuration policy, you may configure 31 different button and action combinations. For each button assignment, the policy can be configured to reset the button to the default action, assign the button to launch a specified application, or set the button to activate a function, including Input Panel, Scroll Down, Scroll Left, Scroll Right, Scroll Up, Start Menu, or Today.

The Programs tab on the policy specifies the applications presented in the Start menu or on the desktop. Each specified shortcut allows you to give the application to launch when selected. The policy can also specify whether other menu or desktop items not specified should be hidden from view.

The Power tab specifies how long the device should run before being turned off, either when the device is on battery power or on external power.

The policy status can display how this policy has been deployed across associated devices. The policy schedule allows the specification of when the policy will be enforced.

WinCE Remote Management Policy

The WinCE Configuration policy allows the administrator to configure if Remote Control is allowed on associated WinCE devices. When you select to administer this policy, you will be presented with a screen shown in Figure 16.5.

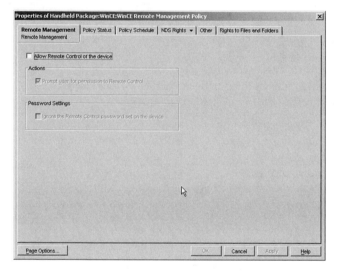

FIGURE 16.5
WinCE Remote Management administration screen.

Check the Allow Remote Control of the Device to activate the remote control capabilities of ZENworks for Handhelds. After this check box has been activated, you can chose any of the following options:

▶ Prompt User for Permission to Remote Control—This causes a prompt to appear on the PDA Device when you request a remote control session with the device. The user will have the option of accepting or declining the remote control session.

▶ Ignore the Remote Control Password Set on the Device—Selecting this will keep the user or administrator from having to know the local security password on the device in order to perform Remote Control functions.

WinCE Security Policy

The WinCE security policy provides configuration settings that give a greater security to the data, through power-on passwords and enforcement of data and application removal should security be compromised.

The Security tab allows you to configure whether a password will be required on the device. On this screen, you can specify some additional requirements to provide a greater measure of security when it comes to the password set on the device. This feature is not available natively on the handheld device and includes minimum password length, alphanumeric mix, password expiration, and unique passwords. Additionally, the policy can specify whether the password should be set as part of power-on sequence, after inactivity for a specified time, or at a specified time. ZENworks enforces this on the device. ZENworks also remembers the last eight passwords to make them unique.

The Self-Destruct tab allows you to specify when the data and applications should be destroyed on the device through a system reset. The self-destruct can be set to occur should the user fail to enter the correct password after a specified number of attempts and/or number of days since the last time the device has synchronized. Should the device not be synchronized after the specified time, or the password fails, the device will be reset and factory restored—removing all data and installed applications.

NOTE The self-destruct feature causes the WinCE device to perform a factory reset, removing all data and applications that have been placed on the device. This could result in all or some of your data being lost. You can restore from your last synchronization, but any changes since then will be lost.

The policy status can display how this policy has been deployed across associated devices. The policy schedule allows the specification of when the policy will be enforced.

This policy can be effective in protecting any sensitive corporate data from being lost or stolen. Should some problem arise and the device be reset inadvertently, the user need only resynchronize with ZENworks to have all associated applications and data restored either through ZENworks or HotSync features.

File Retrieval Policy

The File Retrieval policy is included in the package by clicking the Add button. You can have multiple file retrieval policies in the package.

On the Files tab the policy allows the specification of the files that should be collected from the handheld device. The filenames are case sensitive and can include wildcards. Additionally, this policy specifies the destination directory of the files. As part of the destination path, the policy may refer to specific values, including

- ▶ Device CN—Common name in eDirectory for the handheld device.
- ▶ Device DN—Distinguished name of the eDirectory object for the device.
- ▶ Device User—Username of the device.
- ▶ Retrieval Date—Date when the file was retrieved from the device.
- ▶ Retrieval Time—Time stamp of when the file was retrieved from the device.
- ▶ Device GUID—Unique GUID of the device that is automatically generated when the agents are placed on the device and the device is imported into the system.
- ▶ Server Name—Windows Name of the server that received the data.

The destination filename may also be set as the same as the original or the renamed to another name.

BlackBerry Policies

The BlackBerry policies include the BlackBerry Configuration policy, the BlackBerry Inventory policy, and the BlackBerry Security policy, as shown in Figure 16.6.

The Policies tab allows for the configuration and activation of these policies. The Associations tab allows you to assign this policy to a device, container, or group of handheld devices.

BlackBerry Configuration Policy

The BlackBerry Configuration policy allows the setting of the owner name and owner contact information on the device.

The policy status can display how this policy has been deployed across associated devices. The policy schedule allows the specification of when the policy will be enforced.

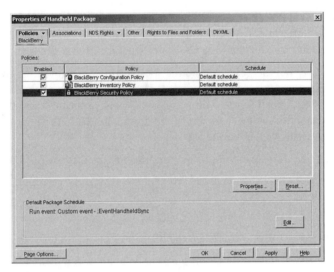

FIGURE 16.6
BlackBerry policies in the handheld policy package.

BlackBerry Inventory Policy

The inventory policy configures whether the hardware and software components of the BlackBerry device should be collected and included in the ZENworks inventory system.

The policy status can display how this policy has been deployed across associated devices. The policy schedule allows the specification of when the inventory will be collected.

BlackBerry Security Policy

The Security policy configures whether the BlackBerry device should require a password. When activated, the associated devices require that a password be set and entered on the device.

The policy status can display how this policy has been deployed across associated devices. The policy schedule allows the specification of when the policy will be enforced.

Handheld Service Package

The Handheld Service package is one of the three types of handheld policy packages. The Handheld Service package is associated with a handheld service object and contains policies enforced as part of the ZENworks Handheld server. The Associations tab allows you to assign this policy to a set of service objects, as shown in Figure 16.7.

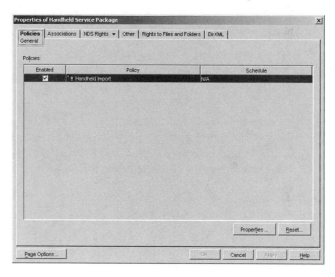

FIGURE 16.7
Handheld Service package.

The only policy currently available for the service is the Handheld Import policy.

The Handheld Import policy configures the behavior of the ZENworks Handheld service when a new handheld device is presented to the system and a handheld object needs to be created in eDirectory.

After you choose the properties of the import policy, the Platforms tab allows the specification as to whether the configuration should be applied to all platforms (General) or to the Palm, WinCE, or BlackBerry devices. Each platform may be individually configured. Regardless of the platform, the configuration is done in the same manner.

The Location tab within the Platforms screen allows the specification of the following:

▶ Allow Importing of Handhelds—Specifies whether the policy should be active and devices be imported into eDirectory.

- ► Create Handheld Objects In—Allows you to select the container where the newly created handheld objects should reside. The choices are

  - ► Selected Container—If chosen, an additional field is activated that allows you to browse to and select the container.

  - ► Server Container—Places the handheld object in the container where the handheld service object is located. An additional field is activated that allows the specification of a relative path from the server container.

  - ► Associated Object Container—Places the handheld device object in the container where the policy is associated. An additional field is activated that allows the specification of a relative path from the associated container.

The Naming tab on this screen allows configuration of the automatically generated name for the handheld device object. The following can be selected as part of the name:

- ► Device—The type of device—Palm, WinCE, or BlackBerry.

- ► Owner—The name entered into the device as owner.

- ► Computer—The name of the synchronized computer. With the BlackBerry device, this is the email service name.

- ► User Defined—A defined string.

A combination of these components can be configured to generate the name of the device.

The Groups tab allows you to specify the groups into which this device should automatically be placed as a member. This allows newly introduced devices to be automatically part of a group, which may have associated policies or applications.

Handheld User Package

The Handheld User package contains the following policies: Palm Access Point Configuration policy, Palm Configuration policy, Palm Security policy, WinCE Access Point Configuration policy, WinCE Configuration policy, WinCE Remote Management policy, WinCE Security policy,

BlackBerry Configuration policy, BlackBerry Inventory policy, and BlackBerry Security policy. Each of these policies is described in other sections earlier in the chapter.

The Handheld User package policies will be enforced over handheld policies should the same policies be activated in each package.

Summary

ZENworks provides several handheld policies that strengthen the security of these devices. Over the last year, more than 250,000 handheld devices were lost in U.S. airports alone. Think of how much corporate confidential information was exposed with these losses. ZENworks helps to manage these devices and keeps your data safe.

Additionally, with ZENworks you can retrieve information and deliver content and applications to handheld devices throughout your corporation, to individual devices, or even to a particular user.

## CHAPTER 17

Setting Up Container Policies

In addition to user and workstation policies discussed in previous chapters, a container policy package can also be created. This package is associated with a container and affects the understanding of policies below the container level. This chapter discusses the container policy package.

What Is a Container Policy Package?

A *container policy package* contains a set of policies associated only with containers. These policies affect the behavior of other ZENworks user and workstation policies and are therefore associated only with containers.

ZENworks agents work in a standard way to search out policies within a tree, starting at either the user or the device object depending on the application of the policy. After the user or device object is located, the ZENworks agents seek out a container policy package. The first container policy package found while the agent is walking up the tree is used to modify the behavior of the search for all other policies. After the container policy package is discovered, the agents use the information in the package to seek other user or device policy packages.

Setting Up a Container Package

To have a container package affect policies, you must first create it. To create a container policy package, do the following:

1. Start ConsoleOne.

2. Browse to the container where you want to have the policy package.

NOTE Remember that you do not have to create the policy package in the container where you are doing the associations. You can associate the same policy package with many containers in your tree.

---

3. Create the policy package by right-clicking and choosing New→Policy Package or by selecting the Policy Package icon on the toolbar.

4. Select the container package object in the wizard panel and click Next.

5. Enter the desired name of the package in the Policy Package Name field and select the container where you want the package to be located. The Container field is already filled in with the selected container, so you should not have to browse to complete this field. If not, click the browse icon button next to the field, browse to and select the container where you want the policy object stored, and click Next.

6. Select the Define Additional Attributes field to go into the properties of your new object and activate some policies and then click Finish.

7. Check and set any policies you want for this container policy package and click OK.

The following sections describe each of the tabs, panels, and options available on the Properties of Container Package window.

Policies Tab

The Policies tab on the Properties of Container Package window lists the set of available policies and those that are active (see Figure 17.1).

Because no platform-specific policies currently exist in the container package, only the General panel of the Policies tab is available.

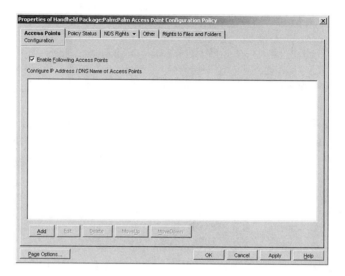

FIGURE 17.1
The Policies tab on the Properties of Container Package page, showing the General panel.

After you have created a container package, you can activate policies. By clicking a policy within the policy package, that policy becomes active. An active policy is designated by a check in the check box (refer to Figure 17.1). The details of any particular policy can be modified by selecting the policy and clicking the Properties button. The Reset button resets the selected policy back to its system defaults.

Associations Tab

The Associations tab on the Properties of Container Package page displays all the locations in the tree (containers) where the policy package has been associated. These associations do not necessarily reflect where the policy package is located in the directory. The agents associated with users or workstations that are in or below those containers have this policy package enforced. Clicking the Add or Remove buttons enables you to add or remove containers in the list associated with this policy.

Search Policy

A search policy governs the behavior of the ZENworks Desktop agents as they search for user and workstation policies. With all the ZENworks agents, there could be some significant walking of the tree as it searches for the policies of the identified user and workstations, especially if the tree is of a significant depth. This is the reason why ZENworks Desktop Management has this search policy.

Often the performance of your network searching with ZENworks is not significant until you cross a partition boundary. When you cross a partition boundary, the system must make a connection and authenticate to another server. This is particularly time consuming should the system need to cross a WAN link.

With the ZENworks Middle Tier, the agents cannot determine where a partition boundary is located. Consequently, in the newer version of ZENworks the policy has been changed to remove the partition boundary option and replace it with the associated container.

The search policy tells the ZENworks agent how far up the tree it should search and what order (object, group, container) should be followed to find the policies.

NOTE The order is significant because often the first policy found governs the behavior of the system.

Search Level Tab

This tab on the Search Policy window (see Figure 17.2) enables the administrator to identify how far up the tree the ZENworks Desktop Management agents should travel in their search for policies.

The following fields may be administered in the search level features on the Search Level tab:

▶ Search for Policies Up To—Enables you to specify the container in the tree at which searching will complete. The choices that can be made through the drop-down list may be any of the following:

   ▶ [Root]—Search up to the root of the tree.

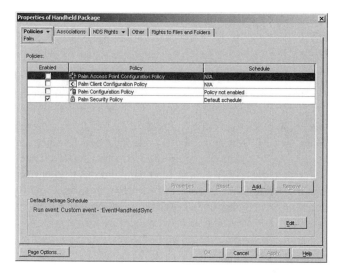

FIGURE 17.2
Search Level tab on the Search Policy window within a container policy
package.

▶ Object Container—Search up to the container that holds the
object associated with the policy. For example, if you were
searching for a user policy package, the object container
would be the context of the user object.

▶ Associated Container—Search up the tree to the container
where the policy is associated.

▶ Selected Container—Searches up to the specified container.
When this option is chosen, the Selected Container field is
activated, and you can browse in this field to the desired
container.

▶ Search Level—Enables you to specify an additional level of container beyond that given in the Search for Policies Up To field. A search
level value of 0 causes searches to be limited to the specified container. A search level of a positive numerical value enables searching the number of containers specified. Should the search level be a
negative number, the search proceeds at the specified level minus
the number specified. For example, if the Object Container value
is selected, the object is in the Provo.Utah.Novell container, and
the search level is 0, the searching stops at the Provo.Utah.Novell

container. If the search level is 2, the searching continues to the Novell container. If the search level is –1, no policy will be found because the object container is already above the search level.

At first it may not be apparent why a negative search level exists, but this value does have a purpose. Suppose, for example, that your tree is set up as Organization.Region.Company, where the organization is the container given to each organization in the company, and the region represents the area of the company. Now suppose that you want policies to be effective only for each organization; you could set up one single search policy at the Region.Company level with a selected container as Region.Company and a search level of –1. This would enable each organization to have a customized policy and ensure that no one organization's policies would impact another's because the search would stop at the organization level.

Search Order Tab

This tab enables the administrator to identify the order that the agents should go looking for policies. The default order is always object, group, and then container. This policy enables the administrator to change this order.

You can modify the search order by selecting the item in the Search Order list and then selecting the up or down arrows to rearrange the list. Clicking the Remove button removes the selected order. Clicking the Add button adds that search order item, if any have been previously deleted.

NOTE Because the first policy found has the greatest significance in the behavior of the system, make sure that you have the order set (from top to bottom) in the way that you want to find that first policy.

Be aware of when it is a good idea to use the search order policy. Because many ZENworks features stop walking up the tree when a policy is found, it would be wise to make policies search in order of object, container, and then group. This is because the proximity of these objects in the tree is always going to be closer to the partition on the server. The object is, obviously, always the closest in the tree to the workstation or user object. Next the container is the closest in the tree-walking scenario because the container must be known for the object to be found in the tree. Consequently, the container is very close in the local replica to the object. Groups, however, can be stored in any container, and they could be in a completely different part of the tree than the object. Therefore, the amount of walking of the tree that is potential with a group is significant. Any significant walking of the tree has a corresponding performance cost, and this should be considered as you manage your tree and search policies.

Refresh Interval Tab

The Refresh Interval tab on the Search Policy window enables the administrator to identify whether the policy manager should refresh the set of policies from eDirectory and how often to check eDirectory for new or changed policies. The policy manager in ZENworks Server Management is an agent that resides on the server and is responsible for getting ZENworks Server Management policies and enforcing them on the server. An option on the Refresh Interval tab gives this refresh interval configuration to this agent. If the check box is off, meaning that the agent should not refresh from eDirectory, the agent gets the policies only at initialization time, or should the server or the agent be restarted. If the check box is on, the agent checks for any changes or new policies every time the interval has passed.

This same behavior is also available in Workstation Manager, the agent that enforces policies on the workstation. It also looks for new policies and scheduled actions, and only does that at boot time and at the identified intervals.

Handheld Application Search Policy

A separate Handheld Application Search policy has been created to manage the way that the handheld device agents search the tree for their applications. This policy has the same options as the general search policy.

Summary

ZENworks allows you to create a container policy package. This package is associated with a container and affects the understanding of policies below the container level.

## CHAPTER 18

Creating Service Location Policies

In addition to user, workstation, and container policies discussed in previous chapters, a service location package also exists. This package is associated with a container and identifies where agents associated with objects below the associated container may locate services they need, such as the database to record events or workstation inventory. This chapter discusses the service location package.

What Is a Service Location Package?

A *service location package* contains a set of policies associated only with containers. These policies are expected to identify the location of resources other ZENworks agents throughout the network need. These resources are associated through the container to all agents working on behalf of the objects in the container or subcontainer.

For example, if you have set up a service location package associated with container A and activated a database location policy specifying that the database is located on server A, all the workstation agents on the PCs whose workstation objects are located in or below container A look in the tree and walk up the tree to find the service location package associated with container A. In this policy, they would find the database where they should store their events or inventory information located on server A because the database location policy in the service location package would be active. The agents would then contact the database on server A and send it their information.

Setting Up a Service Location Package

To have a service location package identify resources in the network, you must first create it. To create a service location package, do the following:

1. Start ConsoleOne.

2. Browse to the container where you want to have the policy package.

NOTE You do not have to create the policy package in the container where you are doing the associations. You can associate the same policy package to many containers in your tree.

---

3. Create the policy package by right-clicking and choosing New→Policy Package or by selecting the Policy Package icon on the toolbar.

4. Select the service location package object in the wizard panel and click Next.

5. Enter the desired name of the package in the Policy Package Name field and select the container where you want the package to be located. The Container field is already filled in with the selected container, so you should not have to browse to complete this field. If it is not filled in, click the browse icon button next to the field, browse to and select the container where you want the policy object stored, and click Next.

6. Select the Define Additional Attributes field to go into the properties of your new object, activate some policies, and click Finish.

7. Check and set any policies you want for this service location package and click OK.

The following sections describe each of the fields, property pages, and tabs available in the service location package.

Policies Tab

All the policies for users are activated within the Policies tab on the Service Location Package page. Initially, the Policies tab displays the General panel. Because in the service location no platform-specific policies currently exist, no drop-down menu is present on the Policies tab. The Policies tab lists the set of available policies and those that are active (see Figure 18.1).

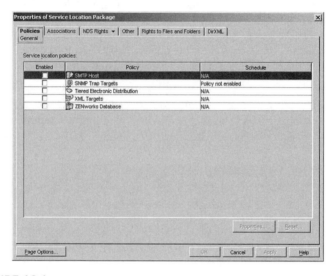

FIGURE 18.1
The Policies tab of the Service Location Package page.

After you have created a service location package, you can activate policies. By clicking on a policy within the policy package, that policy becomes active. An active policy is designated with a check in the check box. The details of any particular policy are modified by selecting the policy and clicking the Properties button.

The Reset button on the Policies page resets the selected policy to the system defaults for that policy.

Associations Tab

The Associations tab of the Service Location Package page displays all the locations in the tree (containers) where the policy package has been associated. These associations do not necessarily reflect where the policy package is located in the directory. The agents associated with users or workstations in or below those containers have this policy package enforced. Clicking the Add or Remove buttons enables you to add or remove containers in the list that are associated with this policy.

SMTP Host Policy

Several features in ZENworks include the capability to have information and events emailed to identified users. To send the email, the agents must contact the SMTP server in your environment, communicate, and send the email through that system. This policy enables you to specify the IP address of the SMTP host that the agents associated with this policy (through inheritance) use.

The SMTP Host tab, accessed from the Service Location Object window in ConsoleOne, enables the administrator to identify the IP address of the SMTP mail server in your environment (see Figure 18.2).

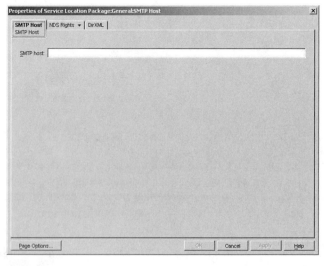

FIGURE 18.2
SMTP Host tab of the SMTP Host policy page.

Just place your cursor in the SMTP Host field and enter the IP address of the SMTP mail host. You must enter the IP address or the DNS name of the host.

SNMP Trap Target Policy

In ZENworks, the Application Launcher has been enhanced to send an SNMP message to a central server that stores these messages and enables you to print reports on the traps. These traps can identify whether an application was successfully distributed; if not, the trap identifies the potential problem with the distribution.

NOTE This policy used to be in the container policy package in previous versions of ZENworks.

The SNMP Trap Target policy identifies the location of the service accepting and recording the SNMP messages from the Application Launcher. In previous versions of ZENworks, you had to place the database service as an SNMP Trap Target policy to receive Application Launcher events. This is no longer necessary because the Application Launcher can write directly to the database.

Figure 18.3 displays the SNMP Trap Policy tab on the SNMP Trap Targets page, accessed from the Service Location Object window in ConsoleOne. The service on the workstation walks the tree to find this policy and uses the service location stored in this policy as the destination for SNMP messages.

After you have brought up the policy page, you can add as many trap targets as you want. The service on the workstation sends the SNMP message to all the specified trap targets. Click the Add button and specify whether the destination can be achieved with an IP address or a DNS name. After selecting the type, a dialog box comes up for you to enter either the address or the DNS name of the target service.

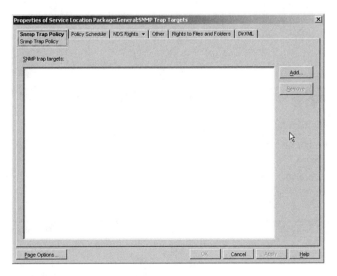

FIGURE 18.3
The SNMP Trap Policy tab of the SNMP Trap Targets policy page.

XML Targets

The XML Targets tab of the XML Targets policy page (see Figure 18.4) allows you to specify the URL(s) used to view information exported from ZENworks Application Management in XML format. XML provides ZENworks with a flexible way to create useful, platform-independent reports. The XML Targets tab can be accessed from the Service Location Object window in ConsoleOne.

Click the Add button to add any URL you want so that you may view exported XML reports from application management.

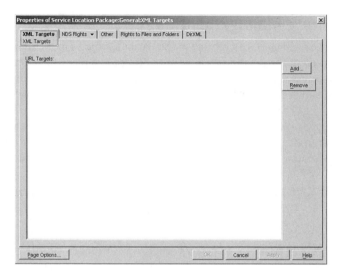

FIGURE 18.4
The XML Target tab of the service location package.

ZENworks Database Policy

Many agents in the system want to record information into the
ZENworks database installed on your system. Previously, agents (such as
the Application Launcher agent) would get their event information into
the database indirectly through SNMP messages. In ZENworks, the
Application Launcher agent and other agents write directly to the database and do not rely on the SNMP system to record events. For these
agents to discover the database they should place their information into,
they walk the tree from the object representing the system they are supporting until they find a service location package with an active
ZENworks database policy.

The database policy then refers to a ZENworks database object in the
directory (created at installation time), which, in turn, contains the
server—or IP address of the server—supporting the database. The system
uses other information in the database object as well.

Inventory Management Page

This page enables you to browse to the database objects in the directory that represent the databases you want to use for inventory management. All agents associated with this policy write their log information into these databases. Figure 18.5 is a snapshot of the Inventory Management that can be accessed from the Service Location Object window in ConsoleOne. From this tab, you can click the browse icon button and navigate to the ZENworks inventory database you want to use for this service location policy.

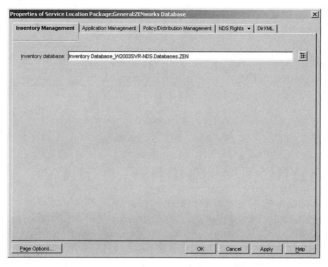

FIGURE 18.5
The Inventory Management tab of the ZENworks Database page.

Application Management Tab

You can also specify the location of the application management database for the service location. From the ZENworks Database page, click the Application Management tab (refer to Figure 18.5); then click the browse icon button to navigate to the ZENworks Application Management database object you want to use for this service location.

Policy/Distribution Management Tab

This section of the policy allows the specification of the database that will hold the Policy and Distribution event and tracking information. Click the browse icon button to navigate and select the ZENworks Server Management database object you want to use for this service location.

Objects associated with this service location object use the inventory or application management databases you assign to store and retrieve data.

Tiered Electronic Distribution Policy

In ZENworks, you can define several configuration items in this policy that are applied to the components in the Tiered Electronic Distribution (TED) system. Using this policy keeps you from having to administer these items in each of the subscribers or distributors you create in the network. This policy is found by association and is not placed in the Distributed Policy Package. This policy will be found by the distributor walking the tree, from the perspective of itself or the subscriber, and then includinge the found policies in the standard distribution.

The Settings Policy Page

This page is found under the General tab and represents some general configuration settings effective for any associated distributors and/or subscribers. Figure 18.6 shows this page.

On this property page, you may enter the following settings:

▶ Input Rate (Kbytes/Sec)—Represents the number of bytes per second that you allow a subscriber to consume for all distributions for input. The default is for the system to send at the maximum rate possible on the server. If you choose to enter 4096, for example, the subscriber will not exceed receiving 4KB per second for incoming messages. This setting does not change the I/O rate for the distributor when gathering distributions via the FTP or HTTP agents, which always consume as much bandwidth as possible.

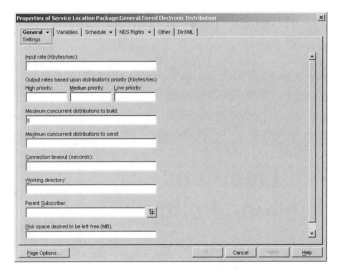

FIGURE 18.6
Settings property page of a Tiered Electronic Distribution policy object.

▶ Output Rates Based upon Distribution's Priority (Kbytes/sec)—
Represents the number of bytes per second that you allow a distributor to consume for all subscriptions based on the distribution's
priority. If you entered 4096 into the Low Priority category, for
example, the distribution whose priority is set for low will not
exceed sending 4KB per second.

▶ Maximum Concurrent Distributions To Build—Each time the system is going to perform a distribution, it creates a Java thread that
handles building of the distribution. This value identifies the maximum number of threads that you allow the distributor to create to
build distributions.

▶ Maximum Concurrent Distributions To Send—Each time the system is going to send a built distribution, it creates a Java thread
that handles sending the distribution to the subscriber. This value
identifies the maximum number of threads that you allow the distributor to create where each can send distributions.

▶ Connection Timeout (Seconds)—The default for this is 300 seconds. You can also enter your own timeout value. When the timeout value is exceeded, the distributor fails the distribution and
retries the distribution every 2 minutes for the next 30 minutes (as

long as it is still in its scheduled window). If, after all 15 retries, the distribution still has not succeeded, the distributor fails, cancels the distribution, and does not attempt to distribute it again until the next scheduled time for the channel to be distributed.

▶ Working Directory—Identifies the directory where the distributor or subscriber stores its distribution files. The agents on the distributor, when they are called to collect the files and compress them into the distribution file, store the files in this working directory. The agents on the subscriber use this working directory to uncompress the files before copying them to their final destination. It is not recommended to use the SYS volume because of the potential system problems should that volume become full.

▶ Parent Subscriber—Enables you to identify whether the associated subscribers should receive distributions from the specified parent subscriber (as opposed to getting them directly from the distributor).

▶ Disk Space Desired to Be Left Free (MB)—Enables you to establish a buffer on your hard drive so that a certain percentage of it will always be free. This is important for large packages so that there is still enough drive space to install the application after it is delivered.

The Messaging Property Page

The Messaging property page is under the General tab and can be configured by clicking the small triangle on the right side of the General tab and selecting Messaging under the drop-down menu that appears. Figure 18.7 shows a sample Messaging page. Unless you are having problems and are diagnosing issues, it is not recommended to request a message level higher than 4.

For each of the appropriate fields, you may enter one of the following message levels:

▶ Level 6—Includes all the other levels plus developer trace information.

▶ Level 5—Includes all Level 4 messages in addition to trace information, which notifies the observer of the modules being executed. This level also captures and displays all Java exceptions.

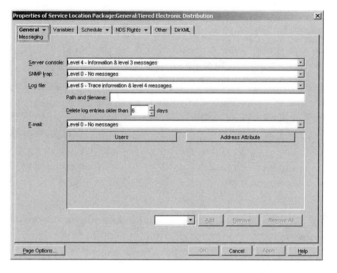

FIGURE 18.7
Messaging property page of a Tiered Electronic Distribution policy object.

► Level 4—Includes all the Level 3 messages and, in addition, informational messages that identify key points in the system.

► Level 3—Displays any warnings encountered in the system in addition to all the Level 2 messages.

► Level 2—Displays the successes satisfied by the system and also includes all the Level 1 messages.

► Level 1—Displays only errors encountered in the system.

► Level 0—Displays no messages.

You can administer the following configuration parameters on the Messaging property page:

► Server Console—Identifies the level of messages displayed on the distributor or subscriber console (not the main server console).

► SNMP Trap—Identifies the level of messages that should be sent as an SNMP trap to the SNMP host. The SNMP Host policy must be defined and active in an effective (for the distributor or subscriber object) Service Location package for traps to be sent.

▶ Log File—Identifies the level of messages that should be stored in the log file. Additionally, you can configure the following about the log file:

    ▶ Path and Filename—The filename of the log file. The default location for a distributor is `SYS:\TED\DIST\DIST.LOG` and `SYS:\TED\SUB\SUB.LOG` for a subscriber. You should probably change the location of the log file because it can grow as well. The log file may adversely affect the system because it is located on the SYS volume by default.

    ▶ Delete Log Entries Older Than X Days—Identifies the number of days (X) worth of log entries that should remain in the log file. The default is 6 days. Therefore, any log entries older than 6 days are cleared from the log file. The process of removing the old entries from the log happens once every 24 hours.

▶ E-mail—Specifies the level of messages sent in an email to the identified users. The SMTP Host policy in the ZENworks for Servers 3 Service Location package must be active, and the package must be effective for the distributor or subscriber object to enable it to discover the address of the SMTP host to send the email. If this is not specified, the email will not be sent.

In addition to identifying the level of messages, you must also specify who should receive these messages. To add users to the list and have them receive the message, you must first click on the drop-down box next to the Add button and select whether you want to add an eDirectory User or Group, or specify an email address in the drop-down menu. When you select a user, you are asked to browse to the user in the directory, and the system takes the email address attribute from the user and uses that as the address for the user. Should you choose a group, all the users in the group are sent the email message, and the email attribute is used for each of those users.

Should you not want to use the email address attribute in the user object, you may select the down arrow in the Address Attribute field (see Figure 18.8) and select which of the eDirectory User attributes you want to identify as containing the email address. It is expected that the attribute you identify will contain a valid email address.

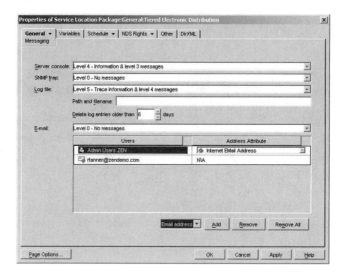

FIGURE 18.8
Email address attribute selection from eDirectory user.

If you choose to enter an explicit email address rather than select a user or a group, click the Add button and choose E-mail Address. You are prompted to enter a valid email address. The entered email address is assumed to be valid and is shown as the User's field in the table with an "N/A" in the Address Attribute field.

The Variables Property Pages

Variables enable you to substitute a name in the distribution with the value specified for the subscriber. When you create a distribution, you can, for example, use variables in the volumes and directory names. When the distribution is sent to the subscriber and the extraction agent is called, the agent replaces these variables with their defined value in the subscriber object. If no value is given, the variable name (including the % [percent sign]) is used for that value.

The variables defined in this policy are additions to the variables defined in any associated subscriber. If you define the same variable in the effective policy and directly in the subscriber object, the variable definition found directly in the subscriber object is used.

Unlike ZENworks Server Management policies and software distribution packages, the TED software performs only basic substitution of variable to value and does not allow you to reference an eDirectory object or its attribute. This is done to eliminate the requirement that the subscriber have access to eDirectory and all the objects in the tree. This would be especially difficult if the subscriber is an external subscriber—not even in the same tree as the distributor!

If you created a distribution and specified %DEST_VOLUME% as the volume name, for example, when the subscriber extracts the files, the agent substitutes the variable DEST_VOLUME defined in this property page with the value. If DEST_VOLUME is not defined, a directory called %DEST_VOLUME% is created in the SYS volume.

Remember to be consistent in your conventions and your variable names. You should probably come up with a set of common variables that you define with each subscriber that you set up. When you create a distribution, you can use these variables in defining the directories in which the distribution will be placed. Remember, the subscribers that receive the distribution are purely based on who subscribes to the channels where you place the distribution. If you are not consistent in your variables across all subscribers, you may inadvertently send a distribution to a subscriber that does not have the variable defined. This results in the distribution being extracted in a place you do not expect (probably on the SYS volume). Some variables that you should consider defining in each of your subscribers are as follows:

▶ DEST_VOLUME—Define this variable as the volume that receives the distribution after it is extracted.

▶ DEST_APPVOL—Define this to be the volume where your applications are stored.

▶ DEST_APPDIR—Define this to be the directory under the application volume where you place your applications.

The Schedule Property Page

This policy page enables you to specify how often the associated distributor software on the server goes to eDirectory and reads the configuration information for itself, the distributions for which it is responsible, the channels with which its distributions are associated, and the subscribers to those channels. The default value is Never, which means that the associated distributors read information from eDirectory only when it is first loaded on the server, anytime you reboot or restart the server or distributor process, or if you explicitly refresh the distributor from the distributor console or from the distributor object in ConsoleOne.

This page enables you to select when the configuration should be read and applied: Never, Daily, Monthly, Yearly, Interval, or Time.

After you select when you want the configuration applied, you have additional fields to select in the lower portion of the screen. The following sections discuss the various options.

Never

This option loads the distributor with the configuration information only when it is first loaded on the server or after each reboot or restart.

Daily

When you choose to have the configuration applied to the system daily, you need to also select when the changes will be made.

This schedule requires that you select the days when you want the configuration applied by clicking the days you want. The selected days appear as depressed buttons.

In addition to the days, you can select the times the configuration is applied. These start and stop times provide a range of time where the configuration will be applied.

You can have the configuration also reapplied within the time frame specified per hour, minute, or second by clicking the Repeat the Action Every field and specifying the time delay.

Monthly

Under the monthly schedule, you can select which day of the month the configuration should be applied, or you can select Last Day of the Month to handle the last day because all months obviously do not end on the same calendar date (that is, 30 days hath September, April, June, and November; all the rest have 31 except for February…).

After you select the day, you can also select the time range when the configurations are reread and applied.

Yearly

Select a yearly schedule if you want to apply the configuration only once a year. On this screen, you must choose the day that you want the configuration to be applied. This is done by selecting the Calendar button to the right of the Date field. This brings up a Monthly dialog box where you can browse through the calendar to select the date you want. This calendar does not correspond to any particular year and may not take into account leap years in its display. This is because you are choosing a date that will come along in the present and future years.

After you select the date, you can also select the time range when the configuration should be read and applied.

To keep all the distributors from simultaneously accessing eDirectory, you can select Randomly Dispatch Policy During Time Period. This causes each server to choose a random time within the time period when the server will retrieve and apply the configuration.

Interval

This schedule type enables you to specify how often to repeatedly read and apply the configuration. You can specify the interval with a combination of days, hours, minutes, and seconds. This type of schedule waits for the interval to pass before applying the configuration for the first time and then for each sequence after that.

Time

This allows you to specify a calendar date and time when the configuration is applied. When the current date on the server is beyond the identified date, the configuration is applied.

Summary

The Service Location package provides policies that can be applied to the containers in your directory to provide configuration information to ZENworks agents throughout your network.

CHAPTER 19

Creating Server Policies

This chapter discusses each of the various policies available to manage the servers in your environment.

What Is a Server Package?

A *server package* contains a set of policies associated with agents that run on servers. These policies are expected to give policy information and configuration behavior to these agents and may be associated with the server, a group of servers, or a container.

The agents follow the expected walking of the tree to locate their server package. Namely, they find the search policy and then use the order specified in the search policy, or they use the default. The default is to search for a server package associated with the server, then search the group of servers, and finally search the container. The first policy package is the one that the agents use.

Previous releases of ZENworks introduced a Distributed Server package. The Distributed Server package is unique to the Server Package because of how the package is delivered to the server. The Distributed Server package is delivered to servers via ZENworks Policy and Distribution Services, namely Tiered Electronic Distribution (see Chapter 25, "Setting Up Tiered Electronic Distribution (TED)" for more information).

The Distributed Server package must be included in a Distribution and then sent to the servers that are to apply the policy. Distributions are sent to servers who subscribe to the channel into which they are placed.

Setting Up a Server Package

To have a server package, you must first create the policy package. To create a server package, do the following:

1. Start ConsoleOne.

2. Browse to the container where you want to have the policy package. Remember that you do not have to create the policy package in the container where you are doing the associations. You can associate the same policy package to many containers in your tree.

3. Create the policy package by right-clicking and choosing New→Policy Package or by selecting the Policy Package icon on the toolbar. This will launch a wizard to help you in the creation of your package.

4. Select the Server Package object and click Next.

5. Enter the desired name of the package in the Policy Package Name field and select the container where you want the package to be located. The Container field is already filled in with the selected container, so you should not have to browse to complete this field. If not, click the browser button next to the field and browse to and select the container where you want the policy object stored. Click Next.

6. Select Define Additional Attributes to go into the properties of your new object and activate some policies. Click Finish.

7. Check and set any policies you want for this server package and click OK.

The following subsections describe each of the fields and property pages available in the server package.

Policies Property Page

All the policies for servers are activated within the Policies property page. Initially the page is on the General policies. As other platforms are selected, additional policies are displayed. You can select which platform to display by placing the mouse over the small triangle on the right side of the Policies tab. This activates a drop-down menu that enables you to select which platform-specific page you want to display.

The following sections briefly discuss each of the policy pages, and then we cover the specifics of each policy.

General Policies

When you first go into the properties of the server package you are presented with the Policies property page. The Policies page first displays the General category. All the policies activated in the General category are active for *all* server platforms supported by ZENworks and associated with the server.

Figure 19.1 shows the initial property page of the server package.

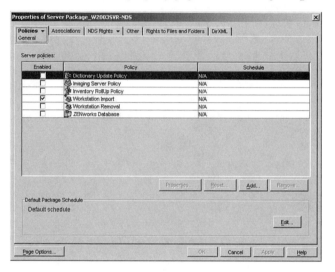

FIGURE 19.1
Server package Policies General property page.

As you can see from Figure 19.1, currently six policies are available to all the platforms supported by ZENworks. They are Dictionary Update policy, Imaging Server policy, Inventory Rollup policy, Workstation Import policy, Workstation Removal policy, and ZENworks Database policy. And if you click the Add button you can include additional Wake on LAN policies. These, as well as all the other policies, are discussed later in this chapter.

To activate a policy you simply need to click on the box to the left of the policy. You can go into the details of the policy and set additional configuration parameters on that specific policy.

Windows Policies

Within the Policies tab you can select the Windows page. This page displays the policies available for your Windows servers. These policies include Dictionary Update policy, Workstation Import policy, Workstation Removal policy, and ZENworks Database policy. See Figure 19.2 for a sample of the Windows page.

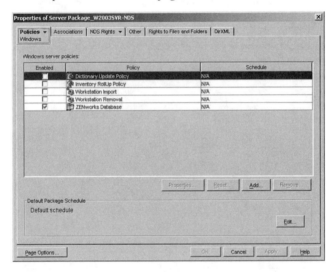

FIGURE 19.2
Server package Windows property page.

As you can see in Figure 19.2, when appropriate, the same policies are under both the General and the Windows properties pages. When you select a policy in the Windows page, it supercedes any selections that may have been on the General page for that platform. The policies will not be merged together; only the platform-specific policy will be used instead of the policy set in the General category. Also, only the policies selected in the platform-specific tab are used in place of the General policies. For example, if the Workstation Import policy is selected in the General page, and the Workstation Removal policy is selected in the Windows page, agents on a Windows Servers system use the General Import policy, and the Windows Removal policy is activated.

NetWare Policies

Within the Policies tab you can select the NetWare page. This page displays the policies available for NetWare servers. These policies include Dictionary Update policy, Inventory RollUp policy, Workstation Import policy, Workstation Removal policy, and ZENworks Database policy. See Figure 19.3 for a sample of the NetWare page.

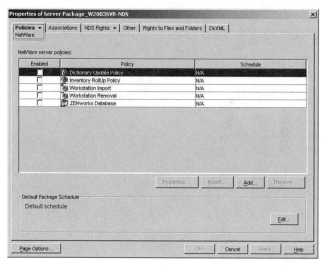

FIGURE 19.3
Server policy package NetWare property page.

As you can see in Figure 19.3, when appropriate, the same policies are under both the General page and the NetWare page. When you select a policy in the NetWare page, it supercedes any selections that may have been on the General page for that platform. The policies will not be merged together; only the platform-specific policy is used instead of the policy set in the General category. Also, only the policies selected in the platform-specific page are used in place of the General policies. For example, if the Workstation Import policy is selected in the General page and the Workstation Removal policy is selected in the NetWare page, agents on a NetWare system use the General Import policy, and the NetWare Removal policy is activated.

Linux Policies

Within the Policies tab you can select the Linux page. This page displays the policies available for Linux servers. These policies include the Dictionary Update policy, Inventory RollUp policy, Server Down Process, Workstation Import policy, Workstation Removal policy, ZENworks Database policy, and ZENworks Server Management policy. See Figure 19.4 for a sample of the Linux page.

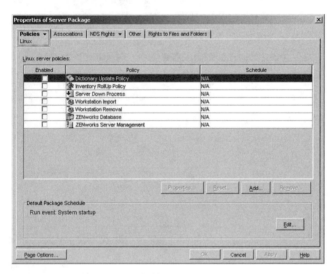

FIGURE 19.4
Server policy package Linux property page.

As you can see in Figure 19.4, when appropriate, the same policies are under both the General page and the Linux page. When you select a policy in the Linux page, it supercedes any selections that might have been on the General page for that platform. The policies will not be merged together; only the platform-specific policy is used instead of the policy set in the General category. Also, only the policies selected in the platform-specific page are used in place of the General policies. For example, if the Workstation Import policy is selected in the General page and the Workstation Removal policy is selected in the Linux page, agents on a Linux system use the General Import policy, and the Linux Removal policy is activated.

Associations Property Page

The Associations page of the server package displays all the locations in the tree (containers) where the policy package has been associated. These associations do not necessarily reflect where the policy package is located in the directory. The agents associated with servers that are in or below those containers have this policy package enforced. Clicking the Add or Remove buttons enable you to add or remove containers in the list associated with this policy.

Setting Up a Distributed Server Package

To create a Distributed Server package, do the following:

1. Start ConsoleOne.

2. Browse to the container where you want to have the policy package. Remember that you do not have to create the policy package in the container where you are doing the associations. You can associate the same policy package to many containers in your tree.

3. Create the policy package by right-clicking and choosing New→Policy Package or by selecting the Policy Package icon on the toolbar. This will launch a wizard to help you in the creation of your package.

4. Select the Distributed Server Package object and click Next.

5. Enter the desired name of the package in the Distributed Policy Package Name field and select the container where you want the package to be located. The Container field is already filled in with the selected container, so you should not have to browse to complete this field. If not, click the browser button next to the field and browse to and select the container where you want the policy object stored. Click Next.

6. Select Define Additional Attributes to go into the properties of your new object and activate some policies. Click Finish.

7. Check and set any policies you want for this server package and click OK.

The following subsections describe each of the fields and property pages available in the server package.

Policies Property Page

All the policies for servers are activated within the Policies property page. Initially the page is on the General policies. As other platforms are selected, additional policies are displayed. You can select which platform to display by placing the mouse over the small triangle on the right side of the Policies tab. This activates a drop-down menu that enables you to select which platform-specific page you want to display.

The following sections briefly discuss each of the policy pages, and then we cover the specifics of each policy.

General Policies

When you first go into the properties of the server package you are presented with the Policies property page. The Policies page first displays the General category. All the policies activated in the General category are active for all server platforms supported by ZENworks and associated with the server.

Currently five policies are available to all the platforms supported by ZENworks. They are Server Inventory Policy, SMTP Host, SNMP Trap Targets, ZENworks Database, and ZENworks Server Management. If you click the Add button, you can include additional Copy Files, Prohibited Files, or Text File Changes policies. These, as well as all the other policies, are discussed later in this chapter.

To activate a policy you simply need to click on the box to the left of the policy. You can go into the details of the policy and set additional configuration parameters on that specific policy.

Windows Policies

Within the Policies tab you can select the Windows page. This page displays the policies available for your Windows servers. These policies include Server Down Policy, Server Inventory Policy, Server Remote Management Policy, SMTP Host, SNMP Trap Targets, ZENworks Database, and ZENworks Server Management. If you click the Add button, you can include additional Copy Files, Prohibited Files, Scheduled Down, Scheduled Load/Unload, Server Scripts, or Text File Changes policies.

The same policies are under both the General and the Windows properties pages. When you select a policy in the Windows page, it supercedes any selections that might have been on the General page for that platform. The policies will not be merged together; only the platform-specific policy will be used instead of the policy set in the General category. Also, only the policies selected in the platform-specific tab are used in place of the General policies. For example, if the Workstation Import policy is selected in the General page, and the Workstation Removal policy is selected in the Windows page, agents on a Windows Servers system use the General Import policy, and the Windows Removal policy is activated.

NetWare Policies

Within the Policies tab you can select the NetWare page. This page displays the policies available for NetWare servers. These policies include Server Down Policy, Server Inventory Policy, SMTP Host, SNMP Trap Targets, ZENworks Database, and ZENworks Server Management. If you click the Add button, you can include additional Copy Files, NetWare Set Paramters, Prohibited Files, Scheduled Down, Scheduled Load/Unload, Server Scripts, or Text File Changes policies.

When appropriate, the same policies are under both the General page and the NetWare page. When you select a policy in the NetWare page, it supercedes any selections that might have been on the General page for that platform. The policies will not be merged together; only the platform-specific policy is used instead of the policy set in the General category. Also, only the policies selected in the platform-specific page are used in place of the General policies. For example, if the Workstation Import policy is selected in the General page and the Workstation Removal policy is selected in the NetWare page, agents on a NetWare system use the General Import policy, and the NetWare Removal policy is activated.

Linux Policies

Within the Policies tab you can select the Linux page. This page displays the policies available for Linux servers. These policies include Server Down Process, SMTP Host, SNMP Trap Targets, and ZENworks Database, ZENworks Server Management. If you click the Add button, you can include additional Copy Files, Prohibited Files, Scheduled Down, Scheduled Load/Unload, Server Scripts, or Text File Changes policies.

When appropriate, the same policies are under both the General page and the Linux page. When you select a policy in the Linux page, it supercedes any selections that might have been on the General page for that platform. The policies will not be merged together; only the platform-specific policy is used instead of the policy set in the General category. Also, only the policies selected in the platform-specific page are used in place of the General policies. For example, if the Workstation Import policy is selected in the General page and the Workstation Removal policy is selected in the Linux page, agents on a Linux system use the General Import policy, and the Linux Removal policy is activated.

Solaris Policies

Within the Policies tab you can select the Solaris page. This page displays the policies available for Linux servers. These policies include Server Down Process, SMTP Host, SNMP Trap Targets, ZENworks Database, and ZENworks Server Management. If you click the Add button, you can include additional Copy Files, Prohibited Files, Scheduled Down, Scheduled Load/Unload, Server Scripts, or Text File Changes policies.

When appropriate, the same policies are under both the General page and the Solaris page. When you select a policy in the Solaris page, it supercedes any selections that might have been on the General page for that platform. The policies will not be merged together; only the platform-specific policy is used instead of the policy set in the General category. Also, only the policies selected in the platform-specific page are used in place of the General policies. For example, if the SMTP Host policy is selected in the General page and the ZENworks Database policy is selected in the Solaris page, agents on a Solaris system use the General SMTP Host policy, and the ZENworks Database policy from the Solaris page is activated.

Distributions Property Page

The Distributions page of the server package displays distributions that contain this policy package. Clicking the Add or Remove buttons enable you to add or remove Distributions in the list associated with this policy.

Copy Files Policy

The Copy Files policy is a policy which enables you to configure ZENworks to copy or move files on a server from one location to another. The Copy Files policy can be an extremely powerful tool that you can use for file distribution or synchronization on a server.

The following is a list of parameters which can be configured from the file copy policy:

- ▶ Source Path—Specifies the full path where the files to be copied are located (you can use the following wildcards in the path: *, ?, ???).

- ▶ Target Path—Specifies the full path where the copied files are to be placed (you can also use wildcards in the target path).

- ▶ Include Subfolders—Tells ZENworks to include all files in all subdirectories beginning from the directory that ends the path. If this box is not checked, only the files in the directory at the end of the path are copied.

- ▶ Maintain Attributes—Tells ZENworks to maintain the file attributes in the target paths file system.

- ▶ Overwrite Destination Files—Specifies whether you want ZENworks to overwrite files of the same name in the destination directories. If this box is not checked, files of the same name are not replaced.

- ▶ Maintain Trustees—Tells ZENworks to maintain the file's trustee attributes. You should plan carefully whether you want ZENworks to maintain the trustees of files, so that users do not gain access to files they should not.

- ▶ Retry Times—If this box is checked, ZENworks will retry overwriting a locked file the number of times specified.

- ▶ Kill Connection of Open Files—If this box is checked, ZENworks kills any connection that has the file open so it can be overwritten. You should use caution when setting this option because it can result in users losing data.

- ▶ Error Processing—Selecting Fail on Error (enabled by default) stops the file copying process when an error is encountered in copying. Selecting Continue on Error causes file copying to continue on with the next file.

▶ Operation—Specifies whether you want ZENworks to copy or move the files identified in the Source Path. Moving has the advantage of freeing up disk space in the source location. However, if you are trying to synchronize or replicate files, you need to use the copy feature.

Make certain that you do not have any read-only files or directories in the copy files locations. ZENworks applies the attributes to the locations prior to copying the files. Therefore, if you set a directory to read-only and ZENworks tries to copy it, ZENworks will create the directory in the destination location, set it to read-only, and then error on every file it tries to copy into that directory.

Dictionary Update Policy

This policy allows you to specify where the source for the software dictionary list is located. A software dictionary contains a list of files that, when found on the drive, constitute a known software package. The software dictionary is stored on each individual workstation as it performs its scanning process for it to determine the software packages present on the workstation.

Occasionally, you may want to update the dictionary to include additional, internal software package files. This policy tells the workstation agents where to find the source and how often to update their individual dictionary files.

Dictionary Update Policy Page

This page allows you to check whether the roll-up server is the source of the dictionary. If the roll-up server has the source, nothing else is needed on this page. If the roll-up server is not the source of the dictionary, you need to configure the remaining components on this page, including

▶ Destination Service Object—The eDirectory object that represents the inventory service running on the target server.

▶ Server IP/DNS Address—Alternatively you may specify the address of the inventory server.

▶ Proxy Server Configuration—ZENworks allows retrieving of the dictionary files through the specified proxy.

Dictionary Update Schedule Page

This page allows you to specify how often and when the dictionary files should be updated on the workstation.

This page enables you to select when the configuration should be read and applied: Never, Daily, Monthly, Yearly, Interval, or Time.

After you select when you want the configuration applied, you have additional fields to select in the lower portion of the screen. The following sections discuss the various options.

Weekly

You can alternatively choose that the policies be applied only weekly. In the Weekly screen you choose on which day of the week you want the policy to be applied. When you select a day, any other selected day is unselected. After you have selected the day, you can also select the time range when the policy may be applied.

To keep all workstations from simultaneously accessing the servers, you can select Randomly Dispatch Policy During Time Period. This causes each workstation to choose a random time within the time period when it will retrieve and apply the policy.

Daily

When you choose to have the configuration applied to the system daily, you need to also select when the changes will be made.

This schedule requires that you select the days when you want the configuration applied by clicking on the days you want. The selected days appear as depressed buttons.

In addition to the days, you can select the times the configuration is applied. These start and stop times provide a range of time where the configuration will be applied.

You can have the configuration also reapplied within the time frame specified per hour, minute, or second by clicking the Repeat the Action Every field and specifying the time delay.

Monthly

Under the monthly schedule, you can select which day of the month the configuration should be applied, or you can select Last Day of the Month to handle the last day because all months obviously do not end on the same calendar date (that is, 30 days hath September, April, June, and November; all the rest have 31 except for February...).

After you select the day, you can also select the time range when the configurations are reread and applied.

Yearly

Select a yearly schedule if you want to apply the configuration only once a year.

On the Yearly screen, you must choose the day that you want the configuration to be applied. This is done by selecting the Calendar button to the right of the Date field. This brings up a Monthly dialog box where you can browse through the calendar to select the date you want. This calendar does not correspond to any particular year and may not take into account leap years in its display. This is because you are choosing a date for each year that will come along in the present and future years.

After you select the date, you can also select the time range when the configuration should be read and applied.

To keep all the distributors from simultaneously accessing eDirectory, you can select Randomly Dispatch Policy During Time Period. This causes each server to choose a random time within the time period when the server will retrieve and apply the configuration.

Never

This option loads the distributor with the configuration information only when it is first loaded on the server or after each reboot or restart.

Imaging Server Policy

ZENworks has the capability to image a workstation and to apply that image back to the original or other workstations. See Chapter 22, "Imaging a Workstation," for more detailed information on the functionality of the ZENworks imaging system.

The placement of an image, associated with an image object in the directory, onto a workstation, may occur five different ways in ZENworks:

▶ Boot the workstation to PXE and have the ZENworks PXE system connect the workstation to the imaging server, bringing down the imaging system and communicating to the imaging agent on the server.

▶ Boot the workstation with the Imaging boot CD that communicates with the imaging server.

▶ Boot the workstation with floppy diskettes that communicate with the imaging agent on the server.

▶ Place a special boot partition on an unregistered workstation that communicates with the imaging agent on the server.

▶ Place a special boot partition on a registered workstation and set the Check for Imaging Work for This Workstation on the Next Boot field in the workstation object. (In this case, the image is determined by an image association or the rules in the Workstation Imaging policy; see Chapter 15, "Setting Up Workstation Policies," for more details.)

Each of these ways results in the workstation being imaged with the image associated with the workstation or determined by the imaging agent that resides on the server. The way that the workstation finds the imaging server is, when the imaging boot media is created, the administrator can specify either an IP address or a DNS name for the server. Additionally, configuration parameters are placed in the PXE system that knows where the imaging server is located.

The imaging policy becomes effective when the workstation is not associated with a workstation object. Because no image is associated with the specific workstation, the imaging server must determine, based on rules, what image to place on the workstation.

This policy enables the administrator to create a set of rules that can govern when a particular image should be used, based on some basic information from the workstation. The imaging server follows the list of rules in the policy until one of the rules is satisfied. The rule that is satisfied results in an associated image that is applied to the workstation.

Imaging Partition

The Imaging Partition page allows you to disable the ZENworks imaging partition if it exists. This is useful if you want to disable imaging on the workstation because no active imaging is occurring on the workstation. For example, you have a one-time image applied to a workstation annually in January. You need the partition to remain intact, but you can disable it the rest of the year. Novell now recommends that the imaging partition be done away with in your environment, replaced with PXE.

PXE Settings

Now that ZENworks Desktop Management ships with PXE-enabled software you also may set the PXE settings for deploying any images. Novell now recommends that the Linux partition on the workstation be removed and that customers should move to the PXE method of image deployment. On the PXE Settings page you may set whether the PXE menu should appear automatically when PXE is launched, and you may also set the values that appear on the menu.

A PXE menu displays, for example, whether to receive an image or take an image.

Rules Page

The Rules page, selected from the Work To Do tab pull-down menu, enables the administrator to input the rules and associated images that the system uses to determine the image to place on a specific type of workstation. Figure 19.5 shows an example of this page.

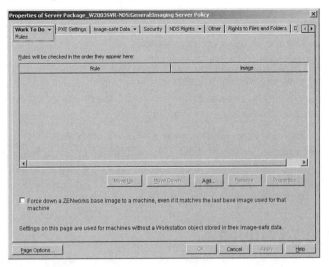

FIGURE 19.5
Rules page for a sample Imaging Server policy of a server package.

You must first click the Add button to add rules to the list. After you have added several rules, you may select a specific rule and change its order in the list, look at its properties, or remove the rule. When you click the Add button, the screen shown in Figure 19.6 appears.

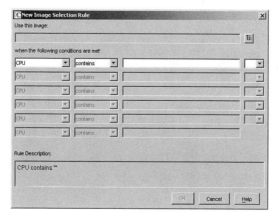

FIGURE 19.6
New Image Selection Rule dialog for a sample Imaging Server policy of a
server package.

You first click the browse button next to the Use This Image field to
browse to an image object in the tree associated with an image file on the
image server. After the image object is selected, you may identify the rule
associated with this image. You may currently only have six key/value
pairs to compare about the workstation to determine what image to use.

In the middle of the dialog box you can see the six potential equations
that you can generate to determine whether the image should be used.
The equation is made up of a series of True/False statements put together
with AND and OR logic. You construct the statement by filling in the
drop-down fields. (The resulting statement is displayed in a more
English-like view to help you understand the equation.)

The logic for the AND and OR operators is strictly left to right in the
equation. In the Rule Description box parentheses are added to the equation to help the administrator understand how the rule is evaluated. You
cannot insert the parentheses; they are automatically inserted as part of
the explanation of the equation and are not under user control.

You first select the key you want to examine by selecting the key via
a drop-down dialog box. The keys that you can choose from are the
following:

▶ CPU—Displays the reported processor. An example would be
   Genuine Intel Mobile Pentium MMX 233 MHZ.

▶ Video—Captures the type of video adapter in the workstation. An example of this would be Trident Cyber9397 (rev 243).

▶ Network—The network adapter for the workstation. An example would be 3Com.

▶ Sound Card—The sound card that has been reported. Often this field results in no sound card being detected. This is because the system sends out a PCI request; if no sound cards respond you get this even though a sound card may be present.

▶ Hard Drive Controller—The type of hard drive in the system. If the hard drive is an IDE device, the value for this field is IDE. If the hard drive is a SCSI device, you get the reported name of the device, such as FUJITSU MHJ2181AT.

▶ MAC Address—The MAC address of the network card. An example of this value would be 00 60 80 03 C2 E7.

▶ IP Address—The assigned IP address of the workstation. This would be reported as the traditional 137.65.237.5.

▶ BIOS Asset Number—Represents the Asset number that may have been placed in the BIOS of the device. Most newer computers have this field in their BIOS that is set by the manufacturer or through a tool.

▶ BIOS Serial Number—Represents the serial number of the device. Most computers now have this field set in their BIOS by the manufacturer.

▶ Hard Drive Size—Reports the disk size in number of megabytes. Therefore, an 8GB hard drive would be reported as 8192MB in this field. The imaging system may not always report the full disk capacity. It is advisable that you use a wide boundary when generating your rules. For example, if you want to look for an 8GB drive, put in the fields so the resulting statement is `Hard drive size >= 8000 MB`.

▶ RAM—The reported amount of RAM in megabyte units. This would be reported as 64MB. This field also may not always report the exact amount of RAM space that you would expect on your workstation. It is advisable that you use a wide boundary when generating your rules. For example, if you want to look for 16MB RAM, put in the field so the resulting statement is `RAM >= 15MB`.

When the workstation is booting the imaging system, it is in reality booting up the Linux operating system and running the tools included in the imaging system. The values for the keys described previously are values that the Linux system can report to the software. To discover what a system reports to Linux, you need to boot a sample workstation with the Imaging system boot disk and run the command `img information`. This displays the information sent to the image server about the workstation. This information is the data values that you put into the key comparison equations for your rules. You can also get this information from an image by opening the image in the ZENworks image editor, right-clicking the image file, and selecting Properties from the menu. See Chapter 22 for more detailed information on the functionality of the ZENworks imaging system.

The next part of the equation is to specify the operator. Two types of operators exist: string and integer. The Hard Drive Size and RAM fields are treated as integers, whereas all the other fields are treated as strings, where a not case-sensitive string compare is done to determine operator results. The string operators are `contains`, `doesn't contain`, `begins with`, and `equals`. The integer operators are =, <>, >, >=, <, and <=.

These operators perform expected comparisons between the key value supplied by the workstation to the imaging server and the value that you place into the value field of the equation. The following meanings are placed with each operator:

- ▶ `contains`—The specified value is a substring anywhere in the reported value.

- ▶ `doesn't contain`—The specified value is not equal to or contained in the reported value.

- ▶ `begins with`—The specified value is represented in the initial character of the reported value.

- ▶ `equals`—The specified value is the same as the reported value.

- ▶ = equals—The specified value is numerically equivalent to the reported value.

- ▶ <> not equal—The specified value is not equal to the reported value.

- ▶ > greater than—The specified value is greater than the reported value.

▶ >= greater than or equal to—The specified value is numerically equal to or greater than the reported value.

▶ < less than—The specified value is less than the reported value.

▶ <= less than or equal to—The specified value is numerically less than or equal to the reported value.

The next field in the operation is where you enter the value that you want to compare. The far right field enables you to extend the operation to additional key/value comparisons. Your choices currently are AND and OR.

The Boolean operators are evaluated strictly from left to right. For example, if the following rules were entered into the policy, the resultant evaluation would be (Hard drive >= 600MB AND RAM < 16MB) OR (RAM > 31MB):

▶ Hard drive size >= 600MB AND

▶ RAM < 16MB OR

▶ RAM > 31MB

This would result in giving the image to any system that has a disk greater than 600MB with less than 16MB RAM. This would also give the image to any system that has more than 31MB RAM regardless of the size of the hard drive.

You can view the precedence of the equation, complete with parentheses, on the bottom half of the screen as you introduce new key/value pairs into your rule.

After your set of key/value pairs has been entered and you have reviewed your equation at the bottom of the screen, click OK to include the rule into the imaging system. You are returned to the original Rules page with the rule that you entered on the screen.

Once again, from this page, after you enter some rules you can specify the order that the rules are evaluated. After selecting a rule, you can move that rule in the order by clicking either the Move Up or the Move Down button. As the imaging server is evaluating the rules, the first rule that results in a TRUE evaluation results in that imaging being supplied to the workstation.

Multicast

The Multicast page allows you to specify whether the imaging server checks first to see whether the workstation should take part in a multicast session prior to checking the image selection rules within this policy. If the Check the Image Selection Rules in This Policy Before Checking Within Multicast Sessions check box is checked, the imaging server will check the image selection rules prior to checking its multicast sessions.

> **NOTE** The Check the Image Selection Rules in This Policy Before Checking Within Multicast Sessions check box will have no effect on workstations configured to serve as session masters because that role takes priority over any other imaging setting.

Image-Safe Data Page

The Image-Safe Data tab is composed of four pages. These pages represent information and data placed or retrieved from the system regardless of the image used. The following sections depict the pages available by selecting the small triangle drop-down menu on the Image-Safe Data tab.

An agent exists that may be placed on the workstation called the Image-Safe Data agent. This agent has the responsibility of moving data between a special sector on the disk used to store configuration information such as IP address or DHCP configuration along with workgroup information. This information on the disk is not affected by an image taken or placed on the drive.

When the Image-Safe Data agent runs on the workstation, it makes sure that the information in the special sector and the operating system are synchronized properly. For example, following an image placement, the agent moves the data from the disk into the operating system, setting up the DHCP and computer name. On a workstation that has not just been imaged, the agent moves the information from the operating system into the sector on the disk so that the data can be restored should a new image be placed on the drive. Should the agent not run, the workstation would be an exact mirror of the image (with the same IP and computer name configuration).

The Image-Safe Data configuration page enables the imaging server to pass this configuration information to the agent via this disk sector.

IP Assignment Log Page

The IP Assignment Log page displays the IP addresses that the imaging server has assigned to any imaged or re-imaged workstations. The available IP addresses can be set in the IP Configuration page described in the following section.

The IP Assignment Log page displays the log of the addresses that have been assigned.

This page can also be used to place an IP address back into the pool of available addresses. If you have an address that you want to place back into the pool, select it from the log list and click the Remove button.

NOTE When you remove a specific IP address it may not be properly represented in the IP Configuration range and therefore will not be reused.

If you specified a range in the IP Configuration page to be the set of IP addresses that you will make available for workstations, when the imaging server uses a portion of the range (at the ends), the range is refreshed on the Configuration page. For example, if the range 123.65.234.1... 123.65.234.100 were in the configuration and IP address 123.65.234.1-10 were assigned, the range would be changed to 123.65.234.11... 123.65.234.100. Consequently, when you go to the IP Assignment Log page and free up IP address 123.65.234.10, the range is not reconfigured, and the freed IP address is not reassigned. You must manually go to the Configuration page and modify the range to include the addresses that you have freed.

IP Configuration Page

The IP Configuration page enables you to specify whether the workstations imaged by the imaging server will obtain their IP address from a DHCP server or via a static assignment that is done as part of the imaging process.

If you select the DHCP option, when the workstation is imaged, the Windows system is told to get IP addresses from a DHCP server. If, however, you select that you want to specify an IP address, the other fields on the page are activated.

To specify a static IP address, you must first enter the subnet mask and default gateway that you want all your imaged workstations (imaged via the image server using this particular policy) to receive. You must also specify the range of IP addresses used by the imaging server and assigned uniquely to each of the imaged workstations. You specify the set of IP addresses by using the Add and Add Range buttons.

When the imaging server is given a request for an image and after the image has been placed onto the workstation, the IP address information is transmitted and assigned to the workstation. That address is logged in the imaging server and not reused for another workstation.

To remove any address or ranges from the possible set, select the item and click the Remove button. These addresses will no longer be in the pool of available addresses for the imaging server to assign.

Windows Networking Page

In the Windows Networking page you can specify the computer name for the workstation and the workgroup for the system.

The computer name prefix that you enter in the field (maximum of seven characters) is prepended to a randomly generated set of characters and numbers to construct the final 15-character computer name for the workstation.

The Make the Computer a Member of the Following Workgroup field enables you to specify the workgroup that you want for the workstation. You select which you prefer by selecting the field and entering the work-group name.

DNS Settings

The DNS Settings page allows you to specify the DNS suffix and name servers that will be used by this policy. Simply type in the suffix you want to use and click the Add button to bring up an IP address dialog box to specify the addresses of name servers. It is important to use the correct suffix and name servers for the ZENworks imaging engine to process imaging operations on a workstation.

Security Page

As part of the imaging system the administrator has the ability to request that the workstation have an image taken of itself and placed onto the server. This is done by checking some fields in the workstation object (see Chapter 22 for more details), which causes the workstation to take an image of itself on its next reboot.

When the workstation takes an image of itself, or when an image is taken when a request is made through the Linux boot system, the image is transmitted to the image server. This image server receives the .ZMG file and places it in the path specified. To protect the system from overwriting any files or to prevent users from placing the image files into inappropriate directories, the imaging server takes the information in the security page and restricts the placement of the image files.

When you check Allow Imaging to Overwrite Existing Files When Uploading, you are enabling the system to overwrite any files that may have the same name as the one specified by the user for the name of the image file.

The Only Allow Uploads to the Following Directories check box activates the requirement that all requested uploads must specify one of the directories identified. If the directory portion of the destination path, specified by the user, does not match one of the directories specified in the list on this page, the request to store the uploaded image is refused. To add paths to the list of accepted destinations, click the Add button and enter in the acceptable path.

Paths in the directories may be one of the following formats:

- *Driveletter:path*
- *Volume\path*
- *NTShare\path*

The system does not, for example, take any UNC path. When the user enters the location of the file, including the path, this information transmits to the imaging server. The server compares the directory portion of the path given with all the strings in this list. If a match occurs (that is, the directory is listed), the operation is accepted, and the image is taken and stored. Otherwise, the operation fails, and the image is not taken.

Inventory Roll-Up Policy

The Inventory Roll-Up policy dictates to the services running on a specific server (such as, inventory server) where they should roll-up or transmit the inventory information that they have received from the various workstations. By doing this, the system receives local inventory information and then moves it up in the tree hierarchy, consolidating inventory information from various remote locations and constructing a more centralized database of inventory information (see Chapter 20, "Using ZENworks Workstation Inventory," for more detailed information).

When the inventory system is installed into the network, the system creates service objects that govern the behavior of the agents working on each of the inventory servers. These agents also respond to this policy to understand to which service agent they should transmit their inventory information. All service agents associated with this policy transmit their inventory information to the same target agent.

Figure 19.7 shows a sample of this page.

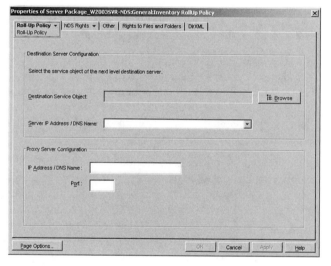

FIGURE 19.7
Inventory Roll-Up policy of a server package.

As you can see in Figure 19.7 the policy simply requests the object eDirectory Distinguished Name of the service where the associated agents should transmit their inventory information. The local agents may keep a copy of the inventory data, if they are a designated database gathering location, but they still transmit an additional copy if they are configured to do so.

In this policy you click the Browse button to the right of the Destination Service Object field and browse the tree to select the service object of the inventory agent that you want to receive the information. You may also specify the DNS or IP address of the server running the service.

Additionally, ZENworks provides the ability to roll up the inventory through a proxy by specifying the IP/DNS name and a port number.

The Roll-Up policy is only read by the service manager agent on startup and then every 1,000 minutes (this is not configurable). So if the policy change needs to be immediately effective, the service manager agent on the server must be stopped and restarted.

NetWare Set Parameters Policy

This policy is a plural policy, which means that you can create multiple instances of this policy in a single policy package. You create this policy by clicking the Add button at the bottom of the main Server Policy Package screen. When you click the Add button, you are prompted to select a policy and to name the policy. You need to select NetWare Set Parameters for the policy and type a unique policy name.

After you have added the policy, you are guided through a wizard to collect potential parameters. Because the set parameters on NetWare are dynamic and can be enhanced by various sets of NLMs, there is not a known set of set parameters. Consequently, ZENworks Server Management walks you through a wizard that goes to an identified NetWare server (the server must be running the ZENworks Server Management Policy engine) and queries the server for the set of parameters. This list is then transmitted back to the wizard.

After the parameters have been imported into the policy, you are able to edit and modify their values, or remove them from the policy. The parameters that remain in the policy will be set on the target server when applied.

Prohibited Files Policy

The Prohibited Files policy will cause the ZENworks Server Management system to, at a scheduled time, search the server file system and remove or move any specified files (by wildcarding) from the the server or to a specified directory. For example, if you don't want MP3 files stored on a specific server, ZENworks can go through the target server and remove all MP3 files from the server with a Prohibited Files policy.

With this policy, you can

- ▶ Specify one or more volumes/drives or directories to monitor. You have the option to include all subdirectories for monitoring.

- ▶ Specify which file types to monitor using wildcard combinations.

- ▶ Specify the action of either Delete or Move to Specified Location for all encountered files.

- ▶ Specify a schedule for enforcement of the policy.

Directories to Monitor

For this instance of the policy, you can specify the paths to be monitored. These directories are used as the source to determine which files are to be deleted or moved in the target locations. You cannot move files to a directory that is being monitored.

Path

This can be a volume, drive, or directory name. It must be the full path when a directory is given. You can add multiple paths. For each path that you enter, files matching the file types that you define in the File Type field are either deleted or moved according to which Action button you select. Variables are supported in the paths.

Subdirectory

Select the check box to specify that all subdirectories be included. If you want only a certain subdirectory, you should create another policy just for that subdirectory by giving its full path in the Path field.

Add

Opens a dialog box where you can enter a path. This field cannot be browsed, so you must know the full path to the files to be moved or deleted.

Edit

Allows you to edit the selected path.

Remove

Removes the selected path entry from the list.

NOTE IMPORTANT: Do not have the directory where the files are to be moved to be beneath the directories that are being monitored.

File Type

You can specify the type of files you want to monitor.

Add

Opens a dialog box where you specify a file type. You can include wild-card characters. This field cannot be browsed, so you must enter the correct information to identify the files to be moved or deleted.

Edit

Allows you to edit the selected file type.

Remove

Removes the selected file type from the list.

Action

You have two options for how to handle the files you have specified in the Directories to Monitor and the File Types fields:

- ▶ Delete Files—Select the option button to delete the specified files from all of the paths that you have identified.

- ▶ Move Files To—Select the option button to move the specified files to the path that you specify in this field. This field cannot be browsed, so you must know the full path to where you want the files to be moved.

CAUTION IMPORTANT: You cannot move files to a directory that is being monitored. If you move files, the full paths of the files are preserved (meaning if the path doesn't exist at the target, it is created there); files are overwritten if they exist in the same path; file or directory attributes and trustees are not transferred; and file ownership is preserved.

When a File Is Locked

Occasionally, files you might be trying to delete or move might be open. For these files, you can specify one of the following resolutions:

- ▶ Retry ___ Times—Select the check box and enter a number for how many times you want to retry deleting or moving the file before continuing on with the next file. Valid entries are from 1 to 10. The time used by each increment depends on the various hardware and software speeds involved in your system.

Use this field to allow enough time for a temporarily opened file to be closed, such as a file that is only opened long enough for the application to either obtain a copy for editing or write a new copy of the file.

▶ Kill Connection of Open Files (NetWare only)—Select the check box to have the file deleted or moved, even if it is opened by a user at the time. It kills the connection that is holding the file open so the file can be deleted or moved.

NOTE IMPORTANT: You can only kill connections to files on workstations. Server files cannot be disconnected from the process that has them open.

Scheduled Down Policy

This policy is a plural policy, which means that you can create multiple instances of this policy in a single policy package. You create this policy by clicking the Add button at the bottom of the main Server Policy Package screen. When you click the Add button, you are prompted to select a policy and to name the policy. You need to select Scheduled Down for the policy and type a unique policy name. After you do this, you can activate and modify the policy.

This policy allows you to schedule that the server reset, restart, or down at a particular time.

You can select one of the following server options:

▶ Reset server—This downs the server and performs a warm boot of the machine.

▶ Restart server—This downs and then restarts the server.

▶ Down server—This downs the server.

On the Policy Schedule page, you may specify the time frame when you want the server to be reset, restarted, or downed.

Scheduled Load/Unload Policy

This policy is a plural policy, which means you can create multiple instances of this policy in a single policy package. You create this policy by clicking the Add button on at the bottom of the main Server Policy Package screen. When you click the Add button, you are prompted to select a policy and to name the policy. You need to select Scheduled Load/Unload for the policy and type a unique policy name. After you do this, you can activate and modify the policy. This policy enables you to specify when you want to have a selected set of NLMs or Java processes loaded or unloaded on the server.

In this policy, you click the Add button and select whether you want to load an NLM or Java class, or unload a process by using the drop-down menu to the left of the Add button. After you make your selection, an entry is placed on the left side of the screen. Corresponding to this entry are some parameters that are displayed and edited on the right. By selecting the entry on the left, you can administer the values on the right. You can edit the entries on the left by selecting the entry (like you do in Windows), and this enables you to change the name to something more useful.

In the fields on the right, you enter the name of the NLM or Java class and any parameters that are needed for the process.

When you are loading a process, you can enter the NLM or class name and also specify the parameters that you want passed to these processes. Additionally, you can specify whether you want to wait for the loaded NLM or Java class to terminate before continuing onto the next item in the list. Make sure you check this box only if you are expecting the process to complete and exit on its own; if you are just loading monitor.nlm, the policy will be waiting for a long time to be able to move onto the next item.

When you are unloading a process, you can enter the name of the NLM or the Java class name. Additionally, you can specify if you should wait for the termination to complete before proceeding in the list.

After you have entered several items in the list, you can select an item and move it up and down the list. This is significant because the items are processed in the order specified, from top to bottom. By selecting any item and moving it about in the list, you can order the loads and unloads in a sequence that is necessary for your process.

On the Policy Schedule page, you can specify the time frame when you want the system to perform this policy.

Server Down Policy

The Server Down Process policy allows you to specify what should happen when the server receives a command to go down. This catches the instances when the user types the down command on the console; this process does not catch any other down request (done programmatically). You can even specify that other servers notify you if the downed server does not come up after a certain amount of time.

Describing the Down Procedure Page

The Down Procedure page enables you to specify the procedure that should be followed when the server is downed.

The following options on the page are activated when the check box is checked:

- ▶ Follow This Procedure When a Down Server Is Triggered—This activates or does not activates the procedure identified on this page. If this check box is not checked, this policy will not be in effect for the associated servers. You can specify, when activated, how many minutes the server must wait before it actually performs the down process.

- ▶ Disable Login Before Downing—This effectively runs the disable logins command on the server, disallowing anyone to be able to log into the server. You can specify how many minutes before the downing process you want to disallow anyone to log into the server. If the number of minutes specified in this field is greater than that specified in the Follow This Procedure When a Down Server Is Triggered field, the disabling of logins occurs immediately when the down request is given.

- ▶ Drop Connections Before Downing—This drops all the current connections on the server before downing the server. You can specify the number of minutes before the actual downing of the server when you want the connections dropped. If the number of minutes specified in this field is greater than that specified in the Follow This Procedure When a Down Server is Triggered field, the connections are dropped immediately when the down request is given.

Discussing the Ordered Unload Page

By selecting the small triangle drop-down control on the Down Process page, you can select the Ordered Unload page. This page enables you to specify a set of NLMs and Java processes that you want killed or unloaded and the order in which to kill or unload them before the downing of the server actually begins.

When you select with the Add button either to unload an NLM or kill a process, a dialog box prompts you to enter the name of the NLM or the process. After entering the name of the NLM or process, click the OK button on the dialog box and the NLM or process name appears in the Ordered Unload page. After you have more than one process or NLM in the list, you can select an item in the list and then move it up or down in the list by clicking the up or down arrows, after selecting an item.

Before the server is downed, these systems are unloaded or killed on the server. This is useful if you have such processes or NLMs as databases or other programs that are caching items in memory and need to flush those buffers onto disk. This can be done, usually, by unloading the process or NLM. This can keep your data integrity solid instead of pulling the server out from under these processes, not allowing them to save their data.

Looking at the Reporting Page

The Reporting page is under the Notification tab. The purpose of this page is to identify some companion servers, whose responsibility it is to send notifications if the server that is associated with this policy does not come up after a specified time. When the server is told to go down, it contacts these companion servers and places a scheduled entry to send a notification message. When the server comes back up and the policy engine is restarted, it contacts these servers again and removes the scheduled entry for the notifications. If the server and the policy engine do not come up in the specified time, these companion servers fire the scheduled entry and send the specified notification messages. These companion servers must also be running the policy engine for this to work.

The Send SNMP Alert if Server Is Not up After a Number of Minutes check box turns on or off the monitoring of the server. You can specify the number of minutes that these other "watcher" servers will wait before they send their SNMP alerts notifying you that the server that was downed is not coming back up.

You then must click the Add button and then browse the tree to identify the servers that are to monitor this behavior. After you specify more than one server, you can order the servers to identify which server has first responsibility to monitor the downed server. When the ZENworks Server Management engine recieves the event that signals the down, it attempts to contact the servers in this list (in order) to notify them to watch for when the server comes back up. If the server in the list cannot be contacted, the engine goes to the next server in the list.

Introducing the Broadcast Message Page

The Broadcast Message page can be found under the Notification tab. This page enables you to specify the broadcast messages that are sent to the connected users as the system is being taken down. You can specify if the message should be sent, how many times you want the message sent before the system goes down, the contents of the message, and an additional trailer that tells the users how long before they will be disconnected from the server.

The number of times to send the message is divided evenly into the number of minutes specified in the Down Procedure page before dropping connections or downing the server (if the Dropping Connections check box is not checked). If, for example, you stated that the server should go down 10 minutes after the request and you specify that the connections should be dropped 4 minutes before downing, the number of minutes that a user has left on the server is 6 minutes (10–4). The number of messages are divided into the 6 minutes and spaced evenly across that time.

If you include the line that states the number of minutes left, the "x" in the line is calculated the same way as above, minus a broadcast cycle. You subtract one cycle so that the last message is displayed at the beginning of the last cycle (rather than the end).

About the Targeted Messages Page

The Targeted Messages page enables you to send specific email messages to a selected set of users to notify them of the downing of the server.

The Send Email to Selected Users When Server Is Going Down check box turns off or on this feature. The Email Message box displays the message that is sent to each of the specified users. You are not able to change or customize the message that is sent.

To add users to the list and have them receive the message, you must click the Add button and select whether you want to add an NDS User or Group, or specify an email address explicitly. When you select User, you are asked to browse to the user in the directory, and the system takes the email address attribute from the user and uses that as the address for the user. Should you choose a group, all of the users in the group are sent the email message and the email attribute is used for each of those users. Should you not want to use the email address attribute in the user object, you may select the down arrow in the Address Attribute field and select which of the NDS User attributes you want to identify as containing the email address. It is expected that the attribute you identify contains a valid email address.

If you choose to enter an email address explicitly, rather than selecting a user or a group, you may choose the Email Address choice from the Add button. You are prompted to enter a valid email address. The entered email address is assumed to be valid and is shown as the User Name field entry in the table with N/A in the Address Attribute field.

You can place any number (based on the limits of NDS) of users, groups, or email addresses into the page and each of them are sent the email message when the server has been requested to go down. The email users recieve just one message at the very beginning of the downing process. This gives these users the maximum amount of time to connect to the server and stop the downing process should they desire. They can connect to the server and, via the policy engine console or via Remote Web Console, cancel the down process.

Exploring the Conditions Page

This page enables you to specify conditions when the down server request should not be honored.

You must check the Use Conditions in Downing Server? check box to make the conditions effective. Then you can add any number of conditions that you want to identify. If any of these conditions are true, the server does not honor the down server request. Select any of the following choices from the drop-down menu:

▶ File Open—Specify if an identified file is currently open on the server. If that file is open, the system does not allow the down request.

▶ NLM or Java Loaded—Specify if a particular NLM or Java application is currently loaded on the server. The system checks to see if the NLM or Java application is loaded before it performs any unload of NLMs or Java applications that were specified in the Ordered Unload page. So, if you have an NLM or Java application in the Unload page and in the conditions, the down is halted if the NLM or Java application is loaded.

▶ Server Connected—If the identified server is currently connected to the server, the down request is denied.

▶ User Connected—If the identified user has a current connection to the server, the down request is denied.

▶ Number of User Connections—Specify the number of active connections whereby, if exceeded, the down will not be allowed. If, for example, you specify 15 as the number of active connections and there are 16 or more connections, the down request is denied.

These are active connections, which include server and agent connections, not just authenticated user connections.

▶ Workstation Connected—Identify the workstation that, when connected, halts the down request. You cannot specify a group of workstations, but must identify them individually.

This feature functions only when you have ZENworks Desktop Management installed in your system.

Server Scripts Policy

This policy is a plural policy, which means you can create multiple instances of this policy in a single policy package. You create this policy by clicking the Add button at the bottom of the main Server Policy Package screen. When you click the Add button, you are prompted to select a policy and to name the policy. You need to select Server Scripts for the policy and enter a unique policy name. After you have done this, you can activate and modify the policy.

This policy enables you to specify a set of scripts that you want to have run on your server.

You add a script to the policy by clicking the Add button. When you click the Add button, an entry is placed in the left window and you can edit the name of the script. After you have named the script, you can choose on the right the type of script that you will be creating. The choices of script types are currently NCF, NETBASIC, and PERL. After you identify the script type, you are free to type in the script in the provided window. ZENworks provides no syntax checking or validation for the script you enter. You may enter ZENworks Server Management variables into the script and they will be processed prior to the script being executed.

You can add multiple scripts of any of the available types into this one policy. The scripts are executed in the order shown on the administration screen (from top to bottom). If you want to reorder the running of the scripts, you must select a script name from the left pane and click the up or down arrows to move the script into a different order.

When the ZENworks policy engine launches this policy, it creates a temporary script file (in its working directory) that contains the specific script, and then launches the corresponding NLM that works with the identified script, passing the NLM the name of the script to run. Consequently, netbasic.nlm and perl.nlm must already exist on the server where the script is to be run. These are normally installed with the standard NetWare server. Regardless of whether a script fails or succeeds, the engine proceeds on to the next script.

On the Policy Schedule page, you may specify the time frame when you want the system to enforce this policy.

Server Inventory Policy

The Server Inventory Policy defines where to locate the ZENworks inventory service that is running, so the server can transmit any inventory information to that service. Additionally, this policy identifies the types of inventory that should be taken and any normalization rules that you want applied.

General Tab

On the General tab you can specify the following:

- ▶ Inventory Service Object DN—Browse to and select the DN that represents the Inventory service that is running on a back-end server. This object was created when you installed the Inventory services from the ZENworks Server Management installation.

- ▶ Server IP Address/DNS Name—Enter the DNS name or the IP address of the server that is hosting the back-end services.

- ▶ Proxy Server Configuration: IP Address/DNS Name—Enter the DNS name or the IP address of any proxy server that you may have set up to receive inventory.

- ▶ Proxy Server Configuration: Port—Enter the Port that is receiving the inventory information.

Software Scan Tab

Check the Enable Software Scan check box to enable scanning the file system to search for application software. Select the Custom Editor button to add entries into the database to describe application software that is not known in the software database.

Configuration Editor Tab

Enter any software rules into the Editor tab. These rules constitute key = value pairs used to normalize the inventory information that is collected through the header data on the software application files. If any of the specified keys are found, they are replaced with the given value. This allows you to normalize your data and represent a particular company, for example, as the same string regardless of the different strings that may have been stored in the executable.

Server Remote Management Policy

This policy allows you to configure how the Remote Management agent should behave on any assigned Windows servers. From this policy you can specify rights configurations and settings for remote control and remote view processes.

General Tab

On the General tab you can set the following options:

- ▶ Enable Session Encryption—This flag allows the configuration as to whether the agent will allow encrypted sessions.

- ▶ Allow User to Request Remote Session—This configuration will allow users on the remote server to request remote control sessions back to the administrator machine. This is necessary if the remote system is behind a NAT and the administrator machine cannot see the remote system on the network.

- ▶ Display Remote Management Agent Icon to Users—This will cause the remote management agent icon to be displayed in the system bar.

Control Tab

This tab allows you to describe how the remote control session behaves. The following options are available:

- ▶ Prompt User for Permission to Remote Control—Configure if the user should be prompted to allow the remote control session to begin.

- ▶ Give User Audible Signal When Remote Controlled—This will cause a beeping to occur on the target device when it is being remote controlled. The additional entry with this line allows you to specify the frequency that the beeping should occur.

- ▶ Give User Visible Signal When Remote Controlled—Configure if the name of the administrator performing the remote control should be displayed on the screen in a title box. Optionally you can specify how often to update the entry.

- ▶ Allow Blanking User's Screen—This will allow the administrator to blank the target screen. This will keep the user from seeing what is happening on the monitor.

- ▶ Allow Locking User's Keyboard and Mouse—This will allow the administrator to lock the user's keyboard and mouse, keeping them from typing and moving the mouse on the screen.

View Tab

This tab allows you to describe how the remote view session behaves. The following options are available:

▶ Prompt User for Permission to Remote View—Configure if the user should be prompted to allow the remote view session to begin.

▶ Give User Audible Signal When Remote Viewed—This will cause a beeping to occur on the target device when it is being remote viewed. The additional entry with this line allows you to specify the frequency that the beeping should occur.

▶ Give User Visible Signal When Remote Viewed—Configure if the name of the administrator performing the remote view should be displayed on the screen in a title box. Optionally you can specify how often to update the entry.

SMTP Host

Several of the features in ZENworks include the capability to have information and events emailed to identified users. In order to send the email, the agents must contact the SMTP server in your environment and will send the email through that system. This policy allows you to specify the IP address of the SMTP host that the agents associated with this policy (through inheritance) will use.

The SMTP Host page allows the administrator to identify the IP address of the SMTP mail server in their environment.

Just place your cursor in the SMTP Host field and type the IP address of the SMTP mail host. This field saves only the IP address. You can type in the DNS name of the SMTP host, but it will be saved as the IP address. The field queries DNS to resolve the IP address and then saves that address here.

SNMP Trap Targets

In ZENworks, several agents send an SNMP message to a central server that stores these messages and enables you to print reports on the traps. These traps can identify whether a policy has been successfully applied, whether a distribution was sent successfully, and other potential successes and failures.

The SNMP Trap Targets policy identifies the location of the service that is accepting and recording the SNMP messages from the server agents.

After you bring up the policy page, you may add as many trap targets as you desire. The service on the server sends the SNMP message to all of the specified trap targets. Click the Add button and specify whether the destination can be achieved with an IP address, an IPX address, or a DNS name. After selecting the type, a dialog box appears in which you can type either the address or the DNS name of the target service.

After you have added the trap targets, you need to specify how often that policy should be applied to the SNMP agents on the service location. From the Policy Schedule tab, you simply identify the policy schedule type that you want to apply. When the scheduled time arrives, the system retrieves the SNMP Trap Targets policy and applies it to the agents on the server.

Text File Changes Policy

This policy is a plural policy, which means you can create multiple instances of this policy in a single policy package. You create this policy by clicking the Add button at the bottom of the main Server Policy Package screen. When you click the Add button, you are prompted to select a policy and to name the policy. You need to select Text File Changes for the policy and enter a unique policy name. After you do this, you can activate and modify the policy.

This policy enables you to specify a set of text changes that you want done on ASCII text files on your server.

You enter a requested text file change by clicking the Add button. After clicking the Add button, you are prompted to identify the name of the text file and the name of the change script. You can have multiple change scripts for each file you identify. Make sure you enter the complete filename (including path) for the name of the text file to change. The changes are applied to the specified file in the order shown. Should you want to change the order of the changes or the order of the files, select the item and move it in the list by clicking the up or down arrows.

The first setting to be done is to choose the change mode that corresponds to this change policy. You may choose either Search File, Prepend to File, or Append to File as one of your modes.

Prepend to File

When you choose to prepend text to the file, the right side of the Administration page changes to display a large text box. You may enter any text strings that you want in the text box. Click OK to store this entry. When the policy is applied, the exact strings that you typed are placed as the first lines in the file.

Append to File

When you choose to append text to the file, the right side of the Administration page changes to display a large text box. You may enter any text strings that you want in the text box. Click OK to store this entry. When the policy is applied, the exact strings that you typed are placed as the last lines in the file.

Search File

Should this change be a Search File change, you need to administer the following additional information to make the change effective:

1. Identify the search type that you need for this change. The search type may be Sub-String, Whole Word, Start of Line, End of Line, or Entire Line. The following describes the meaning of each of these search types.

   ▶ Sub-String—Search for the search string in any of the text. The text specified may be contained anywhere in the file, even in the middle of a word. If you have the substring of "day," for example, the following text would all match with this substring: today, day, yesterday, daytime, and so forth.

   ▶ Whole Word—Search for the string such that it is surrounded by white space or beginning or end of line. If you have the string of "day," for example, only the word *day* would be a match. The words *today*, *yesterday*, *daytime*, and so forth do not constitute a match.

   ▶ Start of Line—This is a successful match if the beginning of a line (first line of file, or characters following a carriage return) starts with the string, regardless of whether the string is a whole word. To continue the example, if you had the string "day," this type would match only with the following lines: daytime is set, day by day, and so forth.

▶ End of Line—This is a successful match if the end of a line (characters preceding the carriage return or end of file) contains the string, regardless of whether the string is a whole word. With the example, if you had the string "day," this type would match only with the following lines: the time to act is today, day by day, and so forth.

▶ Entire Line—The entire specified string must consume the entire line of text (from text following a carriage return, or beginning of the file, to the next carriage return, or end of the file), including any white space. It must be an exact match of every character, other than the carriage returns, on the line. If your string were "day," only a line with the single word *day* on it will would match.

2. Specify the search string you're trying to match. Enter this into the Search String field.

3. Identify if you want the search to be case sensitive by selecting the check box to make the search only match if the case matches.

4. Change the Find All Occurrences field if you want to find only the first occurrence of the string in the file. The default is to have this field checked, meaning that all occurrences in the file will have this policy applied to them.

5. Choose a result action that is applied to the string after it is located in the file. The possible actions are Delete All Lines After, Delete All Lines Before, Prepend to File if Not Found, Append to File if not Found, Replace String, Replace Word, Replace Line, and Append Line. The following describes each of these choices and their resulting action:

   ▶ Delete All Lines After—All lines (characters following the next carriage return) are deleted from the file. The file is basically truncated, ending with the line that held the first matching string. Obviously, searching for all occurrences is not effectual when this is the resulting action, as a match truncates the rest of the file.

   ▶ Delete All Lines Before—All lines (characters before and including the previous carriage return) are deleted from the file. The file is reset such that it begins with the line that held the first matching string. With this result action, another search continues and if another match is found, all the lines before it are deleted as well.

- ▶ Prepend to File If Not Found — This action places the replacement text in the file at the very beginning of the file should the search string not be found. This action only adds text; it does not delete or modify text.

- ▶ Append to File If Not Found—This action places the replacement text at the end of the file should the specified search string not be found. This action only adds text; it does not delete or modify text.

- ▶ Replace String—This action takes the matching string and removes it from the file, placing the replacement string in the exact location of the deleted string. If the replacement string is of a different length than the search string, the surrounding characters are shifted to the left or right depending on whether less or more room is required. Basically, the new text is inserted in the location were the search string was removed.

- ▶ Replace Word—This action takes the word where a substring was matched and replaces the whole word (from space or beginning of line to space or end of line) with the replacement text. If the substring were "day," for example, the following words would be replaced with the replacement text: *day*, *today*, *daytime*, and so forth.

- ▶ Replace Line—This action takes the line where the match has occurred and removes the complete line from the file. The replacement text is placed in the same location where the removed line was located in the file.

- ▶ Append Line—This action appends the replacement string to the line that contained the match. The matching string is not removed from the file; the only change is the addition of text to the end of the line.

6. Specify the new string. In the text box that is provided, you need to supply the text that will be applied to the file, based on the action that was specified.

Wake on LAN Policy

The Wake on LAN policy allows you to manage which managed workstations will be controlled by the Wake on LAN service. The Wake on LAN service allows you to wake up a managed workstation or a set of managed workstations when activity on the LAN is detected. From the Wake on LAN policy page, you can specify objects from the following list of targets:

- ▶ Containers—All workstations in a country, locality, organization, or organizational unit

- ▶ Workstation—A specific workstation object

- ▶ Workstation Group—All workstations associated with a specific workstation group object

A Wake on LAN policy is added to a platform policy by clicking the Add button within a particular server policy list.

Workstation Import Policy

In ZENworks a service that now runs on a NetWare or Windows server automatically receives import requests and immediately creates the workstation object. After the object is created it returns the eDirectory Distinguished Name (DN) to the workstation. To perform these actions, the import service must be running on the server and must be accessible using a registry key on the workstation (`HKEY_LOCAL_MACHINE\ Software\Novell\ZENworks\zenwsreg\ImportServer = IP/DNS`) or the DNS name of `zenwsimport` either through the local host file on each workstation or via a DNS service. Additionally, the import service must have rights in the directory to create the workstation objects. The pages in this policy enable the administrator to grant these create rights to the import service, to specify how to name the workstation objects and in which container to place the objects, and to limit the number of requests that can be satisfied (to keep the system from overloading a server).

The import service can also be configured to ignore the first N requests from a workstation before it creates a workstation object. This can be useful if the workstation needs to pass through several hands to get properly configured and tested before it is actually given to the final end-user. This is to help this process settle before the workstation object is actually created.

NOTE

Your desktops do not import automatically if the workstations are finding a ZENworks 2 search policy in the tree. They must see either no search policy or a ZENworks 6.5 search policy to activate the automatic workstation import. See Chapter 3, "Getting ZENworks Desktop Management 7 Working in Your Environment," for more information.

Sometimes you want to have an import service provide more than one import policy. This can be done by setting the following key on the workstation that requires the nondefault policy:

```
[HKEY_LOCAL_MACHINE\SOFTWARE\Novell\ZENworks\zenwsreg]
"PolicyDN"="policyDN.novell"
```

This allows you to have the import server run various different policies. For example, if you have a single import server, but you want your lab machines to be automatically placed in a different group or have a different naming convention, place this registry key on those images with their policy identified. When the import service runs, it activates the specified policy for the import rules.

The following sections describe each of the pages available with the workstation import process. The NDS Rights, Other, and Rights to Files and Folders pages are described in the "Setting Up a Server Package" section earlier in the chapter.

Containers Page

The Containers page enables the administrator to grant rights to the import service to containers where they must create workstation objects. When you add a container to the list, the system grants rights to the policy object. When the import service needs to perform an import, it logs in as the policy being used, enabling it to obtain rights to create workstation objects in the specified container.

The process of adding and removing containers is familiar. You click the Add button, and you are presented with a dialog that enables you to browse through the tree to select the container you want. When selected, the container is added to the list, and the import service is given a trustee assignment to that container and given the rights to Browse and Create objects.

To remove a container from the list, select the desired container and click the Remove button. This removes the trustee assignment given to the service and deletes it from the displayed list.

Platforms Page

The Platforms page enables you to specify the naming of the workstation objects, the location of the object in the tree, and any workstation groups of which you want the workstation objects to be a member. This can be specified for each of the following categories: General, WinNT, Win2000, WinXP, or Win 9x (for example, Windows 98).

Each of the pages within these categories is identical, with the exception that on the nongeneral pages you have the additional field: Enable Platform Settings to Override General Settings. When this field is checked, the platform-specific configuration parameters are used rather than the general. We only discuss the General pages because they apply to all the other platform pages.

Figure 19.8 displays the first General page available.

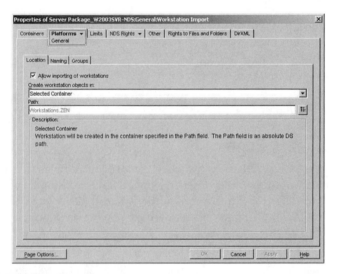

FIGURE 19.8
General page of a sample Workstation Import policy of a server package.

Each page has three tabs that enable you to configure separate options of the import policy. These tabs are Location, Naming, and Groups. Each of the following subsections discusses these tabs.

Location Tab

The Location tab enables the administrator to identify the container in the tree that should hold the workstation object when it is created during the import process. Figure 19.8 displays this screen.

The Allow Importing of Workstations check box enables or disables the ability to import workstations. When this box is checked, the other fields of the page become usable.

The Create Workstation Objects In drop-down box allows the administrator various options for locating the container in which to place the workstation objects. The options are as follows:

- ▶ Server Container—This option is new in ZENworks Desktop Management and when selected tells the system to place the workstation objects in the same container as the server running the import process.

- ▶ User Container—Signals that the container that holds the user object, of the user who logged in to the system when the registration of the workstation occurred, is the container that also holds the workstation object. Remember it is the first user who connects to the system (after the number of ignored connections has passed) that has the association to the workstation. A path may be specified in the Path field that would be considered to be relative to the user's container. The Path field is constructed by entering a relative path. This relative path is constructed by a series of dots and container names. For each dot in the path, the system moves up one level from the associated object container. For example, the path of .Workstations means for the system to go up two levels and in a container called Workstations at that level. If an alternative user is desired, you must run the unregistration tool zwsreg found in Program Files\Novell\ZENworks with the –unreg option.

- ▶ Associated Object Container—Signals that the container that has the policy package associated with it is used as the starting container to place the workstation object. If a path is specified, the associated container is used as the base, and the path is considered a relative path. The path field is constructed by entering a relative path. This relative path is constructed by a series of dots and container names. For each dot in the path, the system moves up one level from the associated object container. For example, the path of .Workstations means for the system to go up two levels and enter a container called Workstations at that level.

▶ Selected Container—Identifies that the specified path is an absolute container path in the tree. The Path field is required with this selection and must identify the specific container that will hold the workstation object.

Workstation Naming Page

On the Workstation Naming page the administrator can describe how the import process should use the information in the registration to craft the name of the workstation object.

The Workstation Name field displays the final combination of registration information that creates the name. In the previous example, the workstation object name is the computer name followed by the MAC address. This is confirmed by the fact that the Workstation Name field contains Computer+MAC Address. If the computer name was Rtanner and the MAC address of the NIC card were 12345, the workstation object name would be Rtanner12345.

The Add Name Fields and Place Them in Order field displays the various components put together to form the workstation name. Each line displayed in this field represents a value that is part of the name. The order of the lines from top to bottom represents the order that they appear in the name. The options that can be placed in the names are as follows:

▶ <User Defined>—Represents an administrator-defined string. When this field is chosen, the administrator is prompted to enter a string into the dialog box. This string is placed into the name. This can be any combination of standard ASCII visible characters including whitespace characters.

▶ Computer—Represents the computer name given to the computer usually during installation of the operating system.

▶ Container—Represents the name of the container into which the workstation object is placed. This name is included in the workstation name.

▶ CPU—Represents the CPU type of the machine. The possible values are 386, 486, and PENTIUM.

▶ DNS—Represents the DNS (Domain Name Services) name of the computer.

▶ IP Address—Represents the IP address of the machine when it is first registered with the tree. In previous versions of ZENworks Desktop Management this was retrieved through the Network Address request and a preferred protocol set to IP.

▶ MAC Address—Represents the address of the machine when it is first registered with the tree. In previous versions of ZENworks Desktop Management this was referred to as the Network Address.

▶ OS—Represents the operating system type of the machine. The expected values would be WINNT or WIN95, for example.

▶ User—The login name of the user connected to the tree when the registration process first executed.

For example, assume that a workstation had been registered with the following values:

```
CPU = PENTIUM
DNS = zen.novell.com
MAC address = 00600803c2e7
IP address = 137.65.61.99
OS = WINNT
Server = ZENSERVER
User = rtanner
Computer = RonComputer
```

Then, if we were to administer the Workstation Import policy with the following naming attributes, the corresponding workstation name would be created, assuming that pieces in quotes are a user-defined string:

```
UserOS = rtannerWINNT
DNSCPU = zen.novell.comPENTIUM
User" "MAC Address = rtanner 00600803c2e7
```

Remember that these values are used only at workstation object creation time. After the object is created, its name never changes. So if you replace the NIC card, although the address of the workstation changes, the name of the workstation does not change. If the name includes the NIC address, the workstation retains the name with the old NIC address.

Workstation Groups

The Workstation Groups page enables you to specify into which groups you want to place the workstation object when it is created. By placing the workstation object into a specific group you can automatically provide policies or rights to the workstation by group associations.

In the Workstation Groups page you may add and remove groups in the list, and the workstation will be made a member of each of the listed groups. The following describes the behavior of each button on the screen:

- ▶ Add—Adds a group to the list. When the button is clicked a dialog box is presented that enables you to browse the tree to identify the group. You browse the tree in the right pane and select the group in the left pane. After a group is selected, it is added to and displayed in the list.

- ▶ Remove—Becomes activated when a group in the window is selected. When a group is selected and Remove is clicked, the group is removed from the list.

- ▶ Remove All—Completely removes all groups from the list and cleans the set from consideration.

Remember that the Workstation Import policy is activated only when a new workstation is imported into the tree. If a workstation created with this policy is associated with a group and you go into the import policy and change the group memberships, the workstations that have already been created retain their group memberships. Only the new workstations created after the change are affected.

Limits Page

On the Limits page the administrator can control when a workstation automatically registers and how the import service on the server behaves. The intention of these fields is to ensure that the performance of the service does not consume a significant amount of processing on the server.

The first portion of the page, the User Login Number field, enables you to configure how many times the workstation must be used (a user logs in to the network via that desktop) before it is registered into the tree. This may be useful if your desktops must pass through several hands (that may connect to the tree) before it gets to its final user destination. Each time the workstation is used and a user is connected to the tree (or the workstation manager agents connects to the tree), the workstation communicates with the workstation import and requests a workstation object. If the number of login times has not been consumed, the service reports that one is not created, and the workstation continues. This repeats until the number of login times has occurred, whereupon the service creates the workstation object and returns the eDirectory Distinguished Name (DN) of the workstation object to the workstation. The desktop records this DN in its registry.

Each time that a user logs in to the workstation, ZENworks updates a count. This count is kept in the workstation registry and is transmitted to the import server, which checks it against the policy. If the count is greater than the policy, the import is performed. This count on the workstation is not reset if the policy changes.

When the Disable History check box is checked, the system will not keep a record of the users who have logged in to this workstation.

Selecting the Limiting the Number of Workstations Imported check box and filling in the Workstations Created Per Hour field enables the administrator to throttle the number of workstations created. This keeps your eDirectory from overloading with a tremendous amount of objects and having to synchronize them around your tree. Imposing this limit forces the service to create only the specified number of workstations in an hour period. As soon as the maximum has been reached within the hour, the workstations are told to proceed without a workstation object. The next time the workstations log in to the network, and the maximum has not been exceeded, the service creates a workstation object for them.

Workstation Removal Policy

Along with the ability to automatically create workstations in the tree, ZENworks provides an automated way to have expired workstation objects removed from the tree. This is to keep the tree from being cluttered with workstations no longer associated with any physical device.

Each time a workstation is used and has been registered in the tree, a service visits the workstation object and time stamps the last visit into the workstation object, along with refreshing several other pieces of information in the workstation object. This time stamp is what the workstation removal service looks at when it determines whether the workstation should be removed.

Containers Page

The Containers page enables the administrator to grant rights to the removal service to containers where they must remove workstation objects. When you add a container to the list, the system grants rights to the policy object. When the removal service needs to perform and delete a workstation object, it logs in as the policy being used, enabling it to obtain rights to remove workstation objects in the specified container.

These containers are the only ones that the service monitors for stale workstation objects.

The process of adding and removing containers is familiar. Click the Add button, and you are presented with a dialog box that enables you to browse through the tree to select the container you want. When selected, the container is added to the list, and the import service is given a trustee assignment to that container and given the rights to Browse and Delete objects.

To remove a container from the list, select the desired container and click the Remove button. This removes the trustee assignment given to the service and deletes it from the displayed list.

Limits Page

The Limits page enables you to specify how stale a workstation object must be before it is considered for removal. Figure 19.9 shows a sample Limits page.

You can use the up and down spinner controls to specify the number of days the workstation should not be connected with a device before it is considered for deletion. When the time stamp in the workstation object is older than the specified number of days on this page, the removal service deletes the object from the directory.

Schedule Page

The Schedule page enables the administrator to identify how often and when the workstation removal service should run on the server.

On this page you may identify the following configuration schedules:

- ▶ Year—The year to begin the launch of the removal service.
- ▶ Date—The calendar date within the year specified in the "Year" field when the removal service will be launched.

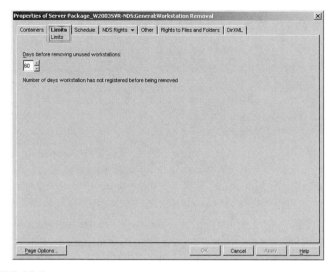

FIGURE 19.9
Workstation Removal policy; Limits page.

▶ Start Time—The time of day when the removal service is available to run.

▶ Duration—How long, after the start time, should the removal service run.

▶ Repeat Interval—How often after the initial start date the removal service should rerun and be made available.

▶ Limit Number of Workstations Removed—In the session value, the maximum number of workstations that should be removed while the removal service is available. When this maximum is reached, the service quits removing workstations until the next specified execution time. This is to keep from consuming a significant amount of processing cycles for eDirectory Distinguished Name to refresh the partitions where the removal has occurred.

The service, when started, calculates based on the start date, how often it should come alive (interval), and which day it should work. If today's the day, the service begins its workstation removal work. This is done so that even if the server needed to be rebooted, the service still would properly calculate the day it should run and not rely on being up the number of days in the interval.

ZENworks Database

Many of the agents in the system want to record information into the ZENworks database that is installed on your system. The ZENworks agents record logging and other information directly to the database and do not rely on the SNMP system to record events. In order for these agents to discover which database they should place their information in, they look for a ZENworks Database policy.

The Database policy then refers to a ZENworks database object in the directory (that was created at installation time), which in turn contains the DN or the IP address of the server that is supporting the database. The system also uses other information in the database object.

The Database page enables you to browse to the database object in the directory that represents the database that you want to use. All policy engines and distributor agents associated with this policy then log information into this database.

To set the Inventory Management database, you must go to the Inventory Database tab, click the Browse button to the right of the field, and then browse to and select the database object that you wishwant. This places the DN of the database object into the field.

To set the Policy/Distribution Management database, you must go to the Policy/Distribution Management Database tab, click the Browse button to the right of the field, and then browse to and select the database object that you want. This places the DN of the database object into the field.

ZENworks Server Management cannot use the database until a database policy is set and sent to the agents from the distributor.

ZENworks Server Management

In a ZENworks Server Management, you can define several configuration items in this policy that are applied to the components in the Policy and Distribution Services system. Using this policy keeps you from having to administer these items in each of the subscribers or distributors that you create in the network.

Defining the Messaging Property Page

The Messaging property page is under the General tab. Unless you are having some problems and are diagnosing some issues, it is not recommended to request a message level higher than 4.

For each of the appropriate fields, you may enter one of the following message levels:

- ▶ Level 6—This level includes all the other levels plus developer trace information.

- ▶ Level 5—This level includes all Level 4 messages in addition to trace information, which notifies the observer of the modules that are being executed. This level also captures and displays all Java exceptions.

- ▶ Level 4—This level includes all the Level 3 messages and, in addition, informational messages that identify key points in the system.

- ▶ Level 3—This level displays any warnings that were encountered in the system in addition to all the Level 2 messages.

- ▶ Level 2—This level displays the successes that were satisfied by the system and will also include all the Level 1 messages.

- ▶ Level 1—This level displays only errors that were encountered in the system.

- ▶ Level 0—This level displays no messages.

You can administer the following configuration parameters on the Message property page:

- ▶ SNMP Trap—This identifies the level of messages that should be sent as an SNMP trap to the SNMP host. The SNMP Host policy must be defined and active in an effective (for the distributor or subscriber object) Service Location package for traps to be sent.

- ▶ Log File—This identifies the level of messages that should be stored in the log file. Additionally, you can configure the following about the log file:

  - ▶ Filename—This is the filename of the log file. The default location for a distributor is SYS:\TED2\DIST\DIST.LOG and SYS:\TED2\SUB\SUB.LOG for a subscriber. You should probably change the location of the log file because it can grow. The log file may adversely affect the system because it is located on the SYS volume by default.

▶ Delete Log Entries Older than X days—In this parameter, you identify the number of days (X) worth of log entries that should remain in the log file. The default is 6 days. Therefore, any log entries that are older than 6 days are cleared from the log file. The process of removing the old entries from the log happens once every 24 hours.

▶ Email—With the email option, you can specify the level of messages that are sent in an email to the identified users. The SMTP Host policy in the ZENworks for Servers 3 Service Location policy package must be active and the package must be effective for the distributor or subscriber object in order to enable it to discover the address of the SMTP host to send the email. If this is not specified, the email will not be sent.

In addition to identifying the level of messages, you must also specify who should receive these messages. To add users to the list and have them receive the message, you must select whether you want to add an NDS User or Group, or specify an email address in the drop-down menu. When you select a user, you are asked to browse to the user in the directory, and the system takes the email address attribute from the user and uses that as the address for the user. Should you choose a group, all the users in the group are sent the email message, and the email attribute is used for each of those users. Should you not want to use the email address attribute in the user object, you may select the down arrow in the Address Attribute field and select which of the NDS User attributes you want to identify as containing the email address. It is expected that the attribute you identify will contain a valid email address.

If you choose to enter an explicit email address, rather than selecting a user or a group, you may choose the Email Address choice from the Add button. You are prompted to enter a valid email address. The entered email address is assumed to be valid and is shown as the User Name field in the table with an "N/A" in the Address Attribute field.

Configuration Page

Under the ZENworks Server Management tab is the Configuration Page. You can administer the following configuration options on this page:

▶ Working Directory—This is for temporary and backup files. The default directory is sys:\zenworks\pds\smanager\working. For NetWare servers, do not use extended or double-byte characters in the path.

▶ Purge Database Entries Older Than X Days—Specify a number for periodic purging of the database file. All Server Management information older than the number of days entered is purged when Server Management is started on the same server where zfslog.db resides.

NOTE IMPORTANT: The database file can be purged only if the Policy/Package Agent is running on the same server where the database file is located.

Port Configuration Page

Under the ZENworks Server Management Port Configuration tab is the Port Configuration Page. This allows you to specify the port that should be used for communications to the services running on the device. The default port is 8089 and can be changed by clicking the up and down arrows.

Summary

This chapter discusses all the policies available in the server package and those that are effective for servers in your network. Using these server policies allows you to efficiently configure your ZENworks system and describe the desired actions and behaviors so that ZENworks automatically manages your systems.

## CHAPTER 20

Using ZENworks Workstation Inventory

ZENworks Desktop Management includes powerful workstation inventory software that allows you to gather complete hardware and software inventory for all managed workstations on your network. After workstations have been imported into eDirectory by ZENworks, the inventory software can be used to collect, store, and report information about the client workstations on your network. This information can be useful in helping to make business decisions on how to manage workstations. The following are some examples of business decisions that can be made from workstation inventory information:

- ▶ Which workstations need new applications
- ▶ Which workstations need updated hardware and drivers
- ▶ Which workstations should receive an application object
- ▶ Which workstations are running the corporate software standard
- ▶ Which workstations conform to the corporate hardware standard

The following sections describe the workstation inventory process, how to set up inventory in your environment, and what tasks can be performed after it has been properly installed and configured.

Understanding Workstation Inventory

To better help you understand how to make the most of the workstation inventory feature of ZENworks Desktop Management, you need to know how the process works and what components are involved. The following sections describe the inventory process, the servers involved, and the roles they play in various inventory database designs.

Understanding the Inventory Process

The inventory process is the act of acquiring hardware and software information from the workstation, relaying that information to the inventory server, and then storing it in a database for later retrieval. The following sections describe how workstations are scanned, how inventory data is rolled up to the database, what information is collected, and the files and directories involved.

Workstation Scanning

Scanning is done by an application that runs on the workstation. The inventory scanner and all necessary components were installed on the workstation when the ZENworks management agent was installed. That application scans the workstation and collects data based on the various configurations of the inventory settings. If the workstation is Desktop Management Interface (DMI) compliant or Web-based Management Interface (WMI) compliant, the scanner can also query the DMI and WMI service layers to collect data.

After the scanner has collected information about the workstation, it stores it in an .STR file in the scan directory of the inventory server. The scanner tracks the changes in the scan data by storing it in the `HIST.INI` file, located in the ZENworks installation directory. Any errors that the scanner reports are stored in the `ZENERRORS.LOG` file, located in the ZENworks installation directory on the workstation.

Workstation inventory scanning uses the following steps to update the inventory server and eDirectory:

1. The inventory policies in eDirectory define the inventory settings, such as scanning time, whether to include software scanning of workstations, and the location of the scan directory.

2. The Scanner reads the settings in the inventory policies and uses them to collect the workstation inventory information.

3. The Scanner stores the scan data of each workstation as an .STR file in the scan directory (**SCANDIR**) at the server.

4. The Scanner also stores a minimal subset of workstation inventory information of the workstation, in the eDirectory workstation object.

5. The Selector, running on the inventory server, validates the .STR file and places the file in the enterprise merge directory (**ENTMERGEDIR**). If a database is attached, the Selector places the files in the Database directory (**DBDIR**).

6. If a database is attached to the server, the server updates the database with the inventory information of the .STR file.

After these steps are complete, the network administrator then can view the inventory information, query the database, and generate inventory reports in ConsoleOne.

Inventory Data Roll-Up

In many networks, one server is not enough to collect and store inventory data for every workstation in the tree. For this reason, multiple servers can be configured to collect inventory data and roll that information up to other servers.

ZENworks uses the following steps to roll scanned data up after it is collected on a server:

1. After the Selector validates the .STR file and places the file in the enterprise merge directory (**ENTMERGEDIR**) for roll-up of scan data, the sending server uses a roll-up policy to identify the server to which it will transmit the scan data. It also reads the roll-up schedule to determine the specified time for roll-up of data.

2. The sending server compresses the .STR files as a .ZIP file and places the .ZIP file in the enterprise push directory (**ENTPUSHDIR**). The Sender then sends the .ZIP file to the receiver on the next-level server.

3. The receiving server on the next level receives the .ZIP file and places the file in **ENTPUSHDIR**. If this server has a database attached to it or if the server is a root server, the compressed files are placed in the database directory (**DBDIR**).

4. The receiving server extracts the .ZIP file containing the .STR files into a temp directory (`DBDIR\TEMP`) and updates the database with the inventory information of the workstation .STR file.

When these steps are complete, the network administrator then can view the inventory information, query the database, and generate inventory reports in ConsoleOne.

What Software Information Is Recorded

The scan program also scans the workstation software for Desktop Management Interface (DMI) software as well as Web-based Management Interface (WMI) systems. If neither of these is present, the scanner contacts the hardware directly and continues to scan the drive for installed software. The software scan performs the following functions based on its setup and configuration:

▶ Check the existence of the software at the workstations and servers.

▶ Gather information about the application file.

▶ Report the information about the scanned software (such as software vendor, software title, file size, and so on).

▶ Check for the software specified in the inventory policy associated with the workstation object.

▶ Customize the software scanning based on the software list configured.

▶ Collect configuration file information and report details and contents of the system files.

▶ Report information about the installed drivers.

Inventory Files and Directories

Workstation inventory uses several files and directories during the scanning and roll-up process. You should be aware of the following files used during the scanning and roll-up process:

▶ `HIST.INI`—Located in the Windows ZENworks directory on the workstation. Contains the history of the scan data for each workstation.

▶ .STR—Formatted: *macaddress_gmt_sequencenumber*`.STR`. Located in the `SCANDIR` directory on the inventory server. Created by the scanning program. Contains all inventory information scanned from the workstation.

▶ .ZIP—Formatted:
scheduletime_inventoryservername_siteID_sitename.ZIP.
Located in the ENTPUSHDIR and DBDIR. Contains the compressed
scan data for several workstations, up to 1,000 .STR files, collected
by a receiving inventory server. Used to transmit the data from one
server to another.

▶ .PRP—Formatted: *scheduletime_inventoryservername*.PRP.
Located in the .ZIP files. Identifies the information for roll-up from
the enterprise push directory to the next-level server. The properties file contains the schedule time, inventory server name, and signature that helps to authenticate the .ZIP file.

After the scan program has run and the hardware and software information about the server has been recorded, that information is stored on the
inventory servers in the following directory locations:

▶ SCANDIR—Contains the .STR files, which is the raw data collected
by the scan programs run at the workstation.

▶ DBDIR—Contains the .STR files for workstations scanned on the
network. The .STR files in the DBDIR directory are used to update
the workstation objects in the database.

▶ ENTMERGEDIR—Stores the .STR files created and transferred by the
workstation scan programs.

▶ EntPushDir—Stores the .STR and .ZIP files used to roll inventory
data up in an enterprise tree.

Understanding Inventory Database Server Types

Data collected from each scan is stored in directories and databases located on inventory servers. The following are the types of servers used in
the inventory process.

Root Server

The root server acts as the highest point in the inventory tree. A root
server, by default, must have a database attached to it. The root server
can collect data from intermediate servers, leaf servers, or from workstations attached to it. A root server can only be configured to receive data,
not to roll it up to another level.

Intermediate Server

The intermediate server acts as a staging server to receive data from a lower server in the tree and send it to another intermediate server or to a root server. By default, the intermediate server does not have a database attached, nor does it have workstations attached. You can, however, configure the intermediate server to have both workstations and a database attached to it. The intermediate server typically receives data from a leaf server or another intermediate server and then rolls it up higher in the tree, eventually to the root server.

Leaf Server

The leaf server acts as the gathering server of inventory information from workstations. By default, the leaf server must have workstations attached but does not have a database attached to it. The leaf server simply gathers data and rolls it up higher in the tree. Typically the data is rolled up to an intermediate server, but a leaf server can also roll data up to a root server.

Standalone Server

The standalone server acts as a single point of inventory data collection for workstations. The standalone server must have both a database and workstations attached to it. The data collected by a standalone server cannot be rolled up to another server, nor can information collected by a leaf server be rolled up to a standalone server. Typically, the standalone server is used in small networks where only one inventory server is needed to collect data.

Understanding Inventory Server Roles

Now that you understand the types of servers used for workstation inventory, you need to know the roles they can provide. Depending on their types, each server can be configured to perform one or both of the following two roles:

▶ Workstations attached

▶ Database attached

Each of these options is explored in the following sections.

Workstations Attached

The first role a server can perform is to have workstations attached. Setting this option for the server means that the server accepts data from the scan programs being run at the workstations. At least one server on the network must perform this role, but usually most of the servers configured for workstation inventory will perform the role of collecting data from the workstations. Leaf servers and standalone servers always have this option set, but you can configure root server and intermediate servers to have workstations attached as well.

Database Attached

The second role a server can perform is to have a database attached to it. Setting this option means that the server is configured to enter the information scanned by the workstation, either locally or up from a server below, into a local database. This means that a database must be running on the server to accept the information from ZENworks. Root servers and standalone servers always have this option set, but you can configure intermediate servers and leaf servers to have a database as well.

Workstation Inventory Design

Now that you understand the types of servers and the roles they play in workstation inventory, you need to design an inventory tree that matches your network. The following sections describe some common designs for generic networks.

Standalone Inventory

The standalone inventory is the simplest design; only one server is involved. That server acts as the collection and storage service for inventory data scanned from workstations. It has an inventory database installed on it and workstations attached.

This type of design is perfect for smaller networks with 5,000 or fewer workstations. It is easy to maintain and configure; however, it is not scalable.

Centralized Inventory

The centralized inventory design, shown in Figure 20.1, is for large networks where all servers are connected on a LAN. In this approach, allowance is made for a large number of users by adding a number of leaf and intermediate servers for workstation scanners to send their data to.

The centralized inventory approach is still fairly easy to maintain; however, roll-up policies must be configured for the intermediate and leaf servers.

Centralized Inventory

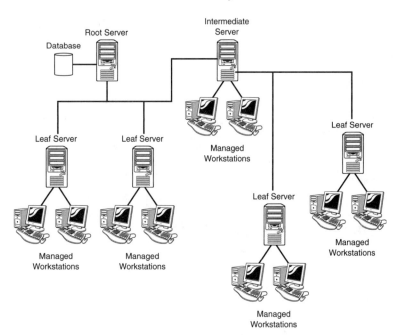

FIGURE 20.1
The centralized workstation inventory design.

Distributed Inventory

The distributed inventory design, shown in Figure 20.2, is for large networks where several remote sites are connected through a WAN. In this approach, allowance is made for a large number of users by creating several root servers, one at each remote site, and then leaf and intermediate servers for workstation scanners to send their data to.

The distributed inventory approach is still much more difficult to maintain because you need to manage several inventory trees. However, the distributed approach overcomes problems that can occur rolling up large numbers of workstations from remote offices.

Enterprise Inventory

The final type of inventory design is the enterprise inventory design shown in Figure 20.3. Most enterprise networks take this approach in one form or another. In the enterprise design, accommodations exist for the large number of users, yet a single management point is made by creating a single root server and interlacing intermediate and leaf servers at strategic locations in the network to ensure optimal performance.

Distributed Inventory

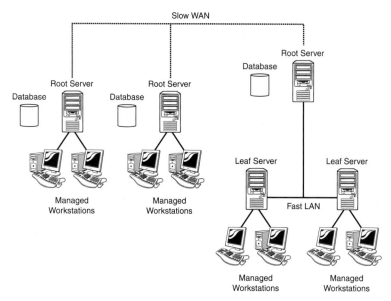

FIGURE 20.2
The distributed workstation inventory design.

The best way to achieve an optimal enterprise design is to follow the steps outlined in the following sections.

List the Sites in the Enterprise

The first step in designing an enterprise workstation inventory tree is to describe the entire network of your company by doing the following:

- ▶ List the various sites in your company (buildings, cities, countries, and so on).

- ▶ List the physical links between the various sites.

- ▶ Identify the type of links in terms of bandwidth and reliability.

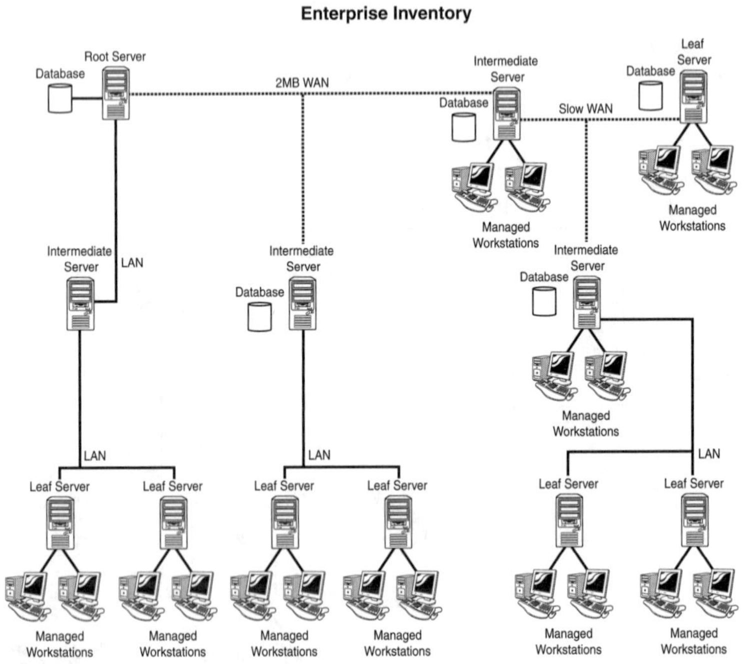

Enterprise Inventory

FIGURE 20.3
The enterprise workstation inventory design.

Determine the Ideal Place for Root Server

After you list the sites in your enterprise network, you need to determine the best place to put the root server. The inventory information stored in the inventory database of the root server consists of all lower-level sites on the network as well as the root server site.

The location of the root server determines the behavior and scalability of your inventory tree. Consider the following factors when determining its location:

▶ The root server should be on the site with high network bandwidth.

▶ A console administrator can collect workstation inventory information from any of the sites connected on high-speed links from the root server, or from the root server level site.

▶ A database server of suitable configuration can be provided for the inventory server. For a network with 250,000 workstations, the recommended configuration for the root server is 25GB of disk space and 1GB RAM.

Determine Requirements for Other Databases

Now that you have determined the location of the root server, you need to determine whether you need to maintain database servers at different sites. You may want to maintain additional databases if sites or subtrees are managed for inventory at different locations over a slow link.

Also consider specific reasons to have a separate database for a single site or a set of sites. There may be some organizational needs of your company to have the database server on different sites.

NOTE For a majority of enterprises, there may be no need to have any other database besides the enterprisewide single database. All site-specific reports can be generated from this database easily.

If you determine that another database is required, consider the following to determine the appropriate location and setup:

▶ Identify the sites that need a database. Additionally, you need to examine whether the database will cater to the local site or a site of sites (subtree). Then identify the sites that require data in each inventory database.

▶ All the sites served by a single database should typically access this database rather than the database at root server for inventory management. This reduces the load on the database at root server.

▶ Database administrators should be available for these sites.

Identify the Route for Inventory Data

After you determine any additional databases needed, you need to identify the routes for inventory data for all sites to the nearest database. From those routes you then need to determine the final route to the database on the root server.

The route plan can become complex, so to help devise a route plan follow these guidelines:

▶ Each route can have an intermediate server at a staging site. The intermediate server receives and transmits the data to the next destination. These are application-layer level routes for inventory data. There can be various network-layer level routes between two adjacent servers, which is determined and managed by the routers in the network.

▶ The route answers the basic question: To which site will the inventory data travel from a particular site so that it eventually reaches the database at the root server, which is its final destination?

▶ There may be multiple routes. Choose the fastest and most reliable route. To determine the route, consider the physical network links.

▶ Routes identified once and made operational can be changed later; although there may be some cost in terms of management and traffic generation. If no intermediate database is involved, you can change the route by changing the eDirectory based policy only.

▶ Put intermediate servers on sites where the link parameters change substantially. Criteria to consider are difference in bandwidth, difference in reliability of the links, and need for different scheduling.

▶ Availability of servers on the intermediate site for staging the inventory data should be considered in deciding the sites for intermediate servers. Provide enough disk space on these servers to store all the inventory data on the disk until the roll-up policy asks to send them to the next destination.

▶ Workstations should not be connected to the inventory server over a WAN because the scanning of workstations should not happen across a WAN.

Identify Servers on Each Site for Inventory, Intermediate, and Database

After you plan the routes that data will take to the root server, you need to identify servers on each site to perform the roles necessary to achieve the route. Specifically, you need to identify servers to act as inventory, intermediate, and database servers.

A single server can have different roles if it has sufficient resources. For example, an inventory server can be a leaf server with database. You could also designate a server as an intermediate server with database, which receives inventory from the workstations and also has an inventory database.

When considering the roles of the server, take into account the following factors:

▶ The number of workstations attached to the server also determines the load.

▶ Take an average of 50KB inventory data from each workstation to calculate the load.

▶ Any inventory server that has workstations attached to it requires 100KB per workstation.

▶ The server that has the inventory database requires 200KB per workstation.

▶ An intermediate server that rolls up data requires 5KB for roll-up of 50KB scan data.

Create the Tree of Servers for Workstation Inventory

After you determine the roles that inventory servers will take at each site, you need to create the tree of servers that will be used for workstation inventory.

After the inventory server tree is designed, make sure that the following are true:

▶ The root of the tree is the root server.

▶ Servers on each site of the tree represent all the sites in the company.

▶ At least one server exists per site.

▶ Assuming that workstations to be scanned exist on each site, there is an inventory server role on each site.

▶ Optimally, database and intermediate servers exist at the appropriate sites.

Create an Implementation Plan

After you design your inventory server tree, you need to create an implementation plan. The implementation plan should cover the phased deployment of inventory throughout the network.

To help with creating an implementation plan use the following guidelines:

▶ Start the deployment from the root server site and flow it down to the servers of other sites that connect to the root server.

▶ Use the number of workstations on each site and server as the main criteria for deployment.

▶ Deploy the product on approximately 5,000 workstations per day.

Setting Up Workstation Inventory

After you install the appropriate components and complete your workstation inventory tree design, you are ready to begin configuring your network to start scanning workstation data and storing it into the inventory database. The following sections describe the configuration necessary to implement your tree design.

Configuring the Settings for the Inventory Service Object

The first step in configuring workstation inventory is to configure the settings for the inventory service object. The inventory service object controls how, when, and where the inventory server collects inventory scan data. The following sections discuss how to configure the inventory service object.

Configuring the Inventory Service Object Properties

The first things you must configure for the inventory service object is the role, scan data time and path in the Inventory Service Object property page.

From within ConsoleOne, right-click the inventory service object and select Properties. Then select the Inventory Service Object Properties tab, as shown in Figure 20.4. The following sections describe the configuration options on the Inventory Service Object property page.

Modify the Role for the Inventory Service Object

Based on the servers that you have deployed for scanning inventory, you must specify the role of the server. You can select root server, intermediate server, leaf server, or standalone server based on your inventory configuration.

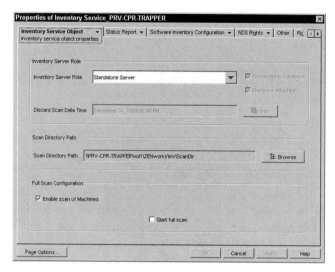

FIGURE 20.4
The Inventory Service Object Properties tab for inventory service objects in ConsoleOne.

Discard Scan Data Files at the Specified Date and Time

Select the time and date. Any scan data files (.ZIP files) that have scan information before this date and time will be discarded. The scan data files are removed from the server at the time specified in the Discard Scan Data Time field. This can be useful in keeping your servers from running out of disk space.

Modify the Path for the Scan Files

When you install ZENworks Desktop Management, you specify the volume on the server for storing the scan data files. If required, you can modify the volume or the directory of the Scan Directory (**SCANDIR**) setting from the Inventory Service Object property page.

To modify the setting you must click on the Browse button to browse to the new **SCANDIR** directory path on the server. The format of the scan directory path is as follows:

```
\\server_name\volumename\path
```

NOTE You cannot modify the server name specified in the SCANDIR path. If you modify the directory, the directory must already exist.

Enable Scanning of Workstations

To select the enable scanning of workstations option to scan the workstations associated with the policy, you must check the Enable Scan of Machines option listed in the Inventory Service Object property page. By default, the scanners collect only hardware information of the workstations.

Enforce Full Scan

When scanning the workstation for the first time the Scanner collects the complete inventory of the workstation. A complete inventory scan of the workstation is referred as a *full scan*.

After the workstation is inventoried, the next time the Scanner runs, it compares the current inventory data to the history data that it maintains. If any changes to the workstation exist, the Scanner creates a *delta scan*, which collects the changes in inventory since the last scan was reported. The Delta scan setting is the default scan operation for each successive scan after the first scanning of the workstation.

If the Status Log reported by the inventory component indicates that the scanning on the workstation is not successful, you can enforce a full scan. This policy's settings are applicable for all workstations associated with it. To override this policy, you set this option for an individual workstation.

Configuring the Inventory Service Sync Schedule

After you configure the settings on the Inventory Service Object Properties page, you need to configure the sync schedule for the inventory service. The Inventory Sync Service runs on all inventory servers that have inventoried workstations attached to them. The Inventory Sync Service is a service loaded by the Inventory Service Manager. It removes the redundant or obsolete inventoried workstations from the Inventory database.

Use the following steps in ConsoleOne to configure the Inventory Sync Service Schedule to schedule the Inventory Sync Service to run:

1. Right-click on the Inventory Service object and select Properties from the pop-up menu.

2. Select Inventory Service Object tab→Inventory Service Sync Schedule shown in Figure 20.5.

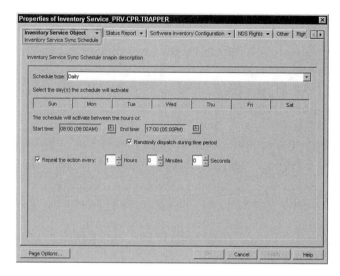

FIGURE 20.5
The Inventory Service Sync Schedule tab for inventory service objects in ConsoleOne.

3. Modify the schedule settings to schedule the Inventory Sync Service to run at the appropriate time.

4. Click OK to apply the settings and close the window.

If your workstation inventory tree design includes multiple levels, you need to configure roll-up of scan data in your inventory setup. You need to specify the details, such as the next-level server for roll-up in the roll-up policy contained in the server package. Use the procedures outlined in the following sections to create and configure a roll-up policy for scan data.

Server Package for Roll-Up

After you configure the inventory service sync schedule, use the following steps to create a server package that contains the roll-up policy for identifying the next-level server for roll-up:

1. In ConsoleOne, right-click the container where you want the policy package created. Click New→Policy Package→Server Package. Then click Next.

2. Type the name for the server package, click Next, and then click Finish.

Enable the Roll-Up Policy

After you configure the next-level server for roll-up, use the following steps to enable the roll-up policy in the server package and associate the server package to eDirectory objects.

1. In ConsoleOne, right-click the Server Package and select Properties→Policies. Then click one of the following subtabs: General, NetWare or Windows.

2. Check the Enabled Column for the Inventory Roll Up Policy box.

3. Click Properties. The Inventory Roll-Up Policy tab appears.

4. Browse to select the DN of the inventory service object and click OK.

5. Select the IP address or DNS name of the inventory server you want to assign the roll-up policy to. You can also specify a proxy server address and port.

At the completion of these steps, click OK to assign the roll-up policy.

Schedule the Roll-Up Time

After you enable the roll-up policy in the server package, use the following steps to schedule the date and time when the roll-up should occur:

1. In ConsoleOne, right-click the Server Package and select Properties. Select Policies and click one of the following subtabs: General, NetWare, or Windows.

2. Select the Roll-Up Policy row and then select Properties. Click the Roll-Up Policy tab and select Roll-Up Schedule. Modify the settings for scheduling the roll-up time and click OK.

NOTE While scheduling the roll-up of data in the inventory policies, we recommend that the roll-up frequency should be at least one day. It is likely that if the roll-up frequency is too low, for example less than one hour, there may be some performance degradation of the inventory server.

Configuring the Policies for the Database

The installation program creates the database object for Sybase and configures the database server. However, you need to set up the associations for the database server.

If you are maintaining the Inventory database in Oracle or MS SQL Server, perform the tasks outlined in the following sections before making the associations.

Configure Database Server Options

The first step in configuring policies for the database is to configure the database server options of the database object. The following steps describe configuring the database server options:

1. In ConsoleOne, right-click the Inventory Database object and select Properties→ZENworks Inventory Database.

2. Browse for the DN of the server or type the server IP address.

3. Type the values for the following options: Database (Read-Write) User Name: **MW_DBA**; Database (Read-Write) Password: *<inventory password>*; Database (Read Only) User Name: **MW_READER**; Database (Read Only) Password: *<inventory password>*; Database (Write Only) User Name: **MW_UPDATER**; Database (Write Only) Password: *<inventory password>*.

4. Click OK.

Configure JDBC Driver Properties

After you configure the database server options of the database object, use the following steps to ensure that the JDBC driver properties are correct as per your database configuration:

1. In ConsoleOne, right-click the database object and select Properties. Then click the Jdbc Driver Information tab.

2. Select Oracle; then populate the fields for an Oracle database as shown in Table 20.1. Then click Populate Now.

3. Click OK.

After you complete the steps for having the Inventory database in Oracle or MS SQL—or if you are simply using the Sybase database—perform the following steps to do the associations for the server.

TABLE 20.1   Database Settings for a Sybase Database, Oracle Database, and an MS SQL Server Database

DATABASE SETTINGS	FOR A SYBASE DATABASE	FOR AN ORACLE DATABASE	FOR AN MS SQL SERVER
Driver	Com.sybase.jdbc.SybDriver	oracle.jdbc.driver.OracleDriver	com.microsoft.jdbc.sqlserver.SQLServerDriver
Protocol	Jdbc:	jdbc:	jdbc:
SubProtocol:	Sybase:	oracle:	microsoft:
SubName:	Tds:	thin:@	sqlserver:11
Port:	2638	1521	1433
Flags:	?ServiceName=mgmtdbs& JCONNECT_VERSION=4	Database Service Name (Service ID of the Oracle database)	-Orcl

Create the Service Location Package

You must set up the ZENworks database policy to establish the location of the database; otherwise, no information can be logged to the database. To establish the service location of the database, use the following steps:

1. In ConsoleOne, right-click the Policy Packages container and select New→Policy Package→click Service Location Package. Then click Next.

2. Type the name for the Service Location Package. Then click Next and click Finish.

Configure the Service Location Policy

1. In ConsoleOne, right-click the Service Location Package and select Properties. Then click the Policies tab.

2. Check the box under the Enabled column for the ZENworks database.

3. Click Properties.

4. Browse to the DN of the ZENworks inventory database object and click OK to accept the object. Click OK again to close the ZENworks database properties window.

5. Select the Associations tab and then click the Add button.

6. Browse to select the container under which the database object is present and click OK twice.

Configuring the Inventory Policies for Workstations

After you configure the server database and service location policies you need to configure the inventory policies for the workstation. In the workstation inventory policy, you configure the following settings for scanning workstations:

▶ Scanning time at the workstations

▶ Inventory server to which the workstations send scanned data

▶ Include software scanning of workstations

▶ List of software applications for scanning

Use the following steps to configure the workstation inventory policy.

Create a Workstation Policy Package

You need to create a policy package for the workstations to configure the inventory policies for them. Use the following steps to create and configure a policy package for the workstations:

1. In ConsoleOne, right-click the container where you want the workstation package and select New→Policy Package.

2. Select Workstation Package from the policy packages list and click Next.

3. Type the name for the workstation package and click Next. Then click Finish.

Enable Workstation Inventory Policy

After you create a policy package for the workstaions, use the following steps to enable and associate the workstation inventory policy:

1. In ConsoleOne, right-click the Workstation Package and select Properties→Policies. Then click one of the following subtabs: Windows 9x, Windows NT-2000-XP, Windows NT, Windows 2000, or Windows XP.

2. Check the Enable the Workstation Inventory Policy box and click Apply.

3. Click the Associations tab and click Add.

At the conclusion of these steps, browse to select the container object under which the workstations are registered and then click OK twice.

Specify Inventory Server

After you enable and associate the workstation inventory policy, use the follwing steps to specify the inventory server to which the scanner sends the workstation scan data:

1. In ConsoleOne, right-click the workstation package and Properties→Policies. Then select one of the following subtabs: Windows 9x, Windows NT-2000-XP, Windows 2000, or Windows XP.

2. Select the Workstation Inventory Policy row. Then select Properties and select the Workstation Inventory tab.

3. Configure the workstation inventory policy as described in the section "Configuring the Workstation Inventory Policy" later in this chapter.

4. Click OK.

Schedule Workstation Scanning

After you specify the inventory server to which the scanner will send the workstation scan data, use the following steps to schedule the time for activating scanning at the workstations:

1. In ConsoleOne, right-click the Workstation Package and select Properties→Policies. Then select one of the following subtabs: Windows 9x, Windows NT-2000-XP, Windows 2000, or Windows XP.

2. Click the Workstation Inventory Policy row and select Properties. Then select the Policy Schedule tab.

3. Modify the settings for scheduling the scan of the workstations. Click OK twice.

Enable Scanning

After you schedule the time for activating scanning at the workstations, use the following steps to ensure that the scanning is enbabled:

1. In the Inventory Service Object property page, you enable the scan of the workstations associated with the selected inventory server.

2. From ConsoleOne, right-click the Inventory Service object (`Inventory servername_ZenInvService`) and select Properties. Then select the Inventory Service Object Properties tab.

3. Check Enable Scan of Machines and click OK.

After you finish configuring the workstation inventory policies for workstations, make the following check in your environment to make sure that the inventory scanning process can complete properly.

If you configured the inventory server that is a Windows server and Windows 98 workstations are present that will send their scan data to that Windows server, you must do the following for the scanners to collect data:

▶ If eDirectory users are present who are also Windows domain users, make sure that the users logged in are valid users of the Windows domain in the existing share created by ZENworks.

▶ If users are logged in to a different domain, make sure that the users are trusted users of the domain in the existing share created by ZENworks.

▶ If eDirectory users are present who are not users of any Windows domain, make sure that the users do not log in to eDirectory during workstation startup. However, these users can log in to eDirectory later.

Configuring the Workstation Inventory Policy

The workstation inventory policy allows you to configure which inventory service the workstations associated with this workstation policy package will use. It also allows you to enable and configure hardware and software scanning.

To configure the server inventory policy for a workstation policy package, right-click on the package and select Properties from the pop-up menu. Then select the Policies tab for the operating system you want to configure. ZENworks Desktop Management allows you to select Windows 9x, Windows NT-2000-XP, Windows 2000, or Windows XP—or General to configure for all those operating systems. Next, enable the workstation inventory policy by checking the box next to it. Finally, select the workstation inventory policy and click the Properties button to bring up the Workstation Inventory Policy Properties window. The following sections discuss how to configure the workstation inventory policy from this window.

Configure General Settings

The first step in configuring the workstation inventory policy is to configure which inventory service workstations associated with this policy will use. Select the General tab in the Workstation Inventory Policy page, as shown in Figure 20.6, and configure the following settings:

▶ Inventory Service Object DN—Use the Browse button to navigate through the eDirectory tree and locate the inventory service policy, the correct roll-up schedules, and locations configured for servers associated with this workstation policy package.

▶ Force Full Scan Schedule—After you select the inventory service object, you need to specify, in the Force Full Scan Schedule field, the number of delta scans that will occur before a full scan is required.

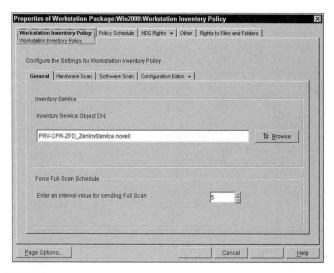

FIGURE 20.6
General settings in the Workstation Inventory Policy page for a workstation policy package.

Configure Hardware Scan

Next you need to configure hardware scanning by selecting the Hardware Scan tab, shown in Figure 20.7, and setting the following options:

▶ Enable DMI Scan—Enables ZENworks to collect hardware inventory data from Windows workstations using the Desktop Management Interface (DMI) 2.0 specification.

▶ Enable WMI Scan—Enables ZENworks Desktop Management to collect hardware inventory data from Windows workstations using the Web-based Management Interface (WMI) 1.5 specification.

▶ Enable Custom Scanning—Allows you to enable custom hardware scanning and specify a custom scan executable to be run on inventoried workstations.

▶ Custom Attribute Editor—Allows you to specify a list of custom hardware attributes that should be scanned for during the workstation scanning process.

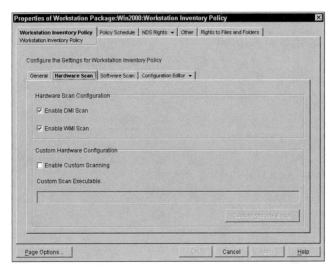

FIGURE 20.7
Hardware scan settings for the workstation inventory policy for a workstation policy package.

Configure Software Scan

Next you need to configure software scanning. From the Software Scan tab, shown in Figure 20.8, you have the option to enable the following software inventory options to use when scanning workstations:

▶ Enable Software Scan—Enables software scanning on workstations associated with this workstation policy package.

▶ Product Identification Number—Scans for product identification numbers of applications installed on inventoried workstations. The product identification number can be useful in sorting and organizing inventory software reports.

▶ Product Location—Allows you to specify software scanning to include scanning of the full path of the product executable installed on the inventoried workstations.

▶ Perform Only Custom Scanning—Allows you to specify software scanning to scan only for the software defined by the custom scan editor.

▶ Custom Scan Editor—Clicking on the Custom Scan Editor button brings up the Custom Scan Editor window.

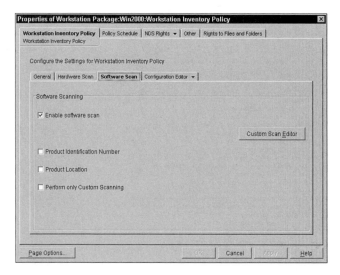

FIGURE 20.8
Software Scan settings for the workstation inventory policy for a workstation policy package.

Configure the Configuration Editor

After you enable and configure software scanning, you can modify the INI file that ZENworks Desktop Management uses when reporting software inventory by selecting the Configuration Editor tab, shown in Figure 20.9. From the Configuration Editor tab, you can edit the SWRules file by clicking on the Set Default button to open the default file and then modifying the entries. ZENworks uses this file when you create inventory reports.

If you are modifying the workstation inventory policy for Windows, the Configuration Editor tab will have a drop-down arrow allowing you to modify the entries' INI files for Zipped Names. This allows you to specify the manufacturers of software being used to zip files as well as the identifiers they are using for the zipped files.

You can also modify the entries in the INI file for Asset Information. You can specify the DMI class names and attributes for things such as a workstation model, model number, serial number, and computer type.

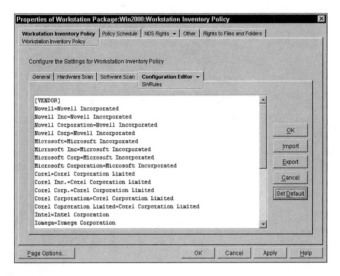

FIGURE 20.9
Configuration Editor for the workstation inventory policy for a workstation policy package.

Workstation Inventory Tasks

After you install, configure, and start the workstation inventory process for your network, you should be aware of several tasks. The following sections describe common tasks that you need to be aware of and perform to use and maintain your workstation inventory.

Optimizing Database Performance

One important task you should be familiar with is improving the database performance by improving database cache size. You can improve the performance of the Inventory database maintained in Sybase on NetWare or Windows servers. The default database cache size is 32MB; however, this database cache size may not be adequate for large databases with more than 10,000 workstations.

You should change the database cache size to an optimum size. We recommend a database cache size that is one-fourth of the database size. You must also consider server memory size while assigning a cache size. For example, if you have 256MB RAM, a cache size of 64MB is recommended.

Use the following steps to change the database cache size on a NetWare server:

1. Close all connections to the Inventory database.

2. Quit the Sybase server.

3. Open the `MGMTDB.NCF` file in the `SYS:\SYSTEM` directory.

4. Modify the `-c` parameter. For example, `-c 64M` sets the cache size to 64MB.

5. Save the file.

6. On the server console, load the Inventory database. Enter **MGMTDBS**.

Use the following steps to change the database cache size on a Windows server:

1. Run the file, `NTDBCONFIG.EXE` from the installation directory on the database server.

2. Modify the `-c` parameter.

3. Save the file.

4. Restart the server so that the Inventory database service (Adaptive Service Anywhere - ZENworks Desktop Management) starts up.

Backing Up the Inventory Database

Another inventory task you should be aware of is backing up the Inventory database. ZENworks Desktop Management provides an option to back up the Inventory database from the server. We recommend that you back up the database weekly. However, if you are tracking the inventory of workstations frequently, increase the frequency of backup.

The Database Backup tool can be run from ConsoleOne by selecting Tools→ZENworks Inventory→Configure DB→ZENworks Database object and clicking OK. Then click Tools→ZENworks Inventory→ Database Backup. Specify the location to back up the database to and then click the Start Backup button.

Use the following steps to restore the database:

1. If the Inventory database server is up, stop the database storing service. At the database server console, enter **StopSer Storer**.

2. Quit from the Sybase database.

3. On NetWare servers, at the database server prompt, enter **q** to stop the Sybase database.

4. On Windows, stop the Sybase service (Adaptive Service Anywhere - ZENworks Desktop Management).

5. Copy the backup files, overwriting the working database files.

6. Restart the database server.

NOTE The backup tool creates a .LOG file located in the ZENworks database directory on NetWare and Windows servers. The log records the status of the backup operation. This file increases in size for every backup operation. Remove the existing contents of the file if you do not need the details.

These steps work for the Sybase database only. For detailed instructions on backing up the Oracle database, refer to the online ZENworks Desktop Management documentation.

Customizing Software Scanning

Another important task you should be familiar with for workstation inventory is how to customize software scanning. You can customize the list of software applications that you want to scan for at the managed workstations by specifying the Software Scan settings in the Workstation Inventory Policy page.

By default, the Scanner does not scan for software applications at the workstation. You must check the Enable Software Scan option in the workstation inventory policy and should use the Custom Scan Editor to configure the list of applications for scanning. The Custom Scan Editor provides a powerful tool to optimize software scanning for your network. Use the Custom Scan Editor to specify the vendor, product name, product version, filename, and file size of the software you want to scan for on servers. This allows you to selectively inventory only software that is important to track, reducing the size of inventory reports as well as network and server utilization.

Use the following steps to configure custom application scanning for workstations:

1. In ConsoleOne, select the Workstation Inventory Policy and click Properties. Select the Software Scan tab of the Workstation

Inventory Policy page and make sure that the Enable Software Scan option is checked.

2. Click the Custom Scan Editor button to bring up the Custom Scan Editor, shown in Figure 20.10.

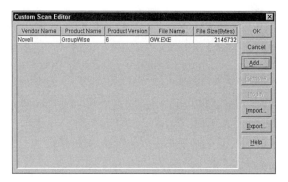

FIGURE 20.10

The Custom Scan Editor window for software scanning in the workstation inventory policy for a workstation policy package.

3. Click the Add button to add a custom application to be scanned for.

4. Fill in the details of the application: Vendor Name, Product Name, Product Version, File Name, and File Size (in Bytes).

5. Click OK.

6. To save the application entry in eDirectory, click OK in the Custom Scan Editor dialog box.

You can also add application entries to the Custom Scan table by importing a file with the list of application entries by using the following steps:

1. Open a text editor.

2. Create a file with the following format:

```
total_ _application_entries_in_Custom_Scan_file>;
total_ _columns_in_the_application_entry
vendor_name;product_name;product_version;file_name;
file_size(in Bytes)
vendor_name;product_name;product_version;file_name;
file_size(in Bytes)
```

3. Save the application as a text file with any extension you want.

4. In ConsoleOne, select the Workstation Inventory Policy and click Properties. Make sure that the Enable Software Scan option is checked.

5. Click Custom Scan Editor.

6. Click Import. To save the application entry in eDirectory, click OK in the Custom Scan Editor dialog box.

Keep the following guidelines in mind if you decide to create your own custom scan files:

▶ The default total number of columns in the application entry is 5.

▶ The separator between the columns is a semicolon (;).

▶ Fill in all the columns for each application entry.

▶ Do not use a comma (,) in the File Size parameter.

Exporting the Inventory Data to XML or CSV Format

ZENworks Desktop Management includes a tool that allows you to customize the inventory data you want from the Inventory database and export it to a file. After you select the inventory components that you need and further filter the data, the export program exports the data into XML or a Comma Separated Value (CSV) file format.

All workstations satisfying the filter you specify in the selected database are exported to an XML or CSV file. If you save the settings, you can later reload the configuration file to export the data. The following sections describe how to set the filters and queries and export the data from either a client or a server.

Exporting Inventory Data from ConsoleOne

The Data Export tool can be run from ConsoleOne by selecting Tools→ ZENworks Inventory→Configure DB→ZENworks Database object and then clicking OK. Then select Tools→ZENworks Inventory→Data Export to open the data export tool.

After the tool is open use the following steps to export the inventory data into an XML or a CSV file:

1. Select Create a New Database Query to open the Defined Query dialog box shown in Figure 20.11. This option lets you add a new

query that defines the inventory fields such as hardware, software, network, and others that you want to export. You can also specify the criteria to limit the workstations and the database to be included in the query. Based on the inventory components and criteria you specify, the inventory data from the database is exported to a CSV file. Click Next.

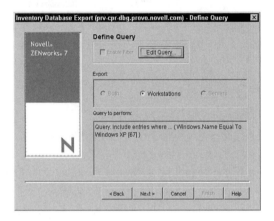

FIGURE 20.11
Defined Query dialog box in the ZENworks Inventory Data Export tool of ConsoleOne.

2. Specify the scope of the query to be Workstations, Servers, or both.

3. Form the query and specify the filter conditions as described in the following section by clicking on the Edit Query button shown in Figure 20.11. Click Next.

4. Configure the database fields that you want to be exported for the workstations that match the criteria you specified in step 3. The fields can be added and removed by navigating the Database Fields and Selected Fields lists, shown in Figure 20.12, and using the arrow button to add and remove entries. Click Next.

5. View the summary data export settings. Click Save Configuration to save the configuration settings to an .EXP file, specify the filename for the .EXP file, and click Save. The configuration file (.EXP) contains the settings such as the inventory components you selected and also the query formed for filtering the workstation data export. You create an .EXP file so that you can reload the configuration

settings and generate the XML or .CSV files any time you need to. Click Next.

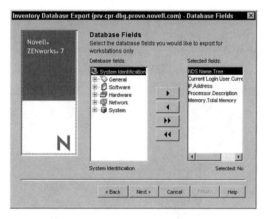

FIGURE 20.12
Database Fields dialog box in the ZENworks Inventory Data Export tool of ConsoleOne.

6. Click Perform the Query from This Computer to run the data export processing from the workstation computer. This option accesses the Inventory database on the specified database server and exports the data into an XML or a .CSV file. Click Finish.

7. Specify the file type and then name the XML or .CSV filename and click OK.

This generates the file in the specified directory. You can then open the XML file in a web browser or other application that supports XML files or the .CSV file in any CSV-supported viewer to view the exported data.

Forming a Query and Setting Filter Conditions
The following sections discuss setting the appropriate query values on the Define Query window shown in Figure 20.13.

Select the Attributes of the Inventory Components
Click the Browse Attribute button to select component attributes in the Select Attribute dialog box shown in Figure 20.14. For example, to specify the version of Bios as a component in the data export, select Bios as the component, and select Version as the component attribute.

Components are as follows: Software, Hardware, Network System, DMI, and General Information.

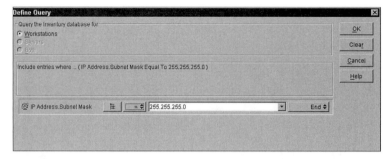

FIGURE 20.13
Define Query dialog box in the ZENworks Inventory Data Export tool of
ConsoleOne.

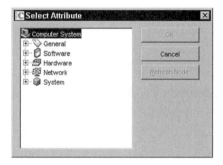

FIGURE 20.14
Select Attribute dialog box in the ZENworks Inventory Data Export tool of
ConsoleOne.

Select the Operator

Relational operators show the relationship between the component and
the value. Use the Matches option to specify the wildcard characters in
the Value field.

Specify the Values for the Inventory Attributes

Description values are the possible values of an inventory component.
For example, 6.0 is a possible value for the DOS-Version attribute.
Description values are not case-sensitive. Use the wildcard character % to
substitute any number of characters, or the ? character to substitute one
character in the Value field.

The list of description values displayed for an Inventory component is
taken from the Inventory database corresponding to the component.

Specify the Query Connectors and Controls

The connectors and controls available for building filter conditions include the following:

▶ AND—The expressions before and after the AND must be true.

▶ OR—Either the expression before the OR or the expression after the OR must be true.

▶ Insert Row—Lets you build the filter condition for this current row.

▶ Delete Row—Deletes the row.

▶ New Group—Lets you form a new filter condition group and specify the criteria for it. This group is combined with the previous group by using the relational operator specified between the groups.

▶ End—Ends the filter condition.

Exporting Inventory Data from the Server

Accessing the Inventory database from a server is recommended if you are exporting data from a large database or if you have specified complex queries for filtering the workstation.

Use the following steps to run the data export program from the server:

1. Make sure that you have generated the data configuration files. Then perform steps 1 through 5 of the "Exporting Inventory Data from ConsoleOne" section of this chapter. Also make sure that you save the settings in the .EXP file.

2. Click Perform the Query on a Remote Server to run the data export program from any server that has workstation inventory components installed. Click Finish.

3. From the server console, run `DBEXPORT.NCF` on NetWare servers or `DBEXPORT.BAT` on Windows servers, by typing **DBEXPORT** **`configuration_filename.exp csv_filename.csv`** where `configuration_filename`.EXP is an existing file that contains the data export settings. The data exported from the database is stored in the `csv_filename.csv`. The corresponding .CFG file for the .EXP file should be in the same folder as the .EXP file. The .CFG file contains the list of the database attributes to be exported.

4. Choose the inventory sites.

5. If you want to export the data from all database sites, satisfying the filter conditions, type **0**.

6. To choose the database sites, type the numbers corresponding to the site names in the displayed list.

7. To select multiple site databases, separate the site numbers corresponding to the site names by commas.

8. The data export displays the number of workstations that satisfy the query and filter conditions for export.

You can now open the .CSV file in Microsoft Excel or any other CSV-supported viewer to view the exported data.

Viewing Inventory Data

Another important inventory task you should be familiar with is viewing the information in the workstation inventory. The following sections describe how to view information about managed workstations.

Viewing Minimal Inventory Information from an eDirectory Object

Workstation inventory scanners store a subset of the scan data directly into the workstation object in eDirectory. You can view that information by right-clicking on the workstation object and selecting Properties. Then click the ZENworks Inventory tab and select Minimal Information.

The minimal view, shown in Figure 20.15, displays the following information about that workstation: Asset Tag, BIOS type, Computer Model, Computer Type, Disk Information, IP Address, IPX Address, Last Scan Date, MAC Address, Memory Size, Model Number, NIC Type, Novell Client, OS Type, OS Version, Processor, Serial Number, Subnet Mask, and Video Type.

Viewing the Workstation Inventory Summary of a Managed Workstation

If the minimal inventory information does not show all you need, you can see the complete listing from ConsoleOne by selecting Tools→ZENworks Inventory→Configure DB and then right-clicking on the workstation object and selecting Actions→Inventory.

The summary view, shown in Figure 20.16, allows you to view the entire listing of the inventory scan data for the workstation object.

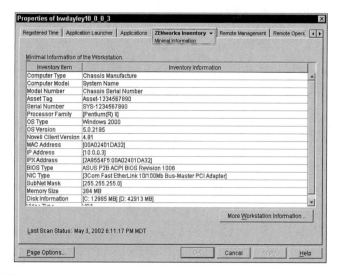

FIGURE 20.15
Minimal view of inventory data for a workstation object in ConsoleOne.

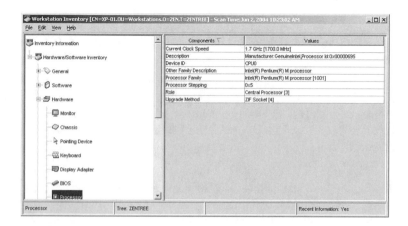

FIGURE 20.16
Summary view of inventory data for a workstation object in ConsoleOne.

If the entire listing for the workstation object is too much for you, you can view only the information that you requested by performing a query. Use the following steps to view the information formed by a query:

1. In ConsoleOne, click a container.

2. Select Tools→ZENworks Inventory→Configure DB.

3. Select Tools→ZENworks Inventory→Inventory Query.

4. From the Inventory Query from Database dialog box, shown in Figure 20.17, specify the criteria for the query. Set the Find In, Search Entire Database, Find Type, Attributes, Operator, Value, and Save options for the query.

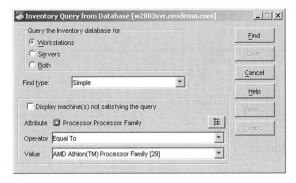

FIGURE 20.17
Inventory Query dialog box for the ZENworks inventory database in ConsoleOne.

5. Click Find.

A query is run on the database, and the results are displayed for you to view.

Creating Inventory Reports

Another inventory task that is useful to know is how to run inventory reports. You can run reports from a predefined list to gather inventory information from the Inventory database. After you run the report, it can be printed or exported as desired.

Use the following steps to generate the inventory report:

1. In ConsoleOne, click a server object.

2. Select Tools→ZENworks Reports.

3. Select the report you want to generate. See Table 20.2 for a list of reports and their descriptions.

4. Specify the Selection Criteria. See Table 20.2 for a list of reports and their criteria.

5. Click the Run Selected Report button.

A status box appears displaying the progress of the report generation. When the report is generated, it appears in the viewer. Use the buttons on the toolbar to page through, print, or export the report.

NOTE Beneath Criteria, in Table 20.2, the IP Address, DN, Distinguished Tree, and DNS name can be used for all workstation inventory reports.

TABLE 20.2 Report Types and Criteria for Inventory Reports

NAME (SIMPLE/COMP)	CRITERIA	DESCRIPTION
Scan Time Listing(S)	Last Scan Date	Date and time of the last inventory scan on each workstation
Operating System Listing(S)	OS Type, OS Version	List of all the workstations with an OS Type, an OS Version, and the total number of such workstations
BIOS Listing(S)	BIOS Install Date	List of all the workstations with a BIOS release date, and the total number of such workstations
Processor Family Listing(S)	Processor Family	List of all the workstations with a processor family (such as Pentium* Pro), and the total number of such workstations
Processor Current Clock Speed(S)	Lower Bound, Upper Bound	List of all the workstations within a range of processor speed (such as 200-1000 MHz), and the total number of such workstations

TABLE 20.2   Continued

NAME (SIMPLE/COMP)	CRITERIA	DESCRIPTION
Processor Maximum Clock Speed(S)	Lower Bound, Upper Bound	List of all the workstations within a range of maximum processor speed (such as 200-1000 MHz), and the total number of such workstations
Monitor Listing(S)	Scope, Machine Name, IP Address, DNS Name, Manufacturer, Manufacture Date, Nominal Size (Lower Bound in inches), and Nominal Size (Upper Bound in inches)	List of all inventoried workstations that match the specified monitor manufacturer's name, manufacture date, and the specified range of monitor's nominal size
Video Adapter Listing(S)	Video Architecture	List of all the workstations with a video adapter (such as MGA 2064W), and the total number of such workstations
Network Adapter Listing(S)	Adapter Name	List of all the workstations with a network adapter (such as 3Com* Fast EtherLink*) and the total number of such workstations
BIOS Listing(S)	Scope, Machine Name, IP Address, DNS Name, BIOS Install Date, and Manufacturer	List of all the inventoried workstations with BIOS manufacturer, BIOS release date, and the total number of such machines
Battery Listing(S)	Scope, Machine Name, IP Address, DNS Name, and Name	List of all inventoried workstations that match the specified battery name

TABLE 20.2   Continued

NAME (SIMPLE/COMP)	CRITERIA	DESCRIPTION
Bus Listing(S)	Scope, Machine Name, IP Address, DNS Name, and Bus Type	List of all inventoried workstations with the selected bus type
CDROM Listing(S)	Scope, Machine Name, IP Address, DNS Name, Caption, Description, and Manufacturer	List of all inventoried workstations that match the specified CD caption, description, and manufacturer's name
Hardware Summary Report(S)	Scope, Machine Name, IP Address, DNS Name, Operating System Type Operating System Version, Processor Family, Curr. Clock Speed (Lower Bound in MHz), Curr. Clock Speed (Upper Bound in MHz), Total Memory (Lower Bound in MB), Total Memory (Upper Bound in MB), Hard Disk Size (Lower Bound in GB), and Hard Disk Size (Upper Bound in GB)	Operating system name, operating system version, processor family, processor current clock speed, memory, and hard disk size for each inventoried workstation
Software Listing(S)	Software Name and Version	List of all the workstations with a software name, version, and the total number of such workstations
Software Summary Listing(S)	Software Name and Version	Lists of the total number of workstations with a particular software and version

TABLE 20.2 Continued

NAME (SIMPLE/COMP)	CRITERIA	DESCRIPTION
Application Software Inventory Report(C)	DN of Workstation	Software information including product name, version, and vendor on each workstation
Asset Management Report(C)	DN of Workstation	Memory, processor, display details, keyboard, pointing device, fixed and removable disk, floppy, CD drive, network adapter, and monitor details for inventoried workstations
System Internal Hardware Report(C)	DN of Workstation	Memory, processor, display details, physical disk drive, and modem for each workstation
Networking Information Report(C)	DN of Workstation	OS Description, MAC address, NIC type, IP address, and network drive mappings for each workstation
Storage Devices Inventory Report(C)	DN of Workstation	Hard disk, removable disk, logical drives, diskette, and CDROM details for each workstation
System Software Inventory Report(C)	DN of Workstation	OS description, display drivers, pointing device drivers, network adapter drivers, and NetWare Client details for each workstation
System Peripherals Inventory Report(C)	DN of Workstation	Computer description, display details, keyboard, pointing device and network adapter detail for each workstation

Using the ZENworks Quick Report to View Inventory Data

ZENworks Desktop Management includes a utility called the Quick Report to simplify using the inventory database schema to retrieve data from the Inventory database.

Quick Report allows administrators to create custom views of the inventory data that contain a custom view name, database query, and custom defined attributes. These views give administrators the ability to quickly query the Inventory database and retrieve and view only the pertinent information they want.

Quick Report created by administrators are stored in the Inventory database. A copy of the data used to define the custom view is also stored in configuration files with the .EXP extension. The custom view configuration files are located in the following directory on the management console by default:

```
Consoleone\1.2\reporting\export
```

Administrators can also specify a different location to store the quick report configuration files.

Starting Quick Report

Quick Report, shown in Figure 20.18, can be started using one of the following two methods from ConsoleOne:

▶ Right-click a database object and then select ZENworks Inventory→Quick Report.

▶ From the main menu, select Tools→ZENworks Inventory→Quick Report.

NOTE You must configure the Inventory database before starting Quick Reports.

Creating a New Quick Report

After you start Quick Report, you can use the following steps in the Create and Manage Quick Reports dialog box to create a new quick report to access inventory data:

1. Click the New button.

2. Specify whether the report should include workstations, servers, or both.

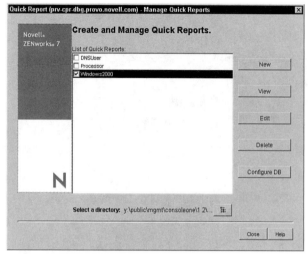

FIGURE 20.18
Main window in ZENworks Quick Report.

3. Click the Edit Query button shown in Figure 20.19.

4. From the Define Query window shown in Figure 20.13, define a query that includes the specific information you need in the custom view and click Next.

5. Select the required attribute field by clicking on the Select Attributes button.

6. Specify the logical operation to apply to the attribute by clicking on the Select Relational Operator button.

7. Specify an appropriate value for the operation on the attribute, and then add additional attributes using the logical operator button to the right of the value text box and repeat steps 5–7.

8. After you have added all attributes to use for the query criteria, click the OK button to return to to Quick Report and click Next.

9. From the Database Fields window, shown in Figure 20.12, add fields that you want to appear in the report.

10. When you have finished selecting fields to apear in the report, click the Save button and specify the name of the report.

11. Click Close.

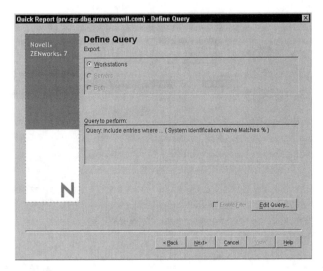

FIGURE 20.19
Define Query window in ZENworks Quick Report.

You have now created a custom Quick Report with which you can easily access inventory data.

Viewing a New Quick Report

After you start Quick Report, you can use the following steps in the Create and Manage Quick Reports dialog box to view Quick Reports that has already been created:

1. Select the report that you wish to view from the List of Quick Reports list, shown in Figure 20.18.

2. Click the View button to view the report.

3. You can also view the report in a web browser by clicking on the View in Browser button in the Quick Report viewer, shown in Figure 20.20.

A useful advantage of using the View in Browser feature of Quick Report is the capability to print directly from the browser in a formatted form, shown in Figure 20.21. The browser file is an XML document, so you also have the capability to use Save As from the browser to store the report for your records.

FIGURE 20.20
ConsoleOne view of an Inventory Query.

FIGURE 20.21
Web Browser view of an Inventory Query.

View the Workstation Inventory Status Logs

Another valuable task that you should use frequently is viewing the status and scan logs generated by workstation inventory. The following sections list the logs, what they contain, and how to access them.

Workstation Scan Log

The workstation scan log monitors information from scan programs and the database storage process on the server. It contains the scanned workstation name, time of scan, inventory component, message type, and status message.

To access the workstation scan log from within ConsoleOne, select the container and then select Tools→ZENworks Inventory→Workstation Scan Log. The workstation scan log, shown in Figure 20.22, displays a listing of inventory scans that have occurred on the configured inventory database.

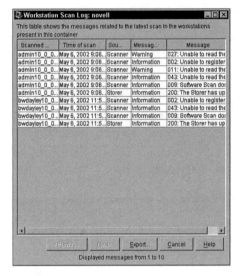

FIGURE 20.22
Workstation scan log for the ZENworks Inventory database in ConsoleOne.

Roll-Up Log

The roll-up log contains information collected from data sending servers, data receiving servers, and the database storage process. The roll-up log contains information about where the roll-up initiated from, roll-up start time, inventory component, message type, and status message.

To access the roll-up log from within ConsoleOne, select the container for the inventory service object and then select Tools→ZENworks Inventory→Roll-Up Log.

Workstation Scan Status

The workstation scan status monitors information from the scan programs and the database storage process. It contains the time of scan and status message.

To access the workstation scan status from within ConsoleOne, right-click the workstation object and select Properties. Then click the ZENworks Inventory tab and select Scan Status. The Scan Status tab, shown in Figure 20.23, displays the time of each scan as well as status messages that occurred during the scan. You can use the up and down arrows to navigate through the status messages.

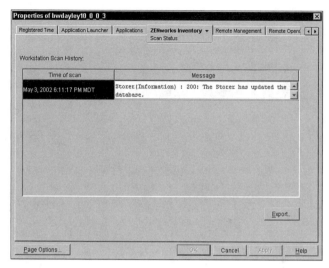

FIGURE 20.23
Scan status of inventory scans that have occurred on a workstation object in ConsoleOne.

Status of Inventory Components on Server

The status of inventory components on the server contains information gathered from sending server, receiving servers, the Selector on the server, the database storing process, the service manager, and the roll-up scheduler. It shows the time of log, source, message type, and a textual message.

To access the status of inventory components on the server from within ConsoleOne, right-click the inventory service object and then select Properties→Status Report→Server Status (see Figure 20.24).

Roll-Up Status

The roll-up status contains information gathered from the sending server, receiving servers, and the database storing process. It shows the roll-up start time and message.

To access the roll-up status from within ConsoleOne, right-click the inventory service object and then select Properties→Status Report→Roll-Up Status.

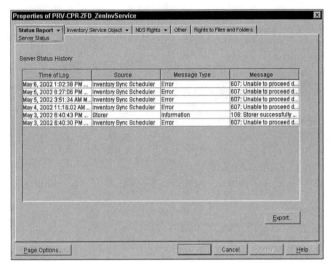

FIGURE 20.24
Inventory server status window for a ZENworks inventory service object in
ConsoleOne.

Summary

This chapter explored the workstation inventory process. It looked at
how to set up inventory in your environment and what tasks can be performed after it has been properly installed and configured.

## CHAPTER 21

Using ZENworks Handheld Inventory

This chapter discusses ZENworks Handheld Inventory: how it is collected and how you can retrieve information from the inventory. ZENworks Handheld Inventory is activated automatically when a workstation receives the agents and is registered with eDirectory. Unlike other components of ZENworks, handheld management does not require that any policies be configured to collect inventory information.

To collect hardware and software information, make sure that the import policy is activated on your handheld services (see Chapter 16, "Setting Up Handheld Policies," for more details).

After the PDA is imported into the system, ZENworks agents begin to transmit the inventory information. ZENworks handheld agents send the information to the specified ZENworks Handheld Access Point. From there, the ZENworks server agents transmit the inventory to the ZENworks Handheld Server. Services on the ZENworks Handheld Server then analyze the data and place the hardware and software information into the handheld inventory database along with updating the handheld object in eDirectory.

Viewing Inventory for a Specific Device

To view the inventory for a specific handheld device, do the following:

1. Open ConsoleOne.

2. Browse to and select the desired handheld object. Right-click and select Properties on the pop-up menu.

   This presents the General information screen of the handheld device shown in Figure 21.1.

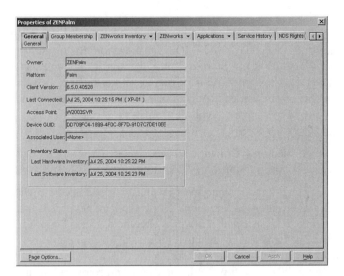

FIGURE 21.1
General information of a ZENworks handheld device.

3. Select the ZENworks Inventory tab to be directed to the inventory information of this device, as shown in Figure 21.2.

   The information in the inventory page in eDirectory is considered the general hardware information for the handheld device. If you want additional, more detailed information, click the Advanced Inventory button.

4. The Advanced Inventory displays the hardware and software information for the selected PDA device (see Figure 21.3).

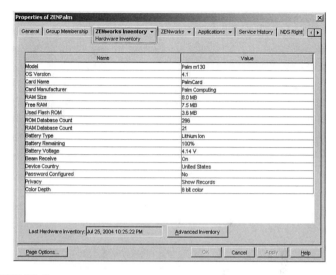

FIGURE 21.2
ZENworks Inventory page from a typical PDA device.

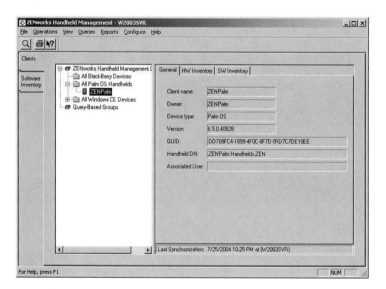

FIGURE 21.3
Advanced Inventory display, where inventory for all devices and reports may be generated.

RIM BlackBerry devices are unique in that they require an inventory policy to collect inventory. The Palm and PocketPC devices automatically collect inventory when they synchronize (unless the schedule is changed). The BlackBerry devices must have a policy associated with them.

The BlackBerry inventory policy can be found under the handheld package type. The inventory policy is under the BlackBerry tab of the handheld package.

To activate the inventory policy, do the following:

1. Create a handheld policy package and activate a BlackBerry inventory policy.

2. Click on the Properties of the inventory policy. You are presented with the General tab (see Figure 21.4).

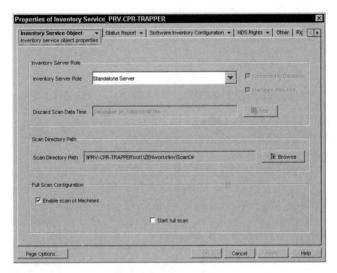

FIGURE 21.4
General tab of RIM BlackBerry inventory policy.

3. Select each of the settings to collect hardware and software information.

4. Select the Policy Schedule tab and adjust the schedule for when you want to collect the inventory. The default schedule of EventHandheldSync results in collecting the inventory once a day (because the BlackBerry is always connected and synchronizing).

5. Click OK to save the configuration settings for the policy.

6. Associate the policy package with your favorite BlackBerry device, device group, or container. Any associated BlackBerry devices will begin to collect inventory based on the schedule configured.

Viewing Software Inventory Across Multiple Devices

From the Advanced Inventory tool you can view inventory information across multiple PDA devices, even devices of different types. You can get to the Advanced Inventory tool by selecting a single handheld object, right-clicking the handheld object to bring up the pop-up menu, and selecting Properties. Then click on the ZENworks Inventory tab, select Hardware Inventory, and click the Advanced Inventory button.

Within the Advanced Inventory tool, select the Software Inventory tab. This displays all the various device types. Selecting a type of device—Palm, for example—displays all the software found on all the Palm devices, as illustrated by Figure 21.5.

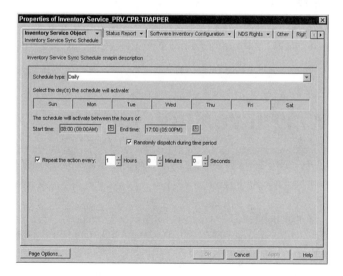

FIGURE 21.5
Multiple devices inventory within the Advanced Inventory tool.

Expanding the folder lists the inventory applications that have been found. Selecting an application displays on the right panel information about the software package and the specific clients that have that software package installed.

For Windows CE devices, the files are grouped and listed by the product information placed in the files. If no product information is in the file, those applications are listed in the unidentified files folder.

You can identify the package that a file is part of by doing the following:

1. Click on the Software Inventory tab.

2. Select the Unidentified Windows CE Files folder.

3. Double-click on a file listed on the right pane and click on Identify File.

4. This brings up a dialog that allows you to specify Name of Application, Version of Application, and Company Name for the application.

5. Optionally, change the identification date and time of the file. If you specify a different date and/or time, only files with those exact specifications will be matched and included in the product listing. Otherwise, the files will be placed in the unidentified file folder.

You can also specify files and packages that you want ignored. Ignored files do not appear in the application view. This is done to keep the view to a manageable amount and not to display standard applications or files that are on all devices.

Viewing Inventory Reports

You can generate reports about the hardware and software on your handheld devices to make it easy to see the applications you have installed, which devices need upgrades, which hardware components are installed, and more.

ZENworks Handheld Management provides predefined reports for information stored in the ZENworks Handheld Management database, including

- ▶ Handheld application objects (status, run time, and so on)

- ▶ Devices (groups belonged to, distributions run, hardware/software inventory)

- ▶ Groups
- ▶ Software inventory (list of all software applications and where they are installed, unidentified files, and so on)
- ▶ Hardware inventory

After they are generated, reports can be viewed online, sent to a printer, or saved to a file in a variety of formats. Figure 21.6 shows a sample report.

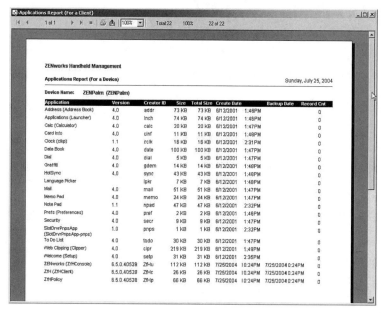

FIGURE 21.6
Sample handheld inventory report.

Running Reports

You generate and view ZENworks Handheld Management reports in the ZENworks Handheld Management Inventory Viewer. To do so, complete the following steps:

1. In ConsoleOne, right-click a handheld device object and select Actions→Inventory.

2. Select Reports and choose the type of report to generate.

3. After choosing a report, you might be prompted to select a device or group before generating the data.

After the report is generated, you can scroll through the report, print it, or export it to many different formats including Excel, HTML, RTF, and so on.

Exporting Reports

After you generate a report, you can export the report to a file or import the data into a database or spreadsheet.

Reports can be exported to formats such as HTML, tab/comma-delimited text files, Microsoft Excel, and so on. After choosing the export format, you can choose the destination, such as a file, a Lotus Notes database, or an email system.

To export a report, follow these steps:

1. Click on the envelope icon on the report output toolbar.

2. Choose the format in which to export the report.

3. Select the destination for the report.

4. Click OK.

You are prompted for additional information based on the format and destination.

Creating Custom Reports

Users who have Crystal Reports can create their own custom reports from the ZENworks Handheld Management database.

NOTE If you create custom reports, the reports must be stored in a shared path if you want them to be accessed by a remote ConsoleOne installation. When saving a custom report, specify a UNC path to the share (do not use local drive letters).

To create a custom report, do the following:

1. Go to the Advanced Inventory tool by right-clicking on any hand-held device object and selecting Actions→Inventory.

2. Select Reports→Custom Report.

3. Click Add.

4. Type a name for the report.

5. Specify a location for the report you created; then click OK.

6. Click Run to generate the report.

The report displays similar to any standard report.

Summary

ZENworks Handheld Management provides comprehensive hardware and inventory collection for all supported PDA devices. ZENworks Handheld Management also includes a powerful reporting tool that allows you to generate reports of all your devices, devices by categories, or individual PDA devices. These reports can help in tracking and understanding upgrade needs for your corporate handhelds.

## CHAPTER 22

Imaging a Workstation

One significant feature of ZENworks Desktop Management is the capability to create and deploy images of workstations throughout the network. With this capability you can provide an additional level of support and service to workstation users by being able to take an image of a golden workstation for your organization and then apply that image to any workstation in the network. This can be used to initially set up workstations in your organization and to restore a workstation to properly functioning status should problems occur that are best repaired by getting the workstation to a known, beginning state.

Workstation Imaging System

The ZENworks Desktop Management system for imaging workstations is made up of the following components: Linux operating system, Linux imaging software, imaging server agents, and Windows workstation image-safe data agent. In addition to these components, ZENworks adds objects in eDirectory, and some administrative tools in ConsoleOne to get the job done.

There may be a Linux partition placed on a workstation (minimum of 100MB) that can hold the Linux OS and the imaging engine. This is ideal to place on workstations that you may want to image on-the-fly (from ConsoleOne) because, when requested, the workstation gets notified of this work and then performs the imaging task. If no work exists for the imaging system to perform, the partition boots into the normal operating system.

The ZENworks Desktop Management imaging system is designed to function in an automatic mode (although it does have a manual mode). The expectation is that you use the system to deploy images to your workstations in the network to set up initial systems or repair systems and get them back online as quickly as possible. Consequently, the system assumes that a workstation that is contacting the imaging server, but is *not* registered in the tree, is requesting an image, and that a registered workstation is contacting the imaging server to see whether any work (indicated by flags in the workstation object) is to be done.

The ZENworks Desktop Management product shipped with the ZENworks Preboot Services product. This allows you to have *PXE* (*Pre-Execution Environment*) support right out of the box! Now you don't have to have a Linux partition on the workstation. Instead, you can boot PXE, and the PXE Server provided in ZENworks Desktop Management will download the ZENworks Imaging Environment (Linux Imaging Software), which then contacts the imaging server for work to do, either to take or receive an image.

Linux Imaging Software

Linux Imaging Software is the Linux application that actually performs actions such as the creation and installation/restoration of images. This software is automatically launched when the workstation is started, prior to booting the Operating System. This allows the software to update workstations with newer images prior to users accessing the system.

This software is not writing bits and bytes on the sectors, but it uses the various supported file system types to read and write files. The supported file system types are FAT16, FAT32, NTFS 4 (Windows NT), and NTFS 5 (Windows 2000/XP/2003).

NOTE If you take the manual approach to restoring the image and the partition is not empty, the currently existing files will be mixed with the files from the restore—which can cause unexpected behavior (OS and driver files can become intermixed, and so on).

NOTE Images always have the suffix .ZMG and may not be compressed. You must have enough room on the destination server to store the entire image, or the image transfer will fail and the partial image will be deleted.

The imaging software can function in one of two modes: automatic and manual. In the automatic mode, the imaging software contacts the imaging server and requests any requests to take or receive an image. If an image must be taken or received, the imaging software begins the process. If no work must be done, the imaging software completes, and the workstation boots to the native operating system.

If the imaging software is in manual mode, the software does not automatically communicate with the imaging server but places a Linux prompt on the workstation screen. From the Linux prompt, you perform specific partitioning and imaging tasks including taking or receiving an image. See the "Advanced Imaging" section later in this chapter to understand the commands you can perform in the manual mode. When the imaging software is finished, the user must manually request the reboot to the native operating system.

ZENworks 7 introduces a new initial screen that allows you to specify the following options as the Imaging Software is loaded:

▶ A

▶ B

ZENworks 7 also introduces a new GUI when operating in manual mode. When executing an 'img' command in manual mode, the new GUI is loaded. From the new GUI you have the option of performing all advanced functions of the Imaging Software. This feature is useful because you can use function keys or the mouse to start operations without having to know command-line commands and parameters. Another useful feature of the new GUI is that it provides a better look and feel; for instance, when creating an image a status bar with the current progress, total time, and file information is displayed.

Imaging Server Agents

An imaging server agent is the agent that runs on the server that is responsible for communicating with the imaging software running on the workstation. These agents tell the workstation whether to take the image or to receive an image and are responsible for walking the eDirectory tree to find the image. This is the agent affected by the imaging server policy in the server policy package. It is responsible for receiving information from the workstation and processing the rules in the policy to find an image object that should be applied to the workstation.

After the image is determined, this agent gets the image file and transmits it to the Linux software residing on the workstation. It is also responsible for receiving any images that the workstation is sending it and storing them onto the server in the specified and approved locations.

The image server is loaded on the NetWare server as `imgserv.nlm`, and the NT/2000/2003 version is a service DLL with the same name. The imaging server has a status screen that tells you some information on the number of requests and images it has received and served. It, unfortunately, does not have any information on the screen on currently receiving or delivering work. You can load the service with a debug option and get it to write a log file called `ZIMGLOG.XML` on the server.

Windows Workstation Image-Safe Data Agent

The Windows Workstation image-safe data agent resides on the Windows workstation and is responsible for receiving image-safe data from the disk and placing it into the Windows Registry. It also makes sure that the information in the Windows Registry is synchronized on the disk.

A special sector on the disk is reserved for placing information that is preserved despite having an image applied to the workstation. This way a workstation keeps its IP address (or DHCP settings), computer name, workstation object, domain, and group names.

eDirectory Objects

Several objects are introduced to the tree to support ZENworks Desktop Management imaging. These objects are the following:

- ▶ Workstation imaging policy—Is in the workstation policy package and represents the policy to determine, for the associated workstations, the image to be used if a reimage is requested. See Chapter 15, "Setting Up Workstation Policies," for more information about this policy.

- ▶ Imaging server policy—Is in the server policy package and represents the policy to determine for the associated imaging servers the image to be used if an image is requested for a nonregistered workstation. See Chapter 19, "Creating Server Policies," for more information about this policy.

- ▶ Image object—An eDirectory object that represents an image that has been taken of a workstation and stored on the imaging server. See the following section, "Image Object," to learn more about the image object.

- ▶ Workstation object: imaging configuration—Some configuration parameters that are part of the workstation object. In this page you can configure whether the workstation should take or receive an image on the next reboot.

Image Object

The image object is created in eDirectory by the administrator and is associated with an image file (.ZMG) that has been taken by the ZENworks Desktop Management imaging system. To properly configure an image object you must do the following:

1. Take an image of a workstation and store that image on an imaging server. See the "Creating a Workstation Image" section later in this chapter.

2. Launch ConsoleOne and browse to the container where you want the image object to reside.

3. Create an image object by selecting the container and then choosing File→New→Object from the menu and selecting Workstation Image object from the list of objects.

4. After the object is created, go into the properties of the object either by selecting additional properties in the create process or by right-clicking on the object and choosing Properties from the menu.

5. Select the Image Files tab and specify whether you want to use a base file image or set up scripted imaging. If you select standard imaging, you must administer the location of the .ZMG files by clicking the Browse button on the Base Image File field. You need to browse to the imaging server and then to the file system on that server to specify the .ZMG file. If you select scripted imaging, you are provided with a text window in which you can specify an imaging command (see "Advanced Imaging" later in this chapter).

6. Choose the file set to bring as part of the image by selecting the Set in the Use File Set parameter at the bottom left side of the screen. You can have up to 10 different file sets.

7. If you are using standard imaging, you can also append additional images to this image by clicking the Add button and placing them in the Add on Image File field. These additional images are included with the base image and placed on the workstation when it is imaged. These additional images could be application object images (see Chapter 11, "Creating and Using Application Objects," for more information).

8. Click OK to save the administrative changes and exit ConsoleOne.

This completes the steps necessary to properly configure an image object.

Administrative Tools

Several tools are available to perform the imaging operation. First are the snap-ins for ConsoleOne that enable you to create image objects, launch tools to create the imaging boot disks, and view and manipulate an image file.

The Boot Disk Creator and the Image Explorer are both Windows programs launched from ConsoleOne from the Tools menu. The Boot Disk Creator creates the Linux diskettes necessary to boot the workstations to communicate with the imaging server and to create and install the images.

The Image Explorer enables you to view the contents of the image file, mark files in the image to be included in various sets of files, remove files, or add files to the image.

An additional graphical interface to the Image Explorer, discussed later in this chapter, has also been added to the ZENworks Suite to provide additional capabilities to better manage workstation images.

Setting Up Workstations for Imaging

The ZENworks Desktop Management imaging engine that performs the actual imaging of the workstation is a Linux application. Therefore, the workstation must be booted to Linux temporarily while the imaging is performed. For a workstation to use ZENworks imaging, you need to prepare a bootable device that has the following components:

▶ Linux kernel—Either a bootable device or partition with Linux installed

▶ Imaging engine—ZENworks Desktop Management imaging software

▶ Network drivers—Drivers to access the network to communicate with the ZENworks Desktop Management imaging server

You can use any of the following methods to load the imaging software on a workstation:

▶ Preboot Services (PXE)

▶ Boot diskettes

▶ Boot CD

▶ Linux partition on a workstation

Each of these methods is discussed in the following sections.

Using Preboot Services with Imaging

When a workstation with PXE support is booted, it searches the network for the server where Preboot Services are installed, as described in Chapter 2, "Installing ZENworks 7 Suite." After it locates the server, it uses a DHCP request to query the server and determine whether there is any imaging work to do. If ZENworks determines that there is imaging work to do, it then downloads the following files to boot the workstation to Linux and performs the imaging operations: LINUX.1, LINUX.2, and LOADLIN.EXE. These files will not be downloaded if ZENworks determines that there is no work to be done.

PXE is an industry-standard protocol that allows a workstation to boot up and execute a program from the network before the workstation operating system starts. ZENworks Workstation Imaging uses Preboot Services to allow imaging operations to occur without having to boot from floppy, CD, or a Linux partition on the workstation. This is extremely useful if you want to quickly throw an image on a workstation that has a blank HD in it. For more information, see "Preboot Services" at the website www.novell.com/products/zenworks/.

Creating Boot Diskettes

Imaging starts by booting up the workstation with a bootable CD, PXE-enabled LAN card or the ZENworks Desktop Management imaging boot disk. To create this disk, do the following:

1. Get a formatted floppy disk. The system does not work properly if you create image disks on previously used floppies without reformatting it first.

2. Launch ConsoleOne.

3. Launch the Boot Disk Creator program (sys:\public\zenworks\ imaging\zimgboot.exe) by going to the Tools menu and selecting the correct option (Tools→ZENworks Utilities→Imaging→Create or Modify Boot Diskette).

4. Within the Boot Disk Creator program choose the options that you want. Figure 22.1 shows a sample of the Boot Disk Creator window.

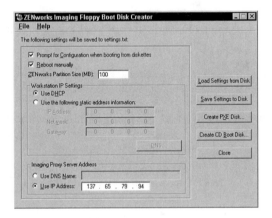

FIGURE 22.1
ZENworks Imaging Boot Disk Creator.

You can make the following choices in the program:

▶ Prompt for Configuration When Booting from Diskettes—
After the boot process is finished, this prompts the screen for
the configuration information included on this screen (such as
Reboot Manually, Proxy Address, Use DHCP, and so on). This
enables you to change these values from the specified defaults
given in this screen. Press Enter when running the imaging
program on the workstation because you want to keep the
defaults that you specify on this screen.

▶ Reboot Manually—This requires that the user request the
reboot (Ctl+Alt+Del) manually at the completion of the imaging process (either take an image or receive an image) instead
of having the program automatically reboot the workstation
when finished.

▶ ZENworks Partition Size—This enables you to specify how
many megabytes you want any Linux partition to be on the
workstation, if you decide to create the partition.

▶ Workstation IP Settings: Use DHCP—Tells the Linux system
to use DHCP to get the workstation's IP address to connect to
the imaging server.

▶ Workstation IP Settings: Use the Following Static Address Information—Enables you to specify the address instead of using DHCP. This is the address used by the workstation to connect to the imaging server.

▶ Imaging Proxy Server Address: Use DNS Name—This flag enables you to select and enter the DNS name of the imaging server. Choose this option only if you have DNS enabled and have entered a record in the DNS system for this server. Be sure and put the full DNS name such as imgsrvr.novell.com.

▶ Imaging Proxy Server Address: Use IP Address—This flag identifies that the system should use the IP address to connect to the imaging server rather than DNS. The address specified should be the address of the server running the imaging service.

5. Put the floppy disk into the disk drive and click the Create CD Boot Diskette button. This writes a compressed file with the Linux boot system and the `setting.txt` file to the floppy. Click Close.

This floppy can now be used to boot the workstation and begin the imaging process.

Creating a Boot CD

If you have systems capable of booting from CD-ROM, you can create a CD with the Linux boot system. With your CD writer software, you need to create a CD using the ISO file called `bootcd.iso` from the `public\zenworks\imaging` directory or from the ZENworks Desktop Management Program CD. You also need the `settings.txt` file, which holds the configuration for the boot CD—such items as prompt, size of Linux partition, and so on. You also need this `settings.txt` file on the CD. If the `settings.txt` file is not added, you will need to copy it to a floppy as described in the previous section, and it will be asked for during the booting process when booting using the CD. Your CD writer software can either include the `settings.txt` file into the ISO image or needs to write a multisession CD. Obviously, your workstations need to support booting from a multisession CD.

The `session.txt` file is an ASCII text file that holds key/value pairs that tell the boot system the configuration settings for the imaging engine. The following is a sample of the `settings.txt` file:

```
# ZENworks Imaging settings.txt
#    denotes a comment

#PROMPT should be set to YES if you want to configure
# various parameters
#PROMPT=YES

#PARTITIONSIZE should be set to the Linux partition size
# in MB, to be created on install
PARTITIONSIZE=15

#IPADDR should be set to the desired ip address of the
# machine. To use DHCP comment out the line, or remove
# it from the file.
#IPADDR=137.65.138.128

#GATEWAY is the router address for this machine. If
# using DHCP, remove this line, or comment it out.
#GATEWAY=137.65.139.254

#NETMASK is this machine's subnet mask. If using DHCP,
# remove or comment out this line.
#NETMASK=255.255.252.0

#PROXYADDR is the address of the server running ZENworks
# Image Server nlm
PROXYADDR=137.65.203.1

#uncomment if you want to reboot manually.
#MANUALREBOOT=YES
```

From this sample file it is possible to see the key/value pairs for the boot system configuration settings used by the imaging engine.

Placing a Linux Partition on a Workstation

The Linux partition is the boot partition, and on boot-up of the workstation, the imaging server is contacted to see whether it has any requested work (based on administration in the workstation object). If it has work, the imaging engine either gets or puts an image. If it has no work, the imaging system continues the boot process, booting the workstation to the native operating system.

If you are placing a Linux partition on a previously functioning system, this process assumes that the workstation has already registered with the network and has an associated workstation object and that the image-safe data agent has run on the workstation. Having the workstation already registered prevents the imaging server from attempting to place a new image on the workstation. However, if you are placing the Linux partition on a new workstation, this process can place a new, standard image on the workstation, preparing it for use in your organization.

The placing of the Linux partition and the ZENworks Desktop Management boot system does not function with booting programs such as System Commander. These systems need to be disabled or marked such that the Linux partition automatically gets booted. The ZENworks Desktop Management boot system functions properly with the Windows Boot manager by configuring the `boot.ini` file to properly boot.

NOTE The imaging system does some special recognition for Compaq systems and does not destroy the Compaq partition used to run machine configurations.

WARNING Placing a Linux partition destroys the disk and all the other partitions unless you take special care in saving the partitions or using another program to create a new partition without destroying the current partitions.

To place a ZENworks Desktop Management Linux imaging partition on a workstation you need to do the following steps. Be sure to save any data on the workstation; any time you are working with partitions you must prepare your data to be able to recover should a failure occur.

One method is to make sure that an empty place exists on the disk that is sufficient to hold the Linux partition (the size was identified in the creation of the boot disks and is 100MB minimum). This could be leftover space or space created by some program such as Partition Magic, which frees up space. If sufficient free space *is* present on the hard drive, the Linux install process should consume that space *only if the free partition is partition 0* (in other words, the first partition in the partition table) and thereby will not destroy any other partitions (although you have to be trusting, and you know how sometimes everything doesn't go perfectly). The following steps describe how to put the Linux partition on without loss of data and without any other tools:

1. Create your ZENworks Desktop Management boot diskettes with the proper configuration, including the setting to Reboot Manually.

2. Boot the workstation with the ZENworks Desktop Management imaging boot diskettes or CD. Make sure that you select manual mode when the system comes up. If you select nothing at the prompt in 60 seconds, the system boots to automatic mode.

3. If this is a previously functioning workstation, take an image of the workstation by entering the following command: **img makep <address/DNS of image server> <filename for image file>**. The address may be an IP address or the DNS name of the image server. The filename is the name of the image file you want to hold the image. The filename must include the following format: *//servername/dir/dir/../filename*.img. The *servername* is actually ignored because the address of the server receiving the image stores the file on its disk. (Redirection of image servers does not work in manual mode.) The new GUI will start a progress bar that allows you to monitor the status of creating the image.

4. Enter **img dump** to view the list of known partitions on the disk. Remember the numbers of the partitions.

5. Enter **/bin/install.s** from the Linux prompt to install the Linux partition on the disk. This destroys all data on the workstation's hard drive. It creates a new Linux partition on the disk the specified size and place of the Linux boot system on that partition. The ZENworks boot loader is automatically installed in this process. A message comes on the screen stating that the boot process could not fully function. This is because Linux creates logical partitions for all the partitions seen at boot time. You just added a new

partition, and it cannot create a logical partition for it. When it reboots, the boot manager system automatically reinstalls itself when it is assumed that all partitions are now present.

6. Enter **img dump** at the Linux prompt to view the list of known partitions. There should be one less partition listed than in step 4 because the Linux partition is hidden from this listing. Also note that all the other partitions are destroyed (in other words, have no file system type associated with them).

7. Perform a reboot of the workstation to make sure that the Linux partition is functioning properly. This can be done by typing **reboot** at the Linux prompt or by turning the workstation off and on. Make sure that you have removed the Linux boot media. This should boot to the Linux partition and get to the Linux prompt (because the system has been configured to not automatically reboot).

8. If you took an image in step 3, bring down the image that was taken by typing **image rp <address of image server> <image filename>**. The image is brought down to the disk. The image is then reduced in size sufficiently to take the remaining space on the disk (we had to take space for the Linux partition). If the image is too big to be reduced, an error occurs. The installing of an image from ZENworks Desktop Management takes special care to not destroy or overwrite the Linux partition. When the image is successfully down, you have the same workstation data and environment with the exception of a new Linux partition.

9. Enter **img dump** at the Linux prompt to view the list of partitions again. There should be the same number as in step 6 (one less than in step 4), and there should now be file system types to the partitions that you have just restored.

10. Reinitialize the boot manager by running **/bin/lilo.s**. You should do this any time you bring down any image to the workstation. In automatic mode, the system performs this automatically.

11. Perform a reboot of the workstation. This can be done by typing **reboot** at the Linux prompt or by turning the workstation off and on. Make sure that you have removed the Linux boot diskettes. This should boot to the Linux partition and get to the Linux prompt (because the system has been configured not to automatically reboot).

12. The workstation should now boot to the Linux partition that goes into automatic mode communicating with the image server. It should find no work if the workstation is registered, and the image configuration flags are off. If the workstation is not registered and you did not lay down an image in step 8, the image server is contacted and goes through its rules processing (see the server policy package, imaging server policy) and determines an image that should be placed on this workstation. If one is found, that image is placed on the workstation. If you manually placed an image down on a workstation that had not been previously registered, the imaging server compares the name of that image file with the image determined by the imaging server. If they are the same, the imaging server does not attempt to lay down a new image. This should result in the workstation having no work and again booting to its native operating system. This completes the steps necessary to put the Linux partition on without any loss of data.

Creating a Workstation Image

Depending on your situation and setup, several ways exist to create a workstation image.

If the workstation is registered in the directory and has a Linux partition on it (see the section "Placing a Linux Partition on a Workstation" earlier in the chapter), you can go to the workstation object in the tree and set a workstation flag (in the ZENworks Imaging Configuration tab) to take an image on the next boot. The next time that the workstation boots, the Linux partition boots, and the imaging engine on the workstation contacts the imaging server. The server notes that the workstation object has the flag set and requests that the workstation send an image. When the image is completed, the flag is reset in the workstation object, and the workstation continues to boot into the native operating system.

Make sure that you disable or remove any boot manager systems such as System Commander. You do not want them included in the image that you take, or when they are placed onto a workstation they overwrite the ZENworks boot system, and the connectivity between the workstation and the imaging server does not occur, keeping you from having the features of automatic execution.

Creating an Image Using a Workstation Object

If the workstation is registered in the directory but does not have a Linux partition, you need to boot from the floppies, PXE, or CD we made previously. When booting from CD or floppies, choose the manual boot method. For PXE, hold down the left Ctrl+Alt keys during the process of loading PXE and then choose Maintenance mode. After the system is booted, you can let Linux proceed in automatic mode. This contacts the image server and takes the image as described in the previous paragraph.

Creating an Image Using a Linux Partition

If the workstation is not registered in the directory but has a Linux partition installed, when the workstation boots into the Linux partition, it contacts the imaging server that runs its rules—attempting to discover a matching image. If one is found, it images the workstation with the matching image. Because of this, you need to boot the workstation from the floppies to get the imaging engine into manual mode and not connect to the imaging server.

Creating an Image Using Bootable Media or PXE

If the workstation is not registered in the directory and does not have a Linux partition you must boot from floppies (or CD) and then type **manual** when the Linux partition is booted. Type **img mp <proxy address> <full path to image>**. Don't forget that the path must use forward slashes and must include the server. The directories in the path must already exist. This takes an image of the workstation and places it on the imaging server.

> **NOTE** Whenever you take an image or place an image on a workstation, the ZENworks imaging engine does *not* take an image of the Linux partition or replace it with an image being brought down. The only way to place a Linux partition on a workstation is via the bootable floppies or another imaging program.

Because the imaging process understands FAT16, FAT32, NTFS 4, and NTFS 5, it reads the files from these systems and includes them in the image on a file-by-file basis. If the imaging system does not understand the partition type, it does a sector-by-sector copy of the partition.

Using the ZENworks Image Explorer Graphical User Interface

After an image is taken on the system and stored on the imaging server, you can examine the contents of an image by running the ZENworks Desktop Management Image Explorer (`\zenworks\imgexp.exe`). When you launch the Image Explorer, you are placed in a Windows program. From there you go to the File menu and open the .ZMG file that holds the workstation image. Figure 22.2 show a sample of an image in the Image Explorer.

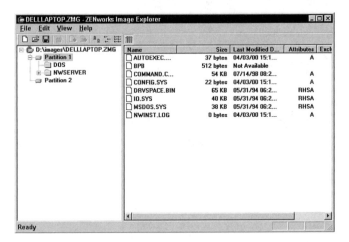

FIGURE 22.2
The ZENworks Image Explorer.

As you can see in Figure 22.3, you can browse the image and discover the partitions and all the files in the image. You can also, using the Image Explorer, look at the information gathered from the workstation such as the hardware configuration. To look at this information, select the .ZMG file in the image editor and select File→Properties, or right-click and select Properties. When you do, the dialog box shown in Figure 22.3 is displayed.

As you can see, this dialog displays the description of the image and all the hardware information on the workstation where the image was captured. (You can use this information to help you construct your rules in the image server policy.) Other fields include when created, the author, and any comments. If you want to modify any of the Description, Author, or Comments fields, just move the cursor to these fields and type in the information you want.

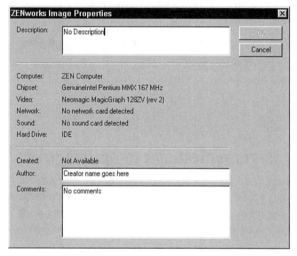

FIGURE 22.3
Image properties from an image in the ZENworks Image Explorer.

Adding and Removing Files and Directories

From within the Image Explorer you can add files or directories of files to the image. ZENworks also allows you to create up to 10 different versions of the file set for the image. This is useful to tailor your images after they have been created or for creating an image from scratch. For example, an administrator may want to have two separate versions of the same workstation images—one for the user's local workstation and one for his remote workstation.

Use the following steps to add files and/or directories to an image object in Image Explorer:

1. Select the partition and, optionally, the directory in the partition where you want to add the files or directories.

2. Choose Image→Add Files or Image→Add Directory.

3. Navigate to the file or directory you want to add to the image and click the Add button.

The files and directories you selected are added to the image.

Use the following steps to create a new directory in an image object from within Image Explorer:

1. Select the partition and, optionally, the directory in the partition where you want to create the directory.

2. Choose Image→Add Directory.

3. Specify the name of the directory, and a new directory is added to the image.

Adding Registry Settings to an Image

Image Explorer also allows you to add a Windows Registry file to an image. This is necessary to add additional Registry entries that may need to be made to keep an image updated. Use the following steps to add a Registry file to an image object from within Image Explorer:

1. Select the partition.

2. Choose Image→Add Registry file.

3. Navigate to the file or directory you want to add to the image and click the Add button.

The files and directories you selected are added to the image. You can remove files from an image; you may also mark files and place them into image sets. These sets consist of a group of files that can then be referenced from the imaging server (for example, place all files in set 1 from image A onto this workstation). By default, all files in the image are included in all sets.

NOTE When the imaging engine requests an image from the imaging server, it automatically requests all files from the image in set 1.

Excluding Files from an Image Variant File Set

When you create a workstation image object in the directory and associate it with the image file, ZENworks allows you to specify, in the object, which set of files to use. See the discussion on image objects in the section, "Image Object" earlier in the chapter.

Use the following steps to exclude files from a file set:

1. Select the file in the view window of Image Explorer.

2. Right-click on the file and select File Sets from the pop-up menu.

3. Select the set from which you want to exclude the file from the pop-up menu listing sets 1 through 10. The file icon will be grayed out.

   You can also click Edit from the pop-up menu, and a dialog box similar to the one shown in Figure 22.4 is displayed. You can specify which sets you want to exclude the file from. This is much faster if you need to specify multiple file sets to exclude the file from.

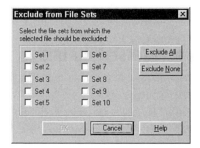

FIGURE 22.4
Image Exclude From File Sets dialog in the ZENworks Image Explorer.

Resizing Partitions in an Image

ZENworks Image Explorer provides the capability to resize partitions inside an image. After an image is created, it may be necessary at some point to increase or decrease the size of a partition within it.

For example, you may start using workstations with larger disk drives that require larger partitions.

Use the following steps to resize a partition in an image from within ZENworks Image Explorer:

1. Right-click a partition in the left frame; then click Properties.

2. Increase or decrease the value in the Original Size text box.

NOTE The Original Size cannot be decreased to a smaller value than what is in the Minimum Size text box.

Viewing Files Inside an Image

ZENworks Image Explorer also provides the capability to view files inside an image using their original applications. This can be useful if you need to determine what text is contained in configuration files because you do not need to manually extract the file from the image to a new location.

Use the following steps to view files from inside the ZENworks Image Explorer:

1. Select the File.

2. Click File→Extract and View.

Compressing a Workstation Image

Another great feature contained in ZENworks Image Explorer is the capability to compress the image by up to 60% of the original file size. This feature provides two benefits. The first is that the image takes up less space on disk. The second is that the image can't be restored to a workstation faster.

Use the following steps to compress an image from inside the ZENworks Image Explorer:

1. Click Tools→Compress Image to bring up the image QuickCompress dialog box shown in Figure 22.5.

2. Browse to a folder, specify a new image filename, and then select a compression option:

   ▶ Optimize for Speed—Takes the least amount of time to compress but creates the largest compressed image file.

▶ Balanced (Recommended)—Represents a compromise between Compression time and image file size. This option is used by default when an image is created.

▶ Optimize for Space—Creates the smallest image file but takes longer to compress.

3. Click Compress.

NOTE If you have used Delete to hide files in the image, they are removed from the image during compression.

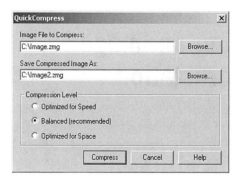

FIGURE 22.5
The image QuickCompress dialog in the ZENworks Image Explorer.

Splitting a Workstation Image

Another great feature contained in ZENworks Image Explorer is the capability to split an image into smaller split image files. This feature allows you to copy large images to CDs for distribution.

Use the following steps to split an image from inside the ZENworks Image Explorer:

1. Click Tools→Split Image to bring up the Image Split Settings dialog box shown in Figure 22.6.

2. Specify an existing base image file to split.

3. Specify the directory in which to store the split images.

4. Specify the maximum file size of each split image file.

5. Click Split.

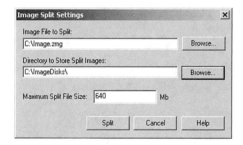

FIGURE 22.6
The Image Split Settings dialog in the ZENworks Image Explorer.

Assigning an Image to a Workstation

Three ways exist in which the workstation automatically discovers the workstation image that it should place onto its hard drive:

▶ The image may be chosen by the imaging server when an unregistered workstation boots the Linux system and contacts the imaging server. The imaging server goes through its rules to determine the image to place on the workstation.

▶ The image may be chosen by the imaging server when a registered workstation boots the Linux system and contacts the imaging server, and the workstation has an associated workstation imaging policy.

▶ If the administrator has configured the workstation object to be associated with a specific image in the directory, when the Linux system is booted and contacts the imaging server, the server looks into the workstation object to see whether it should be re-imaged. If so, it then looks to see whether a specific image file has been specified and sends that file. Otherwise, it performs as described in the preceding option.

Workstation Object

In the workstation object properties, an Image page exists. Within this Image page, you have a couple of settings that you can administer in relationship to the imaging system. The following settings can be applied on the Image page of the workstation object:

▶ Take an Image of This Workstation on the Next Boot—Enables you to specify that on the next reboot of the workstation, the Linux boot system contacts the imaging server and is told to take an image of the workstation. With this field, you also get to specify the name of the image file. The image server saves the image to the specified filename.

▶ Put an Image on This Workstation on the Next Boot—Enables you to signal that the workstation should receive an image on the next boot. When the Linux boot system contacts the imaging server, it is told that it should put down an image. In addition to this field, you can specify the image object that represents the image you want put down on the workstation. Click the Browse button to select the image object in the directory. If no image object is specified, the image server looks for any workstation image policy that may be associated with the workstation. If no workstation image policy is associated with the workstation and the administrator specifies no image, no image is applied to the workstation.

After the workstation reboots and performs the requested action (make or restore an image), these flags are reset so that on the next reboot no work will be done. If the action is not successful, these flags are *not* reset and continue to cause the action to be requested upon each reboot.

Applying Application Objects to an Image

One of the most significant advancements that ZENworks Desktop Management has over your standard imaging systems is the ability for you to include all the files and software associated with an application object into a workstation image. By performing this function, when the image is placed onto the workstation, all the included application object files are installed with the image. When the workstation boots into the native operating system, these application object files are treated as disconnected applications and are available from the workstation.

See Chapter 11 to understand better how the ZENworks Application Window works.

To apply the application objects to an image you need to perform the following steps. These steps assume that you already have an image object representing some base image and an application object in your tree:

1. Launch ConsoleOne.

2. Browse to and select Properties on an application object that you want to include in an image. This application object can be included in any number of images.

3. Go to the Common tab→Imaging property page.

4. On the Imaging property page, you can identify the name of the image file by browsing to an existing file (to be overwritten) or by typing in a new filename to be created. It is recommended that you type in a UNC path so that all machines can get to this image instead of having to have a mapped drive to the identified volume.

5. Select the application object flags at the bottom of the screen that tell the ZENworks Application Window how to handle the application.

6. Click the Create Image button to have the system create an image representation of the application into the specified image file.

7. Close the dialog boxes to get back to the main ConsoleOne screen.

8. Browse to and select the properties of the workstation image object that you want to include the application object.

9. Go to the Images tab.

10. Click the Add button on the screen and enter the server name and path to the image file you want to have added to the image.

11. Click OK to save all the changes and exit ConsoleOne.

Now when the image is applied to a workstation either through the policy or direct association, the base image plus the added image are placed on the workstation.

NOTE **If you update an application object you have to re-create the image file again. You do not have to re-add it to the base image as long as you keep the same image file name.**

Re-Imaging a Workstation

You can re-image the workstation (for example, apply a new image on top of the file system) through manual mode with the boot media or through the automatic method. Applying an image does not overwrite the Linux partition or the image-safe data on the hard drive.

You can automatically apply an image by doing the following. This assumes that the workstation is associated with a workstation object and that an image exists in the tree. The steps to accomplish this are

1. Launch ConsoleOne.

2. Browse and select Properties on the workstation object associated with the desktop.

3. Select the Images tab and select Put an Image on This Workstation on the Next Boot and click the Browse button in the Image File field to select an image to apply.

4. Click OK and exit from ConsoleOne.

5. Request that the user reboot the workstation.

Advanced Imaging

When the workstation boots the Linux imaging software and you request to go into manual mode, several commands, described in the following sections, are available. You only need to type enough of the command to be unique. The following describes only the minimal keystrokes to get the command functional.

Remember that you are running on top of the Linux operating system and that any normal Linux command is valid on the command line. This enables you freedom to use any command to help in the setup and configuration of the workstation. For example, you can see a listing of files (`ls  —FC`) or mount a drive (`mount /dev/hdc /mnt/cdrom`). Also any Linux utility that you may have can be run on the workstation.

Accessing the Imaging Engine Command Menu

You can access operations available in the imaging engine from the command menu. To access the command menu use the **img** command with

no parameters, and a menu will be displayed for you to select the operation you want to perform.

Information Commands

The following commands are general-purpose commands that display
information about the system:

- ▶ `img help [mode]`—Displays a screen of help to assist in reminding
  you about some of the commands. It does not display an exhaus-
  tive list of available commands. The optional mode parameters are
  m, to display information on the Make mode, and **p**, to display
  information on the Partition mode. For example:

  `img help p`

- ▶ `img info [zisd]`—Displays the detected hardware information.
  This is useful to determine the values for the rules in the policies.
  The engine sends this information to the imaging server. The
  optional **zisd** parameter lists the data currently stored in the
  image-safe area on the computer and the last base image that was
  put down to the workstation. For example:

  `img info zisd`

Automation Commands

The auto mode images the computer automatically based on any applicable NDS or eDirectory policies and settings. In this mode, the imaging
engine queries the imaging specifies in the **PROXYADDR** environment variable for any work to do. The imaging server checks the relevant NDS or
eDirectory policies and settings to determine which imaging tasks should
be performed. The following commands cause the imaging engine to
connect to the imaging server and perform any actions specified in NDS
or eDirectory:

- ▶ `img auto`—Sends a request to the imaging server to see whether
  any work needs to be performed. If work must be performed, the
  imaging server immediately performs the work. The following
  codes are returned to the Linux shell on completion: 0—no work
  to perform; 0—successful imaging task completed, no change to
  the hard drive; 1—successfully received one or more images, the
  hard drive has been altered; n—other error codes. For example:

  `img auto`

Partition Commands

The following commands deal with manipulation of the partitions on the workstation:

▶ `img dump`—Displays the partition information of the hard disk. This command is important because the partition numbers displayed from this command are the partition numbers used as parameters to other advanced imaging commands. For example:

`img dump`

▶ `img dump geo`—Displays the partition information of the hard disk and the geometry of the disk. This command is important because the partition numbers displayed from this command are the partition numbers used as parameters to other advanced imaging commands. For example:

`img dump geo`

▶ `img pa<partition number>`—Makes the specified partition the active partition. The partition number is the partition number returned from the `img dump` command. For example:

`img pa2`
`img pa1`

▶ `img pc<partition number> <partition type> [partition size] [cluster=<cluster size>]`—Creates a partition in an empty slot. The partition number is the partition number returned from the `img d` command. The command fails if the partition specified is not empty. The partition type must be one of the following: `fat12`, `fat16`, `fat32`, or `ntfs`. The partition size parameter is optional and represents the number of megabytes requested. If the size is not given, the largest partition size possible for the specified type is created. The cluster size is supported only for NTFS partition types. For the FAT partitions, the cluster size is determined automatically by the size of the partition.

When a partition is created, the ZENworks imaging engine performs some low-level preformatting. This preformatting process depends on the actual file system being created. It is usually a subset of the formatting process performed on new partitions by the various operating systems, but it is not enough to be recognized as a valid partition by those operating systems. It is only formatted enough to enable the imaging engine to start inserting files into the partition. At least one base image must be applied to the partition before it is recognized by the operating system. Some examples follow:

```
img pc2 ntfs 500 c8
img pc3 fat32
img pc4 NTFS 2000 cluster=1
```

▶ `img pd<partition number>`—Deletes the specified partition from the hard drive. For example:

```
img pd3
```

Creating Image Commands

The following commands deal with the creation of workstation images:

▶ `img makel[partition number] <path> [comp=<comp level>] [x<partition number>]`—Makes an image of the disk and places it in the local file system. The optional partition number represents the partition where you want to store the image. This specified partition is *not* included in the image. If no partition is specified, all partitions (except the Linux boot partition) are imaged, and the image is stored on the Linux partition. The path must resolve to a valid path on the system. No directories are automatically created, and any existing file with the same name is overwritten.

By being able to specify the partition number used to store the image, you can have an attached jaz drive, which shows up as a partition and then stores the image of the hard drive on your removable media. The `comp` parameter specifies the amount of compression used when storing the image. Valid compression levels are from 0-9, where, 0 is no compression for optimized speed, and 9 means full compression optimized for space. Use 6 to balance between space and speed. The `x<partition number>` option excludes the partition specified from the image. You can exclude as many partitions as you need to reduce the imaging size and time. Some examples are

```
img makel12 imgdump.zmg
img makel fulldump
img makel /images/wsdump.zmg comp=6 x2 x3
```

▶ img makep <imaging server address> <UNCpath> [comp=<comp level>] [x<partition number]—Takes an image of the workstation and sends that image to the specified imaging server. This imaging server address is the actual IP address (not the DNS name) of the imaging server. The UNC path is where the image is stored on that imaging server. The path must resolve to a valid path on the system—no directories are automatically created, and any existing file with the same name is overwritten. The UNC must have the format of *//server name/dir/dir. . ./filename* (make sure that you use the forward slash). If the suffix .ZMG is not specified, it is automatically appended to the filename. The server name is really ignored because the image is sent and stored on the imaging server specified by the IP address. The `comp` parameter specifies the amount of compression used when storing the image. Valid compression levels are from 0-9, where, 0 is no compression for optimized speed, and 9 means full compression optimized for space. Use 6 to balance between space and speed. The `x<partition number>` option excludes the partition specified from the image. You can exclude as many partitions as you need to reduce the imaging size and time. The server name may be used at some future release. Some examples follow:

```
img makep 137.65.203.1 //zen1/vol1/images/dellb.zmg
img makep 137.65.203.254 //zen2/vol2/ibmlaptop
img makep 137.65.79.123 //zen2/vol2/ntws.zmg comp=9 x2
```

Restoring Image Commands

The following commands deal with the restoring of images onto the workstation. These commands may or may not destroy any previous data on the workstation:

▶ img restorel[partition number] path [s<set number>]— Restores an image from the partition and path specified onto the disk. All partitions on the hard disk, other than the Linux partition, are removed prior to the image being placed on the workstation. The optional partition number specifies the partition (as displayed in the `img d` command) where the image is stored. The path must resolve to a valid image file on the system. If you are restoring from a removable media drive, the partition number is the partition for the jaz or CD-ROM drive. The path must be a valid path and must represent an image file on the specified partition. The optional set number enables you to specify which set of files to include from the image. The sets can be specified in the ZENworks Image Editor program. If the set number is not specified it is assumed that it is set 1. For example:

```
img restorel2 myimage
img restorel theimage.zmg s2
```

▶ `img restorep <proxy IP address> <UNCpath> [s<set number>]`—Rakes an image from the imaging server and puts it on the workstation. The proxy IP address must be the address of the imaging server where the image is stored. You cannot use a DNS name in this field. The UNC path must be a valid path that represents the image file. The path must be in the format `//server name/share/dir/dir. . ./filename` or `//server name/ volume/dir/dir. . ./filename`. The optional set number enables you to specify which set of files to include from the image. The sets can be specified in the ZENworks Image Editor program. If the set number is not specified, it is assumed that it is set 1. Some examples are as follows:

```
img restorep 137.65.200.1 //zen9/image/delllaptop.zmg
img restorep 137.65.200.1 //any/image/delllaptop.zmg s2
```

Advanced Restoring Image Commands

These advanced image restore commands enable you to specify that the partitions on the disk should not be destroyed and how to map the partitions in the image to the partitions on the disk. Additionally, when images are restored, the partitions are automatically resized to fit the archived partition. In these commands, the physical partition can remain larger than the archived partition:

▶ `img restorel[partition number] path [s<set number>] a<archive partition>:p<physical partition>`—Restores an image from the partition and path specified onto the specified partition on disk. This does not destroy the partition but instead takes the archived partition and places its files into the specified partition. Any files already existing on the partition remain; files with the same name are overwritten. The optional partition number specifies the partition (as displayed in the **img d** command) where the image is stored. The path must resolve to a valid image file on the system. If you are restoring from a removable media drive, the partition number is the partition for the jaz or CD-ROM drive. The path must be a valid path and must represent an image file on the specified partition. The optional set number enables you to specify which set of files to include from the image; the sets can be specified in the ZENworks Image Editor program. If the set number is not specified, it is assumed that it is set 1.

The `a<archive partition>:p<physical partition>` enables you to create a mapping between the two drive spaces. You can take archived partition 1 and place it on physical partition 2, for example. You must specify at least one partition mapping to keep from having the default, wipe all partitions, behavior. You may specify as many mappings as are needed, and you may map multiple archive partitions onto a single physical partition. An archive partition cannot be mapped to more than one physical partition. For example:

```
img restore12 myimage a1:p2
img restore13 theimage.zmg s2 a1:p2 a2:p2
```

► `img restorep <proxy IP address> <UNCpath> [s<set number>] a<archive partition>:p<physical partition>`— Takes an image from the imaging server and puts it on the workstation into the specified partition. The proxy IP address must be the address of the imaging server where the image is stored. You cannot use a DNS name in this field. The UNC path must be a valid path that represents the image file. The path must be the format *//server name/share/dir/dir. . ./filename* or *//server name/volume/dir/dir. . ./filename*. The optional set number enables you to specify which set of files to include from the image; the sets can be specified in the ZENworks Image Editor program. If the set number is not specified, it is assumed that it is set 1.

The `a<archive partition>:p<physical partition>` enables you to create a mapping between the two drive spaces. You can take archived partition 1 and place it on physical partition 2, for example. You must specify at least one partition mapping to keep from having the default, wipe all partitions, behavior. You may specify as many mappings as are needed, and you may map multiple archive partitions onto a single physical partition. An archive partition cannot be mapped to more than one physical partition. For example:

```
img restorep 137.65.200.1 //zen9/image/delllaptop.zmg
➥a2:p1
img restorep 137.65.200.1 //any/image/dtop.zmg s2 a2:p2
➥a3:p2
```

ZENPartition Commands

You can use the ZENPartition mode to enable, disable, or remove the installed ZENworks Desktop Management imaging partition from the workstation. This allows you to control the behavior of ZENworks imaging on the workstation.

The following commands are available for the ZENPartition mode:

▶ `zenPartition enable`—Enables the ZENworks imaging partition

▶ `zenPartition disable`—Disables the ZENworks imaging partition to stop imaging on the workstation

▶ `zenPartition remove`—Removes the ZENworks imaging partition from the workstation to permanently stop imaging on it; for example:

```
img zenPartition enable
```

Multicast Commands

You can also set up the ZENworks imaging system to perform multicasting of the image. You can set up a single workstation to act as the master and send its hard drive contents to all the participating slave workstations.

You start the multicast session by entering the following on all workstations participating on the session:

`img session <session name> [option]`

The following options are available for the `img session name`:

▶ name—The name of the multicast session that each computer joining the session will use.

▶ master¦client—Specifies whether this client will be the session master or just a client. If you do not use this parameter, the system waits until a master is found.

▶ `clients=<count>`—Specifies the number of computers that must be registered with the master before imaging begins. After imaging begins, computers attempting to register with the session will be denied.

▶ `t=<minutes>`—Specifies the number of minutes the master computer waits for the next participant to register before starting the imaging process without reaching the number of computers specified by the `clients` option.

The session name must be a unique string to identify this multicast session. The session name string used must be identically entered on *all* workstations (both master and slave) that are going to participate in the session. This string is used to hash a multicast address, so a small chance exists that two different strings may result in the same multicast address. Multicast addresses are class D IP addresses. To ease wire sniffing, troubleshooting, and LAN traffic analysis, the imaging engine always uses 231 as the first octet in its address.

When started, by entering the `img session <name>` command, each workstation waits until the user determines which station will act as the master. The master workstation should be the **SOURCE** workstation; all slave workstations are **DESTINATION** workstations.

To designate the master workstation, go to the workstation that contains the **SOURCE** drive. The workstation should have already had the **session** command started and should be waiting just like all the other workstations. Press the **m** key on the master workstation. This designates that workstation as the master. At this point, all the other workstations attempt to register with the master and receive a unique session identifier. If for some reason a slave station is rebooted before the session starts, it always receives the same identifier.

When the desired number of stations has registered with the master; the master displays a running count of the number of registered slaves and then starts the session by pressing **g** on the master workstation. Any station attempting to join the session after the session has started is denied access. This should now transfer the contents of the master to all the slave workstations.

After the session is over, the master workstation displays a list of the stations that did not successfully complete the image.

> **NOTE** The multicast operations are dependent on the multicast features configured in your network equipment. Possible problems might include the routing of multicast packets not being allowed, stations outside the defined scope of multicast on switches not receiving the packets, and so on.

Script Commands

The following commands perform some type of operation that would normally only be activated when the imaging engine is initially booted in manual mode. These are simple shell scripts that have been created for your convenience and use by the imaging system. Other script files exist, but these are the most useful to you.

▶ `/bin/cdrom.s`—Mounts the `cdrom` drive to `/mnt/cdrom`.

▶ `/bin/config.s`—Enables you to configure the `settings.txt` file for the Linux partition.

▶ `/bin/imaging.s`—Runs the imaging engine in auto mode, just like the `img a` command.

▶ `/bin/install.s`—Creates the Linux partition and installs it onto the hard disk. It removes all partitions *unless* the Linux partition already exists; then it just updates the files.

▶ `/bin/lilo.s`—Installs the ZENworks imaging boot manager system, making sure that this system is booted first on the drive.

Summary

This chapter examined the capability of ZENworks to create and deploy images of workstations throughout the network. This can be useful when you set up workstations initially in your organization as well as when you need to restore a workstation to properly functioning status after problems have occurred.

## CHAPTER 23

Using ZENworks Software Metering

A major advantage included with ZENworks is the capability to do software metering. ZENworks software metering gives organizations the capability to manage software licenses and track software usage through ZENworks application management and Novell's Licensing Services (NLS). Currently NLS cannot be administered in ConsoleOne, requiring that you administer the licensing in NWAdmin while managing ZENworks in ConsoleOne.

After software metering is configured for Application Window, a license is incremented each time a user launches the application. In other words, every time a user runs the application, one license is also in use.

NOTE Applications must be delivered to the user through Application Explorer or Application Window to take advantage of software metering. Application objects must also be associated with license containers.

To set up and use ZENworks software metering you need to become familiar with the procedures discussed in this chapter.

Using NWAdmin to Install and Administer Licenses

NWAdmin is used to install and administer licenses. You should use the NWAdmin utility to create metered certificates as well as to add new ones to existing license containers. You can also use NWAdmin to generate reports and view information about software metering.

To access the licensing features from NWAdmin, select Tools→Novell Licensing Services to open the License Services manager shown in Figure 23.1.

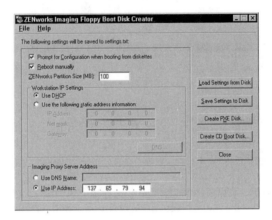

FIGURE 23.1
The licensing options in NWAdmin.

Installing a License Certificate Using NWAdmin

Installing a certificate for an NLS-aware application adds a license container object to the NDS database as well as a license certificate object inside that container object. To install a license certificate in NWAdmin, use the following steps from the tree browse view:

1. Select the container you want to install the license certificate into.

2. Select Tools→Novell Licensing Services→Add Licenses.

3. From the pop-up window, select License File and click OK.

4. A window pops up enabling you to specify the license file you want to install. From this window, navigate to the location of the license file you want to install and select it. Click OK.

5. A window similar to the one shown in Figure 23.2 appears. From this window, browse to the NDS context where the certificate object should be installed (the default is the currently selected container).

After both fields are entered, click the View Policy button to see specific information about the license, or click the Add button to install the license certificate.

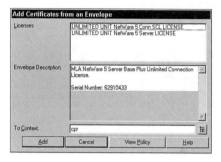

FIGURE 23.2
The Add Certificates from an Envelope window in NWAdmin.

Creating a Metered Certificate Using NWAdmin

Metered certificates enable you to track usage of applications. Using metered certificates enables you to track and manage the licenses for user applications even if they are not NLS aware.

To create a metered certificate using NWAdmin, use the following steps from a tree browse window:

1. Select Tools→Novell Licensing Services→Add Licenses.

2. From the pop-up window, select License Metering and click OK.

3. A screen similar to the one shown in Figure 23.3 appears. From this screen, enter the name of the software publisher.

4. Enter the product name.

5. Enter the version.

6. Change the NDS context for the license certificate if needed (currently selected container is set by default).

7. Set the number of licenses for the certificate.

8. Enter or select the number of grace licenses you will allow.

9. Set whether users will use a single license when launching an application multiple times from one workstation.

10. Click OK to finish.

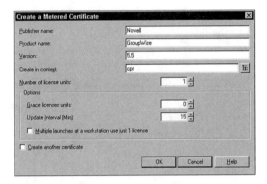

FIGURE 23.3
The Create a Metered Certificate window.

The Grace Licenses Units option enables additional users to run. If you do not enter a number of grace licenses, users will not be allowed to open additional applications beyond the number specified in Number of License Units.

Assigning Licenses to Users Using NWAdmin

When you know how to install license certificates and create metering certificates you need to know how to assign licenses to users using NWAdmin.

The NDS user who installs the license certificate is the owner. An owner can assign the following objects access to the licenses:

- ▶ User
- ▶ Group
- ▶ Organization
- ▶ Organizational unit
- ▶ Server

For example, if an owner assigns a container object to use a certificate, all users in and below that container can use the certificate. After license assignments are made, only those objects assigned to the license certificates can use the license.

To assign and delete access to licenses using NWAdmin, use the following steps from a tree browse window:

1. Select the license certificate that you want users to access.

2. Right-click the license certificate and select Details.

3. Select the Assignments property page.

4. Click Add to add objects.

5. Locate and select the object that enables the correct users to access the certificate's licenses.

Here are the steps for deleting assignments to a license certificate in NWAdmin:

1. Navigate to the Assignments property page of the License Certificate object you want to delete assignments on.

2. Select the user objects and click Remove.

Assigning a New Owner to a License Certificate Using NWAdmin

Because the user who installs a certificate automatically becomes the owner of that certificate, you might want to reassign ownership at a later date. NWAdmin enables you to assign a new owner to a license certificate by using the following steps:

1. Select the license certificate object from a tree browse window in the NWAdmin utility.

2. Right-click the object and select details.

3. Select the Installer property page.

4. From the Installer property page, locate and select the object you want to assign as owner of this certificate.

It is important to know that only a certificate's owner can reassign ownership of the certificate.

Working with Reports in NWAdmin

Because NWAdmin tracks data about licenses and metered products, you can create reports that help you assess and monitor usage and compliance concerning these products for the past 15 months.

These reports can range from information about a single license certificate to information about all license certificates currently being used for a given product.

Creating a Report

To create a report for license certificates, use the following steps from within NWAdmin:

1. Select Tools→Novell Licensing Services→Generate License Reports.

2. From the screen shown in Figure 23.4, you can select to scan either the tree or a predefined catalog to generate the report.

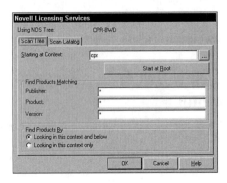

FIGURE 23.4
The Scan Tree tab on the Novell Licensing Services window in NWAdmin.

3. Select a license container you want to begin the scan at; specify any publisher, product, or version filters you want to use for the scan; and click OK.

After the scan is complete a list of license certificates and containers is displayed. To create a report, simply select the license certificate you want to report usage on and select Actions→Create License Usage Report. A screen similar to the one shown in Figure 23.5 appears.

Viewing a Report

After you create a report using NWAdmin, you can toggle between a graphical view of the report and that report's text.

To use the graphical view click Graph, as shown in Figure 23.6, and a graphical representation of the data in the report is displayed onscreen. This view displays the number of license units installed and the number used. The dates along the bottom of the graph show the start and end dates that the report covers. You can change these dates to make the data more informational.

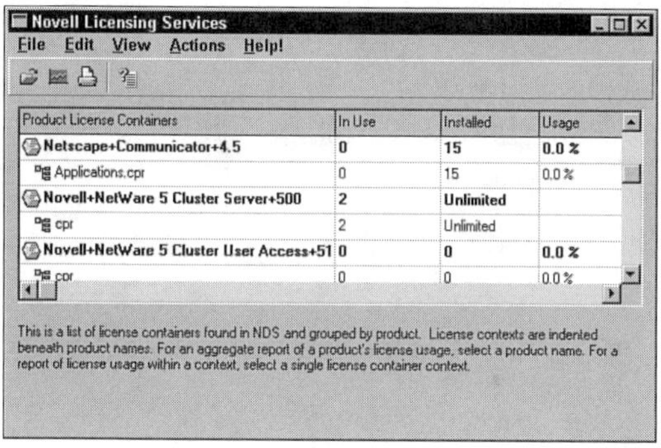

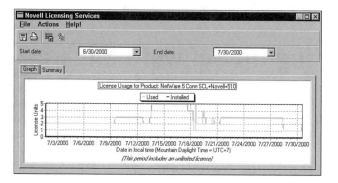

FIGURE 23.5
A metered license certificate report in NWAdmin.

FIGURE 23.6
A metered license certificate usage report graph in NWAdmin.

To use the textual view, click Summary, and a textual representation of the data in the report is displayed onscreen, as shown in Figure 23.7.

The textual view provides the following information:

▶ The date and time you created the report

▶ The product

▶ The location or NDS context of the object

▶ Current number of licenses being used and installed

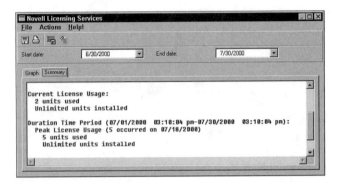

FIGURE 23.7
A metered license certificate usage report summary in NWAdmin.

▶ The range of dates being reported

▶ Peak usage of licenses including date the peak occurred

▶ The number of units used and installed during peak usage

▶ A list of possible dates out of compliance

Setting Up Software Metering

Software metering involves using the following procedures to verify the metering requirements and setting up metering certificates. The following sections describe configuring software metering certificates that allow you to properly meter software on your network.

Verifying Setup Requirements

The first step in setting up software metering is to make sure that you have met the system requirements. The following are the current requirements for setting up software metering:

▶ You should have Supervisor rights to the [ROOT] of the eDirectory tree in which you install the Application Management portion of ZENworks.

▶ Users must have Read and File Scan rights to the directory in which you install NAL.

▶ Users must have sufficient rights to the directories in which you install the applications they can access.

Installing Locally or on the Network?

After the system requirements are met, make sure that the application is delivered to the user through the Application Window via the Application Window or the Application Explorer. Although software metering does not care where an application's executable file is located, the application must be delivered to the user through the Application Window.

Ensuring Users Have Access to NLS

The next step in setting up software metering is to make sure that users have access to NLS. Users must always be attached to a NetWare server that provides licensing services.

TIP By loading NLS on more than one server in your tree and ensuring that users have a connection to one or more servers with NLS loaded, you can make sure that users have access to NLS. If a server running NLS goes down, NLS still works as long as it is running on another server and users have a connection to that server.

Assigning Users to a License Certificate Object

After you verify that the system and setup requirements for software metering are met, you need to assign users to a license. If no object is specifically assigned to a license certificate object, anyone can use the certificate. However, after at least one user is assigned to a license certificate object, only the users, groups, or containers assigned to that license can use the certificate. This limits access to the licenses.

To assign users to a license certificate object use NLS Manager or the following steps in the NWAdmin utility:

1. Double-click a product license container.

2. Select a license certificate object.

3. Right-click and select Details to add users.

Creating a License Container and Metered Certificate Object

To set up software metering, create a license container and metered certificate object. These objects enable ZENworks to track and control access to license objects. The license container is a special container object in NDS to store metered certificate objects.

The metered certificate object contains the information you enter. License containers can contain multiple metered certificate objects. To create a metered certificate object and a license container, use the following steps in the NWAdmin utility:

1. Highlight the container where you want to create a metered certificate.

2. Select Tools→Novell License Metering→Add Licenses then License File.

3. A screen similar to the one shown in Figure 23.8 appears. From this screen, enter information about the application that you want to meter, such as software publisher name, software product name, and version or revision.

4. Click OK.

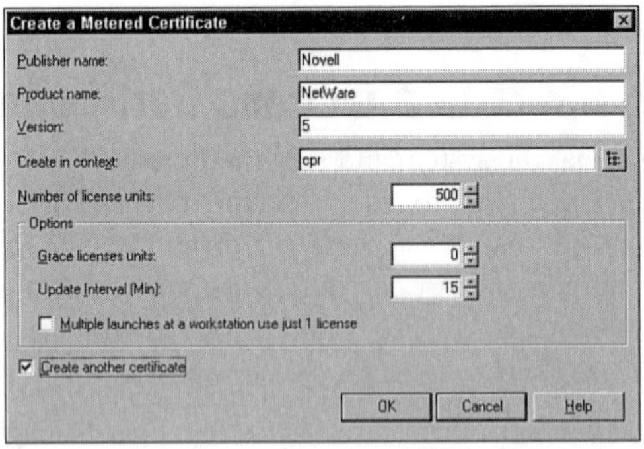

FIGURE 23.8
The Create a Metered Certificate window in NWAdmin.

Adding Additional Licenses (Metered Certificates)

The last procedure you need to be aware of when setting up software metering is adding additional licenses—for example, if you originally installed a 50-user license of an application and want to extend this to a 75-user license. To extend the license of the application, you need to create another metered certificate object.

The license container is a container class object in eDirectory and cannot be renamed. The metered certificate is a leaf object of the license container. The metered certificate basically represents the individual license count. To get a total license count, the license container totals up all leaf metered certificates beneath it.

To add additional licenses, add additional metered certificates using the following steps in the NWAdmin utility:

1. Highlight the container where you want to add a license.

2. Select Tools→Novell License Metering→Add Licenses then License Metering.

3. From the screen that appears, enter the same name as the original license container to which you want to add licenses.

If you enter the same software publisher name, software product name, and version number, a new metered certificate is created below the license container. This metered certificate is added to those already located in the license container to form a new license total.

Summary

This chapter examined ZENworks software metering. This feature gives organizations the capability to manage software licenses and track software usage in NWAdmin and ConsoleOne.

## CHAPTER 24

Integrating ZENworks Desktop Management with ZENworks Server Management Tiered Electronic Distribution

A major advantage included in ZENworks Desktop Management is its capability to integrate into the Tiered Electronic Distribution (TED) system included with ZENworks Server Management. This integration enables you to leverage the powerful TED engine for application distribution, thus enabling you to distribute desktop applications throughout your entire network and across tree boundaries—all from a single source location.

The following sections describe what TED does and how to integrate a ZENworks Desktop Management application object into the TED distribution system to more effectively distribute applications to users on large networks.

How to Use TED with ZENworks Desktop Management

The TED engine in ZENworks Server Management is comprised of three components: the distributor, a subscriber, and proxy agents hosted on NetWare, Linux, Solaris, and Windows servers throughout your tree. When you install ZENworks Server Management, the installation program creates distributor and subscriber objects for the TED agents that you select to install on each server.

After you install TED, you can configure and manage the TED objects from ConsoleOne and iManager, making it easy to distribute files by grouping them into data packages (distributions) and hosting them in distribution channels made up of distributor and subscriber objects. Application objects can be added to the TED distribution system as data packages by using the Desktop Application Distribution Wizard to create a desktop application distribution object.

TED then transfers the desktop application distribution object from single or multiple sources to the subscriber server nodes in the distribution channel. This allows you to schedule distributions to take advantage of off-peak hours. It also sends notification of distribution statuses by sending email messages, displaying real-time messages, logging events, database reporting, or sending SNMP traps.

About the Desktop Application Agent

The TED agent that allows you to distribute ZENworks Desktop Management application objects through the TED channel is the ZENworks Server Management desktop application agent. The desktop application agent is responsible for keeping track of the application object-specific information as the package is distributed through the channel so that it can be maintained when it reaches the destination subscriber.

After you set up the application object through the wizard, the ZENworks Server Management distributor reads the object's properties in eDirectory and determines the location of the source files. Next, it determines the associations with other application objects, application folder objects, chained applications, and containers. It packages the associations data into an XML file and packages it with the application object's source files, including the source files of any associated application objects, into a .CPK file to be distributed though the TED channel.

When the package is distributed through the ZENworks Server Management channel, subscriber servers extract the package including the source files and XML data and replicate the application object in their tree locations. The subscriber could be in a different location of the same tree or in an entirely different tree.

NOTE You must install ZENworks Desktop Management Policy-enabled Distribution Services to have access to the desktop application agent.

Using the Desktop Application Distribution Wizard to Create a Distribution

Now that you understand how the desktop application agent works to distribute a desktop application distribution through a TED channel, you need to know how to create the desktop application distribution object. ZENworks Server Management includes a Desktop Application Distribution Wizard to ease the creation of desktop application distributions. The wizard allows you to specify an application object that you want to distribute and then it allows you to set properties that determine how it is delivered. The following sections discuss creating a distribution object, running the Desktop Application Distribution Wizard to add an application object to it, and setting the properties to distribute the application.

Creating a Distribution Object

The first step in creating a desktop application distribution is to create a TED distribution object. Use the following steps to create a TED distribution object from within ConsoleOne:

1. Select the container in which you want to create the TED distribution object.

2. Select File→New→Object→TED Distribution.

3. Enter the name of the Distribution object in the object creation window shown in Figure 24.1.

4. Use the browse button to select the distributor object that you want to distribute the application. The source files for application objects that will be part of the distribution must exist on the local file system of the distributor you select.

5. Click OK.

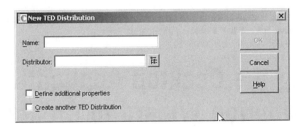

FIGURE 24.1
Distribution object creation window in ConsoleOne.

NOTE The source files for the application objects you add to the distribution must
reside on the distributor's local file system. The subscriber must have access to Novell's
eDirectory to extract the application object and apply it. Only NetWare and Windows subscribers can create application objects.

Configuring Distribution Type

After you create the TED distribution object, you need to define the distribution type as a desktop application so that you can use the Desktop
Application Distribution Wizard to define the desktop application properties and make the TED distribution a desktop application distribution.

Use the following steps to define the distribution type and start the application wizard:

1. Right-click on the TED distribution object you just created and
   select Properties from the pop-up menu.

2. Click on the Type tab, shown in Figure 24.2.

3. Select Desktop Application from the drop-down Type list to set the
   distribution type as a desktop application distribution.

4. Click the Setup button to open the Desktop Application
   Distribution Wizard shown in Figure 24.3.

WARNING Do not edit desktop application distribution objects manually from their
ConsoleOne properties window. Always go through the wizards to make changes to these
objects.

The following sections describe how to navigate through the Desktop
Application Distribution Wizard to define the settings to be used when
distributing the desktop application through the TED channel.

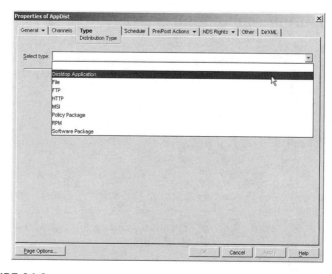

FIGURE 24.2
Type tab for the TED distribution object in ConsoleOne.

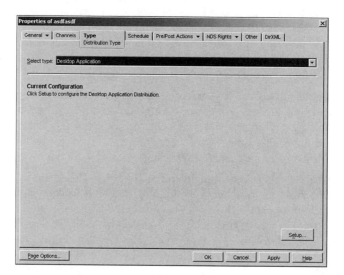

FIGURE 24.3
Desktop Application Distribution Wizard for the desktop application agent
in ConsoleOne.

Configuring Application Source Options

After you click Next from the initial window in the Desktop Application
Distribution Wizard, you see a screen similar to the one in Figure 24.4.
From this screen you can configure settings that control what properties
of the source application object you want to maintain when it is distributed through the TED channel as well as whether load balancing and
fault tolerance should be observed.

The following is a list of the properties that you need to define the application source options screen in the wizard:

▶ Maintain Source Tree Structure—Selecting this option duplicates
the source tree's directory structure at the destination's location,
which is the target subscribers' working context. This tree structure
is then used to create the ZENworks Desktop Management application objects. You must enable this option if you want to use
chained applications.

▶ Source Root Context—This field specifies a container object to be
used as the root container for the ZENworks Desktop Management
application objects. The distributor only records directory data
from that container and its subordinate containers; therefore, when
the subscriber extracts the package it applies the application object
to its working directory as if the container had actually been the
root. You can select application objects from this root container and
its subordinate containers.

▶ Maintain Associations—Selecting this option maintains the group
and container associations of the application object in its source
tree, by replicating the associated groups or containers at the target
location if they do not exist. User and workstation associations in
the source location are not replicated.

▶ Load Balancing and Fault Tolerance Support—This section allows
you to specify whether to use automated load balancing, fault tolerance, or neither. If you select Load Balance, ZENworks automatically spreads the desktop application distributions of the servers being
used. Fault tolerance is automatically accomplished through load
balancing because of multiple servers involved. If you specify Fault
Tolerance, ZENworks allows a server currently being used for desktop application distributions to assume the distribution role of
another server that has gone down, however. If you select None,
you can manually configure each application object for load balancing or fault tolerance.

▶ Rebuild Distribution—This selection configures when the distribution is rebuilt in the system. When checked, the system automatically rebuilds the distribution when the version number of the application object changes or when there is an alteration in the application object list in the actual distribution.

▶ Overwrite Exiting Target Folder Object Attributes—This section configures whether the attributes of the source folder object should be merged into or overwrite the target folder object when there is a folder object referred to by an included application object. When checked, the source folder object will overwite the target. When unchecked, ZENworks will merge the source values into the target folder object.

▶ Always Replicate Association Flags—This selection configures whether the association flags (Force Cache, Force Run, Desktop, and so on) should be replicated from the source to the target application object. When this flag is unchecked, the association flags will only be placed when the target application is first created by a distribution.

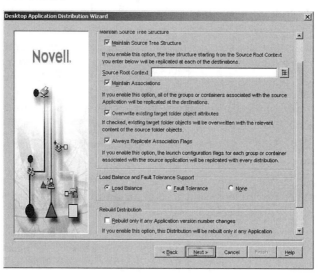

FIGURE 24.4
Application source options screen of the Desktop Application Distribution Wizard in ConsoleOne.

Configuring Application Source Objects

After you configure the options for maintaining information about the
source application object and click the Next button, you see a screen
similar to the one in Figure 24.5. This screen allows you to configure
which application objects you want to be part of the desktop application
distribution.

You must first specify at least one valid ZENworks Desktop Management
application object. ZENworks Server Management TED supports application objects that are chained together. When you add an application
object that is chained, all associated objects in the chain are automatically
included in the distribution.

The Keep the Same Source Paths for the Replicated Objects check box
allows you to retain the source application's file source paths in the desktop application distribution for when a mapped drive designation must
be used by the desktop application that is distributed.

Key points to remember about this option:

▶ Select this option only if the source application's file source path is
  a mapped drive, and you want the path on the replicated application objects to be the same.

▶ If the source applications' file source paths are mapped drives, but
  you want the replicated applications to use a UNC path according
  to the extraction directory, you do not need to select this option, as
  long as you provide a service location package with variables
  defined for the mapped drives and associate the package to the
  distributors.

▶ If this option is selected, only the Application's Default Directory
  Path option is supported.

▶ Enabling this option requires that each application object (and its
  chained applications) contained in the distribution has a mapped
  drive for the source path.

  For example, if the mapped drive source path for a golden application object is `N:\applications\msi\acrobat` and `N:` represents
  the `sys:\public` directory for the distributor server, you must have
  a service location package associated with the parent container of
  the Distributor object. Inside this package, the TED policy must be
  enabled. To do this, open the properties of this policy, click the
  Variables tab, and then enter the variable `N:` and its value
  `sys:\public`. By doing this, the distributor knows where to gather
  the application files from.

▶ Enabling this option requires subscribers to have the corresponding mapped drive defined.

▶ Subscribers use a mapped drive variable if it is defined in either the subscriber's properties or in a TED policy associated with the subscriber's container or any container above it. The value of the mapped drive determines where the application files are copied to.

For example, if the file source path for a source application is `N:\applications\acrobat`, the subscriber objects need to have a variable `N:` defined, such as `data:\public2` for NetWare servers or `public2` as the shared folder for Windows servers.

ZENworks searches the variables to find a match with the source application object's file source path. For example, if the source path in the golden application object is `n:\apps\acrobat`, the following order is searched for a match:

`n:\ N:\ n: N: n N`

However, if the source application object's file source path is `N:\apps\acrobat`, the following order is searched for a match:

`N:\ n:\ N: n: N n`

▶ After you select or deselect this option, the option is disabled for any future updates to the distribution, because of the potential problems associated with alternating between using and not using the application object's mapped drives.

▶ If both the distributor and subscriber use the same mapped drive value, only one service location package is needed. You can associate the same service location package with the parent containers of both the distributors and subscribers. Also, make sure that on the Variables property page for each subscriber, the Include Policy check box is selected so that the subscribers use the variables defined inside the service location package.

▶ If the distributor and subscriber are in the same organizational unit and the subscriber has a different value for the mapped drive, you could add a mapped drive variable in the subscriber object's properties. This takes precedence over the same mapped drive variable defined in the service location package.

From the application source objects screen, shown in Figure 24.5, click the Add button and select application objects to be added to the desktop application distribution.

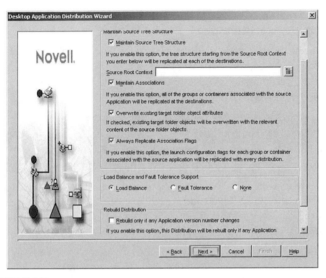

FIGURE 24.5
Application source objects screen of the Desktop Application Distribution
Wizard in ConsoleOne.

Configuring Application Destination Options

After you select the application objects and click the Next button, you
see a screen similar to the one in Figure 24.6. From this screen you can
configure settings that control where the application object's source files
will be extracted to when it has been distributed through the TED channel to a subscriber. It is important for you to verify that the destination
nodes have enough disk space to receive the application objects.

The following is a list of the properties that you need to define the application destination options screen in the wizard:

▶ Destination Volume or Shared Folder—Allows you to specify a
NetWare volume or shared folder that will be used to store the
source files of the application object at the destination subscriber
node. This volume must exist on the destination node. The default
is %DEST_VOLUME%, which is a macro to use the same volume name
as where the source files are stored on the distributor.

▶ Applications' Destination Directory Path—You also have the option
to use the default directory for the application object to store the
application object source files, or you can enter a user-defined

directory. If you select user-defined, the path you enter will be added to the destination path between the destination volume and the parent directory of the application object's default path. For example, if the application object's default path is \APPS\APP1\, and you entered VOL1 as the destination volume and \CTREE\ as a user-defined path, the effective path would be VOL1:\CTREE\APP1\.

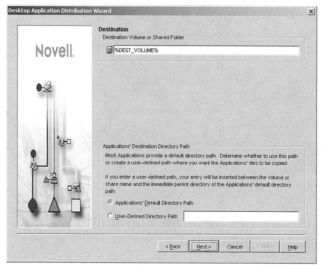

FIGURE 24.6
Application destination options screen of the Desktop Application Distribution Wizard in ConsoleOne.

Viewing the Application Distribution Summary

After you configure the application destination options and click Next, a desktop application distribution summary window similar to the one shown in Figure 24.7 appears.

Review the information on this screen carefully. If any problems exist, you can click the Back button and make changes. Otherwise, click Finish, and the desktop application distribution object is created. If you need to modify these settings, you can run the Desktop Application Distribution Wizard again by clicking on the Modify button on the Type tab of the distribution object.

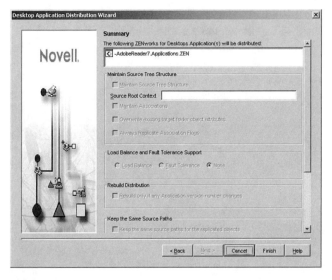

FIGURE 24.7
Site distribution summary in ConsoleOne.

Configuring the Desktop Application Distribution Object

After you set up and configure the TED distribution object to be a desktop application distribution, you need to finish setting up the distribution object and schedule it to be distributed through the TED channel. The following sections discuss configuring the distribution object's settings, channel, and schedule.

Configuring Settings

You can configure the settings for the desktop application distribution object from the General→Settings tab shown in Figure 24.8. From this screen you can specify the following settings that the distribution object will have as it is distributed through the TED channel:

- ▶ Active—Activates or deactivates the distribution. If a distribution is inactive, the distribution is not sent to subscribers even if it is in a channel.

- ▶ Use Digest—Activates the TED system to use a digest on the distribution file.

▶ Encrypt—Activates distribution encryption providing security for the distribution during transit between the distributor and subscriber. Typically, you would only encrypt a distribution sent through a firewall. If you enable encryption, you have the option to select either Strong or Weak encryption.

▶ Maximum Revisions—Enables you to specify the number of revisions of the distribution that you will keep. Each time a distribution is collected and a distribution file is created, this constitutes a revision. When the maximum number of revisions has been created, all previous distributions and delta distributions are deleted, and a new baseline distribution is created and sent. Each subscriber that receives this distribution will keep this number of revisions. This includes subscribers that act as parent subscribers but do not actually subscribe to the channel. You also have the option of selecting to delete previous revisions prior to accepting the next. This is useful in the case of large distributions because the subscriber frees up space for the new version before receiving it.

▶ Priority—Specifies the priority for this distribution that determines how it will be sent in relation to other distributions. A high priority means it will be sent before all medium and low priority distributions.

▶ Distributor—A display-only field that identifies the distributor that performs the collection and transmission of this distribution. This distributor is specified when the distribution object is created. This distributor is the owner of this distribution. The owner of a distribution cannot be changed.

▶ Description—Enables you to have a free-flowing text description of the distribution. This can be used to help in understanding the files and the purpose for the distribution package.

Configuring the Channel

After you configure the general settings for the desktop application distribution object, you need to configure the channel you want it to be distributed through from the Channels tab, shown in Figure 24.9. From the Channels tab you can select the channels that contain this distribution. This distribution can be placed in any number of channels. All the subscribers associated with each channel are sent this distribution by the distributor associated with this distribution object.

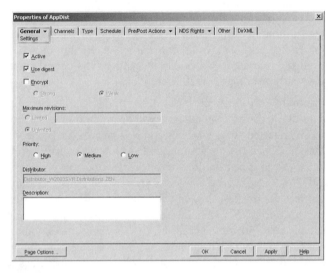

FIGURE 24.8
General Settings tab for the TED distribution object in ConsoleOne.

To add this distribution to a channel, click the Add button and browse
through eDirectory to select the channel. After you select the channel, it
is placed in the list displayed in the Channels box. To delete the channel
from the list (removing the distribution from being distributed), select
the channel and click the Delete button. To go to the property pages of
the channel object, select the object and click the Details button.

Any distributions associated with channels also appear in the channel
object under the Distributions property page.

Configuring the Schedule

After you configure the channels to distribute the desktop application
distribution object through, you need to configure the distribution schedule from the Schedule tab shown in Figure 24.10. The Schedule tab
enables you to specify how often and when this distribution should be
gathered. Each time the server clock hits the specified scheduled time,
the agents are activated and the distribution is gathered and compared
with the previous version to determine whether any changes have been
made. If changes have been made, a new version of the distribution file is
created. The actual distribution of the file occurs based on schedules of
the channels.

The following choices are available for the scheduling of the distribution: Never, Daily, Monthly, Yearly, Interval, Time, or Run Immediately.

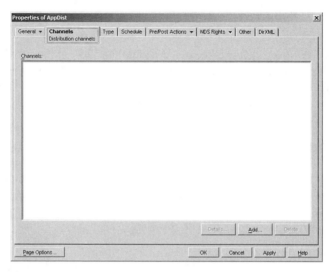

FIGURE 24.9
Channels tab for the TED distribution object in ConsoleOne.

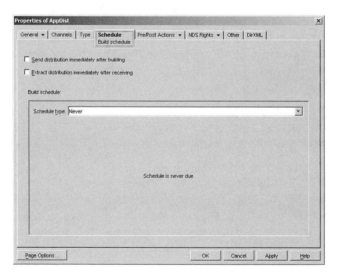

FIGURE 24.10
Schedule tab for the TED distribution object in ConsoleOne.

You can also choose to ignore the schedules of the channel with regard to
sending the distribution by selecting the Send Distribution Immediately
After Building check box. This causes the distributor to collect the distribution and then send it directly to the subscribers regardless of the channel schedule.

You can also override the extraction schedule specified on the subscriber
by checking the Extract Distribution Immediately After Receiving check
box. This causes the subscriber, after it has completed receiving the distribution, to immediately begin the extraction process.

Summary

ZENworks Server Management TED components is a powerful feature of
ZENworks. It allows you to automatically maintain synchronized application files and objects across the various containers of your tree.
Additionally, it allows you to send those applications to other trees in
your environment.

TED also provides an efficient mechanism to transmit applications and
other content files across servers in your enterprise. This can be useful in
sending files and updates across your enterprise and even to partner
companies (not in your tree).

## CHAPTER 25

Setting Up Tiered Electronic Distribution (TED)

This chapter discusses the construction, deployment, and administration of the ZENworks Tiered Electronic Distribution (TED) subsystem. As part of ZENworks, TED provides a mechanism to enable you to reliably transmit files from server to server throughout your entire network, independent of eDirectory trees and server platforms. TED is designed to be a high-end distribution service that can handle the complexity of a large network made up of multiple eDirectory trees as well as NetWare, Linux, Windows, and Solaris servers.

Understanding the General Architecture for TED

To get the most out of ZENworks Tiered Electronic Distribution, you need a high level of understanding about the architecture of TED. This section discusses the components of TED and how to consider placing them into your network.

Introducing the Components of TED

Tiered Electronic Distribution in ZENworks is composed of the following components:

► Distributor—A Java software process that runs as a process on a NetWare server, as a service on a Windows server, and as a daemon on a Linux/Solaris server. This software is responsible for distributing the files to the subscribers in the network. The distributor also calls on some TED agents to collect the files and bundles them into a distribution that can then be sent to the subscribers (see the next item).

▶ Subscriber—A Java software process that runs as a process on a NetWare server, as a service on a Windows server, and as a daemon on a Linux/Solaris server. The subscriber is responsible for receiving software distributions from distributors or parent subscribers. The subscriber also calls TED agents, when appropriate, to perform additional actions on the distributions after they are received.

▶ Parent subscriber—A Java software process that runs as a process on a NetWare server, as a service on a Windows server, and as a daemon on a Linux/Solaris server. This module fulfills two purposes. The parent subscriber is first a subscriber and can receive and extract distributions for the server on which it resides. However, it additionally has the responsibility of forwarding some distributions on to other subscribers, when instructed. This module is the same software as the subscriber; the only difference is that the requests sent have additional information instructing the subscribers to pass the distribution on to at least one other subscriber, thus reducing the number of subscribers a distributor must actually pass the software to. Any subscriber has the potential to become a parent subscriber by simply being listed in the routing hierarchy on a distributor object, or by being listed as a parent subscriber in any subscriber object list.

▶ Routing table—Each distributor has a routing table that contains a hierarchical list of subscribers who can receive distributions as well as pass them on to other subscribers.

▶ TED agents—Java modules that are started by the distributor or the subscriber and have a specific function. For example, there are agents whose job it is to collect files and collapse them into a distribution package suitable for transmission to subscribers. There are also agents responsible for expanding these distributions and placing the extracted files on the servers that received the distribution.

▶ Certificates—Distributors create certificates to provide secure distributions by issuing them to all subscribers receiving distributions from that distributor. For a subscriber to accept distributions from a distributor, it must have a certificate in its security directory from that distributor.

In ZENworks, both the distributor and subscriber are the same Java software component. Whether the component behaves as a logical distributor, parent subscriber, or subscriber depends on the function that it must currently perform. Several logical TED components may reside on the same server. For example, you may have a server that is both a distributor and a subscriber and agents when creating and extracting files from a distribution.

eDirectory Objects

TED uses objects in the directory to help direct and control its configuration and behavior in the network. The following objects are associated with TED components:

▶ Distributor object—May be placed anywhere in the tree and holds the configuration information for the distributor.

▶ Subscriber object—Contains some configuration information that the subscriber uses. This object is never actually accessed by any subscriber (removing the need for a subscriber process to access eDirectory); instead, the distributor reads the configuration information from the subscriber objects and sends this configuration information to the subscriber agents with every distribution.

▶ External subscriber object—Refers to a subscriber outside the distributor's tree. The configuration information for this subscriber is contained in a subscriber object in its own tree or in a local configuration file. This object is used to enable TED to distribute across tree boundaries or to servers that are not in any tree.

▶ Subscriber group—Represents a set of subscriber objects with common channels. You can configure the channels for the subscriber group and then assign subscriber objects as members of the group to share the channels.

▶ Distribution object—Represents the collection of files that you want to transmit as a bundle across the network to various subscribers. A distribution is owned by a single distributor. That distributor is responsible for collecting, packaging, and distributing all the files listed in the distribution object.

▶ Channel object—Represents a set of distributions and subscribers grouped together. When you place a distribution into a channel, all subscribers associated with the channel receive the distribution.

When you place a new subscriber into a channel, all distributions associated with the channel are sent to the subscriber.

When you install TED components, you can specify which servers in the network will be distributors and subscribers. The channel relationship is constructed after the installation process through ConsoleOne.

The following list describes the relationships of the various components of TED:

▶ Distributors create certificates and through ConsoleOne you can copy them to subscribers for distribution security. Distributions are built on the distributor server. The same distributor sends the distribution, regardless, to any of the subscribers (or parent subscribers) that will be receiving the files.

▶ Subscribers subscribe to channels to obtain distributions. A subscriber subscribes to many channels and receives all the distributions placed in each of the channels. External subscribers subscribe to a channel in an eDirectory tree that they do not belong to (for example, to the tree where they get their configuration information).

▶ Parent subscribers are identified as a parent either in the routing hierarchy list in any distributor object or as the parent subscriber in any subscriber object.

▶ Channels are a collection of distributions and subscribers. Subscribers and distributions are associated with the channel. Essentially, the channel describes a set of subscribers that should receive the set of distributions. Distributions from many distributors can be placed in a single channel.

▶ Distributions are collections of files sent in the TED system. Each distribution belongs to a single distributor and can be placed in multiple channels. A distribution may be placed in any number of channels, and the distributor is responsible for sending the distribution to all the subscribers subscribed to the channels.

TED also uses digital certificates and message digests of the distributions to verify the contents and originator of the distributions. When a distributor is doing the gathering process (that is, the agent is actively collecting the files and placing them in the distribution file), it runs a message digest on the distribution. When the distributor is sending the distribution, it sends a header to the subscriber that includes the digest and other information—all digitally signed with the signature of the distributor. When the subscriber receives the header, it checks the digital signature of the distributor with the digital certificate that it has for the server (you need to install this certificate on the subscriber through ConsoleOne or manually). If the signatures match, the subscriber proceeds with the download. When the download is complete, the subscriber runs its own message digest on the file and compares the results with the digest the distributor placed originally in the header. If they match, the file is deemed valid, and the subscriber proceeds to schedule the agents to handle the unpacking of the distribution.

TED Configuration in Your Network

During the planning phase, you need to consider how you want to lay out TED in your tree and network. You need to take into account any WANs that you must use for your distributions and be careful to minimize the amount of traffic transmitted over a WAN link. TEDs from ZENworks are designed to handle anything from small networks to large enterprises and can be configured to help minimize this traffic. However, you must set up TED and administer its functions to get these gains.

A Simple Layout

To help in the explanation, let's take an example of a simple and then a complex tree and discover the best method to lay out TED components to get the best performance for your network. Figure 25.1 shows a simple tree.

As you can see in Figure 25.1, the tree (SIMPLE_TREE) is assumed to represent a single campus where no WANs are involved. The TED configuration for this setup can be fairly simple, because there are only eight servers in the system. To not overburden them, a distributor or parent subscriber should not support more than 40 subscribers. Because there will not be more than eight subscribers in the network, we only need in this simple case a single distributor and eight subscribers (one on each server, including the distribution server).

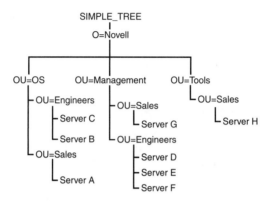

FIGURE 25.1
Simple example tree for TED distribution.

The number of channels that you want is based on the types of distributions you would expect to perform or the time schedules that you want the distribution sent. It is recommended that you base your channels on the types of distributions or schedules you expect to send, rather than the destination. For example, name your channels Sales Data, Base Engineering Apps, Virus Patterns, Europe Off Hours, and so forth. By naming your channels this way (rather than Building1, for example), it will be clear by the name of the channel what type of distributions can be expected to be transmitted to the subscribers attached to the channel. You can have any number of channels in the directory, and a subscriber can subscribe to any number of channels, so there is no reason to limit the channels you create.

In the **SIMPLE_TREE**, we create three channels: Sales Apps, Eng Apps, and Sales Data. We place a distributor on server A because the sales data is written on this server and a distributor on server B because it holds all the golden images of the engineering applications. We place a subscriber on each of the other servers and associate them with the appropriate channels. Figure 25.2 displays the same tree with all the channels, distributors, and subscribers in place. Subscriber H subscribes to channels Sales Data and Sales Apps, whereas subscriber G subscribes only to Sales Apps. Subscribers B, C, E, and F, subscribe to the Eng Apps channel.

This layout is done because of the needs of each of the servers, regardless of their location in the network or the tree.

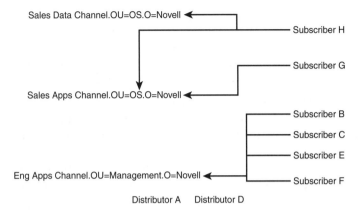

FIGURE 25.2
Channels, subscribers, and distributors for the simple example tree.

A Complex Layout

Now let's take a look at a more complex tree, one that includes some WAN traffic to cross container boundaries. Figure 25.3 is a demonstration of this type of tree.

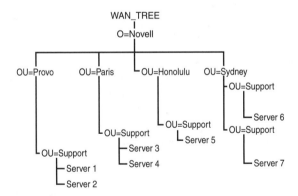

FIGURE 25.3
WAN example tree for TED distribution with channels, subscribers, and distributors.

In the WAN tree you can see Provo, Paris, Honolulu, and Sydney. Let's assume that Provo is in the United States, Paris is in France, and Sydney is in Australia, thus requiring a WAN to interconnect these sites. An added complexity is not shown, and that is to get to Sydney from Provo you must first make a WAN hop in Honolulu and then the final WAN hop to Sydney. To throw in a twist, we'll have a sales server, server 7, in the mix that is getting information from a Sales channel from somewhere in the tree.

Because WANs are involved, you want to minimize the traffic that must go over the WAN lines. This can be accomplished by placing a parent subscriber at each of the WAN sites and then connecting each of the destination subscribers in the target WAN to that parent. In the case of Sydney, we need to have a parent subscriber send the distributions to another parent subscriber in Sydney because it is a two-hop scenario.

Don't forget that eDirectory needs to be contacted by the distributors in our system. Make sure that the partition that contains the description of your distributors and subscribers is accessible to the distributors. Remember that if the partition is not close, the distributor will consume some traffic going to the partition and reading information about its distributor and subscribers.

We only look at two channels, one called Sales Channel (collected and distributed by an unshown distributor) and one called TID Channel that is used to transmit all the TID files collected at the main Provo site and then transmitted to each of the support sites across the world. We want to set up the channels, distributors, and subscribers shown in Figure 25.4 to support the WAN tree.

As you can see, there are two channels; the TID channel in Provo and the Sales channel somewhere in the tree (it is really not relevant where the channel is located). We have connected subscribers 3, 4, 5, and 6 to the TID channel in eDirectory. We have also made sure that subscriber 7 is connected to the Sales channel. The distributor is simply shown to exist in the Provo LAN and is not fully shown in the tree. Suffice it to say that it exists on a server in Provo in the same tree as shown.

Now we must define the parent subscribers in the network for distributor 1 (in the Provo LAN) to be the most efficient in its use of the WANs. If we do not define parent subscribers, the distributor transmits to each subscriber directly. This results in the same files being transmitted to Paris twice, to Honolulu three times, and to Sydney twice, for a total of seven WAN transmissions. Let's see how this would work out by looking at Table 25.1. As you can see, they each take one hop except for Sydney, which requires a hop through Honolulu and then to Sydney.

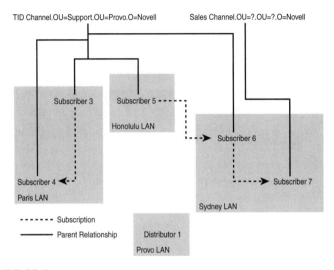

FIGURE 25.4
Subscribers, distributors, and channel configuration for the WAN example tree.

TABLE 25.1 WAN Hops for WAN Tree Transmissions

LAN	#OF WANS	TO SUBSCRIBER
Paris LAN	1	Subscriber 3
Paris LAN	1	Subscriber 4
Honolulu LAN	1	Subscriber 5
Sydney LAN	2	Subscriber 6
Sydney LAN	2	Subscriber 7

Now we can describe in eDirectory the parent subscribers of our network. This can be done in one of two ways: as a routing hierarchy in the distributor object, or as a parent subscriber identification in each child or leaf subscriber (see Figure 25.5).

The quickest way to define this would be to go to distributor 1's object in the tree and define the following routing hierarchy:

1. Subscriber 3

   a. Subscriber 4

2. Subscriber 5

    a. Subscriber 6

      i. Subscriber 7

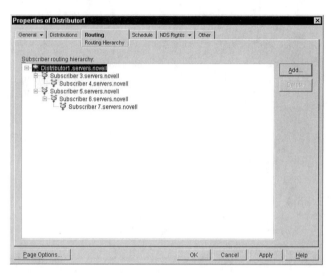

FIGURE 25.5
Subscribers, distributors, and channel configuration for the WAN example
tree.

This would state to the distributor that when it is distributing its collections, subscriber 3 will service subscriber 4, and subscriber 5 will service
subscriber 6, which then services subscriber 7. If we look at the behavior
of TED when this is done, the transmissions listed in Table 25.2
occur over the WAN.

TABLE 25.2   Optimized WAN Hops for WAN Tree Transmissions

LAN	#OF WANS	SUBSCRIBER
Paris LAN	1	Subscriber 3
Local, from subscriber 3	0	Subscriber 4
Honolulu LAN	1	Subscriber 5
Sydney LAN, passed from subscriber 5	1	Subscriber 6
Local, from subscriber 6	0	Subscriber 7

We see now that we will only transmit the files three times over a WAN and will have saved almost 233% of the traffic that we would have consumed had we not done parent subscribers.

One annoyance is, when you define the routing hierarchy in the distributor, *only* that distributor knows of this configuration. You have to go to all the distributors in that LAN and put this same routing hierarchy into their objects. This can also be a great benefit because it enables you to set up different distribution routes depending on the distributor sending the information. For example, you might have a financial information distributor, but you might not want that financial information passing through a certain subscriber. By defining a separate distribution hierarchy on the financial distributor, you can eliminate certain servers from ever getting the financial information. To save you some aggravation with having to describe your whole network, you can leave the leaf node subscribers out of the routing hierarchy definitions and identify their parent in their own object. The distributor automatically discovers this and includes it in the routing list. (See the "Construction of a Routing Hierarchy" section later in this chapter for more information.)

A Tree-Spanning Layout

Now let's take a look at some examples of spanning distributions across tree boundaries. ZENworks also allows you to distribute software independent of trees by using external subscriber objects (discussed later in this chapter).

The following are some examples of how to get benefits from spanning distributions across trees:

- ▶ One example of when you would want to span trees is if you need to maintain similar distributions in each of your trees. Say that you have one tree for your corporate office in Houston and another tree for your manufacturing plant in Detroit. The distance and dissimilar functions of the two sites make having a single tree unreasonable; however, both sites use the same accounting and payroll system that needs to be updated occasionally. The value of an external subscriber is for the occasional use of sending the accounting and payroll distribution from the corporate tree to the manufacturing tree, instead of duplicating the distribution creation work for the same distribution in both trees.

▶ Another example of when you might want to span trees is if you need to send a distribution outside your firewall, perhaps to another business. Say that your business manufactures a product distributed by one company and then sold by a third company. You could create an external subscriber for both the distributor and the reseller. Then you could create a distribution for product schedules and so on. That way a single distribution could update not only the appropriate offices in your own business but also your distributor and reseller as well, and all three companies will stay current.

Examining Capacities and Restrictions

There are some issues you should watch for in your network to make sure that you don't overburden your servers with distribution work. This concern is relative to the number of dependents a distributor must support and where distributors must be in the network.

As mentioned earlier, you should attempt to not overburden any distributor or parent subscriber with more than 40 direct dependents. This can be difficult to manage, and you will need to keep a careful eye on how you configure your subscribers and distributors to keep this from becoming a problem. The issue is that you really don't know at the beginning which distributors will be sending to which subscribers because it is purely based on which channel you chose to place the distribution. The easiest way to keep this all working well is to think about your TED distribution network from the bottom up as you are constructing the system. As you place subscribers into the network, choose a hierarchy of well-known parent subscribers, making sure that no branch of your TED network is overburdened.

For example, say that we start with the TED distribution network shown in Figure 25.6.

In Figure 25.6, we set up subscribers 3 through 63 so that they each use either subscribers 1 or 2 as their parent subscriber. We also set up subscribers 66 through 84 to use subscriber 64 as their parent subscriber. In Figure 25.6, we labeled the levels of the hierarchy (levels 1–4) to help us understand where in the structure each subscriber resides. Now, when we want to add more subscribers, we can either place them hierarchically, under some other subscribers at level 2, or we can create a new level 1 and go from there. Just try to keep the TED distribution hierarchical tree balanced somewhat so as to not overburden any one subscriber or distributor.

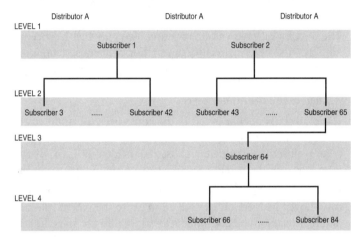

FIGURE 25.6
Phase1 hierarchy of subscribers in TED distribution network.

This leveling approach works well for a single LAN. When you move into multiple LANs and introduce a WAN link, you need to have this leveling in each of the LANs in your network and then describe in the distributors how you may efficiently move from one WAN to the next, based on their location. For example, distributor X may only have one hop to LAN Y, but distributor M may have two. So, the routing hierarchy defined in distributors X and M will be different with regard to how to most efficiently get to LAN Y.

Configuring TED Systems

You should know several algorithms to help determine the best configuration of TED components. The following sections shed some light on how the internals of TED components function.

Construction of a Routing Hierarchy

The distributor is responsible for constructing a routing hierarchy when it sends each distribution. The following describes the steps that the distributor follows to construct the hierarchy:

1. The distributor discovers all the subscribers (that is, leaf subscribers) to receive this distribution.

2. The distributor looks into the routing hierarchy that has been administered in its eDirectory object. For each subscriber, it looks to see whether that subscriber is in its hierarchy list. If it is, it sends the distribution to that subscriber following the routing hierarchy defined in the distributor object.

3. If the subscriber is not found in the administered list, the distributor looks in the subscriber's object to see whether it has identified a parent subscriber. If a parent subscriber is identified, the distributor then looks for the parent subscriber in its routing hierarchy list.

4. If the parent subscriber is in the routing hierarchy list, the distributor follows the hierarchy described to get to the parent subscriber and then tack on the end-node subscriber into the route to get the distribution to the subscriber.

5. If the parent subscriber is not in the distributor's routing hierarchy list, the distributor sends the distribution directly to the identified parent subscriber (identified in the subscriber's object) or directly to the subscriber (when no parent subscriber is identified).

Note that in the algorithm the distributor does not go to the subscriber and get its parent and then go to the parent and get its parent, and so forth, trying to construct the hierarchy of subscribers. The distributor only goes up one level in your TED distribution hierarchy. Therefore, you must, if you have more than one level of subscribers, describe $n - 1$ levels in the routing hierarchy in each distributor object. You can then leave the last level undefined in the distributor, defining it in each subscriber object (or in a TED policy that affects each subscriber) instead.

The following is a list of guidelines you should use when constructing your routing hierarchy:

▶ Include at least one parent subscriber on each LAN segment. This significantly reduces the amount of traffic across a WAN link.

▶ Include multiple parent subscribers on each LAN that has 40 or more subscribers. The performance of distributors and parent subscribers is significantly reduced when they are assigned more than 40 subscribers.

▶ Make sure that any subscribers not included in a distributor's distribution round are assigned to a parent subscriber on the same LAN.

Designing Distribution Routes

Now that you understand how to construct a route hierarchy, consider the following when designing your distributor's routing hierarchy:

▶ Distribution route—Represents the most efficient path to any given segment of your LAN or WAN. A distribution route is made up of a list of parent subscribers responsible for transferring distributions through the channel. The distribution route should use parent subscribers to minimize the workload for a distributor by spreading the workload of distributions.

▶ End-node subscribers—The last subscriber in a distribution route to receive a distribution. End-node subscribers do not need to be added to the routing hierarchy because they only receive the distributions.

▶ Distribution topology—The LAN/WAN topology that the distributions must follow on their assigned routes. Consider your WAN topology design and the number of subscribers on each LAN and then build the routing hierarchy to reflect your network topology.

▶ Multiple distributors—By using multiple distributors you can place the same subscribers under each of them, effectively creating the same distribution route for each distributor.

▶ Reuse subscribers—A subscriber can be used more than once as long as you have multiple distributors to assign it to. However, be careful not to overload the subscriber.

Scheduler Interactions

As you introduce yourself to the various components of the TED system (distributor, subscriber, distribution, channel), you will discover that each component has its own independent scheduler to determine when its work is done. At first look you will say okay, but then confusion will set in as you try to jumble how the schedules of these various components can keep or enable a successful distribution.

Here we examine, briefly, the various schedulers for each component and how they can play together to create a functioning TED system in your network. Let's first look at each of the components and the responsibility the scheduler plays:

▶ Distributor schedule—Determines when the distributor reads eDirectory for the configuration information for itself, its distributions, and any channels and subscribers it interacts with. It discovers the channels and subscribers by looking at any distributions that it has in any channels and the subscribers hooked to these channels. The distributor also looks for the eDirectory objects for any TED policies that may affect the configuration of itself, channels, or subscribers and includes them in its configuration information. The information for a subscriber is collected from eDirectory when the distributor schedule fires, and it reads the information from eDirectory. Any changes to the subscriber objects or policies that affect the subscribers need to be made in eDirectory prior to the distributor refresh schedule firing. This information is then sent on to the subscribers when a distribution is given to them.

▶ Distribution schedule—Determines when the agents on the distributor server will be activated to perform any gathering of the files and compacted into the single distribution file. This process must be completed before the channel begins its processing or the distribution needs to wait until the next channel cycle. The gathering does not occur if the distribution is inactive or does not belong to a channel with active subscribers. ZENworks Server Management has added downstream control that forces all downstream distributors to stop distributions when the send schedule ends. The distributions starts up again the next time the send schedule starts.

▶ Channel schedule—Determines when the distributor transmits any previously constructed distribution files to any destination subscribers. Any distribution files that have not been constructed when the channel is activated (based on the schedule) will have to wait until the next firing of the channel schedule to be transmitted. The transmission is terminated if the time has expired for the channel, and the transmission picks up where it left off on the next scheduled time for the channel.

▶ Subscriber schedule—Determines when the subscriber activates the agents on the subscriber server to extract any files from distributions that have been received and not processed. The extraction continues after it has started on a particular distribution even if the time has expired for the extraction schedule.

Looking at the network, you would want the time frames to occur in your systems as represented in Figure 25.7.

FIGURE 25.7
Schedule coordination time frame.

For example, if you schedule your distributor to refresh the configuration each day at the close of the day (say 5 p.m.), and then schedule the distribution to gather the files at 6 p.m., and then the channels to begin their distributions at 10 p.m. and the subscribers to extract at 4 a.m., the cycle could be completed in the night. This obviously gets more complicated when you cross time zone boundaries. You could simplify this some by having, possibly, channels for each different area of the world, which would have a different local time to begin the distribution such that the remote site and the local site will be busy at appropriate levels.

NOTE The channel schedule is "translated" into the distributor's time zone. For example, if the channel schedule says 3 p.m. MST and the distributor is in California, it starts at 2 p.m. PST. If you have a distributor in New York that also has distributions in this channel, it starts at 5 p.m. EST. This means that all distributors with distributions in a channel start sending at the same time, regardless of time zone.

About the TED Distributor

The TED distributor has the responsibility for transmitting a distribution (collection of files) to subscribers throughout the tree and to external subscribers found outside the distributor's tree. The distributor calls TED agents to collect the files and compact them into a distribution file that is then sent to the appropriate subscribers.

The distributor can also be managed by command-line commands (see the section "ZENworks Distributor/Subscriber Commands" later in this chapter for more details), by iManager web management tool, and by a distributor object placed in the tree. The following sections discuss each of the pages that can be administered on the distributor object. Traditionally, because the distributor is associated with the server (a distributor object is expected for each server running a distributor), it should be named such that the server is clearly known. The default naming by the installation process is `Distributor_<SERVERNAME>`, and the distributor object is created in the same container where specified.

NOTE The TED distributor and subscriber objects should only be created through the installation program on the product CD. This ensures that the NCF files on the servers authenticate with the correct objects in eDirectory. If you move or rename a distributor object, you need to update the `PATH:\ZENWORKS\ZFS-STARTUP.XML` file with the new DN of the distributor object, or it ceases to function. All other TED objects can be moved and renamed, but remember to refresh the distributor after any change to these objects.

The distributor is the only TED component that queries eDirectory and reads its object. The distributor reads its distribution object, the channel objects, and any policies when it starts on the server when requested through the console with a refresh command, by right-clicking the distributor object in ConsoleOne and choosing the Refresh Distributor option, or as scheduled in the distributor object. The distributor also reads any subscriber related to the distribution it is to send and relays any updates in the subscriber object and policies (such as the Tiered Electronic Distribution policy in the Service Location Policy package) to the subscriber when the distribution is sent.

The Settings Property Page

This page is found under the General tab and represents some general configuration settings effective for this distributor. Figure 25.8 shows this screen.

On this property page you may make the following settings:

▶ Input Rate (KBps)—Represents the number of bytes per second that you allow a distributor to consume for all distributions for input (acknowledgments and so forth). The default is for the distributor to send at the maximum rate possible on the server. For example, if you enter 4096, this distributor will not exceed receiving 4KBps for incoming messages. This setting does not affect the rate at which FTP and HTTP distributions are gathered. The distributor always uses as much bandwidth as available when gathering distributions.

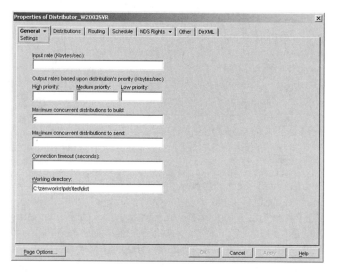

FIGURE 25.8
Settings property page of a distributor object.

▶ High Priority—Represents the number of bytes per second that you allow a distributor to consume for all high priority distributions' output.

▶ Medium Priority—Represents the number of bytes per second that you allow a distributor to consume for all medium priority distributions' output.

▶ Low Priority—Represents the number of bytes per second that you allow a distributor to consume for all low priority distributions' output.

▶ Maximum Concurrent Distributions to Build—Each time a distributor is going to perform a distribution, it creates a Java thread that handles the gathering of the distribution. This value identifies the maximum number of threads that you allow the distributor to create concurrently to service the building of distributions. Valid values are from 1 and 10.

▶ Maximum Concurrent Distributions to Send—Each time a distributor is going to perform a distribution, it creates a Java thread that handles the distribution to the subscriber. This value identifies the maximum number of threads that you allow the distributor to create concurrently to service the sending of distributions. The Maximum Number of Concurrent Distributions to Send value is affected by prioritizing because it is subordinate to the priorities set for the distributions. For example, you have the concurrent distribution number set to 10, and there are 4 high priority distributions, 5 medium priority distributions, and 20 low priority distributions. Initially, the 4 high priority distributions will be sent concurrently, and the 5 medium priority distributions must wait until all 4 high priority distributions are complete. Then the 5 medium priority distributions are sent concurrently, and only when they are complete will 10 of the 20 low priority distributions be sent.

▶ Connection Timeout (Seconds)—The default for this is 300 seconds. You can also enter a timeout value that, when exceeded, the distributor fails the distribution and retries it every two minutes for the next 30 minutes (as long as it is still in its scheduled window). If after the retries the distribution still has not succeeded, the distributor fails the distribution, and at the next scheduled distribution time for the channel, the distributor will reattempt to send the distribution.

▶ Working Directory—This identifies the directory where the distributor stores its distribution files. The agents, when they are called to collect the files and compress them into the distribution file, store the files in this working directory. It is not recommended to use the **SYS** volume because of the potential system problems should that volume become full.

The Messaging Property Page

The Messaging property page is under the General tab and can be configured by selecting the active tab and selecting the Messaging value under the drop-down menu on the tab (by clicking the small triangle in the tab). Figure 25.9 shows a sample Messaging page. Unless you are having some problems and are diagnosing some issues, it is recommended to use level 4 or lower.

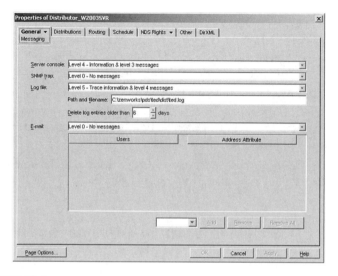

FIGURE 25.9
Messaging property page of a distributor object.

For each of the appropriate fields, you may enter one of the following
message levels:

▶ Level 0—Displays no messages. In the Messaging page, you can
  administer the following items regarding the behavior of the
  distributor.

▶ Level 1—Displays only errors encountered in the system.

▶ Level 2—Displays the successes satisfied by the system and also
  includes all the level 1 messages.

▶ Level 3—Displays any warnings encountered in the system, in
  addition to all the level 2 messages.

▶ Level 4—Includes all the level 3 messages and, in addition, informational messages that identify key points in the system.

▶ Level 5—Includes all level 4 messages in addition to trace information, which notifies the observer of the modules being executed.
  This level also captures and displays all Java exceptions.

▶ Level 6—Includes all the other levels plus developer trace
  information.

You can administer the following configuration parameters on the Message property page:

▶ Server Console—Identifies the level of messages displayed on the distributor server console (not the main server console).

▶ SNMP Trap—Identifies the level of messages sent as an SNMP trap to the SNMP trap target. The SNMP Trap Targets policy must be defined and active in an effective (for the distributor object) Service Location policy for traps to be sent.

▶ Log File—Identifies the level of message that should be stored in the log file. Additionally, you can configure the following about the log file:

   ▶ Path and Filename—The filename of the log file. The default location is `SYS:\ZENworks\TED\DIST\ted.LOG` (`c:\ZENworks\PDS\TED\dist\ted.log` on Windows). You should change the location of the log file because it can grow as well and may adversely affect the system if it is located on the `SYS` volume.

   ▶ Delete Log Entries Older Than X Days—In this parameter you identify the number of days (X) worth of log entries that should remain in the log file. The default is six days. Therefore, any log entries older than six days will be cleared from the log file. The process of scanning for and removing old log entries happens once every 24 hours and is not configurable.

▶ E-mail—Specify the level of messages that will be sent as email to the identified users. The SMTP Host policy in the ZENworks Service Location policy package must be effective for the distributor object to enable it to discover the address for the SMTP host to send the email. If this is not specified, the email will not be sent.

In addition to identifying the level of messages, you must also specify who should receive these messages. To add users to the list and for them to be sent the message, you must select User, Group, or E-mail; click the Add button; and specify the eDirectory user or group or email address. When you select a user, you are asked to browse to the user in the directory, and the system takes the email address attribute from the user and uses that as the address for the user. Should you choose a group, all the users in the group are sent the email message, and the email attribute is used for each of those users. Should you not want to use the email address attribute in the user object, you may select the down arrow in the Address Attribute field and select which of the eDirectory user attributes you want to identify as containing the email address. Many administrators store user email addresses in the Internet E-mail Address attribute instead of the E-mail Address attribute. It is expected that the attribute you identify contains a valid email address.

If you choose to enter an explicit email address, instead of selecting a user or a group, you may choose the E-mail Address choice from the Add button. You are prompted to enter a valid email address. The entered email address is assumed to be valid and is shown as the Username field in the table with an N/A in the Address Attribute field.

The Distributions Property Page

This page of the distributor object identifies the defined distributions that this particular distributor is responsible for collecting and sending. You cannot add distributions on this page; they are only added or deleted in this list when the actual distribution object is created or deleted from eDirectory. You may look at the distribution object, however, by selecting the distribution in the list and clicking the Details button. This launches the property pages for the selected distribution object.

The Routing Hierarchy Property Page

The Routing Hierarchy property page is one of the most important pages to administer, especially if you have WANs in your tree and you want to be efficient in your distribution of files. Figure 25.10 shows a sample of this page.

On this property page you can define the hierarchy associating the distributor to subscribers. This is the path that the distributor uses in sending distributions to the subscribers. As discussed in the "TED Configuration in Your Network" section earlier in this chapter, this page defines the route that you want TED to follow when attempting to transmit a distribution from this distributor to any identified subscriber.

On this page you build a hierarchy tree that describes the routes that the distributor must follow. You place a child in the tree by selecting the parent and clicking the Add button. After the Add button is clicked, you are required to browse the eDirectory tree and identify the subscriber(s) you want to insert. For example, if we wanted the routes shown in Figure 25.4 placed into this distributor, we would perform the following steps:

1. Select the distributor 1 object in the list (the topmost item). Click the Add button.

2. Browse eDirectory and select subscriber 3 in the tree.

3. Select subscriber 3 in the list and click Add.

4. Browse eDirectory and select subscriber 4 in the tree.

5. Select the distributor 1 object in the list and click Add.

6. Browse eDirectory and select subscriber 5 in the tree.

7. Select subscriber 5 in the list on this property page and click Add.

8. Browse eDirectory and select subscriber 6 in the tree.

9. Select subscriber 6 in the list and click Add.

10. Browse eDirectory and select subscriber 7 from the tree.

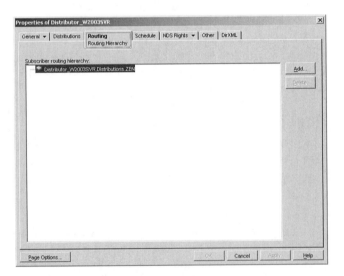

FIGURE 25.10

Routing Hierarchy property page of a distributor object.

The hierarchy shown in Figure 25.11 should be displayed on the Routing Hierarchy page after you have completed the preceding steps.

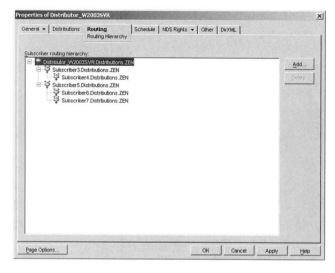

FIGURE 25.11
Routing Hierarchy property page of a distributor object after entering routes.

Using the routing algorithm, the distributor now sends any distributions to subscriber 3 that are bound for either subscriber 3 or 4 and sends any distributions to subscriber 5 that are bound for either subscriber 5, 6, or 7.

NOTE The subscriber can be in the routing table and send distributions to other subscribers even if they are not participating in the channel for the end-target subscriber. They simply forward the distribution on and do not extract it on their local system.

The routing hierarchy must be entered for each distributor object in the tree. If no entries are in the hierarchy, the distributor only relies on the parent subscriber, which can be defined in the subscriber object to give any type of route other than direct. See the routing hierarchy algorithm described previously to understand how the distributor uses the routing hierarchy and the parent subscribers.

The Schedule Property Page

The Schedule property page (shown in Figure 25.12) enables you to specify how often the distributor software on the server will go to eDirectory and read the configuration information in its object, the distributions assigned to the distributor, channel information, and subscriber configuration information. The default value is Never, which means that the distributor only reads its eDirectory object when it first is loaded on the server, or if told to with the console command (refresh), or in ConsoleOne if you right-click the distributor object and choose the Refresh menu option.

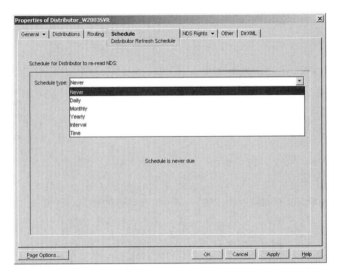

FIGURE 25.12
Schedule property page.

If there is a Tiered Electronic Distribution policy in a Service Location policy package associated with the distributor, the check box for using the policy appears on this page. If there is no policy, the check box is not displayed. When this check box is activated, the schedule described in the policy is used for this distributor. When unchecked, this distributor has its own schedule, and the Schedule Type field is available for administration. By default, this check box is checked if you have a TED policy.

This page enables you to select when the configuration should be read and applied: Never, Daily, Monthly, Yearly, Interval, or Time.

After you select when you want the configuration applied, you have additional fields to select in the lower portion of the screen. The following sections discuss the various options you have.

Never

This option only loads the distributor with the configuration information when it is first loaded on the server or after each reboot or restart.

Daily

When you choose to have the configuration applied to the system daily, you also need to select when the changes will be made.

This schedule requires that you click on the days when you want the configuration applied. The selected days appear as depressed buttons.

In addition to the days, you can select the times the configuration is applied. These times—the start and stop times—provide a range of time when the configuration will be applied.

You can have the configuration also reapplied within the time frame every specified hour, minute, or second by clicking the Repeat the Action Every field and specifying the time delay.

To keep all the distributors from simultaneously accessing eDirectory, you can select the Randomly Dispatch Policy During Time Period option. This causes each server to choose a random time within the time period when it will retrieve and apply the configuration.

Monthly

Under the monthly schedule, you can select which day of the month the configuration should be applied, or you can select Last Day of the Month to handle the last day, because all months obviously do not end on the same calendar date (that is, 30 days hath September, April, June, and November; all the rest have 31 except for February...).

After you select the day, you can also select the time range when the configuration will be reread and applied.

To keep all the distributors from simultaneously accessing eDirectory, you can select the Randomly Dispatch Policy During Time Period option. This causes each server to choose a random time within the time period when it will retrieve and apply the configuration.

Yearly

Select a yearly schedule if you want to apply the configuration only once a year.

On this screen you must choose the day that you want the configuration to be applied. Selecting the Calendar button to the right of the Date field does this. This brings up a Monthly dialog box where you can browse through the calendar to select the date you want. This calendar does not correspond to any particular year and may not take into account leap years in its display. This is because you are choosing a date for each year that will come along in the present and future years.

After you select the date, you can also select the time range when the configuration should be read and applied.

To keep all the distributors from simultaneously accessing eDirectory, you can select the Randomly Dispatch Policy During Time Period. This causes each server to choose a random time within the time period when it will retrieve and apply the configuration.

Interval

This schedule type enables you to specify how often to repeatedly read and apply the configuration. You can specify the interval with a combination of days, hours, minutes, and seconds. This type waits for the interval to pass first before applying the configuration for the first time and then for each sequence after that.

Time

This enables you to specify a calendar date and time when the configuration will be applied. When the current date on the server is beyond the identified date, the configuration will be applied.

The Parent Subscriber

The TED parent subscriber is first a subscriber and can receive distributions if they are subscribed to a channel. A parent subscriber has the additional responsibility to take the distribution and pass it along to a set of designated subscribers. In this manner, a parent subscriber acts as a relay transmitter for the distributor and relays the distribution onto other subscribers. Any subscriber can become a parent subscriber without any software change. The subscriber only needs to be designated a parent in either the distributor's routing hierarchy or in a subscriber object.

No parent subscriber object is created in eDirectory. A subscriber acts as a parent subscriber any time it is identified in either another subscriber object (as that subscriber's parent) or as an entry, with a child subscriber, in the routing hierarchy of any distributor.

A subscriber that receives a route with the distribution that identifies that it should forward the distribution on to other subscribers activates its parent subscriber code and forwards the distribution to all the subscribers in the next level of the route. Identifying a subscriber as a parent only aids the distributor in the construction of the routing for a distribution.

Just like the distributor, a parent subscriber is responsible for sending configuration information to the end-node subscriber. When the distributor sends configuration information to the parent subscriber, it includes all configuration information for any other parent or end-node subscribers that this parent subscriber is responsible for forwarding distributions to. When this parent subscriber has a distribution for a destination subscriber (parent or end node), it bundles the configuration relevant for those destination subscribers and sends it along with the distribution. All configuration information is stored in a configuration file in the TED directory. This file is created or updated when the subscriber process exits.

The TED Subscriber

The TED subscriber is responsible for receiving and extracting distributions, validating that they come from an acceptable distributor and that the distribution file is accurate. The subscriber, when the extraction schedule starts, activates TED agents to unpack the distribution and handle the placement of the data in the distribution. If the subscriber should receive, with the distribution, a route that specifies that it send a distribution to other subscribers, the subscriber forwards the distribution to the next level of specified subscribers.

The subscriber system on a server never accesses eDirectory. The distributor, who is sending a distribution to this subscriber, is responsible for communicating any information from the subscriber object to the subscriber software. The distributor only sends configuration information to the subscriber if the distributor has a newer revision of the subscriber object or the effective policy. The subscriber stores any changes in a configuration file so that the next time it is started it loads the configuration information.

All subscribers must have a copy of the digital certificate of the distributor to receive distributions from the distributor. If there is a distribution in the channel coming from a distributor for which the subscriber does not hold a copy of the distributor's digital certificate, the subscriber rejects the distribution. You can transmit the digital certificate manually, or ConsoleOne will attempt to contact the subscribers with a UNC path when a distribution is placed in a channel from a new distributor or when a subscriber is added to the channel. Over this connection, the digital certificate of all distributors (that currently have distributions in the channel) are sent and placed on the file system of the subscriber. Perform the following steps to secure a copy of the digital certificates of the distributors that may be sent to the subscriber:

1. Launch ConsoleOne.

2. Browse to the distributor object of the distributor whose certificate you want to retrieve. Select the distributor object.

3. Right-click and select Resolve Certificates. You are presented with a dialog box that gives you two radial buttons:

   ▶ Copy Certificates to Subscribers Automatically—This goes to all distributions associated with this distributor and then to all the subscribers associated with all the channels that the distribution is in, and also to all subscribers that act as parent subscribers to pass the distributions to the subscribers associated with the channels. It attempts to gain access to the subscriber file system with a UNC path and write the certificate to the SYS:\ZENWORKS\PDS\TED\security directory (c:\ZENworks\PDS\TED\security on Windows) on the subscriber server.

   ▶ Save Certificates to Disk—This writes the certificates to the directory specified on the disk.

4. Choose Save Certificates to Disk and type in the directory name to copy the certificates on your local drive or floppy. Or, click the browse button to browse to the directory where you want the certificates copied.

5. Click OK. The certificates are placed in the directory specified.

6. Take the files written to the directory and copy them to the directory PATH:\ZENWORKS\TED\SECURITY on the subscriber system.

NOTE You can also use ConsoleOne to automatically resolve certificates for a specific subscriber instead of a distributor. By right-clicking the subscriber object and choosing the Resolve Certificate option, the subscriber receives all certificates for all distributors that have distributions associated with the channels to which the subscriber is subscribed.

The Settings Property Page

This page is found under the General tab and represents some of the configuration settings in effect for this subscriber. Figure 25.13 displays this screen.

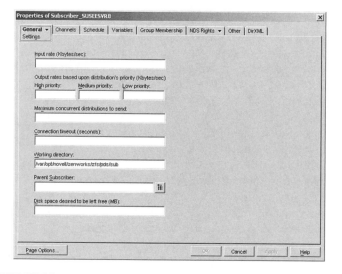

FIGURE 25.13
Settings property page of a subscriber object.

On this property page, you may make the following settings:

▶ Input Rate (KBps)—Represents the number of bytes per second that you allow a subscriber to consume for all subscriptions. The default is for the subscriber to receive at the maximum rate possible on the server. For example, if you choose to enter 4096, this subscriber does not exceed receiving 4KBps from any distributor, regardless of the capacity of the subscriber.

▶ High Priority—Represents the number of bytes per second that you allow a subscriber to consume for all high priority subscriptions' output.

▶ Medium Priority—Represents the number of bytes per second that you allow a subscriber to consume for all medium priority subscriptions' output.

▶ Low Priority—Represents the number of bytes per second that you allow a subscriber to consume for all low priority subscriptions' output.

▶ Maximum Concurrent Distributions to Send—Each time a subscriber is going to relay a distribution (because it is a parent subscriber), it creates a Java thread that handles the sending of the distribution to the child subscriber. This value identifies the maximum number of threads that you will allow the parent subscriber to create to service relaying distributions. The Maximum Number of Concurrent Distributions to Send value is affected by prioritizing because it is subordinate to the priorities set for the distributions. For example, you have the concurrent distribution number set to 10, and there are 4 high priority distributions, 5 medium priority distributions, and 20 low priority distributions. Initially, the 4 high priority distributions will be sent concurrently, and the 5 medium priority distributions must wait until all 4 high priority distributions are complete. Then the 5 medium priority distributions are sent concurrently, and only after they are complete will 10 of the 20 low priority distributions be sent.

NOTE The subscriber always creates all the concurrent receiver threads that it needs regardless of this maximum value. There is currently no method to manage the total number of receiver threads.

▶ Connection Timeout (Seconds)—The default for this is 300 seconds. You can also enter a timeout value that, when exceeded, the parent subscriber fails the distribution and retries the distribution every two minutes for the next 30 minutes (as long as it is still in its scheduled window). If after the retries, the distribution still cannot succeed, the parent subscriber fails the distribution, and the next time it tries is when the distributor reattempts the distribution. This value is also used for the maximum amount of time a subscriber waits between packets while receiving a distribution from a distributor or parent subscriber.

▶ Working Directory—Identifies the directory where the subscriber stores the distribution files it receives. The agents, when they are called to extract the files, go to this directory to find the distribution files. It is not recommended to use the **SYS** volume because of the potential system problems should that volume become full.

▶ Parent Subscriber—Enables you to specify a parent subscriber from which this subscriber should receive all distributions (as opposed to getting it directly from the distributor). This can be overridden on a per-distributor basis by including the subscriber in the routing hierarchy on each distributor (see the "Configuring TED Systems" section earlier in the chapter for more information).

▶ Disk Space to Be Left Free (MB)—Specifies amount of disk space that you want to remain in addition to the size of any distribution to be received. This allows you to enter a value large enough to also allow room for the distribution to be extracted and installed. The subscriber server will only receive the distribution if the amount of free disk space on the subscriber server is equal to or greater than the sum of the compressed distribution and the value you entered here.

Working Context Property Page

On this page you can set the working context of the subscriber to be a container in eDirectory. This context is used in conjunction with the application object distribution type to identify where in the tree the newly replicated application object should be created.

The Messaging Property Page

The Messaging property page is under the General tab and can be configured by selecting the active tab and selecting the Messaging value under the drop-down menu on the tab (by clicking the small triangle in the tab). Figure 25.14 shows a sample Messaging page.

For each of the appropriate fields, you may enter one of the message levels described in the distributor section.

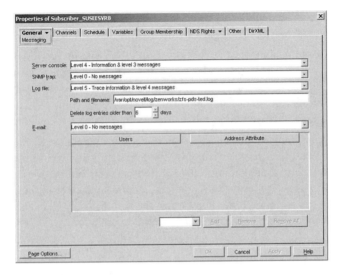

FIGURE 25.14
Messaging property page of a subscriber object.

You can administer the following configuration parameters on the
Messaging property page:

- ▶ Server Console—Identifies the level of messages displayed on the
  subscriber server console (not the main server console).

- ▶ SNMP Trap—Identifies the level of messages sent as an SNMP trap
  being sent to the SNMP trap target. The SNMP Trap Targets policy
  must be set in the Service Location policy package effective for the
  subscriber object. This information is included in the configuration
  information sent to the subscriber from the distributor.

- ▶ Log File—Identifies the level of message that should be stored in
  the log file. Additionally, you can configure the following about the
  log file:

  - ▶ Path and Filename—The filename of the log file. The default
    location is `PATH:\ZENWORKS\PDS\TED\DIST\TED.LOG`. You
    should change the location of the log file because it can grow,
    as well, and may adversely affect the system if it is located on
    the **SYS** volume.

  - ▶ Delete Log Entries Older Than X Days—In this parameter,
    you identify the number of days (X) worth of log entries that
    should remain in the log file. The default is six days.

Therefore, any log entries older than six days will be cleared from the log file. The process of scanning the log for and removing old log entries happens once every 24 hours and is not configurable.

▶ E-mail—You may specify the level of messages that will be sent as an email to the identified users. The SMTP Host policy in the ZENworks Service Location policy package must be effective for the subscriber object to enable it to discover the address for the SMTP host to send the email. If this is not specified, the email will not be sent.

In addition to identifying the level of messages, you must also specify who should receive these messages. To add users to the list and for them to be sent the message, you must select User, Group, or E-mail from the drop-down list; then click the Add button and specify the eDirectory User or Group or email address. When you select a user, you are asked to browse to the user in the directory, and the system takes the email address attribute from the user and uses that as the address for the user. Should you choose a group, all the users in the group are sent the email message, and the email attribute is used for each of those users. Should you not want to use the email address attribute in the user object, you may click the down arrow in the Address Attribute field and select which of the eDirectory user attributes you want to identify as containing the email address. Many administrators store user email addresses in the Internet E-mail Address attribute instead of the E-mail Address attribute. It is expected that the attribute you identify will contain a valid email address.

If you choose to enter an explicit email address rather than select a user or a group, you may choose E-mail from the drop-down list and click the Add button. You are prompted to enter a valid email address. The entered email address is assumed to be valid and is shown as the Username field in the table with an N/A in the Address Attribute field.

The Channels Property Page

This page of the subscriber object identifies the channels that this subscriber is going to receive distributions from. A subscriber may subscribe to many channels. To add a channel to the list, click the Add button and browse in eDirectory to the channel. After this channel is added, it appears on the list.

To delete a channel from the list, you must first select the channel and then click the Delete button. The subscriber will no longer accept distributions from this channel.

You can view or edit the property pages of the channel by selecting the channel and clicking the Details button.

The same distribution may be placed in more than one channel. It is possible that the same subscriber may be subscribed to multiple channels, and that more than one channel may want to distribute the same distribution. The distributor and subscriber keep a version number on each distribution and do not send the same distribution more than once to the same subscriber, no matter how many channels the distribution is in.

The Extract Schedule Property Page

The Extract Schedule property page enables you to specify when and how often the extraction agents are called to dissect the distribution file and extract the files within, placing them in the file system of the server as specified in the distribution. Figure 25.15 shows a sample of this page.

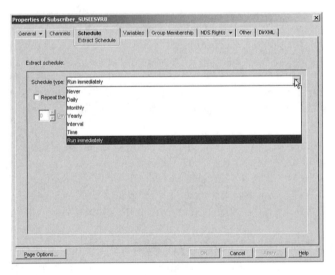

FIGURE 25.15
Extract Schedule property page of a subscriber object.

If there is a Tiered Electronic Distribution policy in a Service Location policy package effective for the subscriber object, the check box for using the policy appears on this page. If there is no effective policy, the check box is not displayed. When this check box is activated, the schedule described in the policy is used for this subscriber. When unchecked, this subscriber has its own schedule, and the Schedule Type field is available for administration. The check box is checked by default if there is an effective TED policy.

This page enables you to select when the extraction agents should do their work on the subscriber server: Never, Daily, Monthly, Yearly, Interval, Time, or Run Immediately.

After you select when you want the configuration applied, you have additional fields to select in the lower portion of the screen.

NOTE The default is Never. Therefore, the subscriber never extracts the files until you change the schedule. Remember, the configuration of the subscriber does not change until the next distribution, when the distributor sends the new configuration.

See the section "About the TED Distributor" earlier in the chapter for an explanation of additional scheduling options beyond the Run Immediately option.

With the Run Immediately schedule type, the first time that the associated object is activated the schedule causes the activity to occur. You may also specify a repeat interval in days, hours, minutes, and seconds. If no repeat interval is specified, the action only runs once, until the object is restarted or refreshed.

Variables Property Pages

Variables enable you to substitute a variable name in the distribution with the value specified in the subscriber. When you create a distribution, you may use variables in the volumes and directory names, for example. When the distribution is sent to the subscriber and the extraction agent is called, the agent replaces these variables with their defined value in the subscriber object. If no value is given, the variable name (including the % [percent sign]) is used for that value.

If there is a Tiered Electronic Distribution policy in a Service Location policy package effective for the subscriber, the check box for using the policy appears on this page. If there is no policy, the check box is not displayed. When this check box is activated, the variables described in the policy are used for this subscriber in addition to the variables that you define in the subscriber. When unchecked, this subscriber has its own independent variables. If there is a duplicate, the subscriber's definition is used. This enables you to override a specific variable from the policy, while still accepting the other variables from the policy.

Unlike ZENworks policies and software distribution packages, the TED software only performs basic substitution of variable to value and does not allow you to reference an eDirectory object or its attribute. This is done to eliminate the requirement that the subscriber have access to eDirectory and all the objects in the tree. This would be especially difficult if the subscriber is an external subscriber—not even in the same tree as the distributor!

For example, if you created a distribution and specified %DEST_VOLUME% as the volume name, when the subscriber extracts the files, the agent substitutes the variable DEST_VOLUME defined in this property page with the value. If DEST_VOLUME is not defined, a directory called %DEST_VOLUME% is created in the SYS volume.

Remember to be consistent in your conventions and your variable names. You should probably come up with a set of common variables that you define with each subscriber that you set up. Then when you create a distribution, you can use these variables in defining the directories where the distribution will be placed. Remember, the subscribers that receive the distribution are purely based on who subscribes to the channels where you place the distribution. If you are not consistent in your variable names across all subscribers, you may inadvertently send a distribution to a subscriber that does not have the variable defined; this results in the distribution being extracted in a place you do not expect (probably on the SYS volume). Some variables that you should consider defining in each of your subscribers are the following:

▶ DEST_VOLUME—Define this variable as the volume that receives the distribution after it is extracted.

▶ DEST_APPVOL—Define this to be the volume where your applications are stored.

▶ DEST_APPDIR—Define this to be the directory under the application volume where you place your applications.

External Subscriber

An *external subscriber* is a TED subscriber that resides on a server not located in the tree of the distributor. The controlling subscriber object of an external subscriber is located in the external tree. The distributor's tree does contain an external subscriber object, which identifies the IP address of the remote subscriber.

An external subscriber object is basically just a pointer to the subscriber service running on a server that has its subscriber object in a different tree. Each subscriber should have exactly one subscriber object, but each may also have many external subscriber objects that reference them. For example, if a subscriber object were in the FORD tree, it would receive its configuration information from a distributor in the FORD tree. There could be an external subscriber object in each of the GM, NISSAN, and BMW trees, but distributors in those trees would only send distribution files, not configuration information, to the subscriber.

The following is a list of important things to note about an external subscriber:

- ▶ A server can be associated with both a subscriber object in one tree and an external subscriber object in another tree.

- ▶ An external subscriber is a server running the subscriber software but does not have a subscriber object in the same eDirectory tree as the distributor from which it will receive a distribution.

- ▶ A server identified in the external subscriber object's properties in Tree A must be a subscriber in Tree B so that it can receive and extract a distribution.

- ▶ An external subscriber must have a parent subscriber in the tree where its external subscriber object resides. In other words, an external subscriber in Tree B cannot receive distributions directly from a distributor in Tree A.

- ▶ External subscribers cannot be used as parent subscribers in the tree where their external subscriber object exists. However, they can be a parent subscriber in their own tree where their subscriber object exists.

▶ A subscriber receives its configuration information from a distributor in its own tree. This is because the subscriber's information is stored in its eDirectory object, which is not accessible to TED agents in another tree. Therefore, a subscriber must have received a distribution from a distributor in its own tree before it can receive a distribution from another tree.

▶ Variables you may be using in the definition of your distributions must be defined in the actual subscriber object because anything defined in the tree where the external subscriber object exists is not passed on as part of distributions sent from distributors in that tree.

The General Property Page

On this page you may identify a parent subscriber for this subscriber. The parent subscriber would be a subscriber object in this tree. Click the browse button to the side of the field and browse eDirectory to select the subscriber to be identified as the parent subscriber.

The Channels Property Page

On this property page you identify the channels from which this external subscriber will receive distributions. As you recall, any distribution placed in a channel subscribed by this external subscriber will be sent.

The Network Address Property Page

On this property page, shown in Figure 25.16, you specify the IP address or DNS name of the server running the external subscriber.

To administer the address, simply place the cursor in the IP Address or DNS Name field and enter the IP address or the DNS name of the server.

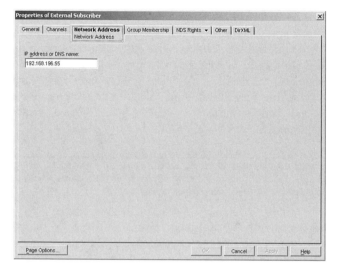

FIGURE 25.16
Network Address property page of an external subscriber object.

TED Distribution

The TED distribution object represents the collection of files compiled into a distribution file and then sent to the subscriber. When at the subscriber, the distribution is extracted from the distribution file and placed in the locations specified in this distribution (with appropriate variable substitution).

All the files specified in a TED distribution must reside on the file system of the distributor, or the server must have access to HTTP and FTP capabilities to retrieve the files for those agents. After the distribution is defined, to get the distribution transmitted to a subscriber, it must be placed into a channel or a set of channels. The files specified in the distribution object are collected by the agents on the distributor system and placed into a single distribution file. This file is then transmitted to all the subscribers subscribed to the channels where the distribution object is placed.

The distribution is a live object. The distribution objects are sent each time the channel schedule is activated. When the gatherer schedule activates this distribution, the agent is called to collect the files specified and compare them to the previous distribution. If differences have occurred in the files, a new delta package, or an entire distribution, of the distribution is generated, and the new revision is sent to the subscribers of the designated channels. This happens each time the gatherer and send schedule activate the distribution. Unless a distribution is expressly identified as a one-time only distribution, it does not become inactive after it has been sent. The distribution continues to be reevaluated, recollected, and redistributed each time the schedule is activated.

NOTE The distribution does not rebuild based on any file system event, such as an update to a file. The distribution rebuilds strictly based on the gatherer schedule in the distribution, whether the files have changed or not.

If there is no subscriber to receive a distribution (that is, no subscribers in the channel), or the distribution is inactive and not associated with any channel, the distribution is never gathered and built, even if the gathering is scheduled.

The General Property Page

The Settings property page of the General property page enables you to specify some settings used in the deployment of the distribution. Figure 25.17 displays a typical snapshot of this page. You may need to scroll the property page in order to see all of the available fields.

You can specify the following settings on this General property page:

▶ Active—Activates or deactivates the distribution. If a distribution is inactive, the distribution is not sent to subscribers even if it is in a channel.

▶ Use Digest—Activates the TED system to use a digest on the distribution file. The digest is used to verify that the contents of the distribution file have not changed from the distributor to the subscriber (during transmission). When the subscriber receives the distribution, it verifies the digest it calculates with the digest that the distributor computes and places in a header. If the digests match, the file is unchanged, and the subscriber accepts the distribution.

NOTE The generation of the message digest may take significant time, particularly with large distribution files. Be aware that this increases the time it takes to gather and create the distribution file.

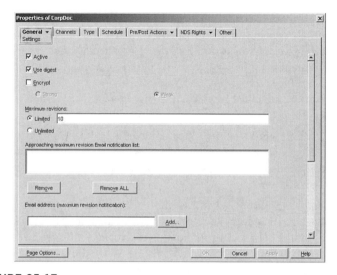

FIGURE 25.17
General property page of a TED distribution object.

▶ Encrypt—Activates distribution encryption providing security for
the distribution during transit between the distributor and subscriber. Typically, you would only encrypt a distribution sent
through a firewall. If you enable encryption, you have the option to
select either Strong or Weak encryption.

▶ Maximum Revisions—Enables you to specify the number of revisions (or unlimited) of the distribution that you will keep. Select
the Limited option and enter the maximum number of revisions, or
select the Unlimited radio button. Each time a distribution is collected and a distribution file is created, this constitutes a revision.
When the maximum number of revisions has been created, the oldest revision is discarded from the disk (unless it is currently being
sent to a subscriber, in which case it is discarded on the next distribution cycle). Each subscriber that receives this distribution will
keep this number of revisions. This includes subscribers that act as
parent subscribers but do not actually subscribe to the channel.

NOTE When the maximum revisions number is reached, the file agent deletes all revisions and creates a new baseline of the distribution.

▶ Approaching Maximum Revision Email Notification List—Set of specified email addresses that will be sent an automated email message from ZENworks notifying them that the maximum revision threshold is about to be reached. Since rebaselining a distribution can result in significant CPU resources and wire traffic, you may want to be notified so you can change when the baselining will occur.

▶ Email Address (Maximum Revision Notification)—Enter in an email address of a recipient to receive the maximum revision notification. Click the Add button to add the entered address to the list of recipients.

▶ Send Notifications When Distributions Revision Is X or Less of Reaching Maximum Revisions—Specifies the number of revisions remaining before the maximum revision threshold is reached and the rebaselining process will be started. When the revision count is within X of reaching the maximum, ZENworks will automatically send email notifications to the specified email list users.

▶ Email Server Address—Specify the SMTP email server address to be used by the system to send the emails.

▶ Priority—Specifies the priority for this distribution that determines how it will be sent in relation to other distributions. A high priority means it will be sent before all medium and low priority distributions.

▶ Distributor—A display-only field that identifies the distributor that performs the collection and transmission of this distribution. This distributor is specified when the distribution object is created. This distributor is the owner of this distribution. The owner of a distribution cannot be changed.

▶ Description—Enables you to have a free-flowing text description of the distribution. This can be used to help in understanding the files and the purpose for the distribution package.

The Restrictions page of the General properties page enables you to specify whether platform restrictions should be specified for the distribution. If there are no restrictions, the distribution is accepted by any subscriber and then extracted on that subscriber. If there are restrictions, uncheck the No Restrictions box and check the boxes that correspond to the platforms that accept this distribution. The distribution only extracts on the platforms with a checked box. ZENworks allows you to specify the following platforms: NetWare All, NetWare 4.x, NetWare 5.0, NetWare 5.1, NetWare 5.x, NetWare 6.x, Windows Server, Solaris, and Linux.

The Channels Property Page

In the Channels property page, the administrator can select the channels that contain this distribution. This distribution can be placed in any number of channels. All the subscribers associated with each channel are sent this distribution by the distributor associated with this distribution object. Figure 25.18 shows this page.

To add this distribution to a channel, click the Add button. You are next presented with a dialog box to browse through eDirectory to select the channel. After you select the channel, it is placed in the list displayed in the Channels box. To delete the channel from the list (removing the distribution from being distributed), select the channel and click the Delete button. To go to the property pages of the channel object, select the object and click the Details button.

Any distributions associated with channels also appear in the channel object under the Distributions property page.

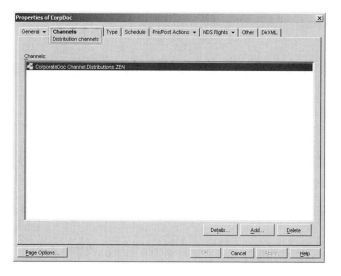

FIGURE 25.18
Channels property page of a TED distribution object.

The Agent Property Page

In the Agent property page you specify the agent and the files that will be sent as part of this distribution. The agent determines the type of distribution (for example, local files from the file agent, remote files from the HTTP or FTP agent, software installations from the server software packages agent, and so forth). Figure 25.19 shows this page. After you select the agent that this distribution will use (you can only select a single agent per distribution), the screen updates, and you need to give files specification details. (See the section "Working with TED Agents" later in the chapter for more details about each agent.)

The Schedule Property Page

This property page enables you to specify how often and when this distribution should be gathered. Each time the server clock hits the specified scheduled time, the agents are activated, and the distribution is gathered and compared with the previous version to determine whether any changes have been made. If there have been changes, a new version of the distribution file is created. The actual distribution of the file occurs based on schedules of the channels. Figure 25.20 displays the TED distribution Schedule page.

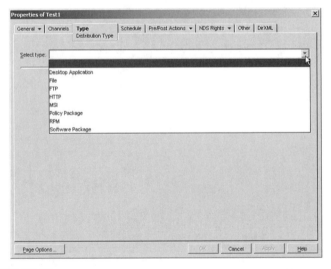

FIGURE 25.19
Agent Type property page of a TED distribution object.

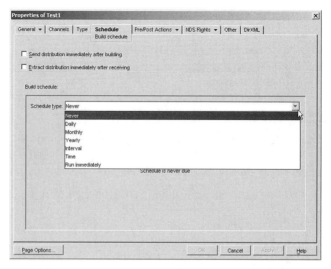

FIGURE 25.20
Schedule property page of a TED distribution object.

The following choices are available to you for the scheduling of the distribution: Never, Daily, Monthly, Yearly, Interval, Time, or Run Immediately. (See the section "About the TED Distributor" earlier in the chapter for an explanation of additional scheduling options beyond the Run Immediately option.)

You can also bypass both the channel schedule and the subscriber schedule by checking the boxes on the page:

▶ Send Distribution Immediately After Building—Results in the channel schedule being ignored and the distribution being sent immediately to all subscribers in the channel.

▶ Extract Distribution Immediately After Receiving—Ignores the subscriber schedule by activating an extraction of the distribution as soon as the target subscriber has received it.

Working with Manual Distribution

TED provides a mechanism for you to send your distributions manually, avoiding the need to contact any subscribers over the wire. You may possibly use this to place a distribution across a WAN link that may not be reliable or where you are going to that location and want to bring the distribution with you. You must first run a wizard to create the distribution file and then rerun the wizard at the destination to bring the distribution into the remote system.

Creating a Manual Distribution

The manual distribution is created through a wizard. Perform the following steps to create the distribution that can be placed on portable media and then manually transported to the destination systems:

1. Launch ConsoleOne, create a normal distribution, and place it into a channel.

2. Make sure that the distributor has gathered the distribution and the distribution file has been created.

TIP The easiest way to know whether a distribution has been created is to go to the distributor's working directory and see whether a subdirectory has been created with the name of the distribution. Inside this directory are subdirectories; each named with a time stamp—for example, SYS:\ZENWORKS\PDS\TED\DIST\<DISTRIBUTION NAME>051400502\. Each of these directories contains the files used in the distribution. The actual distribution file is called distribution.ted.

---

3. Launch ConsoleOne and choose TED Manual Distribution under the Tools menu. This launches the wizard to create the manual distribution media.

4. On the first page of the wizard, choose Export a Distribution from TED and Copy to Disk. Click Next.

5. Use the browse button to select the channel that contains the distribution you want to manually create. After you select the channel, the wizard displays the list of distributions. Select the desired distribution. Click Next.

6. Enter the desired name of the distribution file, including the path. The file should have a .TED extension. You may also click the browse button to select a file that already exists on the disk. Click Next.

7. A summary screen appears. Click Finish. At this time, the wizard creates the distribution file in the directory and with the name specified.

8. Take the file you have created and transport it to the destination location. Perform an import distribution to bring the distribution into the destination subscriber or parent subscriber.

After you have completed these steps, you will have created a manual distribution onto a removable media that is ready to be manually imported into a subscriber.

Importing the Distribution

After you create the distribution and carry it to the destination site (a remote subscriber or parent subscriber), you need to run the wizard again to bring the distribution into the system. Perform the following steps to import the distribution into the remote system:

1. Make sure that the distribution file created with the Export Wizard is accessible to the system. Also, make sure that you have access (through UNC paths) to the destination subscriber or parent subscriber that is to receive the distribution.

2. Launch ConsoleOne and choose TED Manual Distribution under the Tools menu. This launches the wizard to import the manual distribution media.

3. On the first page of the wizard, choose Import a Distribution from Disk to TED. Click Next.

4. Use the browse button to browse to and select the distribution file you have brought to this site. Click Next.

5. This page of the wizard displays all the known subscribers and parent subscribers that have subscribed to the channel that you selected when you created the manual distribution file. Select the subscribers or parent subscribers that you want to receive this distribution. If you select a parent subscriber, it automatically sends the distribution to all its destination subscribers. Click Next.

6. A summary screen appears. Click Finish. At this time, the wizard copies the distribution file to the subscriber's working directory through UNC paths.

The distribution is *not* automatically extracted on the subscriber. It is only extracted by one of the following methods:

▶ The channel schedule fires to send the distribution, and the distribution is administered to have Run Immediately schedule. The distributor connects with the subscriber and sees that the latest version of the distribution is already on the subscriber, so it does not resend the distribution. If it is a Run Immediately selection, the subscriber next extracts the distribution. This is only possible when the distributor can communicate with the subscriber over the wire.

▶ The extraction schedule on the subscriber fires, which causes the subscriber to unpack all distributions that have not been done, including the one you just imported.

▶ The subscriber is restarted. This causes the extraction to occur based on the schedule of the subscriber.

When the preceding steps are completed, the manual distribution that you made and imported into the subscriber will be extracted on the subscriber as if it had been received over a connection.

Working with TED Agents

TED agents are Java modules activated by either a distributor or a subscriber to either pack up or unpack a distribution file. Currently, the following agents are available in ZENworks: the desktop application agent, the HTTP agent, the FTP agent, the software package agent, the policy package agent, the MSI agent, the RPM agent, and the file agent. The following sections discuss each of the agents and what they do for TED.

WARNING After you create a distribution, and the agent performs its gathering process, and then you change the agent used for the distribution (that is, you re-administer the distribution object and change to a different agent type), unpredictable behavior may occur. This can impact the effect of versioning, which can lead to failures. You should, when changing to a different agent, go to the distributor's working directory and locate the subdirectory titled the same as the distribution and then remove all time stamp subdirectories under this distribution directory. This causes the agent to perform a clean build of the distribution, ensuring that the distribution is complete and accurate for the new agent.

About the Desktop Application Agent

The ZENworks desktop application agent allows you to distribute ZENworks Desktop Management application objects through the TED channel. This is useful because this effectively allows you to distribute desktop applications throughout your entire network, across tree boundaries, from a single source location.

NOTE You must install ZENworks Desktop Management and have at least one application object. The source files for the application object must reside on the distributors' local file system. The subscriber must have access to Novell's eDirectory to extract the application object and apply it. ZENworks subscribers on Linux/Unix cannot extract a desktop application distribution; however, they can route it to a NetWare or Windows server that can.

Use the Desktop Application Wizard to create a desktop application distribution. The wizard is started when you select Desktop Application from the distribution type drop-down list. The wizard first asks you to specify an application object that you want to distribute and then it asks you to set properties that determine how it is delivered.

After you set up the application object through the wizard, the ZENworks distributor reads the object's properties in eDirectory and determines the location of the source files. Next, it determines the associations with other application objects, application folder objects, chained applications, and containers. It packages the associations data into an XML file and packages it with the application object's source files, including the source files of any associated application objects, into a CPK file to be distributed though the TED channel.

When the package is distributed through the ZENworks channel, subscriber servers extract the package including the source files and XML data and replicate the application object in their tree locations. The subscriber could be in a different location of the same tree or in an entirely different tree.

The following is a list of the properties that you need to define in the wizard to distribute desktop applications through TED:

▶ Application Object—You must first specify a valid ZENworks desktop application object. After you create the object, all associated objects will be shown on the Type page of the distribution object.

▶ Maintain Source Tree Structure—Selecting this option duplicates the source tree's directory structure at the destination's location, which is the target subscribers' working context. This tree structure is then used to create the ZENworks desktop application objects. You must enable this option if you want to use chained applications.

▶ Source Root Context—This field specifies a container object to be used as the root container for the ZENworks desktop application objects. The distributor only records directory data from that container and its subordinate containers; therefore, when the subscriber extracts the package it applies the application object to its working directory as if the container had actually been the root. You can select application objects from this root container and its subordinate containers.

▶ Maintain Associations—Selecting this option maintains the group and container associations of the application object in its source tree by replicating the associated groups or containers at the target location if they do not exist. User and workstation associations in the source location are not replicated.

▶ Load Balancing and Fault Tolerance—This setting allows you to specify whether to use automated load balancing, fault tolerance, or neither. If you select Load Balance, ZENworks automatically spreads the desktop application distributions of the servers being used. Fault tolerance is effectively automatically accomplished through load balancing because of multiple servers involved. If you specify Fault Tolerance, ZENworks allows a server currently being used for desktop application distributions to assume the distribution role of another server that has gone down, however. If you select None, you can manually configure each application object for load balancing or fault tolerance.

NOTE After you set the distribution type to Desktop Application, you cannot change it to another type.

WARNING Do not edit desktop application distribution objects manually from the ConsoleOne main window. Always go through the wizards to make changes to these objects. The wizards will make all the changes necessary for the application distributions to work properly. Manually creating the application distributions can result in applications that are not properly added to the ZENworks distribution channel.

Understanding the HTTP Agent

The HTTP agent connects to the specified target and attempts to retrieve the specified file via the HTTP protocol. The construction of the destination path is the same as described in the file agent section. The only difference is when an Add File button is clicked, you are prompted for the URL that will reference the file that the agent should retrieve. Multiple

URLs can be added to the list. The HTTP agent cannot authenticate to the HTTP server. Also, it cannot get files over a secure (SSL) connection.

Understanding the FTP Agent

The FTP agent connects to an FTP server, transfers the specified files from that server into the distributor, and then collects these files into a single distribution file to be sent and extracted in the subscriber.

When you begin defining the files for the FTP agent, you must first specify a New FTP Source by clicking this button (see Figure 25.21). This prompts you for a server name, the login, and the password for this server to retrieve FTP files. Then, you continue to add destination folders as described in the section on file agents. When you attempt to add a file, ConsoleOne immediately attempts to connect to the FTP server and enables you to browse the FTP server, selecting the files that you want to gather at the designated time.

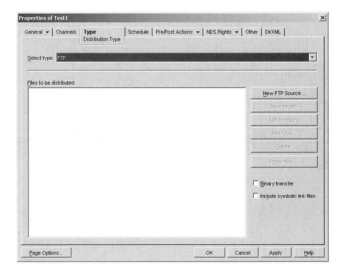

FIGURE 25.21
FTP Agent Distribution Type property page.

By default, the FTP agent retrieves the files in ASCII mode. If you want to retrieve the files in binary mode, which is required when transferring any file that contains nontext characters, you need to select the Binary

Transfer check box. You can only specify binary mode for the entire distribution, so if you need to get some binary files and some text files, you may need to use separate distributions. Using binary mode to transfer text files may corrupt the files if transferring from a Unix FTP server, so be sure to use ASCII mode when getting text files from Unix servers.

Working with the Server Software Package Agent

This agent is responsible for distributing server software packages, specific to ZENworks, which are packages for delivery and installation of software on servers. In Chapter 26, "Understanding and Creating Server Software Packages," Figure 26.25 shows the distribution object. You can identify the set of server software packages that you want included in the distribution. To construct a server software package, see the details described in Chapter 26.

With the server software package agent, you list the individual server software packages that you want delivered and installed on the target servers. Figure 25.22 shows the Distribution Type property page where you can list each of the software packages to deliver and install.

NOTE A subscriber receiving a distribution that is a server software package must have the ZENworks Server Management policy and package agent installed and running (ZFS.NCF). This agent assists in the extraction and installation of these packages.

To add software packages to the distribution, click the Add button and browse to select the .CPK file. When several packages are selected, you can specify the order that the software packages will be applied to the subscriber server. The order can be specified by selecting the package and clicking the Up or Down button to order the packages. To remove packages, select the package and click the Delete button.

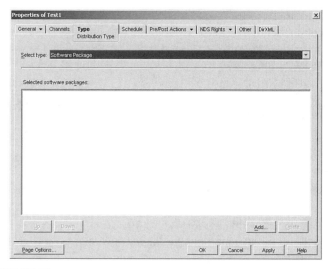

FIGURE 25.22
Server software package agent, distribution agent of a distribution object.

Working with the Policy Package Agent

ZENworks distribution type Policy Package allows you to specify policy packages to be distributed directly to the individual servers where the policies will be enforced. Previously in ZENworks for Servers, you associated a policy package object with eDirectory Server objects and/or container objects so that the policy could be effective for the servers.

The policy package agent allows you to specify which servers are to have a given policy enforced by simply creating a distribution for that policy and distributing it to the selected servers. When a target server has extracted the distribution, the policies contained in the distribution are enforced on that server according to the subscriber's distribution schedule.

To create a policy package distribution simply select Policy Package from the list of distribution types. Then click the Add button to navigate through the eDirectory tree and select policy packages that you want to be enforced on the subscriber servers in the distribution channel.

Understanding the MSI Agent

Another distribution type in ZENworks Server Management is the MSI type. The MSI agent allows you to use TED to distribute packages to a Windows platform. This allows any Microsoft Installer (MSI) packages you have created or collected to be added to a distribution channel and distributed to your Windows servers.

To create an MSI distribution for your MSI package, simply select MSI from the list of distribution types to bring up the MSI Agent page. From this screen click the Add from Distributor button to add an MSI package located on the distributor's file system, or you can click the Add from FTP Site button to log in to an FTP server and select an MSI package located on it.

Working with the RPM Agent

Another distribution type in ZENworks Server Management is the RPM type. The RPM agent allows you to use TED to distribute packages to a Unix platform. This allows any Red Hat Package Manager (RPM) packages you have created to be added to a distribution channel and distributed to your Linux or Solaris servers. Although RPM is not native to all Linux implementations, it is the most commonly used package manager for enterprise environments.

To create an RPM distribution for your RPM package, simply select RPM from the list of distribution types to bring up the RPM Agent page. From this screen click the Add from Distributor button to add an RPM package located on the distributor's file system, or you can click the Add from FTP Site button to log in to an FTP server and select an RPM package located on it.

Understanding the File Agent

This agent enables you to select any file or set of files on the distributor file system and place it in a defined directory on the subscriber system. The directories specified do not have to exist on the target server; they are created at extraction time. Figure 25.23 shows a distribution using the file agent.

You begin identifying the target set of files to include in the distribution by clicking the New Target button. This creates a root node displayed on the left panel. Traditionally, this represents the destination volume for the files. ConsoleOne initially places the string %DEST_VOLUME% in this field. You can change the string by selecting the text and clicking the left mouse button. The field clears, and you can enter any text string you want, including hard-coded volume names (on the target subscribers) or variable names (don't forget the surrounding percent signs).

You then construct a tree of the file system as you want it created on the target subscriber. You can add subdirectories by highlighting a directory in the tree and clicking the Add Folder button. You can then click on the folder name to edit the name of the folder (initially it is set as the string "New Folder").

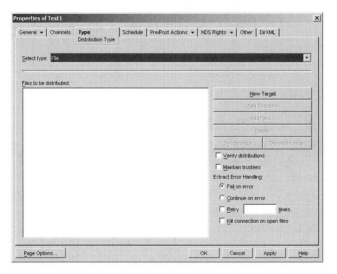

FIGURE 25.23
File agent, distribution agent of a distribution object.

When you want to send a file to the destination subscriber, you first highlight the folder that is the file's parent on the destination subscriber and click the Add File button. This brings up a Browser dialog box, enabling you to browse through the file system of the distributor to the volume you want and then down into the volume file system. Continue browsing until you find the file you want. Select the file by double-clicking the filename, or by selecting the file and clicking OK on the dialog box. The full path name of the file (as found on the distributor) is displayed as the name of the file in the tree. The actual name of the file when it is transmitted and extracted from the distribution is the base name of the file (the filename without any directories), and the file is located under the directories and subdirectories that you have specified in the tree design in the left panel.

Continue doing the preceding steps until all the desired files are selected and placed in the desired locations on the target subscriber. Should you need to delete a file or directory, simply select the item and click Delete. The file and/or the directory and all subdirectories will be removed from the tree display and will not be included in the distribution.

The following configuration flags can be placed on the distribution and only apply when the extraction process is occurring on the subscriber:

▶ Synchronize—Forces the distribution to synchronize the directories specified in the file agent. If this option is set, only the files specified in the agent will be allowed to exist in the directories specified. This is useful if you need to replicate exact directory structures throughout your network.

▶ Desynchronize—Removes the synchronization administration of the directory. The files in the specified directory, on the subscriber, will no longer be synchronized with those on the distributor.

▶ Verify Distributions—Enables the distributor to force the subscriber to extract the current version of the distribution, even if it has already been extracted. This allows the subscriber to refresh the files contained in the current version, eliminating any changes that may have occurred since the original distribution.

▶ Maintain Trustees—Instructs the subscriber to maintain file ownership and trustee data in the files. This option is only valid on distributions between NetWare servers where the distributor and subscriber reside in the same eDirectory tree.

▶ Retry X Times—Attempts to write the file the specified number of times. If the write fails—because the file is open, for example—the agent repeats the attempts the specified number of times before failing.

▶ Kill Connection on Open Files—Enables the process to drop the connections to the subscriber server for the connection that has the file open, preventing the agent from writing the file. This terminates the session for the user currently using the file, and the user will have to log in again to the server.

▶ Fail on Error—Terminates the extraction should a failure occur in writing the files.

WARNING The system does not roll back any files that have been installed at the point of failure.

▶ Continue on Error—Causes the agent to skip the file, logging the error if specified, and continue to extract the other files in the distribution.

These options are for the entire distribution and are not specified on a per-file basis.

WARNING ZENworks creates the directory structure first and applies the attributes to the directories before copying files. Therefore, if you flag a directory that is to be distributed with the read-only flag, the distribution will fail because it cannot copy files to a read-only directory.

The file agent does not create a new distribution file in its entirety. If a previous distribution is available, the agent performs a *file-wise* delta where only changed files are included in the new distribution. When the number of revisions reaches the administered maximum revisions, the agent removes all previously created versions and creates a completely new *baseline* of the distribution consisting of all the files specified in the distribution. This is important because each subscriber must extract the various revisions of the distribution in order.

Understanding the TED Channel

The TED channel basically identifies the group of subscribers that should receive the distributions in the channel. Multiple distributions from multiple distributors can be in the channel. Figure 25.24 displays this object.

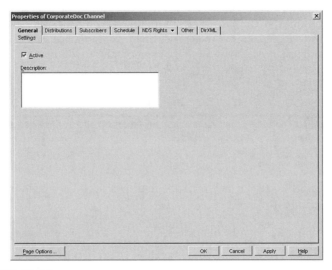

FIGURE 25.24
Channel object.

The Settings Property Page

On the Settings property page you can specify a description of the channel. This hopefully gives an indication of the type of distributions placed in the channel and the type of subscribers. For example, a channel for engineering applications would give a good signal that the distributions are applications used by engineers in the organization.

You can also activate or deactivate a channel. If a channel is active, the distributions are sent per the channel schedule.

The Distributions Property Page

This page enables you to specify the distributions that should be included in the channel. From this page, you can add distributions by clicking the Add button and browsing eDirectory to select the distribution objects. You can also look at the details or remove distributions from the channel in this property page. This can also be done in the distribution objects. If the distribution is associated with the channel in the distribution object, the distribution automatically appears in this list as well.

The Subscribers Property Page

This page enables you to specify the subscribers that should be included in the channel. From this page, you can add subscribers by clicking the Add button and browsing eDirectory to select the subscriber or external subscriber objects. You can also look at the details or remove subscribers from the channel in this property page. This can also be done in the subscriber object. If the subscriber is associated with the channel in the subscriber object, the subscriber automatically appears in this list as well.

The Schedule Property Page

This page enables you to specify the send schedule for all distributions within the channel. The channel schedule determines when the distributions are sent to the subscribers. See the section "About the TED Distributor" earlier in this chapter for more details on the different schedule types available.

NOTE The channel schedule is converted into the time zone of the distributor. All distributors that own distributions that are in this channel start sending at once, regardless of what time zone they are in.

ZENworks Server Management Web-based Management

ZENworks includes a web-based management role snap-in to the Novell iManager utility. This role can be used as an alternative to ConsoleOne for managing TED objects and distributions. This role is covered in more detail in Chapter 33, "Using ZENworks Server Management Web-based Management." We recommend taking some time to become familiar with using this tool because it can be accessed virtually from anywhere you have Internet access to your network.

ZENworks Distributor/Subscriber Commands

Several ZENworks Server Management and Tiered Electronic Distribution processes run on the ZENworks NetWare server. These processes provide independent consoles that allow you to use console commands to check the status and control the behavior of ZENworks Server Management.

The ZENworks policy engine and distributor/subscriber runs on the NetWare server, provides enforcement of server policies, and installs server software packages. The commands listed in Table 25.3 are available from the ZENworks Server Management console. The console is labeled as ZENworks Server Management in the screens list.

TABLE 25.3   Console Commands for ZENworks Server Management

COMMAND	DESCRIPTION
cls	Clears the screen and places the prompt at the top of the screen.
down !	Downs the server, ignoring any downing policy that may be in effect.
down cancel	Cancels the current down process. If the server is still sending out messages and so forth from the down policy, the down is cancelled, the logins are re-enabled, and so forth, to bring the server back to its previous state. Any previously dropped connections will, obviously, be lost.
down reset	Downs the server by performing a reset of the server. If a downing policy is administered, it is enforced.
down restart	Downs the server and restarts the hardware, bringing the system back up. If a downing policy is administered, it is enforced.
down server	Downs the server and does not bring the server back up, enforcing the downing policy if one is administered.
down status	Reports whether the server is in the process of handling a down request. It tells you, for example, how many minutes before the down actually occurs.

TABLE 25.3   Continued

COMMAND	DESCRIPTION
events fire <eventid>	Fires an event as if the event actually happened in the server. The eventid is the exact string displayed on the events list. It is not a number but the name of the class handling the event.
events list	Lists all the events that the ZENworks Server Management system is monitoring and the Java process that is watching for the event.
events status	This command is nonfunctional.
Exit	Terminates the policy engine and unloads the processes. Any other enforcer or other Java processes related to ZENworks Server Management policy management will continue.
Help	Provides help on the ZENworks Server Management console commands. You may also enter help <command> to get more specific help on individual commands.
Listplugins	Lists the plug-ins in the system.
package list	Lists the current set of installed software packages and the dates that they were installed. An asterisk by the item means that requesting a rollback can uninstall that package.
package process <file>	Processes the specified .CPK (software package) file and installs it onto the server.
package rollback	Uninstalls the last package installed (shown with an asterisk in the package list).
policy eventbased	Displays the policies effective on this server that are activated by an event on the server.
policy list	Lists the current effective policies. Also displays a policy number with each effective policy. This number is used in the policy enforce command.

TABLE 25.3 Continued

COMMAND	DESCRIPTION
policy plugins	Displays the current plug-ins in the policy engine. There is a policy plug-in called an *enforcer* for each policy that can be associated with the server. These enforcers are responsible for making the policy effective when launched by the scheduler. This command also lists the event handler that watches events that occur on the server (for example, down server) that may be monitored by the engine because a policy may affect behavior.
policy refresh	Causes the policy engine to refresh its configuration and policy information by going to eDirectory, getting all policies, recaching them internally, and rescheduling any scheduled policies.
policy refreshonly	Retrieves from eDirectory all the effective policies associated with this server and refreshes them into the server's cache of the policies. This does not refresh or reschedule any scheduled policy.
policy rescheduleonly	Retrieves from eDirectory all the scheduled effective policies associated with this server, refreshes them into the server's cache of the policies, and reschedules them.
policy schedules	Displays the policy schedules to be fired on this server.
prompt [new prompt]	Displays the current prompt if none is given on the command line. If a new string prompt is given, the new prompt is set as the prompt for the console. No quotes are required for the parameter. The system automatically tacks on the > character after the prompt.

TABLE 25.3 Continued

COMMAND	DESCRIPTION
Refresh	Manually requests that the server refresh its configuration policy. This does not read all policies—only the ZENworks Server Management policy associated with this server. Use the `policy refresh` command to read all other policies.
setfilelevel [#]	Sets the following level number for the messages to be sent to the log file: 0 = No Messages; 1 = Errors; 2 = Successes & Level 1; 3 = Warnings & Level 2; 4 = Information & Level 3; 5 = Trace information & Level 4; 6 = Developer trace information & Level 5. If no level number is entered, the current level is displayed. This command does not change the messages sent to the console.
showschedule	Displays the current scheduled actions and the Java classes (plug-in) that handle the action when the schedule fires.
Showvars	Lists the current variables defined on the system. This gives the keys and their values.
Status	Displays status information on the policy engine, including base path, number of plug-ins loaded, number of events registered, number of scheduled items, and the current console message level.
Time	Displays the current date and time of the server.
Version	Displays the current version of the ZENworks Server Management Policy Manager.

The commands listed in Table 25.4 are the debug commands available with the policy engine. The debug commands allow you to access some of the debugging features of ZENworks Server Management to troubleshoot problems. These commands are not supported by Novell, Inc., and may not be fully functional. These commands are valid even if debug is not turned on in the console.

TABLE 25.4 Debug Console Commands for ZENworks Server Management NetWare Console

COMMAND	DESCRIPTION
Addtables	Adds tables to the Sybase database for logging policy messages and events.
Debug	Instructs user to use the debugon command to turn on help for debug commands.
Debugoff	Turns off help for debug commands.
Debugon	Turns on help for debug commands.
Deltables	Deletes the log tables created in the Sybase database for logging policy messages and events. All the data in the tables will be lost.
echo <command> <console>	Sends the given command to the specified ZENworks Server Management console, such as distributor or subscriber. echo help distributor, for example, causes the distributor console to execute the help command.
load <module name>	Loads the specified Java class module into the Java engine.
Logconsoleoutputoff	Turns off sending all characters displayed on the console to the log file.
Logconsoleoutputon	Turns on sending all characters displayed on the console to the log file.
Off	Performs a clear screen, just like cls.
resolve [ip address¦dns name]	Resolves a given IP address or DNS name. This returns the IP address and the DNS name known to the system.
send <message>	Performs a broadcast of the message to all connected users.
setconsolelevel [#]	Sets the following level of messages to display on the policy engine console: 0 = No Messages; 1 = Errors; 2 = Successes & Level 1; 3 =

TABLE 25.4   Continued

COMMAND	DESCRIPTION
	Warnings & Level 2; 4 = Information & Level 3; 5 = Trace information & Level 4; 6 = Developer trace information & Level 5. The level is the same as the `setfilelevel` command. The default level is 4, but it can be specified in the ZFS policy. The level is reset back to the level specified on any refresh or restart of the policy engine.
showstates	Displays the various Java components (in policy engine threads) currently active and the state they are in, such as downing in five minutes and so forth.
spc <dn><plugin><cmd><string>	Executes a "server procedure call" to the specified server DN. The call causes the plug-in specified to be loaded and the command with the given string parameters to be launched. This can be used to launch an enforcer on a remote server.
threads	Lists the current threads that the policy engine is managing.

Summary

This chapter discussed the construction, deployment, and administration of the ZENworks Tiered Electronic Distribution (TED) subsystem. TED enables you to reliably transmit files from server to server throughout your entire network, independent of eDirectory trees and server platforms.

## CHAPTER 26

Understanding and Creating Server Software Packages

This chapter discusses the creation of server software packages and how you can use them to manage your servers. With server software packages, you can create a package that runs scripts for pre-installation and post-installation, for loading and unloading of NLMs and Java classes, for installation prerequisites to restrict package installation, and for installing software on your servers.

Understanding Server Software Packages

Server software packages are much like any other installation package that you may be familiar with for other systems. This package system enables you to specify that certain features of the hardware and system need to be present (disk space, OS version, and so forth), and you can look for the existence of particular files and registry keys or set parameters. You may also specify variables that are substituted into the package when installation occurs to enable you to customize the package for several different target machines. Additionally, you may include the loading and unloading of NLMs and Java classes and the execution of specified scripts both before and after the installation of the package.

A software package is made up of a set of components. You can have any number of components within a software package. Within a component, you may have any number of files and folders copied to the server.

Installation Requirements

Before you can install a software package on the server, the server must satisfy the requirements that have been administered as part of the package. In addition to those for the package, each component may have its own set of requirements that must be fulfilled before it's installed. If the requirements are not met for a particular component, it will not be installed.

Consequently, only portions of a software package may actually be installed on the server. Additionally, because of the logic placed in the components and the fact that the package installs the portions in order, you could have components later in the package check to see whether a previous part has been installed. By doing this, you can have subsequent components fail and not be installed if a previous component has not been installed. You could, for example, have component 2 look for the existence of a file on the server that should have been installed if component 1 was successful. If component 1 does not install properly, component 2 will not run because the file from component 1 will not be found on the server.

.SPK and .CPK Files

The specifications you give are all stored in a file with the suffix of .SPK. This file is stored on the file system and contains the configuration information for all components of the package. The .SPK file cannot be sent to a server or installed on a server; it must first be compiled into a .CPK file. At compile time, the ConsoleOne snap-in takes the references to the files in the .SPK file and retrieves these files, placing them into the single .CPK file so that no references are in the file. All the data for the installation is compacted and stored into the single .CPK file. This complete file can then be used to install the features onto your servers.

The compiled .CPK file may be sent over to the servers via the TED distribution system, or it may be manually copied to those servers (through CDs, Jaz drives, a network, and so forth) and then executed locally. The TED system subscribers (see Chapter 25, "Setting Up Tiered Electronic Distribution (TED)," for more information) receive the .CPK file, and, if the ZENworks Policy Manager is running on the server, activate that agent to have it unpack and execute the .CPK file. This can also be done manually by copying the file to the server (or having it accessible from the server drivers—for example, CD-ROM) and then entering the command `PACKAGE PROCESS <path to .CPK file>`. This performs the unpacking and execution of the .CPK file.

Rolling Back Changes

ZENworks Server Management provides the capability to roll back an installation that has occurred via a .CPK file. The rollback can remove any installation changes that have occurred on the last applied package. You can find yourself needing to perform several rollbacks to get back to previous packages. For example, if packages A, B, and C have been applied, you can roll back only C. And after package C has been rolled back, you can roll back package B.

When ZENworks applies a package, it creates a rollback package in the working directory of the policy engine, under the **ROLLBACK** subdirectory. Each rollback file is itself a .CPK file and is named by a GUID (globally unique identifier). When you request that a rollback occur, the rollback .CPK file is processed and then deleted. Rerunning the same installation .CPK file (unchanged version) does not create multiple rollback files. But if you recompile the .SPK file, a new .CPK file is created, even if you give it the same name, and the package will be installed again on the server even though the .SPK file was unchanged.

You can request a rollback by going to the ZENworks console and entering the command **package rollback**. Additionally, you can go through the browser-based management system and request that a rollback occur on the server.

Creating and Managing .SPK Files in ConsoleOne

As mentioned earlier, you can create and manage .SPK files in ConsoleOne. The ZENworks install establishes a new *namespace* in ConsoleOne to manage these packages. A namespace in ConsoleOne results in a new rooted entry under your My World icon, at the same level as eDirectory in the ConsoleOne hierarchy display in the left panel.

When you create or insert an .SPK file, an entry is placed in ConsoleOne configuration files that, when ConsoleOne comes up, displays the known software packages without requiring the namespace to search all possible drives to find the .SPK file. Consequently, if you delete the .SPK file from the file system, ConsoleOne is not aware of this and continues to display the software package entry in the server software packages namespace. But if you attempt to modify the package parameters, an error occurs because the file is not found. You need to manually delete the entry from ConsoleOne by choosing the Remove Package entry from the menu.

NOTE Choosing the Remove Package entry does *not* remove the .SPK or .CPK files associated with the package. You also need to manually remove them from the file system if you no longer want to keep the packages.

Installation Failures

Should the processing of a .CPK run into problems installing the components (for example, running out of file space), the package installation is aborted, an error log is created, and a message is displayed. The components of the package that were installed are automatically rolled back and uninstalled.

Creating a Server Software Package

You can create server software packages inside ConsoleOne. When you installed ZENworks (policies and TED components), a ConsoleOne snap-in registered itself, displaying a new rooted entry under your My World icon in ConsoleOne. The name of this container under My World is called Server Software Packages.

Two methods are used to introduce software packages into ConsoleOne and the system. You may create a new software package, or you may insert a previously constructed software package. When you insert a software package (by right-clicking the Packages container and choosing Insert Package on the pop-up menu), you are prompted through the wizard to specify the location of the .SPK file. This file is then read, and the information is displayed and is modifiable in ConsoleOne as if the package was just created. This is the one way that you can reintroduce a package that you had created and then removed from ConsoleOne.

At a high level, the steps to follow in administering a server software package include

1. Create a server software package and administer any rules associated with installation of the package.

2. Create components in the software package and administer any additional rules (beyond the package rules), if necessary, for the component to install.

3. Compile the package and place the resulting .CPK file on the distribution server.

4. Deliver the package to the target server manually or through Tiered Electronic Distribution (TED).

5. Install the package. Tiered Electronic Distribution services and the ZENworks Server Management agent do this automatically. You can also install the package manually by typing **PACKAGE PROCESS <path to CPK file>** at the ZENworks Server Management console.

Creating a New Server Software Package

To create a new server software package, follow these steps:

1. Launch ConsoleOne.

2. Select the Server Software Packages container in the left panel of ConsoleOne (the hierarchical browser).

3. Right-click the Server Software Package container and select New Package from the menu that appears. This launches the Software Package Wizard that prompts you through the initializations of the .SPK file.

4. Click Next.

5. Specify the name of the package and the filename of the .SPK file. You can browse through the file system to find an existing .SPK file to overwrite or specify the name of a new file. You may give the file any extension you want, but parts of the system expect the extension to be .SPK, so that is your best bet. If you do not enter a suffix, the system automatically puts the .SPK suffix on the package.

6. Click Next. The basic package is created, and an entry is placed in the ConsoleOne Server Software Packages namespace for this new package. The new package is now displayed under the Server Software Packages container.

7. Right-click the new software package. From the menu, you may choose Properties to set up the package requirements and rules, or New Component to add a new component to the package. You may also choose Remove if you want to delete this package from the namespace. Removing this package from the display in ConsoleOne does not remove the associated .SPK and .CPK files from the file system.

The following sections discuss package rule administration and the addition of components to your software packages.

Working with Package Management

When you select a package under the Server Software Packages container, the pathname to the package .SPK file appears in the right view window, and you see the administered description of the package (which is empty the first time). To administer the rules and features of the package as a whole, you must right-click the package in the container to bring up the menu choices. From that menu, select Properties, and the screen shown in Figure 26.1 appears.

The following property pages are available for administration under the package.

Identification Property Page

Under the Identification property page, you may administer the name and the description of the package. The name of the package appears under the Server Software Packages container in ConsoleOne, and the description appears in the right window of ConsoleOne when the package is selected.

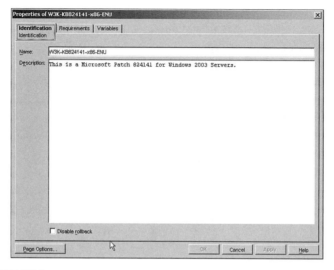

FIGURE 26.1
Property pages for package management.

If you select the Disable Rollback check box, this package will not be available for rollback on the installed servers. It will be installed normally, but the rollback scripts and information associated with them will not be created.

Requirements Property Page

The Requirements property page enables you to specify the requirements that must be satisfied for any portion of the package to be installed. If any requirement is not satisfied, no component will be installed from the package. Figure 26.2 shows a sample of the Requirements page.

Within the Requirements property page, you may set up any number of requirements that must be satisfied for the package to be installed. You may even set up multiples of the same type of rule (such as two file requirements) for the requirements. Be careful not to place contradictory rules. This causes the package to never install because all rules must be satisfied for any portion of the package to be installed on the server.

To add a rule, click the Add button and select the type you want. The rules appear in the left panel. To administer or modify a rule, select the rule on the left and administer its values in the right panel. To remove a rule, select it and then click the Remove button. The types of rules you can choose from are Operating System, Memory, Disk Space, Set Commands, Registry, File, and Products.dat. The following sections describe each type of rule.

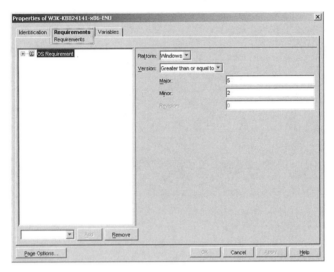

FIGURE 26.2
Requirements property page for server software package management.

The Operating System Rule

Within the Operating System requirement, you may choose from the NetWare, Windows, Solaris, and Linux operating systems.

After you choose an operating system type, you may also keep the default, which states that it will install on any version of the operating system. Should you choose to be selective, you can enter the version number (major, minor, revision) of the operating system and then choose one of the appropriate rules to apply to the comparison between the administered value and the actual version number of the target servers. You may choose one of the following:

- Any—Ignore the version number of the operating system.

- Less Than—The target server version number is less than the entered value.

- Less Than or Equal To—The target server version number is less than or equal to the administered value.

▶ Equal To—The target server version is exactly the same as the administered value.

▶ Greater Than—The target server version is greater than the specified version number.

▶ Greater Than or Equal To—The target server is greater than or equal to the specified version.

The Memory Rule

The Memory rule enables you to specify the amount of RAM that must be present on the server. This is *not* the amount of current free memory space, but the total amount of RAM installed on the server. You may choose the following options on the rule and specify the amount to compare (for example, 128) in megabytes:

▶ Less Than—The target server has less installed memory than the specified amount of RAM.

▶ Less Than or Equal To—The target server has the same or less than the amount of RAM specified.

▶ Greater Than—The target server has more RAM than the specified amount.

▶ Greater Than or Equal To—The target server has as much or more than the RAM specified.

> **NOTE** To get the amount of RAM from the server, enter the **memory** command on the main server console. This gives you the amount of memory in kilobytes, so divide that number by 1,024 to get megabytes.

The Disk Space Rule

This rule enables you to specify the amount of free disk space that must be available on the server prior to the package being installed. The amount of free space is specified in megabytes (MB), and you can specify either the **SYS** volume or a specific volume name. If the specified volume name (for example, **VOL1**) is not found on the server, the package will not be installed on the server. You can choose from the following rules:

▶ Less Than—The target server volume has less space than the specified amount.

▶ Less Than or Equal To—The target server volume has the same or less than the amount of disk space specified.

▶ Greater Than—The target server volume has more space than the specified amount.

▶ Greater Than or Equal To—The target server volume has as much or more than the amount of space specified.

The Set Commands Rule
Within this rule, you can specify the expected value for any of the possible set parameters. When you select this rule, the Set Parameters Wizard walks you through contacting only a NetWare server that is running ZENworks Policy Manager, which retrieves from the specified server the list of potential set parameters. Because different servers with different software installed may have different set commands, the wizard has you browse for a server running ZENworks to use as the model server. The set commands from the server you select should represent the other servers in your network. From this list you may choose which set parameters (by category or specific parameter) you are interested in having contained in the rule. After the list is selected, the wizard terminates, and the list of chosen parameters is displayed on this page.

Then you may create the rule by selecting the parameter and specifying the value that the parameter must have to enable the package to be installed. If any of the specified parameters is not set as administered, no component of the software package will be installed.

The Registry Rule
This page enables you to place a rule on the existence or value of a registry key from the Windows or NetWare registry. You may first select whether the registry interest is either a key, a name, or data. Currently, the data values may only be represented as strings, and an exact match is the only type of compare supported.

When you select a key type, you may choose to accept the installation depending on whether the key exists. Then you must specify the name of the key.

By selecting the name type on this rule, you can also choose to accept the installation based on whether the name exists in the registry. If this is chosen, you must specify the name to be matched.

When you choose to look for a data value, you must specify whether the data value equals the specified value. Then you must specify the key, the name, and the value of the data. The page is set up to enable you to compare based on several different types of values; currently, the only value type is string.

The File Rule

With the File rule, you may specify whether a particular file exists on the server. You specify the name of the file (including the volume; SYS is assumed if not specified) and the flag to succeed if the file exists, or if you want to base the rule on the date of the file. Should you choose to look at the date of the file, you can choose from the following:

▶ Before—The target server file has a date and/or time earlier than the specified date and time.

▶ On or Before—The target server's file has a time stamp that is the same or before the specified date and time.

▶ On—The target server file has the same time stamp as specified.

▶ On or After—The target server file has the same time stamp or later than the one specified.

▶ After—The target server file has a date that is after the given date and/or time.

After choosing the comparison function, click the Calendar button to be given a calendar control enabling you to select a date and enter a time value for the file.

The Products.dat Rule

This rule enables you to match strings stored in the products.dat file on the server. The products.dat file identifies the various features and NetWare components that have been installed on the server.

This rule enables you to specify the name of the product ID and then look at the version and the description of the ID to see whether a match exists. With both the version and the description, you may identify whether the specified value contains, begins with, or matches the entry in the products.dat file. All comparisons of the values, including the ID, use case-sensitive matching. If the matched ID exists and has the value identified, the package satisfies this rule.

Exploring the Variables Property Page

This property page enables you to specify variables used by the installation package to customize the filenames and locations in the software package.

Several variables can be used in this and other places in ZENworks. These variables are enclosed in % (percent signs) and can be either a defined set, an environment variable from the server, an attribute of the server object, or an attribute of a specified eDirectory object. The order that ZENworks uses to recognize environment variables is as follows:

1. If the string between the %s is a predefined variable, that value is placed in that string. Predefined variables are one of the following:

   ▶ **LOAD_DIR**—The directory where the NetWare server was loaded

   ▶ **TREE_NAME**—The name of the tree where ZENworks Server Management is located

   ▶ **WORKING_PATH**—The working directory for the temporary files

   ▶ **SERVER_DN**—eDirectory distinguished object name for the server

   ▶ **IP_ADDRESS**—IP address of the server

   ▶ **BASE_PATH**—The base path showing where the ZENworks Server Management policy engine is located (such as, **SYS:\SMANAGER**)

   ▶ **SERVER_NAME**—Name the server was given at install time

2. If the string has the format **%object distinguished name;attribute%**, the attribute value of the specified object is placed in the string.

3. If the string has no semicolon, the system looks for an environment variable of that name and replaces the value in the string. The system looks in both the NetWare and the Java environments for this variable.

4. If no environment variable exists with that name, the name is assumed to be a server attribute, and the system attempts to place the attribute's value in the string.

5. If the variable is not a server attribute, the unchanged variable string (including the % signs) is used as the value.

Managing Package Components

After you create a package, you need to add components to the package. The components that actually contain the files will be installed on the target server.

To add a component to a package, right-click the package in ConsoleOne to bring up the menu. From the menu, choose the New Component option. After selecting the option, a dialog box prompts you for the name of the component. Remember, multiple files can be installed in a single component, and a component can have its own set of rules to enable it to be installed independently in the package. Choose a name that will help you remember the types of files in the component. When a name is supplied, the component is created and displayed under the package title. When you select the component, its description is displayed in the right pane.

To manage a component, right-click on it and select Properties from the menu. After selecting Properties, you are presented with the property pages for the component. Figure 26.3 shows sample property pages for a component.

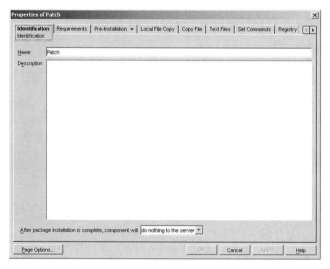

FIGURE 26.3
Property pages for a component of a server software package.

From these property pages you may administer the following pages in the component.

The Identification Property Page

As shown in Figure 26.3, you may administer the name of the component and the description of the component. The name of the component is displayed in ConsoleOne under the package, and the description is displayed in the right panel of ConsoleOne when the component is selected.

Additionally, you can request that an action on the server be performed after the entire package is successfully installed on the server. This is administered at the bottom of the page and has the following values:

▶ Do Nothing to the Server—Continue and perform no particular action

▶ Down the Server—Down the server without restarting system

▶ Restart the Server—Down the server and restart it, which causes the server hardware to be rebooted

▶ Reset the Server—Down the server and reset the server

The Pre-Installation Requirements Property Page

This Requirements property page enables you to specify various requirements that must be met for the component to be installed on the server. No component will be installed if the server does not meet the requirements of the package. In addition to the requirements of the package, the component pre-installation requirements must also be met for the component to be installed. Components may have different requirements, resulting in the possibility of only some components being installed on the server, whereas other components are not installed.

See the section "Working with Package Management" earlier in the chapter, which discusses its property page. The same components are available to the package.

The Pre-Installation Load/Unload Property Page

From this page you can request that the system load or unload an NLM or Java process or a service. Despite what some documentation states, you can unload/kill an NLM process with the unload process request. Figure 26.4 shows a sample of this property page.

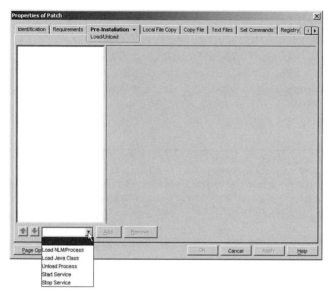

FIGURE 26.4
The Pre-Installation Load/Unload property page for a component of a server software package.

To add an action on this page, click the Add button and select whether you want to load an NLM, load a Java class, or unload a process. When selected, an entry is placed in the left panel. You may edit the name of the entry by selecting the entry and typing in a new name. In the right panel, associated with each entry, you need to provide information such as a filename and any parameters.

Each loading or unloading of processes occurs in the order specified in the left panel. You can rearrange the order by selecting an item in the list and clicking the up and down arrows on the page to move the item either up or down in the list.

Loading an NLM
When you select to have an NLM loaded prior to installation, you need to provide the following information in the right panel:

▸ File Name—Enter the filename to be loaded. Make sure to include the full path if the NLM is not in the **SYS:\SYSTEM** or in the path of the server. The path can include variable names.

▸ Parameters—Enter any parameters that you want to pass to the NLM. These parameters can include variable names.

▸ Wait for Termination—Tells the system to wait until the NLM loads, does its work, and then unloads itself before proceeding in the installation process. If the NLM does not terminate and unload, the installation does not continue until you manually unload the NLM.

NOTE If the software package agent tries to load an NLM that is already loaded on the server, it will fail, and the entire package will be rolled back. It is recommended that you unload the NLM first in the unload parameters (the attempt to unload an NLM not current-ly loaded does not result in a failure) and then ask that it be loaded.

Loading a Java Class

When you select to load a Java class, you must also provide the following information:

▸ File Name—The filename, or traditionally referred to as the class name, to load into the JVM (for example, `com.novell.application.zenworks.ted.Distributor`).

▸ Parameters—The parameters that you want included on the com-mand line when the process is launched (such as `ZENTREE "Distributor_ZEN1.servers.novell"`). This parameter is the parameter passed to the Java process; traditionally, these parameters follow the process name when launching the Java Virtual Machine.

▸ JVM Parameters—The parameters to be passed to the Java virtual machine. Traditionally, these parameters are such items as the class path or other Java configuration parameters. These parameters can include variable names.

▸ Wait for Termination—Tells the system to launch the Java class, wait for it to run, and then terminate. If the class does not self-terminate, the installation will not continue until you manually terminate the Java class.

Unloading a Process

When you choose to unload an NLM or Java process, you must also provide the following information:

▶ File Name—The class name, or NLM filename (with the .NLM extension), of the process that the system should attempt to unload. The system first attempts to unload (as if it was an NLM) the filename you specify, and then the system attempts to perform a `java -kill` by using the name given. If the name matches both an NLM and a Java process, both are terminated. The Java process name must match exactly the process names that appear with the `java -show` command given at the console.

▶ Wait for Termination—Notifies the system to wait until the process is terminated before proceeding. If the process does not unload, the installation process will not continue until you manually terminate the process.

Start Service

ZENworks allows you to start a service on a Windows NT/2000/2003 server when you are distributing a software package to it. This enables you to start any services required for the software package to be applied. When you choose to Start a Service, you must also provide the following information:

▶ Service Name—The name of the Windows server you want to start.

▶ Wait for This Service to Start Before Continuing—Tells ZENworks whether to verify that the service has actually started before applying the software package.

Stop Service

ZENworks allows you to stop a service on a Windows NT/2000/2003 server when you are distributing a software package to it. This enables you to stop any services that will interfere with applying the software package. When you choose to stop a service, you must also provide the following information:

▶ Service Name—The name of the Windows server you want to stop.

▶ Wait for This Service to Stop Before Continuing—Tells ZENworks whether to verify that the service has actually stopped before applying the software package.

The Script Property Page

You add a script to the policy by clicking the Add button on this property page. When you click the Add button, an entry is placed in the left window, and you are allowed to edit the name of the script. After you name the script, you can choose on the right the type of script that you will be creating. The choices of script types are currently NCF, NETBASIC, and PERL. After you identify the script type, you are free to type in the script in the provided window. ZENworks provides no syntax checking or validation for the script you enter.

You can add multiple scripts of any of the available types into this component. The scripts are executed in the order shown on the administration screen (from top to bottom). If you want to reorder the running of the scripts, you must select a script name in the left pane and click the up or down arrows to move the script into a different order.

When the ZENworks policy engine runs the pre-installation scripts of this component, it creates a temporary script file (in its working directory) that contains the specific script and then launches the corresponding NLM that works with the identified script, passing the NLM the name of the script to run. Consequently, `netbasic.nlm` and `perl.nlm` must already exist on the server where the script is to be run. These are installed by default on NetWare servers. Regardless as to whether a script fails or succeeds, the engine proceeds to the next script.

The Local File Copy Property Page

ZENworks allows you to specify local file copy operations to be performed when applying a software package. This can be useful if you need to copy or move files that exist on the local file system to a new directory without making them part of the software package.

For example, suppose that you have configuration files for a software package that are specific to each server, but they need to be moved to a new location for the software package. You can have ZENworks move the files as part of applying the software package to the server.

You can set up a local file copy by selecting the Local File Copy tab of the software package Component object and specifying the following options:

▶ Source Path—Specifies path to the source file(s).

▶ Destination Path—Specifies path to copy the files to.

▶ Include Subdirectories—Indicates whether ZENworks includes any subdirectories located under the source path in the copy.

▶ Maintain Attributes—Indicates whether to maintain the file attributes (read-only, hidden, and so on).

▶ Overwrite Destination Files—Specifies whether ZENworks overwrites files during the copy. This overwrites files regardless of file date.

▶ Maintain Trustees—(NetWare only) Determines whether ZENworks maintains the file system trustees of objects copied. This option is important because improperly setting it could give users access to files that they should not have, or users could lose access to files they need.

▶ Retry When Locked—Specifies whether to retry if the file is locked and, if so, specifies the number of times to retry before failing the copy.

▶ Kill Connection of Opened Files—Allows you to tell ZENworks to kill the connection of a user if a file is locked because they have it opened. Turning on this option has the potential for users to lose data in the file they have opened when their connection is terminated.

▶ Error Processing—Allows you to specify whether ZENworks fails or continues when it encounters an error copying a file. This is useful to allow you to apply the package even if the file copy fails.

▶ Operation—Allows you to specify whether ZENworks moves or copies the file. Use the Move option unless you need to maintain a copy of the file on the system.

The Copy File Property Page

This property page handles the placement of source files onto the server. It places a copy of the specified file (placed into the package) onto the target server. Figure 26.5 displays a sample of this page.

The first step in the Copy File page is to define a file group. A group is a set of files copied onto the server into the same root directory. You may have more than one group in the software package to enable you to copy files to a different root directory. You define a new group by clicking the Add button, and the system prompts you for a group name and a target path. The target path may contain variables. Groups are processed in the order shown in the left panel. If you want to modify the order, select a group and click the up or down arrows to rearrange the order of the groups. Folders and files cannot be reordered.

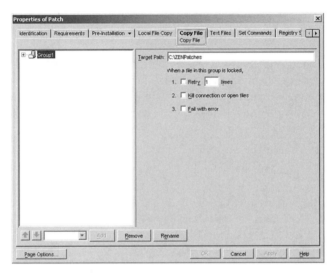

FIGURE 26.5
Copy File property page for a component of a server software package.

After you create a group, you may add files or directories under that file group to have these files and subdirectories created on the target server under the group target path. Select the addition of either subdirectories (folder) or files from the Add menu after your first group is created. You can also select the creation of additional groups through the Add button.

When you create each item, you have the option of naming the folder or file by editing the item name in the left panel. In the right panel, you may choose options with each type to describe how you want to have the system create or delete your files.

Identifying a Folder

A folder identifies a subdirectory under the target path. Select the folder in the left panel with a click of the mouse, and then type in the name you want. The right panel enables you to select whether this folder should be created or deleted. If it is to be created and already exists, nothing happens. If the folder is to be deleted, this folder and all contained files and subfolders are deleted from the server file system.

Identifying a File

Now you may identify a file to be sent to or removed from the target server. Browsing through your file system mapped drives and selecting the file enters the filename. This represents the source path of the file (which can be different from the target path you are generating with the series of paths and folders). In the right pane, you administer the following actions associated with the designated file:

- ▶ Copy Mode—Identifies the method that should be used when copying the file onto the target server from the package. The choices are as follows:

    - ▶ Copy Always—Copies the file onto the target server, either creating the file or overwriting an existing file of the same name.

    - ▶ Copy If Exists—Copies the file only if the file already exists on the server, overwriting the original target file.

    - ▶ Copy If Does Not Exist—Copies the file only if the file does not already exist in the specified location.

    - ▶ Copy If Newer—Copies the file onto a target server only if the file date is newer than the current file on the target server with the same name. If the file does not exist, this will *not* copy the file to the target server.

    - ▶ Copy If Newer and Exists—Copies the file only if it is newer than the existing file or if the file does not exist in the specified target directory.

    - ▶ Delete—Removes the file from the server and does not copy anything from the package.

- ▶ Attributes—Enables you to specify the attributes that should exist on the file after it is placed on the target server. This does not modify any existing file that was not changed in the process. The possible attributes that can be set are Read Only, Archive, Hidden, and Execute.

The Text Files Property Page

This page enables you to enter multiple text file changes into this single package. Text file changes are edits that you want to occur to existing ASCII files on the server. You create the changes by clicking the Add button at the bottom of the screen. When you click the Add button, you are prompted to enter the name of the file (on the target server) to modify. The name should include the full path to the file to ensure that you are modifying the file you want. You can modify more than one text file by selecting Text File from the Add button menu.

You can also make multiple changes to the same text file by selecting the text file, clicking the Add button, and selecting Change. A new change is placed in the left panel with the cursor at the change name, enabling you to edit the name of the change. The changes are applied to the specified file in the order shown. Should you want to change the order of the changes or the order of the files, select the item and move it in the list by clicking the up or down arrow.

After you select a text file to change, choose the corresponding change mode. You may choose either Prepend to File, Append to File, or Search File as one of your modes.

Prepend to File

When you choose to prepend text to the file, the right side of the Administration page changes to display a large text box. You may enter any text strings that you want in the text box and click OK to store this entry. When the change is applied, the exact strings that you typed are placed before the first lines in the existing file.

Append to File

When you choose to append text to the file, the right side of the Administration page changes to display a large text box. You may enter any text strings that you want in the text box and click OK to store this entry. When the change is applied, the exact strings that you typed are placed after the last lines in the existing file.

Search File

If this change is a search file change, you need to administer the following additional information to make the change effective:

1. Identify the search type that you need for this change. The search types are as follows:

▶ Sub-String—Search for the search string in any of the text. The text specified may be contained anywhere in the file, even in the middle of a word. If you have the substring of *day*, the following text would all match with this substring: *today, day, yesterday, daytime,* and so forth.

▶ Whole Word—Search for the string such that it is surrounded by white space or beginning or end of line. If you have the string of *day*, only the word *day* would be a match. The words *today, yesterday, daytime,* and so forth do not constitute a match.

▶ Start of Line—This is a successful match if the beginning of a line (first line of file, or characters following a carriage return) starts with the string, regardless of whether the string is a whole word. If you had the string *day*, this type would match only with the following lines—*daytime is set, day by day,* and so forth.

▶ End of Line—This is a successful match if the end of a line (characters preceding the carriage return or end of file) contains the string, regardless of whether the string is a whole word. If you had the string *day*, this type would match only with the following lines: *the time to act is today, day by day,* and so forth.

▶ Entire Line—The entire specified string must consume the entire line of text (from text following a carriage return, or beginning of the file, to the next carriage return, or end of the file) including any white space. It must be the only characters, other than the carriage returns, on the line. If the string were *day*, only a line with the single word *day* on it would match.

2. Specify the search string you're trying to match. Enter this into the Search String field.

3. Specify whether you want the search to be case-sensitive by checking the box to make the search match only if the case matches.

4. Change the Find all Occurrences field if you want to find only the first occurrence of the string in the file. The default is to have this field checked, meaning that all occurrences in the file will have this policy applied to them.

5. Choose a result action that will be applied to the string after it is located in the file. The possible result actions are as follows:

   ▶ Delete All Lines After—All lines (characters following the next carriage return) are deleted from the file. The file is basically truncated, ending with the line that held the first matching string. Obviously, searching for all occurrences is not effectual when this is the resulting action, as a match truncates the rest of the file.

   ▶ Delete All Lines Before—All lines (characters before and including the previous carriage return) are deleted from the file. The file is reset so that it begins with the line that held the first matching string. With this result action, another search continues, and if another match is found, all the lines before it are deleted as well.

   ▶ Prepend to File If Not Found—This result action places the replacement text in the file at the beginning of the file should the search string not be found in the file. This action only adds text; it doesn't delete or modify text.

   ▶ Append to File If Not Found—This result action places the replacement text at the end of the file should the specified search string not be found. This action only adds text; it doesn't delete or modify text.

   ▶ Replace String—This action takes the matching string and removes it from the file, placing the replacement string in the exact location of the deleted string. If the replacement string is of a different length than the search string, the surrounding characters are shifted to the left or right depending on whether less or more room is required. Basically, the new text is inserted in the location where the search string was removed.

   ▶ Replace Word—This result action takes the word where a substring was matched and replaces the whole word (from beginning of line or space to space or end of line) with the replacement text. If the substring were *day*, the following words would be replaced with the replacement text: *day*, *today*, *daytime*, and so forth.

▶ Replace Line—This action takes the line where the match has occurred and removes the complete line from the file. The replacement text is placed in the same location where the removed line was located in the file.

▶ Append Line—This action appends the replacement string to the line that contained the match. The matching string is not removed from the file; the only change is the addition of text to the end of the line.

6. Specify the new string. In the text box provided, enter the text that will be applied to the file based on the result action specified.

The Set Commands Property Page

This property page enables you to set parameters on the NetWare server as part of the installation of this package. If there is a policy that also modifies a set parameter, the next time that the policy runs it will reset the set parameter to the value defined in the policy.

To add parameters, click the Add button. This activates a wizard to collect potential parameters. Because the set parameters on NetWare are dynamic and can be enhanced by various sets of NLMs, there is not a known set of set parameters. Consequently, ZENworks walks you through a wizard that goes to an identified NetWare server (the server must be running ZENworks Server policy engine) and queries the server for the set of parameters. This list is then transmitted back to the wizard and used as a model for other servers in your network.

To complete the wizard and to add parameters to this component, follow these steps:

1. Click the Add button in the Set Parameters Policy window to activate the wizard.

2. Click the browse button and browse the `EDIRECTORY` tree to the server that has a representative set parameter list. Select that server and click Next. This causes the wizard to query the server and retrieve all possible set parameters.

3. Select the set of parameters that you want to have contained in the component. You can select an entire category by clicking the check box next to the category, or you can open the category and select

individual set parameters. After you select the set of parameters you want to administer with the component, click Finish.

4. You return to the Set Commands property page with the list of only the categories and/or the parameters that you had selected in the wizard. To administer an individual parameter, select the parameter and click the Edit button.

5. When you click Edit, you are presented with a dialog box that is unique for each parameter type. From this dialog box you may administer the value of the parameter. You may also select one of the following choices that administer how the parameter is given to the server:

   ▶ Console—The command is passed to the server console by the policy engine.

   ▶ Autoexec.ncf—In addition to passing the command to the console for immediate activation, the set parameter is placed into the autoexec.ncf file so that following a reboot the server will set the parameter.

   ▶ Startup.ncf—In addition to passing the command to the console for immediate activation, the set parameter is placed into the startup.ncf file so that following a restart the server will set the parameter.

6. Complete the list of parameters and click OK to have these items set as part of the software package.

The Registry Settings Property Page

NetWare 5 introduced a registry to the server; this page enables you to modify or set registry keys into the server. This page is ignored on previous versions of NetWare. This page also allows the setting of registry keys on Windows servers. Figure 26.6 shows this page.

You add a key to the list by clicking the Add button and then selecting the Key menu entry. Each key may have any number of values based on the value syntax. The possible key types are Binary, Expand String, (Default), Dword, Multi-Valued String, and String.

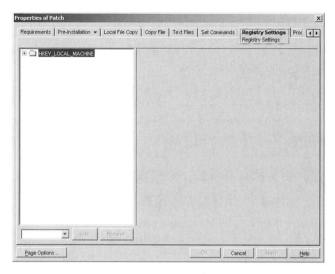

FIGURE 26.6
Registry Settings property page for a component of a server software package.

Each type of key is presented with the value name in the left pane and the actual data value in the right pane. Depending on the type of the value, the right pane will have appropriate fields to enable you to enter the values for the registry key.

You can add multiple values or keys to this property page by continuing to click the Add button and selecting the item you want.

See the section "The `Products.dat` Rule" earlier in this chapter, which discusses the Products.dat property page. The same rules and modifications are available to the component.

Products.dat Property Page

This page allows you to specify any changes you would like to make to the `products.dat` file as a part of this CPK delivery. The choices on this page include no action, add, modify existing entry, or replace existing entry.

- ▶ No Action— No change will be made to the `products.dat` file.

- ▶ Add—This will add the specified entry into the `products.dat` file. When this is chosen, you are prompted to enter the following information: ID, Version, and Desctiption.

▶ Modify Existing Entry—This will search for a specified entry and then modify it with the specified values. When this option is chosen, you must enter the following values: Find Product ID, New Version, and New Description.

▶ Replace Existing Entry—This will search for a specified entry and then replace it with the specified values. When this option is chosen, you must enter the following values: Find Product ID, Find Version, Id, Version, and Description.

Simplifying the Post-Installation Load/Unload Property Page

This identifies the set of NLMs or Java processes that should be loaded or unloaded after the installation process is completed. See the section "The Pre-Installation Load/Unload Property Page" earlier in this chapter for more information.

Outlining Post-Installation Script Property Page

This identifies the set of scripts that should be executed after the installation process is completed. See the section "The Script Property Page" earlier in this chapter for more information.

Compiling the Software Package

After you complete the administration of the software package to include all the files and changes that you want for the installation, you must compile the package before it can be installed on the target server. The compilation process checks the rules and package for any errors and also retrieves the files specified and includes them in the compressed package file. The target package file is expected to have the suffix .CPK. Obviously, because all the files that are to be installed on the target server are contained in the compiled package, the .CPK file will be significantly larger than its .SPK counterpart. So, be prepared to consume some disk space for this process.

To compile a package, right-click the package under the Servers Software Packages container on the ConsoleOne main window and select the

Compile menu choice. This brings up the Compile Wizard that prompts you for the output filename and places the .CPK suffix on that file, if a suffix is not specified. The wizard then compiles the .SPK file into the resulting .CPK file and places it on the disk as specified. The .CPK file can then be installed on the target server after it has been placed on the distribution server and a distribution object has been created and distributed to the target server, or you can copy the .CPK file to the target server manually.

NOTE The files defined in the .SPK are drive dependent, meaning that if you map different drives on another workstation or remap drives, these files may not be found when a compile is requested.

Installing a Server Software Package on the Target Server

After you create a .CPK file by compiling a defined .SPK package, you can place this .CPK file on a target server and request that the ZENworks system install the package and perform the actions specified in the package.

You can get the .CPK file to your target servers a number of different ways: Copy the file to the server, place the file on an external media and take it to the server, or send the .CPK file to the server with TED.

Sending the Compiled File with TED

One alternative is to send your packages through the TED services available through ZENworks. You can create a distribution that contains a server software package and place this distribution into a channel. When the subscriber receives the software package through the channel, it automatically notifies the policy engine (at extraction schedule time) and begins processing the installation package. See Chapter 25 for a more detailed description of how to do this.

Copying the .CPK File Manually

You can get the .CPK file to the server by either creating a movable media that you can then take to your target servers and mount or by copying the file through the file system to a volume on the target server. Be aware that the .CPK file can be extremely large, depending on the files included in it.

After the target server has access to the .CPK file from its local file system, you can request that ZENworks Server Management process the .CPK file by entering the following command on the ZENworks Server Management policy engine console:

```
package process <full path to .CPK file>
```

This spins off a thread that begins the unpacking and installation of the server software package onto the server.

Updating Server Software Packages

When you modify a server software package, the .SPK file automatically updates when you save the changes. The .CPK file, however, is not updated automatically. When you want to update the .CPK file, you need to recompile the package.

If you have set up TED to distribute your software packages, when you update the .CPK file in the same place as listed in TED in a distribution, the package will automatically be sent on the next scheduled update (because it is changed), and the changed package will be installed on the server.

Summary

ZENworks Server Management provides server software packages as a way to deliver and install files onto your servers across your network. You can consider software packages as an installation tool (for example, InstallShield, MSI) for your servers. Software packages are primarily useful for NetWare servers. Windows and Linux servers, although capable of receiving and deploying software packages, have other formats such as MSI and RPM packages, which ZENworks Server Management can deliver and install as well.

## CHAPTER 27

Understanding ZENworks Server Management Services

One of the most difficult tasks network administrators have is to manage large complex networks made up of numerous servers, switches, routers, and other hardware. That task is daunting for most, and for this reason ZENworks Server Management provides a powerful configuration and management engine that can be operated from a centralized location. ZENworks Server Management provides administrators with several monitoring, management, and reporting tools that help them take control of their heterogeneous networks.

This chapter provides an overview of the ZENworks Server Management components and the console interface you use to monitor and manage your network, as well as some strategic planning that you can do to get the most out of ZENworks Server Management services.

Understanding ZENworks Server Management Components

Several different components are provided with ZENworks Server Management, each of which enables you to manage a different aspect of your network. Separately, these components are all useful tools; however, when you use them together they become a powerful management engine. The first step in taking control of your network using ZENworks Server Management is to understand the components that make up ZENworks Server Management services. The following sections cover the main components of ZENworks Server Management services and give you an idea of how they all fit together.

Introducing Management Site Services

The first ZENworks Server Management Service component you need to understand is Management Site Services. Management Site Services is actually a collection of components used to create, monitor, and manage a management site. A *management site* is simply an object in NDS that represents and defines a collection of discovered network objects that together make up a group of resources and services.

Collecting network resources and services together into a single management site allows for easier and more powerful management from a centralized location. The following sections describe the components provided with ZENworks Server Management that are used by Management Site Services.

About Network Discovery

The first component of Management Site Services you need to know is the network discovery component. *Network discovery* is the process of determining the topology of your network by actively probing your network, searching for services and devices that support management information bases (MIB). After you collect the information about the topology of your network, it can be used to enable you to display, monitor, and manage your network from the management console.

For more information about the management console, see the section later in this chapter called, appropriately enough, "About the Management Console."

The following are the two main pieces of software that make up the network discovery component:

▶ Discovery software—A group of modules that run on a management server that searches the network discovering devices to build the network topology. This information is stored in the `NETXPLOR_0.DAT` file.

▶ Consolidator software—Software that runs on the ZENworks Server Management server. It reads data from the NetExplorer data files, which contain all the discovered information from the discovery software. It then interprets the records in the `netxplor.dat` files and populates the ZENworks Server Management database.

Topology Mapping

Now that you understand how the ZENworks Server Management database gets populated, you need to understand the best way to access the information. One of the best tools for accessing information about managed sites is topology mapping through the Atlas Manager. The Atlas Manager is made up of software that reads the ZENworks Server Management database and uses it to create an atlas database and software that displays the network topology in an atlas on the management console. (An *atlas database* is a database that resides on the management server that contains the data used to create the Network Topology view.)

For more information on the management console, see the section "About the Management Console" later in this chapter.

The atlas is a simple view that can be configured to give you the quickest look at your management sites. You can use this atlas of your network topology as a powerful tool to help you monitor your network for heavy usage, outages, and other problems.

About MIB Tools Administration

The next component for ZENworks Server Management site services you should know about is the MIB tools. ZENworks Server Management includes tools to help you monitor and manage all SNMP devices on your network. The following are the two main MIB tools you use to administer SNMP devices:

▶ SNMP MIB Compiler—Parses a set of predefined SNMP MIB files written in ASN.1 and SNMP V2 format, stores the compiled files in the ZENworks Server Management database, and updates trap definitions in the alarm template database. The MIB Compiler also enables you to set new SNMP alarm templates into ZENworks Server Management so that the SNMP alarm templates can be recognized and interpreted as alarms.

▶ SNMP MIB Browser—Takes the compiled MIB and displays the objects in a tree format. The MIB Browser also lets you walk the tree to view and manage the selected MIB objects.

Monitoring SNMP Services

Other components for ZENworks Server Management Site Services you need to know about are the SNMP services that run on managed sites to provide information about connectivity and availability of resources and services within the managed group. These services notify the management console whenever the status of what they are monitoring changes. This gives network administrators fast alarms and information about what is happening on their network.

The following services can be monitored by the ZENworks Server Management SNMP agents:

- ▶ DNS—Domain Name System
- ▶ IP—Internet Protocol
- ▶ DHCP—Dynamic Host Configuration Protocol
- ▶ IPX—Internet Packet Exchange
- ▶ FTP—File Transfer Protocol
- ▶ TFTP—Trivial File Transfer Protocol
- ▶ SMTP—Simple Mail Transfer Protocol
- ▶ SNMP—Simple Network Management Protocol
- ▶ NNTP—Network News Transfer Protocol
- ▶ HTTP—Hypertext Transfer Protocol
- ▶ HTTPS—Hypertext Transfer Protocol Secure
- ▶ NFS—Network File System
- ▶ Echo—Network Echoes
- ▶ Time Service—Network Time Services
- ▶ Wuser—Windows User

Discussing Database Administration

Another important component of Management Site Services is administration of the ZENworks Server Management database. ZENworks Server Management includes a powerful Common Information Model (CIM) compliant database on the management server. The database acts as a repository for server and network data that can be displayed or formatted in various ways to provide specific information you need to manage your network. That information can be displayed or formatted in various ways to provide specific information you need to manage your network. The information ZENworks Server Management collects from your network is stored in the following three logical databases:

- ▶ Topology database—Contains topology, alarms, and map information

- ▶ Inventory database—Contains server inventory data

- ▶ Policy and distribution services database—Logs successes and failures for server policies and Tiered Electronic Distribution components

Using Alarm Management

Another important component of Management Site Services you should be aware of is the ability to manage network alarms throughout the management site. ZENworks Server Management uses alarms to monitor the state of your network and perform predefined actions when an alarm is detected. Alarms recognized by ZENworks Server Management include SNMP traps, connectivity testing, and threshold profiling.

The ZENworks Server Management alarm management system processes SNMP traps and proprietary alarms and then forwards the alarms to subscribing management consoles. You can configure ZENworks Server Management to perform specific actions on an alarm by specifying the desired action in an alarm disposition. The following are some actions that can be automatically performed:

- ▶ Execute a program

- ▶ Send an email notification

- ▶ Create an archive

ZENworks Server Management alarm management enables you to set specific processed alarms to be forwarded to other ZENworks Server Management servers. You can also forward unprocessed SNMP traps directly to a target address of third-party enterprise management applications.

Controlling Your Network with Role-Based Services

The role-based services component of ZENworks Server Management Site Services gives you tight and manageable control of your network. ZENworks Server Management uses role-based services, defined in NDS, to organize ZENworks Server Management tasks into roles and to assign scope information to each role. Role-based services enable you to organize your network management by specifying the tasks each user is authorized to perform.

Reporting

The final component of ZENworks Server Management Site Services you should be aware of is the ability to generate and use reports. ZENworks Server Management provides reporting services for the generation of statistical reports. These reports can be displayed on the management consoles or exported to popular database and Web formats.

ZENworks Server Management reports are powerful tools to understand the state of your network, resolve network problems, and plan for network growth. The following is a list of reports that can be generated by ZENworks Server Management:

- ▶ Health reports—General network health

- ▶ Topology reports—Current network configurations

- ▶ Alarm reports—List of active alarms

- ▶ Server inventory reports—Current server configurations

- ▶ Server policies reports—Current server policy information

- ▶ TED (Tiered Electronic Distribution) reports—Software distribution information

About Server Management

Now that you understand the components involved in ZENworks Server Management Site Services, you need to understand the components specifically for server management. The ZENworks Server Management components enable you to monitor, configure, and control the managed servers and nodes on your network.

ZENworks Server Management is made up of SNMP-based server management agents for NetWare, Windows, and Linux servers, which provide real-time server performance data and information about server alarms and events to network management consoles.

Valuable information about your NetWare, Windows, and Linux servers can be gained by selecting one of the following views from a server or node in ConsoleOne:

- ▶ Console—Provides details about the selected server or node. Enables you to display information about the internal components of the node, such as the devices, operating system, and services available.

▶ Summary—Provides details about the server performance, such as alarms generated by the server, CPU utilization, and available hard drive space. Enables you to view summary information about other components, such as processors, threads, memory, and volumes.

▶ Trend—Displays graphical representations of trend parameters, enabling you to monitor the state of a server over various periods of time. Trend data enables you to track the health status of servers, predict potential problems, and be ready for upgrading your server configurations.

▶ Active Alarms—Displays a list of alarms that are currently active on the server and have not been handled. This allows you to quickly diagnose problems on managed servers.

▶ Alarm History—Displays a list of alarms that have occurred on the managed server, enabling administrators to understand the history of events that have occurred. This can be useful for troubleshooting problems as well as defining deficiencies in the network that need to be addressed.

▶ Conversations—Displays a list of nodes that this server has contacted including the number of packets, bytes, and load percentages. Allows administrators to see which nodes are heavily communicating with the managed server.

ZENworks Server Management components also enable you to configure your NetWare servers as well as execute frequently used commands from the management console.

Analyzing Traffic

In addition to server management, ZENworks Server Management includes powerful tools to help you manage and analyze LAN traffic. The traffic management component provides traffic analysis services that enable a NetWare, Windows, or Linux server to monitor all traffic on an Ethernet, token ring, or FDDI network segment.

ZENworks Server Management traffic analysis tools can be used to understand the general health of your network, predict problem areas, and plan for future growth. The following set of features make up the ZENworks Server Management traffic analysis component:

▶ Standard and enterprise-specific RFC 1757 MIB descriptions for remote network monitoring

▶ Extensions added to NDS, including Remote Network Monitoring (RMON) agent configuration

▶ Network traffic trending and analysis tools to efficiently manage collected data

▶ Canned network health report templates for quick report generation

▶ Integration with topology maps for easy viewing

▶ Performance threshold configuration and profiling for tighter control

▶ A view of conversations on network segment and utilization for problem analysis

▶ Packet capture tools that collect and display LAN packets for problem analysis

Information About Remote Control

Another important component included with ZENworks Server Management is remote control. The remote control component enables remote server management through the management console.

The remote control agent is installed on each NetWare, Windows, or Linux server that you want to remotely control from the management console. The remote control agent ensures that remote control sessions are secure. This enables you to access the NetWare server console or the Windows server and perform maintenance operations without having to be sitting at the machine, thus saving you a considerable amount of time.

Viewing the Server Inventory

Another important component included with ZENworks Server Management is the server inventory. The server inventory component allows you to quickly view the complete hardware and software inventory of all managed servers. ZENworks Server Management server inventory also allows you to query the centralized database of the managed servers to quickly obtain specific information you require.

The server inventory is created by scan programs that identify each managed server by its distinguished name and the tree name and query the server for data. After the scan data is collected, the scan program sends the scan data report to the inventory components on the inventory server. It is stored in the inventory database on the inventory server for later use.

About the Management Console

The most important component of ZENworks Server Management services you should become familiar with is the management console. The management console provides access to all the other components, providing you with a single, centralized location to manage and monitor your network from.

ZENworks Server Management provides several snap-ins to the Novell ConsoleOne management console under the ZENworks Server Management namespace. These snap-ins provide access and control to the ZENworks Server Management services (see the next section for information on how to get the most out of your ZENworks Server Management console).

Using the ZENworks Server Management Console

Now that you understand the components involved with ZENworks Server Management network management services, you need an understanding of how to access, control, and monitor them. ZENworks Server Management includes several snap-ins to the ConsoleOne management tool, which expand its capabilities. This section covers how to use the ConsoleOne snap-ins to manage and monitor your network.

Navigating the ZENworks Server Management Namespace

The first thing you need to understand about the ZENworks Server Management console is how to navigate around the ZENworks Server Management namespace. After ZENworks Server Management services are installed, you have new objects that can be accessed from the main Tree Browse screen in ConsoleOne.

Your network and resources are organized in the namespace as a collection of objects arranged in the following specific hierarchy of objects:

▶ ZENworks Server Management sites object—The ZENworks Server Management namespace container. Resides at the top of the ZENworks Server Management namespace hierarchy. Expanding this object in ConsoleOne displays a list of management sites.

▶ ZENworks Server Management site—Represents a ZENworks Server Management server. It represents an NDS object that defines a collection of discovered objects that collectively make up a group of services. Expanding the site displays an atlas for the services located there.

▶ Atlas—A container object for all objects created during network discovery. Expanding the atlas can show a WAN page, an Area page, and an Islands page, including segments.

▶ Segments—Network objects included within the selected atlas. Expanding a segment reveals a list of server and node objects.

▶ Nodes—Individual network entity. Expanding a node shows you a set of details that describe the node.

▶ Node details—List of system internal components in one of the following three categories: Devices, Operating System, or Services. You can drill down into the server configuration categories further to display more details about the internal components of the server such a CPUs, installed software, volumes, kernel, and adapters.

Setting ZENworks Server Management Console Options

Now that you understand the hierarchy of the ZENworks Server Management namespace in ConsoleOne and can navigate through it to find objects, you need to understand what options you have for managing those objects. From ConsoleOne, you have the ability to view objects in many different ways, set properties for the objects, and perform specific actions on the objects. The following sections describe the various options available from the ZENworks Server Management console.

Understanding Console Views

The first console option you should be aware of is console views. Views are basically different ways of looking at information. ZENworks Server Management provides several different views designed to help you efficiently manage and monitor your network resources. The following is a list of the most common views that you will be using to manage your network:

▶ Atlas—Provides a graphical representation of the discovered network topology, the physical location of nodes, node configuration, and alarm information. This is the easiest view to use to quickly understand the status of your managed network sites.

▶ Console—Displays the objects contained in the selected container object. This is the view to use to navigate the ZENworks Server Management site. It enables you to quickly expand and shrink containers.

▶ Trend—Provides a graphical representation of current and historical trend data by hour, day, week, month, or year. Use this view to monitor network trends, which will help you determine who is using the server and which server is used heavily, troubleshoot network problems, determine how to balance loads across multiple servers, and plan strategies for how to deploy new network resources.

▶ Active Alarms—Provides a tabular display of alarm statistics for all current alarms received from segments or devices, per management site. Use this view to determine any current network alerts because it is updated whenever a new alarm occurs on the network.

▶ Alarm History—Provides a tabular display of all archived alarms, including the handling status of each alarm.

▶ Summary—Provides a tabular view about the selected object's current configuration. The Summary view for a server object, for example, displays information about NLMs, memory usage, adapters, network interfaces, disks and disk controllers, volumes, queues, users, connections, open files, and alarms, as well as installed software.

ZENworks Server Management provides several other views for specific objects in addition to the main views in the preceding list. If you select a memory object, for example, you can select a Disk Cache view that displays utilization for disk cache memory. Similarly, if you select a connections object, you can display an Open Files view that displays information and statistics for the connections on the server.

Setting ZENworks Server Management Properties

ZENworks Server Management provides property pages as well as views for its objects. The property pages enable you to modify settings for each individual object. They are accessed the same way other property pages are accessed in ConsoleOne, by right-clicking the object and selecting Properties. ZENworks Server Management provides property pages at the following levels in its hierarchy:

▶ Site level—Enables you to edit global properties, including alarm dispositions, ZENworks Server Management database settings, SNMP settings, MIB pool entries, and health report profiles.

▶ Server level—Enables you to modify SNMP settings for the managed server.

Performing Actions on Managed Objects

Another option available on some managed objects in the ZENworks Server Management console is the ability to perform an action on the object. The following is a list of actions that you can perform on ZENworks Server Management objects:

▶ Capture packets to and from the server.

▶ Browse the MIB database for the server.

▶ Ping the server's IP address or IPX address.

▶ Perform a connectivity test on the server.

▶ Open a Remote Management Session to load/unload NLMs, mount/dismount volumes, and so on.

▶ Restart the server.

▶ Shut down the server.

▶ Probe manageability of the server.

Managing Console Views

One of the most powerful and important things you should be aware of in the ZENworks Server Management console is the ability to manage the console views. From the management console, you have different options to manage each view based on which of the following types of view it is:

▶ Tabular—Information is organized and displayed in table format. The Console, Active Alarms, and Alarm History are tabular views.

▶ Graphical—The Atlas, Trend, and Summary are graphical views. (The Summary view also contains tabular elements.)

The following sections cover the many options available for you to customize and work with the views to provide you with the most up-to-date and easiest-to-read information about your network.

Changing the Appearance of a View

One of the most useful things you should know about console views is how to modify their appearance. Modifying the appearance can help you make the view easier to read. The following sections cover how to use the ZENworks Server Management console to modify the font, add grid lines, and display the view title.

Changing the Display Font

You may want to change the font in a tabular view to be a different size. If, for example, item names are too long and do not fit in your columns or the columns are too wide for your screen, you may want to make the font size smaller. You may also want to make the font larger to make it more readable.

Follow these steps to change the font used to display text on a tabular view's headings or rows:

1. Select View→Settings→Appearance. The Appearance dialog box appears.

2. Select either the Header Font button or the Row Font button. The Fonts dialog box appears.

3. Select a font from the Font Name list.

4. If you want the font to be displayed in bold or italic, select the appropriate check box.

5. Select the font size from the Size drop-down list.

6. Click OK to close the Fonts dialog box.

7. Click OK to close the Appearance dialog box.

8. If you want to save the changes you've made to the view, select View→Saving→Save.

After you save the settings, the tabular view should begin displaying data with the new font you specified.

Customizing Grid Lines

Although the views displayed by ZENworks Server Management do not contain grid lines, by default, you may want to add them to make the view more readable. Follow these steps to display horizontal and/or vertical grid lines:

1. Select View→Settings→Appearance. The Appearance dialog box appears.

2. Select one of the following grid line styles from the Style drop-down list: No Grid Lines (default), Horizontal Grid Lines Only, Vertical Grid Lines Only, or Vertical and Horizontal Lines.

3. If you want to select a color for the grid lines, click the Color button.

4. Select the color you want to use for the grid lines by using one of the three tab pages; then click OK to close the Color Chooser dialog box.

5. Click OK to close the Appearance dialog box.

6. If you want to save the changes you've made to the view, select View→Saving→Save.

Afte you save the settings, the tabular view should begin displaying data with the new grid lines you specified.

Displaying the View Title

You may want to display the view name in the frame of your current window in ConsoleOne to help you keep track of where you are within the ZENworks Server Management console. To display the view title, select View→Show View Title.

Modifying Columns in Tabular View

Another modification you may want to make to a tabular view is to modify its columns to make it more readable or to fit more data in. The following are operations you can perform on the columns in a tabular view.

Resizing a Column

To resize a column, follow these steps:

1. Move the mouse pointer to the margin between the columns you want to adjust.

2. When the pointer changes to a sizing arrow, click and drag the column to the width you want.

3. If you want to save the changes you've made, select
   View→Saving→Save.

After you save the settings, the tabular view should begin displaying data
with the new column size you specified.

Adding and Removing Columns
To add or remove columns, follow these steps:

1. Select View→Settings→Column Selector.

2. To add a column, select the column name from the Available Fields
   list and click the Add button.

3. To remove a column, select the column name from the Show These
   Fields in This Order list and click the Remove button.

4. Click OK.

5. If you want to save the changes you've made to the view, select
   View→Saving→Save.

After you save the settings, the tabular view should begin displaying data
with the new column list you specified.

Changing the Column Order
To change the column order, follow these steps:

1. Select View→Settings→Column Selector.

2. Select the column you want to move from the Show These Fields in
   This Order lists and then click the Move Up or Move Down button
   to change the location of the column.

3. Click OK.

4. If you want to save the changes you've made to the view, select
   View→Saving→Save.

After you save the settings, the tabular view should begin displaying data
with the new column order you specified.

Limiting Views with Filters
A useful way to manage a tabular view is to filter the entries to limit the
amount of information displayed. You can set up simple filters by selecting a single criterion or more complex filters by using several criteria and
logical relationships as filters.

Follow these steps to set up a filter to limit entries in a tabular view:

1. Select View→Settings→Filter.

2. Select the column by which you want to filter alarms from the first drop-down list.

3. Select an operator from the second drop-down list. The operator defines how to constrain the column you've selected to a value— for example, equal to, not equal to, greater than, less than, greater than or equal to, less than or equal to, contain, or starts with.

4. Select a value for the logical operation set in the previous step.

5. Specify how this filter statement relates to other statements you plan to define by selecting one of the values in the following list from the fourth drop-down list.

6. Click OK when you are finished adding filter statements, and the entries in the view will be filtered according to your criteria.

The following is a list of values that can be used to describe the relationships between different filters for views:

▶ End—Last statement.

▶ New Row—Adds a new line, and you must define a logical relationship between the previous line and the new line.

▶ Delete Row—Removes the current filter row from the filter allowing you to remove unwanted filters without starting over.

▶ And—In the case of a filter statement, both filter statements must be met. In the case of a group of filter statements, the filter statements in both groups must be met.

▶ Or—In the case of a filter statement, at least one of the filter statements must be met. In the case of a group of filter statements, the filter statements in at least one of the groups must be met.

▶ New Group—Begins a new group and a new line that is separated from the rest by an additional drop-down list.

NOTE Filters apply to the current management session only. When you exit the management console, the filters are cleared.

Sorting Views

Another useful way to manage a tabular view is to sort the entries. Sorting the entries can be useful to organize the data obtained from the view.

You can sort the entries based on a single column by simply double-clicking the header of the column you want to use. Double-clicking once sorts the entries in descending order, with the most recent entries first. Double-clicking again sorts the entries in ascending order, with the oldest entries first.

You can also sort a view based on multiple columns by following these steps:

1. Select View→Settings→Sort.

2. Select the first column you want the entries sorted by from the Sort Items By field.

3. Indicate whether you want the entries sorted in ascending or descending order.

4. Select the second column by which you want entries sorted from the Then By field and then select the ascending or descending sort order.

5. Repeat step 4 for each subsequent column for which you want entries sorted.

6. Click OK to finish, and the entries will be sorted based on your criteria.

After you finish, the view should begin displaying data in sorted order based on the settings you specified.

Exporting a View

At any time, you can export a view to a more useful format. This can be useful to put the information on an internal website, to store it in a database, or to use it in a document. The following is a list of formats that ZENworks Server Management views can be exported to by selecting File→Export in ConsoleOne:

▶ HTML

▶ Comma-delimited .CSV file

▶ Tab-delimited text

▶ Blank-space-delimited text

Managing Custom Views

ZENworks Server Management enables you to save and use any customizations that you may have done to views. You should customize ZENworks Server Management views to meet your network's needs and organize them by using the steps in the following sections.

Saving a View

At any time, you can save the changes that you have made to a view by selecting the view you want to save and selecting View→Saving→Save from the main menu. You can also save the view to a different name by selecting View→Saving→Save As and entering a descriptive name.

Deleting/Renaming Customized Views

If you save several views, you may need to delete some or at least rename them to make view management more structured and easier to understand. Follow these steps to either delete or rename a view in ConsoleOne:

1. Click View→Saving→Edit Saved Views.

2. To rename a custom view, select it from the list and click the Rename button.

3. To delete a custom view, select it from the list and click the Delete button.

When you are finished managing the custom views, click the Close button, and the changes you made will be saved.

Planning Your Network Management Services

After you understand the components that make up ZENworks Server Management services and the console used to manage them, you are ready to begin planning a strategy to configure your network to get the most out of ZENworks Server Management. This section covers the steps necessary to understand, plan, and configure your network to maximize the benefits of ZENworks Server Management services.

Defining Management Groups and Needs

The first step you should take in planning for network management is to define what management groups and needs exist in your network. Virtually all organizations are made up of individual groups, each of which requires its own specific information to function. ZENworks Server Management is flexible enough to fit the business needs of each of the groups if you plan your management strategy correctly.

The first step in defining management groups and needs is to identify the individual groups in your organization. These groups should be organized according to management need types. Look for things such as network resources required, management needs, department location, and so forth.

After you identify the groups that require access to network information, you should begin to define the needs each group has. Determine specifically what information each group requires, how often the group accesses the information, and at what times the group accesses it. For example, place servers that require around-the-clock monitoring for critical services into a single group, and place servers used to compile and generate monthly statistical reports into another group.

Planning Your Network Management Strategy

After you define your management groups and needs, you are ready to plan a network management strategy. Your network management strategy should focus on configuring ZENworks Server Management to provide an appropriate level of monitoring for your network with a minimal impact on network performance. This may sound complicated; however, it is really only a matter of organizing the groups you created in the previous step into one of the following categories and then configuring an appropriate polling frequency for each category:

▶ Mission critical—Segments and network devices that need to be actively monitored to ensure high availability. Monitoring on these groups should be set at a high polling frequency.

▶ Crucial—Segments and network devices that need to be actively monitored for availability and usage, or groups that host services that require a balance between polling and network performance. Monitoring on these groups can be set from a few minutes to a few days depending on individual needs.

▶ Common—Segments and network devices that do not need to be actively monitored. Monitoring on these groups should be set to poll infrequently, or can be done manually at the administrator's request.

NOTE Devices that are not polled or are polled infrequently can and should be configured to send alarms to the management server. This ensures that you are notified in the event a critical error occurs on the system; however, your network will not incur a performance hit from active polling.

Configuring Your Network

After you define your network group's needs and plan your network management strategy, configure your network for optimal discovery and monitoring. ZENworks Server Management services rely on standard network protocols to monitor and manage devices on your network. The following sections discuss important considerations to ensure that your network channels are consistent and well configured.

Considerations for IP Addressing

ZENworks Server Management aggressively searches for IP addresses during the discovery process. The following is a list of considerations that you should check for devices you want to be discovered and managed by IP addresses:

▶ The device must have a valid IP address.

▶ TCP/IP must be bound on the designated management console workstations.

▶ IP must be bound on the management server.

▶ A static IP address must be assigned to the management server.

▶ You must verify that a router's addresses are defined in either its management information base (MIB) or seed router table.

▶ Routers must have static IP addresses.

▶ Verify that the subnet mask configuration on all IP networks is correct.

NOTE If a subnet mask is too restrictive, you may not be able to discover all the devices in your management site. The discovery process does not support noncontiguous subnet masks, such as 255.255.0.255.

Identifying IPX Transports

After you verify your IP addressing, look for any software that needs to communicate over IPX. After identifying the IPX transport software, verify that it is configured with an IPX/SPX-compatible transport protocol.

NOTE ZENworks Server Management is fully compatible with the Novell IP compatibility mode driver.

Using IPX Software for NDS and DNS Names Resolution

After you verify your IPX software, check and set up NDS and DNS names for your network devices. ZENworks Server Management uses the server name or hostname instead of the IP or IPX addresses to display maps and configuration views. Set up the most important devices with NDS and DNS names because they are much easier to understand than network addresses. Name resolution can be in the form of local host files, NDS objects, or bindery tables.

Defining Community Names for SNMP Configuration

After setting up your NDS and DNS names, define the community names for your SNMP configuration. SNMP agents and RMON agents, as well as SNMP-enabled devices, require a community name to be identified. You need to configure each SNMP-enabled device with a community name and trap target destination that includes the ZENworks Server Management server.

The community name secures communication channels between the manager and the agent from intruders. The names are set to "public" by default; however, you will want to change the names to something else to prevent outside intruders from accessing information and modifying your system configurations.

Defining Administration Roles

After you configure your network for ZENworks Server Management, you must define roles that will be used to administer it. You can assign administrators specific, defined roles for your organization, which enables you to delegate tasks without compromising network security.

The first step is to define the individuals who will be administering your network. After you have that list of individuals, define a scope for each one based on their access needs to the network. After defining administrators and their scope, they are able to log in and have access to the specific management components that they need to perform their tasks.

The following sections discuss different types of management roles within an organization.

Understanding the ZENworks Server Management Site

The most frequent management role you should use is the management site administrator. The ZENworks Server Management site sets boundaries for access to object data through role-based services. You create roles and tasks that utilize management functions of ZENworks Server Management in the network container space. This defines the level of access to network objects and information.

You need to develop a strategy for creating roles in a management site that reflects your management organization. Use your list of individuals and the scope of their administration needs to plan for roles that manage printers, monitor network traffic, handle alarms, and manage server systems through your network.

NDS user or group objects can be assigned to appropriate roles, thereby acquiring the permissions of the role. The following are the different levels within a role:

- ▶ Roles—Created for the various network management functions in your organization. This simplifies setting permissions and restrictions to management tools and network data.

- ▶ Tasks—Actions performed that utilize components of ZENworks Server Management servers based on assigned responsibility.

- ▶ Component/modules—A specific tool that provides a network management function. (For more information about the components included with ZENworks Server Management services, see the section "Understanding ZENworks Server Management Components" earlier in this chapter.)

Discussing General ZENworks Server Management Roles

After you define the management site roles for your network, take a look at some general roles to cover any individual and management tasks not yet covered.

Several predefined roles exist, or you can define a role by creating an RBS role object in NDS and specifying tasks that the role can perform. The tasks are listed in properties of the RBS task objects in NDS.

The following is a list of predefined roles that ZENworks Server Management creates:

- RBS Admin—Responsible for defining, creating, and administering management roles.

- Segment Administrator—Responsible for administering individual segments, such as adding or deleting users.

- Segment Manager—Responsible for maintaining individual segments, such as adding new workstations or protocols.

- Segment Monitor—Responsible for monitoring network traffic on individual segments.

- Server Administrator—Responsible for administering specific servers, such as adding or deleting users.

- Server Manager—Responsible for maintaining users and applications on specific servers.

- Server Monitor—Responsible for monitoring traffic and services on specific servers.

- Site Database Administrator—Responsible for creating and maintaining ZENworks Server Management database sites.

The following is a list of tasks available to be assigned to role objects:

- Alarm Manager—Gives a role the appropriate rights and assignments to manage alarms raised on a server or segment level.

- Database Object Editor—Gives a role the appropriate rights and assignments to manage ZENworks database objects through the Database Object Editor tool.

- DB_ADMIN_TOOL—Gives a role the appropriate rights and assignments to create and maintain ZENworks databases.

- MIB Browser—Gives a role the appropriate rights and assignments to view MIB objects through MIB Browser.

- MIB Compiler—Gives a role the appropriate rights and assignments to modify and recompile MIBs using MIB compiler.

▶ Node management—Gives a role the appropriate rights and assign-ments to manage individual nodes on a segment.

▶ Remote ping—Gives a role the appropriate rights and assignments to ping nodes on the network remotely.

▶ Traffic management—Gives a role the appropriate rights and assignments to monitor traffic on a server or segment level.

▶ Unified view—Gives a role the appropriate rights and assignments to gain access to the unified view for full network administration.

▶ ZfS maps—Gives a role the appropriate rights and assignments to gain access to the ZfS maps for a complete graphical view of the network.

Summary

This chapter provided an overview of the ZENworks Server Management components and the console interface used to monitor and manage your network. It also looked at some strategic planning topics that you can use to get the most out of ZENworks Server Management services.

## CHAPTER 28

Preparing and Using ZENworks Server Management Network Discovery

Network discovery is one of the first things that must occur before you can begin managing your network with ZENworks Server Management. The manageable devices on the network must be found and stored in the ZENworks Server Management database before they can be configured and managed through ZENworks Server Management. This chapter discusses the discovery process and how to set it up on your network to provide the best topology maps that you can use to manage your network.

Understanding Network Discovery

Network discovery is the process that ZENworks Server Management uses to scan your network and discern its topology. This section discusses the specific components involved in network discovery, the process they use to discover your network topology, and the types of devices discovered.

Understanding the Discovery Components

To understand network discovery, you need to understand the discovery components running on the ZENworks Server Management servers. The discovery components are responsible for scanning your network for devices, collecting data, and transferring that data to NetExplorer.

NetExplorer is the main network discovery module. It is responsible for coordinating the discovery components and collecting their data, which is consolidated into a database where it can be managed and used.

The following sections discuss the main discovery components that make up network discovery: the discovery software, the consolidator software, and the Atlas Manager.

The Discovery Software

The *discovery software* resides on the ZENworks management server. The discovery software is responsible for polling the network and collecting data about devices that exist on the network. The data collected by the discovery software is stored in the `<volume>ZENworks\mms\MMServer\nlmdisk\dat\NETXPLOR.DAT` file.

The discovery software is comprised of the following NLMs that run on the discovery server:

- ▶ `NXPIP.NLM`—Responsible for discovering IP routers on IP networks and sending IP router information to the discovery. It communicates directly with `IPCACHE` and indirectly with `IPGROPER`, which are other discovery modules running on the server, to obtain information.

- ▶ `NXPIPX.NLM`—Responsible for discovering various NetWare systems on IPX networks and sending information about systems to NetExplorer.

- ▶ `IPGROPER.NLM`—Responsible for detecting IP host addresses and services on an IP network, including DHCP services, DNS names, HTTP, SMTP, FTP, SMTP, and telnet.

- ▶ `NXPLANZ.NLM`—Responsible for communicating with traffic analysis agents for NetWare and NT to gather information about all systems communicating on their segments.

NOTE ZENworks Server Management discovery software uses its server and traffic management agents to obtain discovery information. Use these agents throughout your network to improve the speed, reliability, and accuracy of the topology maps.

The server management and traffic analysis agents for NetWare use the Service Advertising Protocol (SAP) to identify themselves to other components. To enable the network discovery component to receive the SAP packets that identify manageable devices on the network, configure your routers so that they are not filtering out the needed SAP packets. Use Table 28.1 to configure your routers.

TABLE 28.1 SAP Numbers for ZENworks Management Devices

COMPONENT	SAP (DECIMAL)	SAP (HEXADECIMAL)
NetExplorer	567	237
NetWare management agent	635	27B
ManageWise agent for Windows Server	651	28B
Traffic analysis agent	570	23A
Print server	7	7
NetWare server	4	4

Understanding the Consolidator Software

Like the discovery software, the consolidator software resides on the ZENworks Server Management server. The consolidator takes the information collected by the discovery software, cleans it up, and stores it in the ZENworks Server Management database for later use.

The following is a list of tasks performed by the consolidator to collect network information and store it in the ZENworks Server Management database:

- ▶ Reads the NETXPLOR.DAT file
- ▶ Interprets the records in the NETXPLOR.DAT file
- ▶ Verifies that the device is not already discovered
- ▶ Queries the bridge management information base (MIB) on IP networks to discover the MAC addresses of all systems on a port
- ▶ Uses the SN3 agent to get the NDS name for network objects
- ▶ Determines whether additional attributes exist in the discovered device
- ▶ Writes the consolidated information to the ZENworks database

The Atlas Manager

The Atlas Manager consists of components that exist both on a server and a client. These components are responsible for reading the ZENworks Server Management database, creating a topology database, and enabling a user to browse and manage the network topology.

The server component runs on the ZENworks Server Management server, where it retrieves discovery information from the ZENworks Server Management database. It then uses that information to create a topology database.

After the topology database is created, the client component of the Atlas Manager can communicate with the Atlas Manager server component. The client component requests topology information from the server component to display topology maps at the client management console. When a user modifies the topology from the client management console, the client component transfers those changes to the server component. The server component then makes the appropriate changes to the topology database.

> **NOTE** For changes made to the network topology from the client to take effect, you must save the database.

Examining Related Components

Other components exist that are not directly discovery components but are used during the discovery process. The following are components that NXPIP.NLM, NXPIPX.NLM, and NXPLANZ.NLM use during the discovery process to obtain a full network topology:

▶ Traffic analysis agent—Discovers all devices on the segments it is monitoring. The NXPLANZ component uses SNMP to query servers running the traffic analysis agent about the devices on their segments.

▶ Server management agent—Respond to SNMP queries from the NXPIPX component. They provide NXPIPX with usernames and addresses of the workstations attached or logged in to them.

▶ NetWare servers—Have internal routing tables stored in their memory. The NXPIPX components query NetWare servers for the information in those tables.

Introducing the Database Object Editor

ZENworks Server Management provides a Database Object Editor (DOE) to supplement the discovery system. Discovery cannot always discover every entity on your network, or it might display incorrect information about some of the entities on your network. The DOE allows you to add the missing entities into the database or edit incorrect information of the entities.

Understanding the Discovery Process

Now that you understand the components that make up network discovery, you need to understand the process that they go through to query your network, collect data about manageable devices, and build a database.

Network discovery occurs in cycles. Each cycle is the process by which one of the discovery modules identifies every device possible, one time. The initial cycle is the first cycle that discovery makes. Although the initial cycle is enough to begin building a topology map, it usually takes several passes to complete the entire network topology.

During the initial discovery cycle, the discovery modules run sequentially; however, after the initial pass, they run independent of each other. The time it takes each module to complete a cycle varies depending on the number of new devices it discovers. When new information is discovered, the discovery modules transfer the data to the NetExplorer, which stores it in a file. Each cycle has the potential to provide the key information NetExplorer needs to identify the device and add it to the database.

The following sections discuss the discovery cycles for each of the discovery modules.

NXPIP

The first sequence in the NetExplorer discovery cycle involves the discovery of IP routers. NXPIP locates its local router by using TCP/IP configuration information and then queries the router for the identity of other routers on the network. NXPIP then queries the MIBs on those routers and collects the IP addresses, interface types, and MAC addresses.

NXPIPX

The NXPIPX discovery begins after NXPIP has completed its first cycle. NXPIPX discovery begins at the management server and uses SNMP, RIP, IPX, and SPX diagnostics to discover attached IPX devices.

NXPIPX begins by examining its own server's routing table and discovers the names of other servers. It then queries each of those servers and repeats the process until no new servers are found.

NXPIPX also reads the connection table of each NetWare server to determine which NetWare clients are logged in to which servers. NXPIPX sends IPX diagnostics packets to the clients to collect additional information about them. NXPIPX also discovers IPX routers in your network.

NOTE If your clients have IPX diagnostics turned off, they will not be discovered.

NXPLANZ
NXPLANZ begins querying after NXPIPX has completed its first cycle. NXPLANZ obtains a list of all traffic analysis agents from NXPIPX and then uses SNMP to query all servers with the traffic analysis agents loaded. It reads the list of workstations that those servers have observed communicating on the network.

NOTE At least one server per network segment should be running the traffic analysis agent for the discovery to be complete.

SNMP Community Name
NetExplorer uses the configured community names from NXPCON each time it attempts to access a system by using SNMP. When it encounters a new system, it runs through the list of names configured in NXPCON until it receives a successful response. After the community name is found, it is stored for later reference.

Understanding What Is Discovered
Now that you understand the process that ZENworks Server Management uses to discover devices on your network, you may want to know what types of devices are being discovered. The devices discovered by ZENworks Server Management can be categorized into either network systems or segments. The following sections discuss the devices discovered by ZENworks Server Management.

Network Systems
The first category of device that the ZENworks Server Management discovery process detects is network systems. Network systems are manageable devices with addresses and/or services associated with them. Network discovery queries the network by using addressing and service requests to find these devices.

The following is a list of network systems discovered by ZENworks Server Management:

▶ Novell Server Management Agent—Service type of 563 decimal (Novell Server Management Agent 1.5 or 1.6) or 635 decimal (Novell Server Management Agent 2.6) or Novell Server Management Agent MIB implemented.

▶ Management Agent for Windows—Management Agent MIB implemented.

▶ Traffic analysis agent for NetWare—Service type of 570 decimal or Traffic Analysis MIB implemented.

▶ Traffic analysis agent for Windows—Traffic Analysis MIB implemented.

▶ Novell NetWare file server—Service type of 4 (file server). NXPIPX discovers all NetWare servers.

▶ Novell NetWare print server—Service type of 71 or 7 decimal.

▶ IPX router—System with more than one adapter connected to different IPX networks.

▶ IP router—System configured as an IP router in MIB-II (IP forwarding enabled).

▶ Novell NetWare client workstation—System that responds to IPX diagnostics requests as an IPX workstation (has the Novell NetWare Shell loaded).

▶ SFT III IOEngine—Discovered by the IPX discovery module; responds with diagnostic information.

▶ SFT III MSEngine—Discovered by the IPX discovery module.

▶ Network printers—Discovered if the printer generates a well-known service type.

▶ Novell NetWare Connect—Service type of 590 decimal.

▶ Novell NetWare communications server—Used by the Novell NetWare for SAA services manager products; has a service type of 304 decimal.

▶ Management server—Running discovery NLM files; has a service type of 567 decimal.

▶ Any system—Any system is discovered if it is connected to a LAN segment being monitored by a traffic analysis agent.

Network Segments

The other category of device that the ZENworks Server Management discovery process detects on your network is network segments. *Network segments* are the communication framework that lies underneath the network systems. The network systems use this framework to communicate with each other. Network discovery detects the different network segment topologies and stores that information in the database. The following sections discuss the different types of network segments discovered by ZENworks Server Management.

LAN and WAN Segments

ZENworks Server Management discovers the typical LAN and WAN segments on your network, provided that they respond with an interface type from the MIB-II RFC 1573 specification. The following is a list of segments known by the ZENworks Server Management database:

▶ ATM—Asynchronous Transfer Mode

▶ FDDI—LAN

▶ Ethernet—LAN

▶ Token ring—LAN

▶ X.25—WAN

▶ PPP—WAN

▶ Frame_Relay—WAN

Source-Route Bridged Token Rings

ZENworks Server Management network discovery also finds source-route bridged token ring segments. How well these segments are discovered and how they appear in your topology map depends on where traffic analysis agents are installed on each of the bridged rings.

NOTE We suggest that you have the traffic analysis agent loaded on at least one NetWare server on each of your bridged rings to provide the best discovery and manageability through ZENworks Server Management.

Transparent Bridges

Network discovery cannot fully discover transparent bridges. Therefore, because they have the same network number, it consolidates groups of transparently bridged segments into a single segment on the topology maps.

Configuration Changes

Network discovery detects most changes in your network topology and relays those changes to the Atlas. But if you remove a device from the network, discovery does not detect the removed device unless it is moved to another location on the network.

Using Network Discovery

Now that you understand the ZENworks Server Management network discovery process, you are ready to begin using it to build a topology database from which you can manage and configure your network.

Configuring and using discovery correctly can improve network bandwidth and make administration much easier. This section covers how to start and stop the network discovery, how to monitor its progress, and how to configure it to correctly discover your network.

Starting and Stopping Network Discovery

The first thing you should know about setting up network discovery is how to start it manually, as well as how to stop it. During the installation, you are prompted whether to start the autodiscovery and back-end services. If you select Yes to those prompts, network discovery automatically launches.

To start the network discovery and load the back-end services on a server, follow these steps:

1. Start the ZENworks Server Management database by entering the **mgmtdbs** command at the ZENworks management server console. This command runs the `mgmtdbs.ncf` file to load the Sybase database engine and the database.

2. Start the rest of the needed ZENworks Server Management processes by entering the **mwserver** command at the server console.

3. Start the autodiscovery process by entering the **netxplor** command at the ZENworks management server console. This command runs the `netxplor.ncf` file, which loads all the discovery modules.

4. Finally, start the basic services on the ZENworks management server by entering the **sloader** command at the console. This command runs the `sloader.ncf` file.

The discovery process runs 24 hours a day while it is loaded. The time required to run the initial discovery and build a complete database of your network varies depending on the size of your network and the load placed on your ZENworks Server Management server.

NOTE The ZENworks Server Management network discovery process occurs in the background on your server. If your server is being heavily used, it takes considerably longer for the network discovery to finish. We suggest that you schedule your network discovery to occur during nonpeak hours—over a weekend, for example.

After the management server is up and running, you can start and stop the discovery process by using the following two commands and the ZENworks Server Management server console:

▶ unxp—An NCF file that unloads the discovery files and halts the discovery process

▶ netxplor—An NCF file that reloads the discovery files, creates a new version of NETXPLOR.DAT, begins the initial discovery process, and processes the discovery data

Checking the Status of the Initial Discovery

After the network discovery process is running, an initial discovery is started. This can take a lengthy amount of time depending on the size of your network. When the initial discovery is completed, your topology maps in the management console reflect the discovered devices while discovery progresses. You must, however, wait for the initial discovery to complete before the topology maps are updated.

The easiest way to determine whether the initial discovery is complete is to use the NXPCON utility on the management server to look at the status of each NetExplorer module. Each module must complete at least one full cycle to complete the initial discovery and draw a complete network map. The following is a list of modules that can be configured to run during discovery:

▶ NXPIP

▶ NXPIPX

▶ NXPLANZ

To view the discovery status, look at the following information displayed on the NetExplorer Console screen, shown in Figure 28.1:

▶ Up Time—Shows the time since the network discovery started running (in Figure 28.1, this is just shown as Up Time).

▶ Status—Shows the overall status of network discovery. If the initial discovery process is still running on at least one module, the value is Initial Cycle in Progress. If the initial discovery process is complete on all modules, the value is Initial Cycle Complete. (In Figure 28.1, the value for this item is 1 Cycle Completed.)

▶ Module Status—Shows the status of each module and the number of cycles each module has completed. In Figure 28.1, note the status listed for NXPIP, NXPIPX, and NXPLANZ.

FIGURE 28.1
Network discovery status on the NetExplorer Console screen.

The following is a list of the different statuses that each module can show and what they mean:

▶ Not Loaded—The module is not loaded. This usually means that this service is not configured for discovery.

▶ Waiting—Module is loaded but is waiting for another module to complete a cycle before it starts.

▶ Running—Module is currently running and collecting network data.

▶ Suspended—Module is suspended because it reached the end of the schedule in which it was running.

▶ Completed—Module completed at least one discovery cycle.

▶ Unknown—NetExplorer cannot obtain the module status. This is either because the module is not loaded, but is configured to run, or because of an internal error inside the module.

Changing the Default Configuration

The ZENworks Server Management network discovery software is installed with configuration defaults designed to work in most network environments. You may, however, want to modify the default configuration to discover more or fewer devices in your network.

To change the default network discovery configuration, you need to use the NXPCON utility on the ZENworks Server Management server. The NXPCON utility is automatically loaded when the NetExplorer software is loaded, or you can load it manually by using the following command at the ZENworks Server Management server console prompt:

```
load nxpcon
```

The following sections describe how you can use the NXPCON utility to choose which discovery modules are loaded, how to change SNMP names, and how to modify the discovery scope to help you optimize the discovery process for your network, and how to ensure workstation discovery.

Choosing Which Modules to Load

After the NXPCON utility is loaded, you can modify which modules are being loaded. If you choose to not load a module, the network discovery is limited to the remaining modules being loaded.

Use the following steps in the NXPCON utility to modify which modules are loaded for network discovery:

1. Select Configuration Options→Discovery Modules.

2. Select the module you want to modify from the Discovery Modules menu, shown in Figure 28.2 and then press Enter.

3. Select No to unload the module or Yes to load the module and then press Enter.

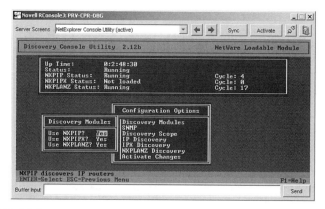

FIGURE 28.2
Network discovery module setting in the NetExplorer Console screen.

   4. Press the Esc key to exit the DiscoveryModules dialog box.

   5. Select Yes.

   6. Unload the NetExplorer software by entering **unxp** at the ZENworks Server Management server's console prompt.

   7. Reload the NetExplorer software by entering **netxplor**, and the changes to network discovery are made.

This allows you to specify the modules of the discovery to load. Next we will discuss the SNMP community names that need to be specified to perform SNMP requests against your systems.

Changing SNMP Community Names

After selecting which modules to load, you may want to change some of the SNMP community names. ZENworks Server Management automatically uses the community name of **public** by default. If your network uses SNMP names other than **public**, you should reconfigure the SNMP names in NXPCON to ensure that your network maintains the proper security.

To view, add, modify, or delete SNMP configuration information from within the NXPCON utility, follow these steps:

   1. Select Configuration Options→SNMP.

   2. Select Edit Community Name List in the SNMP dialog box, shown in Figure 28.3.

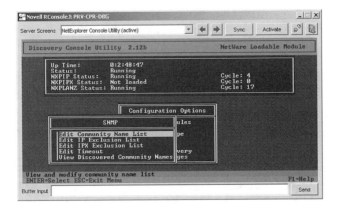

FIGURE 28.3
Network discovery SNMP options dialog box in the NetExplorer Console screen.

3. Select Insert to add a community name; select Delete to delete the highlighted community name; or press Enter to modify the highlighted community name.

4. Press the Esc key to exit from the SNMP dialog box.

5. Select Configuration Options→Activate Changes to update the ZENworks Server Management database.

With these settings accomplished, you should be able to make SNMP requests against your systems. Next we will discuss how to limit the scope that the discovery system uses to find devices in the system.

Changing the Discovery Scope
After you modify your SNMP community names appropriately, you can change the scope of the network discovery. NXPCON is set to discover all IPX and IP networks by default. But if your network is extremely large, you may want to limit the scope of discovery for the following reasons:

▶ Reduce network traffic—Limiting the scope of discovery limits the number of discovery and management packets being sent on your network.

▶ Speed up discovery—Limiting the scope of discovery also speeds up the discovery process by skipping addresses that are not wanted.

▶ Simplify manageability—Limiting the scope of discovery limits the number of objects discovery and thereby reduces the number of objects that appear in the Atlas view. This can make it much easier to navigate the Atlas.

The following two sections discuss how to use the NXPCON utility to modify the network discovery scope.

Changing the IP Discovery Scope

The NXPCON utility enables you to limit the IP discovery scope by address and subnet mask filters. Using these filters enables you to discover only certain segments or addresses.

If you wanted to restrict the discovery scope to your local IP network, for example, you could set a limit to the IP address of your local network and a subnet mask that you want to use. The mask indicates which part of the address needs to match for discovery to proceed on a network segment. The number 0 indicates that no match is required. If your local network IP address were 1.1.x.x, you would use the IP address of 1.1.0.0 and a mask of 255.255.0.0 to capture everything on your local network, but nothing else.

Use the following steps in NXPCON utility to limit the scope of IP discovery:

1. Select Configuration Options→Discovery Scope.

2. Select IP Discovery Scope.

3. Press the Insert key to add a new IP discovery scope entry, press Enter to modify the highlighted scope entry, or press Delete to delete the highlighted scope entry.

4. Enter the address and mask for your discovery, as shown in Figure 28.4.

5. Press the Esc key and select Yes to save the changes to the configuration file.

6. Press the Esc key to exit the Discovery Scope dialog box.

7. Unload the NetExplorer software by typing **unxp** at the console prompt.

8. Reload the NetExplorer software by typing **netxplor** at the console prompt, and the changes will take effect.

FIGURE 28.4
Network IP Discovery Scope dialog box in the NetExplorer Console screen.

This section makes these changes into the IP scope of discovery. The next section discusses how to change the discovery scope for the IPX addresses.

Changing the IPX Discovery Scope

The NXPCON utility enables you to limit the IPX discovery scope by network number and mask filters. Using these filters enables you to discover only certain segments or addresses. A zero in the filter indicates that no match is required.

For example, if you use a specific IPX address on your servers of 1111xxxx, you could limit the scope of your IPX discovery to include only your IPX servers by using the network number of 11110000 and a mask of FFFF0000. Discovery would then pick up only IPX devices whose network number started with 1111.

Use the following steps in the NXPCON utility to limit the scope of IPX discovery:

1. Select Configuration Options→Discovery Scope.

2. Select IPX Discovery Scope.

3. Press the Insert key to add a new IPX discovery scope entry, press Enter to modify the highlighted scope entry, or press Delete to delete the highlighted scope entry.

4. Enter the network number and mask for your discovery, as shown in Figure 28.5.

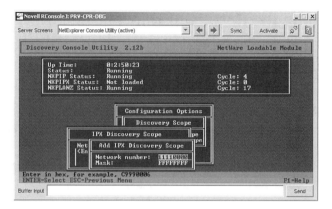

FIGURE 28.5
Network Discovery IPX Mask dialog box in the NetExplorer Console screen.

5. Press the Esc key and select Yes to save the changes to the configuration file.

6. Press the Esc key to exit the Discovery Scope dialog box.

7. Unload the NetExplorer software by typing **unxp** at the console prompt.

8. Reload the NetExplorer software by typing **netxplor** at the console prompt, and the changes will take effect.

This completes the changes in scope for the IPX discovery modules. Now that the scopes are modified for your environment let's verify that we can discover the workstations.

Ensuring Workstation Discovery

After you verify your IPX scopes in the NXPCON utility, you may want to ensure that your IPX workstations will be discovered properly. IPX workstations are discovered with a username if the user is logged in to or attached to a NetWare server running the management agent software. To ensure that your workstations are properly discovered, make sure that the management agent is installed on all NetWare servers that have users attached.

Checking the Results of Network Discovery

You can check the results of the network discovery after the initial discovery is completed and after the ZENworks Server Management database has been updated. Always check your network atlas to determine whether your network topology was accurately discovered.

Your network atlas should have discovered all the servers, desktops, switches, and routers on your network that you configured it for. For each object discovered, the following characteristics are captured:

▶ IP type—IP router, IP host, IP service (HTTP, telnet, SMTP, DNS, FTP, and DHCP)

▶ IPX type—IPX workstation, IPX router, IPX service (file, print, any SAP service)

▶ Subnet mask—Subnet mask used on each segment

▶ NetWare services—Services such as SAP, NCP, and so on

▶ eDirectory names and tree—Full distinguished name of nodes on the network including the tree

If a node is not on your network atlas, check the following things about the device:

▶ Is the device a type that NetExplorer can discover?

▶ Is the node in the incorrect segment? If NetExplorer cannot get enough information about a node, it may simply have been placed in the wrong segment.

▶ Is NetExplorer configured to capture this type of device?

Using the Atlas

After the initial discovery process is complete, you can access the data it collects through the Atlas Manager. The Atlas Manager server component reads the database created by network discovery. It then relays that information to the management console user at the client workstation.

From the client workstation, you can navigate through your network graphically, as shown in Figure 28.6. The following sections discuss using the Atlas to view your discovered network topology.

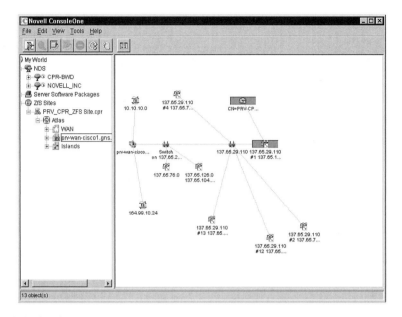

FIGURE 28.6
Graphical Atlas view of a network in ConsoleOne.

Accessing the Atlas

You can use the ConsoleOne utility to access the ZENworks Server
Management network Atlas. The Network Atlas view is a plug-in service
to ConsoleOne that gets installed during the ZENworks Server
Management installation.

To access the Atlas from within ConsoleOne, follow these steps:

1. Double-click the ZENworks Server Management domain. Your
   ZENworks Server Management sites appear.

2. Select the management site you want to view. If the Atlas Manager
   is running on that management server, the Atlas shows up underneath it.

3. Select the Atlas.

4. Right-click the Atlas icon and select Atlas view from the pop-up
   menu. A screen similar to the one shown in Figure 28.7 appears.

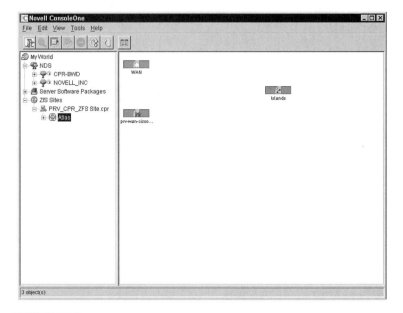

FIGURE 28.7
Atlas view of a network in ConsoleOne.

The initial Atlas screen shows three types of objects, each of which is its own separate Atlas page. These pages represent different views for you to use to see and navigate your network topology. The following list describes the different views you see in each of the three pages:

- ▶ WAN page—Summarizes the entire network by showing the WAN-related network topology. There is usually only one WAN page per network.

- ▶ Area page—Displays the segments on your network. There can be several Area pages on your network, depending on your network configuration as shown in Figure 28.7.

- ▶ Island page—Displays segments with an undetermined connectivity. During discovery, the Island page is a placeholder for network objects not completely discovered. When enough information is obtained about the object, it is moved to an Area or WAN page. There is only one Island page per network.

ZENworks Server Management allows you to perform the following tasks on any of the Atlas pages:

▶ Open—Opens the Atlas page in the view window.

▶ Import—Allows you to insert a wallpaper background for the Atlas view. An example of how this works is to use the `USA.GIF` provided with ZENworks Server Management to display a map of the United States behind your WAN view, allowing you to place your routers and servers on the states that they reside in.

▶ Save—Allows you to save your custom settings for the Atlas view to be used later.

▶ Print—Allows you to print the Atlas view. This feature is useful if you need to take a physical copy of the layout to a planning meeting.

▶ Rename—Allows you to rename the Atlas view to something else. Use names that are as descriptive as possible; you might, for example, use a city name for a router that covers a specific city or a department name for a segment that contains an entire department.

▶ Layout—Changes the focal point and redisplays the page. This is useful if you need to reset the view.

Assigning Management Roles to the Atlas

ZENworks Server Management allows you to assign roles to manage the Atlas, allowing you tighter control over management operations. When you assign a role, you can restrict which operations an operator can perform when managing objects.

You could, for example, restrict a role to a specific segment of the Atlas. Then, when a user accesses the Atlas, the only segment the user can view or manage is that segment. Another example is to restrict a role to adding objects. Anyone using that role can add objects to the Atlas but not delete them.

Using Unified Views

ZENworks Server Management provides a Unified view service that acts as a filter on an Atlas. The Unified view enables you to filter the Atlas based on devices or segments of a particular type. This enables you to easily navigate the Atlas and perform quick operations to check the highest severity of the alarms present in a particular node.

The ZENworks Server Management Unified view service runs on the server and must be running to get the data in the view. Use the `SMGRUI` command at the server console to start and stop the service on the server side. The following sections describe how to use the views after the service is started.

Unified View for Devices

The Unified View for Devices enables you to filter on all manageable or unmanageable devices in the view. This view also displays the MIBs implemented by the device as well as the maximum severity of the alarms against the devices. The following lists the devices that you can filter on from the Unified view:

▶ All (all devices and services)

▶ NetWare servers

▶ Windows devices

▶ Linux devices

▶ IP routers

▶ Routers with unnmbered IP addresses

▶ IPX routers

▶ Switches/bridges

▶ NCP print servers

▶ Printers

▶ TCP services

To filter on specific devices, follow these steps:

1. Right-click the Atlas and select View→Unified View for Devices.

2. From the first drop-down list, select All to list all the devices, select Manageable to list the manageable devices, or select Unmanageable to list the unmanageable devices.

3. From the second drop-down list, select a device.

4. Click the Show button.

This completes the modification of the Unified view for displaying devices. Now let's look at how to modify the view for segments.

Unified View for Segments

The Unified View for Segments enables you to filter on all manageable or unmanageable segments in the view. This view displays the name of the segments as well as the maximum severity of the alarms against the segments. The following lists the segment types you can filter on in the Unified view for segments:

- ▶ All (all types of segments)
- ▶ Ethernet
- ▶ FDDI
- ▶ Token ring
- ▶ Frame Relay
- ▶ X.25
- ▶ ATM
- ▶ PPP
- ▶ IPX compatibility type
- ▶ Unnmbered Network

To filter on specific segments, follow these steps:

1. Right-click the Atlas and select View→Unified View for Segments.

2. From the first drop-down list, select All to list all the segments, select Manageable to list the manageable segments, or select Unmanageable to list the unmanageable segments.

3. Select a segment from the second drop-down list.

4. Click the Show button.

Updating the UNIFIEDVIEW.INI File

ZENworks Server Management allows you to specify your own segment or device types that you want to view in a Unified view. The UNIFIEDVIEW.INI file located in the <vol>:\ZENWORKS\mms\ MWServer\bin\ directory on the server contains details of all the segments and the devices. You can optimize the information that you get from this view by editing this file.

To add a new segment or device type to the Unified view, follow these steps:

1. Open the unifiedview.ini file in a text editor.

2. Add a new entry in the file. The header of the file provides the syntax for adding new entries. The section name should begin with Segment_, and you need to define the values for the properties. The device name should begin with Device_, and you need to define the values for the properties.

3. Save the file.

4. Restart the service, and the changes are implemented.

This makes the changes to your view to ensure that it provides the information you require for your systems. Now let's look at how the Atlas can be used to troubleshoot your systems.

Using the Atlas to Troubleshoot

After the Atlas is up and running, you can use it to monitor and troubleshoot your network. To use the Atlas to troubleshoot your network, you must set alarms for your network devices. When ZENworks Server Management recognizes a critical, major, or even minor alarm on a segment or node, it displays an Alarm icon above the object in the Atlas view.

Using the Database Object Editor

The ZENworks Server Management Database Object Editor (DOE) allows you to perform operations on a segment or on a node object. The DOE server interacts with the consolidator to process information related to the node and segment object, and then populates the CIM table with this information.

The DOE server interacts with the Atlas to process the information related to a page or an atlas object and then populates the MAP table. The DOE client uses the ConsoleOne snap-in to display the user interface; therefore, the user operation is allowed only through the management console view.

Creating a New Segment Using the DOE

The ZENworks Server Management DOE allows you to create your own segments in the Atlas database. This can be useful if you have segments that you need to have in the Atlas but are not being discovered. You could also use this to create segments that you plan to add in the future and to create Atlas views for use in planning. The DOE segment editor, shown in Figure 28.8, enables you to enter the following information about the segments you create:

▶ Segment Name—The name is displayed in the Atlas Manager.

▶ Network Number—The network number associated with the segment.

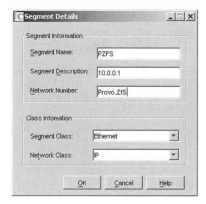

FIGURE 28.8
The Segment Details dialog box for the DOE in ConsoleOne.

▶ Segment Description—A description of the segment. You may, for example, want to include the purpose, location, or other information specific to this segment.

▶ Segment Class—ATM, Ethernet, FDDI, Frame Relay, IPX Compatibility Mode, PPP, Token Ring, Unknown, or X.25.

▶ Network Class—The class of the network the segment is located on.

To create a new segment by using the DOE from the Atlas Manager, follow these steps:

1. Right-click the atlas object you want to create the segment in.

2. Select Database Object Editor→New→Segment from the pop-up menu.

3. Specify the segment settings in the Segment Details dialog box shown previously in Figure 28.8.

4. Click OK to create the object.

This completes the creation of your own customized segment in the Atlas Manager. Now let's review how you can create your own node in the Atlas database.

Creating a New Node Using the DOE

The ZENworks Server Management DOE allows you to create your own node in the Atlas database. This can be useful if you have a workstation or server that you need to have in the Atlas but that is not being discovered. You could also use this to create nodes that you plan to add in the future and to create Atlas views for use in planning.

To create a new node using the DOE from the Atlas Manager, follow these steps:

1. Right-click the atlas object you want to create the node in.

2. Select Database Object Editor→New→Node from the pop-up menu.

3. Specify the node settings in the Node Details dialog box shown in Figures 28.9 through 28.12.

4. Click OK to create the object.

The Node Details windows of the DOE node editor, shown in Figure 28.9, enables you to enter the following information about the nodes you create:

▶ Node Name (mandatory)—The name of the node that appears in the Atlas Manager.

▶ Operating System—The operating system installed on the node.

▶ Type of Node—Node, Router, or Switch.

▶ IP/IPX Router—Selects whether node routes IP, IPX, or both (if the node type is a router).

▶ Prevent Deletion by NetExplorer—Enables you to specify whether NetExplorer will delete the node the next time autodiscovery runs. Check this box if you are adding a node that will not always be available, and you need some specific information in the node object.

The Node Details dialog also provides a list of attributes that are definable for the node you are creating. The following sections describe the options available for each item in the list.

Interface Summary

The Interfaces dialog box (called Interface #1 in Figure 28.10) of the DOE node editor enables you to enter the following information about the nodes you create:

▶ IP Address/IPX Address (mandatory)—Specifies the logical network address of the node. This is an IP address for IP networks or IPX for IPX networks.

FIGURE 28.9
The Node Details dialog box for the DOE in ConsoleOne.

▶ Subnet Mask—Specifies the subnet mask that the node is using to resolve IP.

▶ MAC Address (mandatory)—Specifies the physical MAC address for the network card located in the node.

▶ Network Type—Specifies the type of network the node is located on (IP or IPX).

▶ Interface Type—Specifies the interface type that the node's segment is using.

After you set the preceding information for the node, click OK, and the interface information appears in the Interface Summary list in the Node Details dialog box. You can then add additional interfaces if necessary.

Services
The Available Services and Selected Services lists in the Node Details dialog box of the DOE node editor, shown in Figure 28.11, enable you to enter the services active on the node.

Implemented MIBs
The Implemented MIBs list in the Node Details dialog box of the DOE node editor, shown in Figure 28.12, enables you to enter the MIBs implemented on the node.

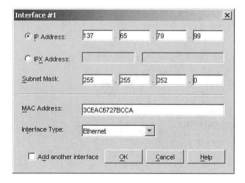

FIGURE 28.10
Interfaces dialog box of the DOE in ConsoleOne.

FIGURE 28.11
Services tab of the Node Details dialog box for the DOE in ConsoleOne.

Switch Summary

The Switch Summary option enables you to specify information specific to nodes that are of switch type. Click the Plus button to bring up the Switch Details dialog box. From this window, you can specify the port number, MAC address, and node information used for switching. To modify the information for a specific port, select the port in the list and click the Details button to bring up the Switch Details dialog box.

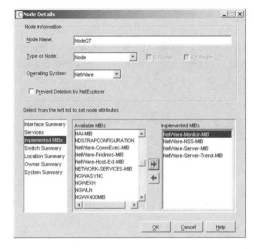

FIGURE 28.12
Implemented MIBs tab of the Node Details dialog box for the DOE in ConsoleOne.

Location Summary

The Location Summary option in the Node Details dialog box of the DOE node editor allows you to specify the location of the node including the address, city, state/region, and country. This can be useful if your network involves multiple buildings or even multiple cities in several countries.

Owner Summary

The Owner Summary option in the Node Details dialog box of the DOE node editor allows you to specify the following information about the person responsible for the node:

▶ Owner Name—Enables you to specify the person who owns or is responsible for the node. This can be the person who uses the node, a supervisor, the IT person responsible, or so on.

▶ Owner Contact—Enables you to specify the contact information for the owner of the node. Usually this is an email address or an office extension.

System Summary

The System Summary option in the Node Details dialog box of the DOE node editor allows you to specify the model, manufacturer, and description of the system. This can be useful in identifying the machines in reports that are run as well as when navigating the Atlas.

Summary

This completes the setting up of network discovery to have ZENworks Server Management automatically find the devices connected in your network. This chapter also demonstrated how to customize the various views available to make the views most effective for you and your environment.

## CHAPTER 29

Using ZENworks Server Management Traffic Analysis

ZENworks Server Management includes LAN traffic analysis tools that help you monitor your LAN traffic, capture traffic data, and collect important statistics of your monitored segments and devices. You can then use the data collected through the LAN traffic tools to understand the usage and performance of your network as well as troubleshoot network issues.

The following sections discuss the different pieces of LAN traffic analysis and how to use them to monitor your managed segments, servers, and other network devices across your multitopology networks.

Understanding LAN Traffic Analysis

ZENworks Server Management LAN traffic analysis is made up of several components that work together to collect, store, and display information about data packets being sent on your network. ZENworks Server Management provides tools that enable you to capture and decode the packets as they are sent from one node to another, giving you the ability to better analyze the traffic. The following sections describe the ZENworks Server Management LAN traffic components, how they communicate, and the functionality of their agents.

Understanding LAN Traffic Components

The ZENworks Server Management LAN traffic analysis system is made up of three main components: the management server, the management console, and the monitoring agent server.

The Management Server

The management server component of ZENworks Server Management LAN traffic analysis is installed on the management site server. It is comprised of a scalable Sybase database that stores static information such as network names and LAN addresses of servers, routers, switches, and other nodes on your network.

The management server components include the NetExplorer, a consolidator, and the Atlas Manager (discussed in Chapter 27, "Understanding ZENworks Server Management Services"). These components gather information about manageable devices on the network and store that information in the management database. The management database is a Common Information Model-2 (CIM-2) database that stores network data used to establish the topology of the network. ZENworks Server Management extends the CIM-2 model to provide the ability to organize the information in the database and create a topology map.

The Management Console

The management console component of ZENworks Server Management LAN traffic analysis is installed on the management client in the form of snap-ins to the ConsoleOne utility. These snap-ins provide an intuitive, graphical method to access data collected by the ZENworks Server Management LAN traffic analysis agents.

The Monitoring Agent Server

The final component of the ZENworks Server Management LAN traffic analysis system is the monitoring agent server. The monitoring agent server is a server with network monitoring agent software installed on it. There must be one monitoring agent server per segment.

The monitoring agent server enables you to analyze a segment by searching the network and gathering information about network traffic. You can then use that information to analyze the LAN traffic on your network.

The network monitoring agents monitor network traffic and capture frames to build a database of objects in the network. Then, network monitoring agent software enables you to use the ZENworks Server Management console traffic analysis tools to maintain your network performance, monitor traffic on your network, and troubleshoot network problems.

Understanding Communication Between Components

Now that you understand what components make up the ZENworks Server Management LAN traffic analysis system, you need to understand how these systems communicate with each other. The management console component communicates with the management server component by using Common Object Request Broker Architecture (CORBA) to obtain static and dynamic information about the managed nodes and devices on your network.

When the management console requests static information from the management server, the management server then communicates with the management database component by using the Java Database Connectivity (JDBC) protocol. It gathers the requested information from the database and relays it back to the management console.

When the management console requests dynamic information from the management server, the management server communicates with the network monitoring agent by using SNMP requests. It gathers the requested information dynamically and relays it back to the management console.

Understanding Agent Functionality

ZENworks Server Management includes several types of monitoring agents to accommodate the various topologies and devices on your network. Network monitoring agents provide the functionality to remotely monitor segments and devices that are SNMP compliant. The agents collect and store statistical and trend information as well as capture real-time data from the managed nodes and devices on your network. The following sections describe the RMON, RMON Lite, RMON Plus, RMON II, and bridge agents to help you decide which one to use based on the size and topology of your network.

RMON Agents

ZENworks Server Management RMON agents use a standard monitoring specification that enables various nodes and console systems on your network to exchange network data. That network data is used to monitor, analyze, and troubleshoot your LAN from a central site.

The RMON agents are typically used to monitor Ethernet, FDDI, and token ring segments. Table 29.1 describes the groups of monitoring elements that make up the RMON agent.

TABLE 29.1 RMON Agent Monitoring Groups

RMON GROUP	DESCRIPTION
Statistics	Records statistics measured by the agents for each monitored interface on the device.
History	Records periodic statistical samples from a network and stores them for later retrieval from the management console.
Alarm	Periodically takes statistical samples from parameters in the agent and compares them with previously configured thresholds. Then, if the monitored parameter crosses a threshold, an alarm event is generated.
Host	Lists the statistics associated with each host discovered on the network.
HostTopN	Prepares tables that describe the hosts that top a list ordered by one of their statistics.
Matrix	Stores statistical information for conversations between two nodes. Creates an entry in its table for each new conversation.
Filters	Enables packets to be matched to a filtered variable. The matched packets form a data stream that may be captured or used to generate events.
Packet Capture	Enables packets to be captured after they flow through a channel.
Events	Controls the generation and notification of events from the device.

RMON Lite Agents
ZENworks Server Management RMON Lite agents also use a standard monitoring specification that enables various devices on your network to exchange network data. The RMON Lite agents are typically used to monitor devices not dedicated for network management, such as a hub or a switch. Table 29.2 describes the groups of monitoring elements that make up the RMON Lite agents.

TABLE 29.2 RMON Lite Agent Monitoring Groups

RMON LITE GROUP	DESCRIPTION
Statistics	Lists statistics measured by the agents for each monitored interface on the device.
History	Records periodic statistical samples from a network and stores them for later retrieval from the management console.
Alarm	Periodically takes statistical samples from parameters in the agent and compares them with previously configured thresholds. Then, if the monitored parameter crosses a threshold, an alarm event is generated.
Events	Controls the generation and notification of events from the device.

RMON Plus Agents

ZENworks Server Management RMON Plus agents are proprietary agents that extend the functionality of the RMON agent. They act exactly the same as the RMON agent and provide the same groups shown in Table 29.1. In addition to providing data collected from the RMON groups, they also provide data collected from the groups shown in Table 29.3.

TABLE 29.3 RMON Plus Agent Monitoring Groups

RMON PLUS GROUP	DESCRIPTION
Buffer	Records the number of octets (excluding framing bits but including frame check sequence octets) in packets captured in the buffer.
Admin	Collects information sent to the agent, such as version number.
HostMonitor	Monitors a set of nodes for a particular host table and sets traps when a host becomes active or inactive.
DuplicateIP	Records and updates lists of packets arriving that contain duplicate IP addresses.
MacToIP	Stores records of the IP addresses associated with host addresses for a host-mapping table.
BoardStatus	Records the status of each logical interface of the RMON or RMON Plus agent.

RMON II Agents

ZENworks Server Management RMON II agents can be used to collect data from nodes and devices in the network and application layers of the network model, unlike the RMON, RMON Lite, and RMON Plus agents, which are used to collect data from nodes and devices in the physical and data link layers of the network model.

RMON II agents can also determine network usage based on the protocol and application used by the nodes in your network. Table 29.4 describes the groups of monitoring elements that make up the RMON II agent.

TABLE 29.4 RMON II Agent Monitoring Groups

RMON II GROUP	DESCRIPTION
Protocol Directory	Creates a table of all identifiable protocols and their descriptions.
Protocol Distribution	Collects statistics for each protocol that the agent is configured to track.
Address Map	Maps a network layer address to the corresponding MAC address.
Network-Layer Host	Collects statistics for each host by network layer address.
Network-Layer Matrix	Collects statistics for each network conversation between pairs of network layer addresses.
Application-Layer Host	Collects statistics on the traffic generated by each host for a specific application layer protocol. The Protocol Directory group can recognize traffic that is broken down by protocols.
Application-Layer Matrix	Collects statistics on conversations between pairs of network layer addresses for a specific application layer protocol. The Protocol Directory group can recognize traffic that is broken down by protocols.
User History	Enables the agent to save samples of RMON II data for any MIB object at specific intervals.
Probe Configuration	Provides remote capability for configuring and querying agent parameters—for example, software updates, IP address changes, resets, and trap destinations.
RMON Conformance	Provides information to the management software regarding the status of support for the group.

Bridge Agents

ZENworks Server Management bridge agents monitor network bridges, enabling you to collect information about switched networks. Table 29.5 describes the groups of monitoring elements that make up the bridge agents.

TABLE 29.5   Bridge Agent Monitoring Groups

BRIDGE GROUP	DESCRIPTION
Base	Stores information about objects applicable to all types of bridges.
Spanning Tree Protocol	Stores information regarding the status of the bridge with respect to the Spanning Tree protocol.
Source Route Bridging	Collects information that describes the status of the device with respect to source route bridging.
Transparent Bridging	Collects information that describes the object's state with respect to transparent bridging.
Static	Collects information that describes the object's state with respect to destination address filtering.

Setting up LAN Traffic Analysis

Now that you understand the components involved in ZENworks Server Management traffic analysis, you are ready to begin setting up traffic analysis on your network. Setting up LAN traffic analysis for ZENworks Server Management involves establishing normal activity for your LAN and then making the necessary configuration changes for the management console to be able to communicate with the management server. The following sections discuss creating a baseline document of normal LAN activity to use as a measurement, selecting the preferred RMON agent, and setting the necessary SNMP parameters for the management console to access the RMON agent.

Creating a Baseline Document

The first step in setting up ZENworks Server Management LAN traffic analysis on your network is to create a baseline document that describes the normal activity and usage of your network. The baseline document should show the normal levels of the most common statistics segments monitored by ZENworks Server Management.

After you create the baseline document, you can use it to identify parts of your network that are experiencing problems, need to be balanced, or need to be upgraded. The following is a list of the most common network statistics that should be used to create a baseline document:

- ▶ Bandwidth utilization—Indicates the percentage of network bandwidth used. Because the network bandwidth tends to be higher at heavy usage times, your baseline document should account for those times—for example, when users are logging on in the morning.

- ▶ Packets per second—Indicates the raw number of packets being transferred on the network. This gives you the best indication of how heavy your network traffic really is.

- ▶ Network error rates—This is also based on heavy usage, so your baseline should take into account periods of the day when heavy usage would cause errors. This helps you identify times when network errors are atypical.

- ▶ Kilobytes per second—Indicates the raw amount of data being transferred on the network. This gives you the best indication of how heavy your network throughput really is.

- ▶ Active servers—Keep track of the three most active servers on the network. This helps you understand where loads need to be balanced and where network upgrades must take place.

Selecting the Preferred RMON Agent

After you create your baseline document, you need to select which remote monitor (RMON) agent you want to monitor each managed segment. The RMON agent is set on the RMON Agent property page for the segment in ConsoleOne. The RMON property page displays the following information, shown in Figure 29.1, about the RMON agent:

- ▶ Preferred—Checked if this server is set as the preferred RMON agent server for the segment.

- ▶ Agent Name—Displays a list of all the servers on which the RMON agent is installed.

▶ Version—Displays the dynamically obtained version number of the RMON agent installed on this server. It is left blank if ZENworks Server Management cannot contact the server to get a version number.

▶ Status—Displays the current status of the RMON agent on the selected segment.

▶ MAC Address—Displays the MAC address of the server.

▶ Interface Index—Displays the number of interface indexes that a server can connect through its network card. Each interface corresponds to a segment.

▶ Available RMON Services—Displays the list of RMON services available from the selected agent (RMON, RMON Plus, or RMON II).

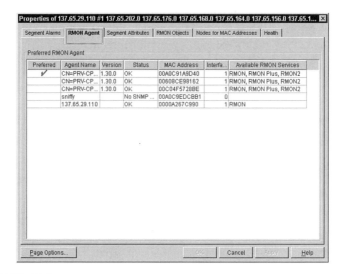

FIGURE 29.1
RMON Agent property page for a segment object in ConsoleOne.

Follow these steps to set an RMON agent as the preferred agent to monitor a segment:

1. Right-click the segment object in ConsoleOne and select Properties from the pop-up menu.

2. Click the RMON Agent tab, as shown in Figure 29.1.

3. Choose a server or workstation name from the list displayed in the properties page and then choose which server acts as the RMON agent for the segment.

4. Click the Apply button to save the settings.

This completes the selection of the RMON agent that will monitor the segment and report the statistics.

Setting Up SNMP Parameters

After you set the preferred RMON agent for each segment, you need to set up the SNMP parameters for the servers hosting your RMON agents. When you request that dynamic information be displayed at the management console, that information is obtained from the monitoring server agents by using SNMP.

Initially, the SNMP communication between the management servers and the management console is based on the default SNMP setting; however, you may want to modify the following settings, as shown in Figure 29.2:

- ▶ SNMP Get (also known as Secure Get)—Encrypts the packets sent by the monitoring agent to the management agent

- ▶ SNMP Set (also known as Secure Set)—Encrypts the packets sent by the management agent to the monitoring agent

- ▶ Community Strings—Community name of the node requesting dynamic data from the agent

- ▶ Number of Retries—Number of times you want the management server to retry connecting to the monitoring agent

- ▶ Timeout in ms—Maximum duration in milliseconds for which the management server should wait for a response from the monitoring agent

- ▶ Port Number—Port on which the management server contacts the monitoring agent

Follow these steps to modify the default SNMP communication for your management servers:

1. Right-click the server object hosting the RMON agent for the segment and select Properties from the pop-up menu.

2. Click the SNMP Settings property page, as shown in Figure 29.2.

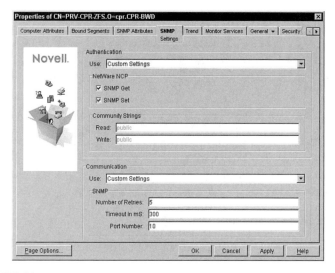

FIGURE 29.2
SNMP Settings tab for a server object in ConsoleOne.

3. Modify the Authentication and Communication settings.

4. Click the Apply button to save your settings.

This completes the configuration of the SNMP parameters necessary to communicate through the system.

Analyzing Network Traffic

After you set up the RMON agents and SNMP parameters for the segments and devices to which you want to analyze traffic, you are ready to begin capturing and analyzing network traffic. ZENworks Server Management enables you to monitor and collect detailed real-time statistics from nodes and segments in your network. That information is displayed back to the management console in the form of tables, graphs, and other graphical displays.

This section discusses how to use the ZENworks Server Management console to monitor and analyze traffic on segments, nodes, protocols, and switches. It also covers how to capture and analyze network packets.

Analyzing Traffic on Network Segments

The most common LAN traffic analysis you will likely be doing is on network segments. You can ensure the most cost-effective, stable, and consistent network by monitoring and managing your segments by using ZENworks Server Management traffic analysis.

ZENworks Server Management provides several different views for analyzing network traffic on segments. The management views translate the data collected by the monitoring agent into an easy to understand graphical and textual form. The following sections discuss how to use the List Segment Statistics, Segment Dashboard, Trend Data, Alarm Statistics, and Summary views on segments to monitor and analyze their traffic.

Viewing Network Statistics for a Segment

The List Segments Statistics view displays a list of segments in your network as well as the following statistical information for each of them, as shown in Figure 29.3:

- ▶ Segment Name—Segment name or address if no name is available.

- ▶ Type—Physical segment type (Ethernet, FDDI, WAN, and so on).

- ▶ Speed (Mbps)—The raw speed of the segment, measured by the speed of the network interface card that attaches the RMON agent to the segment. Cable type is also used to determine the segment speed.

- ▶ Utilization %—Average percentage of the bandwidth currently in use by the traffic on the segment.

- ▶ Packets/s—Average number of packets per second currently being transmitted on the segment.

- ▶ KBytes/s—Average number of kilobytes per second currently being transmitted on the segment.

- ▶ Errors/s—Average number of errors per second the segment is currently incurring.

- ▶ Message—Message describing the current status of the RMON agent on the segment.

Follow these steps from the ZENworks Server Management console to access the List Segments Statistics view:

1. Select a segment or a node from the ZENworks Server Management namespace in the management console.

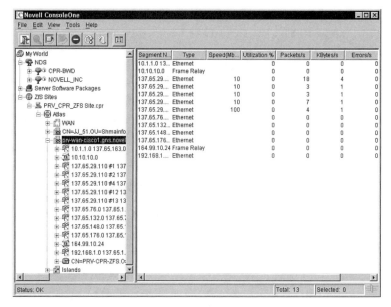

FIGURE 29.3
List Segments Statistics view for a node in ConsoleOne.

2. Select View→List Segment from the main menu, and a screen similar to the one in Figure 29.3 appears.

Determining Individual Segment Performance

The Segment Dashboard view is a graphical view that provides real-time statistical information about an individual monitored segment. Shown in Figure 29.4, it displays four gauges that give the following real-time statistics for that segment, as well as node activity for the top nodes on the segment:

▶ Packets/s—Shows the number of packets per second being transmitted on the segment

▶ Utilization %—Shows the current utilization, compared to the maximum network capacity currently being consumed on the segment

▶ Errors/s—Shows the number of errors per second the segment is currently incurring

▶ Broadcasts/s—Shows the number of broadcast packets per second currently being transmitted on the segment

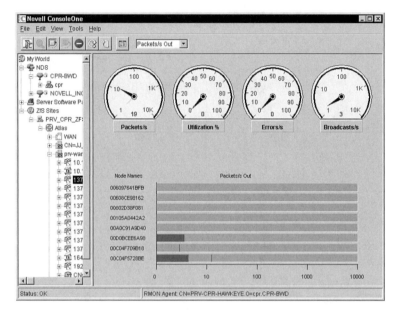

FIGURE 29.4
Segment Dashboard view for a segment in ConsoleOne.

Follow these steps from the ZENworks Server Management console to access the Segment Dashboard view:

1. Select the segment you want to monitor from the ZENworks Server Management namespace in the management console.

2. Select View→Segment Dashboard from the main menu, and a screen similar to the one in Figure 29.4 appears.

Analyzing Segment Trends

Use the Trend Data view in conjunction with the baseline document, discussed earlier in this chapter. The Trend Data view enables you to determine trends of traffic patterns that indicate that a segment is in trouble or needs to be updated or expanded. To access the Trend Data view for a segment from the ZENworks Server Management console, follow these steps:

1. Select the segment you want to monitor from the ZENworks Server Management namespace in the management console.

2. Select View→Segment Trends from the main menu, and a screen similar to the one in Figure 29.5 appears.

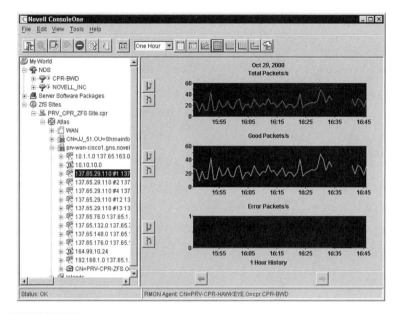

FIGURE 29.5
Trend Data view for a segment in ConsoleOne.

You can configure which statistics to monitor in the Trend Data view.
Follow these steps to configure the statistics that best fit your network:

1. Click the Profile button in the Trend Data view.

2. Select a profile from the Select Profile column in the Edit Profile window.

3. Choose which statistics you want to view in the Select Series column. The available options depend on your network type.

4. Click OK, and the Trend Data view should be updated with your new selections.

This completes how to customize the Trend Data view in a particular segment.

Viewing Alarm Statistics for a Segment

The Alarm Statistics view shows a list of all alarms for the monitored segment along with their threshold and sampling rate. Follow these steps from the ZENworks Server Management console to access the Alarm Statistics view for a segment:

1. Right-click the segment you want to monitor from the ZENworks Server Management namespace in the management console.

2. Select Properties from the pop-up menu.

3. Select the Segment Alarms tab, as shown in Figure 29.6.

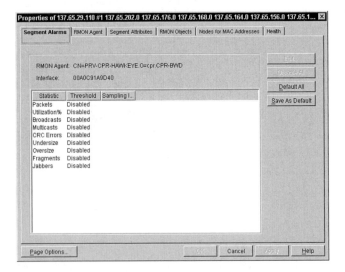

FIGURE 29.6
Segment Alarms tab for a segment object in ConsoleOne.

The alarms can be manually edited by highlighting the alarm and clicking the Edit button, or the Default All button can be used to assign a predefined set of default values to the alarms.

Viewing a Segment Summary

The Segment Summary view is both a graphical and a textual view, which provides a quick summary of the managed segment. This view enables you to quickly assess the current state of the segment. It provides the following static information about the managed segment:

▶ Name—Name or address of the segment

▶ Type—Media type of the segment: Ethernet, token ring, or FDDI

▶ IP Address—IP addresses of the segment

▶ IPX Address—IPX addresses of the segment

▸ Primary Agent—Name of the preferred agent, which is monitoring nodes and traffic on the segment

▸ Agent Status—Current status of the preferred monitoring agent

▸ Nodes—Number of nodes on the segment

▸ IP Nodes—Number of nodes on the segment with IP addresses

▸ IPX Nodes—Number of nodes on the segment with IPX addresses

▸ Servers—Number of NetWare servers on the segment

▸ Workstations—Number of nodes on the segment that are not NetWare servers

▸ Network Probes—Number of monitoring agents available on the segment

▸ Switches—Number of switches on the segment

▸ Routers—Number of routers on the segment

▸ Hubs—Number of hubs on the segment

The Segment Summary view provides the following information about alarms that have occurred on the managed segment:

▸ Severity—Severity level associated with the alarm

▸ From—Network address of the device that sent the alarm to the alarm management system

▸ Summary—Summary of the event, often including the name or address of the object affected by the alarm

▸ Owner—Segment or device affected by the alarm

▸ Received Time—Date and time when the alarm management system received the alarm

▸ Type—Description of the alarm

▸ Category—Category of the alarm based on the MIB

The Segment Summary view provides the following charts and gauges showing you dynamically captured information about the managed segment:

▸ Utilization %—Displays a gauge representing the current real-time usage of the network in relation to the maximum capacity

▸ Packets—Displays a trend graph based on data about packets that have been transmitted on the segment

▶ Protocol Distribution—Displays a pie chart that represents the distribution of protocols on the network

Follow these steps from the ZENworks Server Management console to access the Segment Summary view for a segment:

1. Select the segment you want to monitor from the ZENworks Server Management namespace in the management console.

2. Select View→Segment Summary from the main menu, and a screen similar to the one shown in Figure 29.7 appears.

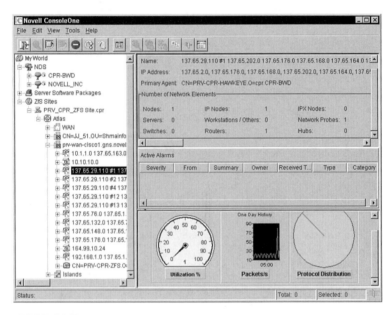

FIGURE 29.7
Segment Summary view for a segment in ConsoleOne.

Analyzing Traffic on Nodes Connected to a Segment

ZENworks Server Management also provides several views to help you monitor and analyze traffic associated with nodes connected to a monitored segment. Monitoring at the segment level gives you a good understanding about the general trends and health of the entire segment. But if you want to analyze traffic at a more granular level, you need to analyze traffic at the node level.

The following sections describe how to use the ZENworks Server Management console to analyze statistics between nodes and to monitor nodes for inactivity.

Analyzing Network Statistics for Stations on a Segment

The first thing that you should do when analyzing traffic of nodes on a segment is to gather information about the most active ones. Viewing the statistics for the most active nodes gives you an indication of how active nodes are on the segment and whether any nodes are exhibiting troubled behavior. ZENworks Server Management provides the Stations view to enable you to view the following statistics on the most active nodes in the segment:

- ▶ MAC Address—Unique physical address of the node
- ▶ Node—Name or address of the node
- ▶ Utilization %—Percentage of maximum network capacity consumed by packets sent from this node
- ▶ Packets/s In—Packets per second received by this node
- ▶ Packets/s Out—Packets per second sent by this node
- ▶ Bytes/s In—Data in bytes per second received by this node
- ▶ Bytes/s Out—Data in bytes per second sent by this node
- ▶ Errors/s—Errors per second received by this node
- ▶ Broadcasts/s—Broadcast packets per second received by this node
- ▶ Multicasts/s—Multicasts per second received by this node
- ▶ Protocols—Types of protocols used by this node
- ▶ First Transmit—Date and time this node first transmitted a packet since the traffic analysis agent was loaded
- ▶ Last Transmit—Date and time this node last transmitted a packet since the traffic analysis agent was loaded

Follow these steps from the ZENworks Server Management console to access the Stations view for a segment:

1. Select the segment you want to monitor nodes on from the ZENworks Server Management namespace in the management console.

2. Select View→Stations from the main menu, and a screen similar to the one in Figure 29.8 appears.

3. Specify what statistic to use in determining a node's activity from the drop-down list at the top of the window.

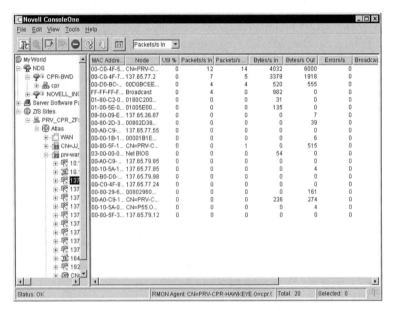

FIGURE 29.8
Segment Stations view for a segment in ConsoleOne.

Analyzing Traffic Between Nodes

The Conversations view is another useful ZENworks Server Management view that allows you to view real-time data showing traffic between a specific node and one or more other nodes on the same segment. Use this information when you need to determine communication activity between specific nodes.

Suppose that you have a database application installed on a node on the segment, and you want to see how traffic from this node behaves when the database is active as opposed to when it is shut down. You would use the Conversations view before and after activating the database and compare the data from each.

The Conversations view provides statistical data on the following characteristics of internode communication:

▶ Node—Name or address of the destination node communicating with the selected node

▶ % Pkt Load—Percentage of the total packet load being used between this node and the destination node

▶ % Byte Load—Percentage of the total byte load being used between this node and the destination node

▶ Pkts/s In—Number of packets received per second by the destination node from this node

▶ Pkts/s Out—Number of packets sent per second from the destination node to this node

▶ Bytes/s In—Number of bytes of data received per second by the destination node from this node

▶ Bytes/s Out—Number of bytes of data sent per second from the destination node to this node

▶ Pkts In—Number of packets received by the destination node from this node since the view was opened

▶ Pkts Out—Number of packets sent by the destination node to this node since the view was opened

▶ KBytes In—Number of kilobytes of data received by the destination node from this node since the view was opened

▶ KBytes Out—Number of kilobytes of data sent by the destination node to this node since the view was opened

▶ Protocols—Protocol packet types used by the destination node to communicate with this node

▶ First Transmit—Date and time that this node first transmitted on the network since the traffic analysis agent was loaded

▶ Last Transmit—Date and time that this node last transmitted on the network since the traffic analysis agent was loaded

Follow these steps from the ZENworks Server Management console to access the Conversations view for a node:

1. Select the node you want to monitor conversations on from the ZENworks Server Management namespace in the management console.

2. Select View→Conversations from the main menu, and a screen similar to the one shown in Figure 29.9 appears.

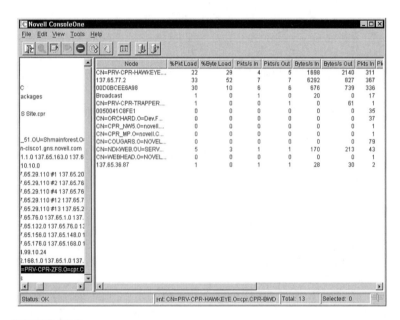

FIGURE 29.9
Conversations view for a node in ConsoleOne.

Monitoring Nodes for Inactivity

Another useful way to monitor network traffic at a node level is to monitor nodes for inactivity. ZENworks Server Management enables you to monitor nodes to determine whether they become inactive and alert you if they do. This does not impact network traffic because the traffic analysis agent does not poll the node to obtain status. Follow these steps from the ZENworks Server Management console to set it to monitor inactivity of a node:

1. Choose View→Monitor Nodes for Inactivity from the menu in ConsoleOne.

2. Click the Add Nodes icon from the icon bar at the top of ConsoleOne. (The Add Nodes icon is a target with a plus sign.)

3. Browse to and select the node you want to add to the list to monitor. Continue to add nodes until you have completed your list.

After you select the nodes that you want to monitor, you can view the following information about them from the Monitor Nodes for Inactivity view:

- ▶ Name—Name of the node being monitored

- ▶ MAC Address—Unique physical address of the node

- ▶ Status—Current status of the node (updated every 60 seconds by default)

Follow these steps from the ZENworks Server Management console to access the Monitor Nodes for Inactivity view:

1. Select the segment for which you want to see a list of nodes monitored for inactivity from the ZENworks Server Management namespace in the management console.

2. Select View→Monitor Nodes for Inactivity from the main menu.

Capturing Packets from the Network

ZENworks Server Management makes it possible for you to be even more detailed than LAN traffic analysis at a node level by enabling you to capture specific sequences of packets from the network. As nodes communicate on a segment, they send packet sequences to each other, which are captured by the RMON agents in a local buffer and can be accessed by the management console.

Packet captures provide much more detail to LAN traffic analysis because they provide information about requests and replies that nodes are making on the network. This can be useful in troubleshooting interserver or client-to-server communication issues.

The following sections describe how to use the ZENworks Server Management console to set up a filter and capture packets from the network.

Setting Up a Capture Filter

The first step in capturing packets from a segment is to set up a filter to limit the number of packets captured. Without a filter, far too many packets would be captured, making it difficult to use the capture.

Filtering enables you to capture only the packets needed. If you are troubleshooting a client-to-server communication issue on an IP application, for example, you would want to capture only IP packets between the client node and the server node.

Follow these steps from the ZENworks Server Management console to define a capture filter:

1. Select a node or a segment from the ZENworks Server Management namespace in ConsoleOne.

2. Select File→Actions→Capture Packets from the main menu. The Packet Capture Setup window, shown in Figure 29.10, appears.

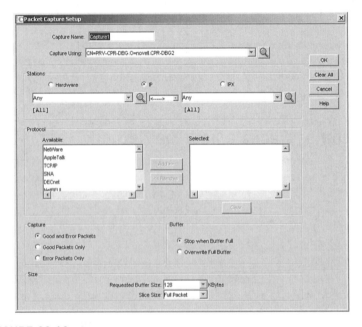

FIGURE 29.10
Packet Capture Setup window for filtering packet captures in ConsoleOne.

3. Type in a descriptive name for the buffer in the Capture Name text box. This typically should describe the purpose of the capture.

4. Select the source and destination nodes from drop-down lists in the Stations box and specify whether you want to capture packets based on an IP, IPX, or hardware address. You can use Any for either the source or destination, or Both to include all nodes. If it's possible, use specific nodes to reduce the size of the capture.

5. Select the direction of traffic flow between nodes. You can select only source to destination, only destination to source, or both directions. This can help limit the capture greatly if you only need one direction.

6. Add protocols to filter on by selecting the protocol in the Selected Protocols list and clicking the Add button. If you do not add protocols to filter on, all protocols are captured.

7. Specify what kind of packets to capture. See Table 29.6 for a list of available statistics by topology.

8. Specify whether you want to overwrite the buffer or stop the capture when the buffer is full. Overwriting the buffer means that the oldest packets are overwritten with the newest ones. If you specify to overwrite, you must manually stop the capture.

9. Specify the buffer size. This depends on what you need to capture and for how long. If you are capturing all packets from all nodes, you need a very large buffer; however, if you only need packets from one node to another one, the default buffer of 129KB is probably enough. Keep in mind that there must be enough free memory at the RMON server to create the buffer.

10. Specify the packet slice size. The Slice Size field specifies the maximum number of bytes of each packet, starting from the packet header, to store in the buffer. This also depends on what you need out of the capture. For header information, you only need 150 bytes or so. But if you need data out of the packet itself, you should select the full packet. This parameter determines the number of packets that a buffer can hold.

11. Click OK, and the filter will be set.

This completes the setup of the capture filter options of the Management and Monitoring system.

TABLE 29.6 Available Statistics to Filter on Based on Segment Type

SEGMENT TYPE	AVAILABLE STATISTICS	DEFAULT STATISTICS
Ethernet	Only good packets, only error packets, both good and error packets	Both good and error packets
FDDI ring	All packets, LLC packets, MAC packets, SMT packets	All packets
Token ring	All packets, non-MAC packets, MAC packets	All packets

Starting a Packet Capture

After you set the filter, you are ready to start the capture. When you click OK from the Packet Capture Filter window, a Capture Status window similar to the one shown in Figure 29.11 appears. The Capture Status window displays the following information about the capture:

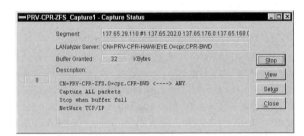

FIGURE 29.11
Packet Capture Status window for packet captures in ConsoleOne.

▶ Segment—Name or address of the segment on which the packet capture is occurring

▶ LANalyzer Server—Name or address of the server running the RMON agent collecting the captured packets

▶ Buffer Granted—Size of the buffer used for the capture

▶ Description—Description of the filter settings for the capture

▶ Count—Incrementing count, shown as 8 in Figure 29.11, for every packet captured

From the Capture Status window, click the Start button to start the capture. If you are trying to capture a specific sequence, start the capture and then perform the sequence—for example, opening a database file or starting an application. When you have captured enough packets, you can click the Stop button to stop the capture, or you can simply wait until the buffer fills up if you specified to stop the capture when the buffer is full.

Analyzing Captured Packets

After you set up a capture filter and capture the sequence of packets, you are ready to begin analyzing them from the management console. The packet captures reside on the server hosting the RMON agent; however, ZENworks Server Management retrieves the packet data from the RMON agent individually as you view each packet.

Viewing Captured Packets

ZENworks Server Management provides a useful Trace Display view to help you view and decode packet data. The Trace Display view, shown in Figure 29.12, provides summary information about the captured packets (top), a decoded view of the selected packet (middle), and a hexadecimal view of the packet (bottom).

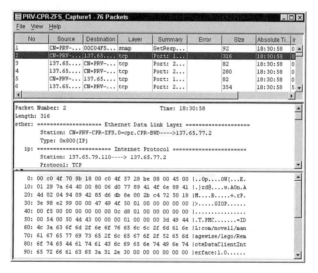

FIGURE 29.12
Packet capture Trace Display view for packet captures in ConsoleOne.

You can open the Trace Display view by clicking the View button on the Capture Status window or by selecting Tools→View Packet File from the main menu in ConsoleOne and then selecting a trace file in the Open dialog box.

The following sections discuss the three different sections of the Trace Display view.

Captured Packet Summary

The summary pane in the Trace Display view displays a list of captured packets providing you with an overview of the communications between source and destination nodes. You can highlight a packet in this pane to display the decoded and hexadecimal packet data in the panes below. The summary pane provides the following statistical information about the captured packets:

▶ No.—Numbers the packets in the order in which they were received at the RMON agent

▶ Source—Name or MAC address of the node from which the packet was sent

▶ Destination—Name or MAC address to which the packet was sent

▶ Layer—Abbreviation of the highest protocol layer in the packet—for example, "ncp" for NetWare Core Protocol or "ether" for Ethernet

▶ Summary—Displays a brief description of the contents of the highest protocol layer

▶ Error—Shows the error type, if any, that occurred in the packet

▶ Size—Displays the number of bytes contained in the packet

▶ Absolute Time—Displays the hardware clock time when the packet arrived

▶ Interpacket Time—Displays the time that elapsed from the end of the preceding packet to the end of the current packet

▶ Relative Time—Displays the time that elapsed since the arrival of the oldest packet still in the buffer

Decoded Packet Data

The decode pane in the Trace Display view displays detailed information about the contents of the selected packet. The packet data is decoded and displayed according to defined protocol fields. This is a useful tool because it tells you information such as the station that sent the packet, protocol, NCP request information, reply results, and so forth. You typically use this field to understand packet sequences and why they failed.

Hexadecimal Packet Data

The hexadecimal pane in the Trace Display view displays the raw packet data in hexadecimal format. The column on the left is the hexadecimal offset from the packet header. The second column is the raw hexadecimal data of the packet. The column on the right is the ASCII form of the hexadecimal data.

You will likely use the hexadecimal display only if you know exactly what you are looking for. If, for example, you know the structure of the data being sent from a client application to a server, you would be able to manually decode the hexadecimal data. The text column of the hexadecimal display, however, is often useful because it shows textual data in the packet. File pathnames, for example, will show up in the ASCII column.

Filtering the Display for Captured Packets

ZENworks Server Management also enables you to filter out packets even after you are viewing the packet trace. This is useful in situations where after you begin viewing a packet trace, you narrow down the problem to a specific node or even a specific request.

Suppose that you originally capture all packets going between a server and all network nodes, but you need to see only the packets going to that server from a specific node. You can filter on only those packets going to the specific node you are troubleshooting.

Another example is if you know the structure of the exact packet type you want to view. You can filter on a value, such as a key sequence, at a specific offset and see only those packets that match.

Follow these steps to set a display filter for captured packets from the Capture Trace view in ConsoleOne:

1. Select View→Filter from the main menu, and the Display Filter dialog box appears.

2. Modify the Stations setting to narrow down to specific stations.

3. Modify the packet direction, if possible, to packets going one way.

4. Add or remove protocols from the selected Protocol list.

5. Set the hexadecimal Offset and the From fields if you are looking for packets containing specific data.

6. Specify the data value and type to search for at the specified offset.

7. Click OK, and your capture display filters on the criteria you have specified.

NOTE If your packet capture is large, you may have to wait a considerable time for the ZENworks Server Management console to be transferred enough of each packet to filter on. This takes up considerable bandwidth. We recommend that you use the capture filter setting to narrow down your captures first.

Highlighting Protocol Fields and Hex Bytes

One of the most valuable features of the Trace Display view is its capability to match data in the decoded pane with the hexadecimal values in the hexadecimal pane. It does this by highlighting the data areas that you select, either in the decode pane, the hexadecimal pane, or in both panes. The following is a list of examples of how you can use the highlighting tool:

- ▶ Highlight a protocol layer in the decode pane and view the hexadecimal bytes in the Hex view.

- ▶ Click a specific field in the decode pane and view the hexadecimal value associated with it.

- ▶ Click a hexadecimal byte in the hexadecimal pane and see which protocol field is associated with it in the decode pane.

- ▶ Click ASCII text in the hexadecimal pane and see the hexadecimal values and the specific decode field associated with it.

NOTE You can save a trace file to a *.tr1 file format so that you can send it to someone else to look at, too, by selecting File→Save Unfiltered Packets or File→Save Filtered Packets.

Analyzing Protocol Traffic

The ZENworks Server Management traffic analysis agent also allows you to monitor statistics of traffic generated by protocols in your network.

Displaying Protocols Used on a Network

The RMON II agent object in the eDirectory tree provides a Protocol Directory property page to view a list of supported and custom protocols used in the network. This is a hierarchical list with the protocols used in the data link layer at the top level. Follow these steps from within ConsoleOne to display the protocols used on your network:

1. Select the node object running the RMON II agent from the ZENworks Server Management namespace.

2. Expand the view by clicking the plus sign next to it.

3. Expand the view for the services object.

4. Right-click the RMON II object under Services and select Properties from the pop-up menu.

5. Select the Protocol Directory tab.

From the Protocol Directory tab, you can also add custom protocols to the supported protocol tree by clicking the Add button. You can also click the Remove button to remove a protocol from being monitored in the tree.

Determining Segment Distribution of Protocols

ZENworks Server Management also enables you to view the distribution of protocols on a segment. This gives the following statistics of the protocol communications in the network layer, transport layer, and application layer that are occurring on your network:

▶ Protocol Name—The name of the protocol

▶ Packets/s—The average number of packets per second being sent using this protocol

▶ Bytes/s—The average number of bytes of data per second being sent using this protocol

▶ Packet Rate %—The percentage of packets transmitted using this protocol, relative to the total percentage of packets transmitted

▶ Byte Rate %—The percentage of bytes of data transmitted using this protocol, relative to the total bytes of data being transmitted

Follow these steps from within the ZENworks Server Management namespace in ConsoleOne to view the distribution of protocols in a segment:

1. Select the managed segment for which you want to view protocols.

2. Select View→Protocol Distribution from the main menu. A window similar to the one shown in Figure 29.13 appears.

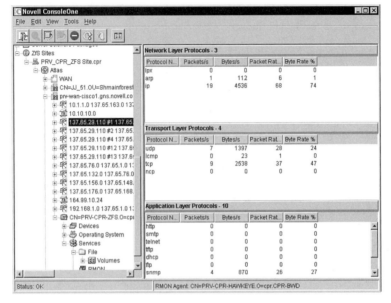

FIGURE 29.13
Protocol Distribution view for a segment object in ConsoleOne.

Analyzing Switch Traffic

The ZENworks Server Management traffic analysis agent also enables you to monitor statistics of traffic generated on switches in your network. This helps you determine the load on workstation and workgroup switches in your network, enabling you to plan for future upgrades.

ZENworks Server Management monitors ports and nodes connected to those ports by using an RMON agent, external RMON agent, or bridge agent. The following sections discuss how to use these agents to display statistics for ports on the switches on your network and to view the summarized information for a specific switch.

Viewing Port Statistics for a Switch

You can view port statistics of a switch by using the ZENworks Server Management Unified Port Traffic view. This view obtains statistical information about every port in your network. It then displays a list of nodes connected to ports on the switch and statistics for each port.

Follow these steps from within the ZENworks Server Management name-space in ConsoleOne to display the Unified Port Traffic view:

1. Select the managed switch on which to view port statistics.

2. Expand the view by clicking the plus sign next to the switch.

3. Expand the view by clicking the plus sign next to Services under the switch.

4. Select Switch/Bridge under Services.

You can now select View→Port Traffic from the main menu to bring up the Unified Port Traffic view.

Viewing Switch Summary Data

ZENworks Server Management also provides a summary view of switch data that provides brief information about the switch. This gives you a quick look at the current status, usage, and alarms generated on the switch. The following statistical information is provided in the Switch Summary view:

▶ Vendor—Name of the manufacturer of the switch

▶ Switch Type—Type of switch: transparent or source route

▶ Number of Ports Active—Number of ports currently active on the switch

▶ Forwarding Table Overflow Count—Number of times the forwarding table has exceeded its capacity

▶ Up Time—Time since the switch was last rebooted

▶ Number of Ports Present—Number of ports that actually exist on the switch

▶ Number of MAC Addresses Learned—Number of MAC addresses dynamically discovered by the switch

Follow these steps from within the ZENworks Server Management name-space in ConsoleOne to display the Switch Summary view:

1. Select the managed switch for which to view the summary.

2. Click View→Switch Summary from the main menu to bring up the Switch Summary view.

Setting Up ZENworks Server Management Traffic Analysis Agents

ZENworks Server Management provides traffic analysis agents and RMON agents for both NetWare and Windows to enable you to monitor heterogeneous LANs. These agents collect information about activity on your network and relay that information back to the management agent, which in turn sends it to the management console for viewing.

The following sections describe how to set up and use the traffic analysis agents for both NetWare and Windows.

Setting Up the Traffic Analysis Agents for NetWare

Take some time to set up the traffic analysis agents on the NetWare servers they are installed on. This involves setting the SNMP parameters, modifying the LANZ.NCF file, and restarting the agents.

Configuring NetWare SNMP Parameters

The fist step in setting up ZENworks Server Management traffic analysis agents on NetWare servers is to configure the SNMP parameters. This involves setting the appropriate read, write, and error-handling options for your agent server.

Follow these steps to configure the SNMP parameters on NetWare servers:

1. At the traffic analysis agent server, load the INETCFG utility.

2. From the Internetworking Configuration screen in the INETCFG utility, select Manage Configuration→Configure SNMP Parameters→Monitor State.

3. From Monitor Community Handling options, select Specified Community May Read, and then enter **public** for the community name and press Enter.

4. Select Control State from the Control Community Handling options, select Specified Community May Write, and then enter **public** for the community name and press Enter.

5. Select Trap State from the Trap Handling options, select Send Traps with Specified Community, and then enter **public** for the community name and press Enter.

6. Press Esc to exit from the SNMP Parameters screen and save changes.

7. Press Esc two more times to exit from the Internetworking Configuration screen and restart the server. These are not changes that the Reinitialize System command makes. For these changes to take place, you have to unload and reload SNMP, and that is done by restarting the server.

This completes the steps for configuring the SNMP parameters on NetWare servers.

Modifying the LANZ.NCF File

The LANZ.NCF file is a script used to launch the traffic analysis agent on NetWare servers. You can modify the LANZ.NCF file to customize agent loading. Use a text editor to modify the commands in Table 29.7 to customize your LANZ.NCF file.

TABLE 29.7   LANZ.NCF File Commands for the Traffic Analysis Agents

COMMAND	DESCRIPTION
LOAD LANZSU DEBUG=1	Enables the LANZ control screen. Add the DEBUG=1 option to turn on the LANZ control screen, which reports significant events for traffic analysis agents on NetWare.
#LOAD LANZFCB	Disables packet capturing to prevent someone from observing secure traffic to and from the server. Comment out the load line for LANZFCB by putting a # sign in front of the statement to disable packet capturing.
LOAD LANZSM DUPIP=0	Disables generation of duplicate IP address alarms to prevent alarm generation in a DHCP environment. Add the DUPIP=0 option to disable duplicate IP address alarms.

TABLE 29.7 Continued

COMMAND	DESCRIPTION
LOAD LANZDI LEVEL=1	Sets packet flow control to yield to other server operations when traffic is high. This reduces the impact of traffic analysis on the server. Add the LEVEL=1 option to enable flow control.
LOAD LANZMEM BOUND=####	Sets the upper limit of available memory to increase the memory that the traffic analysis agents will take. Add the BOUND=#### option to set the amount of memory (####) traffic analysis will use before returning an out-of-memory error.
LOADLANZMEM BOUND=3072 AGE=###	Sets the amount of time the traffic analysis agent will hold data in memory. Add the age to specify the amount of time, measured in hours, that traffic analysis data will be left in memory before it is purged.
LOAD LANZSM TOPN=#	Sorts the number of concurrent sort computations per network adapter. Add the TOPN=# to set the number, between 2 and 10, of sort computations.
LOAD LANZCTL TRAPREG=1	Enables alarms to be sent automatically to the management console. Add the TRAPREG=1 option to tell the traffic analysis agent to automatically send SNMP alarms to management consoles.
LOAD LANZTR POLL=#	Enables/disables polling of source routed bridges on token ring networks. Add the POLL=# option, where # = 0 for off or # = 1 for on, to turn polling of source routed bridges on or off.

Starting/Stopping the Agent

The ZENworks Server Management LAN traffic agents for NetWare are comprised of several modules. The following two script files are included with ZENworks Server Management and should be used to start and stop the LAN traffic agents:

▶ `LANZ.NCF`—Script file that loads the LAN traffic agent NLMs

▶ `ULANZ.NCF`—Script file that unloads the LAN traffic agent NLMs

Using the NetWare LANZCON Utility

The LANZCON utility provided with ZENworks Server Management enables you to configure and view the traffic analysis agents. The LANZCON utility is an NLM installed into the `<ZENworks_Volume>:\` `ZFS_AGNT\ LANZ` directory on the servers in which the traffic analysis agents were installed.

Load the LANZCON utility on your NetWare server with the traffic analysis agents running to view and configure the following items:

▶ Network Adapter Information—Types of items currently being monitored by the adapter. You can also enable or disable an adapter from monitoring the network.

▶ Agent Status—Status of the selected agent and items related to the agent monitoring the segment.

▶ Statistics Information—Packet and event statistics for the selected network adapter.

▶ History Information—Provides sampling information collected at intervals for the networks being monitored by this agent—for example, data source, buckets requested, and buckets granted.

▶ Hosts Information—Statistics about specific host or nodes on the monitored network.

▶ Matrix Information—Consists of three tables that record information about conversations between pairs of nodes on the monitored segment.

Setting Up the Traffic Analysis Agents for Windows NT/2000/2003

After you set up the traffic analysis agent on your NetWare servers, take some time to set up the traffic analysis agents on your Windows NT/2000/2003 servers as well. Once again, this involves setting the SNMP parameters and then restarting the agents.

Configuring NT SNMP Parameters

The first step in setting up ZENworks Server Management traffic analysis agents on NT/2000/2003 servers is to configure the SNMP parameters. This involves setting the appropriate read, write, and error-handling options for your agent server. Follow these steps to configure the SNMP parameters on your Windows NT/2000/2003 servers:

1. Open the Windows Services Manager dialog box. In Windows NT, double-click on Network in the Control Panel and select the Services tab. In Windows 2000/2003, select Start→Program Files→Administrative Services→Services.

2. Select SNMP Services from the list of services.

3. Click the Properties button.

4. Click the Traps tab.

5. From the Accepted Community Names box, click the Add button.

6. Enter **public** in the Service Configuration dialog box.

7. Click the Add button.

8. Enter the DNS names or IP addresses of workstations or servers that should receive traps.

9. Click the Add button.

10. Click the Security tab.

11. From the Accepted Community Names, click the Add button.

12. Enter **public** in the Service Configuration dialog box.

13. Set the rights according to your needs.

14. Click the Add button.

15. Select Accept SNMP Packets from Any Host.

16. Click OK to return to the Network window.

NOTE If SNMP is not already installed on the NT Server, after you install it from the NT Server CD, you have to reboot and get some SNMP errors. To correct this, reapply the NT support pack (whichever one you were on or newer).

Starting/Stopping the SNMP Service

Whenever you make changes to the settings for the SNMP service, you should stop and restart the agent. Follow these steps to stop and restart the traffic analysis agent on a Windows NT/2000/2003 server:

1. Open the Services manager.

2. Select SNMP Services.

3. Click the Stop button.

4. When the agent is stopped, click the Start button.

Using the NT LANZCON Utility

The Windows LANZCON utility provided with ZENworks Server Management enables you to configure and view the traffic analysis agents. The Windows LANZCON utility is an executable installed on the desktop of Windows NT/2000/2003 servers that the traffic analysis agents were installed to. Load the LANZCON utility on your Windows NT/2000/2003 server with the traffic analysis agents running to view and configure the following items:

► Configure LANalyzer Agent—Takes the place of editing the LANZ.NCF file on NetWare servers by letting you enable or disable packet capture and enable/disable station monitoring, and set memory bounds and age (how long to retain packet data before it is too old), concurrent sorting, and duplicate IP address alarms.

► Network Adapter—Displays a list of network adapters discovered by the agent. You can enable or disable a network adapter from monitoring the network.

► Agent Log—Displays a list of significant events and errors that occurred during a session.

► Agent Status—Displays the current status and description of all agents installed on the server.

► RMON Tables—Displays the statistics, history control, history data, host control, host entry, host topN control, host topN entry, matrix control, matrix SD entry, filter, channel, and buffer RMON tables for the network adapter. Also displays the alarm, event, and log RMON tables.

► SNMP Traps—Displays a list of traps that occurred on the managed segment, including the received time and a summary of the trap.

NOTE The ZENworks Server Management traffic analysis agent does not have to be installed on every NetWare and Windows NT/2000/2003 server. You need it installed on only one server (NT/2000/2003 or NetWare) per segment that you want to monitor. This also helps with the discovery process.

Summary

This chapter focused on the different pieces of LAN traffic analysis that exist. It looked at how to use them to monitor your managed segments, servers, and other network devices across your multitopology networks.

## CHAPTER 30

Using ZENworks Server Management Alarm Management

One of the most powerful features of ZENworks Server Management is its capability to make network management much more controlled and easy. ZENworks Server Management adds a powerful alarm management system and a service monitoring system to help you more easily monitor, manage, and control problems on your network.

The ZENworks Server Management alarm management system employs a series of trap and alarm handlers to manage and store information about important events occurring on your network. You can then use tools provided by the ZENworks Server Management console to understand, manage, and resolve those events.

The ZENworks Server Management service monitoring system employs utilities and views from the management console to help you actively test and understand the connectivity between the management console and the monitored services. This feature helps you detect, locate, and understand service and network outages much faster.

The following sections describe the components and utilities that make up the ZENworks Server Management alarm management system and the ZENworks Server Management monitoring services system. They also discuss how to configure and use the services to best detect, diagnose, and resolve network issues.

Understanding Alarm Management Components

The ZENworks Server Management alarm management system comprises several components, each of which has a specific responsibility to either send, receive, transfer, handle, store, or view network alarms. ZENworks Server Management uses these components to alert you when conditions or events occur on the network that require an action on your part to resolve.

The following sections discuss the different components that ZENworks Server Management uses to monitor and manage alarms on your network.

The SNMP Trap Receiver

The *SNMP (Simple Network Management Protocol) trap receiver* is an agent that actively receives SNMP traps from managed servers with SNMP agents loaded on them. When the SNMP trap receiver gets an alarm, it is this agent's responsibility to pass the alarm to the SNMP trap injector component and the SNMP trap forwarder component.

The SNMP Trap Forwarder

The *SNMP trap forwarder* checks traps passed from the SNMP trap receiver against the Alarm Manager database to determine whether the trap has an SNMP trap-forwarding disposition. If the Alarm Manager database has a forwarding disposition for the trap, the SNMP trap forwarder forwards the trap based on the criteria specified by the disposition. If there is no forwarding disposition, the SNMP trap forwarder simply ignores the trap.

The SNMP Trap Injector

The *SNMP trap injector* is responsible for converting the SNMP traps into manageable alarms. After the trap is converted into an alarm, the SNMP trap injector then passes the alarm to the alarm injector.

The Alarm Injector

The *alarm injector* is responsible for collecting alarms from the SNMP trap injector as well as other applications that can transfer alarms to the

ZENworks Server Management system. After it receives an alarm, it then passes it to the inbound processor.

The Three Types of Alarm Processors

The alarm processors are responsible for processing network and server alarms that are added to them by the alarm injector. The following are the three types of alarm processors and their functions:

- ▶ Inbound processor—Receives alarms from the alarm injector and applies a predefined alarm template to them. The alarm template is based on SNMP traps and other proprietary definitions based on specific criteria from the ZENworks Server Management alarm management system. After the inbound processor has applied the template to the alarm, it transfers it to the archive processor.

- ▶ Archive processor—Takes alarms from the inbound processor, adds them to a log, and then stores data about them in the Alarm Manager database. After the alarm data is stored, the archive processor passes the alarm to the outbound processor.

- ▶ Outbound processor—Accepts alarms from the archive processor and then dispatches them to the subscription server and the disposition server.

The Alarm Manager Database

Now that you understand how traps are picked up and converted to alarms and then handled by the processors, you need to understand the Alarm Manager database. The Alarm Manager database is responsible for storing information about processed alarms as well as alarm templates and dispositions. The following sections discuss the different types of alarm information stored in the database.

Processed Alarms

The biggest responsibility of the Alarm Manager database is to store data about alarms that have been handled by the alarm processors. This is the data that you can view at the ZENworks Server Management console via the alarm query server, using the alarm reporting.

Alarm Templates

Another key type of alarm information that is stored in the Alarm Manager database are the templates used by the inbound processor to format the alarm so that it can be properly handled by the ZENworks Server Management alarm management system.

Many SNMP traps, for example, do not have an object ID associated with them. But an object ID is required by the ZENworks Server Management alarm management system to process the alarm. Therefore, a template is applied to the alarm at processing, which associates an object ID with the device or node that triggered the alarm.

Alarm Dispositions

The Alarm Manager database also stores any configured alarm dispositions. Alarm dispositions enable you to configure, prior to the alarm occurring, an automated method of handling the alarm. The alarm dispositions enable you to launch applications, send an email alert, and send console alerts in the form of messages or beeps, forwarding the SNMP traps to other ZENworks Server Management systems or even to other non-ZENworks Server Management systems.

Database Archivers

Now that you understand what information is stored in the Alarm Manager database, you need to know what components are responsible for putting it there. The following is a list of alarm database archivers and their responsibilities:

▶ Alarm archiver—Stores the actual data and statistics about alarms that have occurred on the network. You can configure the alarm archiver to store whatever alarms you want to manage. The default for the alarm archiver is to store all alarms.

▶ Disposition archiver—Receives alarm disposition information from the ZENworks Server Management console and saves it to the Alarm Manager database to be used by the SNMP trap forwarder.

▶ Template archive—Stores changes made to alarm templates by the MIB compiler in the database. ZENworks Server Management includes basic templates for all SNMP traps and proprietary alarms; however, you can reconfigure them by using the MIB compiler.

Alarm Viewers

The final component involved in the ZENworks Server Management alarm management system is the alarm viewers. The alarm viewers are simply different views available at the ZENworks Server Management console.

The ZENworks Server Management console uses alarm queries to the Alarm Manager database to provide you with views on currently active alarms as well as historically archived alarms. You should become familiar with how to view alarm information. The different alarm views are discussed more fully in the next section.

Managing ZENworks Server Management Alarms

Now that you understand the components that make up the ZENworks Server Management alarm management system, you need to know how to begin managing alarms on your network. Alarm management is a process of enabling alarms, monitoring for alarm conditions, handling the alarm situations, and deleting the alarm.

The following sections describe how to use the ZENworks Server Management console to enable alarms, disable alarms, understand alarm indicators, work with alarm views, manage alarms, perform actions on the alarms, and then remove alarms from the system.

Enabling and Disabling Alarms

The first task you must be familiar with when managing the ZENworks Server Management alarm management system is how to enable and disable alarms. Alarm thresholds are associated with each managed server and segment. When an alarm threshold is exceeded, an alarm is generated.

Although server threshold alarms are enabled by default, segment threshold alarms are not. You need to use the ZENworks Server Management console to enable and configure the threshold alarms for your network.

Follow these steps in the management console to enable and disable the alarms for your managed servers and segments to best match your needs:

1. Select the server or segment object to which you want to enable or disable alarms.

2. Right-click the object and select Properties from the pop-up menu.

3. Select the Segment Alarms property tab, shown in Figure 30.1.

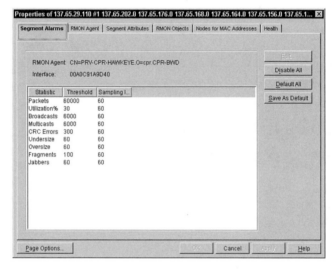

FIGURE 30.1
Segment Alarms property tab for a segment object in ConsoleOne.

4. Select the alarm you want to modify.

5. Click the Edit button, and the Set Alarm Threshold dialog box appears.

6. Select Enable to enable the alarm or deselect Enable to disable the alarm.

7. If you are enabling an alarm, set the threshold value.

8. If you are enabling an alarm, you should also set the amount of time in the Sampling Interval field by which the threshold value must be exceeded to generate the alarm.

After the last step, you can click OK to save your alarm setting and return to the Segment Alarms property tab.

Understanding Alarm Indicators

After enabling, disabling, and configuring the alarm thresholds for the managed servers and segments on you network, ZENworks Server Management starts tracking, storing, and relaying network alarms as they occur. At this point, you need to become familiar with the different alarm indicators so that you can recognize and respond to the alarms as they occur.

The following sections discuss the different indicators that you can watch for when alarms are triggered on your network.

Alarm Icons Anchored to the Affected Object

Alarms that are triggered with a critical, major, or minor severity are displayed in the ZENworks Server Management console in both the Atlas and Console views. When an alarm is triggered on a segment or server being managed by the ZENworks Server Management alarm management system, an Alarm icon is anchored to the object. Therefore, as you browse through the ZENworks Server Management namespace, watch out for Alarm icons.

The Ticker Tape Message on the Status Bar

You can also configure the ZENworks Server Management alarm management system to display alarm messages on the status bar of the management console. This option is on by default. If this option is on, as the alarm management system recognizes an alarm, it displays a descriptive message on the status bar that an alarm has been triggered. This is another thing that you should keep an eye out for. The messages let you know which object is affected so that you can quickly find the problem and resolve it.

The Audible Beep

The final alarm indicator is an audible beep sent to the management console. The alarm management system can be configured to force an audible beep on the management console when an alarm occurs. This is useful if you are not actively browsing or looking for alarms. If you hear a beep on the management console, look for the Alarm icon on your server or segment objects and investigate the alarm.

Working with Alarm Views

Now that you understand the alarm indicators that you should look and listen for, you need to know how to use the views provided with ZENworks Server Management to monitor and manage alarms. The ZENworks Server Management console gives you access to both active and historical data about alarms that are occurring or have occurred on your network.

You can define access restrictions to alarm data and management functions through ZENworks Server Management role-based services. You can also modify the presentation of the alarm data displayed in the views by sorting and filtering on specific data elements.

The following sections discuss the different alarm views provided with ZENworks Server Management and how to use them to monitor and manage alarms.

Monitoring Active Alarms

Active alarms are typically the most important type of alarm that you will encounter. Active alarms indicate that a problem is currently happening on either a monitored segment or a server. The ZENworks Server Management Active Alarm view, shown in Figure 30.2, displays the following alarm statistics for all current alarms for the managed site.

- ▶ Severity—Displays an Alarm icon color coded to indicate the level of alarm severity: Red = Critical, Magenta = Major, Yellow = Minor, Blue = Informational, and White = Unknown.

- ▶ From—Specifies the network address of the device that sent the alarm to the alarm management system.

- ▶ Summary—Displays a summary of the alarm event, including names, addresses, and other information about the alarm.

- ▶ Owner—Specifies the person or group responsible for handling the alarm. SYSTEM is specified until an owner is set.

- ▶ Received Time—Displays the date and time when the alarm management system received the alarm.

- ▶ Type—Specifies the generic type description of the alarm.

- ▶ Category—Specifies the category of the trap-type object identified from its MIB association.

For each of the alarms, the ZENworks Server Management Active Alarm view displays the following alarm-specific data for the selected alarm (refer to Figure 30.2):

- ▶ Alarm ID—Displays the object ID of the alarm in the Alarm Manager database.

- ▶ Alarm State—Displays the current status of the alarm. This tells you if the alarm is currently operational or not.

- ▶ Alarm Severity—Displays the severity of the alarm: Severe, Major, Minor, Informational, or Unknown.

- ▶ Generator Type—Displays the type of agent that activated the alarm.

- ▶ Alarm Category—Displays the category of the trap-type object identified from its MIB association.

▸ Alarm Type—Displays the generic type description of the alarm.

▸ Source Address—Displays the address of the device that triggered the alarm.

▸ Received At—Displays the time at which the alarm management system received the alarm from the agent.

▸ Summary—Gives a descriptive summary of the alarm. This is one of the most useful statistics because the descriptions include node names and specific data about the nature of the alarm.

▸ Number of Variables—Lists the number of variables associated with the alarm.

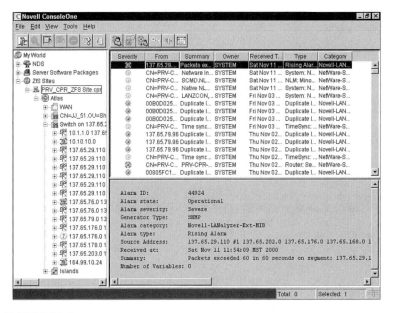

FIGURE 30.2
Active Alarm view for a ZENworks Server Management site management object in ConsoleOne.

Follow these steps from within the ZENworks Server Management console to access the Active Alarm view:

1. Select the ZENworks Server Management site object.

2. Select View→Active Alarms from the main menu in ConsoleOne. The Active Alarm view, shown previously in Figure 30.2, appears.

Displaying Alarm History

In addition to the currently active alarms, ZENworks Server Management also enables you to view data about all archived alarms that have occurred on the network. The Alarm History view is similar to the Active Alarm view. But the Alarm History view includes a Handled status field, shown in Figure 30.3, in addition to the same information about the alarms.

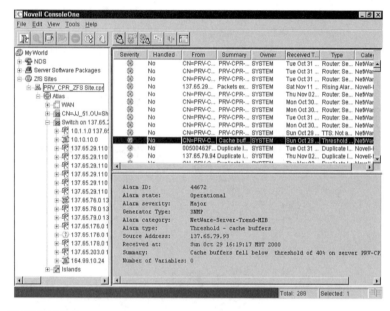

FIGURE 30.3
Alarm History view for a ZENworks Server Management site management object in ConsoleOne.

Follow these steps from within the ZENworks Server Management console to access the Alarm History view:

1. Select the ZENworks Server Management site object.

2. Select View→Alarms History from the main menu in ConsoleOne. The Alarm History view, shown in Figure 30.3, appears.

Sorting Alarms

After bringing up either the Active Alarm or the Alarm History view on the management console, you can change the look of the view by sorting the alarms according to a specific criterion. This enables you to tailor the view to meet the needs of the problem you are trying to resolve or a report that you need to prepare.

The following are the most common criteria you may want to sort alarms on and examples of when to use them:

▶ Received Time—The default sort order. This enables you to see the alarms in the chronological order that they occurred. This is the most useful view in understanding the initial status of the network and when problems started occurring.

▶ Affected Object—Enables you to focus on the specific server or node that triggered the alarm. This is most useful when you are troubleshooting a server or router issue.

▶ Severity—Enables you to focus on a specific level of error. Typically, you sort according to severity when you want to see only the most severe errors that are occurring and resolve them first.

▶ Category—Enables you to focus on specific trap types identified in the MIB. This sorting enables you to focus on a specific alarm. Use this if you are troubleshooting or monitoring a specific router or server issue where you know the specific SNMP trap you are looking for.

▶ Type—Can be useful to troubleshoot some specific issues. If you were watching for hard drive space problems, for example, you may sort by type and bring together all the volume out of disk space alarms.

▶ Owner—Sorting by Owner can be useful to get all the issues sorted by whom the problem belongs to.

Follow these steps from within the ZENworks Server Management console to sort the Active Alarm or the Alarm History view:

1. Open up the alarm view you want to sort.

2. Select View→Settings→Sort from the main menu in ConsoleOne.

3. From the Alarm Sorting dialog box, shown in Figure 30.4, select the criteria by which you want the alarms to be sorted.

4. Select the sort order: Ascending or Descending.

5. Click OK to save your setting. The alarm view should be sorted according to your selections.

This completes the steps for sorting the Active Alarm/Alarm History view.

FIGURE 30.4
Alarm Sorting dialog box for a ZENworks Server Management site management object in ConsoleOne.

Filtering Alarms

ZENworks Server Management also enables you to filter on alarms according to specific criteria after you bring up either the Active Alarm or the Alarm History view on the management console. This enables you even greater control to customize the view to meet more specific needs of the problems you are trying to resolve or reports that you need to prepare.

Table 30.1 shows the available criteria and options that you may want to use to filter alarms in the Active Alarm or Alarm History view.

TABLE 30.1   Criteria Available to Filter Alarm Views On

CRITERIA	OPERATORS	VALUES
Severity	=(equals), !=(does not equal), > or <	Severe, Major, Minor, Informational
Generator type	=(equals) or !=(does not equal)	Only SNMP (unless you have additional alarm generator types on you network).
Alarm category	=(equals) or !=(does not equal)	Any one of the alarm categories available in the MIB—that is, Antivirus-MIB, LANDesk-Alarm-MIB, NetWare-Server-Alarm-MIB, and so on.

TABLE 30.1   Continued

CRITERIA	OPERATORS	VALUES
Alarm type	=(equals) or !=(does not equal)	Any one of the alarm types provided on the alarm system— that is, Threshold—cache buffers, System: Trap NLM Loaded, and so on.
Source address	=(equals) or !=(does not equal)	IP address of source to filter on. This enables you to filter on a specific device.
Affected object	=(equals), !=(does not equal), contains, starts with, or ends with	Full distinguished name of a ZENworks Server Management site server. This lets you filter on a single site if you are using site forwarding.
Alarm owner	=(equals), !=(does not equal), contains, starts with, or ends with	Full distinguished name of a user or group responsible for alarms. This could be used to view the alarms that you are currently responsible for.
Alarm summary	=(equals), !=(does not equal), contains, starts with, or ends with	Any text string that may equal, start, end, or be contained in the alarm summary string. If you were looking at lost connection issues, for example, you could filter on "Lost Connection" and use the contains operator.

Follow these steps from within the ZENworks Server Management console to filter the Active Alarm or the Alarm History view:

1. Bring up the view that you want to filter.

2. Select View→Settings→Filter from the main menu in ConsoleOne. The Alarm Filter dialog box, shown in Figure 30.5, appears.

3. Select the criteria by which you want the alarm management system to filter alarms from the drop-down list on the left.

4. Select an appropriate operator, from Table 30.1, to use from the next drop-down list.

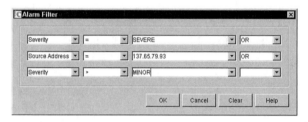

FIGURE 30.5
Alarm Filter dialog box for a ZENworks Server Management site management object in ConsoleOne.

   5. Select an appropriate value from the third drop-down list, or specify a value if one is not provided.

   6. Specify how this specific filter relates to other statements you want to define. You can use the AND, OR, new row, delete row, and new group relationship criteria. This enables you to add multiple filters and groups of filters to the alarm view, as shown in Figure 30.5.

   7. If you defined relationship criteria in step 6, repeat steps 3 through 6.

When you finish specifying filters, click OK. The filter is saved, and the view is adjusted according to your criteria.

Viewing Alarm Summary

ZENworks Server Management allows you to view a summary of the alarms for a managed site. The Alarm Summary view provides concise, but complete, data about the alarms that have occurred on your network over the past day, week, or month.

The following list breaks down the information displayed in the Alarm Summary view shown in Figure 30.6:

   ▶ Severity Distribution—Displays a pie chart breaking out the alarms based on their severity. This information is useful to find out how many critical alarms your network is seeing. You can, for example, view this in terms of days, weeks, and months to determine whether your network is getting healthier or sicker.

   ▶ Category Distribution—Displays a pie chart breaking out the alarms based on the alarms category. This information is useful to help you understand where your network may need to grow or where problems need to be resolved.

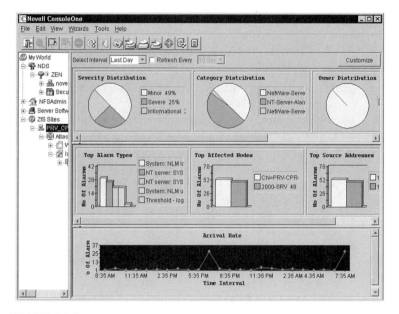

FIGURE 30.6
Alarm Summary view for a ZENworks Server Management site management object in ConsoleOne.

▶ Owner Distribution—Displays a pie chart breaking out the alarms based on the owner of the service that triggered the alarm. This information is useful to know where to begin troubleshooting issues.

▶ State Disposition—Displays a pie chart that breaks down the alarms based on the state that they are in. This information helps you understand the duration of the alarms on your network. If the active state, for example, is the majority of the pie chart, you know that the alarms are active much of the time, and the issues are much more severe.

▶ Top Alarm Types—Displays a bar graph of the alarms triggered most often. This information helps determine which services are being affected most on your network.

▶ Top Affected Nodes—Displays a bar graph of the nodes where alarms are triggered most often. This information helps determine which nodes and/or segments need the most attention in terms of growth and optimization.

▶ Top Source Address—Displays a bar graph of the network address-es where alarms are triggered most often. This information enables you to understand on what segments, routers, and so on problems are occurring.

▶ Arrival Rate—Displays a line graph that shows the number of active alarms based on a time interval. The arrival rate shows you the number of alarms active at any given time. This information is useful to understand network issues that have to do with time. If you are getting numerous alarms at the same time in the morning, for example, you can look at when employees are arriving to work and logging in to the network. You may need to add additional hardware to handle the morning login or perhaps stagger the time employees can log in to the network.

The Alarm Summary page allows you to use the following options from the Alarm Summary view to customize what data is displayed:

▶ Select Interval—This drop-down menu enables you to view data collected from the last day, week, or month. This information is important in giving you an understanding of how the network's sta-tus is changing over a period of time.

▶ Refresh Every—This check box instructs ZENworks to refresh the data every 10 seconds, 30 seconds, or 1 minute.

▶ Customize—Enables you to configure what information is dis-played in the Alarm Summary view. You can disable any of the sta-tistics, and you can set the number of top alarm types, top affected nodes, and top source addresses to display in the bar graphs.

Managing Alarms

Now that you understand how to detect and view network alarms from the ZENworks Server Management console, you need to know how to manage them on large networks. This sort of management is especially important if numerous administrators are managing different aspects of the management site.

ZENworks Server Management adds options to the alarm to enable you to assign, own, and handle alarms. This feature helps you keep track of who is responsible for what issues and which issues have been resolved.

After you select an alarm from the Active Alarm or the Alarm History view, you can manage the alarm by selecting one of the following options for it from the View menu in ConsoleOne:

▶ Assign—Enables you to specify a person or group responsible for handling an alarm. When this option is set, other administrators know that they do not need to respond to it.

▶ Own—Causes the owner that is filed to change to the NDS name you are logged in as. This lets other administrators know that you are handling this alarm. Therefore, they do not need to act on the alarm, and they have a person to contact for estimated resolutions and so forth.

▶ Handle—Removes the alarm from the Active Alarm view. This removes the alarm from active issues that need resolving, enabling administrators to focus on current problems. But the alarm still shows up on the Alarm History view.

▶ Note—Adds any special comments or notes about the alarm. After a note has been added to an alarm, the alarm's icon changes to one with a small icon designating that the alarm has a special note attached to it. The note can be viewed in the alarm information pane when the alarm is selected.

▶ Jump—Use this to jump directly to the object that triggered the alarm. This allows you faster access to the object to troubleshoot issues.

Setting Alarm Actions

One of the most powerful features of the ZENworks Server Management alarm management system is its capability to perform actions automatically to help you manage alarms as they are triggered. You can use the ZENworks Server Management console to configure an alarm to automatically trigger an action when it occurs.

Alarm actions are configured through alarm dispositions. Follow these steps to access the Alarm Disposition page, shown in Figure 30.7, and to configure alarm actions in ConsoleOne:

1. Right-click on the ZENworks Server Management site object to which you want to configure alarm dispositions and select properties.

2. Select the Alarm Disposition tab.

3. Select the Templates tab shown in Figure 30.7.

4. Select the alarm you want to configure from the list.

5. Click the Edit button to bring up the Edit Alarm Disposition dialog box.

This completes the steps for configuring alarm actions in ConsoleOne.

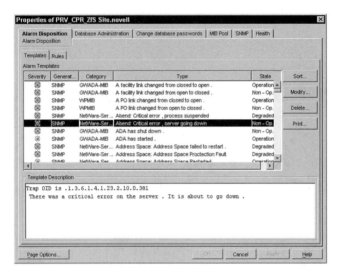

FIGURE 30.7
Alarm Disposition tab for a ZENworks Server Management site management object in ConsoleOne.

ZENworks Server Management has added a Sort button to the Alarm Disposition tab that allows you to define a template for ZENworks to use when sorting alarms. This capability is useful to analyze and understand the nature of alarms occurring on your network. You could, for example, narrow down problem services by setting up a template to sort by the alarm type.

To set up a template to sort alarms, click the Sort button shown in Figure 30.7 to bring up the Template Sorting dialog box. From the Template Sorting dialog box you can define a template to sort based on up to four of the following different criteria types:

▶ Severity—Severity of the alarm

▶ Generator Type—Type of service that generated the alarm

▶ Category—The classification of the alarm

▶ Type—The specific type of the alarm

ZENworks Server Management enables administrators to print the alarm dispositions. The printout of the alarm dispositions can then be saved or taken to use for troubleshooting purposes. Use the following steps to print the alarm dispositions for a ZENworks Server Management site in ConsoleOne:

1. Select the ZENworks Server Management site object you want to print.

2. Select the Alarm Disposition tab, shown previously in Figure 30.7.

3. Select the alarm(s) you want to print.

4. Click the Print button.

5. Set the print properties options and click OK.

ZENworks Server Management also enables administrators to export the alarm dispositions to one of the following file formats:

▶ .HTML—HTML

▶ .CSV—Comma-delimited

▶ .TXT—Tab-delimited

▶ .TXT—Space-delimited

The saved file containing the alarm dispositions can then be used in reports or documenting issues. Use the following steps to export the alarm dispositions for a ZENworks Server Management site in ConsoleOne:

1. Select the ZENworks Server Management site object you want to print.

2. Select the Alarm Disposition tab, shown previously in Figure 30.7.

3. Select the alarm(s) you want to print.

4. Click the Print button.

5. Click the Print to File button.

6. Select the Export file type and specify a filename and location.

7. Click OK.

The following sections discuss the actions to be performed when an alarm is triggered and that are available from the Edit Alarm Disposition dialog box.

Sending Email Notification

The first available option from the Alarm Disposition dialog box is the capability to send an email notification to a user or group. It is useful to be notified when critical alarms occur on the network.

Network administrators use this feature for various kinds of notification. Some have their SMTP mail server configured to page them with the notification email when it is received.

Follow these steps to configure an email notification action for an alarm from the Edit Alarm Disposition dialog box in ConsoleOne:

1. Select the SMTP Mail Notification tab, shown in Figure 30.8.

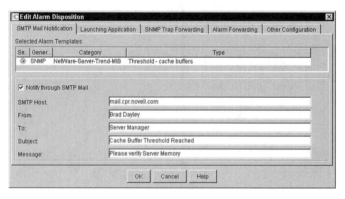

FIGURE 30.8
SMTP Mail Notification tab of an alarm disposition for a site management object in ConsoleOne.

2. Select the Notify Through SMTP Mail check box.

3. In the SMTP Host text box, specify the IP address or DNS name of the SMTP host server that handles incoming and outgoing email. You can also specify a port on the host server by typing a colon and the port number after the IP address.

4. In the From text box, specify the mail ID you want to use. This information is usually important for any additional automation on the back end.

5. In the To text box, specify the mail IDs of the users or groups you want to notify when the alarm is triggered.

6. In the Subject text box, specify the subject line you want to appear on the mail message that is sent. This information is also often important for additional automation on the back end. You can also add variables to the subject line by specifying a % sign in front of them. Use Table 30.2 to specify any variables that might be useful in the email Subject line.

7. In the Message text box, specify the text message you want to appear in the body of the email that is sent. This message should include a description of what the alarm means. You can also add variables to the subject line by specifying a % sign in front of them. Use Table 30.2 to specify any variables that might be useful in the email body.

At the completion of these steps, click OK to save your settings and return to the Alarm Dispositions tab.

TABLE 30.2   Available Variables for Use in the Subject and Message Options for SMTP Mail Notifications

VARIABLES	NAME	DESCRIPTION
a	Alarm ID	Identification number of the alarm as it is stored in the database
c	Affected Class	Class of the device that sent the alarm
n	Affected Object Name	eDirectory Name of the object that sent the alarm
o	Affected Object Number	Identification number, from the database, of the node that generated the alarm
p	Source Address	Address of the device that sent the alarm
s	Alarm Summary String	Message describing the alarm (same message that is displayed in the status bar ticker tape message)

TABLE 30.2 Continued

VARIABLES	NAME	DESCRIPTION
t	Alarm Type String	Description of the alarm (same as the description in the Alarm Type element of the Alarm summary window)
v	Severity Number	Alarm severity level: 1 = Critical 2 = Major 3 = Minor 4 = Informational

Launching an Application

The next option available from the Alarm Disposition dialog box is the ability to launch an application. This option enables you to specify an NLM to be launched when an alarm is triggered on a server.

If your network utilization is too high, for example, you could launch an NLM that shuts down noncritical applications that normally consume high amounts of network bandwidth.

From the Edit Alarm Disposition dialog box in ConsoleOne, follow these steps to configure an external program to be launched when an alarm is triggered:

1. Select the Launching Application tab, shown in Figure 30.9.

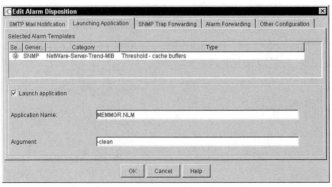

FIGU

Launching Application tab of an alarm disposition for a site management object in ConsoleOne.

2. Select the Launch Application check box.

3. Specify the application path and filename in the Application Name text box.

4. Specify any additional arguments in the Argument text box. You can use variables listed in Table 30.2 as parameters by preceding them with the % sign.

5. Click OK to save your settings and return to the Alarm Dispositions tab.

NOTE The Application Name field cannot exceed 126 characters in total length. The Argument field cannot exceed 119 characters in total length. The combined total of the Application Name and the Argument fields cannot exceed 139 characters in total length.

Forwarding the SNMP Trap

The next option available from the Alarm Dispositions dialog box is the ability to forward the SNMP trap to another management system. This option enables you to specify the IP address of another management station or server to forward the SNMP trap to.

If you had another SNMP management system, for example, in addition to ZENworks Server Management, and wanted that system to receive the trap as well, you could send an SNMP trap to that management system, too.

From the Edit Alarm Disposition dialog box in ConsoleOne, follow these steps to configure an IP address to which the SNMP trap should be forwarded:

1. Select the SNMP Trap Forwarding tab, shown in Figure 30.10.

2. Enter the IP address of the server to which you want to forward the SNMP traps in the SNMP Target Address field. You can also specify a port on the target server by adding a colon and the port number after the IP address.

3. Click Add to add it to the list of targets.

4. Click OK to save your settings and return to the Alarm Dispositions tab.

This completes the steps necessary to configure an IP address to which the SNMP trap should be forwarded.

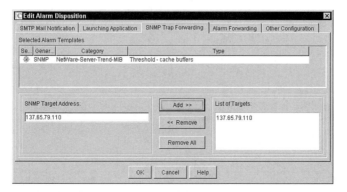

FIGURE 30.10
SMTP Trap Forwarding tab of an alarm disposition for a site management object in ConsoleOne.

Forwarding the Alarm

The next option available from the Alarm Dispositions dialog box is the ability to forward the alarm to another ZENworks Server Management site. This option enables you to specify a ZENworks Server Management site name and hostname in which to forward the alarm.

From the Edit Alarm Disposition dialog box in ConsoleOne, follow these steps to configure another ZENworks Server Management site to which the alarm should be forwarded:

1. Select the Alarm Forwarding tab, shown in Figure 30.11.

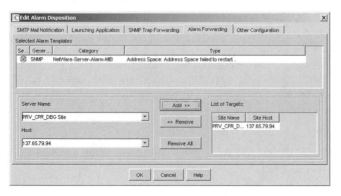

FIGURE 30.11
Alarm Forwarding tab of an alarm disposition for a site management object in ConsoleOne.

2. Enter the ZENworks Server Management site name to which you want to forward the alarm in the Server Name field.

3. Enter the ZENworks Server Management site hostname in the Host field.

4. Click Add to add it to the list of targets.

5. Click OK to save your settings and return to the Alarm Dispositions tab.

Additional Alarm Disposition Actions

The final options panel available from the Edit Alarm Disposition dialog box is the Other Configuration tab, shown in Figure 30.12. This tab enables you to configure the following actions to be performed when an alarm is triggered:

▶ Archive—Stores the statistical data for the alarm instance in the Alarm Manager database on the management server. If you want to see the alarm in the Alarm History view, you need to select this option. It is on by default.

▶ Show on Ticker Bar—Displays a message of the alarm on the status bar of the ZENworks Server Management console to silently notify the administrator of the most recent alarm.

▶ Beep on Console—Sends an audible beep to the ZENworks Server Management console to notify the administrator that an alarm has been triggered.

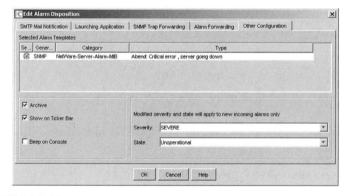

FIGURE 30.12
Other Configuration tab of an alarm disposition for a site management object in ConsoleOne.

Follow these steps to configure additional options for the alarm from the Edit Alarm Disposition dialog box in ConsoleOne:

1. Select the Other Configuration tab (refer to Figure 30.12).

2. Select the Archive check box if you want to save the alarm to the Alarm Manager database.

3. Select the Show on Ticker Bar check box if you want a message to be displayed in the status bar of the management console.

4. Select the Beep on Console check box if you want the alarm to send an audible beep to the management console.

5. Set the Severity of future alarms of this type to Information, Minor, Major, Severe, or Unknown.

6. Set the State of future alarms of this type to Operation, Unoperational, or Degraded.

On completion of these steps, click OK to save your settings and return to the Alarm Dispositions tab.

Configuring Alarm Rules

In addition to assigning actions to specify alarms, ZENworks 7 introduces a powerful feature that allows you to configure rules to define how certain types of alarms are handled automatically.

Use the following steps to configure an alarm rule in ConsoleOne:

1. Right-click on the ZENworks Server Management site object to which you want to configure alarm dispositions and select properties.

2. Select the Alarm Disposition tab.

3. Select the Rules tab shown in Figure 30.13.

4. Click the New button to bring up the New Rule dialog box, shown in Figure 30.14.

The following sections discuss configuring the alarm rules from the New Rule dialog box.

Configure Alarm Rule Properties

You should configure the alarm rule properties first when creating a new alarm by selecting the Properties tab shown in Figure 30.14. From the Properties tab you can specify a rule name and description. This will

allow you and others to identify the type and purpose of the rule and
should be descriptive enough for all alarm administrators to understand.

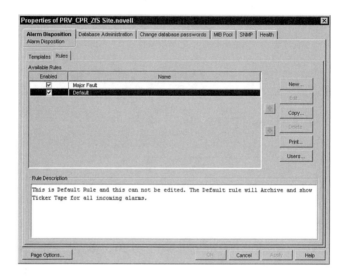

FIGURE 30.13
Alarm Rules tab on the Alarm Disposition page for a ZENworks Server
Management site management object in ConsoleOne.

Configure Alarm Rule Conditions

After you have configured the rule name and description on the
Properties tab, select the Conditions tab shown in Figure 30.14. From
the Conditions tab you can specify the following conditions that determine whether the rule applies to a triggered alarm:

▶ Source Addresses—Allows you to specify a specific IP address or a
range of addresses. This allows you to limit the rule to a specific
device or set of devices.

▶ Alarms—Allows you to specify to which severity/severities, state(s),
or specific alarm(s) the rule should apply. This allows you to limit
to which specific alarms the rule should apply. It also allows you
to limit the rule based on the severity and/or state of the alarms.

▶ Time Intervals—Allows you to specify a specific time interval during which the alarm rule will be enforced. Alarms that occur outside that time interval will not be enforced. This is extremely useful if you need to define rule actions that should not be applied during production hours.

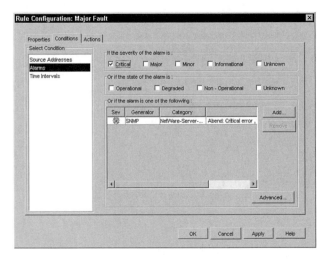

FIGURE 30.14
Conditions tab on the New Rule dialog for an alarm disposition in ConsoleOne.

Configure Alarm Rule Actions

After you have configured the rule conditions on the Conditions tab, select the Actions tab shown in Figure 30.15. From the Actions tab you can specify the following actions if the alarm rule conditions apply to a triggered alarm:

▶ SMTP Mail Notification—Allows you to configure an SMTP mail message that will be sent in the event an alarm is triggered.

▶ Launching Application—Allows you to specify an application and arguments that should be executed in the event a triggered alarm matches the conditions.

▶ SNMP Trap Forwarding—Allows you to specify target addreses and ports that the SNMP Trap should be forwarded to.

▶ Alarm Forwarding—Allows you to forward the alarm to another ZENWorks for Servers site and host.

▶ Miscellaneous—Allows you to specify that the alarm should be archived, that it should be shown on the ticker bar, that the server console should beep, or that the alarm should be automatically handled. It also allows you to change the severity and state of the alarm or assign it to a specific user.

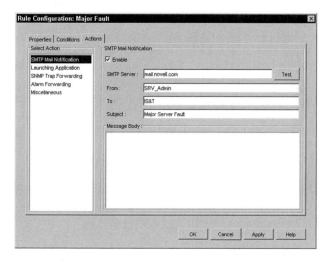

FIGURE 30.15
Actions tab on the New Rule dialog for an alarm disposition in ConsoleOne.

Deleting Alarms

The final task you need to be familiar with when managing ZENworks Server Management alarms is how to remove them when you are completely finished with them. The alarms take up space in the Alarm Manager database until they are removed. If you do not consistently keep the alarms cleaned out of the database, the database can begin to take up an excessive amount of hard drive space.

The following sections discuss how to manually and automatically remove unwanted alarms from the Alarm Manager database.

Deleting Alarms from the Management Console

You can manually delete alarms from the Alarm Manager database by simply deleting them from the ZENworks Server Management console. This is the best way to delete an individual alarm. But if numerous alarms have occurred, this process could be too time-consuming. If you have numerous alarms, instead use the automatic alarm deletion method described in the next section.

Follow these steps to manually delete an alarm from the Alarm Manager database from the management console:

1. Navigate to the server or segment object on which the alarm occurred.

2. Open the Alarm History view to display the alarms.

3. Select the alarm you want to delete.

4. Select View→Delete from the main menu, and the alarm is deleted from the database.

Automating Alarm Deletion

The best way to handle the deletion of alarms is to automate the process by configuring the purge utility to delete the alarms for you. The purge utility is a Java application that runs on the server where the Alarm Manager database is stored.

The purge utility is controlled by a configuration file, AMPURGE.PROPERTY, which defines the criteria for selecting alarms to be purged as well as when to start purging alarms. The first step in using the purge utility to automatically delete alarms is to configure the criteria listed in Table 30.3 according to how long you need the alarms and when to start purging.

TABLE 30.3 Criteria for Purging Alarms Listed in the
AMPURGE.PROPERTY File

CRITERIA SETTING	DESCRIPTION
SeverityInformationalPurgeWait	Specifies the number of days to wait before informational alarms are purged. The default is 7.
SeverityMinorPurgeWait	Specifies the number of days to wait before minor alarms are purged. The default is 7.
SeverityMajorPurgeWait	Specifies the number of days to wait before major alarms are purged. The default is 7.
SeverityCriticalPurgeWait	Specifies the number of days to wait before critical alarms are purged. The default is 7.
SeverityUnknownPurgeWait	Specifies the number of days to wait before unknown alarms are purged. The default is 7.
PurgeStartTime	Specifies the start time hour to begin the daily purge process. Valid values are from 0 (midnight) to 23 (11 p.m.).
AlarmPurgeService	Specifies whether to automatically run the purge process on a daily basis. You can specify either Yes (enable) or No (disable). Omitting this setting also disables it.

After configuring the criteria for purging alarms, you have two options. The first option is to wait for the start time that you specified the purge to begin. The second option is to manually start the purge process.

You may want to manually start the purge process because you turned off the automatic run by setting **AlarmPurgeService** to No, or because the database has grown too rapidly because of a network problem and you need to free up hard drive space.

Use the following command from the console of the server where the Alarm Manager database is stored to start the automatic purge process manually:

```
java com.novell.managewise.am.db.purge.AutoPurgeManager -s
-d <properties_file_directory>
```

The `properties_file_directory` parameter should be replaced with the directory location where the `AMPURGE.PROPERTY` file is located.

NOTE The purge process is highly memory and CPU intensive. Therefore, you should run the purge only during off hours or when it is extremely needed—for example, at night, on weekends, or if the server runs out of disk space.

Using ZENworks Server Management Monitoring Services

In addition to the alarm management services, ZENworks Server Management provides monitoring services to monitor devices on the network. The ZENworks Server Management alarm management system relies on agents either on the device or on the management server to capture events, turn them into alarms, and relay them to the management console.

The ZENworks Server Management monitoring services does the opposite. It enables the management console to check the status of network devices from the point of view of the console itself. This enables you to be immediately notified if connectivity between the console and critical nodes is interrupted.

Use the monitoring service as another option to monitor the status of the critical services on your network. The following sections describe how to define and configure target services you want to monitor.

Monitoring Services on Target Nodes

ZENworks Server Management uses a ping method to monitor service status on target nodes. A ping packet is sent from a remote server to the target node. The remote server then waits for a specific interval. If a reply is received back from the target node before the interval elapses, the status of the server is up. If a reply is not received back from the target node before the interval elapses, the status of the server is down.

The following sections describe the different utilities and views that ZENworks Server Management provides from the management console to monitor servers on one or more target nodes.

Testing a Single Target Node

ZENworks Server Management provides the ping test as a quick method for you to monitor the status of a specific node. Use the ping test if you suspect a problem with a specific node in the network.

The ping test provides the status—up or down—of communication from the management console to the node as well as the round-trip delay for the ping to be received back.

Follow these steps to perform a ping test on a particular node from the management console:

1. Select the node you want to monitor.

2. Select File→Actions→Ping from the main menu. The Ping dialog box, shown in Figure 30.16, appears.

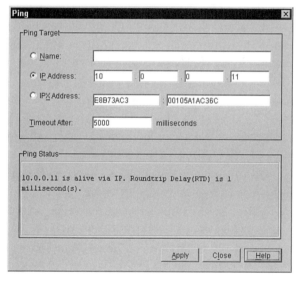

FIGURE 30.16
Ping test results for a monitored server object in ConsoleOne.

3. The IP address should be already displayed for you, if it is the default. But you can also specify a DNS name or IPX address as well at this point. You can also specify a time in milliseconds to wait before timing out. Click the Apply button.

4. View the status in the Ping Status area. The status continues to be updated at a configured interval.

Monitoring Services on Several Nodes

ZENworks Server Management also enables you to monitor the services of several target nodes, from the management console, through the use of a connectivity test utility and Polling view. Each of these options displays the following statistics that are dynamically updated:

- ▶ Target—The name or address of the node for which connectivity to services is being tested.

- ▶ Service—The service being monitored on the target node.

- ▶ Port—The port number of the service on the target node.

- ▶ Status—The status, up or down, for the service. Up means that a ping packet is sent to the service, and a reply is returned; it doesn't necessarily mean that the service is operating normally.

- ▶ Roundtrip Delay—Time interval, in milliseconds, from when the remote ping server sends a ping to the target service and a reply is received back from the target.

- ▶ Packets Sent—Number of packets sent from the remote ping server to the target node.

- ▶ Packets Received—Number of packets received by the remote ping server that were sent from the target node.

- ▶ Packets Lost—Number of ping packets and percentage of total packets lost during the connectivity testing.

- ▶ Interval—Time, in seconds, the remote ping server waits after sending one ping packet before sending the next.

- ▶ Timeout—Time, in milliseconds, the remote ping server waits for a reply from the target node before declaring the service in a down state.

The Polling view displays connectivity statistics for all configured services on the managed segment. This view can give you a quick understanding of the current status of a segment, which can be useful when trying to understand problems such as network outages or LAN overusage. To view the Polling view for a segment, select the desired segment in ConsoleOne; then select View→Polling from the main menu.

The connectivity test utility displays statistics for services from a selective group of nodes. You can tailor the Connectivity view to more closely meet your needs by adding only the most important nodes. Typically, you use the Connectivity view when you are troubleshooting issues on a selective group of servers.

Follow these steps to start the Connectivity view from the management console:

1. Select the segment that contains the nodes in which you want to monitor services.

2. Select the nodes you want to monitor services on in the right pane of the console.

3. Select File→Action→Connectivity Test from the main menu. A screen similar to the one in Figure 30.17 appears.

4. Click the Add button, located in the button bar in Figure 30.17, to add additional services (discussed in the next section) to the view.

Adding Services to the Connectivity Test

After you have the connectivity test utility running, you can add new services to be monitored. This can be useful as you are monitoring connectivity issues on a node because it enables you to check all services on the monitored node to see whether all, some, or only a single service is affected.

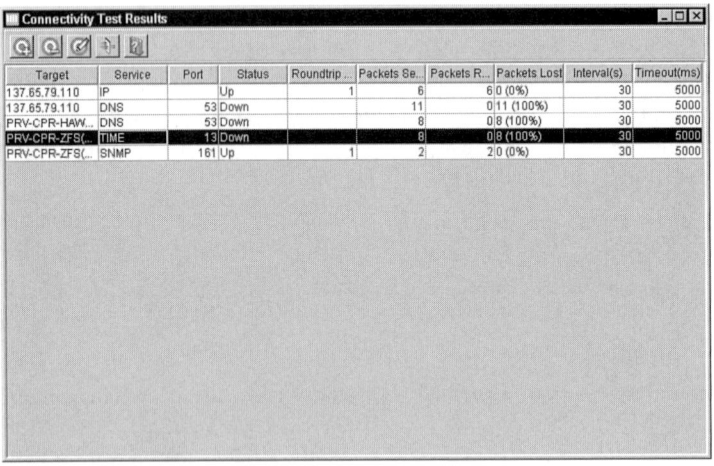

Target	Service	Port	Status	Roundtrip..	Packets Se..	Packets R...	Packets Lost	Interval(s)	Timeout(ms)
137.65.79.110	IP		Up	1	6	6	0 (0%)	30	5000
137.65.79.110	DNS	53	Down		11	0	11 (100%)	30	5000
PRV-CPR-HAW...	DNS	53	Down		8	0	8 (100%)	30	5000
PRV-CPR-ZFS(...	TIME	13	Down		8	0	8 (100%)	30	5000
PRV-CPR-ZFS(...	SNMP	161	Up	1	2	2	0 (0%)	30	5000

FIGURE 30.17
Connectivity test results for a monitored segment object in ConsoleOne.

ZENworks Server Management enables you to monitor the following services on monitored nodes from the management console:

- ▶ IP—Internet Protocol
- ▶ IPX—Internet Packet Exchange
- ▶ DNS—Domain Name System
- ▶ DHCP—Dynamic Host Configuration Protocol
- ▶ ECHO—Echo Protocol
- ▶ FTP—File Transfer Protocol
- ▶ TFTP—Trivial File Transfer Protocol
- ▶ HTTP—Hypertext Transfer Protocol
- ▶ HTTPS—Hypertext Transfer Protocol Secure
- ▶ SNMP—Simple Network Management Protocol
- ▶ SMTP—Simple Mail Transfer Protocol
- ▶ TIME—Time Services
- ▶ WUSER—Windows User
- ▶ NNTP—Network News Transfer Protocol
- ▶ NFS—Network File System

From the connectivity test utility, follow these steps to add services to the Connectivity Test window:

1. Select the target node you want to monitor another service from— or, if you want to add a server from a node not already listed, select any node.

2. Click the Add button. The Add Ping Target(s) dialog box, shown in Figure 30.18, appears.

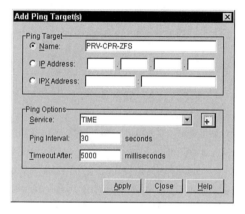

FIGURE 30.18
The Add Ping Target(s) dialog box for the connectivity test on a monitored segment object in ConsoleOne.

3. If you are adding a service from a node not already listed, type the name, IP address, or IPX address in the Ping Target field.

4. Select the service from the drop-down menu, or click the plus sign button next to the Service field and specify a new service and port number.

5. Specify the interval at which you want to ping the service in the Ping Interval field.

6. Specify the amount of time you want to wait for a ping reply before determining that the service is down in the Timeout After field.

On completion of these steps, click the Close button to add the service to the monitor list and close the Add Ping Target(s) dialog box, or click the Apply button to add the service to the list but keep the dialog box open to add additional services.

Setting Up Monitoring Services on Monitored Nodes

You must configure monitoring services on each node you want to monitor from the Polling view in the management console. The connectivity test utility simply uses a list of targets to test; however, the Polling view must read the node object contained within it and check for nodes with monitoring services enabled on them before they can be added to the view.

Follow these steps from the management console to configure and enable monitoring services on nodes you want to monitor:

1. Select the segment in which you want to monitor nodes.

2. Select a node located in the selected segment to which you want to configure monitor services.

3. Right-click the node and select Properties from the pop-up menu.

4. Select the Monitor Services tab, as shown in Figure 30.19.

5. Select the IP or IPX address you want to use for the node. If the node is connected to multiple segments, make sure that you use the address for the segment you want to monitor.

6. Select the services that you want to monitor on the node and click the Add button, or you can also click the Add Service button to specify a new service name and port number.

7. Set the polling interval to ping the server in the Interval field.

8. Set the amount of time to wait for a reply from the service before declaring it down in the Timeout After field.

9. Specify whether to send an alarm if the state changes either from up to down or from down to up.

10. Click the Apply button to save the changes.

This completes the steps for configuring and enabling monitoring services on nodes you want to monitor.

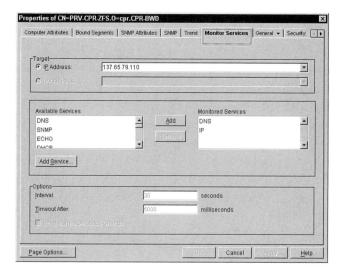

FIGURE 30.19
Monitor Services tab of managed server node object in ConsoleOne.

Summary

This chapter looked at the components and utilities that make up the ZENworks Server Management alarm management system and the ZENworks Server Management monitoring services system. How to configure and use the services to best detect, diagnose, and resolve network issues were discussed.

## CHAPTER 31

Using ZENworks Server Management to Manage Servers

One of the most difficult tasks enterprise network administrators must face is how to manage the numerous servers on their network. ZENworks Server Management includes powerful tools and services that help you manage your network servers, and this chapter discusses them.

Using ZENworks Server Management SNMP Agents

ZENworks Server Management contains two components: Policy and Distribution Services and Management and Monitoring. Included in the Management and Monitoring are several management agents that enable you to configure, monitor, and manage servers from a single console interface. With these agents, you can have the system automatically watch over your servers and networks and alert you when trouble is coming. With ZENworks Server Management and Monitoring you will be ahead of the game and fixing the problem before your users even know it happened.

SNMP-based Server Management

One advantage of using ZENworks Server Management to manage your servers is that its server management agents support the industry standard Simple Network Management Protocol (SNMP). These ZENworks Server Management agents also support the UDP/IP, IPX, and

NCP implementations for packet sending. Therefore, any SNMP console or manager can request information from them.

The ZENworks Server Management agents run on NetWare, Windows, and Linux servers in your network. These agents continuously monitor the servers and collect dynamic data in response to requests from the management console.

ZENworks Server Management uses several different management agents to manage servers:

▶ Monitoring—Provides instant information about the current state of the monitored elements of the server, including CPU utilization, memory size, available cache buffers, connected users, volumes, disks, disk space usage per user, network adapters, available print queues, current print jobs, and NLMs loaded on the server.

▶ Trending—Provides historical data about various server objects and can be displayed in a graphical diagram on the ZENworks Server Management console. The trend data is stored on the managed server, which eliminates the need for extra LAN traffic to poll the SNMP Agent Manager.

▶ Alarm notification—Monitors for predefined alarms or events and then notifies the ZENworks Server Management system (or any SNMP management console). Currently, ZENworks Server Management agents monitor more than 580 different types of alarms or events. Any Windows 2000/2003 system, security, or application event is converted to an SNMP trap and sent to the management system as well.

▶ Configuration management—Enables you to remotely view and modify the NetWare server's configuration from the management console. The configuration management agent enables you to modify 187 SET parameters on the NetWare server to tune performance.

NOTE The ZENworks Server Management SNMP agents must be installed on every server you want to manage.

ZENworks Server Management Views

The ZENworks Server Management agents provide information to the administrator's management console through the use of server management views. You can access the following three main types of server

management views by selecting a server or network node from the
ZENworks Server Management namespace in ConsoleOne:

► Console view—Provides details about the selected server or node.
  You can also drill down into the server configuration to display
  information about the internal component of the server—for example, operating system version, installed devices, and memory.

► Summary view—Provides details about the server's current performance—for example, alarms generated by the server, CPU utilization, and available disk space. Once again, you can drill down
  into the server configuration and view summary information about
  its components—for example, processor, running threads, memory,
  and NetWare volumes.

► Trend view—Provides a graphical representation of the trend
  parameters set up for the server. This enables you to monitor the
  trends of server's state over specific periods of time. Then, using
  this trend data, you can track the general health status of the server
  and predict potential problems and needs for growth.

► Conversations view—Provides information about other nodes that
  the server has been sending and receiving packets from. This can
  help determine network usage being utilized by the managed server.

Tear-Off Views

ZENworks Server Management has added the capability to tear off a view
and place it in its own window in the ConsoleOne Views window shown
in Figure 31.1. This functionality allows administrators to see several
views all at once and quickly switch between them without having to res-
elect objects or menu items in ConsoleOne.

For example, administrators can view a server summary and a segment
summary at the exact same time, comparing information in each to determine whether the health of a server is impacting the health of a segment.

View Builder

ZENworks Server Management has also added a utility called View
Builder to provide administrators the ability to create their own custom
views to monitor specific parameters on managed servers.

View Builder allows you to select specific parameters from the agents that
have SNMP MIBs and traps and display that information as text, tables,
or graphs. For more information about creating custom views, see the
online documentation for ZENworks Server Management.

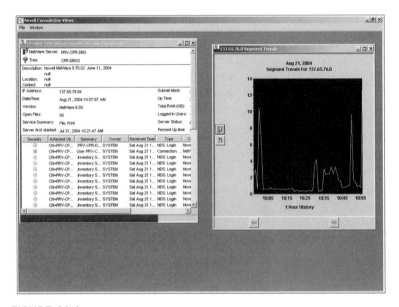

FIGURE 31.1
Server Summary and Segment Trends view in the ConsoleOne Views window.

Planning Server Management

Now that you understand the ZENworks Server Management agents and the console interface used to monitor the state of your server, you need to do a little planning to get the most out of the data that ZENworks Server Management provides you.

This section discusses how to use the data you obtain from the ZENworks Server Management console views to create a baseline document. You then find out how to use that baseline document to monitor, troubleshoot, and optimize your servers.

Creating a Server Baseline Document

Create a baseline document that defines the normal activity and usage of your network servers. This document is later used to identify atypical performance or problems on your servers.

You can create a baseline document either from data out of the Trend view or from a server health report (see the information on health reports in Chapter 32, "Making the Most of ZENworks Server Management

Reporting"). The following elements are vital for every baseline document:

▶ CPU utilization—This statistic indicates how busy the processor is on the server. High CPU utilization greatly impacts the performance of the server. The utilization of the CPU rises and falls with user and network activity throughout each day. CPU utilization, for example, is usually high first thing in the morning when all the users are logging in to the server and reading email, or on Friday when large weekend reports are being run. Create a daily, weekly, and monthly graph for your baseline document, if necessary, to map out an expected CPU utilization pattern.

▶ Cache buffers—These represent the amount of server memory usable for processes. The availability of cache buffers greatly impacts the performance of the server. Once again, the available cache buffers rise and fall during the day based on users and application usage. You should typically have between 65% to 70% of your cache buffers available to applications. Create a daily graph for your baseline document showing the typical trend of cache buffers on your server.

▶ File reads and writes—The file reads and writes by the server should also be graphed into a baseline document. This helps you determine whether a server is performing a high or low number of file I/Os.

▶ Volume utilization—You should also create a graph showing typical volume usage as users create and delete files. This is useful in determining when you must add storage space to a volume.

▶ Running software—Another useful parameter to add to a baseline document is the software running on the server. This helps you in network planning and troubleshooting software issues.

After you complete collecting and understanding this information, create a text document to keep handy that you can refer to, which represents your normal or desired states, as you configure your server management system. You will use information from this document to help you set parameters in the system for when to be notified. For example, if your baseline document states that volumes should always have at least 20% free space, you will probably want to set a threshold alarm in the system to notify you when the server free disk space drops below 25%.

Using a Server Baseline Document

After you create a baseline document, keep it available and up-to-date. The following sections describe situations in which the baseline document can be useful.

Setting Alarm Thresholds

The most useful function of a baseline document is its capability to help you understand what thresholds to set for servers monitored by management agents. You can use the baseline document statistics to set alarm threshold values that alert you when normal server usage is being surpassed—for example, the server starts running out of memory or disk space.

Tracking Server Utilization

Another useful function of a baseline document is to help you track server utilization. You can use the current and past data to evaluate the usage trends of the server and understand needed configuration changes. You can, for example, use the baseline document to predict a volume running out of disk space, available cache buffers insufficient for running software, and so forth.

Server Troubleshooting

The final function of a baseline document is to aid you in troubleshooting your servers. Using the typical data in the baseline document, you can recognize atypical behavior of your servers, which will help you isolate the problem. For example, suppose that a server is running out of memory. When you compare the baseline document to the current state of the server, you notice that the only difference is that a new application is running on the server. The first step in troubleshooting is to remove the application.

Displaying Server Configuration Information

Using the ZENworks Server Management namespace in ConsoleOne, you can display and view critical configuration information about your servers. You can then use this information to manage and control the servers on your managed network. The following is a list of the configuration information components and information that you can retrieve about your managed servers through the ZENworks Server Management namespace:

- ► Processors—Processor number, type, speed, bus, and utilization
- ► LAN adapters—Driver name, adapter number, MAC address, and usage
- ► Disk adapters—Drive number and type
- ► Storage devices—Drive number, vendor name, partition types, size, ID, redirection information, and fault tolerance
- ► OS kernel threads—Thread name, parent NLM, execution time, state, stack size, and affinity
- ► OS kernel interrupts—Interrupt name, number, number of occurrences, execution time, type, processor, service routines, and spurious interrupts
- ► OS kernel memory—Memory type, size, maximum size, and usage
- ► OS kernel address spaces—Space name, number of NLMs loaded, mapped pages, restarted bits, memory, and block usage
- ► Network interfaces—Protocol name, board name, board number, packets out, packets in, address, and descriptions
- ► Network connections—Connection number, username, client address, state, privileges, connection time, bytes read/written, NCP requests, open files, and locked files
- ► Users—Username, disk usage, last login time, account and password status, real name, and bad logins
- ► Installed software—Application name, type, and date installed
- ► NLMs—Filename, version, release date, memory usage, description, copyright, and resource tag information
- ► File services—Volume name, segment number, segment index, logical ID, physical ID, size, fault tolerance, and disk name
- ► RMON services—Agent name and version, IP and/or IPX address, number of interfaces, current status, agent type, resources, owners, and indexes
- ► RMON II services—Agent name and version, IP and/or IPX address, number of interfaces, current status, agent type, resources, owners, and indexes

To access the server configuration from within the ZENworks Server Management namespace in ConsoleOne follow these steps:

1. Locate the server object you want to display configuration information about.

2. Click the plus sign next to the server object to expand the view. The view should expand to reveal the configuration devices, operating system, and services configuration data groups.

3. Click the plus sign next to each of the data groups and data elements to reveal data about each configuration component.

4. You can also get a summary view, shown in Figure 31.2, by selecting View→Summary from the main menu.

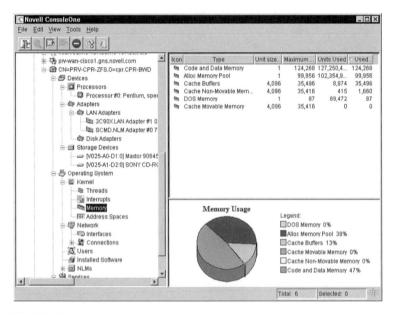

FIGURE 31.2
Server configuration groups and components located in the ZENworks Server Management namespace in ConsoleOne.

Showing Server Summary Data

Displaying the configuration data for each individual component gives you a lot of detailed and useful information. At times, however, you may want to take only a quick look at a server's configuration information. For this reason, ZENworks Server Management also enables you to display a quick summary view of the most vital information about the managed server.

ZENworks Server Management uses a series of SNMP GET requests to the ZENworks Server Management agents to create a quick collection of summary data. ZENworks Server Management dynamically updates summary data as it continuously polls the server.

To access the summary information about a server, right-click the server object and then select Views→Summary from the pop-up menu. A screen similar to the one in Figure 31.3 appears showing the following information about the managed server:

- ▶ Server type—Tells you whether it is a NetWare Windows 2000/2003 or Linux server.

- ▶ Server name—Lets you know which server you are viewing the summary for.

- ▶ Server tree—Useful when troubleshooting eDirectory issues.

- ▶ Description—Tells you the server type, version, and revisions. This is useful in determining whether a support pack has been applied to the server.

- ▶ Location—If a Location field is set up for the server in the management database, that location shows up here. This is essential if you have a WAN with numerous servers located in several different buildings, cities, or countries.

- ▶ Contact—Useful for finding the person responsible for the server because most enterprise networks are partitioned and administered by several different people.

- ▶ IP address—Gives you the IP address and subnet mask for the server.

- ▶ IPX address—Gives you the IPX address and network number for the server.

- ▶ Version—Gives you the OS version of the server.

- ▶ Subnet Mask—Gives you the IP address subnet mask configured for this server.

- ▶ Total RAM—Indicates total RAM installed, which is useful in troubleshooting server problems.

▶ Up time—Useful for things such as knowing when the server was last serviced, if the server has been down recently, or if the server has experienced critical problems and reset itself.

▶ Date/Time—The current time that the server thinks it is. This is helpful if you are having any issues involving time synchronization in eDirectory.

▶ Service summary—Lists the services currently available on the server. This can be helpful if you are browsing servers to find a candidate to take on extra services.

▶ Logged in users—Gives you the number of users currently logged in to the server.

▶ Open files—Gives you the number of files currently open on the server.

▶ Server status—If for any reason the server cannot be contacted, the most recent summary data is collected, and the server shows up as being down.

▶ Managed events—Lists all events monitored by ZENworks Server Management that occur on the server. This list can be useful in understanding the current state of a server because alarms are also listed.

▶ CPU utilization—Displays a speedometer of the current percentage of utilization of the server's CPU.

▶ Volume data—Displays the mount status and free and used space on the server's volumes.

▶ Cache activity—Displays a graph showing the history of the server's cache memory in terms of cache hits and percentage of free cache buffers.

NOTE ZENworks Server Management also enables you to display similar summary data for processors, LAN adapters, disk adapters, storage devices, threads, interrupts, memory, address spaces, interfaces, connections, users, installed software, NLMs, and volumes.

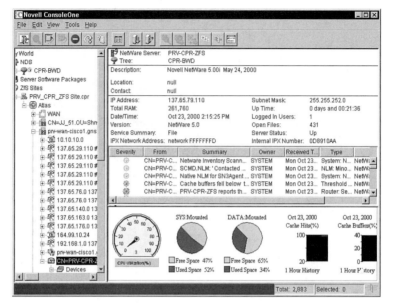

FIGURE 31.3
Server summary of a NetWare server, located in the ZENworks Server Management namespace in ConsoleOne.

Viewing Trend Data

Trend data is another important aspect of your servers that ZENworks Server Management enables you to view and monitor. ZENworks Server Management is continuously gathering data about the trends in CPU usage, memory usage, and network traffic from the managed server as it is operating.

You can view the trend data from the management console in terms of current data or historically by hour, day, week, month, or year. That trend data can be useful in troubleshooting network and server issues, as well as understanding the current workload on the server.

Monitor the trend data to help with making decisions on setting trend alarm thresholds, determining peak usage of the server, balancing server loads, and allocating new resources. To view the trend data from the management console, simply right-click the server you want to monitor and select Views→Trend from the pop-up menu; a screen similar to the one shown in Figure 31.4 should appear.

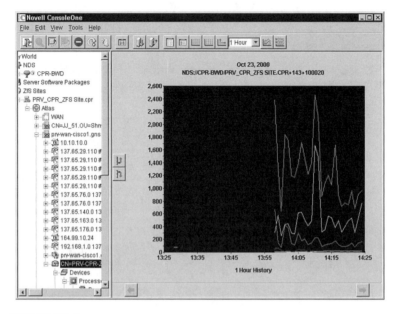

FIGURE 31.4
Trend Data view of a NetWare server, located in the ZENworks Server
Management namespace in ConsoleOne.

ZENworks Server Management enables you to customize the Trend Data
view to give you the maximum use of the data. The following sections
describe how to customize the Trend Data view by displaying the legend,
modifying time spans, displaying grid lines, stacking/unstacking graphs,
and modifying the Trend view profile.

Displaying the Legend

You must display a legend to understand the Trend Data view shown in
Figure 31.4 and use it to understand the current status of the server. The
legend is simply a window that relates the trend data parameters used in
the Trend view with the color of its line shown on the graph. Viewing the
legend helps you understand what trends are being displayed on the
server so that the graph makes sense.

To view the Trend view legend, simply click the Legend icon in the Trend
view toolbar (see Figure 31.4). A pane similar to the one shown in Figure
31.5 appears.

FIGURE 31.5
Legend window for the Trend Data view in ConsoleOne.

Modifying Time Spans

After you view the legend and understand what parameters the graph is showing you, you can modify the time spans for the trend data to best understand how the server is doing. You can modify the time span by clicking the down arrow on the toolbar of the Trend Data view and selecting one of the following time spans:

▶ 1 Hour—Shows you the current status of the server. At 9 a.m., for example, you may want to view the 1 Hour span to see how the server is doing during the morning login.

▶ 1 Day—Shows you how the server did over the past 24 hours. This can be useful to see how the server performed over a workday or overnight while reports and backups were running.

▶ 1 Week—Monitors your servers week to week. This is the most commonly used time span to judge overall usage and performance of a server.

▶ 1 Month—Monitors the long-term performance of your server. This can be helpful in determining increased workload trends.

▶ 1 Year—Compares the usage of your servers over the past year. This can help you determine where more servers are needed or where you can reallocate users.

Displaying Grid Lines

Another task you can perform in the Trend Data view is to display horizontal and vertical grid lines. The grid lines make the graphs easier to read. You can turn the horizontal grid lines on and off by clicking the Horizontal Grid button on the Trend Data view toolbar. Conversely, you can turn the vertical grid lines on and off by clicking the Vertical Grid button on the Trend Data view toolbar.

Stacking and Unstacking Graphs

One of the most useful ways to customize your Trend Data view is to stack and unstack the graphs. Stacking the graphs means that they are laid on top of each other on a single graph with several lines for all parameters. Unstacking the graphs makes several different graphs, each with its own line for a single parameter, as shown in Figure 31.6. (Refer to Figure 31.4 to see what a stacked graph looks like.)

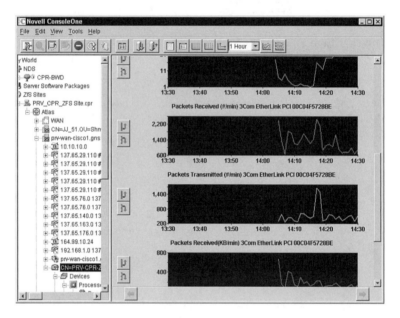

FIGURE 31.6
Unstacked Trend Data view of a NetWare server, located in the ZENworks Server Management namespace in ConsoleOne.

To stack the graphs on top of each other, click the Stack Chart button on the Trend Data view toolbar. To unstack the graphs, click the Strip Chart button on the Trend Data view toolbar.

Modifying the Trend View Profile

The most comprehensive way to modify the Trend Data view is to modify the Trend view profile. The Trend view profile is basically the set of parameters displayed on the Trend view graph. Modify the Trend view profile to best fit your servers and your environment. Follow these steps to modify the Trend view profile:

1. Click the Profile button on the Trend Data view toolbar. A window similar to the one in Figure 31.7 appears.

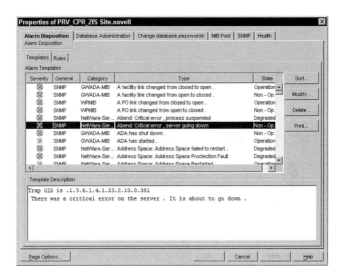

FIGURE 31.7
Trend view profile settings window for the Trend Data view in ConsoleOne.

2. Edit the profile by clicking the parameters to either select or deselect them. Use the Shift+click and Ctrl+click methods to select multiple parameters.

3. Click OK to apply the setting. The Trend Data view should now be updated.

Managing Trend Samplings

Now that you understand how to view the trend data, you need to know how to manage the way the data is collected. ZENworks Server Management enables you to modify the trend data sampling rates and thresholds used to collect the data. The following sections discuss how to use the management console to customize trend sampling to fit your network.

Modifying Trend Samplings and Intervals

The first step in managing trend sampling is to set the sampling and interval rates for trend parameters. Setting the sampling rate effectively determines the duration for which data from a particular parameter is collected by specifying the number of samples to take. Setting the interval rate determines how often data is collected from a particular parameter. Follow these steps to set the sampling and intervals for trend data parameters:

1. Right-click the server object and select Properties from the pop-up menu.

2. Select the Trend tab, as shown in Figure 31.8.

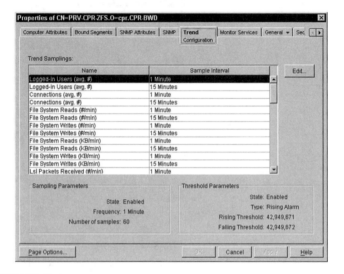

FIGURE 31.8
Trend tab for a managed server object in ConsoleOne.

3. Select the trend parameter you want to modify and click the Edit button. An Edit dialog box appears.

4. From the State drop-down list in the Edit dialog box, shown in Figure 31.9, select Enabled to enable trend sampling for the parameter.

5. Modify the time interval by selecting a value from the Frequency drop-down list. Values are from 5 seconds to one day.

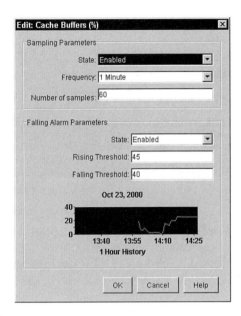

FIGURE 31.9
The Edit dialog box for trend data parameters in ConsoleOne.

6. Specify the duration of time for which to collect samples by entering a value in the Number of Samples field.

7. Click OK, and the parameter is modified.

After these changes are made, the trend information sampling rate will be changed, and the number of data points of information reflected in the trend data will adjust.

Modifying Threshold Alarm Settings

After you set the sampling and interval rates for the trend data parameter, you need to set the threshold alarm settings for the parameter. Modifying the threshold alarm settings for a particular parameter controls the range at which the parameter can operate before triggering an alarm. It also controls the scope of the graph in the Trend Data view. Follow these steps to modify the threshold alarm setting for a trend data parameter:

1. Follow steps 1–3 from the preceding section.

2. From the Edit dialog box, shown previously in Figure 31.9, select Enabled for State in the Alarm section to enable trend sampling for the parameter.

3. Set the Rising Threshold to a value that reflects a safe amount for the parameter.

4. Set the Falling Threshold to a value that reflects an unhealthy state for the parameter.

5. Click OK, and the parameter is modified.

NOTE An alarm is sent the first time the rising threshold is surpassed, and if the parameter never dips back below the falling threshold, an alarm will not be re-sent. In other words, for an alarm to be sent again after it has already been sent once, the current threshold has to dip down below the falling threshold and then surpass the rising threshold again.

Configuring Server Parameters

Another server management innovation that ZENworks Server Management provides is the ability to modify server parameters without being at the server itself or having a remote management session open to it. ZENworks Server Management enables you to modify the managed server's eDirectory object to make changes to its parameters. Follow these steps to modify server parameters from within ConsoleOne:

1. Select the Operating System resource under the NetWare server object in the Atlas namespace.

2. Right-click the Operating System resource and select Properties from the pop-up menu.

3. Select the Set Parameters tab.

4. Click the down arrow and select the category of set parameters you want to change from the drop-down list, as shown in Figure 31.10.

5. Select the specific parameter you want to modify and then click Edit.

6. From the Edit Parameters dialog box, shown in Figure 31.11, enter the new value for the parameter into the field (the field type changes based on the parameter selected).

7. Indicate when you want the change to occur by selecting one of the following times: Now, Until Reboot (the change disappears after the server is rebooted), Only After Reboot (the change does not take effect until the server is rebooted), or Now, and After Reboot (the change is made immediately and permanently).

8. Click OK, and the change to the parameter is made according to the criteria you selected.

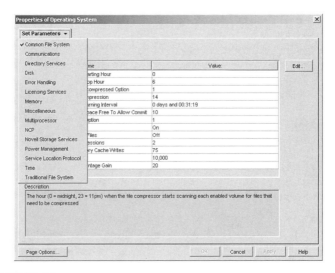

FIGURE 31.10
Set Parameters tab for server objects in the Atlas namespace in
ConsoleOne.

FIGURE 31.11
Edit Parameters dialog box for server set parameters in ConsoleOne.

NOTE The preceding steps are a way to manually change set parameters on a server-by-server basis. If you want to do this on more than one server at a time throughout your network, you would use the Server Policy Package→Set Parameters policy in the policies piece of ZENworks Server Management.

Using this technique, you can modify the system parameters for a specific
NetWare server.

Advanced Trending Agent

The ZENworks advanced trending agent is an application that accumulates and stores the historical trend data for parameters instrumented by an SNMP agent, as long as the parameter is defined by an MIB variable and not just preconfigured MIB variables. Administrators can use the advanced trending agent to manage trends on NetWare, Windows, and Linux platforms.

The advanced trending agent accumulates and stores the samples of the parameters and then exposes that data through an SNMP MIB. The SNMP MIB allows this data to be used to view the long-term trend graphs of the parameters.

Administrators can configure the advanced trending agent using a configuration file or through an SNMP interface. The advanced trending agent also includes a command-line utility that reads the configuration file for any updates.

The advanced trending agent configuration files are located in the following locations:

▶ NetWare—`<installation_path>/advtrend/advtrend.ncf`

▶ Windows—`<installation_path>/advtrend/ini/advtrend.ini`

▶ Linux—`/etc/opt/novell/zenworks/zfs-mms-advtrend.conf`

Administrators can modify the contents to add new parameters to trend on or modify existing ones. The configuration file follows a standard INI format. The section name can contain any value and is typically a meaningful name for the parameter being configured. All the section names in a given file must be distinct.

> **NOTE** You cannot change the name of the section. If you do so, the data for the parameters is lost, and new data is collected. You cannot change the names of the keys. Each key represents a particular configuration that defines the trending activity for that parameter. Certain mandatory keys must be defined for any section. If these keys are not present, the advanced trending agent ignores the entire section.

Executing Server Commands

Another server management innovation that ZENworks Server Management provides is the ability to execute server commands without being at the server itself or having a remote management session open to it.

Earlier in this chapter, you learned how to navigate the server object portion of the ZENworks Server Management namespace to view configuration data. You can also use the server level of the ZENworks Server Management namespace to execute server commands at the server level or below.

ZENworks Server Management enables you to execute the following server commands from the ZENworks Server Management namespace area in ConsoleOne:

▶ Loading and unloading NLMs—You can load or unload an NLM by right-clicking the NLM object in the ZENworks Server Management namespace and selecting Load NLM or Unload NLM from the Actions menu.

▶ Mounting and dismounting volumes—You can mount or dismount a volume by right-clicking the volume object in the ZENworks Server Management namespace and selecting Mount Volume or Dismount Volume from the Actions menu.

▶ Clearing a server connection—You can clear a server connection by right-clicking the connection in the ZENworks Server Management namespace (Server→Operating System→Network→Connections) and selecting Clear Connection from the Actions menu.

▶ Restarting a server—You can restart a server by right-clicking the server object in the ZENworks Server Management namespace and selecting Restart Server from the Actions menu.

▶ Shutting down a server—You can shut down a server by right-clicking the server object in the ZENworks Server Management namespace and selecting Down Server from the Actions menu.

Probing Manageability

Another advanced feature that ZENworks Server Management has is the ability to probe the manageability of servers on the network. This feature allows you to select a server and search for management agents that will allow you to manage the server from the remote mangagement console. When management agents are found, new options will be added to the menus in the console, allowing you to access the server remotely.

Managing Remote Servers

Managing servers remotely has become an industry standard as companies have increased the number of servers, thus requiring large data centers. ZENworks Server Management greatly enhances your ability to remotely manage servers through the addition of applications that enable you to remotely take control of the server.

ZENworks Server Management includes the following features to improve the functionality and reliability of remote server management:

▶ Mirror Driver—Is installed during the ZENworks Remote Management installation on the remote server and provides administrators the ability to select whether an independent driver should be installed and used for remote management sessions rather then the device's video driver. This provides ZENworks the capability to coexist with other remote management products because it has its own video driver to use.

▶ Agent Initiated Connection—Allows a user at a remote server to enter an IP address or DNS name of a remote management console and request a remote session to begin.

▶ Scale to Fit—Allows the remote management operator to scale the remote window to fit the operator's screen.

▶ Block Mouse Movements to Agent—Allows the remote operator the ability to block mouse movements from being seen on the remote server.

▶ Force a 256 Color Palette—Allows the remote operator to force a 256-color palette on the managed server during a remote session, which greatly improves performance over slow connections.

The following sections describe how to use the ZENworks Server Management console to remotely manage a server.

Managing Remote NetWare Servers

ZENworks Server Management includes the capability to use the RCON-SOLEJ utility provided with NetWare to remotely manage a server from the management console. This enables you to manage NetWare servers based on your role in the organization and tasks assigned to you.

You can use the ZENworks Server Management remote management capability to perform the following role-based remote management tasks on a managed NetWare server:

▶ Console commands—Remotely execute console commands as if you were at the server. You may, for example, want to execute a command to start or stop an eDirectory trace.

▶ Scan directories—Scan directories looking for installed software, data files, or file locations.

▶ Edit text files—Edit text files on both NetWare and DOS partitions to modify scripts or other files.

▶ Transfer files—Send files to the server to update an application or data. You cannot transfer files from a server due to security reasons.

▶ Install or upgrade—Perform an install or upgrade. You can, for example, remotely install the latest NetWare support pack to the server.

Follow these steps to begin a remote management session with a NetWare server from the ZENworks Server Management console on an IP-only server:

1. Load the RCONSOLEJ agent (`RCONAG6.NLM`) on the NetWare server.

2. Right-click the server object in ConsoleOne and select Actions→Remote Management from the pop-up menu.

3. Enter the RCONSOLEJ agent password.

4. Enter the TCP port number on which the agent will listen for requests from RCONSOLEJ. (The default value is 2034.)

5. Click the Connect button, and an RCONSOLEJ session similar to the one shown in Figure 31.12 loads.

FIGURE 31.12
RCONSOLEJ remote management session launched from ConsoleOne.

Follow these steps to begin a remote management session with a NetWare server from the ZENworks Server Management console on an IPX-only server:

1. Load the RCONSOLEJ agent (`RCONAG6.NLM`) on the NetWare server.

2. Right-click the server object in ConsoleOne and select Actions→Remote Management from the pop-up menu.

3. Enter the RCONSOLEJ agent password.

4. Enter the TCP port number on which the agent will listen for requests from RCONSOLEJ. (The default value is 2036.)

5. Enter the IP address of the proxy server or choose a proxy server in the Proxy Server options section of the RCONSOLEJ window. The server acting as a proxy server for the RCONSOLEJ session needs to be running both IP and IPX so that it can communicate with both the workstation and the IPX server.

6. Enter the SPX port number on which the agent will listen for requests from the proxy server. (The default value is 16801.)

7. Click the Connect button, and an RCONSOLEJ session similar to the one shown previously in Figure 31.12 loads.

Following the preceding steps will allow you to remotely control a NetWare server from anywhere in your environment.

Managing Remote 2000/2003 Servers

ZENworks Server Management adds the capability to remotely manage a Windows NT/2000/2003 server from the management console. This enables you to manage Windows 2000/2003 servers based on your role in the organization and tasks assigned to you.

You can use the ZENworks Server Management remote management capability to perform the following role-based remote management tasks on a managed Windows 2000/2003 server:

▶ Remote control—Enables you to remotely take control of a Windows 2000/2003 server to resolve any software-related problems and perform any administrative tasks.

▶ Remote view—Enables you to remotely view the desktop of the Windows 2000/2003 server. This enables you to monitor activity on the NT server and see when actions are performed.

Follow these steps to begin a remote management session with a Windows 2000/2003 server from the ZENworks Server Management console:

1. Verify that the remote management agent installed with the ZENworks Server Management install is running on the Windows 2000/2003 server you want to manage.

2. Select the server object from within ConsoleOne.

3. Select Tools→Remote Management→Remote Console→Windows.

4. Specify the agent to use to initiate the remote management session.

5. Select Remote Control or Remote View from the drop-down menu.

6. Enter the password for the ZENworks Server Management remote management agent. The remote management session should activate.

NOTE During a remote management session, the user of the Windows 2000/2003 server receives an audible signal indicating that the server is being accessed. Every five seconds the user receives a visible signal displaying the name of the user accessing the remote server. These settings can be changed by selecting Edit Security Parameters from the Remote Management icon's pop-up menu on the taskbar of the remote server.

Following the preceding steps will allow you to remotely control a Windows server from anywhere in your environment.

Optimizing Server Management

Now that you understand how ZENworks Server Management uses trend data and alarm thresholds to help you manage your servers, you need to know how to optimize the data that ZENworks Server Management gathers for you. When a managed server is first started, agents for trend data, alarm thresholds, and alarm management are loaded and begin collecting data. The best way to optimize server management is to control the initial settings loaded on your servers.

The following sections describe how to modify the configuration files that initialize the server management agents to give you tight control over the information collected and presented at the management console.

Setting Initial Trend Values

The first configuration file you should know how to modify is the trend initialization file. This file sets the initial trends for monitoring a device. Each time a new managed device is discovered on the server, a trend file is created for it.

The trend initialization file is named **NTREND.INI** on a NetWare server and **N_NTREND.INI** on a Windows 2000/2003 server. The following sections describe how to use a text editor to modify the initial trend file shown in Figure 31.13.

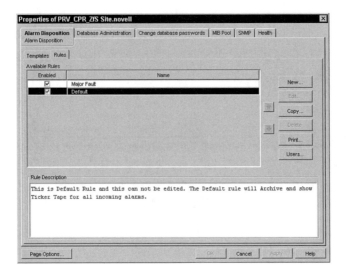

FIGURE 31.13
Trend initialization file for a NetWare server.

Setting the Sample Interval

The first column in the trend initialization file is the parameter name, and the second is the sample interval. The sample interval indicates the frequency that samples of the specified parameter are collected in terms of a time interval between five seconds and one day.

Evaluate each parameter to determine how often it should be sampled. If you sample too often, you run the risk of poor performance. But if you don't sample enough, you run the risk of incomplete or inaccurate information. Use the codes listed in Table 31.1 to set the sample interval for each trend data parameter.

TABLE 31.1 Sample Interval Codes for Trend Initialization

TREND INITIALIZATION CODE	SAMPLE INTERVAL RATE
1	5 seconds
2	10 seconds
3	15 seconds
4	30 seconds
5	1 minute
6	5 minutes
7	15 minutes
8	30 minutes
9	1 hour
10	4 hours
11	8 hours
12	1 day

Setting the Trend Buckets

After you set the sample interval for the trend data parameters, you need to set the number of trend buckets in the third column. Setting the number of trend buckets determines the duration of time for which samples will be collected for the parameter.

If, for example, you want to review the number of users logged in to a server for one day and you set the sample interval to be 30 minutes, you need to specify 48 trend buckets. Each bucket contains one sample taken at a 30-minute interval.

After a particular time duration is exceeded for a file, the oldest trend buckets are emptied and replaced with the most recent samples. Therefore, after the duration has been reached, you will always have samples for that amount of time from the present backward.

Enabling and Disabling Trend Files

The fourth column in the trend initialization file is the Enable Trend Data option. This value can be set to either 0 or 1. Specifying 1 enables the gathering of trend data for this parameter. Specifying 0 disables the gathering of trend data for the parameter.

Setting Initial Threshold Values

After setting up the initial trend values, you need to specify the threshold values for alarm generation. Alarm thresholds control the values at which alarms are generated.

Two values are associated with these thresholds: a rising limit and a falling limit. For rising thresholds, the rising limit is the value at which an alarm is generated for the parameter. The falling limit, for rising thresholds, is the value at which the alarm is reset. They work conversely for falling thresholds. This way, an alarm is generated only when a server goes from a good condition to a bad condition—not if it simply stays in a bad state.

If, for example, you have set a falling threshold on cache buffers and a falling limit of 30% and a rising limit of 50%, the server would send out an alarm if cache buffers got below 30%. If the cache buffers then wavered between 25% and 35%, only the one alarm would be sent. But if the server's cache buffers climbed back up to 60% and then back down to 30%, a second alarm would be sent.

Setting Rising and Falling Thresholds

The fifth and sixth columns in the trend initialization file are the rising and falling limits, respectively. They represent a value that indicates a problem for the trend parameter and a value that indicates that the trend parameter is out of trouble.

Evaluate each parameter to determine the appropriate threshold limits and specify them in their columns. Also specify which type of threshold the parameter has by putting "rising" or "falling" in the Type column of the trend initialization file.

Enabling and Disabling Threshold Traps

After you specify the limits, you can enable or disable the threshold trap by specifying 0 or 1 in the seventh column. Specifying 0 disables alarm generation for the parameter. Specifying 1 enables alarm generation for the parameter.

Configuring Alarm Generation

The next configuration file you should know how to modify is the trap configuration file, which controls alarm generation. The trap configuration file consists of keywords with associated information about alarm generation.

The trap configuration file is located in the following locations on the managed servers:

- NetWare—`SYS:\SYSTEM\NMA\NWTRAP.CFG`
- Windows 2000/2003—`\MW\INI\NTTRAP.INI`

The following sections describe how to modify the trap configuration file, shown in Figure 31.14, to modify the types of alarms forwarded to management consoles, community strings used for sending SNMP traps, traps to be disabled, and specific alarms that you want to prevent from being forwarded.

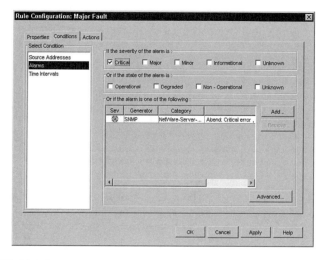

FIGURE 31.14
Trap configuration file, `NWTRAP.CFG`, for a NetWare server.

Setting the Community String
The first thing you can set in a trap configuration file is the community string. The community string is used to generate traps and is restricted to 32 characters. The default community string is `public`.

Setting the Time Interval
After setting the community string, you need to specify the time interval that alarm generation waits before issuing the next alarm. This is to prevent the network and management console from being inundated with identical alarms. The time interval can be any value between 0 and 232.

If, for example, you want to set the amount of time between alarms for traps 5, 10, and 100 to 20 seconds, you would use the following command in the trap configuration file:

```
5 10 100 INTERVAL = 20
```

Configuring Alarm Security Levels

After you specify the time interval for alarms, set the severity levels for alarm generation. Each SNMP alarm has a severity level associated with it. You can specify at what severity level to generate alarms so that only those alarms are actually sent to the management console.

You can use the ENABLE and DISABLE commands, with a severity level code or number, in the alarm configuration file to control which severity levels to pass through. Table 31.2 shows the severity levels for alarm generation and the associated codes for the configuration file.

The following are examples of specifying severity levels in the configuration file:

```
ENABLE SEVERITY >= MINOR
DISABLE SEVERITY <= WARN
```

TABLE 31.2   Severity Levels and Codes for Alarms

NETWARE SEVERITY	SNMP SEVERITY	ZFS SEVERITY	SEVERITY CODE
0—Informational	Informational	Informational	INFORM
1—Warning	Minor	Minor	WARN
2—Recoverable	Major	Major	MINOR
3—Critical	Critical	Critical	MAJOR
4—Fatal	Fatal	Critical	CRITICAL
5—Operation Aborted	Fatal	Critical	CRITICAL
Unrecoverable	Fatal	Critical	CRITICAL

Defining Alarm Recipients

The final configuration file you should know how to modify to optimize server management is the TRAPTARG.CFG file. The TRAPTARG.CFG file is used to send traps to third-party management consoles. It defines recipients of SNMP traps that are detected on the server.

If you plan to use third-party management consoles or utilities to monitor SNMP traps, you need to add their IP address or IPX address to the `TRAPTARG.CFG` file for alarms to be sent to them.

Follow these steps to modify the `TRAPTARG.CFG` file:

1. Open the file in a text editor.

2. Add the IPX network number and MAC address of any management consoles to the IPX section of the `TRAPTARG.CFG` file—for example, **FFFF1111:00001B123456**.

3. Add the IP address or logical name, if you have DNS configured, of any management consoles to the UDP section of the `TRAPTARG.CFG` file—for example, **111.111.5.2**. If DNS is configured in your network, you can use the logical name.

4. Save the file.

5. Unload and reload `NWTRAP.NLM` on the agent server.

When this is completed, the `NWTRAP` system will begin and use the additional addresses placed in the target configuration files as targets for generated alarms.

Using ZENworks Server Management Server Inventory

Another important component of ZENworks Server Management is server inventory. ZENworks Server Management uses inventory scan programs to scan and store hardware and software inventory of your managed servers. The following sections describe the inventory components and discuss how to scan server inventory and customize software scanning.

Understanding Server Inventory Components

To get the most out of ZENworks Server Management server inventory, you need to understand the components that make up the inventory process and roles that inventory servers play in capturing and storing inventory data.

In a small network, one inventory server would be ample to collect, store, and provide access to the inventory data about servers. But in enterprise networks, the number of servers and the amount of inventory data that can be collected and managed becomes complex. For that reason, ZENworks Server Management implements a tree design to allow several inventory servers to be involved in accumulating and distributing the inventory data. The following is a list of the types of inventory servers and their roles in the inventory process:

- ▶ Standalone server—This server is used in small networks where only one server and database are needed for collecting and storing inventory data from the network. The standalone server collects the inventory data and stores it in a local database.

- ▶ Root server—In an enterprise network, you need to implement several inventory servers to collect and store inventory data. The first inventory server you create is a root server that acts as the topmost level for the inventory tree. The root server must have an inventory database stored on it to store data collected from the other inventory servers below it in the tree.

- ▶ Intermediate server—If you have a large network, you also need to create intermediate servers. The intermediate server collects data from servers below and passes that data to either another intermediate server above or to the root server. An intermediate server can have an inventory database attached to it to store inventory information locally, but that is not required.

- ▶ Leaf server—This is the bottommost level of the tree. Leaf servers are responsible for collecting inventory data that has been scanned and then passing that data up to the next level in the inventory tree. The leaf server can send data either to an intermediate server or to the root server. It can also have an inventory database attached to it to store inventory information locally, but that is not required.

Now that you understand the types of inventory servers involved in the server inventory process, you need to understand the components involved. ZENworks Server Management uses several different pieces to scan servers for inventory data, process that information, and then store it in the appropriate location. The following is a list of components that make up the inventory process:

▸ Inventory scanners—Agents that run on managed servers responsible for scanning the server's hardware and software. They collect the data each time they are run and store that data in a file.

▸ Selector—Processes the data scanned by the inventory scanners and selects new data that should be added to the inventory database. It then places those scanned files into appropriate directories.

▸ Sender and receiver—Utilities that run on servers to transfer scanned files from an inventory server to the next level of server in the inventory tree.

▸ Inventory storer—A utility that runs on an inventory server with an inventory database attached. It is responsible for taking the inventory scan files that the server receives and storing the inventory data in the database.

▸ Inventory database—An RDBMS maintained by Oracle or Sybase or a Microsoft SQL Server and acts as the repository for the hardware and software inventory data collected by the inventory scanners. You can access the data in the inventory database through management console reporting as well as through user customized database queries.

Understanding the Scanning Process

Now that you understand the types of inventory servers and the software components involved in ZENworks Server Management server inventory, it is helpful for you to understand the actual process of scanning, collecting, and storing inventory data using ZENworks Server Management.

The first thing that happens in the inventory process is that the inventory scanner agent is activated on a Windows or NetWare server. The agent reads inventory policy settings (discussed later in this chapter) and uses those settings to scan the server. As the scanning agent runs, it collects data about the server's hardware and software and stores that data in .STR files on the server's local file system. The scan collector then transfers those files to the scan directory (\SCANDIR\) of the inventory server defined in the inventory policy.

After the inventory scanner places data in the scan directory, the selector begins to process the .STR files. The selector filters out everything but new inventory data and then stores the new data in the enterprise merge directory (\ENTMERGEDIR\) to be transferred to a higher level and/or to the database directory (\DBDIR\) to be stored in the inventory database, if one is running on the server.

After files are stored in the enterprise merge directory, the sender zips up all the scan data files and sends them to a receiver running on another inventory server, which is defined in the roll-up policy.

The receiver opens the .ZIP files it receives from a sender and copies them to the enterprise merge directory (\ENTMERGEDIR\) to be transferred to a higher level and/or to the database directory (\DBDIR\) to be stored in the inventory database, if one is running on the server. On an intermediate server with an inventory database, for example, the files would be copied to both directories; however, on the root server the files would be copied only to the database directory.

After files are placed, storer opens the .ZIP file, extracts the scan files to a temp directory (\DBDIR\TEMP\), and updates the inventory data with the data in the .STR files. When the database is updated, the administrator can view the new inventory data from the management console.

Setting Up Server Inventory

Now that you understand the components involved in the ZENworks server inventory process, you need to understand how to set up and configure the eDirectory objects that control inventory scanning. You use the management console to define the database types and locations in the inventory tree, as well as their synchronization and roll-up schedules. The following sections discuss the configuration changes you need to make at the management console to configure and customize server inventory.

Configuring the Inventory Service Object

The first object you need to configure for server inventory is the inventory service. You must create an inventory service object for each server on which you install ZENworks Server Management. The inventory service object defines which role that server plays during the server inventory process. (The inventory service object can be created automatically during the installation of ZENworks Server Management.)

To configure the inventory service object for an inventory server, right-click the inventory service object in ConsoleOne and select Properties. Then select Inventory Service Object Properties from the drop-down list of the Inventory Service Object tab, as shown in Figure 31.15.

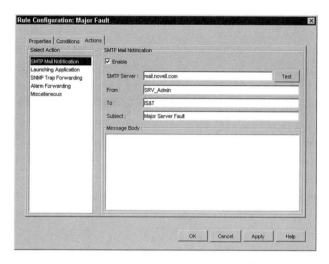

FIGURE 31.15
Inventory service object properties of an inventory service object of a ZENworks Server Management inventory server.

From the Inventory Service Object Properties page, you can configure the following items of the inventory server:

▶ Inventory Server Role—Select the role of the server (Standalone, Root, Intermediate, or Leaf) from the drop-down list. Then you need to define whether it has a database connected by selecting the Connected to Database box (Intermediate and Leaf only). You also need to specify whether machines are connected to this service (Root and Intermediate only).

▶ Discard Scan Data Time—Defines a date and time of when to discard all scan data and start with a fresh copy.

▶ Scan Directory Path—Defines the location on the inventory server where the scan data files are to be stored when a scan is run.

▶ Enable Scan of Machines—Allows you to temporarily disable scanning of machines. This option is useful if you need to reduce server or network traffic for troubleshooting or performance reasons.

ZENworks Server Management enables you to configure the synchronization schedule to synchronize servers being inventoried with the inventory server to which they are associated. To configure the synchronization schedule for an inventory server, right-click the inventory service object in ConsoleOne and select Properties. Then select Inventory Service Sync Schedule from the drop-down list of the Inventory Server Object tab, as shown in Figure 31.16.

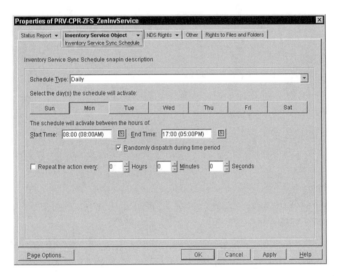

FIGURE 31.16
Inventory Service Sync Schedule page of an inventory service object of a ZENworks Server Management inventory server.

From the Inventory Service Sync Schedule page, you can configure the following synchronization options for the inventory server:

▶ Schedule Type—Determines whether the synchronization is a daily, weekly, or monthly type, or whether it should use the policy package to determine its schedule.

▶ Day(s) the Schedule Will Activate—Allows you to specify, by clicking the day's button, which days the schedule will be active. This is useful for performance reasons. If no changes occur over the weekend, for example, but you are performing network intensive backups, then you would not select Saturday and Sunday.

▶ Start and End Time—Allows you to specify the start and stop time for inventory to occur. This allows you to control what times during the day inventory can run. By setting the stop time to 8 a.m., for example, you could have inventory stop at 8 a.m. before users begin logging in to the network.

▶ Randomly Dispatch During Time Period—Allows you to have ZENworks randomly start the synchronization between the start and end times.

▶ Repeat the Action Every—Allows you to have ZENworks repeat the synchronization at the specified interval. This can be useful if you are watching software inventory that changes frequently.

Configuring the Distributed Server Inventory Policy

After configuring the inventory service object, you need to configure the server inventory policy for distributed server packages that you want to use to collect and distribute inventory data. The server inventory policy enables you to configure which inventory service servers associated with this package will use. It also allows you to enable and configure hardware and software scanning.

To configure the server inventory policy for a distributed server package, right-click the package and select Properties from the drop-down menu. Then select the Policies tab for the operating system you want to configure. ZENworks Server Management enables you to select NetWare, Windows, Linux, Solaris, or General to configure for all those operating systems. Next, enable the server inventory policy by checking the box next to it. Finally, select the server inventory policy and click the Properties button to bring up the Server Inventory Policy Properties window. The following sections discuss how to configure the server inventory policy from this window.

Configuring the Inventory Service for the Server

The first step in configuring the server inventory policy is to configure which inventory service the server associated with this policy will use. Select the General tab in the Server Inventory Policy page, as shown in Figure 31.17, and configure the following settings:

▶ Inventory Service Object DN—Use the Browse button to navigate through the eDirectory tree and locate the inventory service policy, the correct roll-up schedules, and locations configured for servers associated with this distributed server package.

▶ Server IP Address/DNS Name—After selecting the inventory service object, you need to select the IP address or DNS name to use with connecting to the inventory database. Make sure that you select the correct name or address, or the inventory servers will be unable to connect to the inventory service database.

▶ Proxy Server Configuration—Leave this section alone; you do not need to configure it for server inventory. However, if you are using a roll-up of the inventory and the server must roll up the inventory to a server across a firewall, you need to put in the IP address and the port of the proxy server into this field.

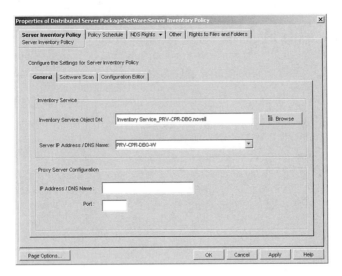

FIGURE 31.17
General panel of the NetWare Inventory Server Policy for a distributed server package.

Configuring Hardware Scan

If you are configuring a server inventory policy for Windows, you need to configure hardware scanning by selecting the Hardware Scan tab and setting the following options:

▶ Enable DMI Scan—Enables ZENworks to collect hardware inventory data from Windows 2000/2003 workstations by using the Desktop Management Interface (DMI) 2.0 specification. (DMI drivers are usually available through the vendor of the hardware platform.)

▶ Enable WMI Scan—Enables ZENworks Server Management to collect hardware inventory data from Windows 2000/2003 workstations by using the Web-based Management Interface (WMI) 1.5 specification (WMI drivers are included in the Windows system).

Configuring Software Scan

Next you need to configure software scanning. Enable software scanning by checking the box next to the Enable Software Scan option and then clicking the Custom Scan Editor button to bring up the Custom Scan Editor window (see Figure 31.18).

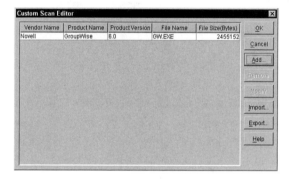

FIGURE 31.18
Custom Scan Editor window for software scanning in the server inventory policy for a distributed server package.

If you are configuring a server inventory policy for Windows, you also have the option to enable ZENworks to scan for product identification numbers of applications installed on inventoried Windows 2000/2003 servers. The product identification number can be useful in sorting and organizing inventory software reports.

From the Custom Scan Editor window, you can create a list of software that ZENworks Server Management will scan for on servers during the inventory process. The Custom Scan Editor provides a powerful tool to optimize software scanning for your network. Use the Custom Scan Editor to specify the vendor, product name, product version, filename, and file size of the software you want to scan for on servers. This allows you to selectively inventory only software that is important to track, reducing the size of inventory reports as well as network and server utilization.

Configuring the Configuration Editor

After you enable and configure software scanning, you can modify the INI file that ZENworks Server Management uses when reporting software inventory by selecting the Configuration Editor tab, as shown in Figure 31.19. From the Configuration Editor tab, you can edit the SWRules file by clicking the Set Default button to open the default file and then modifying the entries. This allows you to modify what information ZENworks includes when you create inventory reports.

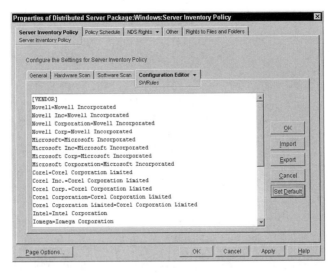

FIGURE 31.19
Configuration Editor page of the server inventory policy for a distributed server package.

If you are modifying the server inventory policy for Windows, the Configuration Editor tab will have a drop-down arrow allowing you to modify the entry's INI files for Zipped Names. This modification enables you to specify the manufacturers of software being used to zip files, as well as the identifiers they are using for the zipped files.

If you are modifying the server inventory policy for Windows, you also can modify the entries in the INI file for Asset Information. You can specify the DMI class names and attributes for things such as server model, model number, serial number, and computer type.

Configuring the Service Location Package

The next step in configuring server inventory is to define the inventory database for the service location package object and associate the database object with the inventory service object.

NOTE If you selected that ZENworks should set up inventory for a standalone server, you don't need to create the database object or do any associations.

This step tells ZENworks which inventory server to use for objects associated with the server package. Follow these steps to configure the server package from within ConsoleOne:

1. Create and/or select the server package.

2. Right-click the server package object and select Properties from the pop-up menu; then select the NetWare or Windows Policies tab.

3. Enable the ZENworks database policy by checking the box next to it. Click the Properties button to open the Database Properties window.

4. Select the Inventory Management Tab; then click the Browse button to find the inventory database object you want to use for the server package. Click OK.

5. When you return to the Properties page for the server package, select the Associations tab.

6. Click the Browse button and select the container that stores the inventory service object you want to associate with the inventory database you defined for the serverpackage. Click OK.

On completion of these steps, click the Apply button to configure the server package.

Configuring the Roll-Up Policy

After configuring the service location package, you need to configure the roll-up policy if this inventory server is a leaf or intermediate server. The roll-up policy controls the flow of scanned data through the inventory tree by determining the next inventory location and schedule-to-roll scan data collected by the current inventory server. Follow these steps to configure the roll-up policy for an inventory server in ConsoleOne:

1. Create and/or select the server package object associated with the inventory server.

2. Right-click the server package object and select Properties from the pop-up menu; then select the NetWare or Windows Policies tab.

3. Enable the inventory roll-up policy by checking the box next to it. Click the Properties button to open the Roll-Up Policy window, as shown in Figure 31.20.

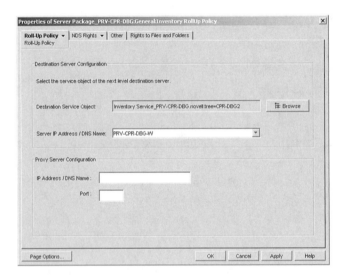

FIGURE 31.20
Roll-Up Policy of a server package object in ConsoleOne.

4. Click the Browse button and navigate to the inventory service object of the intermediate or root server to which you want this server to roll up scan data. Click OK.

5. The IP address or DNS Name should be inserted into the Server IP Address/DNS Name field automatically. If not, select the IP address of the next level inventory server.

6. Select Roll-Up Schedule from the Roll-Up Policy tab and configure the schedule of when to roll scan data collected by this server up to the next level. Keep in mind the synchronization schedule defined for the inventory server when configuring the roll-up schedule so that there are no conflicts and minimal lag time. If the inventory synchronization, for example, only runs monthly, you want the

roll-up to occur after the synchronization is complete to avoid a one-month latency of information being rolled up in the tree. (Refer to the "Configuring the Inventory Service Object" section and Figure 31.15 earlier in this chapter for more information about the schedule page.)

7. Click OK to return to the Server Package Properties page.

8. Select the Associations tab and click the Add button.

9. Browse to the server object you want to associate with this server package. Click OK twice to return to the Server Package Properties page.

On completion of these steps, click Apply to configure the roll-up policy.

Using the ZENworks Quick Report to View Inventory Data

ZENworks Server Management includes a utility called the Quick Report to simplify using the inventory database schema to retrieve data from the Inventory database.

Quick Report allows administrators to create custom views of the inventory data that contain a custom view name, database query, and custom defined attributes. These views give administrators the ability to quickly query the Inventory database and to retrieve and view only the pertinent information they want.

Quick Reports created by administrators are stored in the Inventory database. A copy of the data used to define the custom view is also stored in configuration files with the .EXP extension. The custom view configuration files are located in the following directory on the management console by default:

```
Consoleone\1.2\reporting\export
```

Administrators can also specify a different location to store the Quick Report configuration files.

Starting Quick Report

Quick Report, shown in Figure 31.21, can be started using one of the following two methods from ConsoleOne:

▶ Right-click a database object and then select ZENworks Inventory→Quick Report.

▶ From the main menu, select Tools→ZENworks Inventory→Quick Report.

You must configure the Inventory database before starting Quick Reports.

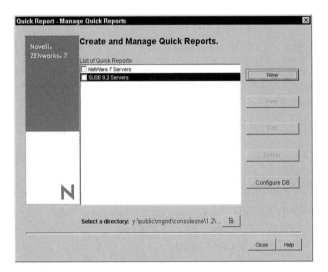

FIGURE 31.21
Main window in ZENworks Quick Reports.

Creating a New Quick Report

After you start Quick Report, you can use the following steps in the Create and Manage Quick Reports dialog box to create a new Quick Report to access inventory data:

1. Click the New button.

2. Specify that the report should include Servers.

3. Click the Edit Query button shown in Figure 31.22.

4. From the Define Query window, define a query that includes the specific information you need in the custom view.

5. Select the required attribute field by clicking on the Select Attribute button.

6. Specify the logical operation to apply to the attribute by clicking on the Select Relational Operator button.

7. Specify an appropriate value for the operation on the attribute, and then add additional attributes using the Logical Operator button to the right of the value textbox and repeating steps 5–7.

8. After you have added all attributes for the query criteria, click the OK button to return to to Quick Report, and then click Next.

9. From the Database Fields window, add fields that you want to appear in the report.

10. When you have finished selecting fields to appear in the report, click the Save button and specify the name of the report.

11. Click Close.

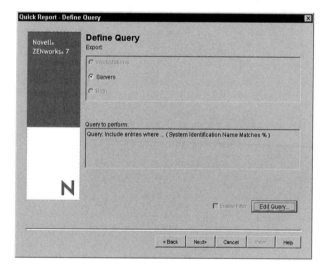

FIGURE 31.22
Define Query window in ZENworks Quick Report.

You have now created a custom Quick Report with which you can easily access inventory data.

Viewing a New Quick Report

After you start Quick Report, you can use the following steps in the
Create and Manage Quick Reports dialog box to view a Quick Report
that has already been created:

1. Select the report that you want to view from the List of Quick
   Reports list by clicking on the check box (refer to Figure 31.21).

2. Click the View button to view the report.

3. You can also view the report in a web browser by clicking on the
   View in Browser button in the Quick Report viewer, shown in
   Figure 31.23.

FIGURE 31.23
ConsoleOne view of an Inventory Query.

Using the View in Browser feature of Quick Report is useful to print
directly from the browser in a formatted form, shown in Figure 31.24.
The browser file is an XML document, so you also have the ability to use
Save As from the browser to store the report for your records.

FIGURE 31.24
Web Browser view of an Inventory Query.

Summary

This chapter focused on how to manage the numerous servers on the network. ZENworks Server Management includes powerful tools and services that help you manage your network servers, and each was discussed in this chapter.

## CHAPTER 32

Making the Most of ZENworks Server Management Reporting

One of the most powerful tools included with ZENworks Server Management is its extensive reporting engine. ZENworks Server Management has the capability to generate reports for you that show you everything from your server inventory to network health. ZENworks Server Management reporting can be a useful tool in helping you understand the condition of your network and plan for future additions. The following sections describe understanding, creating, and using server inventory reports, topology reports, and network health reports to quickly understand and administer your network.

All ZENworks Server Management reports are based on Crystal Reports and are executed through a delivered runtime module. You can design your own reports by creating defined reports through Crystal Reports designer and running them against the ZENworks Server Management database.

Reading ZENworks Server Management Reports

The first step is to understand what types of reports are available and what information can be obtained from them. ZENworks Server Management provides *inventory reports* that enable you to create lists of hardware and services available on your network to use for tracking and planning your network resources. You can use *topology reports*, generated by ZENworks, to understand the layout and design of your network, enabling you to plan for future growth. ZENworks Server Management also includes *health reports* that you can use to understand the overall health of your network and quickly diagnose issues.

Understanding Server Inventory Reports

ZENworks Server Management enables you to create inventory reports of hardware and software located on your managed servers. These reports can be useful if you need to know what hardware or software is on a particular machine.

Suppose, for example, that you want to install new server software that requires a server with a minimum of 256MB of RAM and a processor speed of at least 500MHz. You can use ZENworks Server Management to generate a report of all NetWare servers that are possible candidates for the software. ZENworks Server Management can generate two different types of inventory reports: simple inventory lists and comprehensive inventory lists.

The most common report you will likely use is the simple inventory list report. This report enables you to selectively create reports on every aspect of your server by selecting specific criteria that must be matched.

Simple inventory list reports are usually generated quickly, so the information you need will be almost instantaneously available. You may want to run several different inventory list reports, shown in Table 32.1, depending on what information you need.

The other type of inventory report that you will use is the comprehensive inventory report. The comprehensive inventory report combines several aspects of server inventory into each report. Each report takes considerably longer to generate; however, they are more specific and inclusive. You will typically use one of the comprehensive inventory reports listed in Table 32.1 to help you with business and network planning.

TIP The Software Summary chart might not display properly if too much software data is in your Inventory database. For the chart to display properly, use the selection criteria to restrict the results displayed.

TABLE 32.1   Available Inventory Reports

INVENTORY REPORT GROUP	REPORT NAME	SELECTION CRITERIA	INFORMATION DISPLAYED IN THE INVENTORY REPORT
Hardware Inventory	Asset Management Report	Scope, Machine Name, IP Address, and DNS Name. You can also select to display the following options in the report: Memory, Processor, Display Adapter, Keyboard, Pointing Device, Fixed and Removable Disk, Floppy, CDROM, Network Adapter, and Monitor.	Memory, processor, display details, keyboard, pointing device, fixed and removable disk, floppy, CD drive, network adapter, and monitor details for inventoried servers.
	BIOS Listing	Scope, Machine Name, IP Address, DNS Name, BIOS Install Date, and Manufacturer.	List of all the inventoried servers with BIOS manufacturer, BIOS release date, and the total number of such machines.
	Battery Listing	Scope, Machine Name, IP Address, DNS Name, and Name.	List of all inventoried servers that match the specified battery name.
	Bus Listing	Scope, Machine Name, IP Address, DNS Name, and Bus Type.	List of all inventoried servers with the selected bus type.
	CDROM Listing	Scope, Machine Name, IP Address, DNS Name, Caption, Description, and Manufacturer.	List of all inventoried servers that match the specified CD caption, description, and manufacturer's name.

TABLE 32.1   Continued

INVENTORY REPORT GROUP	REPORT NAME	SELECTION CRITERIA	INFORMATION DISPLAYED IN THE INVENTORY REPORT
	Display Adapter Listing	Scope, Machine Name, IP Address, DNS Name, Video Architecture, and Description.	List of all inventoried servers that match the specified display adapter's video architecture and description.
	Floppy Listing	Scope, Machine Name, IP Address, DNS Name, Manufacturer, and Description.	List of all inventoried servers that match the specified floppy description and manufacturer's name.
	Hardware Summary Report	Scope, Machine Name, IP Address, DNS Name, Operating System Type, Operating System Version, Processor Family, Curr. Clock Speed (Lower Bound in MHz), Curr. Clock Speed (Upper Bound in MHz), Total Memory (Lower Bound in MB), Total Memory (Upper Bound in MB), Hard Disk Size (Lower Bound in GB), and Hard Disk Size (Upper Bound in GB).	Operating system name, operating system version, processor family, processor current clock speed, memory, and hard disk size for each inventoried server.
	Keyboard Listing	Scope, Machine Name, IP Address, DNS Name, Description, and Layout.	List of all inventoried servers that match the specified keyboard description and layout.
	Modem Listing	Scope, Machine Name, IP Address, DNS Name, and Name.	List of all inventoried servers that match the specified modem name.

TABLE 32.1 Continued

INVENTORY REPORT GROUP	REPORT NAME	SELECTION CRITERIA	INFORMATION DISPLAYED IN THE INVENTORY REPORT
	Monitor Listing	Scope, Machine Name, IP Address, DNS Name, Manufacturer, Manufacture Date, Nominal Size (Lower Bound in inches), and Nominal Size (Upper Bound in inches).	List of all inventoried servers that match the specified monitor manufacturer's name, manufacture date, and the specified range of monitor's nominal size.
	Network Adapter Listing	Scope, Machine Name, IP Address, DNS Name, and Name.	List of all inventoried servers that match the specified network adapter's name.
	Physical Disk Listing	Show Chart, Scope, Machine Name, IP Address, DNS Name, Removable, Manufacturer, Description, Total Size (Lower Bound in GB), and Total Size (Upper Bound in GB).	List of all inventoried servers that match the specified physical disk manufacturer's name; description; the specified range of total size; and disks that are fixed, removable, or both. Available Options: pie chart
	Pointing Device Listing	Scope, Machine Name, IP Address, DNS Name, Pointing Device Type, and Pointing Device Name.	List of all inventoried servers that match the specified pointing device type and name.
	Power Supply Listing	Scope, Machine Name, IP Address, DNS Name, and Description.	List of all inventoried machines that match the specified power supply description.

TABLE 32.1 Continued

INVENTORY REPORT GROUP	REPORT NAME	SELECTION CRITERIA	INFORMATION DISPLAYED IN THE INVENTORY REPORT
	Processor Listing	Show Chart, Scope, Machine Name, IP Address, DNS Name, Processor Family, Maximum Speed (Lower Bound in MHz), Maximum Speed (Upper Bound in MHz), Current Speed (Lower Bound in MHz), and Current Speed (Upper Bound in MHz).	List of all the inventoried servers with a processor family (such as Pentium Pro), processor maximum clock speed, and the processor current clock speed of the machines. Available Options: pie chart
	Sound Adapter Listing	Scope, Machine Name, IP Address, DNS Name, and Name.	List of all inventoried servers that match the specified sound adapter name.
	Storage Devices Inventory Report	Scope, Machine Name, IP Address, and DNS Name. Available Options: Fixed and Removable Disk, Logical Disk, Floppy, and CDROM.	Fixed disk, removable disk, logical disk, floppy, and CD drive details for each inventoried server.
	System Chassis Listing	Scope, Machine Name, IP Address, DNS Name, Chassis Type, and Manufacturer.	List of all inventoried servers that match the specified system chassis type and manufacturer's name.

TABLE 32.1 Continued

INVENTORY REPORT GROUP	REPORT NAME	SELECTION CRITERIA	INFORMATION DISPLAYED IN THE INVENTORY REPORT
System Configuration	Inventory Scan Listing	Show Chart, Scope, Machine Name, IP Address, DNS Name, Last Scan Date (On or Before), Inventory Server Name, and Recent Information.	Date and time of the last inventory scan, inventory server name, and recent information on each inventoried server. Available Options: pie chart
	Memory Listing	Show Chart, Scope, Machine Name, IP Address, DNS Name, Total Memory (Lower Bound in MB), and Total Memory (Upper Bound in MB).	List of all the inventoried servers within a range of memory size (such as 200-400MB) and the total number of such machines. Available Options: pie chart
	Networking Information Report	Scope, Machine Name, IP Address, and DNS Name.	Network adapter type, DNS, IP address, MAC address, IPX address, and Windows Domain name for each inventoried server.
	Operating System Listing	Show Chart, Scope, Machine Name, IP Address, DNS Name, Operating System Type, and Operating System Version.	List of all the inventoried servers with an operating system type, an operating system version, and the total number of such servers. Available Options: pie chart.

TABLE 32.1 Continued

INVENTORY REPORT GROUP	REPORT NAME	SELECTION CRITERIA	INFORMATION DISPLAYED IN THE INVENTORY REPORT
	System Information Listing	Scope, Machine Name, IP Address, DNS Name, and Computer Manufacturer.	List of all inventoried servers that match the specified computer manufacturer's name.
	System Internal Hardware Inventory Report	Scope, Machine Name, IP Address, and DNS Name. Available Options: System IRQ, System Cache, System DMA, System Slot, and Motherboard.	IRQ, cache, DMA, slot, and motherboard for each inventoried server.
Software Inventory	Application Software Inventory Report	Scope, Machine Name, IP Address, DNS Name, Software Vendor, Software Name, Software Version, and Scanned From.	Software with product name, version, vendor name, source from where the software was scanned, and recent information for each inventoried server.
	Software Listing	Scope, Machine Name, IP Address, DNS Name, Software Vendor, Software Name, Software Version, and Scanned From.	List of all the inventoried servers that match the specified software vendor, software name, version, source from where the software was scanned, and the total number of such servers.

TABLE 32.1 Continued

INVENTORY REPORT GROUP	REPORT NAME	SELECTION CRITERIA	INFORMATION DISPLAYED IN THE INVENTORY REPORT
	Software Summary Chart	Scope, Software Vendor, Software Name, and Software Version.	Lists the number of inventoried servers with a particular software version.
	Software Summary Listing	Scope, Software Vendor, Software Name, and Software Version.	Lists the number of inventoried servers with a particular software version.
	System Software Inventory Report	Scope, Machine Name, IP Address, and DNS Name. Available Options: Display Driver, Pointing Device Driver, Network Adapter Driver, and NetWare Client.	Drivers (such as pointing device drivers, network adapter drivers, and display drivers) and Novell NetWare Client for each inventoried server.

Analyzing Topology Reports

ZENworks Server Management can also deliver reports on your network topology. These topology reports provide information about the specific topology of selected ZENworks Server Management sites or segments.

ZENworks Server Management can generate two basic types of topology reports. The first is a *site-level report*, which provides details about the discovered devices on each segment included in the ZENworks Server Management site. The second type of report is the *segment-level topology report*, which enables you to narrow the report down to a specific segment in the ZENworks Server Management site.

NOTE Whenever possible, generate a segment-level topology report rather than a site-level topology report. A site-level report takes considerably longer to generate.

The five predefined topology reports that can be generated by ZENworks Server Management are discussed in the following sections.

Computer Systems by Segment Report

The Computer Systems by Segment report can be done at a segment level to get only the systems in that segment; however, it is typically used as a comprehensive report to obtain a list of systems at the management site level.

The Computer Systems by Segment report lists the following information about each node and groups them by segment:

- ▶ System name—Node name. Use descriptive names for your systems to make these reports more useful.

- ▶ MAC address—Physical address.

- ▶ IP address—IP address of node. Useful to match to captured packets and trend data.

- ▶ IPX address—IPX address of node. Useful to match to captured packets and trend data.

- ▶ Services—Network services running on the node. Manageable services for the computer system.

- ▶ MIB services—MIB services running on the node. Manageable MIB services for the device.

- ▶ Community string—Community string defined for SNMP services. SNMP community names associated with this computer system.

NCP Servers Report

When running the NCP Servers report, ZENworks Server Management queries the management site or segment (depending on where the report was run from) and returns the following information for each NetWare server:

- ▶ Server name—Use descriptive names for your servers to make these reports more useful.

- ▶ MAC address—Physical address.

- ▶ IP address—Useful to match to captured packets and trend data.

- ▶ IPX address—Useful to match to captured packets and trend data.

- ▶ Labels—Other names by which the server is known.

- ▶ MIB services—Manageable MIB services for the device.

- ▶ Services—Manageable services for the computer system.

- ▶ Community strings—SNMP community names associated with reads and writes to the server.

Router Report

When running the Router report, ZENworks Server Management queries the management site or segment (depending on where the report was run from) and returns the following information for each router discovered:

- ▶ IPX address—Useful to match to captured packets and trend data.

- ▶ IP address—Useful to match to captured packets and trend data.

- ▶ MAC address—Physical address.

- ▶ Labels—Other names by which the server is known.

- ▶ MIB servers—Manageable MIB services for the device.

- ▶ Services—Manageable services for the computer system.

- ▶ Bound segments—Segments currently bound to the router.

Segment Report

When running the Segment report on a management site, ZENworks Server Management queries the management site and lists the number of computer systems on all segments. If this report is run at the segment level, it lists only the systems on the selected segment. The following information is shown for each computer system listed:

- ▶ IPX address—Useful to match to captured packets and trend data.

- ▶ IP address—Useful to match to captured packets and trend data.

- ▶ Segment type—Whether the segment is IP or IPX.

Segment Topology Report

The Segment Topology report provides network information about routers and bridges in a ZENworks Server Management or segment (depending on where the report is run from).

The following information is shown for each router listed in the report:

- ▶ Router name—Use descriptive names for your routers to make these reports more useful.

- ▶ MAC address—Physical address.

- ▶ IP address—Useful to match to captured packets and trend data.

- ▶ IPX address—Useful to match to captured packets and trend data.

- ▶ MIB services—Manageable MIB services for the device.

- ▶ Community strings—SNMP community names associated with the router.

The following information is shown for each bridge listed in the report:

- ▶ Bridge name—Use descriptive names for your bridges to make these reports more useful.

- ▶ Bridge type—Type of bridge device.

- ▶ IP address—Useful to match to captured packets and trend data.

- ▶ Number of ports—Number of ports on bridge. This is useful when planning for network growth.

- ▶ Port number (attached address)—Useful when troubleshooting software and network problems.

Using Server Management Alarm Reports

ZENworks Server Management alarm reports provide useful information about the alarms received by the ZENworks Server Management server. Alarm reports allow administrators to understand issues and visualize the current status of issues on their network better than any other report.

The three predefined alarm reports that can be generated by ZENworks Server Management are discussed in the following sections.

Alarms Details Report

The Alarms Details report contains the detailed information of the alarms captured on the ZENworks Server Management site. This report is used when you need to know more detailed information about some of the alarms being triggered on your managed server.

The report provides the following information about each managed server:

▶ Alarm severity—Describes how bad the alarm is in terms of how well the node can continue functioning.

▶ Affected object name—Name of the node affected.

▶ Source address—Address of the node affected.

▶ Alarm state—Describes whether the alarm is active.

▶ Alarm category—Describes the categorization of the alarm.

▶ Alarm generator—Describes the trap that triggered the alarm.

▶ Alarm time—Time the alarm was triggered.

▶ Alarm owner—Person responsible for handling the alarm.

▶ Alarm type—Describes what type of alarm was triggered.

▶ Alarm summary—More detailed description of the alarm.

Alarms Summary Report

The Alarms Summary report generates a short summary of the alarms on the site. This report also allows administrators to see a graphical representation of the distribution of alarms based on the selected number of days.

The report provides the following information about each managed server:

▶ Alarm severity—Describes how bad the alarm is in terms of how well the node can continue functioning.

▶ Alarm category—Describes the categorization of the alarm.

▶ Alarm owner—Person responsible for handling the alarm.

▶ Alarm state—Describes whether the alarm is active.

▶ Top alarm types—List the types of the most frequent alarms.

▶ Top affected objects—Lists the names of the nodes most frequently affected by alarms.

▶ Top source address—Lists the addresses of the nodes most frequently triggering alarms.

Available Trap Information Report

The Available Trap Information report lists the information of the SNMP traps currently available on the site server.

The report is generated based on the MIBs compiled on the site server and provides the following information:

▶ Total traps—Lists the total number of traps serviced by the site.

▶ Alarm category—Describes the categorization of the alarms.

▶ Alarm severity—Describes the severity of the alarms.

▶ Alarm type—Describes what type of alarm was triggered.

▶ Trap OID—Lists the MIB object ID for each trap.

▶ Trap description—Describes the trap in a text form.

Understanding Network Health Reports

Network health reports provide information about the overall health of a specified ZENworks Server Management site or managed network segment. ZENworks Server Management uses a predefined health profile to generate health reports. These health profiles define the trend parameters used to calculate the overall health of the segment or site.

The following sections describe the six predefined health profiles provided with ZENworks Server Management.

NetWare Server Profile

The NetWare server profile is used to monitor and understand the basic health of your NetWare servers. It provides graphs and data about the following types of trend parameters used to calculate the overall health of NetWare servers on the managed site or segment:

▶ Cache buffers—Enables you to see the amount of free memory on the server. Low memory is one of the most common symptoms of a sick server.

▶ Cache hits—Enables you to see memory usage to troubleshoot overaggressive applications.

▶ CPU utilization—Enables you to see how hard the server processor is being worked. High utilization for extended periods can lead to server health problems. Watching the server's utilization can help you strategically plan for network growth in overused areas.

▶ Volume free space—Enables you to monitor available disk space on each volume. Low disk space, especially on the **SYS** volume, often causes server and application problems.

Microsoft Windows Profile

ZENworks Server Management uses the Microsoft Windows profile to generate reports that monitor the basic health of your Microsoft Windows servers. It provides graphs and data about the following types of trend parameters used to calculate the overall health of Microsoft Windows servers on the managed site or segment:

▶ Available memory—Enables you to see the amount of free memory on the Windows server. Low memory is one of the most common symptoms of a sick server.

▶ Cache hits—Enables you to see memory usage to troubleshoot overaggressive Windows applications.

▶ CPU utilization—Enables you to see how hard the Windows server processor is being worked. High utilization for extended periods can lead to server health problems. Watching the Microsoft Windows server's utilization can help you strategically plan for network growth in overused areas.

▶ Disk free space—Enables you to monitor available disk space on each disk. Low disk space, especially on the Windows drive, often causes Windows server and application problems. A health report is generated for this parameter but no trend graph.

Linux Server Profile

ZENworks Server Management uses the Linux server profile to generate reports that monitor the basic health of your Linux servers. These reports provide data that allow administrators to quickly determine the overall health of their Linux servers.

Health reports can be generated automatically on a daily, weekly, monthly, or yearly basis using the Linux server profile.

The Linux server profile uses the processor utilization trend parameter to calculate the overall status of the Linux server; however, disk reads, disk block writes, and logged-in users are also displayed on the report.

Ethernet Network Profile

The Ethernet network profile is used to monitor and understand the basic health of your network. It provides graphs and data about the following types of trend parameters used to calculate the overall health of your Ethernet network on the managed site or segment:

- ▶ Total errors—Enables you to see the number of network errors occurring on your managed site or segment. This helps you troubleshoot problem networks.

- ▶ Network utilization—Enables you to see the current usage of your Ethernet networks. This can help you understand which segments are being overused and help you plan for future expansion.

- ▶ Total packets—Enables you to monitor the packets being sent on your managed Ethernet networks. A health report is generated for this parameter but no trend graph.

- ▶ Good packets—Enables you to see the good packets being sent on your managed Ethernet networks. Combined with the total packets, this can help you troubleshoot network problems and overusage. A health report is generated for this parameter but no trend graph.

Token Ring Network Profile

The token ring network profile is used to monitor and understand the basic health of your token ring network. It provides graphs and data about the following types of trend parameters used to calculate the overall health of your token ring network on the managed site or segment:

- ▶ Total errors—Enables you to see the number of token ring network errors occurring on your managed site or segment. This helps you troubleshoot problems on your token ring networks.

- ▶ Network utilization—Enables you to see the current usage of your token ring networks. This can help you understand which segments are being overused and help you plan for future expansion.

FDDI Network Profile

Finally, the FDDI network profile is used to monitor and understand the basic health of your FDDI network. It provides graphs and data about the following types of trend parameters used to calculate the overall health of your FDDI network on the managed site or segment:

▶ Total errors—Enables you to see the number of FDDI network errors occurring on your managed site or segment. This helps you troubleshoot problems on your FDDI networks.

▶ Network utilization—Enables you to see the current usage of your FDDI networks. This can help you understand which segments are being overused and help you plan for future expansion.

▶ Total packets—Enables you to monitor the total packets being sent on your managed FDDI networks. A health report is generated for this parameter but no trend graph.

Using ZENworks Server Management Reports

Now that you understand the types of reports that ZENworks Server Management can generate and the trend profiles it uses to calculate health, you need to understand how you use the ZENworks Server Management console to create, view, and manage those reports. The following sections discuss how to use the three types of ZENworks Server Management reports to monitor and maintain your network health.

Generating Server Inventory Reports

The Server Inventory report enables you to create inventory reports of hardware and software located on your managed servers, as discussed earlier in this chapter. The following sections describe how to create, customize, print, and export the Server Inventory reports.

Creating and Viewing Inventory Reports

The first step in using Server Inventory reports is knowing how to generate them. Follow these steps to generate and view the inventory report from within ConsoleOne:

1. Right-click the ZENworks Server Management site or managed segment.

2. Select Reporting from the pop-up menu.

3. Select a report category from the Available Reports window, shown in Figure 32.1.

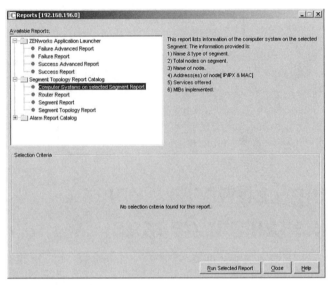

FIGURE 32.1
Server Inventory reports list in ConsoleOne.

4. Specify any additional options you want to use as filters when generating the report. Each report will have different options available to filter the report and reduce the number of entries.

5. Click the Run Selected Report button. A report similar to the one shown in Figure 32.2 appears.

After you generate the report, it's displayed in a window similar to the one shown in Figure 32.2. You can now view the information ZENworks Server Management collected. Notice that the report in Figure 32.2 is a software by machine listing. Listed are the server name, the software title, version (if available), and the number of servers with this software installed. The left and right arrow buttons enable you to navigate from page to page in a multipage report.

Filtering Inventory Reports

ZENworks Server Management enables you to customize the provided reports by filtering certain parameters. This is vital in large managed sites because it enables you to reduce the number of entries returned in the report. If wildcards are allowed, the report will show filter options and state that wildcard characters are allowed, as shown for the Software List report in Figure 32.1.

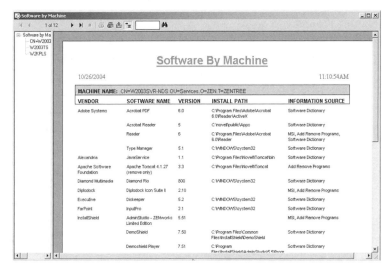

FIGURE 32.2
Software by Machine Inventory report in ConsoleOne.

Table 32.2 lists several character filters you can use to narrow down your report.

TABLE 32.2   Character Filters

CHARACTER	PURPOSE
*	Selects all items for the criteria (* picks up all; PRV-* picks up all objects that begin with "PRV-"—that is, PRV-SERV1, PRV-HOST2, and so on).
?	Uses all items that match the rest of the criteria (PRV-APP? picks up PRV-APP1, PRV-APP2, but not PRV-HOST2).
%	Is the SQL equivalent of the * character.
_	Is the SQL equivalent of the ? character.
Specific name	Filters on a specific name for the criteria (PRV-APP1 picks up only objects with that name for the criteria).

Printing Inventory Reports

After you generate the report, you may want to make a hard copy for later reference. To print the report, simply click the Printer icon shown in Figure 32.2. The Print dialog box comes up, enabling you to print the report.

Exporting Inventory Reports

You also have the option to export the report to a file. Exporting the report can be useful if you want to publish the report in a presentation or on the Web, or import it into another database.

To export a report select File→Export Report from the menu when you have the report up. From the dialog box shown in Figure 32.3, specify the destination as Disk file; then select one of the following or any other of the 30 supported types of files to which ZENworks Server Management should export the report:

- ▶ Text—Exports the report to a simple text file that can be imported into a word processor for a status report.

- ▶ HTML—Exports the report directly to HTML format. This can be useful to publish server status directly to an internal website automatically.

- ▶ PDF—Exports the report to an Adobe Acrobat format. This can be useful when preparing a presentation or publishing it on the Web.

- ▶ SDF—Exports the report to a Standard Delimited Format (SDF). This is useful to import the report into another database for tracking purposes. You must specify a common delimiter such as a comma, space, or tab.

- ▶ XML—Exports the report to an XML document that can be distributed and read from a variety of XML interfaces.

FIGURE 32.3
ZENworks Server Management report exporting options in ConsoleOne.

Creating Topology Reports

ZENworks Server Management also enables you to generate topology reports that can help you understand the status and infrastructure of your network. You can generate two types of reports, one based at a managed site level and the other based at a segment level. The segment level reports provide information about managed devices on the selected segment only.

Follow these steps to generate and view one of the types of topology reports from within ConsoleOne:

1. Right-click the ZENworks Server Management site or managed segment.

2. Select Reporting from the pop-up menu.

3. Select a topology report category from the Reports window, shown in Figure 32.4.

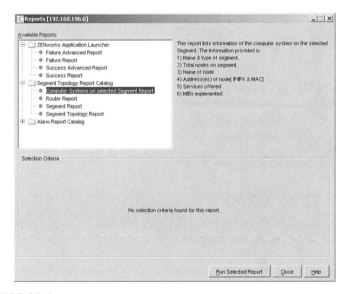

FIGURE 32.4
Topology reports list in ConsoleOne.

4. Click the Run Selected Report button. A report similar to the one shown in Figure 32.5 appears.

After you generate the topology report, it's displayed in a Report window similar to the one shown in Figure 32.5. You can now view the information collected by ZENworks Server Management, such as segment names, addresses, and nodes. The left and right arrow buttons enable you to navigate from page to page in a multipage report. You also have the same options to export and print the report as you do with inventory reports.

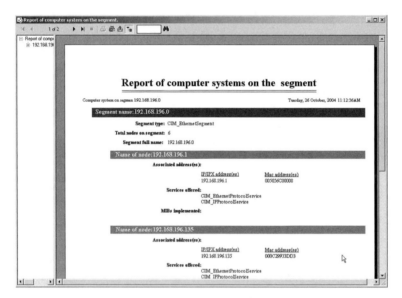

FIGURE 32.5
Computer systems on the segment topology report in ConsoleOne.

Generating Network Health Reports

The final type of ZENworks Server Management report is the Network and Server Management health report. You should become familiar with this report. The six standard profiles used by ZENworks Server Management to generate health reports were discussed earlier in the chapter:

- ▶ NetWare server profile
- ▶ Linux server profile
- ▶ Microsoft server profile
- ▶ Ethernet server profile

▶ Token ring network profile

▶ FDDI network profile

The following sections discuss using those six basic profiles, as well as customizing profiles of your own to schedule, run, and view health reports.

Customizing Health Profiles

The first step when working with network health reports is learning how to customize one of the existing health profiles that you use to generate a health report. Customizing an existing health profile means modifying the trend parameters, discussed earlier in the chapter, to more accurately reflect the health of the monitored devices.

Follow these steps to customize one of the existing health profiles from within ConsoleOne:

1. Right-click the ZENworks Server Management managed site object and select Properties from the pop-up menu.

2. Select the Health Profiles tab.

3. Select the health profile you want to customize and click the Edit button, as shown in Figure 32.6. If you do not want to edit one but want to create a new one, click the New button (discussed in the next section).

4. From the Edit profile box, shown in Figure 32.7, you can modify the directory location to which reports generated by this profile should be published by typing a network path in the Publish Directory box.

5. Modify the trend parameters used to calculate health by either checking or unchecking the In Health Calculation box next to them. This adds or removes the parameter from a list used to calculate the health of the device or segment.

6. Modify the rank of importance of each of the selected trend parameters by specifying a value in the Weight field. You may enter any whole number in the Weight field. ZENworks Server Management uses the number you specify to determine how important the parameter is in calculating the overall health of the device or segment. Larger numbers mean more weight is given to the trend parameter when calculating health of the device.

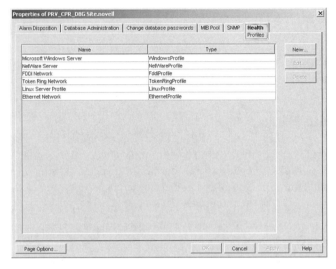

FIGURE 32.6
Available health profiles in the Health Profiles tab for a managed site
object in ConsoleOne.

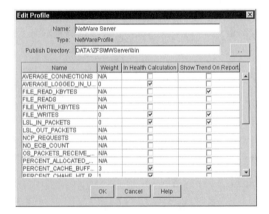

FIGURE 32.7
Health trend parameters in the Edit Profile dialog box in ConsoleOne.

   7. Modify the trend parameters you want to see rendered graphically
   in the health report. Data from the parameters selected will be calculated and graphically represented on the health report.

On completion of these steps, click OK to save your changes.

Adding New Health Profiles

Adding a new health profile means defining the location of the report, the type of report, the trend parameters, and the weights to parameters used to generate a health report of the monitored device. Follow these steps to add a new health profile from within ConsoleOne:

1. Right-click the ZENworks Server Management managed site object and select Properties from the pop-up menu.

2. Select the Health Profiles tab.

3. Select the health profile you want to customize and click the New button, as shown previously in Figure 32.6.

4. From the New Profile dialog box, shown in Figure 32.8, type in the name of the new profile.

5. Select the type of device or segment to which the profile applies from the drop-down list, as shown in Figure 32.8.

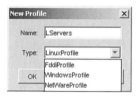

FIGURE 32.8
Drop-down list of health profile types shown in the New Profile dialog box in ConsoleOne.

6. Click OK. The Edit Profile dialog box appears.

7. From the Edit Profile box, shown in Figure 32.9, you can modify the directory location to which reports generated by this profile should be published by typing a network path in the Publish Directory box.

8. Select the trend parameters used to calculate health by either checking or unchecking the In Health Calculation box next to them. This adds or removes the parameter from a list used to calculate the health of the device or segment.

9. Enter the rank of importance of each of the selected trend parameters by specifying a value in the Weight field. You may enter any whole number in the Weight field. ZENworks Server Management uses the number you specify to determine how important the

parameter is in calculating the overall health of the device or segment. Larger numbers mean more weight is given to the trend parameter when calculating health of the device.

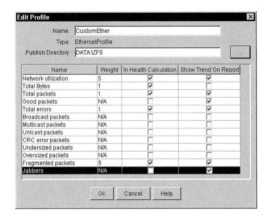

FIGURE 32.9
The Edit Profile dialog box showing the health trend parameters and location for the new health profile in ConsoleOne.

10. Select which of the trend parameters you want to see rendered graphically in the health report. Data from the parameters selected will be calculated and graphically represented on the health report.

On completion of these steps, click OK to save your changes.

Creating and Scheduling Health Reports

After you create and customize the health profiles for your managed network devices and segments, you need to know how to create and schedule a health report to run. You must tell ZENworks Server Management which devices you want a health report to be run on, what type of report to run, and when to run it.

Follow these steps in ConsoleOne to create and schedule a health report:

1. Right-click the ZENworks Server Management managed site object or a container object in the ZENworks Server Management namespace and select Properties from the pop-up menu.

2. Select the Health Reports tab, as shown in Figure 32.10.

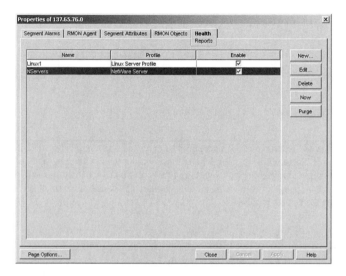

FIGURE 32.10
Drop-down list of health profiles enabled.

3. Click the New button. The Edit Report dialog box appears.

4. From the Edit Report dialog box, shown in Figure 32.11, enter the name you want to call the report.

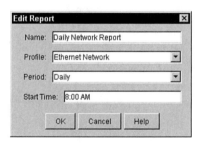

FIGURE 32.11
The Edit Profile dialog box showing the health trend parameters and location for the new health profile in ConsoleOne.

5. Select the profile that you want ZENworks Server Management to use when generating the health report by selecting one of the available types from the Profile drop-down list.

6. Set the frequency that you want to run by selecting Daily, Weekly, or Monthly from the Period drop-down list.

7. Set the time that you want the health report to be generated by entering the appropriate values in the Start Time field.

8. Click OK. The report will be generated by using the date and time that you entered for the report.

TIP Schedule reports to run at optimal times to balance data gathering and network performance. Some of the segment reports, for example, tend to be somewhat network intensive; therefore, you may not want to run them at 9 a.m., when all users are logging in and network usage is at its peak. It could be more advantageous to run them at 1:00 a.m. when the system is slow.

Forcing Health Reports to Run

Now that you understand how to schedule health reports to run, you should also be familiar with how to force them to run. Although health reports are scheduled to run on a daily, weekly, or monthly basis at pre-defined times, you may also need to run them at unscheduled times.

You may, for example, want to force a report to run if you are troubleshooting a network problem, or if you need to know the current health of a segment of servers before upgrading them.

Follow these steps in ConsoleOne to force a health report to run:

1. Right-click the ZENworks Server Management managed site object or a managed container object and select Properties from the pop-up menu.

2. Select the Health Reports tab, shown earlier in Figure 32.10.

3. Select the report to which you want to force generation.

4. Click the Now button, and the report is saved to the publish directory specified in the health profile for the report.

Viewing Health Reports

Now that you understand how to schedule a health report or force one to run, you need to know how to actually view it. After ZENworks Server Management creates the health report, it will be automatically published to a directory specified by its controlling profile.

Also located in the published directory is an HTML document named INDEX.HTM that is associated with the health report. The INDEX.HTM file is an HTML document that contains a Java application that provides access to all the reports stored in the directory.

Follow these steps to view a health report after ZENworks Server Management generates it:

1. From your console workstation, browse to the directory where the health reports for the associated profile are stored.

2. Open the INDEX.HTM file located in the directory specified in the controlling profile. The left column of INDEX.HTM lists the report hierarchy based on profiles and your network topology.

3. Click the plus sign next to the health profile associated with the health report you want to view. The profile object expands to display a list of container objects.

4. Click the plus sign next to the container object associated with the health report you want to view. The container object should expand and display a list of report names associated with it.

5. Click the plus sign next to the report you want to view. The report object expands to display a list of instances of that particular report. A report scheduled to run daily, for example, would have one instance for each day the report was run. The date and time at which the report was run is used to generate the report's name. A report generated on October 11, 2005, at 5:05:00 Mountain Daylight Time would have a name of 2005.10.11_05.05.00_MDT.

6. Click the plus sign next to the report name to display a list of individual report pages. The number of report pages depends on which profile you selected and which managed device or segment the report was generated for.

7. Click the individual report page to display the health report in the right frame, as shown in Figure 32.12. The top of the report displays statistical information about the segment or device and provides an overall calculation of health. The trend parameters specified in the report's health profile are listed with trend data. Below the statistical information are trend graphs depicting health based on the trend data selections in the health profile.

You can now click the Print button at the bottom of the left frame to print the report if you need a hard copy.

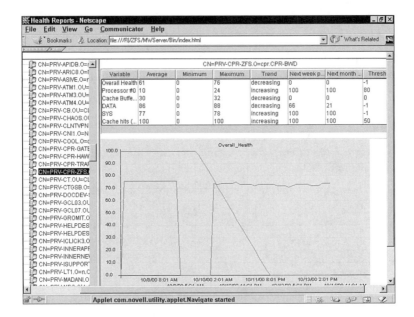

FIGURE 32.12
Navigating and viewing a health report in a Web browser.

NOTE The Java application in the INDEX.HTM file for health reports requires that the Java 1.1.2 plug-in for your Web browser be installed prior to viewing the report. If you do not have the plug-in, you cannot view the report. Also, if there has not been a report fully generated in that directory yet, the Java application will fail to initialize.

Summary

This chapter focused on three types of reports: server inventory reports, topology reports, and network health reports. You can easily design your own reports by creating defined reports through Crystal Reports designer and running them against the ZENworks Server Management database.

## CHAPTER 33

Using ZENworks Server Management Web-based Management

The ZENworks Server Management provides web-based management components that plug-in to the Novell iManager utility. These components allow you to use Novell iManager as an alternative to ConsoleOne for managing TED (Tiered Electronic Distribution) objects and distributions.

The following sections discuss how to access the ZENworks web-based management role and how to use it to administer TED objects. The tiered distribution view is also discussed and how to use it to track distributions throughout your network. You also learn about the Remote Web Console and how to use it to monitor and maintain the distribution agent, subscriber agent, and policy/package agent.

> **NOTE** The ZENworks Server Management installation guide discusses how to set up the necessary components in your network to install the web components for Policy-Enabled Server Management. The installation can be somewhat picky, so you should spend some time understanding the installation steps to make sure that they are followed correctly.

Accessing the ZENworks Web-based Management Role

After you have correctly configured and set up the web-based management components on a NetWare, Windows, Linux, or Solaris server, you can access the iManager interface by simply opening the following URL in your web browser:

   http://server_name_or_IP_address/nps

Where *server_name_or_IP_address* is the name or IP address of the server that has the web-based management components installed on it.

The first web page you see is a login screen prompting you for login information to authenticate to Novell eDirectory. After you log in, you see a page similar to the one shown in Figure 33.1. Expand the ZENworks Server Management section by clicking on the plus sign next to it, and you have access to the ZENworks Server Management web-based management tool.

If you do not see the ZENworks Server Management section, the web-based management components are not properly installed. You might need to install the plug-in by clicking on the configuration button in iManager and selecting Available Novell Plug-in Modules from the Module Installation option. If the ZENWorks 7.0 Server management module is listed, select it and click Install. After you have installed the plug-in, you need to restart Tomcat and Apache for the module to be available.

One specific feature of iManager you should become familiar with is the object selector icon, shown in Figure 33.2. This icon is displayed next to fields that require a Novell eDirectory object. If you do not know the exact Distinguished Name (DN) of the object, you can click on the object selector icon and bring up the Object Selector window shown in Figure 33.3.

The object selector allows you to navigate through the eDirectory tree and select objects you need to fill out forms in the iManager interface. You will use the object selector frequently when managing TED through the web-based management role.

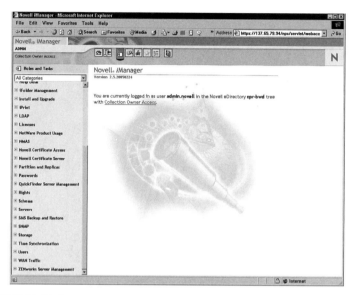

FIGURE 33.1
ZENworks Server Management Roles and Tasks in iManager.

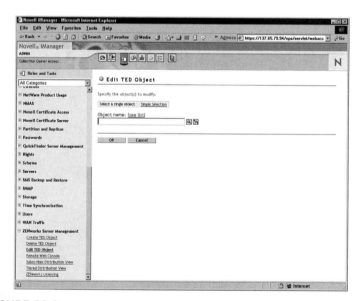

FIGURE 33.2
The object selector icon in iManager on the Edit TED Object page.

FIGURE 33.3
Object selector page in iManager.

Administering TED Objects

A great feature that the web-based management tool offers is the ability to quickly administer TED objects even when ConsoleOne is not available. This can be useful for an administrator who needs to make changes while traveling or working from home. The following sections discuss using the web-based management tool to create, edit, and delete TED objects.

Creating TED Objects

To create a TED object from the web-based management tool, click on the Create TED Object option under the ZENworks Server Management section from the main page shown previously in Figure 33.1. A new page, shown in Figure 33.4, opens in your browser. From this page, you have the option of creating a channel, distribution, subscriber group, or external subscriber.

NOTE A distributor or subscriber is created at the time that ZENworks Server Management software is installed on the server.

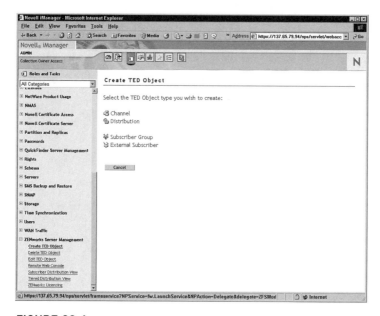

FIGURE 33.4
Creation page for the ZENworks Server Management role in iManager.

When you select the type of object you want to create from the creation page (refer to Figure 33.4), a new page is opened in your browser allowing you to enter the information required to create the type of object you selected. Figure 33.5 shows the object creation page for a distribution object. After you fill out the form with the required information, click OK, and the object is created.

Editing TED Objects

You can edit TED objects in the web-based management tool in two ways. The first way is to click on the Edit TED Object option under the ZENworks Server Management section from the main page. The second way is to select a TED object in the tiered distribution view and click the eDirectory button (see Figure 33.10).

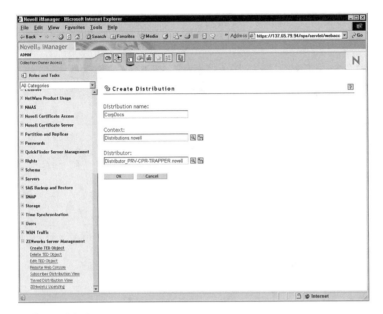

FIGURE 33.5
Creation page to create a distribution in the ZENworks Server Management role in iManager.

When you click on the Edit TED Object option under ZENworks Server Management, you are prompted to enter the object name or use the object selector to specify the TED object you want to edit, as shown in Figure 33.6.

After you select the object and click OK, the edit page for the object is displayed in your browser, as shown in Figure 33.7. From this edit page you can select tabs and different pages that allow you to configure the object's properties. The edit screens try to mimic the look and functionality of ConsoleOne as much as possible.

Figure 33.7 shows the General Settings edit page for a distribution object. Notice that it has the same settings as the Settings property page for the General tab of a distribution object in the ConsoleOne interface.

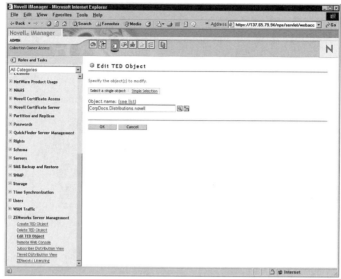

FIGURE 33.6
Editing page for the ZENworks Server Management role in iManager.

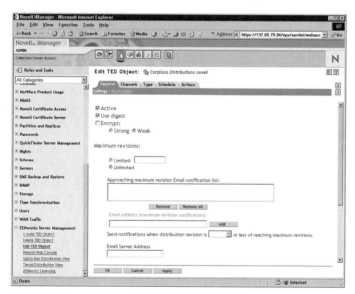

FIGURE 33.7
Editing a distribution object in ZENworks Server Management role in iManager.

Deleting TED Objects

Deleting TED objects from the web-based management tool is quick and simple. First, click on the Delete TED Object option under the ZENworks Server Management section from the main page. Next, from the Delete page, shown in Figure 33.8, click on the object selector icon and find the object you want to delete. After it is selected, simply click OK, and the object is deleted.

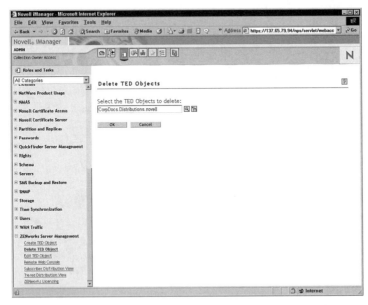

FIGURE 33.8
Deletion page for ZENworks Server Management role in iManager.

Monitoring Tiered Distributions

One of the most useful tools provided with ZENworks Server Management web-based management is the ability to monitor TED distributions. You can use this tool to track the progress of distributions down through the channel and determine which subscriber servers have received the distribution, which distributor sent it to them, and when they received it.

To monitor a TED distribution from the web-based management tool, click on the Tiered Distribution View option under the ZENworks Server Management section from the main page shown previously in Figure 33.1. A new page, shown in Figure 33.9, opens in your browser. From this page, simply click on the object selector and select the distribution that you want to monitor.

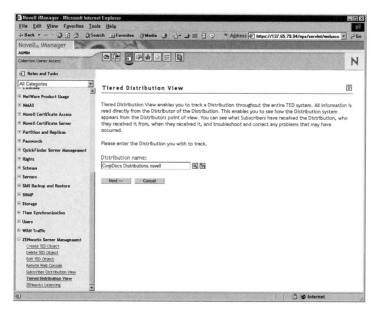

FIGURE 33.9
Select Distribution page for tiered distribution view of the ZENworks Server Management role in iManager.

After you select the distribution you want to monitor, click Next, and select the channel on which you want to monitor the distribution. After you have selected a channel, click Next, and the tiered distribution view, shown in Figure 33.10, displays the status of the distribution. From this page you can specify a browser refresh frequency that allows you to keep the page up and monitor the progress of the distribution in real-time.

You also have the following three options from the tiered distribution view:

▶ Remote Web Console—Brings up the Remote Web Console page (discussed later in the chapter) for the object that you have selected in the distribution screen.

▶ eDirectory Configuration—Brings up the edit page (discussed earlier) for the object that you have selected in the distribution screen.

▶ Expand All—Provides a quick way to expand all the entries in the distribution screen. This is useful to quickly get a picture of the entire distribution.

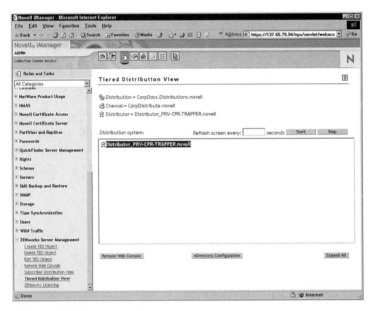

FIGURE 33.10
Tiered distribution view of a TED distribution in the ZENworks Server Management role in iManager.

Monitoring Subscriber Distributions

Another powerful tool provided with ZENworks Server Management web-based management is the ability to monitor TED distributions at the subscriber level. You can use this tool to track the status of distributions on a set of watched subscribers.

To monitor the status of distributions for specific subscribers from the web-based management tool, click on the Subscriber Distribution View option under the ZENworks Server Management section from the main page shown previously in Figure 33.1. A new page, shown in Figure 33.11, displays the status of the distributions on the subscribers that have been added to the watch list.

From this page you can specify a browser refresh frequency that allows you to keep the page up and monitor the progress of the distribution in real-time.

You also have the following options available by clicking the buttons below the subscriber distribution watch list:

▶ Remote Web Console—Brings up the Remote Web Console page (discussed later in the chapter) for the object that you have selected in the distribution screen.

▶ eDirectory Configuration—Brings up the edit page (discussed earlier) for the object that you have selected in the distribution screen.

▶ Expand All—Provides a quick way to expand all the entries in the distribution screen. This is useful to quickly get a picture of the entire distribution.

▶ Add—Allows you to add a subscriber to the watch list.

▶ Remove—Allows you to remove a subscriber from the watch list.

▶ Remove All—Allows you to quickly remove all subscribers from the watch list.

Using the Remote Web Console Tool

Another useful tool provided with ZENworks Server web-based management is the Remote Web Console tool. The Remote Web Console tool allows you to monitor and maintain the distribution agent, subscriber agent, and policy/package agent from a web browser. This allows you to view configurations, distributions, schedules, events, and so on, about the agents for one easy-to-access location.

FIGURE 33.11
Subscriber distribution view of a TED distribution in the ZENworks Server
Management role in iManager.

You access the Remote Web Console in the web-based management tool
in two ways. The first way is to click on the Remote Web Console option
under the ZENworks Server Management section from the main page.
The second way is to select a TED object in the tiered distribution view
and click the Remote Web Console button (see Figure 33.10).

When you click on the Remote Web Console option under ZENworks
Server Management, you are prompted to enter the name of the object or
use the object selector to specify the TED or policy/package agent you
want to monitor.

The following sections discuss using the ZENworks Server Remote Web
Console tool to monitor policy/package agents and TED agents.

Monitoring Policy/Package Agents from the Remote Web Console

The Remote Web Console tool is easily accessible and useful for quickly
viewing configuration and schedule information for policies and software
packages in your tree.

The following sections discuss the type of policy/package information
you can monitor from the Remote Web Console.

When you first enter Remote Web Console, it automatically displays the
information regarding Tiered Electronic Distribution on that server. You
need to first select the Policy Package Agent in the Display field at the
top of the page (see Figure 33.12).

Configuration

The Configuration tab, shown in Figure 33.12, displays the configuration
information about the selected agent. The information shown includes
such items as the version, events registered, console level, and variables.

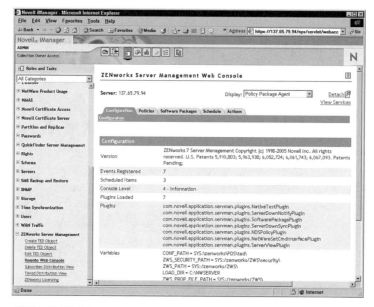

FIGURE 33.12
Configuration page for a policy/package in the Remote Web Console tool
in iManager.

Policies

The Policies tab of a policy/package agent in the Remote Web Console
view displays all policies associated with the agent and allows you to
enforce, refresh, and reschedule them. This page also displays a list of
scheduled policies, including their schedules, and a list of enforcers for
the agent.

Software Packages

The Software Packages tab of a policy/package agent in the Remote Web Console view displays a list of the package name, install date, status, and available actions for all software packages managed by the agent. It also allows you to add a software package.

Schedule

The Schedule tab (see Figure 33.13) of a policy/package agent in the Remote Web Console view displays the scheduled classes and times for the agent. It also displays the name, type, parameters, repeats, time, and actions for each time a schedule is run. You can also add a Java class, script, or executable to the agent's schedule from this page.

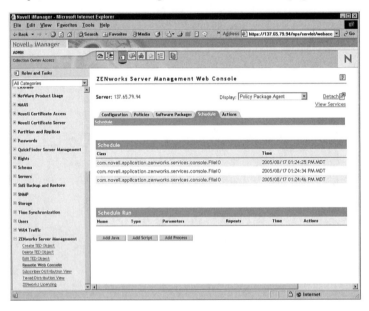

FIGURE 33.13
Schedule page for a policy package in the Remote Web Console tool in iManager.

Actions

The Actions tab of a policy/package agent in the Remote Web Console view gives you the option to perform "down server" and refresh actions on the server that the agent is running.

Monitoring Tiered Electronic Distribution Agents from the Remote Web Console

The Remote Web Console also allows you to monitor and maintain the TED distribution and subscriber agents running on your network. From the Tiered Electronic Distribution Agents view in the Remote Web Console, you can quickly see the configuration and status of distributors and subscribers, distributions, channels, and security as well as events for both successful and unsuccessful distributions occurring in your distribution channel.

The following sections discuss the type of policy/package information that you can monitor from the Remote Web Console.

Configuration

The Configuration tab of a TED agent in the Remote Web Console view displays the configuration information about the distributor or subscriber selected. The following is a list of pages under the Configuration tab for a TED agent:

- ▶ Configuration—Shows the object name, object revision, current working directory, distribution timeout, concurrent distributions, console messaging level, logging level, log file path, I/O rates, schedule, variables, and so on for a distributor or subscriber agent's server. This is a fast way to view the entire configuration for a distributor or subscriber.

- ▶ Subordinate Configuration—Shows the object name, object revision, current working directory, distribution timeout, concurrent distributions, console messaging level, logging level, log file path, I/O rates, schedule, variables, and so on for a subordinate subscriber agent's server.

- ▶ Threads—Displays TED thread information on the agent's server.

- ▶ Route to Subscriber (distributor only)—Shows the routing hierarchy to subscriber servers.

- ▶ Database (distributor only)—Displays information about the ZENworks Server Management database used by the distributor agent.

- ▶ Refresh Distributor (distributor only)—Allows you to force the distributor to refresh the configuration information it holds (distributor, subscribers, channels, and so on). Remember that this causes "Run Immediately" distributions to be regathered and possibly re-sent.

Distributions

The Distributions tab of a TED agent in the Remote Web Console view displays the distribution information about the distributor or subscriber selected. The following is a list of pages under the Distributions tab for a TED agent:

▶ Received Distributions—Displays a list of all distributions that this agent has received. You have the option of selecting a distribution from that list, clicking OK, and then being presented with status information about the selected distribution.

▶ Active Distributions—Displays a list of the ingoing and a list of the outgoing distributions for the agent. From this page, you can view the IP address of the agent sending or receiving the distribution, whether the distribution is currently active, its priority, the version number, distribution, channel, bytes sent or received, total size, heartbeat status, and actions.

▶ Distribution Information (distributor only)—Allows you to view information about any distribution on the agent.

▶ Build Distribution (distributor only)—Allows you to rebuild on the distributor and create a new version, if required (see Figure 33.14).

Channels

The Channels tab of a TED agent in the Remote Web Console view displays the channel information for distributions on the distributor agent selected. The following is a list of pages under the Channels tab for a TED distributor agent:

▶ Channel Information—Allows you to view the configuration of the channel for distributions on the agent.

▶ Distribute Channel—Allows you to select a channel object and send it.

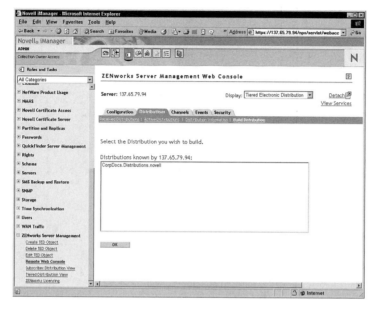

FIGURE 33.14
Distributions page for TED in the Remote Web Console tool in iManager.

Events

The Events tab of a TED agent in the Remote Web Console view displays the distribution events on the subscriber or distributor agent selected. The following is a list of pages under the Events tab for a TED agent:

- ▶ Subscriber Event Log—Displays a list, including severity, time, and message, for all events that have occurred on the subscriber, shown in Figure 33.15.

- ▶ Distributor Event Log—Displays a list, including severity, time, and message, for all events that have occurred on the distributor.

- ▶ Scheduled Events—Displays a list of events scheduled on the TED Agent.

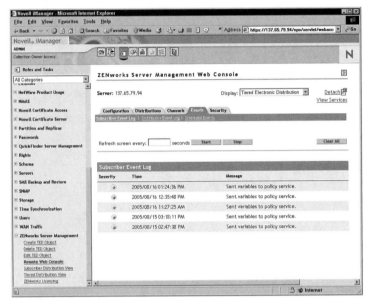

FIGURE 33.15
Subscriber Events page for a policy package in the Remote Web Console tool in iManager.

Security

The Security tab of a TED agent in the Remote Web Console displays the certificates of trusted distributors for distributions on the subscriber or distributor agent selected. The following is a list of pages under the Security tab for a TED agent:

▶ Show Certificates—Displays the data for all certificates on the agent, including who issued the certificate, subject, date/time created, and date/time that it expires.

▶ Sign CSR (distributor only)—Allows you to have the distributor agent sign a Certificate Signing Request (CSR).

Summary

This chapter discusses the administrative interfaces for ZENworks available in the iManager web console. Currently only a few of the ZENworks Server Management functions are available through the web interface.

INDEX

Note: Page numbers with the prefix *DVD:* are located on the accompanying DVD. For example, *ACCESS DENIED error, DVD:1036* is located on page 1036 of the DVD.

A

B

J-K

M

Q-R

V

X-Y-Z